1978	1979	1980	1981	1982	1983	1984	1985	1986	1987	1988	1989	1990
2,294.7	2,563.3	2,789.5	3,128.4	3,255.0	3,536.7	3,933.2	4,220.3	4,462.8	4,739.5	5,103.8	5,484.4	5,803.1
5,672.8	5,850.1	5,834.0	5,982.1	5,865.9	6,130.9	6,571.5	6,843.4	7,080.5	7,307.0	7,607.4	7,879.2	8,027.1
5.6	3.2	−0.2	2.5	−1.9	4.5	7.2	4.1	3.5	3.4	4.1	3.5	1.9
1,428.5	1,592.2	1,757.1	1,941.1	2,077.3	2,290.6	2,503.3	2,720.3	2,899.7	3,100.2	3,353.6	3,598.5	3,839.9
438.0	492.9	479.3	572.4	517.2	564.3	735.6	736.2	746.5	785.0	821.6	874.9	861.0
453.6	500.8	566.2	627.5	680.5	733.5	797.0	879.0	949.3	999.5	1,039.0	1,099.1	1,180.2
7.6	11.3	13.5	10.3	6.2	3.2	4.3	3.6	1.9	3.6	4.1	4.8	5.4
357.3	381.8	408.5	436.7	474.8	521.4	551.6	619.8	724.6	750.2	786.6	792.8	824.8
7.91	11.20	13.35	16.39	12.24	9.09	10.23	8.10	6.80	6.66	7.57	9.21	8.10
9.06	12.67	15.26	18.87	14.85	10.79	12.04	9.93	8.33	8.21	9.32	10.87	10.01
222.6	225.1	227.8	230.0	232.2	234.3	236.3	238.5	240.7	242.8	245.0	247.3	250.1
601.4	460.3	530.6	596.6	594.1	559.8	543.9	570.0	601.7	601.5	643.0	1,091.0	1,536.5
102.3	105.0	106.9	108.7	110.2	111.6	113.5	115.5	117.8	119.9	121.7	123.9	125.8
96.0	98.8	99.3	100.4	99.5	100.8	105.0	107.2	109.6	112.4	115.0	117.3	118.8
6.1	5.8	7.1	7.6	9.7	9.6	7.5	7.2	7.0	6.2	5.5	5.3	5.6
−59.2	−40.7	−73.8	−79.0	−128.0	−207.8	−185.4	−212.3	−221.2	−149.7	−155.2	−152.6	−221.1
776.6	829.5	909.0	994.8	1,137.3	1,371.7	1,564.6	1,817.4	2,120.5	2,346.0	2,601.1	2,867.8	3,206.3
14.95	25.10	37.42	35.75	31.83	29.08	28.75	26.92	14.44	17.75	14.87	18.33	23.19
5.87	6.33	6.84	7.43	7.86	8.19	8.48	8.73	8.92	9.13	9.43	9.80	10.19
35.8	36.6	35.2	35.2	34.7	34.9	35.1	34.9	34.7	34.7	34.6	34.5	34.3
5.4	5.7	4.8	4.7	3.5	4.1	4.6	3.8	3.7	4.9	5.9	4.9	3.9
32.2	37.1	43.2	43.2	57.2	63.7	73.1	82.4	85.9	90.2	94.9	99.9	107.4
25.2	27.4	16.1	26.9	23.8	14.3	26.0	28.5	31.1	38.0	39.6	46.5	46.3
2.65	2.90	3.10	3.35	3.35	3.35	3.35	3.35	3.35	3.35	3.35	3.35	3.80
11.4	11.7	13.0	14.0	15.0	15.2	14.4	14.0	13.6	13.4	13.0	12.8	13.5
0.402	0.404	0.403	0.406	0.412	0.414	0.415	0.419	0.425	0.426	0.427	0.431	0.428
1.1	0.0	−0.2	2.1	−0.8	3.6	2.7	2.3	3.0	0.6	1.5	1.0	2.0
−29.8	−24.6	−19.4	−16.2	−24.2	−57.8	−109.1	−121.9	−138.5	−151.7	−114.6	−93.1	−80.9

CONNECT | ECONOMICS

INSTRUCTORS...

Would you like your **students** to show up for class **more prepared**?
(Let's face it, class is much more fun if everyone is engaged and prepared...)

Want an **easy way to assign** homework online and track student **progress**?
(Less time grading means more time teaching...)

Want an **instant view** of student or class performance?
(No more wondering if students understand...)

Need to **collect data and generate reports** required for administration or accreditation? *(Say goodbye to manually tracking student learning outcomes...)*

Want to **record and post your lectures** for students to view online?

With **McGraw-Hill's** *Connect* **Plus Economics,**

INSTRUCTORS GET:

- Simple **assignment management**, allowing you to spend more time teaching.
- **Auto-graded** assignments, quizzes, and tests.
- **Detailed Visual Reporting** where student and section results can be viewed and analyzed.
- Sophisticated **online testing** capability.
- A **filtering and reporting** function that allows you to easily assign and report on materials that are correlated to accreditation standards, learning outcomes, and Bloom's taxonomy.
- An easy-to-use **lecture capture** tool.
- The option to **upload course documents** for student access.
- Assign all of the end-of-chapter problems as ready-made **pre-built assignments** with the simple click of a button.

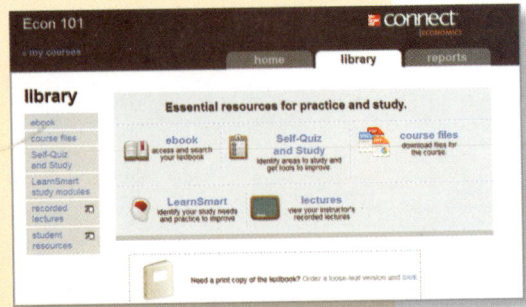

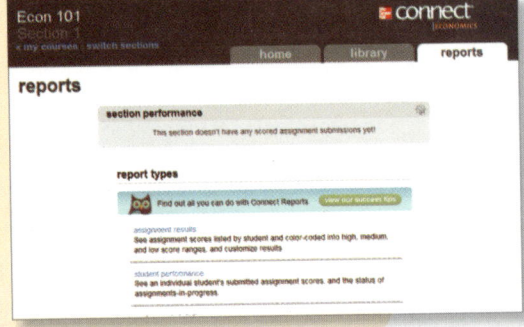

 **STUDENTS...**

Want to get **better grades**? *(Who doesn't?)*

Prefer to do your **homework online**? *(After all, you are online anyway...)*

Need **a better way** to **study** before the big test?
(A little peace of mind is a good thing...)

 With **McGraw-Hill's** *Connect® Plus Economics,*

STUDENTS GET:

- **Easy online access** to homework, tests, and quizzes assigned by your instructor.

- **Immediate feedback** on how you're doing. (No more wishing you could call your instructor at 1 a.m.)

- **Quick access** to lectures, practice materials, e-book, and more. (All the material you need to be successful is right at your fingertips.)

- LearnSmart—intelligent flash cards that adapt to your specific needs and provide you with customized learning content based on your strengths and weaknesses.

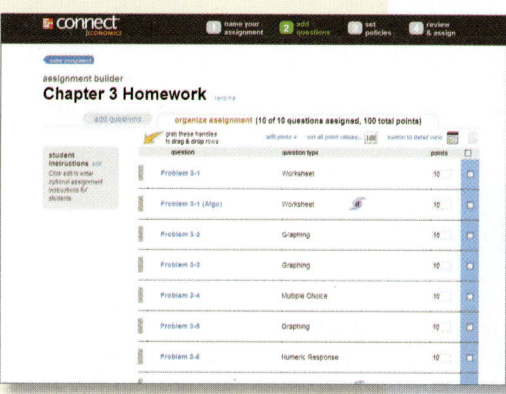

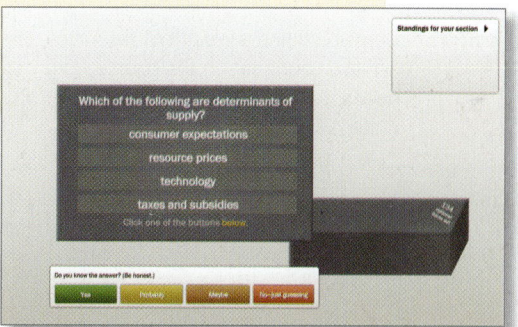

Want an online, **searchable version** of your textbook?

Wish your textbook could be **available online** while you're doing your assignments?

Connect® Plus Economics e-book

If you choose to use *Connect® Plus Economics*, you have an affordable and searchable online version of your book integrated with your other online tools.

Connect® Plus Economics e-book offers features like:

- Topic search
- Direct links from assignments
- Adjustable text size
- Jump to page number
- Print by section

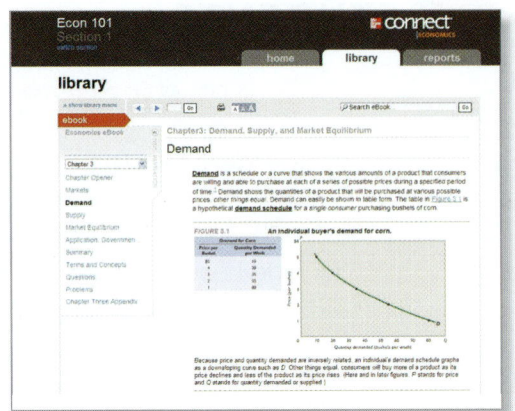

Want to get more **value** from your textbook purchase?

Think learning economics should be a bit more **interesting**?

Check out the STUDENT RESOURCES section under the *Connect®* Library tab.

Here you'll find a wealth of resources designed to help you achieve your goals in the course. Every student has different needs, so explore the STUDENT RESOURCES to find the materials best suited to you.

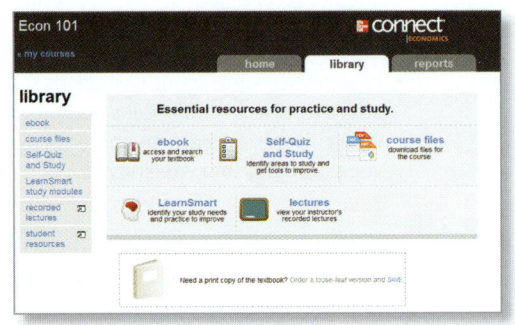

Essentials of
ECONOMICS

The McGraw-Hill Series in Economics

Essentials of
ECONOMICS

Third edition

Stanley L. Brue
Pacific Lutheran University

Campbell R. McConnell
University of Nebraska at Lincoln

Sean M. Flynn
Scripps College

With the special assistance of
Randy R. Grant
Linfield College

McGraw-Hill
Irwin

McGraw-Hill Irwin

ESSENTIALS OF ECONOMICS

Published by McGraw-Hill/Irwin, a business unit of The McGraw-Hill Companies, Inc., 1221 Avenue of the Americas, New York, NY, 10020. 2014 by The McGraw-Hill Companies, Inc. All rights reserved. Printed in the United States of America. Previous editions © 2010 and 2007. No part of this publication may be reproduced or distributed in any form or by any means, or stored in a database or retrieval system, without the prior written consent of The McGraw-Hill Companies, Inc., including, but not limited to, in any network or other electronic storage or transmission, or broadcast for distance learning.

Some ancillaries, including electronic and print components, may not be available to customers outside the United States.

This book is printed on acid-free paper.

5 6 7 8 9 0 DOW/DOW 1 0 9 8 7 6 5

ISBN   978-0-07-351145-0
MHID   0-07-351145-5

Senior Vice President, Products & Markets: *Kurt L. Strand*
Vice President, General Manager, Products & Markets: *Brent Gordon*
Vice President, Content Production & Technology Services: *Kimberly Meriwether David*
Managing Director: *Douglas Reiner*
Brand Manager: *Scott Smith*
Executive Director of Development: *Ann Torbert*
Managing Development Editor: *Christina Kouvelis*
Editorial Coordinator: *Casey Rasch*
Director of Digital Content: *Doug Ruby*
Marketing Manager: *Katie White*
Project Manager: *Pat Frederickson*
Content Project Manager: *Emily Kline*
Buyer II: *Debra R. Sylvester*
Senior Designer: *Matt Diamond*
Senior Content Licensing Specialist: *Keri Johnson*
Photo Researcher: *Michelle Buhr*
Typeface: *10/12 Jansen*
Compositor: *Aptara,® Inc.*
Printer: *R. R. Donnelley*

Library of Congress Cataloging-in-Publication Data

Brue, Stanley L., 1945-
    Essentials of economics/Stanley L. Brue, Pacific Lutheran University, Campbell R. McConnell,
University of Nebraska at Lincoln, Sean M. Flynn, Scripps College; With the special assistance of
Randy R. Grant, Linfield College.—Third edition.
        pages cm.—(The McGraw-Hill series in economics)
    Includes index.
    ISBN 978-0-07-351145-0 (alk. paper)—ISBN 0-07-351145-5 (alk. paper)
    1. Economics. I. McConnell, Campbell R. II. Flynn, Sean Masaki. III. Title.
HB171.B778 2014
330—dc23

                                    2012045332

www.mhhe.com

About the Authors

Stanley L. Brue

Stanley L. Brue did his undergraduate work at Augustana College (S.D.) and received its Distinquished Achievement Award in 1991. He received his Ph.D. from the University of Nebraska–Lincoln. He is a professor at Pacific Lutheran University, where he has been honored as a recipient of the Burlington Northern Faculty Achievement Award. Professor Brue has also received the national Leavey Award for excellence in economic education. He has served as national president and chair of the Board of Trustees of Omicron Delta Epsilon International Economics Honorary. He is coauthor of *Economics*, Nineteenth Edition (McGraw-Hill/Irwin), *Economic Scenes*, Fifth Edition (Prentice-Hall), *Contemporary Labor Economics*, Eighth Edition (McGraw-Hill/Irwin), and *The Evolution of Economic Thought*, Eighth Edition (South-Western). For relaxation, he enjoys international travel, attending sporting events, and skiing with family and friends.

Campbell R. McConnell

Campbell R. McConnell earned his Ph.D. from the University of Iowa after receiving degrees from Cornell College and the University of Illinois. He taught at the University of Nebraska–Lincoln from 1953 until his retirement in 1990. He is coauthor of *Economics*, Nineteenth Edition (McGraw-Hill/Irwin), *Contemporary Labor Economics*, Eighth Edition (McGraw-Hill/Irwin), and has edited readers for the principles and labor economics courses. He is a recipient of both the University of Nebraska Distinguished Teaching Award and the James A. Lake Academic Freedom Award and is past president of the Midwest Economics Association. Professor McConnell was awarded an honorary Doctor of Laws degree from Cornell College in 1973 and received its Distinguished Achievement Award in 1994. His primary areas of interest are labor economics and economic education. He has an extensive collection of jazz recordings and enjoys reading jazz history.

Sean M. Flynn

Sean M. Flynn did his undergraduate work at the University of Southern California before completing his Ph.D. at U.C. Berkeley, where he served as the Head Graduate Student Instructor for the Department of Economics after receiving the Outstanding Graduate Student Instructor Award. He teaches at Scripps College in Claremont, California and is also the author of *Economics for Dummies* (Wiley) and coauthor of *Economics*, Nineteenth Edition (McGraw-Hill/Irwin). His research interests include finance and behavioral economics. An accomplished martial artist, he has represented the United States in international aikido tournaments and is the author of *Understanding Shodokan Aikido* (Shodokan Press). Other hobbies include running, travel, and ethnic food.

Brief Contents

Contents

PART THREE

Product Markets

Resource Markets

Preface

Welcome to the third edition of *Essentials of Economics*, a one-semester principles of economics text derived from McConnell-Brue-Flynn *Economics*, the best-selling two-semester economics textbook. Over the years numerous instructors have requested a short, one-semester version of *Economics* that would cover both microeconomics and macroeconomics. While some other two-semester books simply eliminate chapters, renumber those that remain, and offer the "cut and splice" version as a customized book, this methodology does not fit with our vision of a tightly focused, highly integrated book. We built this text from scratch, incorporating the core content from *Economics* in a format designed specifically for the one-semester course. This book has the clear and careful language and the balanced approach that has made its two-semester counterpart a best-seller, but the pedagogy and topic discussion are much better suited to the needs of the one-semester course.

We think *Essentials of Economics* will fit nicely in various one-term courses. It is sufficiently lively and focused for use in principles courses populated primarily by nonbusiness majors. Also, it is suitably analytical and comprehensive for use in combined micro and macro principles courses for business and potential economics majors. Finally, we think this book—if supplemented with appropriate lecture and reading assignments—will work well in refresher courses for students returning to MBA programs.

However the book is used, our goals remain the same:

- Help the student master the principles essential for understanding the economic problem, specific economic issues, and policy alternatives.
- Help the student understand and apply the economic perspective and reason accurately and objectively about economic matters.
- Promote a lasting student interest in economics and the economy.

What's New and Improved?

One of the benefits of writing a successful text is the opportunity to revise—to delete the outdated and install the new, to rewrite misleading or ambiguous statements, to introduce more relevant illustrations, to improve the organizational structure, and to enhance the learning aids. We trust that you will agree that we have used this opportunity wisely and fully.

Streamlined Coverage

As part of our ongoing effort to streamline presentation, respond to reviewer input, and keep costs down for students, we have moved some material from the previous edition to our website, **www.brue3e.com**. The Chapter One appendix on **Graphs and Their Meaning** and the resource market chapters on **Wage Determination** and **Income Inequality and Poverty** (formerly Chapters 10 and 11, respectively) have been moved to the web. Instructors who cover these chapters will find them easily accessible and that updates of the content and supplements have received the same careful attention as the rest of the book.

New Discussions of the Financial Crisis and the Recession

In this edition, we have focused on incorporating an analysis of the financial crisis, the recession, and the hesitant recovery into our discussions of macroeconomics. Although we found many ways to work the recession into our macro chapters, we are confident that our basic macroeconomic models will serve equally well in explaining economic recovery and expansion back to the economy's historical growth path. The new inclusions relating to the recession simply help students see the relevance of the models to what they are seeing in the news and perhaps experiencing in their own lives. The overall tone of the book, including the macro, continues to be optimistic with respect to the long-term growth prospects of market economies.

Reworked End-of-Chapter Questions and Problems

We have extensively reworked the end-of-chapter questions, and we have added new problems to each chapter. The questions are analytic and often ask for free responses, whereas the problems are mainly quantitative. We have aligned the questions and problems with the learning objectives presented at the beginning of the chapters. All of the questions and problems are assignable through McGraw Hill's *Connect Economics*, and many contain additional algorithmic variations and can be automatically graded within the system.

Chapter-by-Chapter Changes

In addition to the changes and new features listed above, chapter-specific revisions include:

Chapter 1: Limits, Alternatives, and Choices features updated discussion of the 2007–2009 recession and streamlined coverage of the main concepts. The **Chapter One Appendix: Graphs and Their Meaning** has been moved to our website, **www.brue3e.com**.

Chapter 2: The Market System and the Circular Flow includes an improved discussion of the circular flow model, additional coverage of property rights, and updated global data.

Chapter 3: Demand, Supply, and Market Equilibrium begins with a revised introduction to supply and demand and contains additional clarifications of key concepts.

Chapter 4: Elasticity of Demand and Supply provides an updated discussion of elasticity.

Chapter 5: Market Failures: Public Goods and Externalities features improved coverage of market failures, enhanced discussion of public versus private goods, a new

"Illustrating the Idea" piece on the Coase Theorem, and a more complete discussion of correcting for externalities.

Chapter 6: Businesses and Their Costs includes an improved discussion of costs and a new "Applying the Analysis" piece that discusses rising gas prices.

Chapter 7: Pure Competition features revised discussions of pure competition in the long run and efficiency in pure competition, plus an expanded figure illustrating a competitive firm and market in long-run equilibrium.

Chapter 8: Pure Monopoly contains an updated figure showing the inefficiency of pure monopoly relative to a purely competitive industry and a revised discussion of efficiency.

Chapter 9: Monopolistic Competition and Oligopoly includes a revised introduction, an updated figure illustrating the inefficiency of monopolistic competition, and an improved discussion of cartels and collusion.

Chapter 10: GDP and Economic Growth includes a revised discussion of GDP accounting and updated coverage of productivity changes.

Chapter 11: Business Cycles, Unemployment, and Inflation contains a new chapter introduction, an improved discussion of business cycles and their causes, and detailed coverage of current unemployment rates and inflation throughout the world.

Chapter 12: Aggregate Demand and Aggregate Supply features detailed discussion, application, and analysis of the recession of 2007–2009.

Chapter 13: Fiscal Policy, Deficits, and Debt includes important updates related to the recession, the subsequent policy response, and the debt debate.

Chapter 14: Money, Banking, and Financial Institutions provides an extensive discussion of the 2007–2008 financial crisis and the postcrisis financial services industry.

Chapter 15: Interest Rates and Monetary Policy features updated coverage of recent U.S. monetary policy, a new explanation of the liquidity trap, a new discussion of the Fed's response to the financial crisis, and a new "Applying the Analysis" piece on the Fed's balance sheet and its extensive growth.

Chapter 16: International Trade and Exchange Rates includes updated material on recent U.S. trade deficits and a revised discussion related to changes in the relative value of the U.S. dollar.

Chapters on Wage Determination and Income Inequality and Poverty have been relocated to our website, **www.brue3e.com**. Revisions include improved discussion and significant updates to the data on distribution of income, poverty, and income maintenance programs.

Distinguishing Features and Third Edition Changes

Essentials of Economics includes several features that we think add up to a unique whole.

State-of-the-Art Design and Pedagogy

Essentials incorporates a single-column design with a host of pedagogical aids, including a strategically placed "To the Student" statement, chapter opening objectives, definitions in the margins, combined tables and graphs, complete chapter summaries, lists of key terms, carefully constructed study questions, connections to our

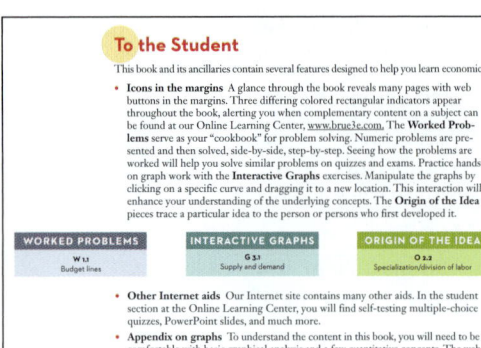

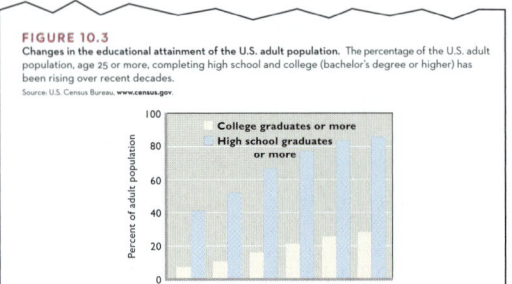

FIGURE 10.3
Changes in the educational attainment of the U.S. adult population. The percentage of the U.S. adult population, age 25 or more, completing high school and college (bachelor's degree or higher) has been rising over recent decades.
Source: U.S. Census Bureau, www.census.gov.

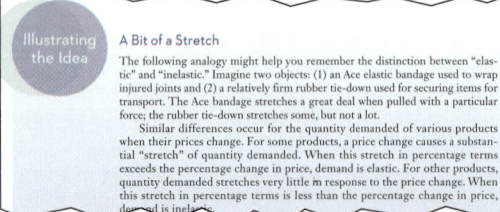

website, an appendix on graphs and a web appendix on additional examples of demand and supply, an extensive glossary, and historical statistics on the inside covers.

Focus on Core Models

Essentials of Economics shortens and simplifies explanations where appropriate but stresses the importance of the economic perspective, including explaining and applying core economic models. Our strategy is to develop a limited set of essential models, illustrate them with analogies or anecdotes, explain them thoroughly, and apply them to real-world situations. Eliminating unnecessary graphs and elaborations makes perfect sense in the one-semester course, but cutting explanations of the truly *essential* graphs does not. In dealing with the basics, brevity at the expense of clarity is false economy.

We created a student-oriented one-semester textbook that draws on the methodological strengths of the discipline and helps students improve their analytical reasoning skills. Regardless of students' eventual majors, they will discover that such skills are highly valuable in their workplaces.

Illustrating the Idea

We include numerous analogies, examples, and anecdotes to help drive home central economic ideas in a lively, colorful, and easy-to-remember way. For instance, elastic versus inelastic demand is illustrated by comparing the stretch of an Ace bandage and that of a tight rubber tie-down. Student exam scores help demonstrate the difference between marginal product and average product. Public goods and the free-rider problem are illustrated by public art, while a pizza analogy walks students through the equity-efficiency trade-off. Inflation as a hidden tax is illustrated by a story of the prince of the realm clipping coins. These brief vignettes flow directly from the preceding content and segue to the content that follows, rather than being "boxed off" away from the flow and therefore easily overlooked.

New to this edition is an *Illustrating the Idea* piece about beekeepers that is used to explain the Coase Theorem.

Applying the Analysis

A glance though this book's pages will demonstrate that this is an application-oriented textbook. *Applying the Analysis* pieces immediately follow the development of economic analysis and are part of the flow of the chapters, rather than segregated from the main-body discussion in a traditional boxed format. For example, the basics of the economic perspective are applied to why customers tend to try to wait in the shortest checkout lines. The book illustrates inelasticity of demand (with changing supply) with an explanation of fluctuating farm income. Differences in elasticity of supply are contrasted by the changing prices of antiques versus reproductions. Hidden car-retrieval systems (such as Lojack) explain the concept of positive externalities. The book describes the principal-agent problem via the problems of corporate accounting and financial fraud. The idea of minimum efficient scale is applied to ready-mix concrete plants and assembly plants for large commercial airplanes. The difference in adult and child pricing for tickets to a ballgame compared to the pricing at the concession stands illustrates the concept of price discrimination. The aggregate demand model is applied to specific periods of inflation and recession, while the trade theory discussion touches on the issue of the offshoring of U.S. jobs. These and many other applications clearly demonstrate to beginning students the relevance and usefulness of mastering the basic economic principles and models.

Applications covering rising gasoline prices, the Federal Reserve's balance sheet, and the financial crisis have been added to this edition.

> **Price Floors on Wheat**
>
> A **price floor** is a minimum price fixed by the government. A price at or above the price floor is legal; a price below it is not. Price floors above equilibrium prices are usually invoked when society feels that the free functioning of the market system has not provided a sufficient income for certain groups of resource suppliers or producers. Supported prices for agricultural products and current minimum wages are two examples of price (or wage) floors. Let's look at the former.
>
> Suppose that many farmers have extremely low incomes when the price of wheat is at its equilibrium value of $2 per bushel. The government decides to help out by establishing a legal price floor (or "price support") of $3 per bushel.
>
> What will be the effects? At any price above the equilibrium price, quantity supplied will exceed quantity demanded—that is, there will be a persistent surplus of the product. Farmers will be willing to produce and offer for sale more wheat than private buyers are willing to buy at the $3 price floor. As we saw
>
> *Applying the Analysis*
>
> **price floor** A legally established minimum (above-equilibrium) price for a product.

Photo Ops

Photo sets called *Photo Ops* are included throughout the book to add visual interest, break up the density, and highlight important distinctions. Just a few of the many examples are sets of photos on complements versus substitutes in consumption, homogeneous versus differentiated products, economic stocks versus economic flows, substitute resources versus complementary resources, consumer durables versus nondurables versus services, and intermediate versus final goods.

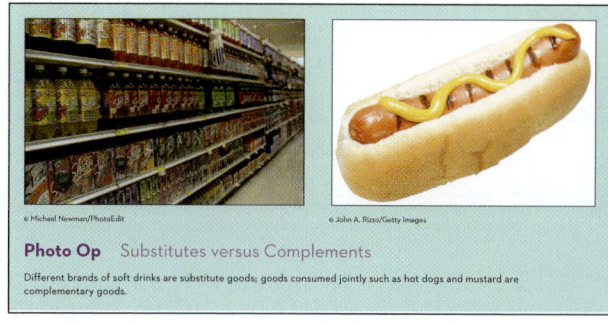

© Michael Newman/PhotoEdit   © John A. Rizzo/Getty Images

Photo Op   Substitutes versus Complements

Different brands of soft drinks are substitute goods; goods consumed jointly such as hot dogs and mustard are complementary goods.

Photo Ops on traffic congestion and holiday lighting contrast negative and positive externalities, large- and small-scale production activities illustrate economies and diseconomies of scale, and Social Security checks and food stamps highlight the differences between social insurance and public assistance.

Web Buttons

We link the book directly to our website, **www.brue3e.com**, via icons that appear throughout the book to indicate that additional content on a subject can be found online. There are three Button types:

INTERACTIVE GRAPHS

G 13.1
Crowding out

ORIGIN OF THE IDEA

O 13.1
Crowding out

- The teal rectangle to the left directs students to **Interactive Graphs.** Developed under the supervision of Norris Peterson of Pacific Lutheran University, this interactive feature depicts major graphs and instructs students to shift the curves, observe the outcomes, and derive relevant generalizations. This hands-on graph work will greatly reinforce the main graphs and their meaning.

- The green rectangle directs students to **Origins of the Idea.** These brief histories, written by Randy

> **Crowding-Out Effect**
>
> **crowding-out effect** A decrease in private investment caused by higher interest rates that result from the federal government's increased borrowing to finance deficits (or debt).
>
> Another potential flaw of fiscal policy is the so-called **crowding-out effect:** An expansionary fiscal policy (deficit spending) may increase the interest rate and reduce investment spending, thereby weakening or canceling the stimulus of the expansionary policy. The rising interest rate might also potentially crowd out interest-sensitive consumption spending (such as purchasing automobiles on credit). But since investment is the most volatile component of GDP, the crowding-out effect focuses its attention on investment and whether the stimulus provided by deficit spending may be partly or even fully neutralized by an offsetting reduction in investment spending.
>
> To see the potential problem, realize that whenever the government borrows money (as it must if it is deficit spending), it increases the overall demand for money. If the monetary authorities are holding the money supply constant, this increase in demand will raise the price paid for borrowing money: the interest rate. Because investment spending varies inversely with the interest rate, some investment will
>
>
>
> **INTERACTIVE GRAPHS**
> G 13.1
> Crowding out
>
> **ORIGIN OF THE IDEA**
> O 13.2
> Crowding out

WORKED PROBLEMS

W 1.1
Budget lines

Grant of Linfield College (OR), examine the origins of scores of major ideas identified in the book. Students will find it interesting to learn about the economists who first developed such ideas as opportunity costs, equilibrium price, creative destruction, comparative advantage, and elasticity.

- The blue rectangle to the left is our web button that directs students to **Worked Problems.** Written by Norris Peterson, these pieces consist of side-by-side computational questions and computational procedures used to derive the answers. From a student perspective, they provide "cookbook" help for problem solving.

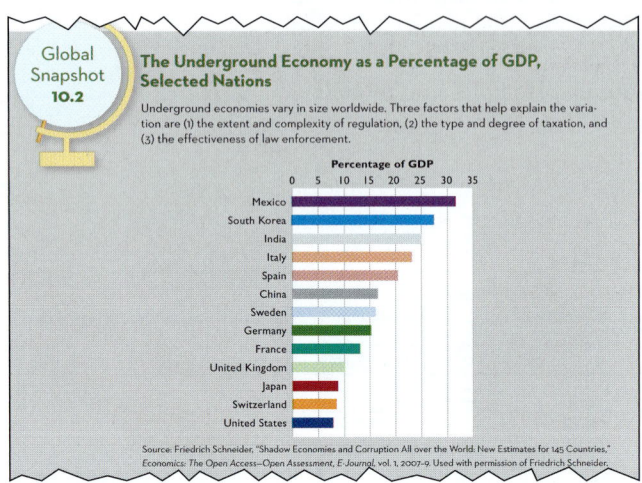

Global Snapshot 10.2

The Underground Economy as a Percentage of GDP, Selected Nations

Underground economies vary in size worldwide. Three factors that help explain the variation are (1) the extent and complexity of regulation, (2) the type and degree of taxation, and (3) the effectiveness of law enforcement.

Source: Friedrich Schneider, "Shadow Economies and Corruption All over the World: New Estimates for 145 Countries," *Economics: The Open Access–Open Assessment, E-Journal,* vol. 1, 2007–9. Used with permission of Friedrich Schneider.

Global Snapshots

Global Snapshot pieces show bar charts and line graphs that compare data for a particular year or other time period among selected nations. Examples of lists and comparisons include income per capita, the world's 10 largest corporations, the world's top brand names, standardized budget deficits or surpluses, the index of economic freedom, sizes of underground economies, rates of economic growth, exports as percentages of GDP, and so forth. These Global Snapshots join other significant international content to help convey that the United States operates in a global economy.

Pedagogical Aids
Supplements for Students

Essentials of Economics, 3e is accompanied by many high-quality supplements that help students master the subject.

- ***Study Guide*** One of the world's leading experts on economic education—William Walstad of the University of Nebraska at Lincoln—has prepared the *Study Guide.* Each chapter contains an introductory statement, a checklist of behavioral objectives, an outline, a list of important terms, fill-in questions, problems and projects, objective questions, and discussion questions. The text's glossary is repeated in the *Study Guide* so that the student does not have to go back and forth between books. Many students will find this printed "portable tutor" indispensable.
- ***Online Learning Center*** (**www.brue3e.com**) Along with the *Interactive Graphs, Worked Problems,* and *Origin of the Idea* pieces, the student portion of the website includes many learning aids for students. For example, there are web-based study questions, self-grading quizzes updated and revised by Emilio Gomez of Palomar College, learning objectives, and PowerPoint presentations—all specific to *Essentials of Economics,* 3e. Students can also access the Solman videos, a set of more than 250 minutes of video created by Paul Solman of *The News Hour with Jim Lehrer.* These videos cover core economic concepts such as elasticity, deregulation, and perfect competition. Students can watch this material on their computers or download the content to a smartphone or tablet.

Digital Solutions

McGraw-Hill's Connect™ Economics

Less Managing. More Teaching. Greater Learning. McGraw-Hill's *Connect Economics* is a web-based assignment and assessment platform that connects students with the tools and resources they'll need to achieve success. *Connect Economics* helps prepare students for their future by enabling faster learning, more efficient studying, and higher retention of knowledge. *Connect Economics* offers a number of powerful tools and features to make managing assignments easier, so faculty can spend more time teaching. With *Connect Economics*, students can engage with their coursework anytime and anywhere, making the learning process more accessible and efficient. *Connect Economics* offers the features as described here.

Simple Assignment Management With *Connect Economics*, creating assignments is easier than ever, so you can spend more time teaching and less time managing. The assignment management function enables you to

- Create and deliver assignments easily with selectable end-of-chapter questions and test bank items.
- Streamline lesson planning, student progress reporting, and assignment grading to make classroom management more efficient than ever.
- Go paperless with the e-book and online submission and grading of student assignments.

Smart Grading When it comes to studying, time is precious. *Connect Economics* helps students learn more efficiently by providing feedback and practice material when they need it, where they need it. When it comes to teaching, your time also is precious. The grading function enables you to

- Score assignments automatically, giving students immediate feedback on their work and side-by-side comparisons with correct answers.
- Access and review each response; manually change grades or leave comments for students to review.
- Reinforce classroom concepts with practice tests and instant quizzes.

Instructor Library The *Connect Economics* Instructor Library is your repository for additional resources to improve student engagement in and out of class. You can select and use any asset that enhances your lecture.

Student Study Center The *Connect Economics* Student Study Center is the place for students to access additional resources. The Student Study Center

- Offers students quick access to lectures, practice materials, e-book, and more.
- Provides instant practice material and study questions, easily accessible on the go.
- Gives students access to the Self-Quiz and Study described below.

LearnSmart: Diagnostic and Adaptive Learning of Concepts Students want to make the best use of their study time. The LearnSmart adaptive self-study technology within *Connect Economics* provides students with a seamless combination of practice, assessment, and remediation for the most important concepts in the course. LearnSmart's intelligent software adapts to every student response and automatically delivers concepts that advance the student's understanding while reducing time devoted to the concepts already mastered. The result for every student is the fastest path to mastery of core concepts. LearnSmart

- Applies an intelligent concept engine to identify the relationships between concepts and to serve new concepts to each student only when he or she is ready.
- Adapts automatically to each student, so students spend less time on the topics they understand and practice more those they have yet to master.
- Provides continual reinforcement and remediation, but gives only as much guidance as students need.
- Integrates diagnostics as part of the learning experience.
- Enables you to assess which concepts students have efficiently learned on their own, thus freeing class time for more applications and discussion.

Self-Quiz and Study   The Self-Quiz and Study (SQS) connects each student to the learning resources needed for success in the course. For each chapter, students

- Take a practice test to initiate the Self-Quiz and Study.
- Immediately upon completing the practice test, see how their performance compares to chapter Learning Objectives to be achieved within each section of the chapter.
- Receive a Study Plan that recommends specific readings from the text, supplemental study material, and practice work that will improve their understanding and mastery of each learning objective.

Student Progress Tracking   *Connect Economics* keeps instructors informed about how each student, section, and class are performing, allowing for more productive use of lecture and office hours. The progress-tracking function enables you to

- View scored work immediately and track individual or group performance with assignment and grade reports.
- Access an instant view of student or class performance relative to learning objectives.
- Collect data and generate reports required by many accreditation organizations, such as AACSB.

Lecture Capture   Increase the attention paid to lecture discussion by decreasing the attention paid to note taking. For an additional charge, Lecture Capture offers new ways for students to focus on the in-class discussion, knowing they can revisit important topics later. Lecture Capture enables you to

- Record and distribute your lecture with a click of a button.
- Record and index PowerPoint presentations and anything shown on your computer so it is easily searchable, frame by frame.
- Offer access to lectures anytime and anywhere by computer, iPod, or mobile device.
- Increase intent listening and class participation by easing students' concerns about note-taking.

Lecture Capture will make it more likely you will see students' faces, not the tops of their heads.

- To learn more about Tegrity, watch a 2-minute Flash demo at **http://tegritycampus. mhhe.com.**

McGraw-Hill's Connect™ Plus Economics   McGraw-Hill reinvents the text-book learning experience for the modern student with *Connect Plus Economics*. A seamless integration of an e-book and *Connect Economics*, *Connect Plus Economics* provides all of the features mentioned above plus the following:

- An integrated e-book, allowing for anytime, anywhere access to the textbook.
- Dynamic links between the problems or questions you assign to your students and the location in the e-book where that problem or question is covered.
- A powerful search function to pinpoint and connect key concepts in a snap.

In short, *Connect Economics* offers you and your students powerful tools and features that optimize your time and energies, enabling you to focus on course content, teaching, and student learning.

For more information about Connect, please visit **www.mcgrawhillconnect.com,** or contact your local McGraw-Hill sales representative.

McGraw-Hill Customer Care Contact Information

At McGraw-Hill, we understand that getting the most from new technology can be challenging. That's why our services don't stop after you purchase our products. You can e-mail our Product Specialists 24 hours a day to get product-training online. Or you can search our knowledge bank of frequently asked questions on our support website. For customer support, call **800-331-5094,** e-mail hmsupport@mcgraw-hill.com, or visit **www.mhhe.com/support.** One of our technical support analysts will be able to assist you in a timely fashion.

CourseSmart

CourseSmart is a new way for faculty to find and review e-textbooks. It's also a great option for students who are interested in accessing their course materials digitally. CourseSmart offers thousands of the most commonly adopted textbooks across hundreds of courses from a wide variety of higher education publishers. It is the only place for faculty to review and compare the full text of a textbook online. At CourseSmart, students can save up to 50 percent off the cost of a print book, reduce their impact on the environment, and gain access to powerful web tools for learning including full text search, notes and highlighting, and e-mail tools for sharing notes between classmates. Your e-book also includes tech support in case you ever need help. Finding your e-book is easy. Visit **www.CourseSmart.com** and search by title, author, or ISBN.

Online Learning Center

At **www.brue3e.com** students have access to several learning aids. Along with the Interactive Graphs, Worked Problems, and Origin of the Idea pieces, the student portion of the website includes web-based study questions, self-grading quizzes, and PowerPoint presentations. For math-minded students, there is a "See the Math" section, written by Norris Peterson, where the mathematical details of the concepts in the text can be explored.

The password-protected instructor's side of the Online Learning Center holds all of the supplementary instructor resource materials.

Premium Content

The Premium Content, available at the Online Learning Center, enables students to study and self-test on their computer or on the go.

- One of the world's leading experts on economic education—William Walstad of the University of Nebraska at Lincoln—has prepared the *Study Guide*. Each chapter contains an introductory statement, a checklist of behavioral objectives, an outline, a list of important terms, fill-in questions, problems and projects, objective questions, and discussion questions. Many students will find this "digital tutor" indispensable.

- The Solman Videos, a set of more than 250 minutes of video created by Paul Solman of *The News Hour with Jim Lehrer*, cover core economic concepts such as elasticity, deregulation, and perfect competition.

Supplements for Instructors

Instructor's Manual

Amy Stapp of Cuesta College prepared the Instructor's Manual. It includes chapter learning objectives, outlines, and summaries; numerous teaching suggestions; discussions of "student stumbling blocks;" listings of data and visual aid sources with suggestions for classroom use; and sample chapter quizzes. Available in MS Word on the instructor's side of the website, the manual enables instructors to print portions of the contents, complete with their own additions and alterations, for use as student handouts or in whatever ways they wish.

Test Bank

The *Essentials of Economics* Test Bank, originally written by William Walstad and newly compiled and updated by Mark Wilson of West Virginia University and Jeffrey Phillips of Colby-Sawyer College, contains multiple choice and true-false questions. Each question is tied to a learning objective, topic, and AACSB Assurance of Learning and Bloom's Taxonomy guidelines. While crafting tests in EZTest Online, instructors can use the whole chapter, scramble questions, and narrow the group by selecting the criteria. The Test Bank is also available in MS Word on the instructor's side of the website.

PowerPoint Presentations

Amy Chataginer of Mississippi Gulf Coast Community College created these in-depth slides to accompany lectures. The slides highlight all the main points of each chapter and include all of the figures and key tables from the text, as well as additional discussion notes. Each slide is tied to a learning objective.

Digital Image Library

Every graph and table in the text is available on the website. These figures allow instructors to create their own PowerPoint presentations and lecture materials.

Computerized Test Bank Online

A comprehensive bank of test questions is provided within McGraw-Hill's flexible electronic testing program EZ Test Online, **www.eztestonline.com.** EZ Test Online allows instructors to simply and quickly create tests or quizzes for their students. Instructors can select questions from multiple McGraw-Hill test banks or author their own, and then either print the finalized test or quiz for paper distribution or publish it online for access via the Internet.

This user-friendly program allows instructors to sort questions by format; select questions by learning objectives or Bloom's taxonomy tags; edit existing questions or add new ones; and scramble questions for multiple versions of the same test. Instructors can export their tests for use in WebCT, Blackboard, and PageOut, making it easy to share assessment materials with colleagues, adjuncts, and TAs. Instant scoring and feedback are provided, and EZ Test Online's record book is designed to easily export to instructor gradebooks.

Assurance of Learning Ready

Many educational institutions today are focused on the notion of *assurance of learning*, an important element of many accreditation standards. *Essentials of Economics*, 3rd edition is designed specifically to support your assurance of learning initiatives with a simple, yet powerful, solution.

Each chapter in the book begins with a list of numbered learning objectives, which appear throughout the chapter as well as in the end-of-chapter content. Every Test Bank question for *Essentials of Economics* maps to a specific chapter learning objective in the textbook. Each Test Bank question also identifies topic area, level of difficulty, Bloom's Taxonomy level, and AACSB skill area. You can use our Test Bank software, *EZ Test* and *EZ Test Online*, or *Connect Economics* to easily search for learning objectives that directly relate to the learning objectives for your course. You can then use the reporting features of *EZ Test* to aggregate student results in similar fashion, making the collection and presentation of Assurance of Learning data simple and easy.

AACSB Statement

McGraw-Hill/Irwin is a proud corporate member of AACSB International. Understanding the importance and value of AACSB accreditation, *Essentials of Economics* recognizes the curriculum guidelines detailed in the AACSB standards for business accreditation by connecting selected questions in the text and the Test Bank to the general knowledge and skill guidelines in the AACSB standards.

The statements contained in *Essentials of Economics* are provided only as a guide for the users of this textbook. The AACSB leaves content coverage and assessment within the purview of individual schools, the mission of the school, and the faculty. While *Essentials of Economics* and the teaching package make no claim of any specific AACSB qualification or evaluation, we have, within *Essentials of Economics*, labeled selected questions according to the six general knowledge and skills areas.

Acknowledgments

We give special thanks to Randy R. Grant of Linfield College, who not only wrote the Origin of the Idea pieces on our website but also served as the content coordinator for

Essentials of Economics. Professor Grant modified and seamlessly incorporated appropriate new content and revisions that the authors made in the nineteenth edition of *Economics* into *Essentials.* He also updated the tables and other information in *Essentials of Economics* and made various improvements that he deemed helpful or were suggested to him by the authors, reviewers, and publisher.

We also want to acknowledge Norris Peterson of Pacific Lutheran University, who created the See the Math pieces and the Worked Problem pieces on our website. Professor Peterson also oversaw the development of the Interactive Graph pieces that are on the site. Finally, we wish to acknowledge William Walstad and Tom Barbiero (the coauthor of the Canadian edition of *Economics*) for their ongoing ideas and insights.

We are greatly indebted to an all-star group of professionals at McGraw-Hill—in particular Douglas Reiner, Christina Kouvelis, Casey Rasch, and Pat Frederickson, Katie White, and Brent Gordon for their publishing and marketing expertise. We thank Keri Johnson and Michelle Buhr for their selection of Photo Op images. Matt Diamond provided the vibrant interior design and cover.

The third edition has benefited from a number of perceptive formal reviews. The reviewers, listed at the end of the preface, were a rich source of suggestions for this revision. To each of you, and others we may have inadvertently overlooked, thank you for your considerable help in improving *Essentials of Economics.*

Stanley L. Brue
Sean M. Flynn
Campbell R. McConnell

Contributors

Reviewers

Mark Abajian, *San Diego City College*
Rebecca Arnold, *San Diego Mesa College*
Benjamin Artz, *University of Wisconsin, Milwaukee*
Clare Battista, *California Polytechnic State University*
Derek Berry, *Calhoun Community College*
Laura Jean Bhadra, *Northern Virginia Community College, Manassas*
Philip Bohan, *Ventura College*
Kalyan Chakraborty, *Emporia State University*
Jan Christopher, *Delaware State University*
Donald Coffin, *Indiana University Northwest*
Diana Denison, *Red Rocks Community College*
John Allen Deskins, *Creighton University, Omaha*
Caf Dowlah, *Queensborough Community College*
Mariano Escobedo, *Columbus State Community College*
Charles Fairchild, *Northern Virginia Community College, Manassas*
Charles Fraley, *Cincinnati State Tech and Community College*
Amy Gibson, *Christopher Newport University*
John Gibson, *Indiana University Northwest*

Robert Harris, *IUPUI, Indianapolis*
Mark Healy, *William Rainey Harper College*
Melinda Hickman, *Doane College*
Glenn Hsu, *Kishwaukee College*
Scott Hunt, *Columbus State Community College*
John Ifcher, *Santa Clara University*
Vani Kotcherlakota, *University of Nebraska, Kearney*
Marie Kratochvil, *Nassau Community College*
Teresa Laughlin, *Palomar College*
Melissa Lind, *University of Texas, Arlington*
Keith Malone, *University of North Alabama*
Khalid Mehtabdin, *College of Saint Rose*
Jennifer Kelleher Michaels, *Emmanuel College*
Babu Nahata, *University of Louisville*
Jim Payne, *Calhoun Community College*
Michael Petrowsky, *Glendale Community College*
Mitchell Redlo, *Monroe Community College*
Belinda Roman, *Palo Alto College*
Dave St. Clair, *California State University, East Bay*
Courtenay Stone, *Ball State University*
Gary Stone, *Winthrop University*
Anh Le Tran, *Lasell College*
Miao Wang, *Marquette University*
Timothy Wunder, *University of Texas, Arlington*

To the Student

This book and its ancillaries contain several features designed to help you learn economics:

- **Icons in the margins** A glance through the book reveals many pages with web buttons in the margins. Three differing colored rectangular indicators appear throughout the book, alerting you when complementary content on a subject can be found at our Online Learning Center, **www.brue3e.com.** The **Worked Problems** serve as your "cookbook" for problem solving. Numeric problems are presented and then solved, side-by-side, step-by-step. Seeing how the problems are worked will help you solve similar problems on quizzes and exams. Practice hands-on graph work with the **Interactive Graphs** exercises. Manipulate the graphs by clicking on a specific curve and dragging it to a new location. This interaction will enhance your understanding of the underlying concepts. The **Origin of the Idea** pieces trace a particular idea to the person or persons who first developed it.

WORKED PROBLEMS	INTERACTIVE GRAPHS	ORIGIN OF THE IDEA
W 1.1 Budget lines	**G 3.1** Supply and demand	**O 2.2** Specialization/division of labor

- **Other Internet aids** Our Internet site contains many other aids. In the student section at the Online Learning Center, you will find self-testing multiple-choice quizzes, PowerPoint slides, and much more.

- **Appendix on graphs** To understand the content in this book, you will need to be comfortable with basic graphical analysis and a few quantitative concepts. The web appendix for Chapter 1 reviews graphing and slopes of curves. Be sure not to skip it.

- **Key terms** Key terms are set in boldface type within the chapters, defined in the margins, listed at the end of each chapter, and again defined in the Glossary toward the end of the book.

- **"Illustrating the Idea" and "Applying the Analysis"** These sections flow logically and smoothly from the content that precedes them. They are part and parcel of the development of the ideas and cannot be skipped. Each "Illustrating the Idea" and "Applying the Analysis" section is followed by a question.

- **Questions and Problems** The end of each chapter features separate sections of Questions and Problems. The Questions are analytic and often ask for free responses, while the Problems are more computational. Each is keyed to a particular learning objective (LO) in the list of LOs at the beginning of the chapter. At the Online Learning Center, there are multiple-choice quizzes and one or more web-based questions for each chapter.

- **Study Guide** We enthusiastically recommend the *Study Guide* accompanying this text. This "portable tutor" contains not only a broad sampling of various kinds of questions but a host of useful learning aids.

Our two main goals are to help you understand and apply economics and help you improve your analytical skills. An understanding of economics will enable you to comprehend a whole range of economic, social, and political problems that otherwise would seem puzzling and perplexing. Also, your study will enhance reasoning skills that are highly prized in the workplace.

Good luck with your study. We think it will be well worth your time and effort.

CHAPTER ONE

Limits, Alternatives, and Choices

After reading this chapter, you should be able to:

1. Define economics and the features of the economic perspective.

2. Describe the role of economic theory in economics.

3. Distinguish microeconomics from macroeconomics.

4. List the categories of scarce resources and delineate the nature of the economizing problem.

5. Apply production possibilities analysis, increasing opportunity costs, and economic growth.

6. (Web appendix) Understand graphs, curves, and slopes as they relate to economics.

(An appendix on understanding graphs can be found on the textbook website. If you need a quick review of this mathematical tool, you might benefit by reading the appendix first.)

Economics is about wants and means. Biologically, people need only air, water, food, clothing, and shelter. But in modern society people also desire goods and services that provide a more comfortable or affluent standard of living. We want bottled water, soft drinks, and fruit juices, not just water from the creek. We want salads, burgers, and pizzas, not just berries and nuts. We want jeans, suits, and coats, not just woven reeds. We want apartments, condominiums, or houses, not just mud huts. And, as the saying goes, "That's not the half of it." We also want flat-panel TVs, Internet service, education, homeland security, cell phones, and much more.

Fortunately, society possesses productive resources such as labor and managerial talent, tools and machinery, and land and mineral deposits. These resources, employed in the economic system (or simply the economy), help us produce goods and services that satisfy many of our economic wants. But the blunt reality is that our economic wants far exceed the productive capacity of our scarce (limited) resources. We are forced to make choices. This unyielding truth underlies the definition of **economics,** which is the social science concerned with how individuals, institutions, and society make choices under conditions of scarcity.

ORIGIN OF THE IDEA
O 1.1
Origin of the term "economics"

The Economic Perspective

economics
The study of how people, institutions, and society make economic choices under conditions of scarcity.

Economists view things through a particular perspective. This **economic perspective,** or economic way of thinking, has several critical and closely interrelated features.

Scarcity and Choice

From our definition of economics, it is easy to see why economists view the world through the lens of scarcity. Scarce economic resources mean limited goods and services. Scarcity restricts options and demands choices. Because we "can't have it all," we must decide what we will have and what we must forgo.

economic perspective
A viewpoint that envisions individuals and institutions making rational decisions by comparing the marginal benefits and marginal costs of their actions.

At the core of economics is the idea that "there is no free lunch." You may be treated to lunch, making it "free" to you, but someone bears a cost. Because all resources are either privately or collectively owned by members of society, ultimately, scarce inputs of land, equipment, farm labor, the labor of cooks and waiters, and managerial talent are required. Because these resources could have been used to produce something else, society sacrifices those other goods and services in making the lunch available. Economists call such sacrifices **opportunity costs:** To obtain more of one thing, society forgoes the opportunity of getting the next best thing. That sacrifice is the opportunity cost of the choice.

opportunity cost
The value of the good, service, or time forgone to obtain something else.

Illustrating the Idea

Did Gates, Winfrey, and Rodriguez Make Bad Choices?

The importance of opportunity costs in decision making is illustrated by different choices people make with respect to college. College graduates usually earn about 50 percent more during their lifetimes than persons with just high school diplomas. For most capable students, "Go to college, stay in college, and earn a degree" is very sound advice.

Yet Microsoft cofounder Bill Gates and talk-show host Oprah Winfrey* both dropped out of college, and baseball star Alex Rodriguez ("A-Rod") never even bothered to enroll. What were they thinking? Unlike most students, Gates faced enormous opportunity costs for staying in college. He had a vision for his company, and his starting work young helped ensure Microsoft's success. Similarly, Winfrey landed a spot in local television news when she was a teenager, eventually producing and starring in the *Oprah Winfrey Show* when she was 32 years old. Getting a degree in her twenties might have interrupted the string of successes that made her famous talk show possible. And Rodriguez knew that professional athletes have short careers. Therefore, going to college directly after high school would have taken away four years of his peak earning potential.

So Gates, Winfrey, and Rodriguez understood opportunity costs and made their choices accordingly. The size of opportunity costs greatly matters in making individual decisions.

Question:
Professional athletes sometimes return to college after they retire from professional sports. How does that college decision relate to opportunity costs?

* Winfrey eventually went back to school and earned a degree from Tennessee State University when she was in her thirties.

Purposeful Behavior

Economics assumes that human behavior reflects "rational self-interest." Individuals look for and pursue opportunities to increase their **utility:** pleasure, happiness, or satisfaction. They allocate their time, energy, and money to maximize their satisfaction. Because they weigh costs and benefits, their decisions are "purposeful" or "rational," not "random" or "chaotic."

utility
The satisfaction obtained from consuming a good or service.

Consumers are purposeful in deciding what goods and services to buy. Business firms are purposeful in deciding what products to produce and how to produce them. Government entities are purposeful in deciding what public services to provide and how to finance them.

> **ORIGIN OF THE IDEA**
> **O 1.2**
> Utility

"Purposeful behavior" does not assume that people and institutions are immune from faulty logic and therefore are perfect decision makers. They sometimes make mistakes. Nor does it mean that people's decisions are unaffected by emotion or the decisions of those around them. People sometimes are impulsive or emulative. "Purposeful behavior" simply means that people make decisions with some desired outcome in mind.

Nor is rational self-interest the same as selfishness. We will find that increasing one's own wage, rent, interest, or profit normally requires identifying and satisfying somebody else's want. Also, many people make personal sacrifices to others without expecting any monetary reward. They contribute time and money to charities because they derive pleasure from doing so. Parents help pay for their children's education for the same reason. These self-interested, but unselfish, acts help maximize the givers' satisfaction as much as any personal purchase of goods or services. Self-interested behavior is simply behavior designed to increase personal satisfaction, however it may be derived.

Marginalism: Comparing Benefits and Costs

The economic perspective focuses largely on **marginal analysis**—comparisons of marginal benefits and marginal costs. To economists, "marginal" means "extra," "additional," or "a change in." Most choices or decisions involve changes in the status quo, meaning the existing state of affairs.

marginal analysis
The comparison of marginal ("extra" or "additional") benefits and marginal costs, usually for decision making.

Should you attend school for another year? Should you study an extra hour for an exam? Should you supersize your fries? Similarly, should a business expand or reduce its output? Should government increase or decrease its funding for a missile defense system?

Each option involves marginal benefits and, because of scarce resources, marginal costs. In making choices rationally, the decision maker must compare those two amounts. Example: You and your fiancée are shopping for an engagement ring. Should you buy a $\frac{1}{2}$-carat diamond, a $\frac{5}{8}$-carat diamond, a $\frac{3}{4}$-carat diamond, a 1-carat diamond, or something even larger? The marginal cost of a larger-size diamond is the added expense beyond the cost of the smaller-size diamond. The marginal benefit is the perceived greater lifetime pleasure (utility) from the larger-size stone. If the marginal benefit of the larger diamond exceeds its marginal cost (and you can afford it), buy the larger stone. But if the marginal cost is more than the marginal benefit, you should buy the smaller diamond instead—even if you can afford the larger stone!

> **ORIGIN OF THE IDEA**
> **O 1.3**
> Marginal analysis

In a world of scarcity, the decision to obtain the marginal benefit associated with some specific option always includes the marginal cost of forgoing something else. The money spent on the larger-size diamond means forgoing some other product. An opportunity cost, the value of the next best thing forgone, is always present whenever a choice is made.

Applying the Analysis

Fast-Food Lines

The economic perspective is useful in analyzing all sorts of behaviors. Consider an everyday example: the behavior of fast-food customers. When customers enter the restaurant, they go to the shortest line, believing that line will minimize their time cost of obtaining food. They are acting purposefully; time is limited, and people prefer using it in some way other than standing in a long line.

If one fast-food line is temporarily shorter than other lines, some people will move to that line. These movers apparently view the time saving from the shorter line (marginal benefit) as exceeding the cost of moving from their present line (marginal cost). The line switching tends to equalize line lengths. No further movement of customers between lines occurs once all lines are about equal.

Fast-food customers face another cost-benefit decision when a clerk opens a new station at the counter. Should they move to the new station or stay put? Those who shift to the new line decide that the time saving from the move exceeds the extra cost of physically moving. In so deciding, customers must also consider just how quickly they can get to the new station compared with others who may be contemplating the same move. (Those who hesitate in this situation are lost!)

Customers at the fast-food establishment do not have perfect information when they select lines. Thus, not all decisions turn out as expected. For example, you might enter a short line and find someone in front of you is ordering hamburgers and fries for 40 people in the Greyhound bus parked out back (and the employee is a trainee)! Nevertheless, at the time you made your decision, you thought it was optimal.

Finally, customers must decide what food to order when they arrive at the counter. In making their choices, they again compare marginal costs and marginal benefits in attempting to obtain the greatest personal satisfaction for their expenditure.

Economists believe that what is true for the behavior of customers at fast-food restaurants is true for economic behavior in general. Faced with an array of choices, consumers, workers, and businesses rationally compare marginal costs and marginal benefits in making decisions.

Question:
Have you ever gone to a fast-food restaurant only to observe long lines and then leave? Use the economic perspective to explain your behavior.

scientific method
The systematic pursuit of knowledge by observing facts and formulating and testing hypotheses to obtain theories, principles, and laws.

Theories, Principles, and Models

Like the physical and life sciences, as well as other social sciences, economics relies on the **scientific method.** That procedure consists of several elements:

• Observing real-world behavior and outcomes.

- Based on those observations, formulating a possible explanation of cause and effect (hypothesis).
- Testing this explanation by comparing the outcomes of specific events to the outcome predicted by the hypothesis.
- Accepting, rejecting, or modifying the hypothesis, based on these comparisons.
- Continuing to test the hypothesis against the facts. As favorable results accumulate, the hypothesis evolves into a *theory*. A very well-tested and widely accepted theory is referred to as a *law* or *principle*. Combinations of such laws or principles are incorporated into *models*, which are simplified representations of how something works, such as a market or segment of the economy.

Economists develop theories of the behavior of individuals (consumers, workers) and institutions (businesses, governments) engaged in the production, exchange, and consumption of goods and services. Economic theories and **principles** are statements about economic behavior or the economy that enable prediction of the probable effects of certain actions. They are "purposeful simplifications." The full scope of economic reality itself is too complex and bewildering to be understood as a whole. In developing theories and principles, economists remove the clutter and simplify.

Economic principles and models are highly useful in analyzing economic behavior and understanding how the economy operates. They are the tools for ascertaining cause and effect (or action and outcome) within the economic system. Good theories do a good job of explaining and predicting. They are supported by facts concerning how individuals and institutions actually behave in producing, exchanging, and consuming goods and services.

There are some other things you should know about economic principles:

- *Generalizations* Economic principles are *generalizations* relating to economic behavior or to the economy itself. Economic principles are expressed as the tendencies of typical or average consumers, workers, or business firms. For example, economists say that consumers buy more of a particular product when its price falls. Economists recognize that some consumers may increase their purchases by a large amount, others by a small amount, and a few not at all. This "price-quantity" principle, however, holds for the typical consumer and for consumers as a group.
- *Other-things-equal assumption* Like other scientists, economists use the *ceteris paribus* or **other-things-equal assumption** to construct their theories. They assume that all variables except those under immediate consideration are held constant for a particular analysis. For example, consider the relationship between the price of Pepsi and the amount of it purchased. It helps to assume that, of all the factors that might influence the amount of Pepsi purchased (for example, the price of Pepsi, the price of Coca-Cola, and consumer incomes and preferences), only the price of Pepsi varies. The economist can then focus on the relationship between the price of Pepsi and purchases of Pepsi in isolation without being confused by changes in other variables.
- *Graphical expression* Many economic models are expressed graphically. Be sure to read the special web appendix for this chapter as a review of graphs.

ORIGIN OF THE IDEA

O 1.4
Ceteris paribus

principles
Statements about economic behavior that enable prediction of the probable effects of certain actions.

other-things-equal assumption
The assumption that factors other than those being considered do not change.

Microeconomics and Macroeconomics

Economists develop economic principles and models at two levels.

Microeconomics

microeconomics
The part of economics concerned with individual decision-making units, such as a consumer, a worker, or a business firm.

Microeconomics is the part of economics concerned with decision making by individual consumers, households, and business firms. At this level of analysis, we observe the details of their behavior under a figurative microscope. We measure the price of a specific product, the number of workers employed by a single firm, the revenue or income of a particular firm or household, or the expenditures of a specific firm, government entity, or family.

Macroeconomics

macroeconomics
The part of economics concerned with the economy as a whole or major components of the economy.

aggregate
A collection of specific economic units treated as if they were one unit.

Macroeconomics examines either the economy as a whole or its basic subdivisions or aggregates, such as the government, household, and business sectors. An **aggregate** is a collection of specific economic units treated as if they were one unit. Therefore, we might lump together the millions of consumers in the U.S. economy and treat them as if they were one huge unit called "consumers."

In using aggregates, macroeconomics seeks to obtain an overview, or general outline, of the structure of the economy and the relationships of its major aggregates. Macroeconomics speaks of such economic measures as total output, total employment, total income, aggregate expenditures, and the general level of prices in analyzing various economic problems. Very little attention is given to specific units making up the various aggregates.

© Robert Holmes/CORBIS

© IMS Communications, Ltd. All rights reserved.

Photo Op Micro versus Macro

Figuratively, microeconomics examines the sand, rock, and shells, not the beach; in contrast, macroeconomics examines the beach, not the sand, rocks, and shells.

Individual's Economic Problem

It is clear from our previous discussion that both individuals and society face an **economic problem:** They need to make choices because economic wants are unlimited, but the means (income, time, resources) for satisfying those wants are limited. Let's first look at the economic problem faced by individuals. To explain the idea, we will construct a very simple microeconomic model.

economic problem
The need for individuals and society to make choices because wants exceed means.

Limited Income

We all have a finite amount of income, even the wealthiest among us. Sure Bill Gates earns a bit more than the rest of us, but he still has to decide how to spend his money! And the majority of us have much more limited means. Our income comes to us in the form of wages, interest, rent, and profit, although we may also receive money from government programs or family members. As Global Snapshot 1.1 shows, the average income of Americans in 2010 was $47,390. In the poorest nations, it was less than $500.

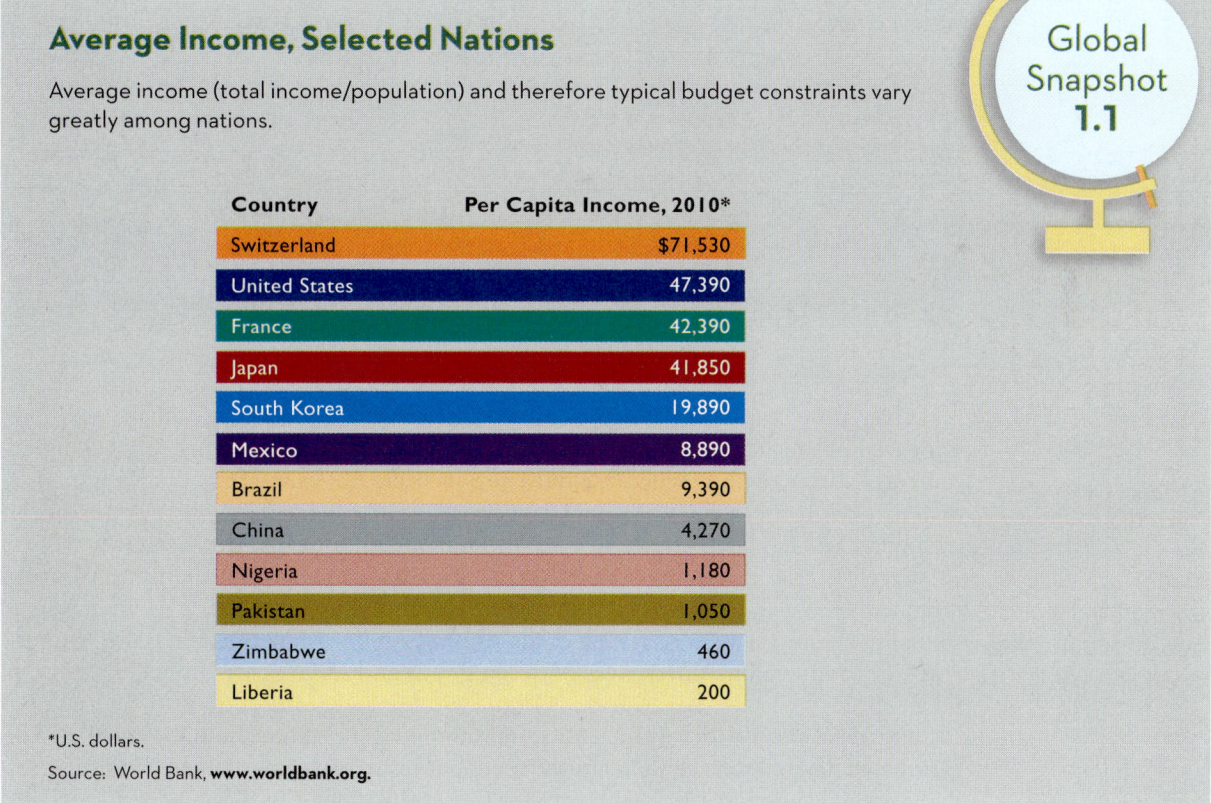

Average Income, Selected Nations

Average income (total income/population) and therefore typical budget constraints vary greatly among nations.

Global Snapshot 1.1

Country	Per Capita Income, 2010*
Switzerland	$71,530
United States	47,390
France	42,390
Japan	41,850
South Korea	19,890
Mexico	8,890
Brazil	9,390
China	4,270
Nigeria	1,180
Pakistan	1,050
Zimbabwe	460
Liberia	200

*U.S. dollars.
Source: World Bank, **www.worldbank.org.**

Unlimited Wants

For better or worse, most people have virtually unlimited wants. We desire various goods and services that provide utility. Our wants extend over a wide range of products, from *necessities* (food, shelter, clothing) to *luxuries* (perfumes, yachts, sports cars). Some wants such as basic food, clothing, and shelter have biological roots. Other wants, for example, specific kinds of food, clothing, and shelter, arise from the conventions and customs of society.

© Bill Aron/PhotoEdit   © F. Schussler/PhotoLink/Getty Images

Photo Op Necessities versus Luxuries

Economic wants include both necessities and luxuries. Each type of item provides utility to the buyer.

Over time, economic wants tend to change and multiply, fueled by new and improved products. Only recently have people wanted iPods, Internet service, digital cameras, or camera phones because those products did not exist a few decades ago. Also, the satisfaction of certain wants may trigger others: The acquisition of a Ford Focus or a Honda Civic has been known to whet the appetite for a Lexus or a Mercedes.

Services, as well as goods, satisfy our wants. Car repair work, the removal of an inflamed appendix, legal and accounting advice, and haircuts all satisfy human wants. Actually, we buy many goods, such as automobiles and washing machines, for the services they render. The differences between goods and services are often smaller than they appear to be.

For most people, the desires for goods and services cannot be fully satisfied. Bill Gates may have all that he wants for himself, but his massive charitable giving suggests that he keenly wants better health care for the world's poor. Our desires for a *particular* good or service can be satisfied; over a short period of time we can surely obtain enough toothpaste or pasta. And one appendectomy is plenty. But our broader desire for more goods and services and higher-quality goods and services seems to be another story.

Because we have only limited income but seemingly insatiable wants, it is in our self-interest to economize: to pick and choose goods and services that maximize our satisfaction, given the limitations we face.

A Budget Line

The economic problem facing individuals can be depicted as a **budget line** (or, more technically, *budget constraint*). It is a schedule or curve that shows various combinations of two products a consumer can purchase with a specific money income.

To understand this idea, suppose that you received a Barnes & Noble gift card as a birthday present. The $120 card is soon to expire. You take the card to the store and confine your purchase decisions to two alternatives: DVDs and paperback books. DVDs are $20 each, and paperback books are $10 each. Your purchase options are shown in the table in Figure 1.1.

At one extreme, you might spend all of your $120 "income" on 6 DVDs at $20 each and have nothing left to spend on books. Or, by giving up 2 DVDs and thereby gaining $40, you can have 4 DVDs at $20 each and 4 books at $10 each. And so on to the other extreme, at which you could buy 12 books at $10 each, spending your entire gift card on books with nothing left to spend on DVDs.

The graph in Figure 1.1 shows the budget line. As elsewhere in this book, we represent discrete (separate element) numbers in tables as points on continuous-data smooth curves. Therefore, note that the line (curve) in the graph is not restricted to whole units of DVDs and books as is the table. Every point on the line represents a possible combination of DVDs and books, including fractional quantities. The slope of the graphed budget line measures the ratio of the price of books (P_b) to the price of DVDs (P_{dvd}); more precisely, the slope is $P_b/P_{dvd} = \$-10/\$+20 = -\frac{1}{2}$ or $-.5$. So you must forgo 1 DVD (measured on the vertical axis) to buy 2 books (measured on the horizontal axis). This yields a slope of $-\frac{1}{2}$ or $-.5$.

The budget line illustrates several ideas.

budget line
A line that shows various combinations of two products a consumer can purchase with a specific money income, given the products' prices.

FIGURE 1.1

A consumer's budget line. The budget line (or budget constraint) shows all the combinations of any two products that can be purchased, given the prices of the products and the consumer's money income.

The Budget Line: Whole-Unit Combinations of DVDs and Paperback Books Attainable with an Income of $120		
Units of DVDs (Price = $20)	Units of Books (Price = $10)	Total Expenditure
6	0	$120 = ($120 + $0)
5	2	$120 = ($100 + $20)
4	4	$120 = ($80 + $40)
3	6	$120 = ($60 + $60)
2	8	$120 = ($40 + $80)
1	10	$120 = ($20 + $100)
0	12	$120 = ($0 + $120)

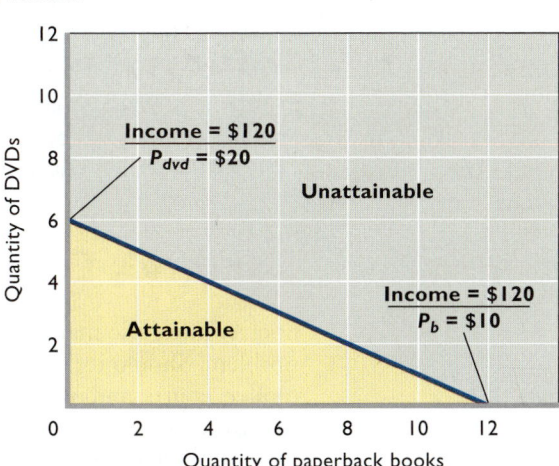

Attainable and Unattainable Combinations

All the combinations of DVDs and books on or inside the budget line are *attainable* from the $120 of money income. You can afford to buy, for example, 3 DVDs at $20 each and 6 books at $10 each. You also can obviously afford to buy 2 DVDs and 5 books, thereby using up only $90 of the $120 available on your gift card. But to achieve maximum utility, you will want to spend the full $120. The budget line shows all combinations that cost exactly the full $120.

In contrast, all combinations beyond the budget line are *unattainable*. The $120 limit simply does not allow you to purchase, for example, 5 DVDs at $20 each and 5 books at $10 each. That $150 expenditure would clearly exceed the $120 limit. In Figure 1.1, the attainable combinations are on and within the budget line; the unattainable combinations are beyond the budget line.

Trade-offs and Opportunity Costs

The budget line in Figure 1.1 illustrates the idea of trade-offs arising from limited income. To obtain more DVDs, you have to give up some books. For example, to acquire the first DVD, you trade off 2 books. So the opportunity cost of the first DVD is 2 books. To obtain the second DVD, the opportunity cost is also 2 books. The straight-line budget constraint, with its constant slope, indicates **constant opportunity cost.** That is, the opportunity cost of 1 extra DVD remains the same (= 2 books) as more DVDs are purchased. And, in reverse, the opportunity cost of 1 extra book does not change (= $\frac{1}{2}$ DVD) as more books are bought.

> **ORIGIN OF THE IDEA**
>
> **O 1.5**
> Opportunity cost

constant opportunity cost
An opportunity cost that remains the same as consumers shift purchases from one product to another along a straight-line budget line.

Choice

Limited income forces people to choose what to buy and what to forgo to fulfill wants. You will select the combination of DVDs and paperback books that you think is "best." That is, you will evaluate your marginal benefits and your marginal costs (here, product price) to make choices that maximize your satisfaction. Other people, with the same $120 gift card, would undoubtedly make different choices.

Income Changes

The location of the budget line varies with money income. An increase in money income shifts the budget line to the right; a decrease in money income shifts it to the left. To verify this, recalculate the table in Figure 1.1, assuming the card value (income) is (a) $240 and (b) $60, and plot the new budget lines in the graph. No wonder people like to have more income: That shifts their budget lines outward and enables them to buy more goods and services. But even with more income, people will still face spending trade-offs, choices, and opportunity costs.

> **WORKED PROBLEMS**
>
> **W 1.1**
> Budget lines

Society's Economic Problem

Society must also make choices under conditions of scarcity. It, too, faces an economic problem. Should it devote more of its limited resources to the criminal justice system (police, courts, and prisons) or to education (teachers, books, and schools)? If it decides to devote more resources to both, what other goods and services does it forgo? Health care? Homeland security? Energy development?

Scarce Resources

Society's economic resources are limited or scarce. By **economic resources** we mean all natural, human, and manufactured resources that go into the production of goods and services. That includes the entire set of factory and farm buildings and all the equipment, tools, and machinery used to produce manufactured goods and agricultural products; all transportation and communication facilities; all types of labor; and land and mineral resources.

economic resources
The land, labor, capital, and entrepreneurial ability used in the production of goods and services.

Resource Categories

Economists classify economic resources into four general categories.

Land   Land means much more to the economist than it does to most people. To the economist **land** includes all natural resources ("gifts of nature") used in the production process. These include mineral and oil deposits, arable land, forests, and water resources.

land
Natural resources ("gifts of nature") used to produce goods and services.

Labor   The resource **labor** consists of the physical actions and mental activities that people contribute to the production of goods and services. The work-related activities of a logger, retail clerk, machinist, teacher, professional football player, and nuclear physicist all fall under the general heading "labor."

labor
The physical and mental talents and efforts of people used to produce goods and services.

Capital   For economists, **capital** (or *capital goods*) includes all manufactured aids used in producing consumer goods and services. Included are all factory, storage, transportation, and distribution facilities, as well as all tools and machinery. Economists use the term **investment** to describe spending that pays for the production and accumulation of capital goods.

Capital goods differ from consumer goods because consumer goods satisfy wants directly, while capital goods do so indirectly by aiding the production of consumer goods. For example, large commercial baking ovens (capital goods) help make loaves of bread (consumer goods). Note that the term "capital" as used by economists refers not to money but to tools, machinery, and other productive equipment. Because money produces nothing, economists do not include it as an economic resource. Money (or money capital or financial capital) is simply a means for purchasing goods and services, including capital goods.

capital
Human-made resources (buildings, machinery, and equipment) used to produce goods and services.

investment
The purchase of capital resources.

Entrepreneurial Ability   Finally, there is the special human resource, distinct from labor, called **entrepreneurial ability.** The entrepreneur performs several socially useful functions:

entrepreneurial ability
The human talent that combines the other resources to produce a product, make strategic decisions, and bear risks.

- The entrepreneur takes the initiative in combining the resources of land, labor, and capital to produce a good or a service. Both a spark plug and a catalyst, the entrepreneur is the driving force behind production and the agent who combines the other resources in what is hoped will be a successful business venture.
- The entrepreneur makes the strategic business decisions that set the course of an enterprise.
- The entrepreneur innovates. He or she commercializes new products, new production techniques, or even new forms of business organization.

- The entrepreneur bears risk. Innovation is risky, as nearly all new products and ideas are subject to the possibility of failure as well as success. Progress would cease without entrepreneurs who are willing to take on risk by devoting their time, effort, and ability—as well as their own money and the money of others—to commercializing new products and ideas that may enhance society's standard of living.

© Lester Lefkowitz/CORBIS   © Lance Nelson/Stock Photos/zefa/CORBIS   © Creatas/PunchStock   © Neville Elder/Corbis

Photo Op Economic Resources

Land, labor, capital, and entrepreneurial ability all contribute to producing goods and services.

factors of production
Economic resources: land, labor, capital, and entrepreneurial ability.

Because land, labor, capital, and entrepreneurial ability are combined to produce goods and services, they are called the **factors of production** or simply inputs.

Production Possibilities Model

Society uses its scarce resources to produce goods and services. The alternatives and choices it faces can best be understood through a macroeconomic model of production possibilities. To keep things simple, we assume:

- *Full employment* The economy is employing all of its available resources.
- *Fixed resources* The quantity and quality of the factors of production are fixed.
- *Fixed technology* The state of technology (the methods used to produce output) is constant.
- *Two goods* The economy is producing only two goods: food products and manufacturing equipment. Food products symbolize **consumer goods,** products that satisfy our wants directly; manufacturing equipment symbolizes **capital goods,** products that satisfy our wants indirectly by making possible more efficient production of consumer goods.

consumer goods
Products and services that directly satisfy consumer wants.

capital goods
Items that are used to produce other goods and therefore do not directly satisfy consumer wants.

Production Possibilities Table

A production possibilities table lists the different combinations of two products that can be produced with a specific set of resources, assuming full employment. Figure 1.2 contains such a table for a simple economy that is producing food products and manufacturing equipment; the data are, of course, hypothetical. At alternative A, this economy would be devoting all its available resources to the production of manufacturing

FIGURE 1.2

The production possibilities curve. Each point on the production possibilities curve represents some maximum combination of two products that can be produced if resources are fully and efficiently employed. When an economy is operating on the curve, more manufacturing equipment means less food products, and vice versa. Limited resources and a fixed technology make any combination of manufacturing equipment and food products lying outside the curve (such as at *W*) unattainable. Points inside the curve are attainable, but they indicate that full employment is not being realized.

	Production Alternatives				
Type of Product	**A**	**B**	**C**	**D**	**E**
Food products (hundred thousands)	0	1	2	3	4
Manufacturing equipment (thousands)	10	9	7	4	0

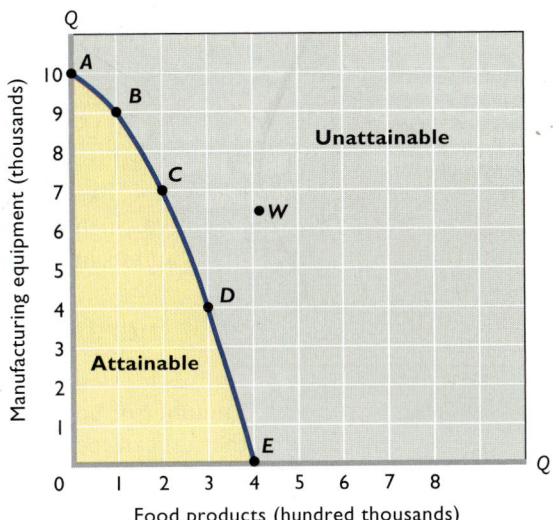

equipment (capital goods); at alternative E, all resources would go to food-product production (consumer goods). Those alternatives are unrealistic extremes; an economy typically produces both capital goods and consumer goods, as in B, C, and D. As we move from alternative A to E, we increase the production of food products at the expense of the production of manufacturing equipment.

Because consumer goods satisfy our wants directly, any movement toward E looks tempting. In producing more food products, society increases the satisfaction of its current wants. But there is a cost: More food products mean less manufacturing equipment. This shift of resources to consumer goods catches up with society over time because the stock of capital goods expands more slowly, thereby reducing potential future production. By moving toward alternative E, society chooses "more now" at the expense of "much more later."

By moving toward A, society chooses to forgo current consumption, thereby freeing up resources that can be used to increase the production of capital goods. By building up its stock of capital this way, society will have greater future production and, therefore, greater future consumption. By moving toward A, society is choosing "more later" at the cost of "less now."

Generalization: At any point in time, a fully employed economy must sacrifice some of one good to obtain more of another good. Scarce resources prohibit such an economy from having more of both goods. Society must choose among alternatives. There is no such thing as a free bag of groceries or a free manufacturing machine. Having more of one thing means having less of something else.

Production Possibilities Curve

The data presented in a production possibilities table can also be shown graphically. We arbitrarily represent the economy's output of capital goods (here, manufacturing equipment) on the vertical axis and the output of consumer goods (here, food products) on the horizontal axis, as shown in Figure 1.2.

Each point on the **production possibilities curve** represents some maximum output of the two products. The curve is a "constraint" because it shows the limit of attainable outputs. Points on the curve are attainable as long as the economy uses all its available resources. Points lying inside the curve are also attainable, but they reflect less total output and therefore are not as desirable as points on the curve. Points inside the curve imply that the economy could have more of both manufacturing equipment and food products if it achieved full employment. Points lying beyond the production possibilities curve, like *W*, would represent a greater output than the output at any point on the curve. Such points, however, are unattainable with the current availability of resources and technology.

INTERACTIVE GRAPHS

G 1.1
Production possibilities curve

Law of Increasing Opportunity Costs

Figure 1.2 clearly shows that more food products mean less manufacturing equipment. The number of units of manufacturing equipment that must be given up to obtain another unit of food products, of course, is the opportunity cost of that unit of food products.

In moving from alternative A to alternative B in the table in Figure 1.2, the cost of 1 additional unit of food products is 1 less unit of manufacturing equipment. But when additional units are considered—B to C, C to D, and D to E—an important economic principle is revealed: The opportunity cost of each additional unit of food products is greater than the opportunity cost of the preceding one. When we move from A to B, just 1 unit of manufacturing equipment is sacrificed for 1 more unit of food products; but in going from B to C, we sacrifice 2 additional units of manufacturing equipment for 1 more unit of food products; then 3 more of manufacturing equipment for 1 more of food products; and finally 4 for 1. Conversely, confirm that as we move from E to A, the cost of an additional unit of manufacturing equipment (on average) is $\frac{1}{4}$, $\frac{1}{3}$, $\frac{1}{2}$, and 1 unit of food products, respectively, for the four successive moves.

Our example illustrates the **law of increasing opportunity costs:** The more of a product that society produces, the greater is the opportunity cost of obtaining an extra unit.

Shape of the Curve   The law of increasing opportunity costs is reflected in the shape of the production possibilities curve: The curve is bowed out from the origin of the graph. Figure 1.2 shows that when the economy moves from *A* to *E*, it must give up successively larger amounts of manufacturing equipment (1, 2, 3, and 4) to acquire equal increments of food products (1, 1, 1, and 1). This is shown in the slope of the production possibilities curve, which becomes steeper as we move from *A* to *E*.

Economic Rationale   The law of increasing opportunity costs is driven by the fact that economic resources are not completely adaptable to alternative uses. Many resources are better at producing one type of good than at producing others. Consider land. Some land is highly suited to growing the ingredients necessary for pizza production. But as pizza production expands, society has to start using land that is less

WORKED PROBLEMS

W 1.2
Production possibilities

production possibilities curve
A curve showing the different combinations of goods and services that can be produced in a fully employed economy, assuming the available supplies of resources and technology are fixed.

law of increasing opportunity costs
The principle that as the production of a good increases, the opportunity cost of producing an additional unit rises.

bountiful for farming. Other land is rich in mineral deposits and therefore well-suited to producing the materials needed to make manufacturing equipment. That land will be the first land devoted to the production of manufacturing equipment. But as society steps up the production of manufacturing equipment, it must push resources that are less and less suited to making that equipment into its production.

If we start at A and move to B in Figure 1.2, we can shift resources whose productivity is relatively high in food production and low in manufacturing equipment. But as we move from B to C, C to D, and so on, resources highly productive of food products become increasingly scarce. To get more food products, resources whose productivity in manufacturing equipment is relatively great will be needed. It will take increasingly more of such resources, and hence greater sacrifices of manufacturing equipment, to achieve each 1-unit increase in food products. This lack of perfect flexibility, or interchangeability, on the part of resources is the cause of increasing opportunity costs for society.

Optimal Allocation

Of all the attainable combinations of food products and manufacturing equipment on the curve in Figure 1.2, which is optimal (best)? That is, what specific quantities of resources should be allocated to food products and what specific quantities to manufacturing equipment in order to maximize satisfaction?

Recall that economic decisions center on comparisons of marginal benefits (MB) and marginal costs (MC). Any economic activity should be expanded as long as marginal benefit exceeds marginal cost and should be reduced if marginal cost exceeds marginal benefit. The optimal amount of the activity occurs where MB = MC. Society needs to make a similar assessment about its production decision.

Consider food products. We already know from the law of increasing opportunity costs that the marginal cost of additional units of food products will rise as more units are produced. At the same time, we need to recognize that the extra or marginal benefits that come from producing and consuming food products decline with each successive unit of food products. Consequently, each successive unit of food products brings with it both increasing marginal costs and decreasing marginal benefits.

The optimal quantity of food production is indicated by the intersection of the MB and MC curves: 200,000 units in Figure 1.3. Why is this amount the optimal quantity? If only 100,000 units of food products were produced, the marginal benefit of an extra unit of them would exceed its marginal cost. In money terms, MB is $15, while MC is only $5. When society gains something worth $15 at a marginal cost of only $5, it is better off. In Figure 1.3, net gains of decreasing amounts can be realized until food-product production has been increased to 200,000.

In contrast, the production of 300,000 units of food products is excessive. There the MC of an added unit is $15 and its MB is only $5. This means that 1 unit of food products is worth only $5 to society but costs it $15 to obtain. This is a losing proposition for society!

So resources are being efficiently allocated to any product when the marginal benefit and marginal cost of its output are equal (MB = MC). Suppose that by applying the above analysis to manufacturing equipment, we find its optimal (MB = MC) quantity is 7000. This would mean that alternative C (200,000 units of food products and 7000 units of manufacturing equipment) on the production possibilities curve in Figure 1.2 would be optimal for this economy.

FIGURE 1.3
Optimal output:
MB = MC. Achieving
the optimal output re-
quires the expansion of
a good's output until its
marginal benefit (MB)
and marginal cost (MC)
are equal. No resources
beyond that point
should be allocated to
the product. Here,
optimal output occurs
when 200,000 units
of food products are
produced.

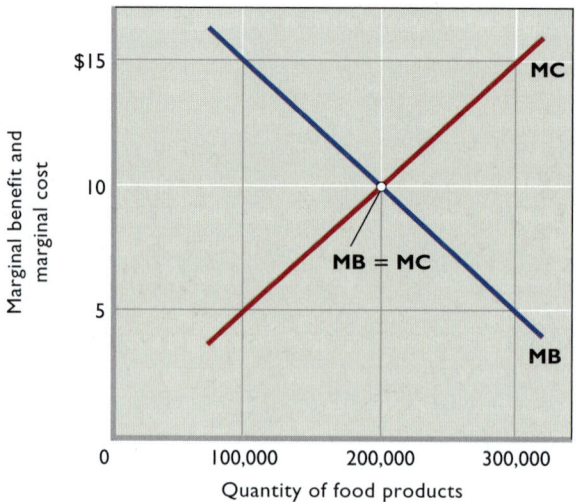

Applying the Analysis

The Economics of War

Production possibilities analysis is helpful in assessing the costs and benefits of waging the war on terrorism, including the wars in Afghanistan and Iraq. At the end of 2011, the estimated cost of these efforts exceeded $1.29 trillion.

If we categorize all of U.S. production as either "defense goods" or "civilian goods," we can measure them on the axes of a production possibilities diagram such as that shown in Figure 1.2. The opportunity cost of using more resources for defense goods is the civilian goods sacrificed. In a fully employed economy, more defense goods are achieved at the opportunity cost of fewer civilian goods—health care, education, pollution control, personal computers, houses, and so on. The cost of waging war is the other goods forgone. The benefits of these activities are numerous and diverse but clearly include the gains from protecting against future loss of American lives, assets, income, and well-being.

Society must assess the marginal benefit (MB) and marginal cost (MC) of additional defense goods to determine their optimal amounts—where to locate on the defense goods–civilian goods production possibilities curve. Although estimating marginal benefits and marginal costs is an imprecise art, the MB-MC framework is a useful way of approaching choices. Allocative efficiency requires that society expand production of defense goods until MB = MC.

The events of September 11, 2001, and the future threats they posed increased the perceived marginal benefits of defense goods. If we label the horizontal axis in Figure 1.3 "defense goods" and draw in a rightward shift of the MB curve, you will see that the optimal quantity of defense goods rises. In view of the concerns relating to September 11, the United States allocated more of its resources to defense. But the MB-MC analysis also reminds us we can spend too much on defense, as well as too little. The United States should not expand defense goods beyond the point where MB = MC. If it does, it will be sacrificing civilian goods of greater value than the defense goods obtained.

Question:
Would society's costs of war be lower if it drafted soldiers at low pay rather than attracted them voluntarily to the military through market pay?

Unemployment, Growth, and the Future

In the depths of the Great Depression of the 1930s, one-quarter of U.S. workers were unemployed and one-third of U.S. production capacity was idle. Subsequent downturns have been much less severe. During the deep 2007–2009 recession, for instance, production fell by a comparably smaller 5.1 percent, and 1 in 10 workers was without a job.

Almost all nations have experienced widespread unemployment and unused production capacity from business downturns at one time or another. Since 2000, for example, several nations—including Argentina, Germany, Japan, Mexico, and South Korea—have had economic downturns and unemployment.

How do these realities relate to the production possibilities model? Our analysis and conclusions change if we relax the assumption that all available resources are fully employed. The five alternatives in the table of Figure 1.2 represent maximum outputs; they illustrate the combinations of food products and manufacturing equipment that can be produced when the economy is operating at full employment. With unemployment, this economy would produce less than each alternative shown in the table.

Graphically, we represent situations of unemployment by points inside the original production possibilities curve (reproduced in Figure 1.4). Point *U* is one such point. Here the economy is falling short of the various maximum combinations of food products and manufacturing equipment represented by the points on the production possibilities curve. The arrows in Figure 1.4 indicate three possible paths back to full employment. A move toward full employment would yield a greater output of one or both products.

A Growing Economy

When we drop the assumptions that the quantity and quality of resources and technology are fixed, the production possibilities curve shifts positions, and the potential maximum output of the economy changes.

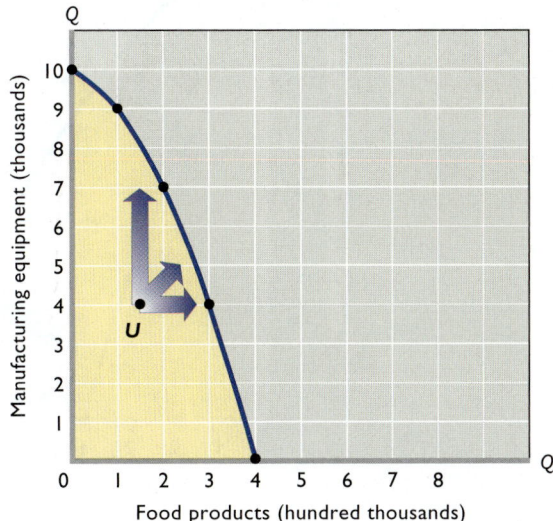

FIGURE 1.4
Unemployment and the production possibilities curve. Any point inside the production possibilities curve, such as *U*, represents unemployment or a failure to achieve full employment. The arrows indicate that, by realizing full employment, the economy could operate on the curve. This means it could produce more of one or both products than it is producing at point *U*.

Increases in Resource Supplies

Although resource supplies are fixed at any specific moment, they change over time. For example, a nation's growing population brings about increases in the supplies of labor and entrepreneurial ability. Also, labor quality usually improves over time. Historically, the economy's stock of capital has increased at a significant, though unsteady, rate. And although some of our energy and mineral resources are being depleted, new sources are also being discovered. The development of irrigation systems, for example, adds to the supply of arable land.

The net result of these increased supplies of the factors of production is the ability to produce more of both consumer goods and capital goods. Thus, 20 years from now, the production possibilities in Figure 1.5 may supersede those shown in Figure 1.2. The greater abundance of resources will result in a greater potential output of one or both products at each alternative. The economy will have achieved economic growth in the form of expanded potential output. Thus, when an increase in the quantity or quality of resources occurs, the production possibilities curve shifts outward and to the right, as illustrated by the move from the inner curve to curve *A′ B′ C′ D′ E′* in Figure 1.5. This sort of shift represents growth of economic capacity, which, when used, means **economic growth**: a larger total output.

economic growth
An outward shift of the production possibilities curve that results from an increase in resource supplies or quality or an improvement in technology.

Advances in Technology

An advancing technology brings both new and better goods and improved ways of producing them. For now, let's think of technological advance as being only improvements in the methods of production, for example, the

---

FIGURE 1.5

Economic growth and the production possibilities curve. The increase in supplies of resources, the improvements in resource quality, and the technological advances that occur in a dynamic economy move the production possibilities curve outward and to the right, allowing the economy to have larger quantities of both types of goods.

Type of Product	Production Alternatives				
	A′	B′	C′	D′	E′
Food products (hundred thousands)	0	2	4	6	8
Manufacturing equipment (thousands)	14	12	9	5	0

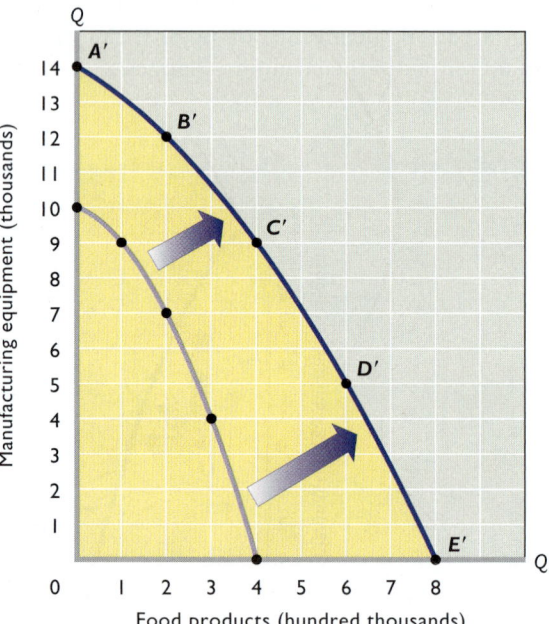

introduction of computerized systems to manage inventories and schedule production. These advances alter our previous discussion of the economic problem by allowing society to produce more goods with available resources. As with increases in resource supplies, technological advances make possible the production of more manufacturing equipment *and* more food products.

Information Technology and Biotechnology

Applying the Analysis

A real-world example of improved technology is the recent surge of new technologies relating to computers, communications, and biotechnology. Technological advances have dropped the prices of computers and greatly increased their speed. Improved software has greatly increased the everyday usefulness of computers. Cellular phones and the Internet have increased communications capacity, enhancing production and improving the efficiency of markets. Advances in biotechnology have resulted in important agricultural and medical discoveries. These and other new and improved technologies have contributed to U.S. economic growth (outward shifts of the nation's production possibilities curve).

Question:
How have technological advances in medicine helped expand production possibilities in the United States?

Conclusion: Economic growth is the result of (1) increases in supplies of resources, (2) improvements in resource quality, and (3) technological advances. The consequence of growth is that a full-employment economy can enjoy a greater output of both consumption goods and capital goods. While static, no-growth economies must sacrifice some of one good to obtain more of another; dynamic, growing economies can have larger quantities of both goods.

Present Choices and Future Possibilities

An economy's current choice of positions on its production possibilities curve helps determine the future location of that curve. Let's designate the two axes of the production possibilities curve as "goods for the future" and "goods for the present," as in Figure 1.6. Goods for the future are such things as capital goods, research and education, and preventive medicine. They increase the quantity and quality of property resources, enlarge the stock of technological information, and improve the quality of human resources. As we have already seen, goods for the future, such as capital goods, are the ingredients of economic growth. Goods for the present are consumer goods such as food, clothing, and entertainment.

Now suppose there are two hypothetical economies, Presentville and Futureville, that are initially identical in every respect except one: Presentville's current choice of positions on its production possibilities curve strongly favors present goods over future goods. Point *P* in Figure 1.6a indicates that choice. It is located quite far down the curve to the right, indicating a high priority for goods for the present, at the

FIGURE 1.6

Present choices and future locations of production possibilities curves. A nation's current choice favoring "present goods," as made by Presentville in (a), will cause a modest outward shift of the production possibilities curve in the future. A nation's current choice favoring "future goods," as made by Futureville in (b), will result in a greater outward shift of the curve in the future.

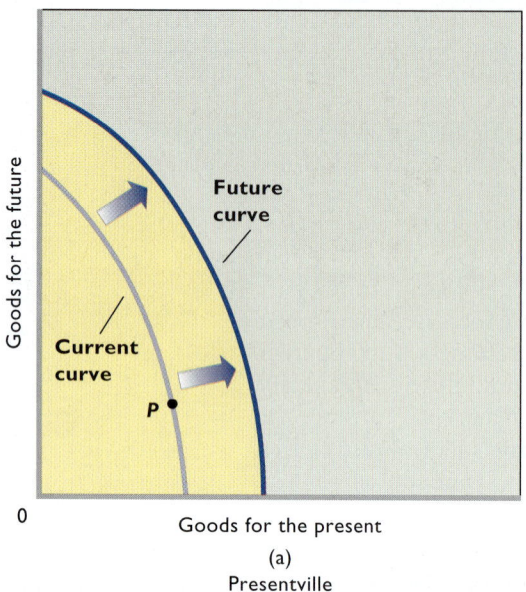

(a)
Presentville

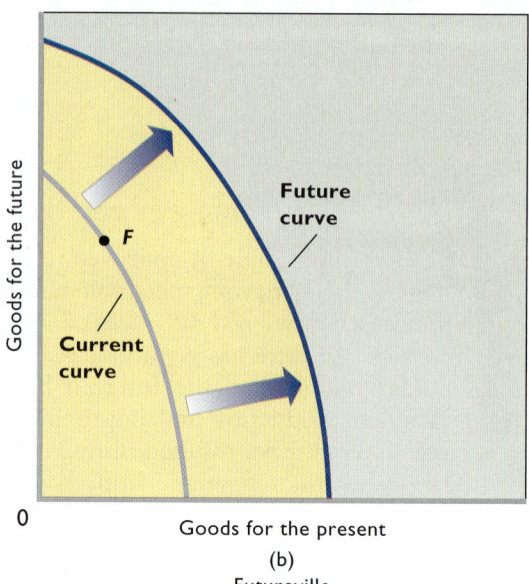

(b)
Futureville

expense of less goods for the future. Futureville, in contrast, makes a current choice that stresses larger amounts of future goods and smaller amounts of present goods, as shown by point *F* in Figure 1.6b.

Now, other things equal, we can expect Futureville's future production possibilities curve to be farther to the right than Presentville's future production possibilities curve. By currently choosing an output more favorable to technological advances and to increases in the quantity and quality of resources, Futureville will achieve greater economic growth than Presentville. In terms of capital goods, Futureville is choosing to make larger current additions to its "national factory" by devoting more of its current output to capital than does Presentville. The payoff from this choice for Futureville is greater future production capacity and economic growth. The opportunity cost is fewer consumer goods in the present for Futureville to enjoy.

Is Futureville's choice thus necessarily "better" than Presentville's? That, we cannot say. The different outcomes simply reflect different preferences and priorities in the two countries. But each country will have to live with the consequences of its choice.

INTERACTIVE GRAPHS

G 1.2
Present choices and future possibilities

Summary

1. Economics is the social science that studies how people, institutions, and society make choices under conditions of scarcity. Central to economics is the idea of opportunity cost: the value of the good, service, or time forgone to obtain something else.

2. The economic perspective includes three elements: scarcity and choice, purposeful behavior, and marginalism. It sees individuals and institutions making rational decisions based on comparisons of marginal costs and marginal benefits.

3. Economists employ the scientific method, in which they form and test hypotheses of cause-and-effect relationships to generate theories, laws, and principles. Economists often combine theories into representations called models.

4. Microeconomics examines the decision making of specific economic units or institutions. Macroeconomics looks at the economy as a whole or its major aggregates.

5. Individuals face an economic problem. Because their wants exceed their incomes, they must decide what to purchase and what to forgo. Society also faces an economic problem. Societal wants exceed the available resources necessary to fulfill them. Society therefore must decide what to produce and what to forgo.

6. Graphically, a budget line (or budget constraint) illustrates the economic problem for individuals. The line shows the various combinations of two products that a consumer can purchase with a specific money income, given the prices of the two products.

7. Economic resources are inputs into the production process and can be classified as land, labor, capital, and entrepreneurial ability. Economic resources are also known as factors of production or inputs.

8. Society's economic problem can be illustrated through production possibilities analysis. Production possibilities tables and curves show the different combinations of goods and services that can be produced in a fully employed economy, assuming that resource quantity, resource quality, and technology are fixed.

9. An economy that is fully employed and thus operating on its production possibilities curve must sacrifice the output of some types of goods and services to increase the production of others. The gain of one type of good or service is always accompanied by an opportunity cost in the form of the loss of some of the other type.

10. Because resources are not equally productive in all possible uses, shifting resources from one use to another results in increasing opportunity costs. The production of additional units of one product requires the sacrifice of increasing amounts of the other product.

11. The optimal point on the production possibilities curve represents the most desirable mix of goods and is determined by expanding the production of each good until its marginal benefit (MB) equals its marginal cost (MC).

12. Over time, technological advances and increases in the quantity and quality of resources enable the economy to produce more of all goods and services, that is, to experience economic growth. Society's choice as to the mix of consumer goods and capital goods in current output is a major determinant of the future location of the production possibilities curve and thus of the extent of economic growth.

Terms and Concepts

economics	macroeconomics	investment
economic perspective	aggregate	entrepreneurial ability
opportunity cost	economic problem	factors of production
utility	budget line	consumer goods
marginal analysis	constant opportunity cost	capital goods
scientific method	economic resources	production possibilities curve
principles	land	law of increasing opportunity costs
other-things-equal assumption	labor	economic growth
microeconomics	capital	

Questions

1. Ralph Waldo Emerson once wrote: "Want is a growing giant whom the coat of have was never large enough to cover." How does this statement relate to the definition of economics? **LO1**

2. "Buy 2, get 1 free." Explain why the "1 free" is free to the buyer but not to society. **LO1**

3. Which of the following decisions would entail the greater opportunity cost: allocating a square block in the heart of New York City for a surface parking lot or allocating a square block at the edge of a typical suburb for such a lot? Explain. **LO1**

4. What is meant by the term "utility," and how does it relate to purposeful behavior? **LO1**

5. Cite three examples of recent decisions that you made in which you, at least implicitly, weighed marginal cost and marginal benefit. **LO1**

6. What are the key elements of the scientific method, and how does this method relate to economic principles and laws? **LO2**

7. Indicate whether each of the following statements applies to microeconomics or macroeconomics: **LO3**
   a. The unemployment rate in the United States was 9.0% in April 2011.
   b. A U.S. software firm discharged 15 workers last month and transferred the work to India.
   c. An unexpected freeze in central Florida reduced the citrus crop and caused the price of oranges to rise.
   d. U.S. output, adjusted for inflation, grew by 2.9% in 2010.
   e. Last week Wells Fargo Bank lowered its interest rate on business loans by one-half of 1 percentage point.
   f. The consumer price index rose by 1.6% in 2010.

8. What are economic resources? What categories do economists use to classify them? Why are resources also called factors of production? Why are they called inputs? **LO4**

9. Why isn't money considered a capital resource in economics? Why is entrepreneurial ability considered a category of economic resource, distinct from labor? What are the major functions of the entrepreneur? **LO4**

10. Specify and explain the typical shapes of marginal-benefit and marginal-cost curves. How are these curves used to determine the optimal allocation of resources to a particular product? If current output is such that marginal cost exceeds marginal benefit, should more or fewer resources be allocated to this product? Explain. **LO5**

11. Explain how (if at all) each of the following events affects the location of a country's production possibilities curve: **LO5**
    a. The quality of education increases.
    b. The number of unemployed workers increases.
    c. A new technique improves the efficiency of extracting copper from ore.
    d. A devastating earthquake destroys numerous production facilities.

12. Suppose that, on the basis of a nation's production possibilities curve, an economy must sacrifice 10,000 pizzas domestically to get the 1 additional industrial robot it desires but that it can get the robot from another country in exchange for 9000 pizzas. Relate this information to the following statement: "Through international specialization and trade, a nation can reduce its opportunity cost of obtaining goods and thus 'move outside its production possibilities curve.'" **LO5**

Problems

1. Potatoes cost Janice $1 per pound, and she has $5.00 that she could possibly spend on potatoes or other items. If she feels that the first pound of potatoes is worth $1.50, the second pound is worth $1.14, the third pound is worth $1.05, and all subsequent pounds are worth $0.30, how many pounds of potatoes will she purchase? What if she only had $2 to spend? **LO1**

2. Pham can work as many or as few hours as she wants at the college bookstore for $9 per hour. But due to her hectic schedule, she has just 15 hours per week that she can spend working at either the bookstore or at other potential jobs. One potential job, at a café, will pay her $12 per hour for up to 6 hours per week. She has another job offer at a garage that will pay her $10 an hour for up to 5 hours per week. And she has a potential job at a day care center that will pay her $8.50

   per hour for as many hours as she can work. If her goal is to maximize the amount of money she can make each week, how many hours will she work at the bookstore? **LO1**

3. Suppose you won $15 on a lotto ticket at the local 7-Eleven and decided to spend all the winnings on candy bars and bags of peanuts. The price of candy bars is $.75 and the price of peanuts is $1.50. **LO4**
   a. Construct a table showing the alternative combinations of the two products that are available.
   b. Plot the data in your table as a budget line in a graph. What is the slope of the budget line? What is the opportunity cost of one more candy bar? Of one more bag of peanuts? Do these opportunity costs rise, fall, or remain constant as each additional unit of the product is purchased?

c. How, in general, would you decide which of the available combinations of candy bars and bags of peanuts to buy?

d. Suppose that you had won $30 on your ticket, not $15. Show the $30 budget line in your diagram. Why would this budget line be preferable to the old one?

4. Suppose that you are on a desert island and possess exactly 20 coconuts. Your neighbor, Friday, is a fisherman, and he is willing to trade 2 fish for every 1 coconut that you are willing to give him. Another neighbor, Kwame, is also a fisherman, and he is willing to trade 3 fish for every 1 coconut. **LO4**

a. On a single figure, draw budget lines for trading with Friday and for trading with Kwame. (Put coconuts on the vertical axis.)

b. What is the slope of the budget line from trading with Friday?

c. What is the slope of the budget line from trading with Kwame?

d. Which budget line features a larger set of attainable combinations of coconuts and fish?

e. If you are going to trade coconuts for fish, would you rather trade with Friday or Kwame?

5. Below is a production possibilities table for consumer goods (automobiles) and capital goods (forklifts): **LO5**

Type of Production	Production Alternatives				
	A	B	C	D	E
Automobiles	0	2	4	6	8
Forklifts	30	27	21	12	0

a. Show these data graphically. Upon what specific assumptions is this production possibilities curve based?

b. If the economy is at point C, what is the cost of two more automobiles? Of six more forklifts? Explain how the production possibilities curve reflects the law of increasing opportunity costs.

c. If the economy characterized by this production possibilities table and curve were producing 3 automobiles and 20 forklifts, what could you conclude about its use of its available resources?

d. What would production at a point outside the production possibilities curve indicate? What must occur before the economy can attain such a level of production?

6. Referring to the table in problem 5, suppose improvement occurs in the technology of producing forklifts but not in the technology of producing automobiles. Draw the new production possibilities curve. Now assume that a technological advance occurs in producing automobiles but not in producing forklifts. Draw the new production possibilities curve. Now draw a production possibilities curve that reflects technological improvement in the production of both goods. **LO5**

7. On average, households in China save 40 percent of their annual income each year, whereas households in the United States save less than 5 percent. Production possibilities are growing at roughly 9 percent annually in China and 3.5 percent in the United States. Use graphical analysis of "present goods" versus "future goods" to explain the differences in growth rates. **LO5**

FURTHER TEST YOUR KNOWLEDGE AT
www.brue3e.com

At the text's Online Learning Center, **www.brue3e.com,** you will find one or more web-based questions that require information from the Internet to answer. We urge you to check them out, since they will familiarize you with websites that may be helpful in other courses and perhaps even in your career. The OLC also features multiple-choice quizzes that give instant feedback and provides other helpful ways to further test your knowledge of the chapter.

Graphs and Their Meaning

CHAPTER TWO

The Market System and the Circular Flow

After reading this chapter, you should be able to:

1. Differentiate between a command system and a market system.
2. List the main characteristics of the market system.
3. Explain how the market system answers the four fundamental questions.
4. Discuss how the market system adjusts to change and promotes progress.
5. Describe the mechanics of the circular flow model.

You are at the mall. Suppose you were assigned to compile a list of all the individual goods and services there, including the different brands and variations of each type of product. That task would be daunting and the list would be long! And even though a single shopping mall contains a remarkable quantity and variety of goods, it is only a tiny part of the national economy.

Who decided that the particular goods and services available at the mall and in the broader economy should be produced? How did the producers determine which technology and types of resources to use in producing these particular goods? Who will obtain these products? What accounts for the new and improved products among these goods? This chapter will answer these questions.

Economic Systems

economic system
A particular set of institutional arrangements and a coordinating mechanism for producing goods and services.

Every society needs to develop an **economic system**—a particular set of institutional arrangements and a coordinating mechanism—to respond to the economic problem. The economic system has to determine what goods are produced, how they are produced, who gets them, and how to promote technological progress.

Economic systems differ as to (1) who owns the factors of production and (2) the method used to motivate, coordinate, and direct economic activity. There are two general types of economic systems: the command system and the market system.

The Command System

command system
An economic system in which most property resources are owned by the government and economic decisions are made by a central government body.

The **command system** is also known as *socialism* or *communism*. In a command system, government owns most property resources and economic decision making occurs through a central economic plan. A central planning board appointed by the government makes nearly all the major decisions concerning the use of resources, the composition and distribution of output, and the organization of production. The government owns most of the business firms, which produce according to government directives. The central planning board determines production goals for each enterprise and specifies the amount of resources to be allocated to each enterprise so that it can reach its production goals. The division of output between capital and consumer goods is centrally decided, and capital goods are allocated among industries on the basis of the central planning board's long-term priorities.

A pure command economy would rely exclusively on a central plan to allocate the government-owned property resources. But, in reality, even the preeminent command economy—the Soviet Union—tolerated some private ownership and incorporated some markets before its collapse in 1992. Recent reforms in Russia and most of the eastern European nations have to one degree or another transformed their command economies to capitalistic, market-oriented systems. China's reforms have not gone as far, but they have greatly reduced the reliance on central planning. Although there is still extensive government ownership of resources and capital in China, the nation has increasingly relied on free markets to organize and coordinate its economy. North Korea and Cuba are the last remaining examples of largely centrally planned economies. Global Snapshot 2.1 reveals how North Korea's centrally planned economy compares to the market economy of its neighbor, South Korea. Later in this chapter, we will explore the main reasons for the general demise of the command systems.

The Market System

market system
An economic system in which property resources are privately owned and markets and prices are used to direct and coordinate economic activities.

The polar alternative to the command system is the **market system,** or *capitalism*. The system is characterized by the private ownership of resources and the use of markets and prices to coordinate and direct economic activity. Participants act in their own self-interest. Individuals and businesses seek to achieve their economic goals through their own decisions regarding work, consumption, or production. The system allows for the

ORIGIN OF THE IDEA

O 2.1
Laissez-faire

private ownership of capital, communicates through prices, and coordinates economic activity through *markets*—places where buyers and sellers come together to buy and sell goods, services, and resources. Goods and services are produced and resources are supplied by whoever is willing and able to do so. The result is competition among independently acting buyers and sellers of each product and resource. Thus, economic decision making is widely dispersed. Also, the high potential monetary rewards create powerful incentives for existing firms to innovate and entrepreneurs to pioneer new products and processes.

In *pure* capitalism—or *laissez-faire* capitalism—government's role would be limited to protecting private property and establishing an environment appropriate to the operation of the market system. The term "laissez-faire" means "let it be," that is, keep government from interfering with the economy. The idea is that such interference will disturb the efficient working of the market system.

But in the capitalism practiced in the United States and most other countries, government plays a substantial role in the economy. It not only provides the rules for economic activity but also promotes economic stability and growth, provides certain goods and services that would otherwise be underproduced or not produced at all, and modifies the distribution of income. The government, however, is not the dominant economic force in deciding what to produce, how to produce it, and who will get it. That force is the market.

The Two Koreas

Global Snapshot 2.1

North Korea is one of the few command economies still standing. After the Second World War, Korea was divided into North Korea and South Korea. North Korea, under the influence of the Soviet Union, established a command economy that emphasized government ownership and central government planning. South Korea, protected by the United States, established a market economy based upon private ownership and the profit motive. Today, the differences in the economic outcomes of the two systems are striking:

	North Korea	South Korea
GDP	$40 billion*	$1.6 trillion*
GDP per capita	$1800*	$31,700*
Exports	$2.6 billion	$559 billion
Imports	$3.5 billion	$525 billion
Agriculture as % of GDP	21 percent	3 percent

*Based on purchasing power equivalencies to the U.S. dollar.
Source: *CIA World Fact Book,* 2011, **www.cia.gov.**

Characteristics of the Market System

It will be very instructive to examine some of the key features of the market system in more detail.

Private Property

private property
The right of persons and firms to obtain, own, control, employ, dispose of, and bequeath land, capital, and other property.

In a market system, private individuals and firms, not the government, own most of the property resources (land and capital). It is this extensive private ownership of capital that gives capitalism its name. This right of **private property,** coupled with the freedom to negotiate binding legal contracts, enables individuals and businesses to obtain, use, and dispose of property resources as they see fit. The right of property owners to designate who will receive their property when they die sustains the institution of private property.

The most important consequence of property rights is that they encourage people to cooperate by helping to ensure that only *mutually agreeable* economic transactions take place. In a world without legally enforceable property rights, the strong could simply take whatever they wanted from the weak without giving them any compensation. But in a world of legally enforceable property rights, any person wanting something from you has to get you to agree to give it to them. And you can say no. The result is that if that person really wants what you have, she must offer you something that you value more highly in return. That is, she must offer you a mutually agreeable economic transaction—one that benefits you as well as her.

Property rights also encourage investment, innovation, exchange, maintenance of property, and economic growth. Why would anyone stock a store, build a factory, or clear land for farming if someone else, or the government itself, could take that property for his or her own benefit?

Property rights also extend to intellectual property through patents, copyrights, and trademarks. Such long-term protection encourages people to write books, music, and computer programs and to invent new products and production processes without fear that others will steal them and the rewards they may bring.

Moreover, property rights facilitate exchange. The title to an automobile or the deed to a cattle ranch assures the buyer that the seller is the legitimate owner. Also, property rights encourage owners to maintain or improve their property so as to preserve or increase its value. Finally, property rights enable people to use their time and resources to produce more goods and services, rather than using them to protect and retain the property they have already produced or acquired.

Freedom of Enterprise and Choice

freedom of enterprise
The freedom of firms to obtain economic resources, to use those resources to produce products of the firms' own choosing, and to sell their products in markets of their choice.

freedom of choice
The freedom of owners of resources to employ or dispose of their resources as they see fit, and the freedom of consumers to spend their incomes in a manner they think is appropriate.

Closely related to private ownership of property is freedom of enterprise and choice. The market system requires that various economic units make certain choices, which are expressed and implemented in the economy's markets:

- **Freedom of enterprise** ensures that entrepreneurs and private businesses are free to obtain and use economic resources to produce their choice of goods and services and to sell them in their chosen markets.
- **Freedom of choice** enables owners to employ or dispose of their property and money as they see fit. It also allows workers to enter any line of work for which they are qualified. Finally, it ensures that consumers are free to buy the goods and services that best satisfy their wants.

Index of Economic Freedom, Selected Economies

Global Snapshot 2.2

The Index of Economic Freedom measures economic freedom using 10 broad categories such as trade policy, property rights, and government intervention, with each category containing more than 50 specific criteria. The index then ranks 184 economies according to their degree of economic freedom. A few selected rankings for 2012 are listed below.

FREE

| 1 Hong Kong |
| 3 Australia |
| 5 Switzerland |

MOSTLY FREE

| 10 United States |
| 22 Japan |
| 28 Austria |

MOSTLY UNFREE

| 116 Nigeria |
| 138 China |
| 144 Russia |

REPRESSED

| 171 Iran |
| 174 Venezuela |
| 179 North Korea |

Source: The Heritage Foundation, **www.heritage.org**.

These choices are free only within broad legal limitations, of course. Illegal choices such as selling human organs or buying illicit drugs are punished through fines and imprisonment. (Global Snapshot 2.2 reveals that the degree of economic freedom varies greatly from nation to nation.)

Self-Interest

In the market system, **self-interest** is the motivating force of the various economic units as they express their free choices. Self-interest simply means that each economic unit tries to achieve its own particular goal, which usually requires delivering something of value to others. Entrepreneurs try to maximize profit or minimize loss. Property owners try to get the highest price for the sale or rent of their resources. Workers try to maximize their utility (satisfaction) by finding jobs that offer the best combination of wages, hours, fringe benefits, and working conditions. Consumers try to obtain

self-interest
The most-advantageous outcome as viewed by each firm, property owner, worker, or consumer.

the products they want at the lowest possible price and apportion their expenditures to maximize their utility. The motive of self-interest gives direction and consistency to what might otherwise be a chaotic economy.

Competition

The market system depends on **competition** among economic units. The basis of this competition is freedom of choice exercised in pursuit of a monetary return. Very broadly defined, competition requires

- Independently acting sellers and buyers operating in a particular product or resource market.
- Freedom of sellers and buyers to enter or leave markets, on the basis of their economic self-interest.

Competition diffuses economic power within the businesses and households that make up the economy. When there are independently acting sellers and buyers in a market, no one buyer or seller is able to dictate the price of the product or resource because others can undercut that price.

> **ORIGIN OF THE IDEA**
> **O2.2**
> Self-interest

Competition also implies that producers can enter or leave an industry; there are no insurmountable barriers to an industry's expanding or contracting. This freedom of an industry to expand or contract provides the economy with the flexibility needed to remain efficient over time. Freedom of entry and exit enables the economy to adjust to changes in consumer tastes, technology, and resource availability.

The diffusion of economic power inherent in competition limits the potential abuse of that power. A producer that charges more than the competitive market price will lose sales to other producers. An employer who pays less than the competitive market wage rate will lose workers to other employers. A firm that fails to exploit new technology will lose profits to firms that do. And a firm that produces shoddy products will be punished as customers switch to higher-quality items made by rival firms. Competition is the basic regulatory force in the market system.

Markets and Prices

Markets and prices are key components of the market system. They give the system its ability to coordinate millions of daily economic decisions. A **market** is an institution or mechanism that brings buyers ("demanders") and sellers ("suppliers") into contact. A market system conveys the decisions made by buyers and sellers of products and resources. The decisions made on each side of the market determine a set of product and resource prices that guide resource owners, entrepreneurs, and consumers as they make and revise their choices and pursue their self-interest.

Just as competition is the regulatory mechanism of the market system, the market system itself is the organizing mechanism. It is an elaborate communication network through which innumerable individual free choices are recorded, summarized, and balanced. Those who respond to market signals and heed market dictates are rewarded with greater profit and income; those who do not respond to those signals and choose to ignore market dictates are penalized. Through this mechanism society decides what the economy should produce, how production can be organized efficiently, and how the fruits of production are to be distributed among the various units that make up the economy.

Technology and Capital Goods

In the market system, competition, freedom of choice, self-interest, and personal reward provide the opportunity and motivation for technological advance. The monetary rewards for new products or production techniques accrue directly to the innovator. The market system therefore encourages extensive use and rapid development of complex capital goods: tools, machinery, large-scale factories, and facilities for storage, communication, transportation, and marketing.

Advanced technology and capital goods are important because the most direct methods of production are often the least efficient. The only way to avoid that inefficiency is to rely on capital goods. It would be ridiculous for a farmer to go at production with bare hands. There are huge benefits to be derived from creating and using such capital equipment as plows, tractors, storage bins, and so on. The more efficient production means much more abundant outputs.

Specialization

The extent to which market economies rely on **specialization** is extraordinary. Specialization is using the resources of an individual, region, or nation to produce one or a few goods or services rather than the entire range of goods and services. Those goods and services are then exchanged for a full range of desired products. The majority of consumers produce virtually none of the goods and services they consume, and they consume little or nothing of the items they produce. The person working nine to five installing windows in commercial aircraft may rarely fly. Many farmers sell their milk to the local dairy and then buy margarine at the local grocery store. Society learned long ago that self-sufficiency breeds inefficiency. The jack-of-all-trades may be a very colorful individual but is certainly not an efficient producer.

> **specialization**
> The use of resources of an individual, region, or nation to produce one or a few goods and services rather than the entire range of goods and services.

Division of Labor   Human specialization—called the **division of labor**—contributes to a society's output in several ways:

- *Specialization makes use of differences in ability*   Specialization enables individuals to take advantage of existing differences in their abilities and skills. If Peyton is strong, athletic, and good at throwing a football and Beyoncé is beautiful, is agile, and can sing, their distribution of talents can be most efficiently used if Peyton plays professional football and Beyoncé records songs and gives concerts.
- *Specialization fosters learning by doing*   Even if the abilities of two people are identical, specialization may still be advantageous. By devoting time to a single task rather than working at a number of different tasks, a person is more likely to develop the skills required and to improve techniques. You learn to be a good lawyer by studying and practicing law.
- *Specialization saves time*   By devoting time to a single task, a person avoids the loss of time incurred in shifting from one job to another.

> **division of labor**
> The separation of the work required to produce a product into a number of different tasks that are performed by different workers.

> **ORIGIN OF THE IDEA**
> **O 2.3**
> Specialization: Division of labor

For all these reasons, specialization increases the total output society derives from limited resources.

© Brent Smith/Reuters/Corbis   © PRNewsFoto/Diamond information Center

Photo Op Peyton Manning and Beyoncé Knowles

It makes economic sense for Peyton Manning and Beyoncé Knowles to specialize in what they do best.

Geographic Specialization   Specialization also works on a regional and international basis. It is conceivable that oranges could be grown in Nebraska, but because of the unsuitability of the land, rainfall, and temperature, the costs would be very high. And it is conceivable that wheat could be grown in Florida, but such production would be costly for similar geographical reasons. So Nebraskans produce products—wheat in particular—for which their resources are best suited, and Floridians do the same, producing oranges and other citrus fruits. By specializing, both economies produce more than is needed locally. Then, very sensibly, Nebraskans and Floridians swap some of their surpluses—wheat for oranges, oranges for wheat.

Similarly, on an international scale, the United States specializes in producing such items as commercial aircraft and computers, which it sells abroad in exchange for video recorders from Japan, bananas from Honduras, and woven baskets from Thailand. Both human specialization and geographic specialization are needed to achieve efficiency in the use of limited resources.

Use of Money

medium of exchange
Any item sellers generally accept and buyers generally use to pay for goods and services.

A rather obvious characteristic of any economic system is the extensive use of money. Money performs several functions, but first and foremost it is a **medium of exchange.** It makes trade easier.

Specialization requires exchange. Exchange can, and sometimes does, occur through **barter**—swapping goods for goods, say, wheat for oranges. But barter poses serious problems because it requires a *coincidence of wants* between the buyer and the seller. In our example, we assumed that Nebraskans had excess wheat to trade and wanted oranges. And we assumed that Floridians had excess oranges to trade and wanted wheat. So an exchange occurred. But if such a coincidence of wants is missing, trade is stymied.

Suppose that Nebraska has no interest in Florida's oranges but wants potatoes from Idaho. And suppose that Idaho wants Florida's oranges but not Nebraska's wheat. And, to complicate matters, suppose that Florida wants some of Nebraska's wheat but none of Idaho's potatoes. We summarize the situation in Figure 2.1.

In none of the cases shown in the figure is there a coincidence of wants. Trade by barter clearly would be difficult. Instead, people in each state use **money**, which is simply a convenient social invention to facilitate exchanges of goods and services. Historically, people have used cattle, cigarettes, shells, stones, pieces of metal, and many other commodities, with varying degrees of success, as money. To serve as money, an item needs to pass only one test: It must be generally acceptable to sellers in exchange for their goods and services. Money is socially defined; whatever society accepts as a medium of exchange *is* money.

Today, most economies use pieces of paper as money. The use of paper dollars (currency) as a medium of exchange is what enables Nebraska, Florida, and Idaho to overcome their trade stalemate, as demonstrated in Figure 2.1.

On a global basis, specialization and exchange are complicated by the fact that different nations have different currencies. But markets in which currencies are bought and sold make it possible for people living in different countries to exchange goods and services without resorting to barter.

barter
The exchange of one good or service for another good or service.

money
Any item that is generally acceptable to sellers in exchange for goods and services.

FIGURE 2.1

Money facilitates trade when wants do not coincide. The use of money as a medium of exchange permits trade to be accomplished despite a noncoincidence of wants. (1) Nebraska trades the wheat that Florida wants for money from Floridians; (2) Nebraska trades the money it receives from Florida for the potatoes it wants from Idaho; (3) Idaho trades the money it receives from Nebraska for the oranges it wants from Florida.

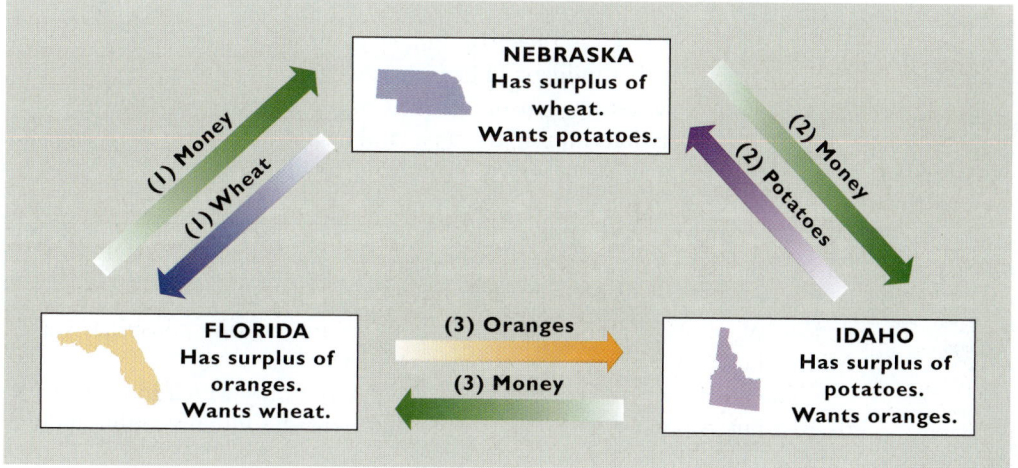

Active, but Limited, Government

An active, but limited, government is the final characteristic of market systems in real-life advanced industrial economies. Although a market system promotes a high degree of efficiency in the use of its resources, it has certain inherent shortcomings. We will discover in Chapter 5 that government can increase the overall effectiveness of the economic system in several ways.

Four Fundamental Questions

The key features of the market system help explain how market economies respond to four fundamental questions:

- What goods and services will be produced?
- How will the goods and services be produced?
- Who will get the goods and services?
- How will the system promote progress?

These four questions highlight the economic choices underlying the production possibilities curve discussed in Chapter 1. They reflect the reality of scarce resources in a world of unlimited wants. All economies, whether market or command, must address these four questions.

What Will Be Produced?

How will a market system decide on the specific types and quantities of goods to be produced? The simple answer is this: The goods and services that can be produced at a continuing profit will be produced, while those whose production generates a continuing loss will be discontinued. Profits and losses are the difference between the total revenue (TR) a firm receives from the sale of its products and the total cost (TC) of producing those products. (For economists, total costs include not only wage and salary payments to labor, and interest and rental payments for capital and land, but also payments to the entrepreneur for organizing and combining the other resources to produce a product.)

Continuing economic profit (TR > TC) in an industry results in expanded production and the movement of resources toward that industry. The industry expands. Continuing losses (TC > TR) in an industry leads to reduced production and the exit of resources from that industry. The industry contracts.

In the market system, consumers are sovereign (in command). **Consumer sovereignty** is crucial in determining the types and quantities of goods produced. Consumers spend their income on the goods they are most willing and able to buy. Through these **"dollar votes"** they register their wants in the market. If the dollar votes for a certain product are great enough to create a profit, businesses will produce that product and offer it for sale. In contrast, if the dollar votes do not create sufficient revenues to cover costs, businesses will not produce the product. So the consumers are sovereign. They collectively direct resources to industries that are meeting consumer wants and away from industries that are not meeting consumer wants.

The dollar votes of consumers determine not only which industries will continue to exist but also which products will survive or fail. Only profitable industries, firms, and products survive.

consumer sovereignty
Determination by consumers of the types and quantities of goods and services that will be produced with the economy's scarce resources.

dollar votes
The "votes" that consumers and entrepreneurs cast for the production of consumer and capital goods when they purchase them in product and resource markets.

McHits and McMisses

McDonald's has introduced several new menu items over the decades. Some have been profitable "hits," while others have been "misses." Ultimately, consumers decide whether a menu item is profitable and therefore whether it stays on the McDonald's menu.

- Hulaburger (1962)—McMiss
- Filet-O-Fish (1963)—McHit
- Strawberry shortcake (1966)—McMiss
- Big Mac (1968)—McHit
- Hot apple pie (1968)—McHit
- Egg McMuffin (1975)—McHit
- Drive-thru (1975)—McHit
- Chicken McNuggets (1983)—McHit
- Extra Value Meal (1991)—McHit
- McLean Deluxe (1991)—McMiss
- Arch Deluxe (1996)—McMiss
- 55-cent special (1997)—McMiss
- Big Xtra (1999)—McHit
- McSalad Shaker (2000)—McMiss
- McGriddle (2003)—McHit
- Snack Wrap (2006)—McHit

Question:
Do you think McDonald's premium salads will be a lasting McHit, or do you think they eventually will become a McMiss?

Source: Dyan Machan, "Polishing the Golden Arches," *Forbes*, June 15, 1998, pp. 42–43, updated. Used with permission of Forbes Media LLC © 2011.

How Will the Goods and Services Be Produced?

What combinations of resources and technologies will be used to produce goods and services? How will the production be organized? The answer: In combinations and ways that minimize the cost per unit of output. This is true because inefficiency drives up costs and lowers profits. As a result, any firm wishing to maximize its profits will make great efforts to minimize production costs. These efforts will include using the right mix of labor and capital, given the prices and productivity of those resources. They also mean locating production facilities optimally to hold down production and transportation expenses. Finally, it means using the most appropriate technology in producing and distributing output.

Those efforts will be intensified if the firm faces competition, as consumers strongly prefer low prices and will shift their purchases over to the firms that can produce a quality product at the lowest possible price. Any firm foolish enough to use higher-cost production methods will go bankrupt as it is undersold by its more efficient competitors who can still make a profit when selling at a lower price. Simply stated: Competition eliminates high-cost producers.

Who Will Get the Output?

The market system enters the picture in two ways when determining the distribution of total output. Generally, any product will be distributed to consumers on the basis of their ability and willingness to pay its existing market price. If the price of some product, say, a small sailboat, is $3000, then buyers who are willing and able to pay that price will "sail, sail away." Consumers who are unwilling or unable to pay the price will "sit on the dock of the bay."

The ability to pay the prices for sailboats and other products depends on the amount of income that consumers have, along with the prices of, and preferences for, various goods. If consumers have sufficient income and want to spend their money on a particular good, they can have it. And the amount of income they have depends on (1) the quantities of the property and human resources they supply and (2) the prices those resources command in the resource market. Resource prices (wages, interest, rent, profit) are key in determining the size of each household's income and therefore each household's ability to buy part of the economy's output.

How Will the System Promote Progress?

Society desires economic growth (greater output) and higher standards of living (greater output *per person*). How does the market system promote technological improvements and capital accumulation, both of which contribute to a higher standard of living for society?

Technological Advance   The market system provides a strong incentive for technological advance and enables better products and processes to supplant inferior ones. An entrepreneur or firm that introduces a popular new product will gain revenue and economic profit at the expense of rivals. Firms that are highly profitable one year may find they are in financial trouble just a few years later.

Technological advance also includes new and improved methods that reduce production or distribution costs. By passing part of its cost reduction on to the consumer through a lower product price, the firm can increase sales and obtain economic profit at the expense of rival firms.

Moreover, the market system promotes the *rapid spread* of technological advance throughout an industry. Rival firms must follow the lead of the most innovative firm or else suffer immediate losses and eventual failure. In some cases, the result is **creative destruction:** The creation of new products and production methods completely destroys the market positions of firms that are wedded to existing products and older ways of doing business. Example: The advent of compact discs largely demolished long-play vinyl records, and iPods and other digital technologies are now supplanting CDs.

creative destruction
The idea that the creation of new products and production methods may simultaneously destroy the market power of existing firms.

Capital Accumulation   Most technological advances require additional capital goods. The market system provides the resources necessary to produce additional capital through increased dollar votes for those goods. That is, the market system acknowledges dollar voting for capital goods as well as for consumer goods.

But who counts the dollar votes for capital goods? Answer: Entrepreneurs and business owners. As receivers of profit income, they often use part of that income to purchase capital goods. Doing so yields even greater profit income in the future if the technological innovation that required the additional capital goods is successful. Also, by paying interest or selling ownership shares, the entrepreneur and firm can attract some of the income of households to cast dollar votes for the production of more capital goods.

The "Invisible Hand"

In his 1776 book *The Wealth of Nations*, Adam Smith first noted that the operation of a market system creates a curious unity between private interests and social interests. Firms and resource suppliers, seeking to further their own self-interest and operating within the framework of a highly competitive market system, will simultaneously, as though guided by an **"invisible hand,"** promote the public or social interest. For example, we have seen that in a competitive environment, businesses seek to build new and improved products to increase profits. Those enhanced products increase society's well-being. Businesses also use the least costly combination of resources to produce a specific output because it is in their self-interest to do so. To act otherwise would be to forgo profit or even to risk business failure. But, at the same time, to use scarce resources in the least costly way is clearly in the social interest as well. It "frees up" resources to produce something else that society desires.

Self-interest, awakened and guided by the competitive market system, is what induces responses appropriate to the changes in society's wants. Businesses seeking to make higher profits and to avoid losses, and resource suppliers pursuing greater monetary rewards, negotiate changes in the allocation of resources and end up with the output that society wants. Competition controls or guides self-interest such that self-interest automatically and quite unintentionally furthers the best interest of society. The invisible hand ensures that when firms maximize their profits and resource suppliers maximize their incomes, these groups also help maximize society's output and income.

Question:
Are "doing good for others" and "doing well for oneself" conflicting ideas, according to Adam Smith?

"invisible hand"
The tendency of firms and resource suppliers that are seeking to further their own self-interest in competitive markets to also promote the interest of society as a whole.

The Demise of the Command Systems

Now that you know how the market system answers the four fundamental questions, you can easily understand why command systems of the Soviet Union, eastern Europe, and prereform China failed. Those systems encountered two insurmountable problems.

The first difficulty was the *coordination problem*. The central planners had to coordinate the millions of individual decisions by consumers, resource suppliers, and businesses. Consider the setting up of a factory to produce tractors. The central planners had to establish a realistic annual production target, for example, 1000 tractors. They then had to make available all the necessary inputs—labor, machinery, electric power, steel, tires, glass, paint, transportation—for the production and delivery of those 1000 tractors.

Because the outputs of many industries serve as inputs to other industries, the failure of any single industry to achieve its output target caused a chain reaction of repercussions. For example, if iron mines, for want of machinery or labor or transportation, did not supply the steel industry with the required inputs of iron ore, the steel mills were unable to fulfill the input needs of the many industries that depended on steel. Those steel-using industries (such as tractor, automobile, and transportation) were unable to fulfill their planned production goals. Eventually the chain reaction spread to all firms that used steel as an input and from there to other input buyers or final consumers.

The coordination problem became more difficult as the economies expanded. Products and production processes grew more sophisticated, and the number of industries requiring planning increased. Planning techniques that worked for the simpler economy proved highly inadequate and inefficient for the larger economy. Bottlenecks and production stoppages became the norm, not the exception.

A lack of a reliable success indicator added to the coordination problem in the Soviet Union and prereform China. We have seen that market economies rely on profit as a success indicator. Profit depends on consumer demand, production efficiency, and product quality. In contrast, the major success indicator for the command economies usually was a quantitative production target that the central planners assigned. Production costs, product quality, and product mix were secondary considerations. Managers and workers often sacrificed product quality because they were being awarded bonuses for meeting quantitative, not qualitative, targets. If meeting production goals meant sloppy assembly work, so be it.

It was difficult at best for planners to assign quantitative production targets without unintentionally producing distortions in output. If the production target for an enterprise manufacturing nails was specified in terms of *weight* (tons of nails), the producer made only large nails. But if its target was specified as a *quantity* (thousands of nails), the producer made all small nails, and lots of them!

The command economies also faced an *incentive problem*. Central planners determined the output mix. When they misjudged how many automobiles, shoes, shirts, and chickens were wanted at the government-determined prices, persistent shortages and surpluses of those products arose. But as long as the managers who oversaw the production of those goods were rewarded for meeting their assigned production goals, they had no incentive to adjust production in response to the shortages and surpluses. And there were no fluctuations in prices and profitability to signal that more or less of certain products was desired. Thus, many products were unavailable or in short supply, while other products were overproduced and sat for months or years in warehouses.

The command systems of the Soviet Union and prereform China also lacked entrepreneurship. Central planning did not trigger the profit motive, nor did it reward innovation and enterprise. The route for getting ahead was through participation in the political hierarchy of the Communist Party. Moving up the hierarchy meant better housing, better access to health care, and the right to shop in special stores. Meeting production targets and maneuvering through the minefields of party politics were measures of success in "business." But a definition of business success based solely on political savvy is not conducive to technological advance, which is often disruptive to existing products, production methods, and organizational structures.

Question:
In market economies, firms rarely worry about the availability of inputs to produce their products, whereas in command economies input availability was a constant concern. Why the difference?

The Circular Flow Model

The dynamic market economy creates continuous, repetitive flows of goods and services, resources, and money. The **circular flow diagram,** shown in Figure 2.2, illustrates those flows for a simplified economy in which there is no government. Observe that in the diagram we group this economy's decision makers into *businesses* and *households*. Additionally, we divide this economy's markets into the *resource market* and the *product market*.

circular flow diagram
The flow of resources from households to firms and of products from firms to households.

Households

The blue rectangle on the right side of the circular flow diagram in Figure 2.2 represents **households,** which are defined as one or more persons occupying a housing unit. There are currently about 119 million households in the U.S. economy. Households buy the goods and services that businesses make available in the product market. Households obtain the income needed to buy those products by selling resources in the resource market.

households
One or more persons occupying a housing unit that provide resources to the economy and use income received to purchase goods and services that satisfy economic wants.

All the resources in our no-government economy are ultimately owned or provided by households. For instance, the members of one household or another directly provide all of the labor and entrepreneurial ability in the economy. Households also own all of the land and all of the capital in the economy either directly, as personal property, or indirectly, as a consequence of owning all of the businesses in the economy (and thereby controlling all of the land and capital owned by businesses). Thus, all of the income in the economy—all wages, rents, interest, and profits—flow to households because they provide the economy's labor, land, capital, and entrepreneurial ability.

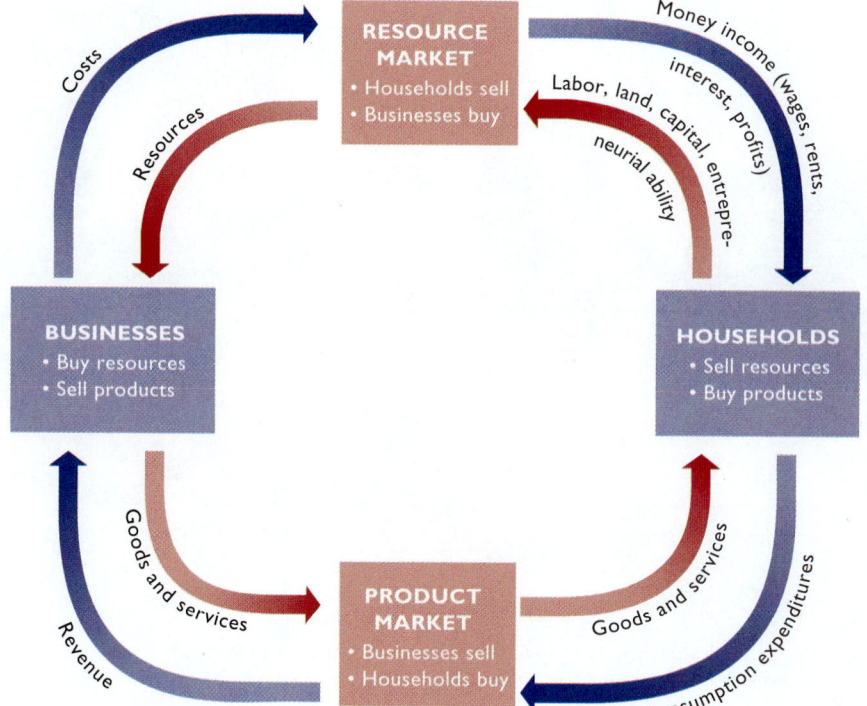

FIGURE 2.2
The circular flow diagram. Products flow from businesses to households through the product market, and resources flow from households to businesses through the resource market. Opposite those real flows are monetary flows. Households receive income from businesses (their costs) through the resource market, and businesses receive revenue from households (their expenditures) through the product market.

Businesses

businesses
Firms that purchase resources and provide goods and services to the economy.

The blue rectangle on the left side of the circular flow diagram represents **businesses,** which are commercial establishments that attempt to earn profits for their owners by offering goods and services for sale. Businesses sell goods and services in the product market in order to obtain revenue, and they incur costs in the resource markets when they purchase the labor, land, capital, and entrepreneurial ability that they need to produce their respective goods and services.

Product Market

product market
A market in which goods and services (products) are sold by firms and bought by households.

The red rectangle at the bottom of the diagram represents the **product market,** the place where goods and services produced by businesses are bought and sold. Households use the income they receive from the sale of resources to buy goods and services. The money that consumers spend on goods and services flows to businesses as revenue. Businesses compare those revenues to their costs in determining profitability and whether or not a particular good or service should continue to be produced.

Resource Market

resource market
A market in which households sell and firms buy economic resources.

Finally, the red rectangle at the top of the circular flow diagram represents the **resource market** in which households sell resources to businesses. The households sell resources to generate income, and the businesses buy resources to produce goods and services. The funds that businesses pay for resources are costs to businesses but are flows of wage, rent, interest, and profit income to the household. Productive resources therefore flow from households to businesses, and money flows from businesses to households.

© T. O'Keefe/PhotoLink/Getty Images

© Royalty Free/CORBIS

Photo Op Resource Markets and Product Markets

The sale of a grove of orange trees would be a transaction in the resource market; the sale of oranges to final consumers would be a transaction in the product market.

The circular flow model depicts a complex, inter-related web of decision making and economic activity involving businesses and households. For the economy, it is the circle of life. Businesses and households are both buyers and sellers. Businesses buy resources and sell products. Households buy products and sell resources. As shown in Figure 2.2, there is a counterclockwise *real flow* of economic resources and finished goods and services and a clockwise *money flow* of income and consumption expenditures.

Applying the Analysis

Some Facts About U.S. Businesses

Businesses constitute one part of the private sector. The business population is extremely diverse, ranging from giant corporations such as Walmart, with 2011 sales of $422 billion and 2.1 million employees, to neighborhood specialty shops with one or two employees and sales of only $200 to $300 per day. There are three major legal forms of businesses: sole proprietorships, partnerships, and corporations.

A *sole proprietorship* is a business owned and operated by one person. Usually, the proprietor (the owner) personally supervises its operation. In a *partnership*, two or more individuals (the partners) agree to own and operate a business together.

A *corporation* is a legal creation that can acquire resources, own assets, produce and sell products, incur debts, extend credit, sue and be sued, and perform the functions of any other type of enterprise. A corporation sells stocks (ownership shares) to raise funds but is legally distinct and separate from the individual stockholders. The stockholders' legal and financial liability is limited to the loss of the value of their shares. Hired executives and managers operate corporations on a day-to-day basis.

Figure 2.3a shows how the business population is distributed among the three major legal forms. About 72% of firms are sole proprietorships, whereas only 18%

FIGURE 2.3

The business population and shares of total revenue. (a) Sole proprietorships dominate the business population numerically, but (b) corporations dominate total sales revenue (total output).

Source: U.S. Census Bureau, **www.census.gov**.

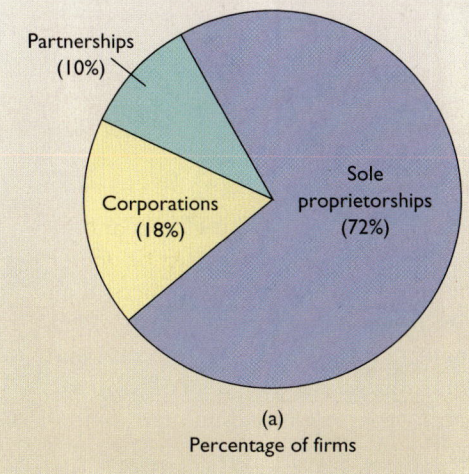
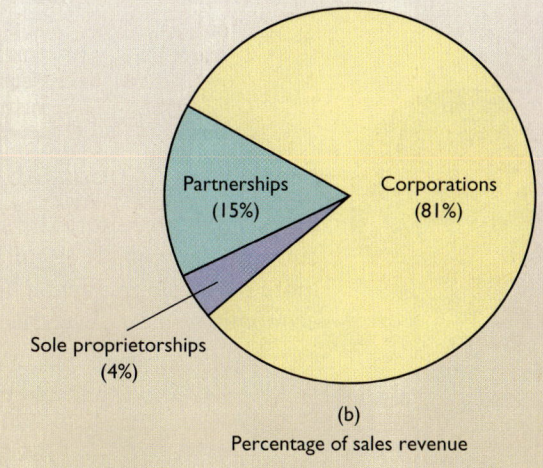

(a)
Percentage of firms

(b)
Percentage of sales revenue

are corporations. But as Figure 2.3b indicates, corporations account for 81% of total sales revenue (and therefore total output) in the United States. Virtually all the nation's largest business enterprises are corporations. Global Snapshot 2.3 lists the world's largest corporations.

Question:
Why do you think sole proprietorships and partnerships typically incorporate (become corporations) when they experience rapid and sizable increases in their production, sales, and profits?

Global Snapshot 2.3

The World's 10 Largest Corporations

Six of the world's ten largest corporations, based on dollar revenue in 2011, were headquartered in the United States or China. Japan, Britain, and The Netherlands account for the rest of the top ten.

Walmart (USA) $422 billion
Royal Dutch Shell (Netherlands) $378 billion
ExxonMobil (USA) $355 billion
BP (Britain) $309 billion
Sinopec (China) $273 billion
China National Petroleum (China) $240 billion
State Grid (China) $226 billion
Toyota Motor (Japan) $222 billion
Japan Post Holdings (Japan) $204 billion
Chevron (USA) $196 billion

Source: "Global 500," Fortune Magazine, July 25, 2011. © Time Inc., used under license.

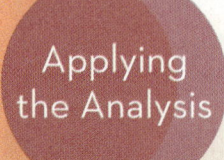

Applying the Analysis

Some Facts About U.S. Households

Households constitute the second part of the private sector. The U.S. economy currently has about 119 million households. These households consist of one or more persons occupying a housing unit and are both the ultimate suppliers of all economic resources *and* the major spenders in the economy.

The nation's earned income is apportioned among wages, rents, interest, and profits. *Wages* are paid to labor; *rents* and *interest* are paid to owners of property resources; and *profits* are paid to the owners of corporations and unincorporated businesses.

Figure 2.4a shows the categories of U.S. income earned in 2010. The largest source of income for households is the wages and salaries paid to workers. Notice that the bulk of total U.S. income goes to labor, not to capital. Proprietors' income— the income of doctors, lawyers, small-business owners, farmers, and owners of other unincorporated enterprises—also has a "wage" element. Some of this income is payment for one's own labor, and some of it is profit from one's own business.

The other three types of income are self-evident: Some households own corporate stock and receive dividend incomes as their share of corporate profits. Many households also own bonds and savings accounts that yield interest income. And some households receive rental income by providing buildings and natural resources (including land) to businesses and other individuals.

U.S. households use their income to buy (spend), save, and pay taxes. Figure 2.4b shows how households divide their spending among three broad categories of goods and services: *consumer durables* (goods such as cars, refrigerators, and personal computers that have expected lives of 3 years or longer), *nondurables* (goods such as food, clothing, and gasoline that have lives of less than 3 years), and *services* (the work done by people such as lawyers, physicians, and recreational workers). Observe that approximately 65% of consumer spending is on services. For this reason, the United States is known as a *service-oriented economy*.

Question:
Over the past several decades, the service share of spending in the United States has increased relative to the goods share. Why do you think that trend has occurred?

FIGURE 2.4

Sources of U.S. income and the composition of spending. (a) Sixty-eight percent of U.S. income is received as wages and salaries. Income to property owners—corporate profit, interest, and rents—accounts for about 23% of total income. (b) Consumers divide their spending among durable goods, nondurable goods, and services. Roughly 65% of consumer spending is for services; the rest is for goods.

Source: Bureau of Economic Analysis, **www.bea.gov.**

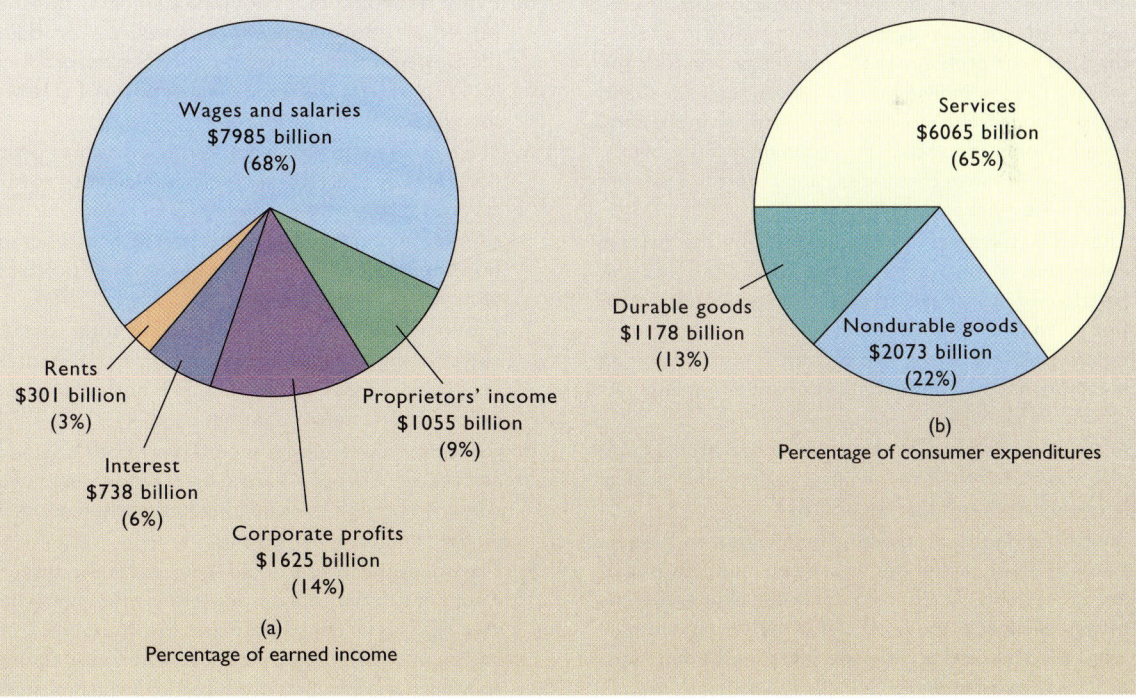

© PRNewsFoto/Whirlpool Corporation

© Ed Carey/Cole Group/Getty Images

© Royalty-Free/CORBIS

Photo Op Durable Goods, Nondurable Goods, and Services

Consumers collectively spend their income on durable goods (such as the washer-dryer combo), nondurable goods (such as the pizza), and services (such as hair care).

Summary

1. The market system and the command system are the two broad types of economic systems used to address the economic problem. In the market system (or capitalism), private individuals own most resources, and markets coordinate most economic activity. In the command system (or socialism or communism), government owns most resources, and central planners coordinate most economic activity.

2. The market system is characterized by the private ownership of resources, including capital, and the freedom of individuals to engage in economic activities of their choice to advance their material well-being. Self-interest is the driving force of such an economy, and competition functions as a regulatory or control mechanism.

3. In the market system, markets, prices, and profits organize and make effective the many millions of individual economic decisions that occur daily.

4. Specialization, use of advanced technology, and the extensive use of capital goods are common features of market systems. Functioning as a medium of exchange, money eliminates the problems of bartering and permits easy trade and greater specialization, both domestically and internationally.

5. Every economy faces four fundamental questions: (a) What goods and services will be produced? (b) How will the goods and services be produced? (c) Who will get the goods and services? (d) How will the system promote progress?

6. The market system produces products whose production and sale yield total revenue sufficient to cover total cost. It does not produce products for which total revenue continuously falls short of total cost. Competition forces firms to use the lowest-cost production techniques.

7. Economic profit (total revenue minus total cost) indicates that an industry is prosperous and promotes its expansion. Losses signify that an industry is not prosperous and hasten its contraction.

8. Consumer sovereignty means that both businesses and resource suppliers are subject to the wants of consumers. Through their dollar votes, consumers decide on the composition of output.

9. The prices that a household receives for the resources it supplies to the economy determine that household's income. This income determines the household's claim on the economy's output. Those who have income to spend get the products produced in the market system.

10. The market system encourages technological advance and capital accumulation, both of which raise a nation's standard of living.
11. Competition, the primary mechanism of control in the market economy, promotes a unity of self-interest and social interests. As if directed by an invisible hand, competition harnesses the self-interested motives of businesses and resource suppliers to further the social interest.
12. The circular flow model illustrates the flows of resources and products from households to businesses and from businesses to households, along with the corresponding monetary flows. Businesses are on the buying side of the resource market and the selling side of the product market. Households are on the selling side of the resource market and the buying side of the product market.

Terms and Concepts

economic system

command system

market system

private property

freedom of enterprise

freedom of choice

self-interest

competition

market

specialization

division of labor

medium of exchange

barter

money

consumer sovereignty

dollar votes

creative destruction

"invisible hand"

circular flow diagram

households

businesses

product market

resource market

Questions

1. Contrast how a market system and a command economy try to cope with economic scarcity. **LO1**
2. How does self-interest help achieve society's economic goals? Why are there such a wide variety of desired goods and services in a market system? In what way are entrepreneurs and businesses at the helm of the economy but commanded by consumers? **LO2**
3. Why is private property, and the protection of property rights, so critical to the success of the market system? How do property rights encourage cooperation? **LO2**
4. What are the advantages of using capital in the production process? What is meant by the term "division of labor"? What are the advantages of specialization in the use of human and material resources? Explain why exchange is the necessary consequence of specialization. **LO2**
5. What problem does barter entail? Indicate the economic significance of money as a medium of exchange. What is meant by the statement "We want money only to part with it"? **LO2**
6. Evaluate and explain the following statements: **LO2**
   a. The market system is a profit-and-loss system.
   b. Competition is the disciplinarian of the market economy.
7. In the 1990s thousands of "dot-com" companies emerged with great fanfare to take advantage of the Internet and new information technologies. A few, like Google, eBay, and Amazon, have generally thrived and prospered, but many others struggled and eventually failed. Explain these varied outcomes in terms of how the market system answers the question "What goods and services will be produced?" **LO3**
8. Some large hardware stores such as Home Depot boast of carrying as many as 20,000 different products in each store. What motivated the producers of those individual products to make them and offer them for sale? How did the producers decide on the best combinations of resources to use? Who made those resources available, and why? Who decides whether these particular hardware products should continue to be produced and offered for sale? **LO3**
9. What is meant by the term "creative destruction"? How does the emergence of MP3 (or iPod) technology relate to this idea? **LO3**
10. In a sentence, describe the meaning of the phrase "invisible hand." **LO4**
11. Distinguish between the resource market and the product market in the circular flow model. In what way are businesses and households both sellers and buyers

in this model? What are the flows in the circular flow model? **LO5**

12. What are the three major legal forms of business enterprises? Which form is the most prevalent in terms of numbers? Which form is dominant in terms of total sales revenues? **LO5**

13. What are the major forms of household income? Contrast the wage and salary share to the profit share in terms of relative size. Distinguish between a durable consumer good and a nondurable consumer good. How does the combined spending on both types of consumer goods compare to the spending on services? **LO5**

Problems

1. Suppose Natasha currently makes $50,000 per year working as a manager at a cable TV company. She then develops two possible entrepreneurial business opportunities. In one, she will quit her job to start an organic soap company. In the other, she will try to develop an Internet-based competitor to the local cable company. For the soap-making opportunity, she anticipates annual revenue of $465,000 and costs for the necessary land, labor, and capital of $395,000 per year. For the Internet opportunity, she anticipates costs for land, labor, and capital of $3,250,000 per year as compared to revenues of $3,275,000 per year. (a) Should she quit her current job to become an entrepreneur? (b) If she does quit her current job, which opportunity would she pursue? **LO5**

2. With current technology, suppose a firm is producing 400 loaves of banana bread daily. Also assume that the least-cost combination of resources in producing those loaves is 5 units of labor, 7 units of land, 2 units of capital, and 1 unit of entrepreneurial ability, selling at prices of $40, $60, $60, and $20, respectively. If the firm can sell these 400 loaves at $2 per unit, what is its total revenue? Its total cost? Its profit or loss? Will it continue to produce banana bread? If this firm's situation is typical for the other makers of banana bread, will resources flow toward or away from this bakery good? **LO3**

3. Let's put dollar amounts on the flows in the circular flow diagram of Figure 2.2. **LO5**

   a. Suppose that businesses buy a total of $100 billion of the four resources (labor, land, capital, and entrepreneurial ability) from households. If households receive $60 billion in wages, $10 billion in rent, and $20 billion in interest, how much are households paid for providing entrepreneurial ability?

   b. If households spend $55 billion on goods and $45 billion on services, how much in revenues do businesses receive in the product market?

FURTHER TEST YOUR KNOWLEDGE AT
www.brue3e.com

At the text's Online Learning Center, **www.brue3e.com**, you will find one or more web-based questions that require information from the Internet to answer. We urge you to check them out, since they will familiarize you with websites that may be helpful in other courses and perhaps even in your career. The OLC also features multiple-choice quizzes that give instant feedback and provides other helpful ways to further test your knowledge of the chapter.

CHAPTER THREE

Demand, Supply, and Market Equilibrium

After reading this chapter, you should be able to:

1. Describe *demand* and explain how it can change.
2. Describe *supply* and explain how it can change.
3. Relate how supply and demand interact to determine market equilibrium.
4. Explain how changes in supply and demand affect equilibrium prices and quantities.
5. Identify what government-set prices are and how they can cause product surpluses and shortages.

The model of supply and demand is the economics profession's greatest contribution to human understanding because it explains the operation of the markets on which we depend for nearly everything that we eat, drink, or consume. The model is so powerful and so widely used that to many people it *is* economics.

Markets bring together buyers ("demanders") and sellers ("suppliers") and exist in many forms.

ORIGIN OF THE IDEA

O 3.1
Demand and supply

The corner gas station, an e-commerce site, the local music store, a farmer's roadside stand—all are familiar markets. The New York Stock Exchange and the Chicago Board of Trade are markets where buyers and sellers of stocks and bonds and farm commodities from all over the world communicate with one another to buy and sell. Auctioneers bring together potential buyers and sellers of art, livestock, used farm equipment, and, sometimes, real estate.

Some markets are local, while others are national or international. Some are highly personal, involving face-to-face contact between demander and supplier; others are faceless, with buyer and seller never seeing or knowing each other. But all competitive markets involve demand and supply, and this chapter discusses how the model works to explain both the *quantities* that are bought and sold in markets as well as the *prices* at which they trade.

Demand

Demand is a schedule or a curve that shows the various amounts of a product that consumers will purchase at each of several possible prices during a specified period of time.[1] The table in Figure 3.1 is a hypothetical demand schedule for a *single consumer* purchasing a particular product, in this case, lattes. (For simplicity, we will categorize all espresso drinks as "lattes" and assume a highly competitive market.)

The table reveals that, if the price of lattes were $5 each, Joe Java would buy 10 lattes per month; if it were $4, he would buy 20 lattes per month; and so forth.

The table does not tell us which of the five possible prices will actually exist in the market. That depends on the interaction between demand and supply. Demand is simply a statement of a buyer's plans, or intentions, with respect to the purchase of a product.

To be meaningful, the quantities demanded at each price must relate to a specific period—a day, a week, a month. Here that period is 1 month.

> **demand**
> A schedule or curve that shows the various amounts of a product that consumers will buy at each of a series of possible prices during a specific period.

Law of Demand

A fundamental characteristic of demand is this: Other things equal, as price falls, the quantity demanded rises, and as price rises, the quantity demanded falls. In short, there is an *inverse* relationship

----

[1] This definition obviously is worded to apply to product markets. To adjust it to apply to resource markets, substitute the word "resource" for "product" and the word "businesses" for "consumers."

FIGURE 3.1

Joe Java's demand for lattes. Because price and quantity demanded are inversely related, an individual's demand schedule graphs as a downsloping curve such as *D*. Other things equal, consumers will buy more of a product as its price declines and less of the product as its price rises. (Here and in later figures, *P* stands for price and *Q* stands for quantity demanded or supplied.)

Joe Java's Demand for Lattes	
Price per Latte	**Quantity Demanded per Month**
$5	10
4	20
3	35
2	55
1	80

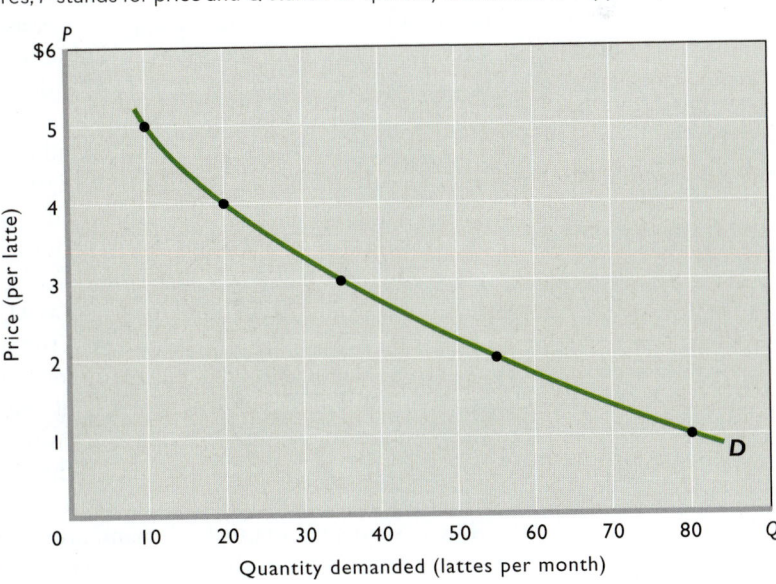

between price and quantity demanded. Economists call this inverse relationship the **law of demand.**

The other-things-equal assumption is critical here. Many factors other than the price of the product being considered affect the amount purchased. The quantity of lattes purchased will depend not only on the price of lattes but also on the prices of such substitutes as tea, soda, fruit juice, and bottled water. The law of demand in this case says that fewer lattes will be purchased if the price of lattes rises while the prices of tea, soda, fruit juice, and bottled water all remain constant.

The law of demand is consistent with both common sense and observation. People ordinarily *do* buy more of a product at a low price than at a high price. Price is an obstacle that deters consumers from buying. The higher that obstacle, the less of a product they will buy; the lower the obstacle, the more they will buy. The fact that businesses reduce prices to clear out unsold goods is evidence of their belief in the law of demand.

The Demand Curve

The inverse relationship between price and quantity demanded for any product can be represented on a simple graph, in which, by convention, we measure *quantity demanded* on the horizontal axis and *price* on the vertical axis. In Figure 3.1 we have plotted the five price-quantity data points listed in the table and connected the points with a smooth curve, labeled *D*. This is a **demand curve.** Its downward slope reflects the law of demand: People buy more of a product, service, or resource as its price falls. They buy less as its price rises. There is an inverse relationship between price and quantity demanded.

The table and graph in Figure 3.1 contain exactly the same data and reflect the same inverse relationship between price and quantity demanded.

Market Demand

So far, we have concentrated on just one consumer, Joe Java. But competition requires that more than one buyer be present in each market. By adding the quantities demanded by all consumers at each of the various possible prices, we can get from *individual* demand to *market* demand. If there are just three buyers in the market (Joe Java, Sarah Coffee, and Mike Cappuccino), as represented by the table and graph in Figure 3.2, it is relatively easy to determine the total quantity demanded at each price. We simply sum the individual quantities demanded to obtain the total quantity demanded at each price. The particular price and the total quantity demanded are then plotted as one point on the market demand curve in Figure 3.2.

Competition, of course, ordinarily entails many more than three buyers of a product. To avoid hundreds or thousands of additions, let's simply suppose that the table and curve D_1 in Figure 3.3 show the amounts all the buyers in this market will purchase at each of the five prices.

In constructing a demand curve such as D_1 in Figure 3.3, economists assume that price is the most important influence on the amount of any product purchased. But economists know that other factors can and do affect purchases. These factors, called **determinants of demand,** are held constant when a demand curve like D_1 is drawn. They are the "other things equal" in the relationship between price and quantity demanded. When any of these determinants changes, the demand curve will shift to the right or left. For this reason, determinants of demand are sometimes referred to as *demand shifters*.

The basic determinants of demand are (1) consumers' tastes (preferences), (2) the number of consumers in the market, (3) consumers' incomes, (4) the prices of related goods, and (5) expected prices.

FIGURE 3.2

Market demand for lattes, three buyers. We establish the market demand curve D by adding horizontally the individual demand curves (D_1, D_2, and D_3) of all the consumers in the market. At the price of $3, for example, the three individual curves yield a total quantity demanded of 100 lattes.

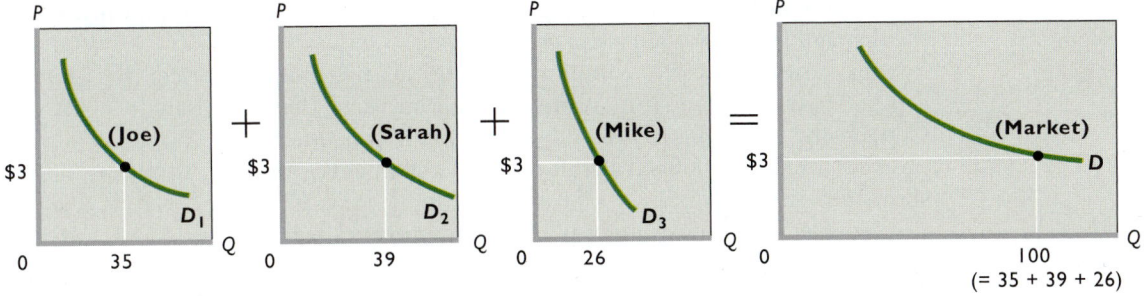

	Market Demand for Lattes, Three Buyers						
Price per Latte	Joe Java		Sarah Coffee		Mike Cappuccino		Total Quantity Demanded per Month
$5	10	+	12	+	8	=	30
4	20	+	23	+	17	=	60
3	35	+	39	+	26	=	100
2	55	+	60	+	39	=	154
1	80	+	87	+	54	=	221

FIGURE 3.3

Changes in the demand for lattes. A change in one or more of the determinants of demand causes a change in demand. An increase in demand is shown as a shift of the demand curve to the right, as from D_1 to D_2. A decrease in demand is shown as a shift of the demand curve to the left, as from D_1 to D_3. These changes in demand are to be distinguished from a change in *quantity demanded*, which is caused by a change in the price of the product, as shown by a movement from, say, point a to point b on fixed demand curve D_1.

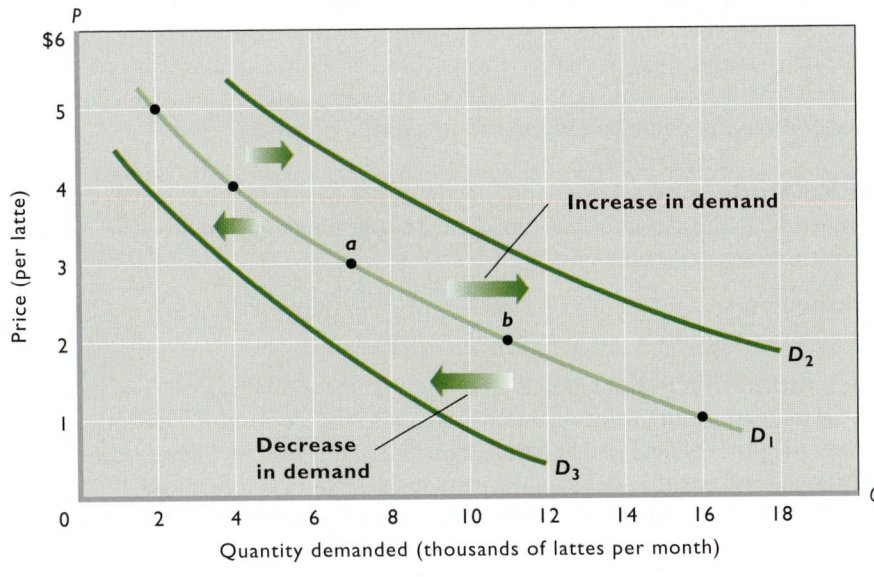

Market Demand for Lattes (D)	
(1)	(2)
Price per Latte	Total Quantity Demanded per Month
$5	2000
4	4000
3	7000
2	11,000
1	16,000

Changes in Demand

A change in one or more of the determinants of demand will change the underlying demand data (the demand schedule in the table) and therefore the location of the demand curve in Figure 3.3. A change in the demand schedule or, graphically, a shift in the demand curve is called a *change in demand.*

If consumers desire to buy more lattes at each possible price, that *increase in demand* is shown as a shift of the demand curve to the right, say, from D_1 to D_2. Conversely, a *decrease in demand* occurs when consumers buy fewer lattes at each possible price. The leftward shift of the demand curve from D_1 to D_3 in Figure 3.3 shows that situation.

Now let's see how changes in each determinant affect demand.

Tastes   A favorable change in consumer tastes (preferences) for a product means more of it will be demanded at each price. Demand will increase; the demand curve will shift rightward. For example, greater concern about the environment has increased the demand for hybrid cars and other "green" technologies. An unfavorable change in consumer preferences will decrease demand, shifting the demand curve to the left. For example, the recent popularity of low-carbohydrate diets has reduced the demand for bread and pasta.

Number of Buyers   An increase in the number of buyers in a market increases product demand. For example, the rising number of older persons in the United States in recent years has increased the demand for motor homes and retirement communities. In contrast, the migration of people away from many small rural communities has reduced the demand for housing, home appliances, and auto repair in those towns.

Income   The effect of changes in income on demand is more complex. For most products, a rise in income increases demand. Consumers collectively buy more airplane tickets, 3D TVs, and gas grills as their incomes rise. Products whose demand increases or decreases *directly* with changes in income are called *superior goods*, or **normal goods.**

Although most products are normal goods, there are a few exceptions. As incomes increase beyond some point, the demand for used clothing, retread tires, and soy-enhanced hamburger may decline. Higher incomes enable consumers to buy new clothing, new tires, and higher-quality meats. Goods whose demand increases or decreases *inversely* with money income are called **inferior goods.** (This is an economic term; we are not making personal judgments on specific products.)

Prices of Related Goods   A change in the price of a related good may either increase or decrease the demand for a product, depending on whether the related good is a substitute or a complement:

- A **substitute good** is one that can be used in place of another good.
- A **complementary good** is one that is used together with another good.

Beef and chicken are substitute goods or, simply, *substitutes.* When two products are substitutes, an increase in the price of one will increase the demand for the other. For example, when the price of beef rises, consumers will buy less beef and increase their demand for chicken. So it is with other product pairs such as Nikes and Reeboks, Budweiser and Miller beer, or Colgate and Crest toothpaste. They are *substitutes in consumption.*

normal good
A good (or service) whose consumption rises when income increases and falls when income decreases.

inferior good
A good (or service) whose consumption declines when income rises and rises when income decreases.

substitute good
A good (or service) that can be used in place of some other good (or service).

complementary good
A good (or service) that is used in conjunction with some other good (or service).

© Bambu Producoes/Getty Images   © Doug Menuez/Getty Images

Photo Op Normal versus Inferior Goods

New television sets are normal goods. People buy more of them as their incomes rise. Hand-pushed lawn mowers are inferior goods. As incomes rise, people purchase gas-powered mowers instead.

Complementary goods (or, simply, *complements*) are products that are used together and thus are typically demanded jointly. Examples include computers and software, cell phones and cellular service, and snowboards and lift tickets. If the price of a complement (for example, lettuce) goes up, the demand for the related good (salad dressing) will decline. Conversely, if the price of a complement (for example, tuition) falls, the demand for a related good (textbooks) will increase.

The vast majority of goods that are unrelated to one another are called *independent goods*. There is virtually no demand relationship between bacon and golf balls or pickles and ice cream. A change in the price of one will have virtually no effect on the demand for the other.

Expected Prices   Changes in expected prices may shift demand. A newly formed expectation of a higher price in the future may cause consumers to buy now in order to "beat" the anticipated price rise, thus increasing current demand. For example, when freezing weather destroys much of Brazil's coffee crop, buyers may conclude that the price of coffee beans will rise. They may purchase large quantities now to stock up on beans. In contrast, a newly formed expectation of falling prices may decrease current demand for products.

© Michael Newman/PhotoEdit   © John A. Rizzo/Getty Images

Photo Op Substitutes versus Complements

Different brands of soft drinks are substitute goods; goods consumed jointly such as hot dogs and mustard are complementary goods.

Changes in Quantity Demanded

change in demand
A change in the quantity demanded of a product at every price; a shift of the demand curve to the left or right.

Be sure not to confuse a *change in demand* with a *change in quantity demanded*. A **change in demand** is a shift of the demand curve to the right (an increase in demand) or to the left (a decrease in demand). It occurs because the consumer's state of mind about purchasing the product has been altered in response to a change in one or more of the determinants of demand. Recall that "demand" is a schedule or a curve; therefore, a "change in demand" means a change in the schedule and a shift of the curve.

change in quantity demanded
A movement from one point to another on a fixed demand curve.

In contrast, a **change in quantity demanded** is a movement from one point to another point—from one price-quantity combination to another—on a fixed demand curve. The cause of such a change is an increase or decrease in the price of the product under consideration. In the table in Figure 3.3, for example, a decline in the price of lattes from $5 to $4 will increase the quantity of lattes demanded from 2000 to 4000.

In the graph in Figure 3.3, the shift of the demand curve D_1 to either D_2 or D_3 is a change in demand. But the movement from point *a* to point *b* on curve D_1 represents a change in quantity demanded: Demand has not changed; it is the entire curve, and it remains fixed in place.

Supply

supply
A schedule or curve that shows the amounts of a product that producers are willing to make available for sale at each of a series of possible prices during a specific period.

Supply is a schedule or curve showing the amounts of a product that producers will make available for sale at each of a series of possible prices during a specific period.[2] The table in Figure 3.4 is a hypothetical supply schedule for Star Buck, a single supplier of lattes. Curve *S* incorporates the data in the table and is called a *supply curve*. The

---

[2]This definition is worded to apply to product markets. To adjust it to apply to resource markets, substitute "resource" for "product" and "owners" for "producers."

FIGURE 3.4

Star Buck's supply of lattes. Because price and quantity supplied are directly related, the supply curve for an individual producer graphs as an upsloping curve. Other things equal, producers will offer more of a product for sale as its price rises and less of the product for sale as its price falls.

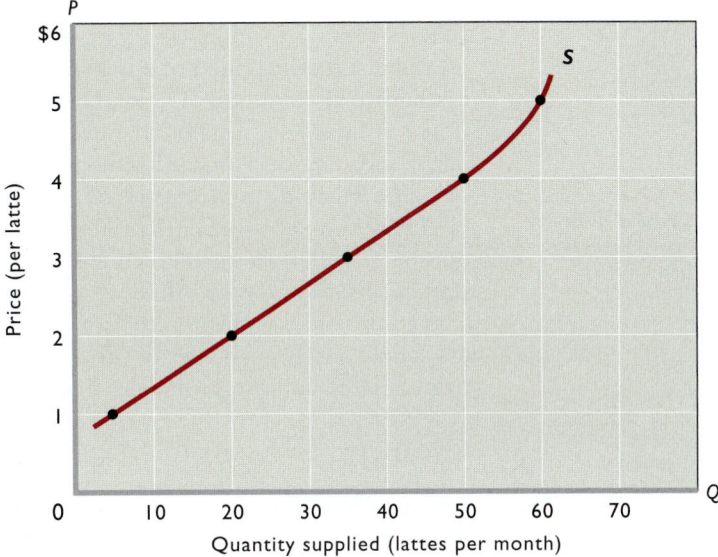

Star Buck's Supply of Lattes	
Price per Latte	Quantity Supplied per Month
$5	60
4	50
3	35
2	20
1	5

schedule and curve show the quantities of lattes that will be supplied at various prices, other things equal.

Law of Supply

Figure 3.4 shows a positive or direct relationship that prevails between price and quantity supplied. As price rises, the quantity supplied rises; as price falls, the quantity supplied falls. This relationship is called the **law of supply.** A supply schedule or curve reveals that, other things equal, firms will offer for sale more of their product at a high price than at a low price. This, again, is basically common sense.

    Price is an obstacle from the standpoint of the consumer (for example, Joe Java), who is on the paying end. The higher the price, the less the consumer will buy. But the supplier (for example, Star Buck) is on the receiving end of the product's price. To a supplier, price represents *revenue*, which is needed to cover costs and earn a profit. Higher prices therefore create a profit incentive to produce and sell more of a product. The higher the price, the greater this incentive and the greater the quantity supplied.

law of supply
The principle that, other things equal, as price rises, the quantity supplied rises, and as price falls, the quantity supplied falls.

Market Supply

Market supply is derived from individual supply in exactly the same way that market demand is derived from individual demand (Figure 3.2). We sum (not shown) the quantities supplied by each producer at each price. That is, we obtain the market **supply curve** by "horizontally adding" (also not shown) the supply curves of the individual producers. The price and quantity-supplied data in the table in Figure 3.5 are for an assumed 200 identical producers in the market, each willing to supply lattes according to the supply schedule shown in Figure 3.4. Curve S_1 is a graph of the market supply data. Note that the axes in Figure 3.5 are the same as those used in our

supply curve
A curve illustrating the direct relationship between the price of a product and the quantity of it supplied, other things equal.

graph of market demand (Figure 3.3). The only difference is that we change the label on the horizontal axis from "quantity demanded" to "quantity supplied."

Determinants of Supply

In constructing a supply curve, we assume that price is the most significant influence on the quantity supplied of any product. But other factors (the "other things equal") can and do affect supply. The supply curve is drawn on the assumption that these other things are fixed and do not change. If one of them does change, a *change in supply* will occur, meaning that the entire supply curve will shift.

determinants of supply
Factors other than price that locate the position of the supply curve.

The basic **determinants of supply** are (1) resource prices, (2) technology, (3) taxes and subsidies, (4) prices of other goods, (5) expected price, and (6) the number of sellers in the market. A change in any one or more of these determinants of supply, or *supply shifters*, will move the supply curve for a product either right or left. A shift to the *right*, as from S_1 to S_2 in Figure 3.5, signifies an *increase* in supply: Producers supply larger quantities of the product at each possible price. A shift to the *left*, as from S_1 to S_3, indicates a *decrease* in supply: Producers offer less output at each price.

Changes in Supply

Let's consider how changes in each of the determinants affect supply. The key idea is that costs are a major factor underlying supply curves; anything that affects costs (other than changes in output itself) usually shifts the supply curve.

Resource Prices   The prices of the resources used in the production process help determine the costs of production incurred by firms. Higher *resource* prices raise production costs and, assuming a particular *product* price, squeeze profits. That reduction

FIGURE 3.5

Changes in the supply of lattes. A change in one or more of the determinants of supply causes a change in supply. An increase in supply is shown as a rightward shift of the supply curve, as from S_1 to S_2. A decrease in supply is depicted as a leftward shift of the curve, as from S_1 to S_3. In contrast, a change in the *quantity supplied* is caused by a change in the product's price and is shown by a movement from one point to another, as from a to b on fixed supply curve S_1.

Market Supply of Lattes (S_1)	
(1) Price per Latte	**(2)** Total Quantity Supplied per Month
$5	12,000
4	10,000
3	7000
2	4000
1	1000

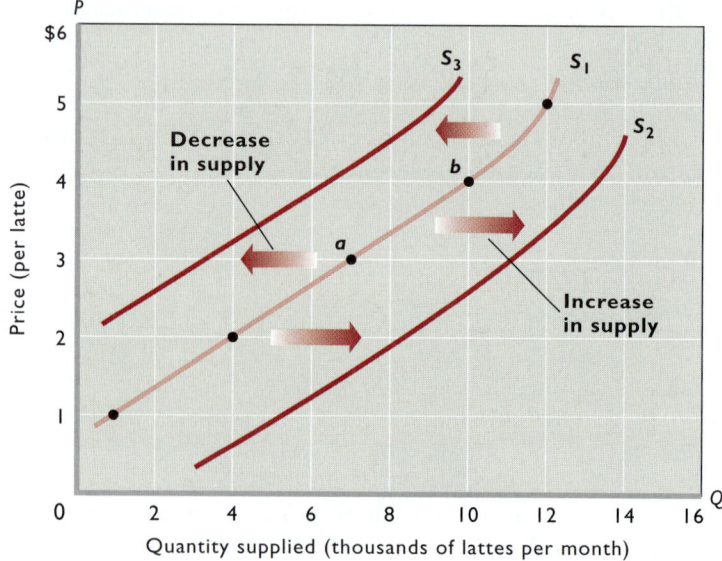

in profits reduces the incentive for firms to supply output at each product price. For example, an increase in the prices of coffee beans and milk will increase the cost of making lattes and therefore reduce their supply.

In contrast, lower *resource* prices reduce production costs and increase profits. So when resource prices fall, firms supply greater output at each product price. For example, a decrease in the prices of sand, gravel, and limestone will increase the supply of concrete.

Technology   Improvements in technology (techniques of production) enable firms to produce units of output with fewer resources. Because resources are costly, using fewer of them lowers production costs and increases supply. Example: Technological advances in producing flat-panel computer monitors have greatly reduced their cost. Thus, manufacturers will now offer more such monitors than previously at the various prices; the supply of flat-panel monitors has increased.

Taxes and Subsidies   Businesses treat sales and property taxes as costs. Increases in those taxes will increase production costs and reduce supply. In contrast, subsidies are "taxes in reverse." If the government subsidizes the production of a good, it in effect lowers the producers' costs and increases supply.

Prices of Other Goods   Firms that produce a particular product, say, soccer balls, can usually use their plant and equipment to produce alternative goods, say, basketballs and volleyballs. The higher prices of these "other goods" may entice soccer ball producers to switch production to those other goods in order to increase profits. This *substitution in production* results in a decline in the supply of soccer balls. Alternatively, when basketballs and volleyballs decline in price relative to the price of soccer balls, firms will produce fewer of those products and more soccer balls, increasing the supply of soccer balls.

Expected Prices   Changes in expectations about the future price of a product may affect the producer's current willingness to supply that product. It is difficult, however, to generalize about how a new expectation of higher prices affects the present supply of a product. Farmers anticipating a higher wheat price in the future might withhold some of their current wheat harvest from the market, thereby causing a decrease in the current supply of wheat. In contrast, in many types of manufacturing industries, newly formed expectations that price will increase may induce firms to add another shift of workers or to expand their production facilities, causing current supply to increase.

Number of Sellers   Other things equal, the larger the number of suppliers, the greater the market supply. As more firms enter an industry, the supply curve shifts to the right. Conversely, the smaller the number of firms in the industry, the less the market supply. This means that as firms leave an industry, the supply curve shifts to the left. Example: The United States and Canada have imposed restrictions on haddock fishing to replenish dwindling stocks. As part of that policy, the federal government has bought the boats of some of the haddock fishers as a way of putting them out of business and decreasing the catch. The result has been a decline in the market supply of haddock.

Changes in Quantity Supplied

The distinction between a *change in supply* and a *change in quantity supplied* parallels the distinction between a change in demand and a change in quantity demanded. Because supply is a schedule or curve, a **change in supply** means a change in the schedule and a shift of the curve. An increase in supply shifts the curve to the right; a decrease in supply shifts it to the left. The cause of a change in supply is a change in one or more of the determinants of supply.

In contrast, a **change in quantity supplied** is a movement from one point to another on a fixed supply curve. The cause of such a movement is a change in the price of the specific product being considered. In Figure 3.5, a decline in the price of lattes from $4 to $3 decreases the quantity of lattes supplied per month from 10,000 to 7000. This movement from point *b* to point *a* along S_1 is a change in quantity supplied, not a change in supply. Supply is the full schedule of prices and quantities shown, and this schedule does not change when the price of lattes changes.

Market Equilibrium

With our understanding of demand and supply, we can now show how the decisions of Joe Java and other buyers of lattes interact with the decisions of Star Buck and other sellers to determine the price and quantity of lattes. In the table in Figure 3.6, columns 1 and 2 repeat the market supply of lattes (from Figure 3.5), and columns 2 and 3 repeat the market demand for lattes (from Figure 3.3). We assume this is a competitive market, so neither buyers nor sellers can set the price.

Equilibrium Price and Quantity

We are looking for the equilibrium price and equilibrium quantity. The **equilibrium price** (or *market-clearing price*) is the price at which the intentions of buyers and sellers match. It is the price at which quantity demanded equals quantity supplied. The table in Figure 3.6 reveals that at $3, *and only at that price*, the number of lattes that sellers wish to sell (7000) is identical to the number that consumers want to buy (also 7000). At $3 and 7000 lattes, there is neither a shortage nor a surplus of lattes. So 7000 lattes is the **equilibrium quantity:** the quantity at which the intentions of buyers and sellers match so that the quantity demanded and the quantity supplied are equal.

Graphically, the equilibrium price is indicated by the intersection of the supply curve and the demand curve in Figure 3.6. (The horizontal axis now measures both quantity demanded and quantity supplied.) With neither a shortage nor a surplus at $3, the market is *in equilibrium*, meaning "in balance" or "at rest."

To better understand the uniqueness of the equilibrium price, let's consider other prices. At any above-equilibrium price, quantity supplied exceeds quantity demanded. For example, at the $4 price, sellers will offer 10,000 lattes, but buyers will purchase only 4000. The $4 price encourages sellers to offer lots of lattes but discourages many consumers from buying them. The result is a **surplus** or *excess supply* of 6000 lattes. If latte sellers made them all, they would find themselves with 6000 unsold lattes.

Surpluses drive prices down. Even if the $4 price existed temporarily, it could not persist. The large surplus would prompt competing sellers to lower the price to encourage buyers to stop in and take the surplus off their hands. As the price fell, the incentive to produce lattes would decline and the incentive for consumers to buy lattes would increase. As shown in Figure 3.6, the market would move to its equilibrium at $3.

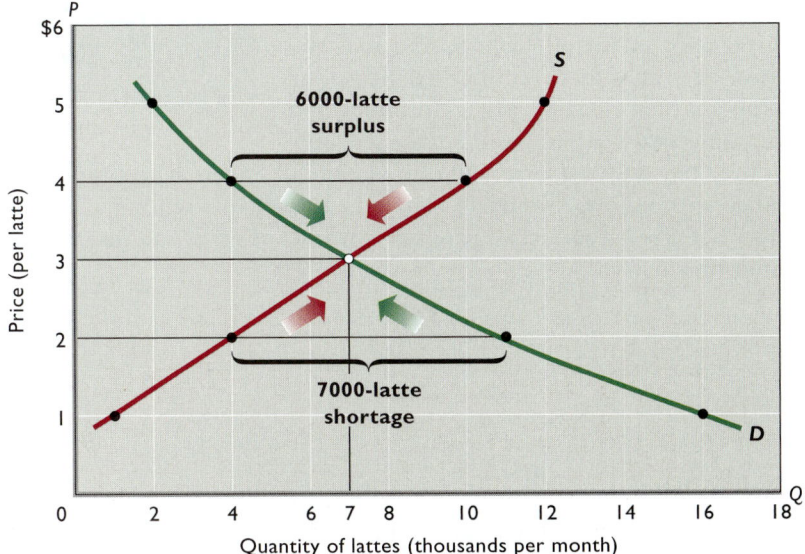

FIGURE 3.6
**Equilibrium price and
quantity.** The intersection
of the downsloping
demand curve D and
the upsloping supply
curve S indicates the
equilibrium price and
quantity, here $3 and
7000 lattes. The short-
ages of lattes at below-
equilibrium prices (for
example, 7000 at $2)
drive up price. The
higher prices increase
the quantity supplied
and reduce the quantity
demanded until equilib-
rium is achieved. The
surpluses caused by
above-equilibrium
prices (for example,
6000 lattes at $4) push
price down. As price
drops, the quantity
demanded rises and the
quantity supplied falls
until equilibrium is established. At the equilibrium
price and quantity, there
are neither shortages
nor surpluses of lattes.

Market Supply of and Demand for Lattes			
(1) Total Quantity Supplied per Month	**(2)** Price per Latte	**(3)** Total Quantity Demanded per Month	**(4)** Surplus (+) or Shortage (−)*
12,000	$5	2000	+10,000 ↓
10,000	4	4000	+6000 ↓
7000	**3**	**7000**	**0**
4000	2	11,000	−7000 ↑
1000	1	16,000	−15,000 ↑

*Arrows indicate the effect on price.

Any price below the $3 equilibrium price would create a shortage; quantity de-
manded would exceed quantity supplied. Consider a $2 price, for example. We see in
column 4 of the table in Figure 3.6 that quantity demanded exceeds quantity supplied
at that price. The result is a **shortage** or *excess demand* of 7000 lattes. The $2 price
discourages sellers from devoting resources to lattes and encourages consumers to
desire more lattes than are available. The $2 price cannot persist as the equilibrium
price. Many consumers who want to buy lattes at this price will not obtain them. They
will express a willingness to pay more than $2 to get them. Competition among these
buyers will drive up the price, eventually to the $3 equilibrium level. Unless disrupted
by supply or demand changes, this $3 price of lattes will continue.

Rationing Function of Prices

The ability of the competitive forces of supply and demand to establish a price
at which selling and buying decisions are consistent is called the *rationing function
of prices*. In our case, the equilibrium price of $3 clears the market, leaving no

shortage
The amount by which
the quantity demanded
of a product exceeds
the quantity supplied
at a specific (below-
equilibrium) price.

burdensome surplus for sellers and no inconvenient shortage for potential buyers. And it is the combination of freely made individual decisions that sets this market-clearing price. In effect, the market outcome says that all buyers who are willing and able to pay $3 for a latte will obtain one; all buyers who cannot or will not pay $3 will go without one. Similarly, all producers who are willing and able to offer a latte for sale at $3 will sell it; all producers who cannot or will not sell for $3 will not sell their product.

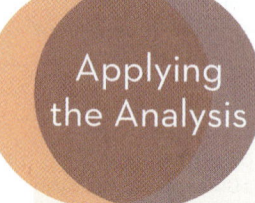

Applying
the Analysis

Ticket Scalping

Ticket prices for athletic events and musical concerts are usually set far in advance of the events. Sometimes the original ticket price is too low to be the equilibrium price. Lines form at the ticket window, and a severe shortage of tickets occurs at the printed price. What happens next? Buyers who are willing to pay more than the original price bid up the equilibrium price in resale ticket markets. The price rockets upward.

Tickets sometimes get resold for much greater amounts than the original price—market transactions known as "scalping." For example, an original buyer may resell a $75 ticket to a concert for $200. The media sometimes denounce scalpers for "ripping off" buyers by charging "exorbitant" prices.

But is scalping really a rip-off? We must first recognize that such ticket resales are voluntary transactions. If both buyer and seller did not expect to gain from the exchange, it would not occur! The seller must value the $200 more than seeing the event, and the buyer must value seeing the event at $200 or more. So there are no losers or victims here: Both buyer and seller benefit from the transaction. The "scalping" market simply redistributes assets (game or concert tickets) from those who would rather have the money (other things) to those who would rather have the tickets.

Does scalping impose losses or injury on the sponsors of the event? If the sponsors are injured, it is because they initially priced tickets below the equilibrium level. Perhaps they did this to create a long waiting line and the attendant media publicity. Alternatively, they may have had a genuine desire to keep tickets affordable for lower-income, ardent fans. In either case, the event sponsors suffer an opportunity cost in the form of less ticket revenue than they might have otherwise received. But such losses are self-inflicted and quite separate and distinct from the fact that some tickets are later resold at a higher price.

So is ticket scalping undesirable? Not on economic grounds! It is an entirely voluntary activity that benefits both sellers and buyers.

Question:
Why do you suppose some professional sports teams have set up legal "ticket exchanges" (at buyer- and seller-determined prices) at their Internet sites? (Hint: For the service, the teams charge a percentage of the transaction price of each resold ticket.)

Changes in Demand, Supply, and Equilibrium

We know that prices can and do change in markets. For example, demand might change because of fluctuations in consumer tastes or incomes, changes in expected price, or variations in the prices of related goods. Supply might change in response to changes in resource prices, technology, or taxes. How will such changes in demand and supply affect equilibrium price and quantity?

Changes in Demand

Suppose that the supply of some good (for example, health care) is constant and the demand for the good increases, as shown in Figure 3.7a. As a result, the new intersection of the supply and demand curves is at higher values on both the price and the quantity axes. Clearly, an increase in demand raises both equilibrium price and equilibrium quantity. Conversely, a decrease in demand, such as that shown in Figure 3.7b, reduces both equilibrium price and equilibrium quantity.

Changes in Supply

What happens if the demand for some good (for example, cell phones) is constant but the supply increases, as in Figure 3.7c? The new intersection of supply and demand is located at a lower equilibrium price but at a higher equilibrium quantity. An increase in supply reduces equilibrium price but increases equilibrium quantity. In contrast, if supply decreases, as in Figure 3.7d, equilibrium price rises while equilibrium quantity declines.

Complex Cases

When both supply and demand change, the effect is a combination of the individual effects.

Supply Increase; Demand Decrease   What effect will a supply increase for some good (for example, apples) and a demand decrease have on equilibrium price? Both changes decrease price, so the net result is a price drop greater than that resulting from either change alone.

   What about equilibrium quantity? Here the effects of the changes in supply and demand are opposed: The increase in supply increases equilibrium quantity, but the decrease in demand reduces it. The direction of the change in equilibrium quantity depends on the relative sizes of the changes in supply and demand. If the increase in supply is larger than the decrease in demand, the equilibrium quantity will increase. But if the decrease in demand is greater than the increase in supply, the equilibrium quantity will decrease.

Supply Decrease; Demand Increase   A decrease in supply and an increase in demand for some good (for example, gasoline) both increase price. Their combined effect is an increase in equilibrium price greater than that caused by either change separately. But their effect on the equilibrium quantity is again indeterminate, depending on the relative sizes of the changes in supply and demand. If the decrease in supply is larger than the increase in demand, the equilibrium quantity will decrease. In contrast, if the increase in demand is greater than the decrease in supply, the equilibrium quantity will increase.

FIGURE 3.7

Changes in demand and supply and the effects on price and quantity. The increase in demand from D_1 to D_2 in (a) increases both equilibrium price and equilibrium quantity. The decrease in demand from D_3 to D_4 in (b) decreases both equilibrium price and equilibrium quantity. The increase in supply from S_1 to S_2 in (c) decreases equilibrium price and increases equilibrium quantity. The decrease in supply from S_3 to S_4 in (d) increases equilibrium price and decreases equilibrium quantity. The boxes in the top right summarize the respective changes and outcomes. The upward arrows in the boxes signify increases in equilibrium price (P) and equilibrium quantity (Q); the downward arrows signify decreases in these items.

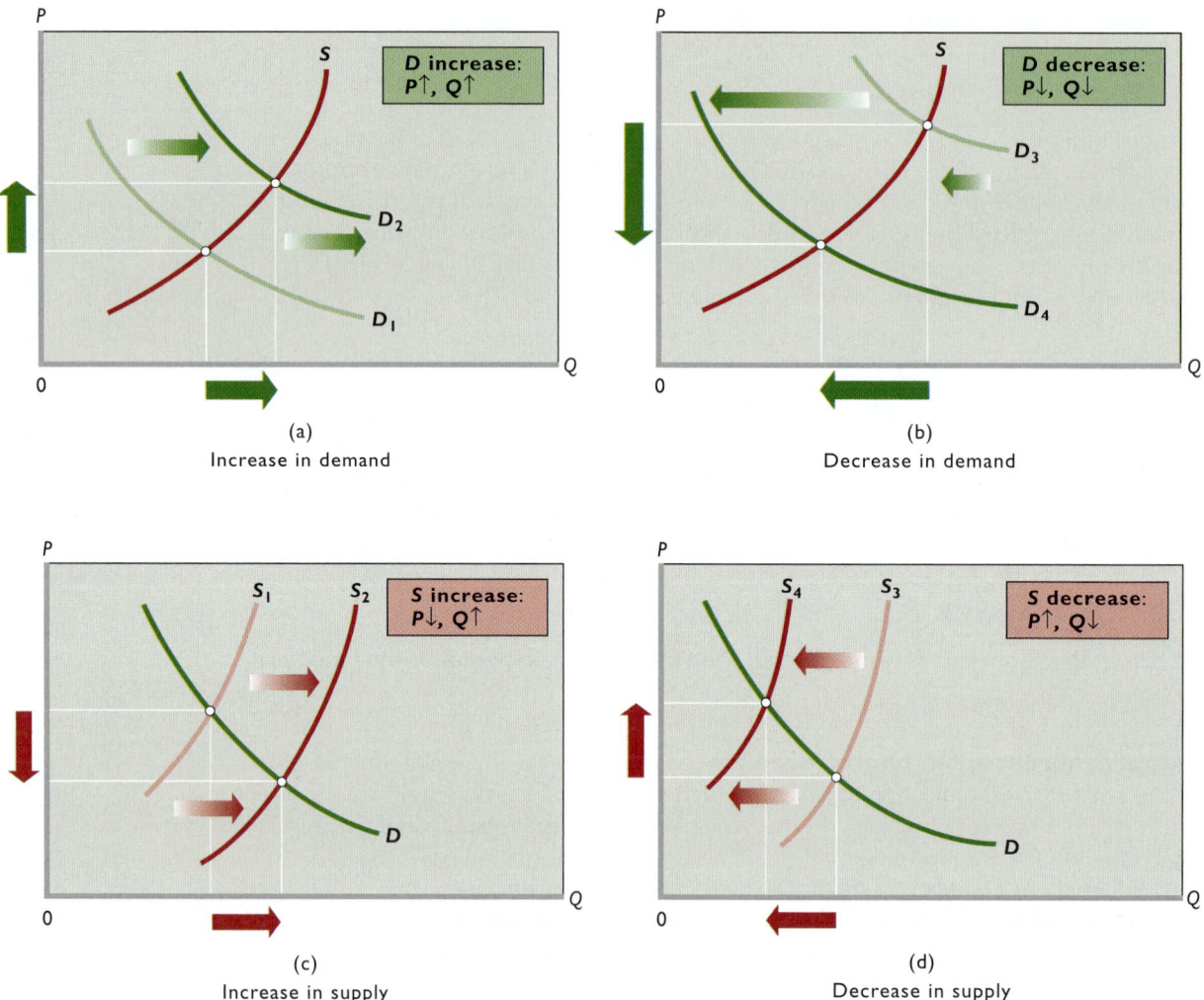

Supply Increase; Demand Increase   What if supply and demand both increase for some good (for example, sushi)? A supply increase drops equilibrium price, while a demand increase boosts it. If the increase in supply is greater than the increase in demand, the equilibrium price will fall. If the opposite holds, the equilibrium price will rise. If the two changes are equal and cancel out, price will not change.

The effect on equilibrium quantity is certain: The increases in supply and in demand both raise the equilibrium quantity. Therefore, the equilibrium quantity will increase by an amount greater than that caused by either change alone.

Supply Decrease; Demand Decrease   What about decreases in both supply and demand for some good (for example, new homes)? If the decrease in supply is greater than the decrease in demand, equilibrium price will rise. If the reverse is true, equilibrium price will fall. If the two changes are of the same size and cancel out, price will not change. Because the decreases in supply and demand both reduce equilibrium quantity, we can be sure that equilibrium quantity will fall.

Government-Set Prices

In most markets, prices are free to rise or fall with changes in supply or demand, no matter how high or low those prices might be. However, government occasionally concludes that changes in supply and demand have created prices that are unfairly high to buyers or unfairly low to sellers. Government may then place legal limits on how high or low a price or prices may go. Our previous analysis of shortages and surpluses helps us evaluate the wisdom of government-set prices.

Applying the Analysis

Price Ceilings on Gasoline

A **price ceiling** sets the maximum legal price a seller may charge for a product or service. A price at or below the ceiling is legal; a price above it is not. The rationale for establishing price ceilings (or ceiling prices) on specific products is that they purportedly enable consumers to obtain some "essential" good or service that they could not afford at the equilibrium price.

price ceiling
A legally established maximum (below-equilibrium) price for a product.

Figure 3.8 shows the effects of price ceilings graphically. Let's look at a hypothetical situation. Suppose that rapidly rising world income boosts the purchase of automobiles and increases the demand for gasoline so that the equilibrium or market price reaches $5 per gallon. The rapidly rising price of gasoline greatly burdens low- and moderate-income households, which pressure government to "do something." To keep gasoline prices down, the government imposes a ceiling price of $4 per gallon. To impact the market, a price ceiling must be below the equilibrium price. A ceiling price of $6, for example, would have no effect on the price of gasoline in the current situation.

What are the effects of this $4 ceiling price? The rationing ability of the free market is rendered ineffective. Because the $4 ceiling price is below the $5 market-clearing price, there is a lasting shortage of gasoline. The quantity of gasoline demanded at $4 is Q_d and the quantity supplied is only Q_s; a persistent excess demand or shortage of amount $Q_d - Q_s$ occurs.

The $4 price ceiling prevents the usual market adjustment in which competition among buyers bids up the price, inducing more production and rationing some buyers out of the market. That process would normally continue until the shortage disappeared at the equilibrium price and quantity, $5 and Q_0.

How will sellers apportion the available supply Q_s among buyers, who want the greater amount Q_d? Should they distribute gasoline on a first-come, first-served basis, that is, to those willing and able to get in line the soonest or stay in line the longest? Or should gas stations distribute it on the basis of favoritism? Since an unregulated shortage does not lead to an equitable distribution of gasoline, the government must establish some formal system for rationing it to consumers. One option is to issue ration coupons, which authorize bearers to purchase

FIGURE 3.8

A price ceiling.
A price ceiling is a maximum legal price, such as $4, that is below the equilibrium price. It results in a persistent product shortage, here shown by the distance between Q_d and Q_s.

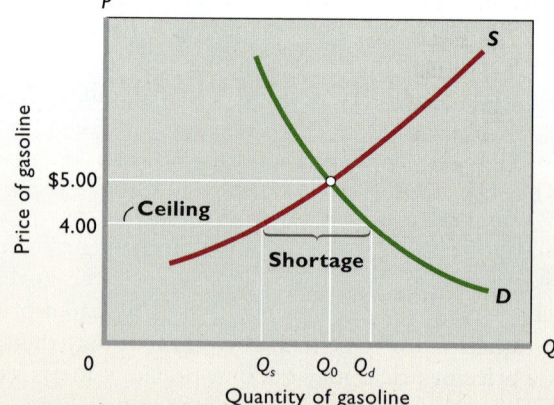

a fixed amount of gasoline per month. The rationing system might entail first the printing of coupons for Q_s gallons of gasoline and then the equal distribution of the coupons among consumers so that the wealthy family of four and the poor family of four both receive the same number of coupons.

But ration coupons would not prevent a second problem from arising. The demand curve in Figure 3.8 reveals that many buyers are willing to pay more than the $4 ceiling price. And, of course, it is more profitable for gasoline stations to sell at prices above the ceiling. Thus, despite a sizable enforcement bureaucracy that would have to accompany the price controls, *black markets* in which gasoline is illegally bought and sold at prices above the legal limits will flourish. Counterfeiting of ration coupons will also be a problem. And since the price of gasoline is now "set by government," there might be political pressure on government to set the price even lower.

Question:
Why is it typically difficult to end price ceilings once they have been in place for a long time?

Applying the Analysis

Rent Controls

About 200 cities in the United States, including New York City, Boston, and San Francisco, have at one time or another enacted price ceilings in the form of rent controls—maximum rents established by law—or, more recently, have set maximum rent increases for existing tenants. Such laws are well intended. Their goals are to protect low-income families from escalating rents caused by demand increases that outstrip supply increases. Rent controls are designed to alleviate perceived housing shortages and make housing more affordable.

What have been the actual economic effects? On the demand side, the below-equilibrium rents attract a larger number of renters. Some are locals seeking to move into their own places after sharing housing with friends or family. Others are outsiders attracted into the area by the artificially lower rents. But a large problem occurs on the supply side. Price controls make it less attractive for landlords to offer housing on the rental market. In the short run, owners may sell their rental units or convert them to condominiums. In the long run, low rents make it unprofitable for owners to repair or renovate their rental units. (Rent controls are one cause of the many abandoned apartment buildings found in some larger cities.) Also, insurance companies, pension funds, and other potential new investors in housing will find it more profitable to invest in office buildings, shopping malls, or motels, where rents are not controlled.

In brief, rent controls distort market signals, and thus resources are misallocated: Too few resources are allocated to rental housing, and too many to alternative uses. Ironically, although rent controls are often legislated to lessen the effects of perceived shortages, controls in fact are a primary cause of such shortages. For that reason, most American cities either have abandoned rent controls or are gradually phasing them out.

Question:
Why does maintenance tend to diminish in rent-controlled apartment buildings relative to maintenance in buildings where owners can charge market-determined rents?

Price Floors on Wheat

A **price floor** is a minimum price fixed by the government. A price at or above the price floor is legal; a price below it is not. Price floors above equilibrium prices are usually invoked when society feels that the free functioning of the market system has not provided a sufficient income for certain groups of resource suppliers or producers. Supported prices for agricultural products and current minimum wages are two examples of price (or wage) floors. Let's look at the former.

Suppose that many farmers have extremely low incomes when the price of wheat is at its equilibrium value of $2 per bushel. The government decides to help out by establishing a legal price floor (or "price support") of $3 per bushel.

What will be the effects? At any price above the equilibrium price, quantity supplied will exceed quantity demanded—that is, there will be a persistent surplus of the product. Farmers will be willing to produce and offer for sale more wheat than private buyers are willing to buy at the $3 price floor. As we saw with a price ceiling, an imposed legal price disrupts the rationing ability of the free market.

Figure 3.9 illustrates the effect of a price floor graphically. Suppose that S and D are the supply and demand curves for wheat. Equilibrium price and quantity are $2 and Q_0, respectively. If the government imposes a price floor of $3, farmers will produce Q_s, but private buyers will purchase only Q_d. The surplus is the excess of Q_s over Q_d.

Applying the Analysis

price floor
A legally established minimum (above-equilibrium) price for a product.

FIGURE 3.9

A price floor. A price floor is a minimum legal price, such as $3, that results in a persistent product surplus, here shown by the distance between Q_s and Q_d.

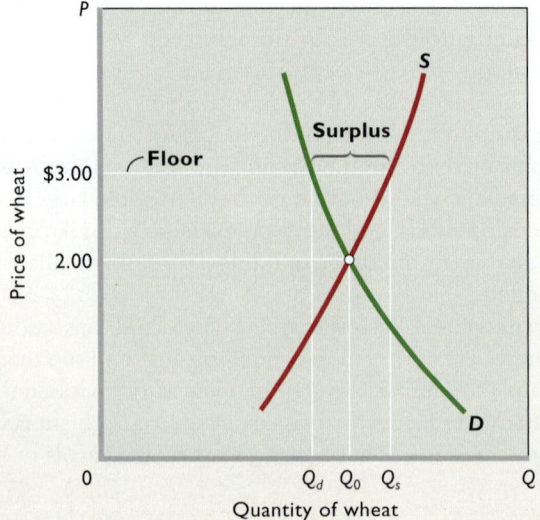

The government may cope with the surplus resulting from a price floor in two ways:

- It can restrict supply (for example, by instituting acreage allotments by which farmers agree to take a certain amount of land out of production) or increase demand (for example, by researching new uses for the product involved). These actions may reduce the difference between the equilibrium price and the price floor and that way reduce the size of the resulting surplus.
- If these efforts are not wholly successful, then the government must purchase the surplus output at the $3 price (thereby subsidizing farmers) and store or otherwise dispose of it.

Price floors such as $3 in Figure 3.9 not only disrupt the rationing ability of prices but also distort resource allocation. Without the price floor, the $2 equilibrium price of wheat would cause financial losses and force high-cost wheat producers to plant other crops or abandon farming altogether. But the $3 price floor allows them to continue to grow wheat and remain farmers. So society devotes too many scarce resources to wheat production and too few to producing other, more valuable, goods and services. It fails to achieve an optimal allocation of resources.

That's not all. Consumers of wheat-based products pay higher prices because of the price floor. Taxpayers pay higher taxes to finance the government's purchase of the surplus. Also, the price floor causes potential environmental damage by encouraging wheat farmers to bring hilly, erosion-prone "marginal land" into production. The higher price also prompts imports of wheat. But, since such imports would increase the quantity of wheat supplied and thus undermine the price floor, the government needs to erect tariffs (taxes on imports) to keep the foreign wheat out. Such tariffs usually prompt other countries to retaliate with their own tariffs against U.S. agricultural or manufacturing exports.

Question:
To maintain price floors on milk, the U.S. government has at times bought out and destroyed entire dairy herds from dairy farmers. What's the economic logic of these actions?

It is easy to see why economists "sound the alarm" when politicians advocate imposing price ceilings or price floors such as price controls, rent controls, interest-rate lids, or agricultural price supports. In all these cases, good intentions lead to bad economic outcomes. Government-controlled prices lead to shortages or surpluses, distort resource allocations, and cause negative side effects.

*For additional examples of demand and supply, view the Chapter 3 web appendix at **www.brue3e.com**. There, you will find examples relating to such diverse products as lettuce, corn, salmon, gasoline, sushi, and Olympic tickets. Several of the examples depict simultaneous shifts in demand and supply curves—circumstances that often show up in exam questions!*

> **INTERACTIVE GRAPHS**
>
> **G 3.2**
> Price floors and ceilings

Summary

1. Demand is a schedule or curve representing the willingness of buyers in a specific period to purchase a particular product at each of various prices. The law of demand implies that consumers will buy more of a product at a low price than at a high price. So, other things equal, the relationship between price and quantity demanded is inverse and is graphed as a downsloping curve.

2. Market demand curves are found by adding horizontally the demand curves of the many individual consumers in the market.

3. Changes in one or more of the determinants of demand (consumer tastes, the number of buyers in the market, the money incomes of consumers, the prices of related goods, and expected prices) shift the market demand curve. A shift to the right is an increase in demand; a shift to the left is a decrease in demand. A change in demand is different from a change in the quantity demanded, the latter being a movement from one point to another point on a fixed demand curve because of a change in the product's price.

4. Supply is a schedule or curve showing the amounts of a product that producers are willing to offer in the market at each possible price during a specific period. The law of supply states that, other things equal, producers will offer more of a product at a high price than at a low price. Thus, the relationship between price and quantity supplied is positive or direct, and supply is graphed as an upsloping curve.

5. The market supply curve is the horizontal summation of the supply curves of the individual producers of the product.

6. Changes in one or more of the determinants of supply (resource prices, production techniques, taxes or subsidies, the prices of other goods, expected prices, or the number of suppliers in the market) shift the supply curve of a product. A shift to the right is an increase in supply; a shift to the left is a decrease in supply. In contrast, a change in the price of the product being considered causes a change in the quantity supplied, which is shown as a movement from one point to another point on a fixed supply curve.

7. The equilibrium price and quantity are established at the intersection of the supply and demand curves. The interaction of market demand and market supply adjusts the price to the point at which the quantities demanded and supplied are equal. This is the equilibrium price. The corresponding quantity is the equilibrium quantity.

8. A change in either demand or supply changes the equilibrium price and quantity. Increases in demand raise both equilibrium price and equilibrium quantity; decreases in demand lower both equilibrium price and equilibrium quantity. Increases in supply lower equilibrium price and raise equilibrium quantity; decreases in supply raise equilibrium price and lower equilibrium quantity.

9. Simultaneous changes in demand and supply affect equilibrium price and quantity in various ways, depending on their direction and relative magnitudes.

10. A price ceiling is a maximum price set by government and is designed to help consumers. Effective price ceilings produce persistent product shortages, and if an equitable distribution of the product is sought, government must ration the product to consumers.

11. A price floor is a minimum price set by government and is designed to aid producers. Price floors lead to persistent product surpluses; the government must either purchase the product or eliminate the surplus by imposing restrictions on production or increasing private demand.

12. Legally fixed prices stifle the rationing function of prices and distort the allocation of resources.

Terms and Concepts

demand	change in demand	change in quantity supplied
law of demand	change in quantity demanded	equilibrium price
demand curve	supply	equilibrium quantity
determinants of demand	law of supply	surplus
normal good	supply curve	shortage
inferior good	determinants of supply	price ceiling
substitute good	change in supply	price floor
complementary good		

Questions

1. Explain the law of demand. Why does a demand curve slope downward? How is a market demand curve derived from individual demand curves? **LO1**

2. What are the determinants of demand? What happens to the demand curve when any of these determinants changes? Distinguish between a change in demand and a change in the quantity demanded, noting the cause(s) of each. **LO1**

3. What effect will each of the following have on the demand for small automobiles such as the Mini Cooper and Smart car? **LO1**
   a. Small automobiles become more fashionable.
   b. The price of large automobiles rises (with the price of small autos remaining the same).
   c. Income declines and small autos are an inferior good.
   d. Consumers anticipate that the price of small autos will greatly come down in the near future.
   e. The price of gasoline substantially drops.

4. Explain the law of supply. Why does the supply curve slope upward? How is the market supply curve derived from the supply curves of individual producers? **LO2**

5. What are the determinants of supply? What happens to the supply curve when any of these determinants changes? Distinguish between a change in supply and a change in the quantity supplied, noting the cause(s) of each. **LO2**

6. What effect will each of the following have on the supply of auto tires? **LO2**
   a. A technological advance in the methods of producing tires.
   b. A decline in the number of firms in the tire industry.
   c. An increase in the price of rubber used in the production of tires.
   d. The expectation that the equilibrium price of auto tires will be lower in the future than currently.

   e. A decline in the price of the large tires used for semi trucks and earth-hauling rigs (with no change in the price of auto tires).
   f. The levying of a per-unit tax on each auto tire sold.
   g. The granting of a 50-cent-per-unit subsidy for each auto tire produced.

7. "In the latte market, demand often exceeds supply and supply sometimes exceeds demand." "The price of a latte rises and falls in response to changes in supply and demand." In which of these two statements are the concepts of supply and demand used correctly? Explain. **LO4**

8. In 2001 an outbreak of hoof-and-mouth disease in Europe led to the burning of millions of cattle carcasses. What impact do you think this had on the supply of cattle hides, hide prices, the supply of leather goods, and the price of leather goods? **LO4**

9. Critically evaluate: "In comparing the two equilibrium positions in Figure 3.7a, I note that a larger amount is actually demanded at a higher price. This refutes the law of demand." **LO4**

10. For each stock in the stock market, the number of shares sold daily equals the number of shares purchased. That is, the quantity of each firm's shares demanded equals the quantity supplied. So, if this equality always occurs, why do the prices of stock shares ever change? **LO4**

11. Suppose the total demand for wheat and the total supply of wheat per month in the Kansas City grain market are as shown in the table on the following page. Suppose that the government establishes a price ceiling of $3.70 for wheat. What might prompt the government to establish this price ceiling? Explain carefully the main effects. Demonstrate your answer graphically. Next, suppose that the government establishes a price floor of $4.60 for wheat. What will be the main effects of this price floor? Demonstrate your answer graphically. **LO5**

Thousands of Bushels Demanded	Price per Bushel	Thousands of Bushels Supplied
85	$3.40	72
80	3.70	73
75	4.00	75
70	4.30	77
65	4.60	79
60	4.90	81

Problems

1. Suppose there are three buyers of candy in a market: Tex, Dex, and Rex. The market demand and the individual demands of Tex, Dex, and Rex are shown below. **LO1**

a. Fill in the table for the missing values.

b. Which buyer demands the least at a price of $5? The most at a price of $7?

c. Which buyer's quantity demanded increases the most when the price is lowered from $7 to $6?

d. Which direction would the market demand curve shift if Tex withdrew from the market? What if Dex doubled his purchases at each possible price?

e. Suppose that at a price of $6, the total quantity demanded increases from 19 to 38. Is this a "change in the quantity demanded" or a "change in demand"?

Price per Candy	Individual Quantities Demanded						Total Quantity Demanded
	Tex		Dex		Rex		
$8	3	+	1	+	0	=	—
7	8	+	2	+	—	=	12
6	—	+	3	+	4	=	19
5	17	+	—	+	6	=	27
4	23	+	5	+	8	=	—

2. The figure below shows the supply curve for tennis balls, S_1, for Drop Volley Tennis, a producer of tennis equipment. Use the figure and the table to the right to give your answers to the following questions. **LO2**

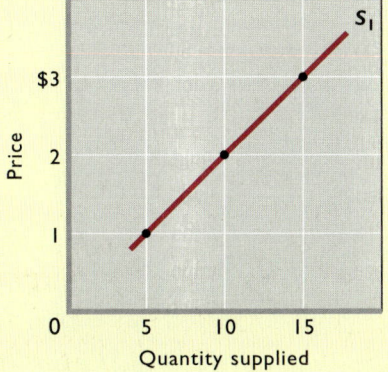

12. What do economists mean when they say "price floors and ceilings stifle the rationing function of prices and distort resource allocation"? **LO5**

a. Use the figure to fill in the quantity supplied on supply curve S_1 for each price in the table below.

Price	S_1 Quantity Supplied	S_2 Quantity Supplied	Change in Quantity Supplied
$3	—	4	—
2	—	2	—
1	—	0	—

b. If production costs were to increase, the quantities supplied at each price would be as shown by the third column of the table ("S_2 Quantity Supplied"). Use those data to draw supply curve S_2 on the same graph as supply curve S_1.

c. In the fourth column of the table, enter the amount by which the quantity supplied at each price changes due to the increase in product costs. (Use positive numbers for increases and negative numbers for decreases.)

d. Did the increase in production costs cause a "decrease in supply" or a "decrease in quantity supplied"?

3. Refer to the expanded table below from question 11. **LO3**

a. What is the equilibrium price? At what price is there neither a shortage nor a surplus? Fill in the surplus-shortage column and use it to confirm your answers.

b. Graph the demand for wheat and the supply of wheat. Be sure to label the axes of your graph correctly. Label equilibrium price P and equilibrium quantity Q.

c. How big is the surplus or shortage at $3.40? At $4.90? How big a surplus or shortage results if the price is 60 cents higher than the equilibrium price? 30 cents lower than the equilibrium price?

Thousands of Bushels Demanded	Price per Bushel	Thousands of Bushels Supplied	Surplus (+) or Shortage (−)
85	$3.40	72	—
80	3.70	73	—
75	4.00	75	—
70	4.30	77	—
65	4.60	79	—
60	4.90	81	—

4. How will each of the following changes in demand and/or supply affect equilibrium price and equilibrium quantity in a competitive market; that is, do price and quantity rise, fall, or remain unchanged, or are the answers indeterminate because they depend on the magnitudes of the shifts? Use supply and demand to verify your answers. **LO4**

   a. Supply decreases and demand is constant.
   b. Demand decreases and supply is constant.
   c. Supply increases and demand is constant.
   d. Demand increases and supply increases.
   e. Demand increases and supply is constant.
   f. Supply increases and demand decreases.
   g. Demand increases and supply decreases.
   h. Demand decreases and supply decreases.

5. Use two market diagrams to explain how an increase in state subsidies to public colleges might affect tuition and enrollments in both public and private colleges. **LO4**

6. **ADVANCED ANALYSIS** Assume that demand for a commodity is represented by the equation $P = 10 - .2Q_d$ and supply by the equation $P = 2 + .2Q_s$, where Q_d and Q_s are quantity demanded and quantity supplied, respectively, and P is price. Using the equilibrium condition $Q_s = Q_d$, solve the equations to determine equilibrium price. Now determine equilibrium quantity. **LO4**

7. Suppose that the demand and supply schedules for rental apartments in the city of Gotham are as given in the following table. **LO5**

Monthly Rent	Apartments Demanded	Apartments Supplied
$2500	10,000	15,000
2000	12,500	12,500
1500	15,000	10,000
1000	17,500	7500
500	20,000	5000

   a. What is the market equilibrium rental price per month and the market equilibrium number of apartments demanded and supplied?
   b. If the local government can enforce a rent-control law that sets the maximum monthly rent at $1500, will there be a surplus or a shortage? Of how many units? And how many units will actually be rented each month?
   c. Suppose that a new government is elected that wants to keep out the poor. It declares that the minimum rent that can be charged is $2500 per month. If the government can enforce that price floor, will there be a surplus or a shortage? Of how many units? And how many units will actually be rented each month?
   d. Suppose that the government wishes to decrease the market equilibrium monthly rent by increasing the supply of housing. Assuming that demand remains unchanged, by how many units of housing would the government have to increase the supply of housing in order to get the market equilibrium rental price to fall to $1500 per month? To $1000 per month? To $500 per month?

FURTHER TEST YOUR KNOWLEDGE AT
www.brue3e.com

At the text's Online Learning Center, **www.brue3e.com,** you will find one or more web-based questions that require information from the Internet to answer. We urge you to check them out, since they will familiarize you with websites that may be helpful in other courses and perhaps even in your career. The OLC also features multiple-choice quizzes that give instant feedback and provides other helpful ways to further test your knowledge of the chapter.

Additional Examples of Supply and Demand

CHAPTER FOUR

Elasticity of Demand and Supply

After reading this chapter, you should be able to:

1. Discuss price elasticity of demand and how it can be measured.
2. Explain how price elasticity of demand affects total revenue.
3. Describe price elasticity of supply and how it can be measured.
4. Apply price elasticity of demand and supply to real-world situations.
5. Explain income elasticity of demand and cross-elasticity of demand and how they can be applied.

Why do buyers of some products respond to price increases by substantially reducing their purchases while buyers of other products respond by only slightly cutting back their purchases? Why do price hikes for some goods cause producers to greatly increase their output while price hikes on other products barely cause any output increase? Why does the demand for some products rise a great deal when household incomes increase while the demand for other products rises just a little? How can we tell whether a given pair of goods are complements, substitutes, or unrelated to each other?

Elasticity extends our understanding of markets by letting us know the degree to which changes in prices and incomes affect supply and demand. Sometimes the responses are substantial, other times minimal or even nonexistent. But by knowing what to expect, businesses and the government can do a much better job in deciding what to produce, how much to charge, and, surprisingly, what items to tax.

Price Elasticity of Demand

The law of demand tells us that, other things equal, consumers will buy more of a product when its price declines and less of it when its price increases. But how much more or less will they buy? The amount varies from product to product and over different price ranges for the same product. And such variations matter. For example, a firm contemplating a price hike will want to know how consumers will respond. If they remain highly loyal and continue to buy, the firm's revenue will rise. But if consumers defect en masse to other sellers or other products, its revenue will tumble.

The responsiveness of the quantity of a product demanded by consumers when the product price changes is measured by a product's **price elasticity of demand.** For some products (for example, restaurant meals), consumers are highly responsive to price changes. Modest price changes cause very large changes in the quantity purchased. Economists say that the demand for such products is *relatively elastic* or simply *elastic.*

For other products (for example, medical care), consumers pay much less attention to price changes. Substantial price changes cause only small changes in the amount purchased. The demand for such products is *relatively inelastic* or simply *inelastic.*

price elasticity of demand
A measure of the responsiveness of the quantity of a product demanded by consumers when the product price changes.

The Price-Elasticity Coefficient and Formula

Economists measure the degree of price elasticity or inelasticity of demand with the coefficient E_d, defined as

$$E_d = \frac{\text{percentage change in quantity demanded of X}}{\text{percentage change in price of X}}$$

The percentage changes in the equation are calculated by dividing the *change* in quantity demanded by the original quantity demanded and by dividing the *change* in price by the original price. So we can restate the formula as

$$E_d = \frac{\text{change in quantity demanded of X}}{\text{original quantity demanded of X}} \div \frac{\text{change in price of X}}{\text{original price of X}}$$

Using Averages Unfortunately, an annoying problem arises in computing the price-elasticity coefficient. A price change from, say, $4 to $5 along a demand curve is a 25 percent (=$1/$4) increase, but the opposite price change from $5 to $4 along the same curve is a 20 percent (=$1/$5) decrease. Which percentage change in price should we use in the denominator to compute the price-elasticity coefficient? And when quantity changes, for example, from 10 to 20, it is a 100 percent (=10/10) increase. But when quantity falls from 20 to 10 along the identical demand curve, it is a 50 percent (=10/20) decrease. Should we use 100 percent or 50 percent in the numerator of the elasticity formula? Elasticity should be the same whether price rises or falls!

The simplest solution to the problem is to use the averages of the two prices and the two quantities as the reference points for computing the percentages. That is

$$E_d = \frac{\text{change in quantity}}{\text{sum of quantities/2}} \div \frac{\text{change in price}}{\text{sum of prices/2}}$$

For the same $5–$4 price range, the price reference is $4.50 [= ($5 + $4)/2], and for the same 10–20 quantity range, the quantity reference is 15 units [= (10 + 20)/2]. The percentage change in price is now $1/$4.50, or about 22 percent, and the percentage change in quantity is 10/15, or about 67 percent. So E_d is about 3. This solution eliminates the "up versus down" problem. All the elasticity coefficients that follow are calculated using averages, also known as the *midpoints approach*.

Elimination of Minus Sign   Because demand curves slope downward, the price-elasticity coefficient of demand E_d will always be a negative number. As an example, if price declines, quantity demanded will increase. This means that the numerator in our formula will be positive and the denominator negative, yielding a negative E_d. For an increase in price, the numerator will be negative but the denominator positive, again producing a negative E_d.

Economists usually ignore the minus sign and simply present the absolute value of the elasticity coefficient to avoid an ambiguity that might otherwise arise. It can be confusing to say that an E_d of -4 is greater than one of -2. This possible confusion is avoided when we say an E_d of 4 reveals greater elasticity than an E_d of 2. In what follows, we ignore the minus sign in the coefficient of price elasticity of demand and show only the absolute value.

Interpretations of E_d

We can interpret the coefficient of price elasticity of demand as follows.

elastic demand
Product demand for which price changes cause relatively larger changes in quantity demanded.

Elastic Demand   Demand is **elastic** if a specific percentage change in price results in a larger percentage change in quantity demanded. In such cases, E_d will be greater than 1. Example: Suppose that a 2 percent decline in the price of cut flowers results in a 4 percent increase in quantity demanded. Then demand for cut flowers is elastic and

$$E_d = \frac{.04}{.02} = 2$$

inelastic demand
Product demand for which price changes cause relatively smaller changes in quantity demanded.

Inelastic Demand   If a specific percentage change in price produces a smaller percentage change in quantity demanded, demand is **inelastic.** In such cases, E_d will be less than 1. Example: Suppose that a 2 percent decline in the price of tea leads to only a 1 percent increase in quantity demanded. Then demand is inelastic and

$$E_d = \frac{.01}{.02} = .5$$

Unit Elasticity   The case separating elastic and inelastic demands occurs where a percentage change in price and the resulting percentage change in quantity demanded are the same. Example: Suppose that a 2 percent drop in the price of chocolate causes a 2 percent increase in quantity demanded. This special case is termed **unit elasticity** because E_d is exactly 1, or unity. In this example,

unit elasticity
Product demand for which relative price changes and changes in quantity demanded are equal.

$$E_d = \frac{.02}{.02} = 1$$

Extreme Cases   When we say demand is "inelastic," we do not mean that consumers are completely unresponsive to a price change. In that extreme situation, where a price change results in no change whatsoever in the quantity demanded, economists say that demand is **perfectly inelastic.** The price-elasticity coefficient is zero because there is no response to a change in price. Approximate examples include an acute diabetic's demand for insulin or an addict's demand for heroin. A line parallel to the vertical axis, such as D_1 in Figure 4.1a, shows perfectly inelastic demand graphically.

perfectly inelastic demand
Product demand for which quantity demanded does not respond to a change in price.

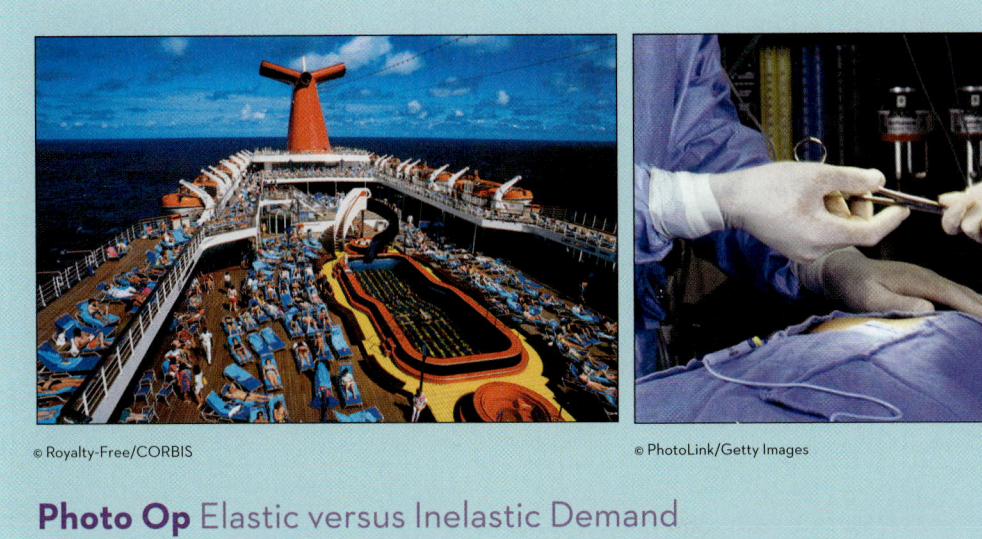

© Royalty-Free/CORBIS   © PhotoLink/Getty Images

Photo Op Elastic versus Inelastic Demand

The demand for expensive leisure activities such as cruise vacations is elastic; the demand for surgery or other nonelective medical care is inelastic.

Conversely, when we say demand is "elastic," we do not mean that consumers are completely responsive to a price change. In that extreme situation, where a small price reduction causes buyers to increase their purchases from zero to all they can obtain, the elasticity coefficient is infinite (∞) and economists say demand is **perfectly elastic.** A line parallel to the horizontal axis, such as D_2 in Figure 4.1b, shows perfectly elastic demand. Such a demand curve, for example, faces wheat growers who can sell all or none of their wheat at the equilibrium market price.

perfectly elastic demand
Product demand for which quantity demanded can be any amount at a particular price.

FIGURE 4.1

Perfectly inelastic and elastic demands. Demand curve D_1 in (a) represents perfectly inelastic demand ($E_d = 0$). A price increase will result in no change in quantity demanded. Demand curve D_2 in (b) represents perfectly elastic demand. A price increase will cause quantity demanded to decline from an infinite amount to zero ($E_d = \infty$).

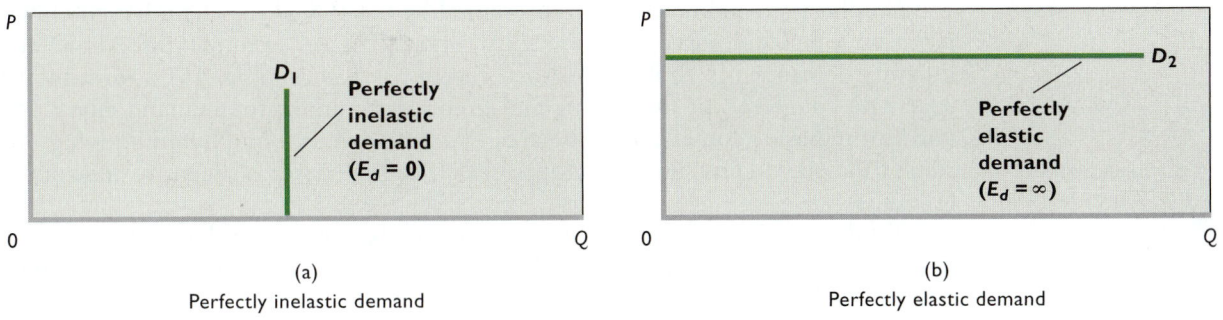

(a)
Perfectly inelastic demand

(b)
Perfectly elastic demand

A Bit of a Stretch

The following analogy might help you remember the distinction between "elastic" and "inelastic." Imagine two objects: (1) an Ace elastic bandage used to wrap injured joints and (2) a relatively firm rubber tie-down used for securing items for transport. The Ace bandage stretches a great deal when pulled with a particular force; the rubber tie-down stretches some, but not a lot.

Similar differences occur for the quantity demanded of various products when their prices change. For some products, a price change causes a substantial "stretch" of quantity demanded. When this stretch in percentage terms exceeds the percentage change in price, demand is elastic. For other products, quantity demanded stretches very little in response to the price change. When this stretch in percentage terms is less than the percentage change in price, demand is inelastic.

In summary:

- Elastic demand displays considerable "quantity stretch" (as with the Ace bandage).
- Inelastic demand displays relatively little "quantity stretch" (as with the rubber tie-down).

And through extension:

- Perfectly elastic demand has infinite quantity stretch.
- Perfectly inelastic demand has zero quantity stretch.

Question:
Which do you think has the most quantity stretch, given an equal percentage increase in price—toothpaste or townhouses?

The Total-Revenue Test

The importance of elasticity for firms relates to the effect of price changes on total revenue and thus on profits (total revenue minus total costs).

total revenue (TR)
The total number of dollars received by a firm from the sale of a product in a particular period.

Total revenue (TR) is the total amount the seller receives from the sale of a product in a particular time period; it is calculated by multiplying the product price (P) by the quantity demanded and sold (Q). In equation form:

$$TR = P \times Q$$

total-revenue test
A test that determines elasticity by examining what happens to total revenue when price changes.

Graphically, total revenue is represented by the $P \times Q$ rectangle lying below a point on a demand curve. At point a in Figure 4.2a, for example, price is $2 and quantity demanded is 10 units. So total revenue is $20 (= $2 × 10), shown by the rectangle composed of the yellow and green areas under the demand curve. We know from basic geometry that the area of a rectangle is found by multiplying one side by the other. Here, one side is "price" ($2) and the other is "quantity demanded" (10 units).

Total revenue and the price elasticity of demand are related. In fact, the easiest way to infer whether demand is elastic or inelastic is to employ the **total-revenue test.**

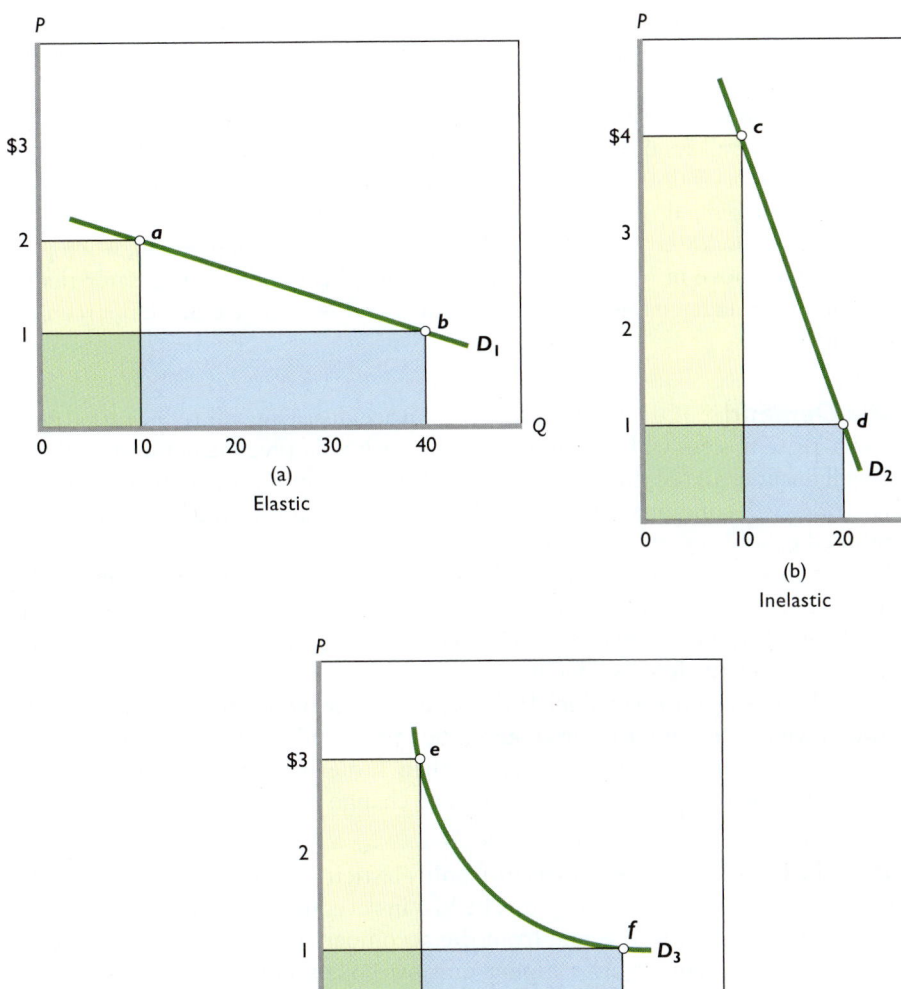

FIGURE 4.2
The total-revenue test for price elasticity.
(a) Price declines from $2 to $1, and total revenue increases from $20 to $40. So demand is elastic. The gain in revenue (blue area) exceeds the loss of revenue (yellow area). (b) Price declines from $4 to $1, and total revenue falls from $40 to $20. So demand is inelastic. The gain in revenue (blue area) is less than the loss of revenue (yellow area). (c) Price declines from $3 to $1, and total revenue does not change. Demand is unit-elastic. The gain in revenue (blue area) equals the loss of revenue (yellow area).

Here is the test: Note what happens to total revenue when price changes. If total revenue changes in the opposite direction from price, demand is elastic. If total revenue changes in the same direction as price, demand is inelastic. If total revenue does not change when price changes, demand is unit-elastic.

Elastic Demand   If demand is elastic, a decrease in price will increase total revenue. Even though a lesser price is received per unit, enough additional units are sold to more than make up for the lower price. For an example, look at demand curve D_1 in Figure 4.2a. We have already established that at point a, total revenue is $20 (= \$2 \times 10$), shown as the yellow plus green area.

If the price declines from $2 to $1 (point b), the quantity demanded becomes 40 units and total revenue is $40 (= \$1 \times 40$). As a result of the price decline,

WORKED PROBLEMS

W 4.2
Total-revenue test

total revenue has increased from $20 to $40. Total revenue has increased in this case because the $1 decline in price applies to 10 units, with a consequent revenue loss of $10 (the yellow area). But 30 more units are sold at $1 each, resulting in a revenue gain of $30 (the blue area). Visually, it is apparent that the gain of the blue area exceeds the loss of the yellow area. As indicated, the overall result is a net increase in total revenue of $20 (= $30 − $10).

The analysis is reversible: If demand is elastic, a price increase will reduce total revenue. The revenue gained on the higher-priced units will be more than offset by the revenue lost from the lower quantity sold. Bottom line: Other things equal, when price and total revenue move in opposite directions, demand is elastic. E_d is greater than 1, meaning the percentage change in quantity demanded is greater than the percentage change in price.

Inelastic Demand   If demand is inelastic, a price decrease will reduce total revenue. The increase in sales will not fully offset the decline in revenue per unit, and total revenue will decline. To see this, look at demand curve D_2 in Figure 4.2b. At point c on the curve, price is $4 and quantity demanded is 10. So total revenue is $40, shown by the combined yellow and green rectangle. If the price drops to $1 (point d), total revenue declines to $20, which obviously is less than $40. Total revenue has declined because the loss of revenue (the yellow area) from the lower unit price is larger than the gain in revenue (the blue area) from the accompanying increase in sales. Price has fallen, and total revenue has also declined.

Our analysis is again reversible: If demand is inelastic, a price increase will increase total revenue. So, other things equal, when price and total revenue move in the same direction, demand is inelastic. E_d is less than 1, meaning the percentage change in quantity demanded is less than the percentage change in price.

Unit Elasticity   In the special case of unit elasticity, an increase or a decrease in price leaves total revenue unchanged. The loss in revenue from a lower unit price is exactly offset by the gain in revenue from the accompanying increase in sales. Conversely, the gain in revenue from a higher unit price is exactly offset by the revenue loss associated with the accompanying decline in the amount demanded.

In Figure 4.2c (demand curve D_3), we find that at the $3 price, 10 units will be sold, yielding total revenue of $30. At the lower $1 price, a total of 30 units will be sold, again resulting in $30 of total revenue. The $2 price reduction causes the loss of revenue shown by the yellow area, but this is exactly offset by the revenue gain shown by the blue area. Total revenue does not change. In fact, that would be true for all price changes along this particular curve.

Other things equal, when price changes and total revenue remains constant, demand is unit-elastic (or unitary). E_d is 1, meaning the percentage change in quantity equals the percentage change in price.

Price Elasticity along a Linear Demand Curve

Now a major confession! Although the demand curves depicted in Figure 4.2 nicely illustrate the total-revenue test for elasticity, two of the graphs involve specific movements along linear (straight-line) demand curves. That presents no problem for explaining the total-revenue test. However, you need to know that elasticity typically varies over different price ranges of the same demand curve. (The exception is the curve in Figure 4.2c. Elasticity is 1 along the entire curve.)

(1) Total Quantity of Tickets Demanded per Week, Thousands	(2) Price per Ticket	(3) Elasticity Coefficient (E_d)	(4) Total Revenue, (1) × (2)	(5) Total-Revenue Test
1	$8		$ 8000	
		5.00		Elastic
2	7		14,000	
		2.60		Elastic
3	6		18,000	
		1.57		Elastic
4	5		20,000	
		1.00		Unit elastic
5	4		20,000	
		0.64		Inelastic
6	3		18,000	
		0.38		Inelastic
7	2		14,000	
		0.20		Inelastic
8	1		8000	

FIGURE 4.3

Price elasticity of demand along a linear demand curve as measured by the elasticity coefficient and the total-revenue test. Demand curve *D* is based on columns (1) and (2) of the table and is labeled to show that the hypothetical weekly demand for movie tickets is elastic at higher price ranges and inelastic at lower price ranges. That fact is confirmed by the elasticity coefficients (column 3) as well as the total-revenue test (columns 4 and 5) in the table.

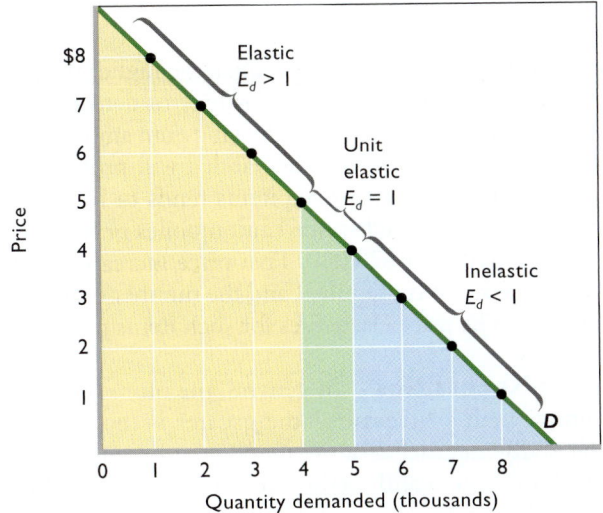

Consider columns 1 and 2 of the table in Figure 4.3, which shows hypothetical data for movie tickets. We plot these data as demand curve *D* in the accompanying graph. The notation above the curve correctly suggests that demand is more price-elastic toward the upper left (here, the $5–$8 price range of *D*) than toward the lower right (here, the $4–$1 price range of *D*). This fact is confirmed by the elasticity coefficients in column (3) of the table: The coefficients decline as price falls. Also, note from column (4) that total revenue first rises as price falls and then eventually declines as price falls further. Column (5) employs the total-revenue test to show that elasticity declines as price falls along a linear demand curve.

INTERACTIVE GRAPHS

G 4.1

Elasticity and revenue

The demand curve in Figure 4.3 illustrates that the slope of a demand curve (its flatness or steepness) is an unreliable basis for judging elasticity. The slope of the curve is computed from *absolute* changes in price and quantity, while elasticity involves *relative* or *percentage* changes in price and quantity. The demand curve in Figure 4.3 is linear, which means its slope is constant throughout. But this linear curve is elastic in its high-price ($8–$5) range and inelastic in its low-price ($4–$1) range.

Determinants of Price Elasticity of Demand

We cannot say what will determine the price elasticity of demand in each individual situation, but the following generalizations are often helpful.

Substitutability   Generally, the larger the number of substitute goods that are available, the greater is the price elasticity of demand. Mercedes, BMWs, and Lincolns are effective substitutes for Cadillacs, making the demand for Cadillacs elastic. At the other extreme, we saw earlier that the diabetic's demand for insulin is highly inelastic because there simply are no close substitutes.

The elasticity of demand for a product depends on how narrowly the product is defined. Demand for Reebok sneakers is more elastic than is the overall demand for shoes. Many other brands are readily substitutable for Reebok sneakers, but there are few, if any, good substitutes for shoes.

Proportion of Income   Other things equal, the higher the price of a product relative to one's income, the greater the price elasticity of demand for it. A 10 percent increase in the price of low-priced pencils or chewing gum amounts to a very small portion of most people's incomes, and quantity demanded will probably decline only slightly. Thus, price elasticity for such low-priced items tends to be low. But a 10 percent increase in the price of relatively high-priced automobiles or houses means additional expenditures of perhaps $3000 or $20,000. That price increase is a significant fraction of the incomes and budgets of most families, and the number of units demanded will likely diminish significantly. The price elasticities for such items tend to be high.

Luxuries versus Necessities   In general, the more that a good is considered to be a "luxury" rather than a "necessity," the greater is the price elasticity of demand. Electricity is generally regarded as a necessity; it is difficult to get along without it. A price increase will not significantly reduce the amount of lighting and power used in a household. (Note the very low price-elasticity coefficient of these goods in Table 4.1.) An extreme case: A person does not decline emergency heart bypass surgery because the physician's fee has just gone up by 10 percent.

On the other hand, vacation travel and jewelry are luxuries that can easily be forgone. If the prices of vacation travel and jewelry rise, a consumer need not buy them and will suffer no great hardship without them.

What about the demand for a common product like salt? It is highly inelastic on three counts: There are few good substitutes available; salt is a negligible item in the family budget; and it is a "necessity" rather than a luxury.

Time   Generally, product demand is more elastic the longer the time period under consideration. Consumers often need time to adjust to changes in prices. For example, consumers may not immediately reduce their purchases very much when the price of beef rises by 10 percent, but in time they may shift to chicken, pork, or fish.

TABLE 4.1
Selected Price Elasticities of Demand

Product or Service	Coefficient of Price Elasticity of Demand (E_d)	Product or Service	Coefficient of Price Elasticity of Demand (E_d)
Newspapers	.10	Milk	.63
Electricity (household)	.13	Household appliances	.63
Bread	.15	Liquor	.70
Major-league baseball tickets	.23	Movies	.87
Cigarettes	.25	Beer	.90
Telephone service	.26	Shoes	.91
Sugar	.30	Motor vehicles	1.14
Medical care	.31	Beef	1.27
Eggs	.32	China, glassware, tableware	1.54
Legal services	.37	Residential land	1.60
Automobile repair	.40	Restaurant meals	2.27
Clothing	.49	Lamb and mutton	2.65
Gasoline	.60	Fresh peas	2.83

Source: Compiled from numerous studies and sources reporting price elasticity of demand.

Another consideration is product durability. Studies show that "short-run" demand for gasoline is more inelastic ($E_d = .2$) than is "long-run" demand ($E_d = .7$). In the short run, people are "stuck" with their present cars and trucks, but with rising gasoline prices they eventually replace them with smaller, more fuel-efficient vehicles.

Table 4.1 shows estimated price-elasticity coefficients for a number of products. Each reflects some combination of the elasticity determinants just discussed.

Price Elasticity of Demand and College Tuition

For some goods and services, for-profit firms or not-for-profit institutions may find it advantageous to determine differences in price elasticity of demand for different groups of customers and then charge different prices to the different groups. Price increases for groups that have inelastic demand will increase total revenue, as will price decreases for groups that have elastic demand.

It is relatively easy to observe differences between group elasticities. Consider tuition pricing by colleges and universities. Prospective students from low-income families generally have more elastic demand for higher education than similar students from high-income families. This is true because tuition is a much larger proportion of household income for a low-income student or family than for his or her high-income counterpart. Desiring a diverse student body, colleges charge different *net* prices (= tuition *minus* financial aid) to the two groups on the basis of elasticity of demand. High-income students pay full tuition, unless they receive merit-based scholarships. Low-income students receive considerable financial aid in addition to merit-based scholarships and, in effect, pay a lower *net* price.

Applying the Analysis

It is common for colleges to announce a large tuition increase and immediately cushion the news by emphasizing that they also are increasing financial aid. In effect, the college is increasing the tuition for students who have inelastic demand by the full amount and raising the *net* tuition of those with elastic demand by some lesser amount or not at all. Through this strategy, colleges boost revenue to cover rising costs while maintaining affordability for a wide range of students.

Question:
What are some other examples of charging different prices to different groups of customers on the basis of differences in elasticity of demand? (*Hint:* Think of price discounts based on age or time of purchase.)

Applying the Analysis

Decriminalization of Illegal Drugs

In recent years proposals to legalize drugs have been widely debated. Proponents contend that drugs should be treated like alcohol; they should be made legal for adults and regulated for purity and potency. The current war on drugs, it is argued, has been unsuccessful, and the associated costs—including enlarged police forces, the construction of more prisons, an overburdened court system, and untold human costs—have increased markedly. Legalization would allegedly reduce drug trafficking significantly by taking the profit out of it. Crack cocaine and heroin, for example, are cheap to produce and could be sold at low prices in legal markets. Because the demand of addicts is highly inelastic, the amounts consumed at the lower prices would increase only modestly. Addicts' total expenditures for cocaine and heroin would decline, and so would the street crime that finances those expenditures.

Opponents of legalization say that the overall demand for cocaine and heroin is far more elastic than proponents think. In addition to the inelastic demand of addicts, there is another market segment whose demand is relatively elastic. This segment consists of the occasional users or "dabblers," who use hard drugs when their prices are low but who abstain or substitute, say, alcohol when their prices are high. Thus, the lower prices associated with the legalization of hard drugs would increase consumption by dabblers. Also, removal of the legal prohibitions against using drugs might make drug use more socially acceptable, increasing the demand for cocaine and heroin.

Many economists predict that the legalization of cocaine and heroin would reduce street prices by up to 60 percent, depending on if and how much they were taxed. According to one study, price declines of that size would increase the number of occasional users of heroin by 54 percent and the number of occasional users of cocaine by 33 percent. The total quantity of heroin demanded would rise by an estimated 100 percent, and the quantity of cocaine demanded would rise by 50 percent.* Moreover, many existing and first-time dabblers might in time become addicts. The overall result, say the opponents of legalization, would be higher social costs, possibly including an increase in street crime.

Question:
In what ways do drug rehabilitation programs increase the elasticity of demand for illegal drugs?

*Henry Saffer and Frank Chaloupka, "The Demand for Illegal Drugs," *Economic Inquiry*, July 1999, pp. 401–411.

Excise Taxes and Tax Revenue

Applying the Analysis

The government pays attention to elasticity of demand when it selects goods and services on which to levy *excise taxes* (taxes levied on the production of a product or on the quantity of the product purchased). If a $1 tax is levied on a product and 10,000 units are sold, tax revenue will be $10,000 (= $1 × 10,000 units sold). If the government raises the tax to $1.50, but the higher price that results reduces sales (quantity demanded) to 4000 because demand is elastic, tax revenue will decline to $6000 (= $1.50 × 4000 units sold). So a higher tax on a product that has an elastic demand will bring in less tax revenue.

In contrast, if demand is inelastic, the tax increase from $1 to $1.50 will boost tax revenue. For example, if sales fall from 10,000 to 9000, tax revenue will rise from $10,000 to $13,500 (= $1.50 × 9000 units). Little wonder that legislatures tend to seek out products such as liquor, gasoline, cigarettes, and phone service when levying and raising taxes. Those taxes yield high tax revenues.

Question:
Under what circumstance might a reduction of an excise tax actually produce more tax revenue?

Fluctuating Farm Income

Applying the Analysis

Inelastic demand for farm products and year-to-year changes in farm supply combine to produce highly volatile farm prices and incomes. Let's see why.

In industrially advanced economies, the price elasticity of demand for agricultural products is low. For farm products in the aggregate, the elasticity coefficient is between .20 and .25. These figures suggest that the prices of agricultural products would have to fall by 40 to 50 percent for consumers to increase their purchases by a mere 10 percent. Consumers apparently put a low value on additional farm output compared with the value they put on additional units of alternative goods.

Why is this so? Recall that a basic determinant of elasticity of demand is substitutability. When the price of one product falls, the consumer tends to substitute that product for other products whose prices have not fallen. But in relatively wealthy societies, this substitution is very modest for food. Although people may eat more, they do not switch from three meals a day to, say, five or six meals a day in response to a decline in the relative prices of farm products. Real biological factors constrain an individual's capacity to substitute food for other products.

Farm supply tends to fluctuate from year to year, mainly because farmers have limited control over their output. Floods, droughts, unexpected frost, insect damage, and similar disasters can mean poor crops, while an excellent growing season means bumper crops (extraordinarily large crops). Such natural phenomena are beyond the control of farmers, yet those phenomena exert an important influence on output.

In addition to natural phenomena, the highly competitive nature of agriculture makes it difficult for farmers to form huge combinations to control production. If the thousands of widely scattered and independent producers happened to plant an unusually large or an abnormally small portion of their land one year, an extra-large or a very small farm output would result even if the growing season were normal.

Combining inelastic demand with the instability of supply, we can see why farm prices and incomes are unstable. Even if the market demand for some crop such as barley remains fixed, its price inelasticity will magnify small changes in output into relatively large changes in farm prices and income. For example, suppose that a "normal" barley crop of 100 million bushels results in a "normal" price per bushel of $3 and a "normal" farm income of $300 million (= $3 × 100 million).

A bumper crop of barley will cause large deviations from these normal prices and incomes because of the inelasticity of demand. Suppose that a good growing season occurs and that the result is a large crop of 110 million bushels. As farmers watch their individual crops mature, little will they realize that their collectively large crop, when harvested, will drive the price per bushel down to, say, $2.50. Their revenue will fall from $300 million in the normal year to $275 million (= $2.50 × 110 million bushels) this year. When demand is inelastic, an increase in the quantity sold will be accompanied by a more-than-proportionate decline in price. The net result is that total revenue, that is, total farm income, will decline disproportionately.

Similarly, a small crop of 90 million bushels, perhaps caused by drought, might boost the price to $3.50. Total farm income will rise to $315 million (= $3.50 × 90 million bushels) from the normal level of $300 million. A decline in supply will cause a more-than-proportionate increase in price and in income when demand is inelastic. Ironically, for farmers as a group, a poor crop may be a blessing and a bumper crop a hardship.

Question:
How might government programs that pay farmers to take land out of production in order to achieve conservation goals (such as erosion control and wildlife protection) increase crop prices and farm income?

Price Elasticity of Supply

The concept of price elasticity also applies to supply. If the quantity supplied by producers is relatively responsive to price changes, supply is elastic. If it is relatively insensitive to price changes, supply is inelastic.

ORIGIN OF THE IDEA

O 4.2
Price elasticity of supply

We measure the degree of price elasticity or inelasticity of supply with the coefficient E_s, defined almost like E_d except that we substitute "percentage change in quantity supplied" for "percentage change in quantity demanded":

$$E_s = \frac{\text{percentage change in quantity supplied of X}}{\text{percentage change in price of X}}$$

For reasons explained earlier, the averages, or midpoints, of the before and after quantities supplied and the before and after prices are used as reference points for the percentage changes. Suppose an increase in the price of a good from $4 to

© Royalty-Free/CORBIS   © The Art Archive/Corbis

Photo Op Elastic versus Inelastic Supply

The supply of automobiles is elastic, whereas the supply of Monet paintings is inelastic.

$6 increases the quantity supplied from 10 units to 14 units. The percentage change in price would be 2/5, or 40 percent, and the percentage change in quantity would be 4/12, or 33 percent:

$$E_s = \frac{.33}{.40} = .83$$

In this case, supply is inelastic because the price-elasticity coefficient is less than 1. If E_s is greater than 1, supply is elastic. If it is equal to 1, supply is unit-elastic. Also, E_s is never negative, since price and quantity supplied are directly related. Thus, there are no minus signs to drop, as was necessary with elasticity of demand.

The degree of **price elasticity of supply** depends mainly on how easily and quickly producers can shift resources between alternative uses to alter production of a good. The easier and more rapid the transfers of resources, the greater is the price elasticity of supply. Take the case of a producer of surfboards. The producer's response to an increase in the price of surfboards depends on its ability to shift resources from the production of other products such as wakeboards, skateboards, and snowboards (whose prices we assume remain constant) to the production of surfboards. And shifting resources takes time: The longer the time, the greater the transferability of resources. So there will be a greater production response, and therefore greater elasticity of supply, the longer a firm has to adjust to a price change.

In analyzing the impact of time on elasticity, economists distinguish among the immediate market period, the short run, and the long run.

price elasticity of supply
A measure of the responsiveness of the quantity of a product supplied by sellers when the product price changes.

Price Elasticity of Supply: The Market Period

The **market period** is the period that occurs when the time immediately after a change in market price is too short for producers to respond with a change in the amount they supply. Suppose a farmer brings to market one truckload of tomatoes that

market period
A period in which producers of a product are unable to change the quantity produced in response to a change in price.

FIGURE 4.4

Time and the elasticity of supply. The greater the amount of time producers have to adjust to a change in demand, here from D_1 to D_2, the greater will be their output response. In the immediate market period (a) there is insufficient time to change output, and so supply is perfectly inelastic. In the short run (b) plant capacity is fixed, but changing the intensity of its use can alter output; supply is therefore more elastic. In the long run (c) all desired adjustments, including changes in plant capacity, can be made, and supply becomes still more elastic.

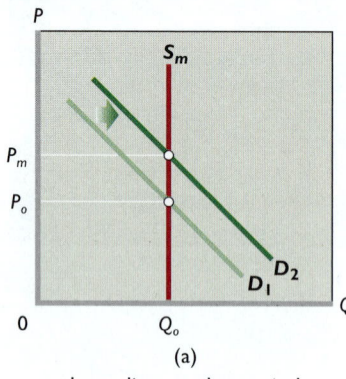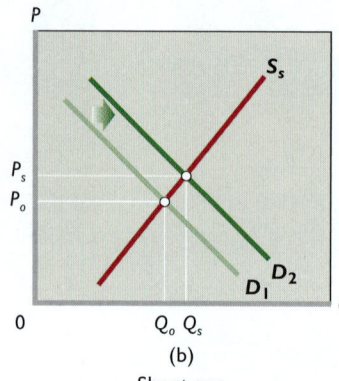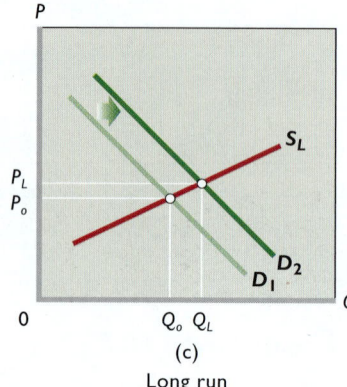

is the entire season's output. The supply curve for the tomatoes is perfectly inelastic (vertical); the farmer will sell the truckload whether the price is high or low. Why? Because the farmer can offer only one truckload of tomatoes even if the price of tomatoes is much higher than anticipated. The farmer might like to offer more tomatoes, but tomatoes cannot be produced overnight. Another full growing season is needed to respond to a higher-than-expected price by producing more than one truckload. Similarly, because the product is perishable, the farmer cannot withhold it from the market. If the price is lower than anticipated, the farmer will still sell the entire truckload.

The farmer's costs of production, incidentally, will not enter into this decision to sell. Though the price of tomatoes may fall far short of production costs, the farmer will nevertheless sell everything brought to market to avoid a total loss through spoilage. In the market period, both the supply of tomatoes and the quantity of tomatoes supplied are fixed. The farmer offers only one truckload, no matter how high or low the price.

Figure 4.4a shows the farmer's vertical supply curve during the market period. Supply is perfectly inelastic because the farmer does not have time to respond to a change in demand, say, from D_1 to D_2. The resulting price increase from P_0 to P_m simply determines which buyers get the fixed quantity supplied; it elicits no increase in output.

However, not all supply curves are perfectly inelastic immediately after a price change. If the product is not perishable and the price rises, producers may choose to increase quantity supplied by drawing down their inventories of unsold, stored goods. This will cause the market supply curve to attain some positive slope. For our tomato farmer, the market period may be a full growing season; for producers of goods that can be inexpensively stored, there may be no market period at all.

Price Elasticity of Supply: The Short Run

short run
A period in which producers are able to change the quantities of some but not all the resources they employ.

The **short run** in microeconomics is a period of time too short to change plant capacity but long enough to use the fixed-size plant more or less intensively. In the short run, our farmer's plant (land and farm machinery) is fixed. But he does have time in the short run to cultivate tomatoes more intensively by applying more labor and more fertilizer and pesticides to the crop. The result is a somewhat greater output in response to a presumed increase in demand; this greater output is reflected in a more elastic supply of tomatoes, as shown by S_s in Figure 4.4b. Note now that the increase in demand from D_1 to D_2 is met by an increase in quantity (from Q_0 to Q_s), so there is a smaller price adjustment (from P_0 to P_s) than would be the case in the market period. The equilibrium price is therefore lower in the short run than in the market period.

Price Elasticity of Supply: The Long Run

The **long run** in microeconomics is a time period long enough for firms to adjust their plant sizes and for new firms to enter (or existing firms to leave) the industry. In the "tomato industry," for example, our farmer has time to acquire additional land and buy more machinery and equipment. Furthermore, other farmers may, over time, be attracted to tomato farming by the increased demand and higher price. Such adjustments create a larger supply response, as represented by the more elastic supply curve S_L in Figure 4.4c. The outcome is a smaller price rise (P_0 to P_L) and a larger output increase (Q_0 to Q_L) in response to the increase in demand from D_1 to D_2.

There is no total-revenue test for elasticity of supply. Supply shows a positive or direct relationship between price and amount supplied; the supply curve is upsloping. Regardless of the degree of elasticity or inelasticity, price and total revenue always move together.

long run
A period long enough to enable producers of a product to change all the resources they employ.

Antiques and Reproductions

The *Antiques Road Show* is a popular PBS television program in which people bring antiques to a central location for appraisal by experts. Some people are pleased to learn that their old piece of furniture or funky folk art is worth a large amount, say, $30,000 or more.

The high price of a particular antique is due to strong demand and limited, highly inelastic supply. Because a genuine antique can no longer be reproduced, its quantity supplied either does not rise or rises only slightly as its price goes up. The higher price might prompt the discovery of a few more of the remaining originals and thus add to the quantity available for sale, but this quantity response is usually quite small. So the supply of antiques and other collectibles tends to be inelastic. For one-of-a-kind antiques, the supply is perfectly inelastic.

Factors such as increased population, higher income, and greater enthusiasm for collecting antiques have increased the demand for antiques over time. Because the supply of antiques is limited and inelastic, those increases in demand have greatly boosted the prices of antiques.

Contrast the inelastic supply of original antiques with the elastic supply of modern "made-to-look-old" reproductions. Such faux antiques are quite popular and widely available at furniture stores and knickknack shops. When the demand for reproductions increases, the firms making them simply boost production. Because the supply of reproductions is highly elastic, increased demand raises their prices only slightly.

Applying the Analysis

Question:
How does the reluctance to sell antiques add to their inelastic supply?

Volatile Gold Prices

The price of gold is quite volatile, sometimes rocketing upward one period and plummeting downward the next. The main sources of these fluctuations are shifts in demand and highly inelastic supply. Gold production is a costly and time-consuming process of exploration, mining, and refining. Moreover, the physical availability of gold is highly limited. For both reasons, increases in gold prices do not elicit substantial increases in quantity supplied. Conversely, gold mining is costly to shut down, and existing gold bars are expensive to store. Price decreases therefore do not produce large drops in the quantity of gold supplied. In short, the supply of gold is inelastic.

The demand for gold is partly derived from the demand for its uses, such as for jewelry, dental fillings, and coins. But people also demand gold as a speculative financial investment. They increase their demand for gold when they fear general inflation or domestic or international turmoil that might undermine the value of currency and more traditional investments. They reduce their demand when events settle down. Because of the inelastic supply of gold, even relatively small changes in demand produce relatively large changes in price.

Question:
What is the current price of gold? (See www.goldprices.com.) What were the highest and the lowest prices over the last 12 months?

Income Elasticity of Demand

income elasticity of demand
A measure of the responsiveness of the quantity of a product demanded to changes in consumer income.

Income elasticity of demand measures the degree to which the quantity of a product demanded responds, positively or negatively, to a change in consumers' incomes. The coefficient of income elasticity of demand E_i is determined with the formula

$$E_i = \frac{\text{percentage change in quantity demanded}}{\text{percentage change in income}}$$

Normal Goods

For most goods, the income-elasticity coefficient E_i is positive, meaning that more of them are demanded as income rises. Such goods are called *normal* or *superior goods* (and were first described in Chapter 3). But the value of E_i varies greatly among normal goods. For example, income elasticity of demand for automobiles is about +3, while income elasticity for most farm products is only about +.20.

Inferior Goods

A negative income-elasticity coefficient designates an inferior good. Used mattresses, long-distance bus tickets, used clothing, and some frozen meals are likely candidates. Consumers decrease their purchases of inferior goods as their incomes rise.

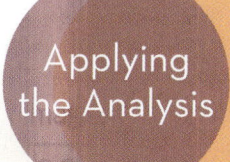

Which Consumer Products Suffer the Greatest Demand Decreases during Recessions?

Coefficients of income elasticity of demand provide insights into how recessions impact the sales of different consumer products. A recession is defined as two or more consecutive quarters (six months) of falling real output, and is typically characterized by rising unemployment rates, lower profits for business firms, falling consumer incomes, and weaker demand for products. In December 2007, the U.S. economy entered its tenth recession since 1950. Because of a worsening mortgage debt crisis, the recession continued through 2008 and into 2009. When recessions occur and incomes fall, coefficients of income elasticity of demand help predict which products will experience more rapid declines in demand than other products.

Products with relatively high income elasticity coefficients such as automobiles ($E_i = +3$), housing ($E_i = +1.5$), and restaurant meals ($E_i = +1.4$) are generally hit hardest by recessions. Those with low or negative income elasticity coefficients are much less affected. For example, food products ($E_i = +.20$) respond relatively little to income fluctuations. When incomes drop, purchases of food (and toothpaste and toilet paper) drop little compared to purchases of movie tickets, luxury vacations, and wide-screen TVs. Products we view as essential tend to have lower income elasticity coefficients than products we view as luxuries. When our incomes fall, we cannot easily eliminate or postpone the purchase of essential products.

Question:
Why did discount clothing stores (such as Kohl's) suffer less than high-end clothing stores (such as Nordstrom) during the 2007–2009 U.S. recession?

Cross-Elasticity of Demand

Cross-elasticity of demand measures how the quantity of a product demanded (say, X) responds to a change in the price of some other product (say, Y). We calculate the coefficient of cross-elasticity of demand E_{xy} just as we do the coefficient of simple price elasticity, except that we relate the percentage change in the consumption of X to the percentage change in the price of Y:

$$E_{xy} = \frac{\text{percentage change in quantity demanded of product X}}{\text{percentage change in price of product Y}}$$

This cross-elasticity (or cross-price-elasticity) concept allows us to quantify and more fully understand substitute and complementary goods, introduced in Chapter 3.

**cross-elasticity
of demand**
A measure of the
responsiveness of the
quantity demanded of one
product to a change in the
price of another product.

Substitute Goods

If cross-elasticity of demand is positive, meaning that sales of X move in the same direction as a change in the price of Y, then X and Y are substitute goods. An example is Evian water (X) and Dasani water (Y). An increase in the price of Dasani causes consumers to buy more Evian, resulting in a positive cross-elasticity. The larger the positive cross-elasticity coefficient, the greater is the substitutability between the two products.

Complementary Goods

When cross-elasticity is negative, we know that X and Y "go together"; an increase in the price of one decreases the demand for the other. This indicates that the two are complementary goods. For example, a decrease in the price of digital cameras will increase the number of memory sticks purchased. The larger the negative cross-elasticity coefficient, the greater is the complementarity between the two goods.

Independent Goods

A zero or near-zero cross-elasticity suggests that the two products being considered are unrelated or independent goods. An example is textbooks and plums: We would not expect a change in the price of textbooks to have any effect on purchases of plums, and vice versa.

Applying the Analysis

Using Cross-Elasticity to Make Business and Regulatory Decisions

The degree of substitutability of products, measured by the cross-elasticity coefficient, is important to businesses and government. For example, suppose that Coca-Cola is considering whether or not to lower the price of its Sprite brand. Not only will it want to know something about the price elasticity of demand for Sprite (will the price cut increase or decrease total revenue?), but it also will be interested in knowing if the increased sales of Sprite will come at the expense of its Coke brand. How sensitive are the sales of one of its products (Coke) to a change in the price of another of its products (Sprite)? By how much will the increased sales of Sprite "cannibalize" the sales of Coke? A low cross-elasticity would indicate that Coke and Sprite are weak substitutes for each other and that a lower price for Sprite would have little effect on Coke sales.

Government also implicitly uses the idea of cross-elasticity of demand in assessing whether a proposed merger between two large firms will substantially reduce competition and therefore violate the antitrust laws. For example, the cross-elasticity between Coke and Pepsi is high, making them strong substitutes for each other. In addition, Coke and Pepsi together sell about 75 percent of all carbonated cola drinks consumed in the United States. Taken together, the high cross-elasticities and the large market shares suggest that the government would likely block a merger between Coke and Pepsi because the merger would substantially lessen competition. In contrast, the cross-elasticity between cola and gasoline is low or zero. A merger between Coke and Shell Oil Company would have a minimal effect on competition. So government would let that merger happen.

Question:
Prior to the 2007–2009 recession, why did sales of sport utility vehicles (SUVs) decline dramatically, while sales of hybrid vehicles rose significantly? Relate your answer to cross-elasticity of demand.

Summary

1. Price elasticity of demand measures the responsiveness of the quantity of a product demanded when the price changes. If consumers are relatively sensitive to price changes, demand is elastic. If they are relatively unresponsive to price changes, demand is inelastic.

2. The price-elasticity coefficient E_d measures the degree of elasticity or inelasticity of demand. The coefficient is found by the formula

$$E_d = \frac{\text{percentage change in quantity demanded of X}}{\text{percentage change in price of X}}$$

Economists use the averages of prices and quantities under consideration as reference points in determining percentage changes in price and quantity. If E_d is greater than 1, demand is elastic. If E_d is less than 1, demand is inelastic. Unit elasticity is the special case in which E_d equals 1.

3. Perfectly inelastic demand is graphed as a line parallel to the vertical axis; perfectly elastic demand is shown by a line above and parallel to the horizontal axis.

4. Total revenue (TR) is the total number of dollars received by a firm from the sale of a product in a particular period. It is found by multiplying price times quantity. Graphically, TR is shown as the $P \times Q$ rectangle under a point on a demand curve.

5. If total revenue changes in the opposite direction from price, demand is elastic. If price and total revenue change in the same direction, demand is inelastic. Where demand is of unit elasticity, a change in price leaves total revenue unchanged.

6. Elasticity varies at different price ranges on a demand curve, tending to be elastic in the upper-left segment and inelastic in the lower-right segment. Elasticity cannot be judged by the steepness or flatness of a demand curve.

7. The number of available substitutes, the size of an item's price relative to one's budget, whether the product is a luxury or a necessity, and the length of time to adjust are all determinants of elasticity of demand.

8. The elasticity concept also applies to supply. The coefficient of price elasticity of supply is found by the formula

$$E_s = \frac{\text{percentage change in quantity supplied of X}}{\text{percentage change in price of X}}$$

The averages of the prices and quantities under consideration are used as reference points for computing percentage changes.

9. Elasticity of supply depends on the ease of shifting resources between alternative uses, which varies directly with the time producers have to adjust to a price change.

10. Income elasticity of demand indicates the responsiveness of consumer purchases to a change in income. The coefficient of income elasticity of demand is found by the formula

$$E_i = \frac{\text{percentage change in quantity demanded}}{\text{percentage change in income}}$$

The coefficient is positive for normal goods and negative for inferior goods.

11. Cross-elasticity of demand indicates the responsiveness of consumer purchases of one product (X) to a change in the price of some other product (Y). The coefficient of cross-elasticity is found by the formula

$$E_{xy} = \frac{\text{percentage change in quantity demanded of product X}}{\text{percentage change in price of product Y}}$$

The coefficient is positive if X and Y are substitute goods and negative if X and Y are complements.

Terms and Concepts

price elasticity of demand	perfectly elastic demand	short run
elastic demand	total revenue (TR)	long run
inelastic demand	total-revenue test	income elasticity of demand
unit elasticity	price elasticity of supply	cross-elasticity of demand
perfectly inelastic demand	market period	

Questions  economics

1. What is the formula for measuring price elasticity of demand? What does it mean (in terms of relative price and quantity changes) if the price-elasticity coefficient is less than 1? Equal to 1? Greater than 1? **LO1**

2. Graph the accompanying demand data, and then use the price-elasticity formula (midpoints approach) for E_d to determine price elasticity of demand for each of the four possible $1 price changes. What can you conclude about the relationship between the slope of a curve and its elasticity? **LO1**

Product Price	Quantity Demanded
$5	1
4	2
3	3
2	4
1	5

3. What are the major determinants of price elasticity of demand? Use those determinants and your own reasoning in judging whether demand for each of the following products is probably elastic or inelastic: (a) bottled water; (b) toothpaste; (c) Crest toothpaste; (d) ketchup; (e) diamond bracelets; (f) Microsoft Windows operating system. **LO1**

4. What effect would a rule stating that university students must live in university dormitories have on the price elasticity of demand for dormitory space? What impact might this in turn have on room rates? **LO1**

5. Calculate total-revenue data from the demand schedule in question 2. Referring to changes in price and total revenue, describe the total-revenue test for elasticity. **LO2**

6. How would the following changes in price affect total revenue? That is, would total revenue increase, decrease, or remain unchanged? **LO2**
   a. Price falls and demand is inelastic.
   b. Price rises and demand is elastic.
   c. Price rises and supply is elastic.
   d. Price rises and supply is inelastic.
   e. Price rises and demand is inelastic.
   f. Price falls and demand is elastic.
   g. Price falls and demand is of unit elasticity.

7. You are chairperson of a state tax commission responsible for establishing a program to raise new revenue through excise taxes. Why would elasticity of demand be important to you in determining the products on which the taxes should be levied? **LO4**

8. In 2006, Willem de Koonig's abstract painting *Woman III* sold for $137.5 million. Portray this sale in a demand and supply diagram, and comment on the elasticity of supply. Comedian George Carlin once mused, "If a painting can be forged well enough to fool some experts, why is the original so valuable?" Provide an answer. **LO4**

9. Because of a legal settlement over state health care claims, in 1999 the U.S. tobacco companies had to raise the average price of a pack of cigarettes from $1.95 to $2.45. The decline in cigarette sales was estimated at 8 percent. What does this imply for the elasticity of demand for cigarettes? Explain. **LO4**

10. The income elasticities of demand for movies, dental services, and clothing have been estimated to be +3.4, +1, and +.5, respectively. Interpret these coefficients. What does it mean if an income-elasticity coefficient is negative? **LO5**

11. Suppose the cross-elasticity of demand for products A and B is +3.6, and for products C and D is −5.4. What can you conclude about how products A and B are related? Products C and D? **LO5**

Problems

1. Look at the demand curve in Figure 4.2a. Use the midpoint formula and points a and b to calculate the elasticity of demand for that range of the demand curve. Do the same for the demand curves in Figures 4.2b and 4.2c using, respectively, points c and d for Figure 4.2b and points e and f for Figure 4.2c. **LO1**

2. Investigate how demand elasticities are affected by increases in demand. Shift each of the demand curves in Figures 4.2a, 4.2b, and 4.2c to the right by 10 units. For example, point a in Figure 4.2a would shift rightward from location (10 units, $2) to (20 units, $2), while point b would shift rightward from location (40 units, $1) to (50 units, $1). After making these shifts, apply the midpoint formula to calculate the demand elasticities for the shifted points. Are they larger or smaller than the elasticities you calculated in problem 1 for the original points? In terms of the midpoint formula, what explains the change in elasticities? **LO1**

3. Suppose that the total revenue received by a company selling basketballs is $600 when the price is set at $30 per basketball and $600 when the price is set at $20 per basketball. Without using the midpoint formula, can you tell whether demand is elastic, inelastic, or unit-elastic over this price range? **LO2**

4. Danny "Dimes" Donahue is a neighborhood's 9-year old entrepreneur. His most recent venture is selling home-made brownies that he bakes himself. At a price of $1.50 each, he sells 100. At a price of $1.00 each, he sells 300. Is demand elastic or inelastic over this price range? *If* demand had the same elasticity for a price decline from $1.00 to $0.50 as it does for the decline from $1.50 to $1.00, would cutting the price from $1.00 to $0.50 increase or decrease Danny's total revenue? **LO2**

5. What is the formula for measuring the price elasticity of supply? Suppose the price of apples goes up from $20 to $22 a box. In direct response, Goldsboro Farms supplies 1200 boxes of apples instead of 1000 boxes. Compute the coefficient of price elasticity (midpoints approach) for Goldsboro's supply. Is its supply elastic, or is it inelastic? **LO3**

6. **ADVANCED ANALYSIS** Currently, at a price of $1 each, 100 popsicles are sold per day in the perpetually hot town of Rostin. Consider the elasticity of supply. In the short run, a price increase from $1 to $2 is unit-elastic ($E_s = 1.0$). So how many popsicles will be sold each day in the short run if the price rises to $2 each? In the long run, a price increase from $1 to $2 has an elasticity of supply of 1.50. So how many popsicles will be sold per day in the long run if the price rises to $2 each? (Hint: Apply the midpoints approach to the elasticity of supply.) **LO3**

7. Lorena likes to play golf. The number of times per year that she plays depends on both the price of playing a round of golf as well as Lorena's income and the cost of other types of entertainment—in particular, how much it costs to go see a movie instead of playing golf. The three demand schedules in the table below show how many rounds of golf per year Lorena will demand at each price under three different scenarios. In scenario D_1, Lorena's income is $50,000 per year and movies cost $9 each. In scenario D_2, Lorena's income is also $50,000 per year, but the price of seeing a movie rises to $11. And in scenario D_3, Lorena's income goes up to $70,000 per year, while movies cost $11. **LO5**

	Quantity Demanded		
Price	D_1	D_2	D_3
$50	15	10	15
35	25	15	30
20	40	20	50

a. Using the data under D_1 and D_2, calculate the cross-elasticity of Lorena's demand for golf at all three prices. (To do this, apply the midpoints approach to the cross-elasticity of demand.) Is the cross-elasticity the same at all three prices? Are movies and golf substitute goods, complementary goods, or independent goods?

b. Using the data under D_2 and D_3, calculate the income elasticity of Lorena's demand for golf at all three prices. (To do this, apply the midpoints approach to the income elasticity of demand.) Is the income elasticity the same at all three prices? Is golf an inferior good?

FURTHER TEST YOUR KNOWLEDGE AT
www.brue3e.com

At the text's Online Learning Center, **www.brue3e.com,** you will find one or more web-based questions that require information from the Internet to answer. We urge you to check them out, since they will familiarize you with websites that may be helpful in other courses and perhaps even in your career. The OLC also features multiple-choice quizzes that give instant feedback and provides other helpful ways to further test your knowledge of the chapter.

CHAPTER FIVE

Market Failures: Public Goods and Externalities

After reading this chapter, you should be able to:

1. Differentiate between demand-side market failures and supply-side market failures.
2. Identify how public goods are distinguished from private goods, and explain the method for determining the optimal quantity of a public good.
3. Explain how positive and negative externalities cause under- and overallocations of resources, and how they might be corrected.
4. Describe the differences between the benefits-received and ability-to-pay principles of taxation.
5. Distinguish between proportional, progressive, and regressive taxes.

Competitive markets usually do a remarkable job of allocating society's scarce resources to their highest-valued uses. But markets have certain limitations. In some circumstances, economically desirable goods are not produced at all. In other situations, they are either overproduced or underproduced. This chapter examines **market failure,** which occurs when the competitive market system (1) does not allocate any resources whatsoever to the production of certain goods or (2) either underallocates or overallocates resources to the production of certain goods.

market failure
The inability of a market to produce a desirable product or produce it in the "right" amount.

Where private markets fail, an economic role for government may arise. In this chapter, we will examine that role as it relates to public goods and so-called externalities—situations where market failures lead to suboptimal outcomes that the government may be able to improve upon by using its powers to tax, spend, and regulate. We conclude the chapter by noting potential government inefficiencies that can hinder government's economic efforts.

Market Failures in Competitive Markets[1]

Competitive markets usually produce an assignment of resources that is "right" from an economic perspective. Unfortunately, the presence of robust competition involving many buyers and many sellers may not be enough to guarantee that a market will allocate resources correctly. Market failures sometimes happen in competitive markets. The focus of this chapter is to explain how and why such market failures can arise and how they might be corrected.

Fortunately, the broad picture is simple. Market failures in competitive markets fall into just two categories:

- **Demand-side market failures** happen when demand curves do not reflect consumers' full willingness to pay for a good or service.
- **Supply-side market failures** occur when supply curves do not reflect the full cost of producing a good or service.

Demand-Side Market Failures

Demand-side market failures arise because it is impossible in certain cases to charge consumers what they are willing to pay for a product. Consider outdoor fireworks displays. People enjoy fireworks and would therefore be *willing* to pay to see a fireworks display if the only way to see it was to have to pay for the right to do so. But because such displays are outdoors and in public, people don't actually *have* to pay to see the display because there is no way to exclude those who haven't paid from also enjoying the show. Private firms will therefore be unwilling to produce outdoor fireworks displays, as it will be nearly impossible for them to raise enough revenue to cover production costs.

Supply-Side Market Failures

Supply-side market failures arise in situations in which a firm does not have to pay the full cost of producing its output. Consider a coal-burning power plant. The firm running the plant will have to pay for all of the land, labor, capital, and entrepreneurship that it uses to generate electricity by burning coal. But if the firm is not charged for the smoke that it releases into the atmosphere, it will fail to pay another set of costs—the costs that its pollution imposes on other people. These include future harm from global warming, toxins that affect wildlife, and possible damage to agricultural crops downwind.

A market failure arises because it is not possible for the market to correctly weigh costs and benefits in a situation in which some of the costs are completely unaccounted for. The coal-burning power plant produces more electricity and generates more pollution than it would if it had to pay for each ton of smoke that it released into the atmosphere. The extra units that are produced are units of output for which the costs are *greater than* the benefits. Obviously, these units should not be produced.

demand-side market failures
Underallocations of resources that occur when private demand curves understate consumers' full willingness to pay for a good or service.

supply-side market failures
Overallocations of resources that occur when private supply curves understate the full cost of producing a good or service.

---

[1]Other market failures arise when there are not enough buyers or sellers to ensure competition. In those situations, the lack of competition allows either buyers or sellers to restrict purchases or sales below optimal levels for their own benefit. As an example, a monopoly—a firm that is the only producer in its industry—can restrict the amount of output that it supplies in order to drive up the market price and thereby increase its own profit.

Efficiently Functioning Markets

The best way to understand market failure is to first understand how properly functioning competitive markets achieve economic efficiency.

A competitive market not only makes private goods available to consumers but also allocates society's resources efficiently to the particular product. Competition among producers forces them to use the best technology and right mix of productive resources. Otherwise, lower-cost producers will drive them out of business. The result is **productive efficiency**: the production of any particular good in the least costly way. When society produces, say, bottled water at the lowest achievable per-unit cost, it is expending the smallest amount of resources to produce that product and therefore is making available the largest amount of resources to produce other desired goods. Suppose society has only $100 worth of resources available. If it can produce a bottle of water using only $1 of those resources, then it will have available $99 of resources to produce other goods. This is clearly better than producing the bottle of water for $5 and having only $95 of resources available for alternative uses.

productive efficiency
The production of a good in the least costly way.

Competitive markets also produce **allocative efficiency**: the *particular mix* of goods and services most highly valued by society (minimum-cost production assumed). For example, society wants high-quality mineral water to be used for bottled water, not for gigantic blocks of refrigeration ice. It wants MP3 players (such as iPods), not phonographs and 45-rpm records. Moreover, society does not want to devote all its resources to bottled water and MP3 players. It wants to assign some resources to automobiles and personal computers. Competitive markets make those proper assignments, as we will demonstrate.

allocative efficiency
The production of the "right" mix of goods and services (minimum-cost production assumed).

Two conditions must hold if a competitive market is to produce efficient outcomes: The demand curve in the market must reflect consumers' full willingness to pay and the supply curve in the market must reflect all the costs of production. If these conditions hold, then the market will produce only units for which benefits are at least equal to costs.

Private and Public Goods

Demand-side market failures arise in competitive markets when demand curves fail to reflect consumers' full willingness to pay for a good or service. In such situations, markets fail to produce all of the units for which there are net benefits because demand curves underreport how much consumers are willing and able to pay. This underreporting problem reaches its most extreme form in the case of a public good: Markets may fail to produce *any* of the public good because its demand curve may reflect *none* of its consumers' willingness to pay.

To understand public goods, we first need to understand the characteristics that define private goods.

private goods
Goods that people individually buy and consume and that private firms can profitably provide because they keep people who do not pay from receiving the benefits.

Private Goods Characteristics

Certain goods called **private goods** are produced through the market system. Private goods encompass the full range of goods offered for sale in stores and shops. Examples include automobiles, clothing, personal computers, household appliances, and sporting goods. Private goods have two characteristics: rivalry and excludability.

- *Rivalry* (in consumption) means that when one person buys and consumes a product, it is not available for another person to buy and consume. When Adams purchases and drinks a bottle of mineral water, it is not available for Benson to purchase and consume.
- *Excludability* means that sellers can keep people who do not pay for a product from obtaining its benefits. Only people who are willing and able to pay the market price for bottles of water can obtain these drinks and the benefits they confer.

Profitable Provision

Consumers fully express their personal demands for private goods in the market. If Adams likes bottled mineral water, that fact will be known by her desire to purchase the product. Other things equal, the higher the price of bottled water, the fewer bottles she will buy. So Adams' demand for bottled water will reflect an inverse relationship between the price of bottled water and the quantity of it demanded. This is simply *individual* demand, as described in Chapter 3.

The *market* demand for a private good is the horizontal summation of the individual demand schedules (review Figure 3.2). Suppose there are just two consumers in the market for bottled water and the price is $1 per bottle. If Adams will purchase 3 bottles and Benson will buy 2, the market demand will reflect that consumers demand 5 bottles at the $1 price. Similar summations of quantities demanded at other prices will generate the market demand schedule and curve.

Suppose the equilibrium price of bottled water is $1. Adams and Benson will buy a total of 5 bottles, and the sellers will obtain total revenue of $5 (= $1 × 5). If the sellers' cost per bottle is $.80, their total cost will be $4 (= $.80 × 5). So sellers charging $1 per bottle will obtain $5 of total revenue, incur $4 of total cost, and earn $1 of profits for the 5 bottles sold.

Because firms can profitably "tap market demand" for private goods, they will produce and offer them for sale. Consumers demand private goods, and profit-seeking suppliers produce goods that satisfy the demand. Consumers willing to pay the market price obtain the goods; nonpayers go without. A competitive market not only makes private goods available to consumers but also allocates society's resources efficiently to the particular product. There is neither underproduction nor overproduction of the product.

Public Goods Characteristics

Public goods have the opposite characteristics of private goods. Public goods are distinguished by nonrivalry and nonexcludability.

- *Nonrivalry* (in consumption) means that one person's consumption of a good does not preclude consumption of the good by others. Everyone can simultaneously obtain the benefit from a public good such as a global positioning system, national defense, street lighting, and environmental protection.
- *Nonexcludability* means there is no effective way of excluding individuals from the benefit of the good once it comes into existence.

These two characteristics create a **free-rider problem.** Once a producer has provided a public good, everyone including nonpayers can obtain the benefit. Because most people do not voluntarily pay for something that they can obtain for free, most

public goods
Goods that everyone can simultaneously consume and from which no one can be excluded, even if they do not pay.

free-rider problem
The inability of a firm to profitably provide a good because everyone, including nonpayers, can obtain the benefit.

people become free riders. Free riders would be willing to pay for the public good if producers could somehow force them to pay—but nonexcludability means that there is no way for producers to withhold the good from the free riders without also denying it to the few who do pay. As a result, free riding means that the willingness to pay of the free riders is not expressed in the market. From the viewpoint of producers, free riding reduces demand. The more free riding, the less demand. And if all consumers free ride, demand will collapse all the way to zero.

© Steven P. Lynch/The McGraw-Hill Companies, Inc.

© S. Solum/PhotoLink/Getty Images

Photo Op Private versus Public Goods

Apples, distinguished by rivalry (in consumption) and excludability, are examples of private goods. In contrast, streetlights, distinguished by nonrivalry (in consumption) and nonexcludability, are examples of public goods.

The low or even zero demand caused by free riding makes it virtually impossible for private firms to profitably provide public goods. With little or no demand, firms cannot effectively "tap market demand" for revenues and profits. As a result, they will not produce public goods. Society will therefore suffer efficiency losses because goods for which marginal benefits exceed marginal costs are not produced. Thus, if society wants a public good to be produced, it will have to direct government to provide it. Because the public good will still feature nonexcludability, the government won't have any better luck preventing free riding or charging people for it. But because the government can finance the provision of the public good through the taxation of other things, the government does not have to worry about profitability. It can therefore provide the public good even when private firms can't.

A significant example of a public good is homeland defense. The vast majority of Americans think this public good is economically justified because they perceive the benefits as exceeding the costs. Once homeland defense efforts are undertaken, however, the benefits accrue to all Americans (nonrivalry). And there is no practical way to exclude any American from receiving those benefits (nonexcludability).

No private firm will undertake overall homeland defense because the free-rider problem means that benefits cannot be profitably sold. So here we have a service that yields substantial net benefits but to which the market system will not allocate sufficient resources. Like national defense in general, homeland defense is a public good. Society signals its desire for such goods by voting for particular political candidates who support their provision. Because of the free-rider problem, government provides these goods and finances them through compulsory charges in the form of taxes.

Optimal Quantity of a Public Good   If consumers need not reveal their true demand for a public good in the marketplace, how can society determine the optimal amount of that good? The answer is that the government has to try to estimate the demand for a public good through surveys or public votes. It can then compare the marginal benefit of an added unit of the good against the government's marginal cost of providing it. Adhering to the MB = MC rule, it can provide the "right" amount of the public good.

Art for Art's Sake

Suppose an enterprising sculptor creates a piece of art costing $600 and, with permission, places it in the town square. Also suppose that Jack gets $300 of enjoyment from the art and Diane gets $400. Sensing this enjoyment and hoping to make a profit, the sculptor approaches Jack for a donation equal to his satisfaction. Jack falsely says that, unfortunately, he does not particularly like the piece. The sculptor then tries Diane, hoping to get $400 or so. Same deal: Diane professes not to like the piece either. Jack and Diane have become free riders. Although feeling a bit guilty, both reason that it makes no sense to pay for something when anyone can receive the benefits without paying for them. The artist is a quick learner; he vows never to try anything like that again.

Question:
What is the rationale for government funding for art placed in town squares and other public spaces?

Measuring Demand   Suppose that Adams and Benson are the only two people in the society and that their willingness to pay for a public good, this time the war on terrorism, is as shown in columns 1 and 2 and columns 1 and 3 in Table 5.1. Economists might have discovered these schedules through a survey asking hypothetical questions about how much each citizen was willing to pay for various types and amounts of public goods rather than go without them.

Notice that the schedules in the first four columns of Table 5.1 are price-quantity schedules, meaning they are demand schedules. Rather than depicting demand in the usual way—the quantity of a product someone is willing to buy at each possible price—these schedules show the price someone is willing to pay for the extra unit of each possible quantity. That is, Adams is willing to pay $4 for the first unit of the public good, $3 for the second, $2 for the third, and so on.

TABLE 5.1

Optimal Quantity of a
Public Good, Two
Individuals

(1) Quantity of Public Good	(2) Adams' Willingness to Pay (Price)		(3) Benson's Willingness to Pay (Price)		(4) Collective Willingness to Pay (Price)	(5) Marginal Cost
1	$4	+	$5	=	$9	$3
2	3	+	4	=	7	4
3	2	+	3	=	5	5
4	1	+	2	=	3	6
5	0	+	1	=	1	7

Suppose the government produces 1 unit of this public good. Because of nonrivalry, Adams' consumption of the good does not preclude Benson from also consuming it, and vice versa. So both people consume the good, and neither volunteers to pay for it. But from Table 5.1 we can find the amount these two people would be willing to pay, together, rather than do without this 1 unit of the good. Columns 1 and 2 show that Adams would be willing to pay $4 for the first unit of the public good, whereas columns 1 and 3 reveal that Benson would be willing to pay $5 for it. Adams and Benson therefore are jointly willing to pay $9 (= $4 + $5) for this first unit.

For the second unit of the public good, the collective price they are willing to pay is $7 (= $3 from Adams + $4 from Benson); for the third unit they will pay $5 (= $2 + $3); and so on. By finding the collective willingness to pay for each additional unit (column 4), we can construct a collective demand schedule (a willingness-to-pay schedule) for the public good. Here we are *not* adding the quantities demanded at each possible price, as with the market demand for a private good. Instead, we are adding the prices that people are willing to pay for the last unit of the public good at each possible quantity demanded.

What does it mean in columns 1 and 4 of Table 5.1 that, for example, Adams and Benson are collectively willing to pay $7 for the second unit of the public good? It means that they jointly expect to receive $7 of extra benefit or utility from that unit. Column 4, in effect, reveals the collective marginal benefit of each unit of the public good.

Comparing Marginal Benefit and Marginal Cost

Now let's suppose the marginal cost of providing the public good is as shown in column 5 of Table 5.1. As explained in Chapter 1, marginal cost tends to rise as more of a good is produced. In view of the marginal-cost data shown, how much of the good should government provide? The optimal amount occurs at the quantity where marginal benefit equals marginal cost. In Table 5.1 that quantity is 3 units, where the collective willingness to pay for the third unit—the $5 marginal benefit—just matches that unit's $5 marginal cost. As we saw in Chapter 1, equating marginal benefit and marginal cost efficiently allocates society's scarce resources.

WORKED PROBLEMS

W 5.1
Optimal amount of a public good

Cost-Benefit Analysis

The above example suggests a practical means, called **cost-benefit analysis,** for deciding whether to provide a particular public good and how much of it to provide. Like our example, cost-benefit analysis (or marginal-benefit–marginal-cost analysis) involves a comparison of marginal costs and marginal benefits.

Suppose the federal government is contemplating a highway construction plan. Because the economy's resources are limited, any decision to use more resources in the public sector will mean fewer resources for the private sector. There will be both a cost and a benefit. The cost is the loss of satisfaction resulting from the accompanying decline in the production of private goods; the benefit is the extra satisfaction resulting from the output of more public goods. Should the needed resources be shifted from the private to the public sector? The answer is yes if the benefit from the extra public goods exceeds the cost that results from having fewer private goods. The answer is no if the cost of the forgone private goods is greater than the benefit associated with the extra public goods.

Cost-benefit analysis, however, can indicate more than whether a public program is worth doing. It can also help the government decide on the extent to which a project should be pursued. Real economic questions cannot usually be answered simply by "yes" or "no" but, rather, involve questions such as "how much" or "how little."

Roads and highways can be run privately, as excludability is possible with toll gates. However, the federal highway system is almost entirely nonexclusive because anyone with a car can get on and off most federal highways without restriction anytime they want. Federal highways therefore satisfy one characteristic of a public good: nonexcludability. The other characteristic, nonrivalry, is also satisfied by the the fact that unless a highway is already extremely crowded, one person's driving on the highway does not preclude another person's driving on the highway. Thus, the federal highway system is effectively a public good. This leads us to ask: Should the federal government expand the federal highway system? If so, what is the proper size or scope for the overall project?

Table 5.2 lists a series of increasingly ambitious and increasingly costly highway projects: widening existing two-lane highways; building new two-lane highways; building new four-lane highways; building new six-lane highways. The extent to which government should undertake highway construction depends on the costs and benefits. The costs are largely the costs of constructing and maintaining the highways; the benefits are improved flows of people and goods throughout the nation.

The table shows that total annual benefit (column 4) exceeds total annual cost (column 2) for plans A, B, and C, indicating that some highway construction is economically justifiable. We see this directly in column 6, where total costs (column 2) are subtracted from total annual benefits (column 4). Net benefits are positive for plans A, B, and C. Plan D is not economically justifiable because net benefits are negative.

But the question of optimal size or scope for this project remains. Comparing the marginal cost (the change in total cost) and the marginal benefit (the change in total benefit) relating to each plan determines the answer. The guideline is well known to you from previous discussions: Increase an activity, project, or output as long as the marginal benefit (column 5) exceeds the marginal cost (column 3).

cost-benefit analysis
The formal comparison of marginal costs and marginal benefits of a government project to decide whether it is worth doing and to what extent resources should be devoted to it.

TABLE 5.2

Cost-Benefit Analysis for a National Highway Construction Project (in Billions)

(1) Plan	(2) Total Cost of Project	(3) Marginal Cost	(4) Total Benefit	(5) Marginal Benefit	(6) Net Benefit (4) − (2)
No new construction	$ 0		$ 0		$ 0
A: Widen existing highways	4	$ 4	5	$ 5	1
B: New 2-lane highways	10	6	13	8	3
C: New 4-lane highways	**18**	8	**23**	10	**5**
D: New 6-lane highways	28	10	26	3	−2

Stop the activity at, or as close as possible to, the point at which the marginal benefit equals the marginal cost. Do not undertake a project for which marginal cost exceeds marginal benefit.

In this case plan C (building new four-lane highways) is the best plan. Plans A and B are too modest; the marginal benefits exceed the marginal costs. Plan D's marginal cost ($10 billion) exceeds the marginal benefit ($3 billion) and therefore cannot be justified; it overallocates resources to the project. Plan C is closest to the theoretical optimum because its marginal benefit ($10 billion) still exceeds marginal cost ($8 billion) but approaches the MB = MC (or MC = MB) ideal.

This marginal-cost–marginal-benefit rule tells government which plan provides the maximum excess of total benefits over total costs or, in other words, the plan that provides society with the maximum net benefit. You can confirm directly in column 6 that the maximum net benefit ($5 billion) is associated with plan C.

Question:
Do you think it is generally easier to measure the costs of public goods or their benefits? Explain your reasoning.

Externalities

In addition to providing public goods, governments also can improve the allocation of resources in the economy by correcting for market failures caused by externalities. An *externality* occurs when some of the costs or the benefits of a good or service are passed onto or "spill over" to someone other than the immediate buyer or seller. Such spillovers are called externalities because they are benefits or costs that accrue to some third party that is external to the market transaction.

Negative Externalities

negative externalities
Spillover production or consumption costs imposed on third parties without compensation to them.

Production or consumption costs inflicted on a third party without compensation are called **negative externalities** or *spillover costs*. Environmental pollution is an example. When a chemical manufacturer or a meatpacking plant dumps its wastes into a lake or river, water users such as swimmers, fishers, and boaters suffer negative externalities. When a petroleum refinery pollutes the air with smoke or a paper mill creates obnoxious odors, the community experiences negative externalities for which it is not compensated.

FIGURE 5.1

Negative externalities and positive externalities. (a) With negative externalities borne by society, the producers' supply curve S is to the right of (below) the total-cost supply curve S_t. Consequently, the equilibrium output Q_e is greater than the optimal output Q_o. (b) When positive externalities accrue to society, the market demand curve D is to the left of (below) the total-benefit demand curve D_t. As a result, the equilibrium output Q_e is less than the optimal output Q_o.

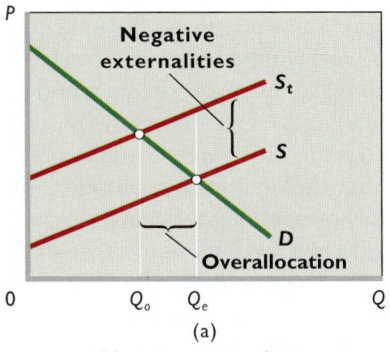

(a)

Negative externalities

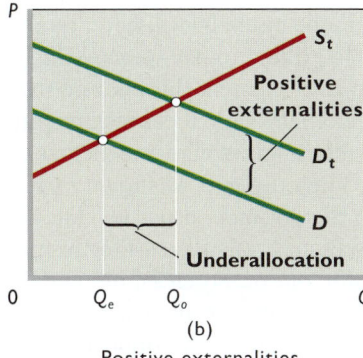

(b)

Positive externalities

Figure 5.1a illustrates how negative externalities affect the allocation of resources. When producers shift some of their costs onto the community as spillover costs, producers' marginal costs are lower than they would be if they had to pay for these costs. So their supply curves do not include or "capture" all the costs legitimately associated with the production of their goods. A supply curve such as S in Figure 5.1a therefore understates the total cost of production for a polluting firm. Its supply curve lies to the right of (or below) the full-cost supply curve S_t, which would include the negative externality. Through polluting and thus transferring cost to society, the firm enjoys lower production costs and has the supply curve S.

> **INTERACTIVE GRAPHS**
>
> **G 5.1**
>
> Externalities

The resource allocation outcome is shown in Figure 5.1a, where equilibrium output Q_e is larger than the optimal output Q_o. This is a market failure because resources are *overallocated* to the production of this commodity; too many units of it are produced. In fact, there is a net loss to society for every unit from Q_o to Q_e because, for those units, the supply curve that accounts for all costs, S_t, lies above the demand curve. Therefore, marginal cost (MC) exceeds marginal benefit (MB) for those units. The resources that went into producing those units should have been used elsewhere in the economy to produce other things.

Positive Externalities

Sometimes spillovers appear as external benefits. The production or consumption of certain goods and services may confer spillover or external benefits on third parties or on the community at large without compensating payment. Immunization against measles and polio results in direct benefits to the immediate consumer of those vaccines. But it also results in widespread substantial positive externalities to the entire community.

Education is another example of **positive externalities.** Education benefits individual consumers: Better-educated people generally achieve higher incomes than less-well-educated people. But education also benefits society through a more versatile and more productive labor force, on the one hand, and smaller outlays for crime prevention, law enforcement, and welfare programs, on the other.

positive externalities
Spillover production or consumption benefits conferred on third parties without compensation from them.

Figure 5.1b shows the impact of positive externalities on resource allocation. When positive externalities occur, the market demand curve D lies to the left of (or below) the full-benefits demand curve, D_t. That is, D does not include the positive externalities of the product, whereas D_t does. Consider inoculations against a communicable disease. When John gets vaccinated against a disease, this is a benefit not only to himself (because he can no longer contract the disease) but also to everyone else around him (because they know that in the future he will never be able to infect them). These other people would presumably be willing to pay some positive amount of money for the benefit they receive when John is vaccinated. But because there is no way to make them pay, the market demand curve reflects only the direct, private benefits to John. It does not reflect the positive externalities—the spillover benefits—to those around John, which are included in D_t.

The outcome, as shown in Figure 5.1b, is that the equilibrium output Q_e is less than the optimal output Q_o. The market fails to produce enough vaccinations, and resources are *underallocated* to this product. The underproduction implies that society is missing out on potential net benefits. For every unit from Q_e to Q_o, the demand curve that accounts for all benefits, D_t, lies above the supply curve that accounts for all costs—including the opportunity cost of producing other items with the resources that would be needed to produce these units. Therefore, MB exceeds MC for each of these units and society should redeploy some of its resources away from the production of other things in order to produce these units that generate net benefits.

Economists have explored several approaches to the problems of negative and positive externalities. Sometimes private parties work out their own solutions to externality problems; other times government intervention is warranted.

> **ORIGIN OF THE IDEA**
>
> **O 5.1**
> Externalities

© Paul Taylor/Photolibrary

© Charles Smith/Corbis

Photo Op Positive and Negative Consumption Externalities

Homeowners create positive externalities when they put up nice holiday lighting displays. Not only does the homeowner benefit from consuming the sight, but so do people who pass by the house. In contrast, when people consume roads (drive) during rush hour, it creates a negative externality. This takes the form of traffic congestion, imposing time and fuel costs on other drivers.

Beekeepers and the Coase Theorem

Illustrating the Idea

Economist Ronald Coase received the Nobel Prize for his so-called **Coase theorem,** which pointed out that under the right conditions, private individuals could often negotiate their own mutually agreeable solutions to externality problems through *private bargaining* without the need for government interventions like pollution taxes.

Coase theorem
The idea that externality problems can be resolved through private negotiations by the affected parties when property rights are clearly established.

This is a very important insight because it means that we shouldn't automatically call for government intervention every time we see a potential externality problem. Consider the positive externalities that bees provide by pollinating farmers' crops. Should we assume that beekeeping will be underprovided unless the government intervenes with, for instance, subsidies to encourage more hives and hence more pollination?

As it turns out, no. Research has shown that farmers and beekeepers long ago used private bargaining to develop customs and payment systems that avoid free riding by farmers and encourage beekeepers to keep the optimal number of hives. Free riding is avoided by the custom that all farmers in an area simultaneously hire beekeepers to provide bees to pollinate their crops. And farmers always pay the beekeepers for their pollination services because if they didn't, then no beekeeper would ever work with them in the future—a situation that would lead to massively reduced crop yields due to a lack of pollination.

ORIGIN OF THE IDEA

O 5.2
Coase theorem

The "Fable of the Bees" is a good reminder that it is a fallacy to assume that the government must always get involved to remedy externalities. In many cases, the private sector can solve both positive and negative externality problems on its own.

Question:
Suppose that in a town a large number of home gardeners need pollination services for their fruit and vegetable crops, but none can individually afford to pay a professional beekeeper. How might that affect the contracting of beekeepers? Would it suggest a possible role for government?

Government Intervention

Government intervention may be called upon to achieve economic efficiency when externalities affect large numbers of people or when community interests are at stake. Government can use direct controls and taxes to counter negative externalities (spillover costs); it may provide subsidies or public goods to deal with positive externalities (spillover benefits).

Direct Controls   The direct way to reduce negative externalities from a certain activity is to pass legislation limiting that activity. Such direct controls force the offending firms to incur the actual costs of the offending activity. To date, this approach has dominated public policy in the United States. Clean-air legislation has created uniform emission standards—limits on allowable pollution—and has forced factories and businesses to install "maximum achievable control technology" to reduce emissions

FIGURE 5.2

Correcting for negative externalities. (a) Negative externalities (spillover costs) result in an overallocation of resources. (b) Government can correct this overallocation in two ways: (1) using direct controls, which would shift the supply curve from S to S_t and reduce output from Q_e to Q_o, or (2) imposing a specific tax T, which would also shift the supply curve from S to S_t, eliminating the overallocation of resources.

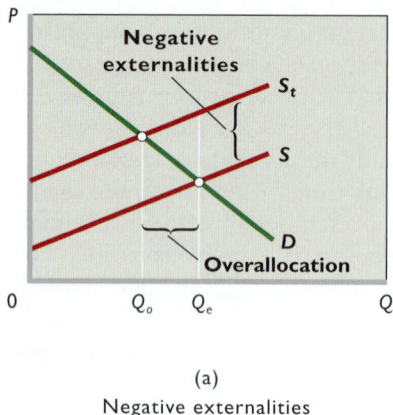

(a)

Negative externalities

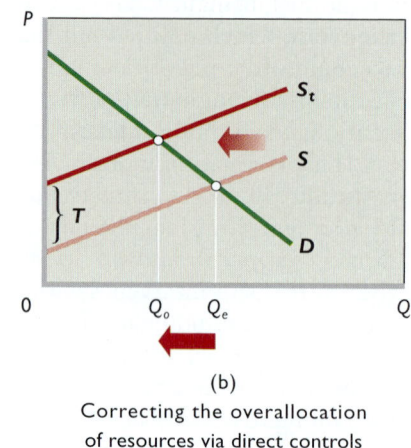

(b)

Correcting the overallocation
of resources via direct controls
or via a tax

of toxic chemicals. It has also mandated reductions in (1) tailpipe emissions from automobiles, (2) use of chlorofluorocarbons (CFCs) that deplete the ozone layer, and (3) emissions of sulfur dioxide by coal-burning utilities to prevent the acid-rain destruction of lakes and forests. Also, clean-water legislation has limited the amounts of heavy metals and detergents that firms can discharge into rivers and bays. Toxic-waste laws dictate special procedures and dump sites for disposing of contaminated soil and solvents. Violating these laws means fines and, in some cases, imprisonment.

Direct controls raise the marginal cost of production because the firms must operate and maintain pollution-control equipment. The supply curve S in Figure 5.2b, which does not reflect the negative externalities, shifts leftward (upward) to the full-cost supply curve, S_t. Product price increases, equilibrium output falls from Q_e to Q_o, and the initial overallocation of resources shown in Figure 5.2a is corrected.

Specific Taxes   A second policy approach to negative externalities is for government to levy taxes or charges specifically on the related good. For example, the government has placed a manufacturing excise tax on CFCs, which deplete the stratospheric ozone layer protecting the earth from excessive solar ultraviolet radiation. Facing such an excise tax, manufacturers must decide whether to pay the tax or expend additional funds to purchase or develop substitute products. In either case, the tax raises the marginal cost of producing CFCs, shifting the private supply curve for this product leftward (or upward).

In Figure 5.2b, a tax equal to T per unit increases the firm's marginal cost, shifting the supply curve from S to S_t. The equilibrium price rises, and the equilibrium output declines from Q_e to the economically efficient level Q_o. The tax thus eliminates the initial overallocation of resources associated with the negative externality.

Subsidies and Government Provision   What policies might be useful in dealing with *positive* externalities? Where positive externalities are large and diffuse, as in our earlier example of inoculations, government has three options for correcting the underallocation of resources:

- *Subsidies to buyers* Figure 5.3a again shows the supply-demand situation for positive externalities. Government could correct the underallocation of resources, for example, to inoculations, by subsidizing consumers of the product. It could give each new mother in the United States a discount coupon to be used to obtain a series of inoculations for her child. The coupon would reduce the "price" to the mother by, say, 50 percent. As shown in Figure 5.3b, this program would shift the demand curve for inoculations from too low D to the appropriate D_t. The number of inoculations would rise from Q_e to the economically optimal Q_o, eliminating the underallocation of resources shown in Figure 5.3a.

- *Subsidies to producers* A subsidy to producers is a tax in reverse. Taxes impose an extra cost on producers, while subsidies reduce producers' costs. As shown in Figure 5.3c, a subsidy of U per inoculation to physicians and medical clinics would reduce their marginal costs and shift their supply curve rightward from S_t to S_t'. The output of inoculations would increase from Q_e to the optimal level Q_o, correcting the underallocation of resources shown in Figure 5.3a.

- *Government provision* Finally, where positive externalities are extremely large, the government may decide to provide the product for free or for a minimal charge. Government provides many goods that could be produced and delivered in such a way that exclusion would be possible. Such goods, called **quasi-public goods,** include education, streets and highways, police and fire protection, libraries and museums, preventive medicine, and sewage disposal. They could all be priced and provided by private firms through the market system because the free-rider problem would be minimal. But, because spillover benefits extend well beyond the individual buyer, the market system may underproduce them. Therefore, government often provides quasi-public goods.

quasi-public goods
Goods for which exclusion could occur but which government provides because of perceived widespread and diffuse benefits.

FIGURE 5.3

Correcting for positive externalities. (a) Positive externalities (spillover benefits) result in an underallocation of resources. (b) Government can correct this underallocation through a subsidy to consumers, which shifts market demand from D to D_t and increases output from Q_e to Q_o. (c) Alternatively, government can eliminate the underallocation by giving producers a subsidy of U, which shifts their supply curve from S_t to S_t', increasing output from Q_e to Q_o.

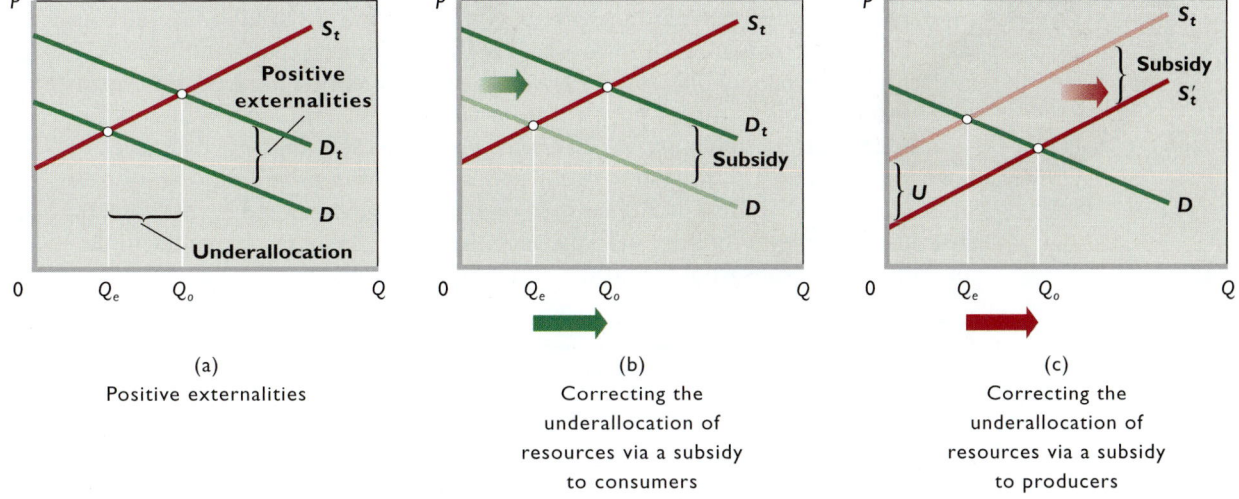

Lojack: A Case of Positive Externalities

Economists Ayres and Levitt point out that some forms of private crime prevention simply redistribute crime rather than reduce it. For example, car alarm systems that have red blinking warning lights may simply divert professional auto thieves to vehicles that do not have such lights and alarms. The owner of a car with such an alarm system benefits through reduced likelihood of theft but imposes a cost on other car owners who do not have such alarms. Their cars are more likely to be targeted for theft by thieves because other cars have visible security systems.

In contrast, some private crime prevention measures actually reduce crime, rather than simply redistribute it. One such measure is installation of a Lojack (or some similar) car retrieval system. Lojack is a tiny radio transmitter that is hidden in one of many possible places within the car. When an owner reports a stolen car, the police can remotely activate the transmitter. Police then can determine the car's precise location and track its subsequent movements.

The owner of the car benefits because the 95 percent retrieval rate on cars with the Lojack system is higher than the 60 percent retrieval rate for cars without the system. But, according to a study by Ayres and Levitt, the benefit to the car owner is only 10 percent of the total benefit. Ninety percent of the total benefit is external; it is a spillover benefit to other car owners in the community.

There are two sources of this positive externality. First, the presence of the Lojack device sometimes enables police to intercept the car while the thief is still driving it. For example, in California the arrest rate for cars with Lojack was three times greater than that for cars without it. The arrest puts the car thief out of commission for a time and thus reduces subsequent car thefts in the community. Second, and far more important, the device enables police to trace cars to "chop shops," where crooks disassemble cars for resale of the parts. When police raid the chop shop, they put the entire theft ring out of business. In Los Angeles alone, Lojack has eliminated 45 chop shops in just a few years. The purging of the chop shop and theft ring reduces auto theft in the community. So auto owners who do not have Lojack devices in their cars benefit from car owners who do. Ayres and Levitt estimate the *marginal social benefit* of Lojack—the marginal benefit to the Lojack car owner *plus* the spillover benefit to other car owners—is 15 times greater than the marginal cost of the device.

We saw in Figure 5.3a that the existence of positive externalities causes an insufficient quantity of a product and thus an underallocation of scarce resources to its production. The two general ways to correct the outcome are to subsidize the consumer, as shown in Figure 5.3b, or to subsidize the producer, as shown in Figure 5.3c. Currently, there is only one form of government intervention in place: state-mandated insurance discounts for people who install auto retrieval systems such as Lojack. In effect, those discounts on insurance premiums subsidize the consumer by lowering the "price" of the system to consumers. The lower price raises the number of systems installed. But, on the basis of their research, Ayres and Levitt contend that the current levels of insurance discounts are far too small to correct the underallocation that results from the positive externalities created by Lojack.

Question:
Other than mandating lower insurance premiums for Lojack users, what might government do to increase the use of Lojack devices in automobiles?

Source: Based on Ian Ayres and Steven D. Levitt, "Measuring Positive Externalities from Unobservable Victim Precaution: An Empirical Analysis of Lojack," *Quarterly Journal of Economics*, February 1998, pp. 43–77. The authors point out that Lojack did not fund their work nor do they have any financial stake in Lojack.

Reducing Greenhouse Gases

Climate change, to the extent it is caused by human-generated greenhouse gases, is a negative externality problem. Suggested policies to reduce carbon emissions, a major greenhouse gas, include carbon taxes and a cap-and-trade program.

A tax imposed on each ton of carbon emitted would increase the marginal cost of production to all firms that release carbon into the air through their production processes. Because of the added marginal cost, the supply curves within affected markets would shift to the left (as illustrated by the move from S to S_t in Figure 5.1). The reduced market supply would increase equilibrium price and reduce equilibrium quantity. With the lower output, carbon emissions in these industries would fall.

A carbon tax would require minimum government interference in the economy once the tax was in place. The federal government could direct the revenues from the tax to research on cleaner production technologies or simply use the new revenues to reduce other taxes. But there would be no free lunch here: According to a 2007 study, a proposed $15 tax per ton of carbon dioxide emitted would add an estimated 14 cents to a gallon of gasoline, 1.63 cents to a kilowatt hour of electricity, $28.50 to a ton of coal, and $6.48 to a barrel of crude oil.

An alternative approach is a cap-and-trade program, which creates a market for the right to discharge a particular pollutant into the air or water. These rights, allocated in the form of a fixed quantity of pollution permits, can be bought or sold in a permit market. Each permit specifies the amount of the pollutant that can be emitted. The decision to buy or sell permits depends on how costly it is for a company to reduce its pollution relative to the market price of the permits. Permit buyers, for example, are those whose costs to reduce emissions exceed the costs of the permits that allow them to pollute.

As it currently does with sulfur dioxide emissions, the federal government could place a cap or lid on total carbon emissions and then either hand out emission rights or auction them off. In ways previously discussed, the cap-and-trade program would reduce society's overall cost of lowering carbon emissions. In that regard, it would be more efficient than direct controls requiring each producer of greenhouse gas to reduce emissions by a fixed percentage amount. Existing cap-and-trade programs—including current European markets for carbon certificates—prove that this program can work. But such programs require considerable government oversight and enforcement of the rules.

Question:
Why would rising prices of emission rights increase the incentive for firms to use cleaner production methods?

Table 5.3 lists several methods for correcting externalities, including those we have discussed thus far.

Society's Optimal Amount of Externality Reduction

Negative externalities such as pollution reduce the utility of those affected. These spillovers are not economic goods but economic "bads." If something is bad, shouldn't society eliminate it? Why should society allow firms or municipalities to discharge *any* impure waste into public waterways or to emit *any* pollution into the air?

TABLE 5.3

**Methods for Dealing
with Externalities**

Problem	Resource Allocation Outcome	Ways to Correct
Negative externalities (spillover costs)	Overproduction of output and therefore overallocation of resources	1. Private bargaining 2. Liability rules and lawsuits 3. Tax on producers 4. Direct controls 5. Market for externality rights
Positive externalities (spillover benefits)	Underproduction of output and therefore underallocation of resources	1. Private bargaining 2. Subsidy to consumers 3. Subsidy to producers 4. Government provision

Economists answer these questions by pointing out that reducing pollution and negative externalities is not free. There are costs as well as benefits to reducing pollution. As a result, the correct question to ask when it comes to cleaning up negative externalities is not, "Do we pollute a lot or pollute zero?" That is an all-or-nothing question that ignores marginal costs and marginal benefits. Instead, the correct question is, "What is the optimal amount to clean up—the amount that equalizes the marginal cost of cleaning up with the marginal benefit of a cleaner environment?"

Reducing a negative externality has a "price." Society must decide how much of a reduction it wants to "buy." High costs may mean that totally eliminating pollution might not be desirable, even if it is technologically feasible. Because of the law of diminishing returns, cleaning up the second 10 percent of pollutants from an industrial smokestack normally is more costly than cleaning up the first 10 percent. Eliminating the third 10 percent is more costly than cleaning up the second 10 percent, and so on. Therefore, cleaning up the last 10 percent of pollutants is the most costly reduction of all.

The marginal cost to the firm and hence to society—the opportunity cost of the extra resources used—rises as pollution is reduced more and more. At some point MC may rise so high that it exceeds society's marginal benefit of further pollution abatement (reduction). Additional actions to reduce pollution will therefore lower society's well-being; total cost will rise more than total benefit.

MC, MB, and Equilibrium Quantity   Figure 5.4 shows both the rising marginal-cost curve, MC, for pollution reduction and the downsloping marginal-benefit curve, MB, for pollution reduction. MB slopes downward because of the law of diminishing marginal utility: The more pollution reduction society accomplishes, the lower the utility (and benefit) of the next unit of pollution reduction.

**optimal reduction
of an externality**
The reduction of a
negative externality to the
level at which the marginal
benefit and marginal cost
of reduction are equal.

The **optimal reduction of an externality** occurs when society's marginal cost and marginal benefit of reducing that externality are equal (MC = MB). In Figure 5.4 this optimal amount of pollution abatement is Q_1 units. When MB exceeds MC, additional abatement moves society toward economic efficiency; the added benefit of cleaner air or water exceeds the benefit of any alternative use of the required resources. When MC exceeds MB, additional abatement reduces economic efficiency; there would be greater benefits from using resources in some other way than to further reduce pollution.

In reality, it is difficult to measure the marginal costs and benefits of pollution control. Figure 5.4 demonstrates that some pollution may be economically efficient.

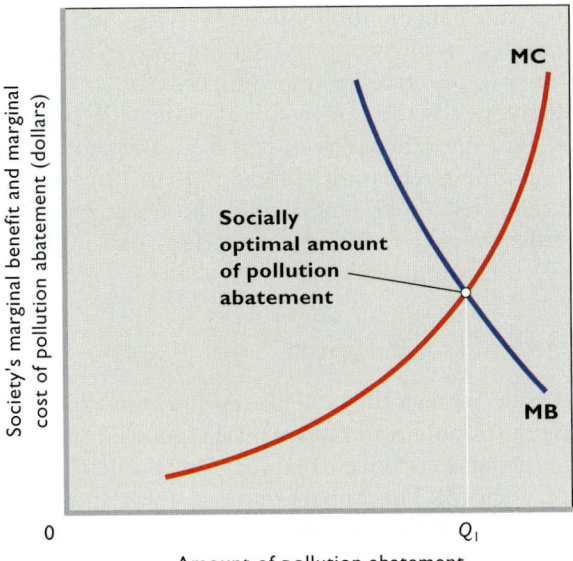

FIGURE 5.4
Society's optimal amount of pollution abatement. The optimal amount of externality reduction—in this case, pollution abatement—occurs at Q_1, where society's marginal cost MC and marginal benefit MB of reducing the spillover are equal.

This is so not because pollution is desirable but because beyond some level of control, further abatement may reduce society's net well-being. As an example, it would cost the government billions of dollars to clean up every last piece of litter in America. Thus, it would be better to tolerate some trash blowing around if the money saved by picking up less trash would yield larger net benefits when spent on other things.

Shifts in Locations of the Curves   The locations of the marginal-cost and marginal-benefit curves in Figure 5.4 are not forever fixed. They can, and probably do, shift over time. For example, suppose that the technology of pollution-control equipment improved noticeably. We would expect the cost of pollution abatement to fall, society's MC curve to shift rightward, and the optimal level of abatement to rise. Or suppose that society were to decide that it wanted cleaner air and water because of new information about the adverse health effects of pollution. The MB curve in Figure 5.4 would shift rightward and the optimal level of pollution control would increase beyond Q_1. Test your understanding of these statements by drawing the new MC and MB curves in Figure 5.4.

Financing the Public Sector: Taxation

How are resources reallocated from the production of private goods to the production of public goods (and quasi-public goods)? How are government programs to deal with externalities funded? If the resources of the economy are fully employed, government must free up resources from the production of private goods and make them available for producing public and quasi-public goods. It does so by reducing the demand for private goods. And it does that by levying taxes on households and businesses, taking some of their income out of the circular flow. With lower incomes and therefore reduced purchasing power, households and businesses must curtail their spending.

As a result, the private demand for goods and services declines, as does the private demand for resources. So by diverting purchasing power from private spenders to government, taxes remove resources from private use.

Government then spends the tax proceeds to provide public and quasi-public goods and services. Taxation releases resources from the production of private consumer goods (food, clothing, television sets) and private investment goods (printing presses, boxcars, warehouses). Government shifts those resources to the production of public and quasi-public goods (post offices, submarines, parks), changing the composition of the economy's total output.

Apportioning the Tax Burden

Once government has decided on the total tax revenue it needs to finance its activities, including the provision of public and quasi-public goods, it must determine how to apportion the tax burden among the citizens. (By "tax burden" we mean the total cost of taxes imposed on society.) This apportionment question affects each of us. The overall level of taxes is important, but the average citizen is much more concerned with his or her share of taxes.

Benefits Received versus Ability to Pay

Two basic philosophies coexist on how the economy's tax burden should be assigned.

benefits-received principle
The idea that people who receive the benefits from government-provided goods and services should pay the taxes required to finance them.

Benefits-Received   The **benefits-received principle** of taxation states that households and businesses should purchase the goods and services of government in the same way they buy other commodities. Those who benefit most from government-supplied goods or services should pay the taxes necessary to finance them. A few public goods are now financed on this basis. For example, money collected as gasoline taxes is typically used to finance highway construction and repairs. Thus people who benefit from good roads pay the cost of those roads. Difficulties immediately arise, however, when we consider widespread application of the benefits-received principle:

- How will the government determine the benefits that individual households and businesses receive from national defense, education, the court system, and police and fire protection? Recall that public goods are characterized by nonrivalry and nonexcludability. So benefits from public goods are especially widespread and diffuse. Even in the seemingly straightforward case of highway financing it is difficult to measure benefits. Good roads benefit the owners of cars in different degrees. But others also benefit. For example, businesses benefit because good roads bring them workers and customers.
- Government cannot logically apply the benefits-received principle to some government programs such as "safety net" programs. It would be absurd to ask poor families to pay the taxes needed to finance their welfare payments. It would be ridiculous to think of taxing only unemployed workers to finance the unemployment compensation payments they receive.

ability-to-pay principle
The idea that people who have greater income should pay a greater proportion of it as taxes than those who have less income.

Ability to Pay   The **ability-to-pay principle** of taxation states that government should apportion the tax burden according to taxpayers' income. In the United States this means that individuals and businesses with larger incomes should pay more taxes in both absolute and relative terms than those with smaller incomes.

The rationale of ability-to-pay taxation is the proposition that each additional dollar of income received by a household yields a smaller amount of satisfaction or marginal utility when it is spent. Because consumers act rationally, the first dollars of income received in any time period will be spent on high-urgency goods that yield the greatest marginal utility. Successive dollars of income will go for less urgently needed goods and finally for trivial goods and services. This means that a dollar taken through taxes from a poor person who has few dollars represents a greater utility sacrifice than a dollar taken through taxes from a rich person who has many dollars. To balance the sacrifices that taxes impose on income receivers, taxes should be apportioned according to the amount of income a taxpayer receives.

This argument is appealing, but application problems arise here too. Although we might agree that the household earning $100,000 per year has a greater ability to pay taxes than a household receiving $10,000, we don't know exactly how much more ability to pay the first family has. Should the wealthier family pay the same percentage of its larger income, and hence a larger absolute amount, as taxes? Or should it be made to pay a larger fraction of its income as taxes? And how much larger should that fraction be? Who is to decide?

There is no scientific way of making utility comparisons among individuals and thus of measuring someone's relative ability to pay taxes. That is the main problem. In practice, the solution hinges on guesswork, expediency, the tax views of the political party in power, and how urgently the government needs revenue.

Progressive, Proportional, and Regressive Taxes

Any discussion of taxation leads ultimately to the question of tax rates. The **marginal tax rate** is the rate paid on each additional dollar of income (or purchases). The **average tax rate** is the total tax paid as a percentage of income.

Taxes are classified as progressive, regressive, or proportional taxes, depending on the relationship between average tax rates and taxpayer incomes. We focus on incomes because all taxes, whether on income or on a product or a building or a parcel of land, are ultimately paid out of someone's income.

- A tax is **progressive** if its average rate increases as income increases. Such a tax claims not only a larger absolute (dollar) amount but also a larger percentage of income as income increases.
- A tax is **regressive** if its average rate declines as income increases. Such a tax takes a smaller proportion of income as income increases. A regressive tax may or may not take a larger absolute amount of income as income increases. (You may want to derive an example to substantiate this conclusion.)
- A tax is **proportional** if its average rate remains the same regardless of the size of income.

We can illustrate these ideas with the personal income tax. Suppose tax rates are such that a household pays 10 percent of its income in taxes regardless of the size of its income. This is a proportional income tax. Now suppose the rate structure is such that a household with an annual taxable income of less than $10,000 pays 5 percent in income taxes; a household with an income of $10,000 to $19,999 pays 10 percent; one with a $20,000 to $29,999 income pays 15 percent; and so forth. This is a progressive income tax. Finally, suppose the rate declines as taxable income rises: You pay 15 percent if you earn less than $10,000; 10 percent if you earn $10,000 to $19,999; 5 percent if you earn $20,000 to $29,999; and so forth. This is a regressive income tax.

marginal tax rate
The tax rate paid on each additional dollar of income.

average tax rate
The total tax paid divided by total taxable income, as a percentage.

progressive tax
A tax whose average tax rate increases as the taxpayer's income increases.

regressive tax
A tax whose average tax rate decreases as the taxpayer's income increases.

proportional tax
A tax whose average tax rate remains constant as the taxpayer's income increases.

TABLE 5.4

Federal Personal Income Tax Rates, 2012*

(1) Total Taxable Income	(2) Marginal Tax Rate, %	(3) Total Tax on Highest Income in Bracket	(4) Average Tax Rate on Highest Income in Bracket, % (3) ÷ (1)
$1–$17,400	10.0	$ 1740	10.0
$17,401–$70,700	15.0	9735	13.8
$70,701–$142,700	25.0	27,735	19.4
$142,701–$217,450	28.0	48,665	22.4
$217,451–$388,350	33.0	105,062	27.1
Over $388,350	35.0		

* For a married couple filing a joint return.

In general, progressive taxes are those that fall relatively more heavily on people with high incomes; regressive taxes are those that fall relatively more heavily on the poor.

Tax Progressivity in the United States

The progressivity or regressivity of taxes varies by type of tax in the United States. As shown in Table 5.4, the federal *personal income tax* is progressive. Marginal tax rates (column 2)—those assessed on additional income—ranged from 10 to 35 percent in 2012. Rules that allow individuals to deduct from income interest on home mortgages and property taxes and that exempt interest on state and local bonds from taxation tend to make the tax less progressive than these marginal rates suggest. Nevertheless, average tax rates (column 4) rise with income.

At first thought, a *general sales tax* with, for example, a 5 percent rate would seem to be proportional. But in fact it is regressive with respect to income (rather than purchases). A larger portion of a low-income person's income is exposed to the tax than is the case for a high-income person; the rich pay no tax on the part of income that is saved, whereas the poor are unable to save. Example: "Low-income" Smith has an income of $15,000 and spends it all. "High-income" Jones has an income of $300,000 but spends only $200,000 and saves the rest. Assuming a 5 percent sales tax applies to all expenditures of each individual, we find that Smith pays $750 (= 5 percent of $15,000) in sales taxes and Jones pays $10,000 (= 5 percent of $200,000). But Smith pays $750/$15,000, or 5 percent of income, as sales taxes, while Jones pays $10,000/$300,000, or 3.3 percent of income. The general sales tax therefore is regressive.

Federal *corporate income tax* rates vary from 15 to 39 percent, depending on the level of income and type of corporation. This makes them progressive for some corporations and proportional for others, but how this affects the general population is more complex. In the short run, the corporate owners (shareholders) bear the tax through lower dividends and share values, making it generally progressive. However if the tax burden is passed on to consumers through higher prices, the tax may be regressive, just like a sales tax. In the long run, workers may bear some of the tax since it reduces the return on investment and therefore slows capital accumulation. It also causes corporations to relocate to other countries that have lower tax rates. With less capital per worker, U.S. labor productivity may decline and wages may fall. This would also make the corporate income tax somewhat regressive.

Payroll taxes (Social Security and Medicare) are regressive because the Social Security tax applies to only a fixed amount of income. For example, in 2012 the Social Security tax rate on employees was 4.2 percent, but only of the first $110,100 of a person's wage income. The Medicare tax was 1.45 percent of all wage income. Someone earning exactly $110,100 would pay $6221, or 5.65 percent (4.2 percent + 1.45 percent) of his or her income. Someone with twice that wage income, or $220,200, would pay $7817 (= $6221 on the first $110,100 + $1596 on the second $110,100), which is less than 4 percent of his or her wage income. So the average payroll tax falls as income rises, confirming that the payroll tax is regressive.

Most economists conclude that *property taxes* on buildings are regressive for the same reasons as are sales taxes. First, property owners add the tax to the rents they charge tenants. Second, property taxes, as a percentage of income, are higher for low-income families than for high-income families because the poor must spend a larger proportion of their incomes for housing. This alleged regressivity of property taxes may be increased by differences in property-tax rates from locality to locality. In general, property-tax rates are higher in poorer areas, to make up for lower property values.

Is the overall U.S. tax structure—federal, state, and local taxes combined—progressive, proportional, or regressive? This question is difficult to answer. Estimates of the distribution of the total tax burden depend on the extent to which the various taxes are shifted to others, and who bears the ultimate burden is subject to dispute. But the majority view of economists is as follows:

- The federal tax system is progressive. In 2007 (the latest year for which data have been compiled), the 20 percent of households with the lowest income paid an average federal tax rate (on federal income, payroll, and excise taxes) of 4.0 percent. The 20 percent with the highest income paid a 25.1 percent average rate; the top 10 percent paid 27.9 percent; and the top 1 percent paid 29.5 percent.[2]
- The state and local tax structures are largely regressive. As a percentage of income, property taxes and sales taxes fall as income rises. Also, state income taxes are generally less progressive than the federal income tax.
- The overall U.S. tax system is slightly progressive. Higher-income people carry a slightly larger tax burden, as a percentage of their income, than do lower-income people.

Government's Role in the Economy

Along with providing public goods and correcting externalities, government's economic role includes setting the rules and regulations for the economy, redistributing income when desirable, and taking macroeconomic actions to stabilize the economy.

Market failures can be used to justify government interventions in the economy. The inability of private-sector firms to break even when attempting to provide public goods and the over- and underproduction problems caused by positive and negative externalities mean that government can have an important role to play if society's resources are to be efficiently allocated to the goods and services that people most highly desire.

Correcting for market failures is not, however, an easy task. To begin with, government officials must correctly identify the existence and the cause of any given market failure. That by itself may be difficult, time-consuming, and costly. But even if a market failure is correctly identified and diagnosed, government may still fail to take

[2]*Average Federal Tax Rates in 2007*, Congressional Budget Office, June 2010.

appropriate corrective action due to the fact that government undertakes its economic role in the context of politics.

To serve the public, politicians need to get elected. To stay elected, officials (presidents, senators, representatives, mayors, council members, school board members) need to satisfy their particular constituencies. At best, the political realities complicate government's role in the economy; at worst, they produce undesirable economic outcomes.

In the political context, overregulation can occur in some cases; underregulation, in others. Some public goods and quasi-public goods can be produced not because their benefits exceed their costs but because their benefits accrue to firms located in states served by powerful elected officials. Inefficiency can easily creep into government activities because of the lack of a profit incentive to hold down costs. Policies to correct negative externalities can be politically blocked by the very parties that are producing the spillovers. Income can be redistributed to such an extent that incentives to work, save, and invest suffer. In short, the economic role of government, although critical to a well-functioning economy, is not always perfectly carried out.

Economists use the term "government failure" to describe economically inefficient outcomes caused by shortcomings in the public sector.

Summary

1. A market failure happens in a particular market when the market produces an equilibrium level of output that either overallocates or underallocates resources to the product being traded in the market. In competitive markets that feature many buyers and many sellers, market failures can be divided into two types: Demand-side market failures occur when demand curves do not reflect consumers' full willingness to pay; supply-side market failures occur when supply curves do not reflect all production costs, including those that may be borne by third parties.

2. Properly functioning competitive markets ensure that private goods are (a) available, (b) produced in the least costly way, and (c) produced and sold in the "right" amounts.

3. Public goods are distinguished from private goods. Private goods are characterized by rivalry (in consumption) and excludability. One person's purchase and consumption of a private good precludes others from also buying and consuming it. Producers can exclude nonpayers (free riders) from receiving the benefits. In contrast, public goods are characterized by nonrivalry (in consumption) and nonexcludability. Public goods are not profitable to private firms because nonpayers (free riders) can obtain and consume those goods without paying. Government can, however, provide desirable public goods, financing them through taxation.

4. The collective demand schedule for a particular public good is found by summing the prices that each individual is willing to pay for an additional unit. The optimal quantity of a public good occurs where the society's willingness to pay for the last unit—the marginal benefit of the good—equals the marginal cost of the good.

5. Externalities cause the output of certain goods to vary from society's optimal output. Negative externalities (spillover costs) result in an overallocation of resources to a particular product. Positive externalities (spillover benefits) are accompanied by an underallocation of resources to a particular product.

6. Direct controls and specific taxes can improve resource allocation in situations where negative externalities affect many people and community resources. Both direct controls (for example, smokestack emission standards) and specific taxes (for example, taxes on firms producing toxic chemicals) increase production costs and hence product price. As product price rises, the externality and overallocation of resources are reduced since less of the output is produced.

7. Government can correct the underallocation of resources in a particular market either by subsidizing consumers (which increases market demand) or by subsidizing producers (which increases market supply). Such subsidies increase the equilibrium output, reducing or eliminating the positive externality and consequent underallocation of resources.

8. The Coase theorem suggests that under the right circumstances private bargaining can solve externality problems. Thus, government intervention is not always needed to deal with externality problems.

9. The socially optimal amount of externality abatement occurs where society's marginal cost and marginal benefit of reducing the externality are equal. With pollution, for example, this optimal amount of pollution abatement is likely to be less than a 100 percent reduction. Changes in technology or changes in society's attitudes toward pollution can affect the optimal amount of pollution abatement.

10. Government reallocates resources from the private sector to the public sector through taxation, which decreases after-tax income and therefore reduces the demand for private goods. Government then uses the tax revenues to finance the provision of public goods and quasi-public goods.

11. The benefits-received principle of taxation states that those who receive the benefits of goods and services provided by government should pay the taxes required to finance them. The ability-to-pay principle states that those who have greater income should be taxed more, absolutely and relatively, than those who have less income.

12. The federal income tax is progressive (average tax rate rises as income rises). The corporate income tax is roughly proportional (average tax rate remains constant as income rises). General sales, excise, payroll, and property taxes are regressive (average tax rate falls as income rises). Overall, the U.S. tax system is slightly progressive.

13. Market failures present government with opportunities to improve the allocation of society's resources and thereby enhance society's total well-being. But even when government correctly identifies the existence and cause of a market failure, political pressures may make it difficult or impossible for government officials to implement a proper solution.

Terms and Concepts

market failures	free-rider problem	benefits-received principle
demand-side market failures	cost-benefit analysis	ability-to-pay principle
supply-side market failures	negative externality	marginal tax rate
productive efficiency	positive externality	average tax rate
allocative efficiency	Coase theorem	progressive tax
private goods	quasi-public goods	regressive tax
public goods	optimal reduction of an externality	proportional tax

Questions

1. Explain the two causes of market failures. Given their definitions, could a market be affected by both types of market failures simultaneously? **LO1**

2. Contrast the characteristics of public goods with those of private goods. Why won't private firms produce public goods? **LO2**

3. Draw a production possibilities curve with public goods on the vertical axis and private goods on the horizontal axis. Assuming the economy is initially operating on the curve, indicate how the production of public goods might be increased. How might the output of public goods be increased if the economy is initially operating at a point inside the curve? **LO2**

4. Use the distinction between the characteristics of private and public goods to determine whether the following should be produced through the market system or provided by government: (a) French fries, (b) airport screening, (c) court systems, (d) mail delivery, and (e) medical care. State why you answered as you did in each case. **LO2**

5. What divergences arise between equilibrium output and efficient output when (a) negative externalities and (b) positive externalities are present? How might government correct these divergences? Cite an example (other than the text examples) of an external cost and an external benefit. **LO3**

6. Why are spillover costs and spillover benefits also called negative and positive externalities? Show graphically how a tax can correct for a negative externality and how a subsidy to producers can correct for a positive externality. How does a subsidy to consumers differ from a subsidy to producers in correcting for a positive externality? **LO3**

7. An apple grower's orchard provides nectar to a neighbor's bees, while the beekeeper's bees help the apple grower by pollinating his apple blossoms. Use Figure 5.1b to explain why this situation of dual positive externalities might lead to an underallocation of resources to both apple growing and beekeeping. How might this

underallocation get resolved via the means suggested by the Coase theorem? **LO3**

8. Explain the following statement, using the MB curve in Figure 5.4 to illustrate: "The optimal amount of pollution abatement for some substances, say, dirty water from storm drains, is very low; the optimal amount of abatement for other substances, say, cyanide poison, is close to 100 percent." **LO3**

9. Explain why zoning laws, which allow certain land uses only in specific locations, might be justified in dealing with a problem of negative externalities. Explain why in areas where buildings sit close together tax breaks to property owners for installing extra fire prevention equipment might be justified in view of positive externalities. Explain why excise taxes on beer might be justified in dealing with a problem of external costs. **LO3**

10. Distinguish between the benefits-received and the ability-to-pay principles of taxation. Which philosophy is more evident in our present tax structure? Justify your answer. To which principle of taxation do you subscribe? Why? **LO4**

11. What is meant by a progressive tax? A regressive tax? A proportional tax? Comment on the progressivity or regressivity of each of the following taxes, indicating in each case where you think the tax incidence lies: (a) the federal personal income tax, (b) a 4 percent state general sales tax, (c) a federal excise tax on automobile tires, (d) a municipal property tax on real estate, (e) the federal corporate income tax, (f) the portion of the payroll tax levied on employers. **LO5**

12. Is it possible for a country with a regressive tax system to have a tax-spending system that transfers resources from the rich to the poor? **LO5**

13. Does a progressive tax system by itself guarantee that resources will be redistributed from the rich to the poor? Explain. Is the tax system in the United States progressive, regressive, or proportional? **LO5**

Problems

1. The accompanying table relating to a public good provides information on the prices Young and Zorn are willing to pay for various quantities of that public good. These two people are the only members of society. Determine the price that society is willing to pay for the public good at each quantity of output. If the government's marginal cost of providing this public good is constant at $7, how many units of the public good should government provide? **LO2**

	Young		Zorn		Society	
P	**Q_d**	**P**	**Q_d**	**P**	**Q_d**
$8	0	$8	1	$_	1
7	0	7	2	_	2
6	0	6	3	_	3
5	1	5	4	_	4
4	2	4	5	_	5
3	3	3	6	_	6
2	4	2	7	_	7
1	5	1	8	_	8

2. The accompanying table shows the total costs and total benefits in billions for four different antipollution programs of increasing scope. Use cost-benefit analysis to determine which program should be undertaken. **LO2**

Program	Total Cost	Total Benefit
A	$3	$7
B	7	12
C	12	16
D	18	19

3. On the basis of the three individual demand schedules in the table below, and assuming these three people are the only ones in the society, determine (a) the market demand schedule on the assumption that the good is a private good and (b) the collective demand schedule on the assumption that the good is a public good. **LO2**

P	$Q_d(D_1)$	$Q_d(D_2)$	$Q_d(D_3)$
$8	0	1	0
7	0	2	0
6	0	3	1
5	1	4	2
4	2	5	3
3	3	6	4
2	4	7	5
1	5	8	6

4. Use your demand schedule for a public good, determined in problem 3, and the following supply schedule to ascertain the optimal quantity of this public good. **LO2**

P	Q_s
$19	10
16	8
13	6
10	4
7	2
4	1

5. Look at the following tables, which show, respectively, the willingness to pay and willingness to accept of buyers and sellers of bags of oranges. For the following questions, assume that the equilibrium price and quantity will depend on the indicated changes in supply and demand. Assume that the only market participants are those listed by name in the two tables. **LO3**

Person	Maximum Price Willing to Pay	Actual Price (Equilibrium Price)
Bob	$13	$8
Barb	12	8
Bill	11	8
Bart	10	8
Brent	9	8
Betty	8	8

Person	Minimum Acceptable Price	Actual Price (Equilibrium Price)
Carlos	$3	$8
Courtney	4	8
Chuck	5	8
Cindy	6	8
Craig	7	8
Chad	8	8

a. What are the equilibrium price and quantity for the data displayed in the two tables?

b. What if, instead of bags of oranges, the data in the two tables dealt with a public good like fireworks displays? If all the buyers free ride, what will be the quantity supplied by private sellers?

c. Assume that we are back to talking about bags of oranges (a private good), but that the government has decided that tossed orange peels impose a negative externality on the public that must be rectified by imposing a $2-per-bag tax on sellers. What are the new equilibrium price and quantity? If the new equilibrium quantity is the optimal quantity, by how many bags were oranges being overproduced before?

6. Suppose a tax is such that an individual with an income of $10,000 pays $2000 of tax, a person with an income of $20,000 pays $3000 of tax, a person with an income of $30,000 pays $4000 of tax, and so forth. What is each person's average tax rate? Is this tax regressive, proportional, or progressive? **LO5**

7. Suppose in Fiscalville there is no tax on the first $10,000 of income, but Fiscalville imposes a 20 percent tax on earnings between $10,000 and $20,000 and a 30 percent tax on income between $20,000 and $30,000. Any income above $30,000 is taxed at 40 percent. If your income is $50,000, how much will you pay in taxes? Determine your marginal and average tax rates. Is this a progressive tax? **LO5**

8. For tax purposes, "gross income" is all the money a person receives in a given year from any source. But income taxes are levied on "taxable income" rather than on gross income. The difference between the two is the result of many exemptions and deductions. To see how they work, suppose you made $50,000 last year in wages and $10,000 from investments, and you were given $5000 as a gift by your grandmother. Also assume that you are a single parent with one small child living with you. **LO5**

a. What is your gross income?

b. Gifts of up to $13,000 per year from any person are not counted as taxable income. Also, the "personal exemption" allows you to reduce your taxable income by $3700 for each member of your household. Given these exemptions, what is your taxable income?

c. Next, assume you paid $700 in interest on your student loans last year, put $2000 into a health savings account (HSA), and deposited $4000 into an individual retirement account (IRA). These expenditures are all tax exempt, meaning that any money spent on them reduces taxable income dollarfor-dollar. Knowing that fact, what is now your taxable income?

d. Next, you can either take the so-called standard deduction or apply for itemized deductions (which involve a lot of tedious paperwork). You opt for the standard deduction that allows you as head of your household to exempt another $8500 from your taxable income. Taking that into account, what is your taxable income?

e. Apply the tax rates shown in Table 5.4 to your taxable income. How much federal tax will you owe? What is the marginal tax rate that applies to your last dollar of taxable income?

f. As the parent of a dependent child, you qualify for the government's $1000-per-child "tax credit." Like all tax credits, this $1000 credit "pays" for $1000 of whatever amount of tax you owe. Given this credit, how much money will you actually have to pay in taxes? Using that actual amount, what is your average tax rate relative to your taxable income? What about your average tax rate relative to your gross income?

FURTHER TEST YOUR KNOWLEDGE AT
www.brue3e.com

At the text's Online Learning Center, **www.brue3e.com,** you will find one or more web-based questions that require information from the Internet to answer. We urge you to check them out, since they will familiarize you with websites that may be helpful in other courses and perhaps even in your career. The OLC also features multiple-choice quizzes that give instant feedback and provides other helpful ways to further test your knowledge of the chapter.

CHAPTER SIX

Businesses and Their Costs

After reading this chapter, you should be able to:

1. Identify features of the corporate form of business organization that have made it so dominant.
2. Explain why economic costs include both explicit (revealed and expressed) costs and implicit (present but not obvious) costs.
3. Relate the law of diminishing returns to a firm's short-run production costs.
4. Describe the distinctions between fixed and variable costs and among total, average, and marginal costs.
5. Use economies of scale to link a firm's size and its average costs in the long run.

In market economies, a wide variety of businesses produce an even greater variety of goods and services. Each of those businesses needs economic resources in order to produce its product. In obtaining and using resources, a business makes monetary payments to resource owners (for example, workers) and incurs opportunity costs when using resources that it already owns (for example, entrepreneurial talent). Those payments and opportunity costs constitute the firm's *costs of production.*

This chapter describes the U.S. business population and identifies the costs faced by firms in producing products. Then, in the next several chapters, we bring demand, product price, and revenue into the analysis and explain how businesses compare revenues and costs to decide how much to produce. Our ultimate purpose is to show how those comparisons relate to profits, losses, and allocative efficiency.

The Business Population

Like households, businesses are a major element in the circular flow diagram that we discussed in Chapter 2. In discussing businesses, it will be useful to distinguish among a plant, a firm, and an industry:

- A *plant* is an establishment—a factory, farm, mine, store, website, or warehouse—that performs one or more functions in fabricating and distributing goods and services.
- A *firm* is an organization that employs resources to produce goods and services for profit and operates one or more plants.
- An *industry* is a group of firms that produce the same, or similar, products.

The organizational structures of firms are often complex and varied. *Multi-plant firms* may be organized horizontally, with several plants performing much the same function. Examples are the multiple bottling plants of Coca-Cola and the many individual Walmart stores. Firms also may be *vertically integrated*, meaning they own plants that perform different functions in the various stages of the production process. For example, oil companies such as Shell own oil fields, refineries, and retail gasoline stations. Some firms are *conglomerates*, so named because they have plants that produce products in several separate industries. For example, Pfizer makes prescription medicines (Lipitor, Viagra) but also chewing gum (Trident, Dentyne), razors (Schick), cough drops (Halls), breath mints (Clorets, Certs), and antacids (Rolaids).

The business population ranges from giant corporations such as Walmart, Exxon, and IBM, with hundreds of thousands of employees and billions of dollars of annual sales, to neighborhood specialty shops with one or two employees and daily sales of only a few hundred dollars. As shown in Figure 2.3 (page 43), only 18 percent of U.S. firms are corporations, yet they account for 82 percent of all sales (output).

Advantages of Corporations

Certain advantages of the corporate form of business enterprise have catapulted it into a dominant sales and profit position in the United States. The corporation is by far the most effective form of business organization for raising money to finance the expansion of its facilities and capabilities. The corporation employs unique methods of finance—the selling of stocks and bonds—that enable it to pool the financial resources of large numbers of people.

A common **stock** represents a share in the ownership of a corporation. The purchaser of a stock certificate has the right to vote for corporate officers and to share in dividends. If you buy 1000 of the 100,000 shares issued by OutTell, Inc. (OT), then you own 1 percent of the company, are entitled to 1 percent of any dividends declared by the board of directors, and control 1 percent of the votes in the annual election of corporate officials.

In contrast, a corporate **bond** does not bestow any corporate ownership on the purchaser. A bond purchaser is simply lending money to a corporation. A bond is an IOU, in acknowledgment of a loan, whereby the corporation promises to pay the holder a fixed amount set forth on the bond at some specified future date and other fixed amounts (interest payments) every year up to the bond's maturity date. For example, you might purchase a 10-year OutTell bond with a face value of $1000 and a 5 percent rate of interest. This means that, in exchange for your $1000, OT promises

stocks
Ownership shares of a corporation.

bonds
Certificates indicating obligations to pay the principal and interest on loans at a specific time in the future.

you a $50 interest payment for each of the next 10 years and then repays your $1000 principal at the end of that period.

Financing through sales of stocks and bonds also provides other advantages to those who purchase these *corporate securities.* An individual investor can spread risks by buying the securities of several corporations. And it is usually easy for holders of corporate securities to sell their holdings. Organized stock exchanges and bond markets simplify the transfer of securities from sellers to buyers. This "ease of sale" increases the willingness of savers to make financial investments in corporate securities. Besides, corporations have easier access to bank credit than do other types of business organizations. Corporations are better risks and are more likely to become profitable clients of banks.

limited liability
Restriction of the maximum loss to a shareholder to the amount paid for the stock.

Corporations provide **limited liability** to owners (stockholders), who risk only what they paid for their stock. Their personal assets are not at stake if the corporation defaults on its debts. Creditors can sue the corporation as a legal entity but cannot sue the owners of the corporation as individuals.

Because of their ability to attract financial capital, successful corporations can easily expand the scope of their operations and realize the benefits of expansion. For example, they can take advantage of mass-production technologies and division of labor. A corporation can hire specialists in production, accounting, and marketing functions and thus improve efficiency.

As a legal entity, the corporation has a life independent of its owners and its officers. Legally, at least, corporations are immortal. The transfer of corporate ownership through inheritance or the sale of stock does not disrupt the continuity of the corporation. Corporations have permanence that lends itself to long-range planning and growth.

The Principal-Agent Problem

Many of the world's corporations are extremely large. In 2011, 484 of the world's corporations had annual sales of more than $20 billion, 165 firms had sales exceeding $50 billion, and 51 firms had sales greater than $100 billion. U.S.-based Walmart alone had sales of nearly $422 billion in 2011.

But large size creates a potential problem. In sole proprietorships and partnerships, the owners of the real and financial assets of the firm enjoy direct control of those assets. But ownership of large corporations is spread over tens or hundreds of thousands of stockholders. The owners of a corporation usually do not manage it—they hire others to do so.

ORIGIN OF THE IDEA

O 6.1
Principal-agent problem

principal-agent problem
A conflict of interest that occurs when agents (managers) pursue their own objectives to the detriment of the principals' (stockholders') goals.

That practice can create a **principal-agent problem.** The *principals* are the stockholders who own the corporation and who hire executives as their *agents* to run the business on their behalf. But the interests of these managers (the agents) and the wishes of the owners (the principals) do not always coincide. The owners typically want maximum company profit and stock price. However, the agents may want the power, prestige, and pay that often accompany control over a large enterprise, independent of its profitability and stock price.

So a conflict of interest may develop. For example, executives may build expensive office buildings, enjoy excessive perks such as corporate jets, and pay too much to acquire other corporations. Consequently, the firm's costs will be excessive, and the firm will fail to maximize profits and stock prices for its owners.

Unprincipled Agents

In the 1990s many corporations addressed the principal-agent problem by providing a substantial part of executive pay either as shares of the firm's stock or as stock options. *Stock options* are contracts that allow executives or other key employees to buy shares of their employers' stock at fixed, lower prices when the stock prices rise. The idea was to align the interest of the executives and other key employees more closely with those of the broader corporate owners. By pursuing high profits and share prices, the executives would enhance their own wealth as well as that of all the stockholders.

This "solution" to the principal-agent problem had an unexpected negative side effect. It prompted a few unscrupulous executives to inflate their firm's share prices by hiding costs, overstating revenues, engaging in deceptive transactions, and, in general, exaggerating profits. These executives then sold large quantities of their inflated stock, making quick personal fortunes. In some cases, "independent" outside auditing firms turned out to be "not so independent" because they held valuable consulting contracts with the firms being audited.

When the stock market bubble of the late 1990s burst, many instances of business manipulations and fraudulent accounting were exposed. Several executives of large U.S. firms were indicted, and a few large firms collapsed, among them Enron (energy trading), WorldCom (communications), and Arthur Andersen (business consulting). General stockholders of those firms were left holding severely depressed or even worthless stock.

In 2002 Congress strengthened the laws and penalties against executive misconduct. Also, corporations have improved their accounting and auditing procedures. But the revelations of recent wrongdoings make it clear that the principal-agent problem is not an easy problem to solve.

Question:
Why are accurate accounting and independent auditing so crucial in reducing the principal-agent problem?

Economic Costs

Firms face costs because the resources they need to produce their products are scarce and have alternative uses. Because of scarcity, firms wanting a particular resource have to bid it away from other firms. That process is costly for firms because it requires a payment to the resource owner. This reality causes economists to define **economic cost** as the payment that must be made to obtain and retain the services of a resource. It is the income the firm must provide to resource suppliers to attract resources away from alternative uses.

This section explains how firms incorporate opportunity costs to calculate economic costs. If you need a refresher on opportunity costs, a brief review of the section on opportunity costs in Chapter 1 might be useful before continuing on with the rest of this section.

economic cost
A payment that must be made to obtain and retain the services of a resource.

Explicit and Implicit Costs

To properly calculate a firm's economic costs, you must remember that *all* of the resources used by the firm have an opportunity cost. This is true both for the resources

127

that a firm purchases from outsiders as well as for the resources that it already owns. As a result, *all* of the resources that a firm uses have economic costs. Economists refer to these two types of economic costs as *explicit costs* and *implicit costs:*

explicit costs
The monetary payments a firm must make to an outsider to obtain a resource.

- A firm's **explicit costs** are the monetary payments it makes to those from whom it must purchase resources that it does not own. Because these costs involve an obvious cash transaction, they are referred to as explicit costs. Be sure to remember that explicit costs are opportunity costs because every monetary payment used to purchase outside resources necessarily involves forgoing the best alternatives that could have been purchased with the money.

implicit costs
The monetary income a firm sacrifices when it uses a resource it owns rather than supplying the resource in the market.

- A firm's **implicit costs** are the opportunity costs of using the resources that it already owns to make the firm's own product rather than selling those resources to outsiders for cash. Because these costs are present but not obvious, they are referred to as implicit costs.

A firm's economic costs are the sum of its explicit costs and its implicit costs:

$$\frac{\text{Economic}}{\text{costs}} = \frac{\text{explicit}}{\text{costs}} + \frac{\text{implicit}}{\text{costs}}$$

The following example makes clear how both explicit costs and implicit costs affect firm profits and firm behavior.

Accounting Profit and Normal Profit

Suppose that after working as a sales representative for a large T-shirt manufacturer, you decide to open your own retail T-shirt shop. As we explain in Chapter 2, you will be providing two different economic resources to your new enterprise: labor and entrepreneurial ability. The part of your job that involves providing labor includes routine tasks that help run the business—things like answering customer e-mails, taking inventory, and sweeping the floor. The part of your job that involves providing entrepreneurial ability includes any nonroutine tasks involved with organizing the business and directing its strategy—things like deciding how to promote your business, what to include in your product mix, and how to decorate your store to maximize its appeal to potential customers.

You begin providing entrepreneurial ability to your new firm by making some initial organizational decisions. You decide to work full time at your new business, so you quit your old job that paid you $22,000 per year. You invest $20,000 of savings that has been earning $1000 per year. You decide that your new firm will occupy a small retail space that you own and had been previously renting out for $5000 per year. Finally, you decide to hire one clerk to help you in the store. She agrees to work for you for $18,000 per year.

After a year in business, you total up your accounts and find the following:

Total sales revenue	$120,000
Cost of T-shirts $40,000	
Clerk's salary 18,000	
Utilities.................................. 5000	
Total (explicit) costs	63,000
Accounting profit	$ 57,000

accounting profit
The total revenue of a firm less its explicit costs.

These numbers look very good. In particular, you are happy with your $57,000 **accounting profit**, the profit number that accountants calculate by subtracting total explicit costs from total sales revenue. This is the profit (or net income) that would appear on your accounting statement and that you would report to the government for tax purposes.

But don't celebrate yet! Your $57,000 accounting profit overstates the economic success of your business because it ignores your implicit costs. The true measure of success is doing as well as you possibly can—that is, making more money in your new venture selling T-shirts than you could pursuing any other business venture.

To figure out whether you are achieving that goal, you must take into account *all* of your opportunity costs—both your implicit costs as well as your explicit costs. Doing so will indicate whether your new business venture is earning more money than what you could have earned in any other business venture.

To see how these calculations are made, let's continue with our example.

By providing your own financial capital, retail space, and labor, you incurred three different implicit costs during the year: $1000 of forgone interest, $5000 of forgone rent, and $22,000 of forgone wages. But don't forget that there is another implicit cost that you must also take account of—how much income you chose to forgo by applying your entrepreneurial abilities to your current retail T-shirt venture rather than applying them to other potential business ventures.

But what dollar value should we place on the size of the profits that you might have made if you had provided your entrepreneurial ability to one of those other ventures?

The answer is given by estimating a **normal profit**, the typical (or "normal") amount of accounting profit that you would most likely have earned in your next-best-alternative business venture. For the sake of argument, let us assume that with your particular set of skills and talents your entrepreneurial abilities would have on average yielded a normal profit of $5000 in one of the other potential ventures. Knowing that value, we can take all of your implicit costs properly into account by subtracting them from your accounting profit:

normal profit
A payment that must be made by a firm to obtain and retain entrepreneurial ability.

Accounting profit	$57,000
Forgone interest . . . . $ 1000	
Forgone rent 5000	
Forgone wages 22,000	
Forgone entrepreneurial income 5000	
Total implicit costs	33,000
Economic profit	$24,000

Economic Profit

After subtracting your $33,000 of implicit costs from your accounting profit of $57,000, we are left with an *economic profit* of $24,000.

Please distinguish clearly between accounting profit and economic profit. Accounting profit is the result of subtracting only explicit costs from revenue: *Accounting Profit = Revenue − Explicit Costs*. By contrast, **economic profit** is the result of subtracting all of your economic costs—both explicit costs and implicit costs—from revenue: *Economic Profit = Revenue − Explicit Costs − Implicit Costs*.

By subtracting all of your economic costs from your revenue, you determine how your current business venture compares with your best alternative business venture. In our example, the fact that you are generating an economic profit of $24,000 means that you are making $24,000 more than you could expect to make in your best alternative business venture.

> **WORKED PROBLEMS**
>
> **W 6.1**
> Economic profit

economic profit
A firm's total revenue less its total cost (= explicit cost + implicit cost).

By contrast, suppose that you had instead done poorly in business, so that this year your firm generated an economic loss (a negative economic profit) of $8000. This would mean that you were doing worse in your current venture than you could have done in your best alternative venture. You would, as a result, wish to switch to that alternative.

Generalizing this point, we see that there is an important behavioral threshold at $0 of economic profit. If a firm is breaking even (that is, earning exactly $0 of economic profit), then its entrepreneurs know that they are doing exactly as well as they could expect to do in their best alternative business venture. They are earning enough to cover all their explicit and implicit costs, including the normal profit that they could expect to earn in other business ventures. Thus, they have no incentive to change. By contrast, entrepreneurs running a positive economic profit know they are doing better than they could in alternative ventures and will want to continue doing what they are doing or maybe even expand their business. And entrepreneurs running an economic loss (a negative economic profit) know that they could do better by switching to something else.

It is for this reason that economists focus on economic profits rather than accounting profits. Simply put, economic profits direct how resources are allocated in the economy. Entrepreneurs running economic losses close their current businesses, thereby freeing up the land, labor, capital, and entrepreneurial ability that they had been using. These resources are freed up to be used by firms that are generating positive economic profits or that are at least breaking even. Resources thus flow from producing goods and services with lower net benefits toward producing goods and services with higher net benefits. Allocative efficiency increases as firms are led by their profit signals to produce more of what consumers want the most.

Figure 6.1 shows the relationship among the various cost and profit concepts that we have just discussed. To test yourself, you might want to enter cost data from our example in the appropriate blocks.

Short Run and Long Run

When the demand for a firm's product changes, the firm's profitability may depend on how quickly it can adjust the amounts of the various resources it employs. It can

FIGURE 6.1

Economic profit versus accounting profit. Economic profit is equal to total revenue less economic costs. Economic costs are the sum of explicit and implicit costs and include a normal profit to the entrepreneur. Accounting profit is equal to total revenue less accounting (explicit) costs.

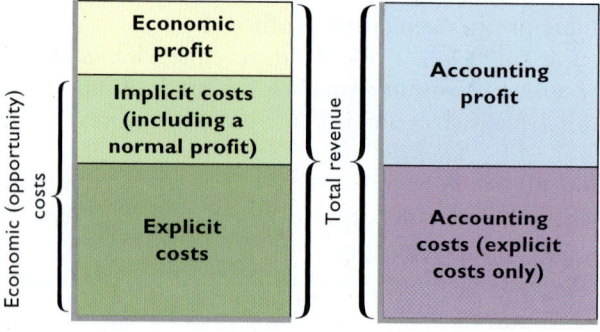

easily and quickly adjust the quantities employed of many resources such as hourly labor, raw materials, fuel, and power. It needs much more time, however, to adjust its *plant capacity*—the size of the factory building, the amount of machinery and equipment, and other capital resources. In some heavy industries such as aircraft manufacturing, a firm may need several years to alter plant capacity. Because of these differences in adjustment time, economists find it useful to distinguish between two conceptual periods: the short run and the long run. We will discover that costs differ in these two time periods.

Short Run: Fixed Plant   In microeconomics, the **short run** is a period too brief for a firm to alter its plant capacity yet long enough to permit a change in the degree to which the fixed plant is used. The firm's plant capacity is fixed in the short run. However, the firm can vary its output by applying larger or smaller amounts of labor, materials, and other resources to that plant. It can use its existing plant capacity more or less intensively in the short run.

short run
A time period in which producers are able to change the quantities of some but not all of the resources they employ.

If Boeing hires 1000 extra workers for one of its commercial airline plants or adds an entire shift of workers, we are speaking of the short run. Both are *short-run adjustments*.

Long Run: Variable Plant   From the viewpoint of an existing firm, the **long run** is a period long enough for it to adjust the quantities of all the resources that it employs, including plant capacity. From the industry's viewpoint, the long run also includes enough time for existing firms to dissolve and leave the industry or for new firms to be created and enter the industry. While the short run is a "fixed-plant" period, the long run is a "variable-plant" period. If Boeing adds a new production facility or merges with a supplier, we are referring to the long run. Both are *long-run adjustments*.

long run
A time period sufficiently long to enable producers to change the quantities of all the resources they employ.

© Viviane Moos/CORBIS

© Richard Klune/CORBIS

Photo Op Long-Run Adjustments by Firms

An apparel manufacturer can make long-run adjustments to add production capacity in a matter of days by leasing another building and ordering and installing extra sewing machines. In contrast, an oil firm may need 2 to 3 years to construct a new refinery to increase its production capacity.

The short run and the long run are conceptual periods rather than calendar time periods. As indicated in the Photo Op, light-manufacturing industries can accomplish changes in plant capacity almost overnight. But for heavy industry the long run is a different matter. A firm may require several years to construct a new facility.

Short-Run Production Relationships

A firm's costs of producing a specific output depend on the prices of the needed resources and the quantities of those resources (inputs) needed to produce that output. Resource supply and demand determine resource prices. The technological aspects of production, specifically the relationships between inputs and output, determine the quantities of resources needed. Our focus will be on the *labor*-output relationship, given a fixed plant capacity. But before examining that relationship, we need to define three terms:

total product (TP)
The total output of a particular good or service produced by a firm.

- **Total product (TP)** is the total quantity, or total output, of a particular good or service produced.
- **Marginal product (MP)** is the extra output or added product associated with adding a unit of a variable resource, in this case labor, to the production process. Thus,

$$\text{Marginal product} = \frac{\text{change in total product}}{\text{change in labor input}}$$

marginal product (MP)
The extra output or added product associated with adding a unit of a variable resource (labor) to the production process.

- **Average product (AP),** also called *labor productivity*, is output per unit of labor input:

$$\text{Average product} = \frac{\text{total product}}{\text{units of labor}}$$

average product (AP)
The total output divided by the quantity of the resource employed (labor).

In the short run, a firm for a time can increase its output by adding units of labor to its fixed plant. But by how much will output rise when it adds the labor? Why do we say "for a time"?

Law of Diminishing Returns

law of diminishing returns
The principle that as successive units of a variable resource are added to a fixed resource, the marginal product of the variable resource will eventually decline.

The answers are provided in general terms by the **law of diminishing returns.** This law assumes that technology is fixed and thus the techniques of production do not change. It states that as successive units of a variable resource (say, labor) are added to a fixed resource (say, capital or land), beyond some point the extra, or marginal, product that can be attributed to each additional unit of the variable resource will decline. For example, if additional workers are hired to work with a constant amount of capital equipment, output will eventually rise by smaller and smaller amounts as more workers are hired. Diminishing returns will eventually occur.

Relevancy for Firms

The law of diminishing returns is highly relevant for production within firms. As producers add successive units of a variable input such as labor to a fixed input such as capital, the marginal product of labor eventually declines. Diminishing returns will occur sooner or later. Total product eventually will rise at a diminishing rate, then reach a maximum, and finally decline.

ORIGIN OF THE IDEA

O 6.2
Law of diminishing returns

Diminishing Returns from Study

The following noneconomic example of a relationship between "inputs" and "output" may help you better understand the idea. Suppose for an individual that

> Total course learning = f(intelligence, quality of course materials, instructor effectiveness, class time, and study time)

where f means "function of" or "depends on." So this relationship supposes that total course learning depends on intelligence (however defined), the quality of course materials such as the textbook, the effectiveness of the instructor, the amount of class time, and the amount of personal study time outside the class.

For analytical purposes, let's assume that one's intelligence, the quality of course materials, the effectiveness of the instructor, and the amount of class time are *fixed*—meaning they do not change over the length of the course. Now let's add units of study time per day over the length of the course to "produce" greater course learning. The first hour of study time per day increases total course learning. Will the second hour enhance course learning by as much as the first? By how much will the third, fourth, fifth, . . . or fifteenth hour of study per day contribute to total course learning relative to the *immediately previous hour?*

We think you will agree that eventually diminishing returns to course learning will set in as successive hours of study are added each day. At some point the marginal product of an extra hour of study time will decline and, at some further point, become zero.

Question:
Given diminishing returns to study time, why devote any extra time to study?

What is true for study time is true for producers. Suppose a farmer has a fixed resource—80 acres of land—planted in corn. If the farmer does not cultivate the cornfields (clear the weeds) at all, the yield will be 40 bushels per acre. If he cultivates the land once, output may rise to 50 bushels per acre. A second cultivation may increase output to 57 bushels per acre, a third to 61, and a fourth to 63. Succeeding cultivations will add less and less to the land's yield. If this were not so, the world's needs for corn could be fulfilled by extremely intense cultivation of this single 80-acre plot of land. Indeed, if diminishing returns did not occur, the world could be fed out of a flowerpot. Why not? Just keep adding more seed, fertilizer, and harvesters!

The law of diminishing returns also holds true in nonagricultural industries. Assume a wood shop is manufacturing furniture frames. It has a specific amount of equipment such as lathes, planers, saws, and sanders. If this shop hired just one or two workers, total output and productivity (output per worker) would be very low. The workers would have to perform many different jobs, and the advantages of specialization would not be realized. Time would be lost in switching from one job to another, and machines would stand idle much of the time. In short, the plant would be understaffed, and production would be inefficient because there would be too much capital relative to the amount of labor.

The shop could eliminate those difficulties by hiring more workers. Then the equipment would be more fully used, and workers could specialize in doing a single job. Time would no longer be lost switching from job to job. As more workers were added, production would become more efficient and the marginal product of each succeeding worker would rise.

But the rise could not go on indefinitely. Beyond a certain point, adding more workers would cause overcrowding. Since workers would then have to wait in line to use the machinery, they would be underused. Total output would increase at a diminishing rate because, given the fixed size of the plant, each worker would have less capital equipment to work with as more and more labor was hired. The marginal product of additional workers would decline because there would be more labor in proportion to the fixed amount of capital. Eventually, adding still more workers would cause so much congestion that marginal product would become negative and total product would decline. At the extreme, the addition of more and more labor would exhaust all the standing room, and total product would fall to zero.

Note that the law of diminishing returns assumes that all units of labor are of equal quality. Each successive worker is presumed to have the same innate ability, motor coordination, education, training, and work experience. Less-skilled or less-energetic workers are not the cause of diminishing returns. Rather, marginal product ultimately diminishes because more workers are being used relative to the amount of plant and equipment available.

Tabular and Graphical Representations

The table at the top of Figure 6.2 is a numerical illustration of the law of diminishing returns. Column 2 shows the total product, or total output, resulting from combining each level of a variable input (labor) in column 1 with a fixed amount of capital, using the existing technology.

Column 3 shows the marginal product (MP), the change in total product associated with each additional unit of labor. Note that with no labor input, total product is zero; a plant with no workers will produce no output. The first 3 units of labor reflect

> **WORKED PROBLEMS**
>
> **W 6.2**
>
> Total, marginal, and average product

increasing marginal returns, with marginal products of 10, 15, and 20 units, respectively. But beginning with the fourth unit of labor, marginal product diminishes continuously, becoming zero with the seventh unit of labor and negative with the eighth.

Average product, or output per labor unit, is shown in column 4. It is calculated by dividing total product (column 2) by the number of labor units needed to produce it (column 1). At 5 units of labor, for example, AP is 14 (=70/5).

Figure 6.2 also shows the diminishing-returns data graphically and further clarifies the relationships between total, marginal, and average products. (Marginal product in Figure 6.2b is plotted halfway between the units of labor, since it applies to the addition of each labor unit.)

Note first in Figure 6.2a that total product, TP, goes through three phases: It rises initially at an increasing rate; then it increases, but at a diminishing rate; finally, after reaching a maximum, it declines.

Geometrically, marginal product—shown by the MP curve in Figure 6.2b—is the slope of the total-product curve. Marginal product measures the change in total product associated with each succeeding unit of labor. Thus, the three phases of total product are also reflected in marginal product. Where total product is increasing at an increasing rate, marginal product is rising. Here, extra units of labor are adding larger and larger amounts to total product. Similarly, where total product is increasing but at a decreasing rate, marginal product is positive but falling. Each additional unit of labor

(1) Units of the Variable Resource (Labor)	(2) Total Product (TP)	(3) Marginal Product (MP), Change in (2)/ Change in (1)		(4) Average Product (AP), (2)/(1)
0	0	10 ⎤ Increasing		–
1	10	15 ⎬ marginal		10.00
2	25	20 ⎦ returns		12.50
3	45	15 ⎤ Diminishing		15.00
4	60	10 ⎬ marginal		15.00
5	70	5 ⎦ returns		14.00
6	75	0 ⎤ Negative		12.50
7	75	–5 ⎬ marginal		10.71
8	70	returns		8.75

FIGURE 6.2

The law of diminishing returns. (a) As a variable resource (labor) is added to fixed amounts of other resources (land or capital), the total product that results will eventually increase by diminishing amounts, reach a maximum, and then decline. (b) Marginal product is the change in total product associated with each new unit of labor. Average product is simply output per labor unit. Note that marginal product intersects average product at the maximum average product.

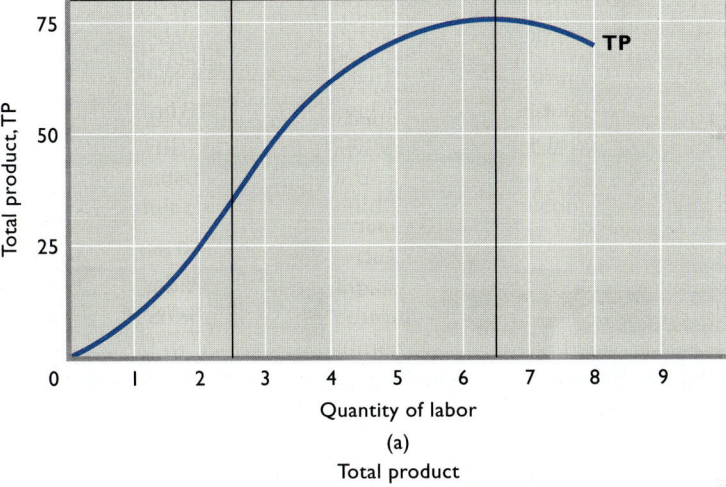

(a)
Total product

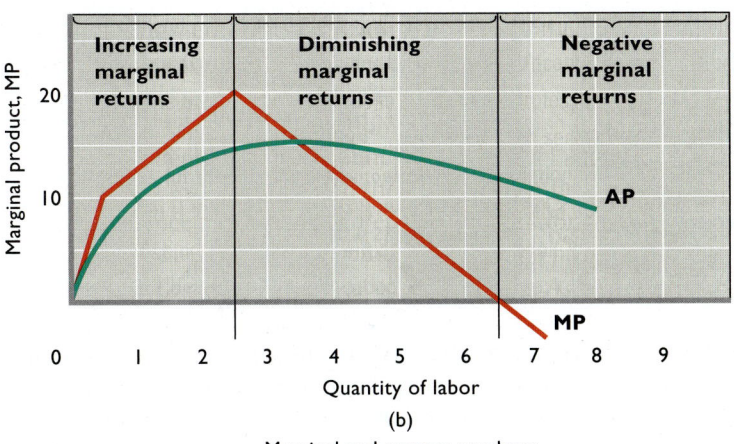

(b)
Marginal and average products

adds less to total product than did the previous unit. When total product is at a maximum, marginal product is zero. When total product declines, marginal product becomes negative.

Average product, AP (Figure 6.2b), displays the same tendencies as marginal product. It increases, reaches a maximum, and then decreases as more and more units of labor are added to the fixed plant. But note the relationship between marginal product and average product: Where marginal product exceeds average product, average product rises. And where marginal product is less than average product, average product declines. It follows that marginal product intersects average product where average product is at a maximum.

> **ORIGIN OF THE IDEA**
>
> **O 6.3**
> Production relationships

Illustrating the Idea

Exam Scores

The relationship between "marginal" and "average" shown in Figure 6.2b is a mathematical necessity. If you add to a total a number larger than the current average of that total, the average must rise. And if you add to a total a number smaller than the current average of that total, the average must fall. You raise your average examination grade only when your score on an additional (marginal) examination is greater than the average of all your past scores. You lower your average when your grade on an additional exam is below your current average. In our production example, when the amount an extra worker adds to total product exceeds the average product of all workers currently employed, average product will rise. Conversely, when the amount an extra worker adds to total product is less than the current average product, average product will decrease.

Question:
Suppose your average exam score for the first three exams is 80 and you receive a 92 on your fourth exam. What is your marginal score? What is your new average score? Why did your average go up?

Short-Run Production Costs

Production information such as that in Figure 6.2 must be coupled with resource prices to determine the total and per-unit costs of producing various levels of output. We know that in the short run, resources associated with the firm's plant are fixed. Other resources, however, are variable in the short run. As a result, short-run costs can be either fixed or variable.

Fixed, Variable, and Total Costs

Let's see what distinguishes fixed costs, variable costs, and total costs from one another.

fixed costs
Costs that do not change in total when the firm changes its output.

Fixed Costs   **Fixed costs** are costs that do not vary with changes in output. Fixed costs are associated with the very existence of a firm's plant and therefore must be paid even if its output is zero. Such costs as rental payments, interest on a firm's debts, a portion of depreciation on equipment and buildings, and insurance premiums are generally fixed costs; they are fixed and do not change even if a firm produces more. In column 2 of Figure 6.3's table, we assume that the firm's total fixed cost is $100. By definition, this fixed cost is incurred at all levels of output, including zero. The firm cannot avoid paying fixed costs in the short run.

FIGURE 6.3

A firm's cost curves. Average fixed cost (AFC) falls as a given amount of fixed costs is apportioned over a larger and larger output. Average variable cost (AVC) initially falls because of increasing marginal returns but then rises because of diminishing marginal returns. The marginal-cost (MC) curve eventually rises because of diminishing returns and cuts through the average-total-cost (ATC) curve and the AVC curve at their minimum points.

Total-Cost Data				Average-Cost Data			Marginal Cost
(1)	(2)	(3)	(4)	(5)	(6)	(7)	(8)
Total Product (Q)	Total Fixed Cost (TFC)	Total Variable Cost (TVC)	Total Cost (TC) $TC = TFC + TVC$	Average Fixed Cost (AFC) $AFC = \frac{TFC}{Q}$	Average Variable Cost (AVC) $AVC = \frac{TVC}{Q}$	Average Total Cost (ATC) $ATC = \frac{TC}{Q}$	Marginal Cost (MC) $MC = \frac{\text{change in TC}}{\text{change in Q}}$
0	$100	$ 0	$ 100				
1	100	90	190	$100.00	$90.00	$190.00	$ 90
2	100	170	270	50.00	85.00	135.00	80
3	100	240	340	33.33	80.00	113.33	70
4	100	300	400	25.00	75.00	100.00	60
5	100	370	470	20.00	74.00	94.00	70
6	100	450	550	16.67	75.00	91.67	80
7	100	540	640	14.29	77.14	91.43	90
8	100	650	750	12.50	81.25	93.75	110
9	100	780	880	11.11	86.67	97.78	130
10	100	930	1030	10.00	93.00	103.00	150

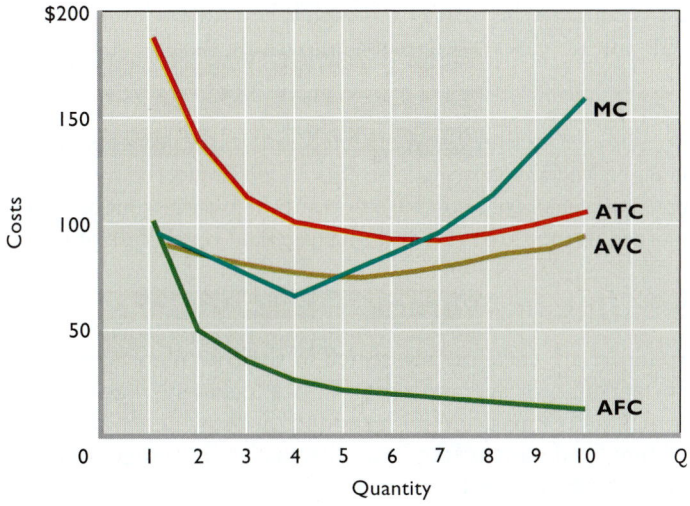

variable costs
Costs that increase or decrease with a firm's output.

Variable Costs   Unlike fixed costs, **variable costs** are costs that change with the level of output. They include payments for materials, fuel, power, transportation services, most labor, and similar variable resources. In column 3 of the table in Figure 6.3, we find that the total of variable costs changes directly with output.

Applying the Analysis

Sunk Costs

Some of a firm's costs are not only *fixed* (recurring, but unrelated to the level of output) but *sunk* (unrecoverable). Such costs are like sunken ships on the ocean floor: Once these costs are incurred, they cannot be recovered. For example, suppose a firm spends $1 million on R&D to bring out a new product, only to discover that the product sells very poorly. Should the firm continue to produce the product at a loss even when there is no realistic hope for future success? Obviously, it should not. In making this decision, the firm realizes that the amount it has spent in developing the product is irrelevant; it should stop production of the product and cut its losses. In fact, many firms have dropped products after spending millions of dollars on their development. For example, in 2007 Pfizer withdrew its novel insulin inhaler from the market because of poor sales and concerns about long-term side effects. The product had cost an estimated $2.8 billion to develop and market.

In short, a firm should ignore any cost that it cannot partly or fully recoup through a subsequent choice. Such costs are sunk costs. They are irrelevant in making future-oriented business decisions. Or, as the saying goes, don't cry over spilt milk.

Question:
Which is a sunk cost, rather than simply a recurring fixed cost: (1) a prior expenditure on a business computer that is now outdated or (2) a current monthly payment on an equipment lease that runs for 6 more months? Explain.

total cost
The sum of fixed cost and variable cost.

Total Cost   **Total cost** is the sum of fixed cost and variable cost at each level of output. It is shown in column 4 of the table in Figure 6.3. At zero units of output, total cost is equal to the firm's fixed cost. Then for each unit of the 10 units of production, total cost increases by the same amount as variable cost.

$$TC = TFC + TVC$$

The distinction between fixed and variable costs is significant to the business manager. Variable costs can be controlled or altered in the short run by changing production levels. Fixed costs are beyond the business manager's current control; they are incurred in the short run and must be paid regardless of output level.

Per-Unit, or Average, Costs

Producers are certainly interested in their total costs, but they are equally concerned with per-unit, or average, costs. In particular, average-cost data are more meaningful for making comparisons with product price, which is always stated on a per-unit basis. Average fixed cost, average variable cost, and average total cost are shown in columns 5 to 7 of the table in Figure 6.3.

AFC Average fixed cost (AFC) for any output level is found by dividing total fixed cost (TFC) by that output (Q). That is,

$$AFC = \frac{TFC}{Q}$$

Because the total fixed cost is, by definition, the same regardless of output, AFC must decline as output increases. As output rises, the total fixed cost is spread over a larger and larger output. When output is just 1 unit in Figure 6.3's table, TFC and AFC are the same at $100. But at 2 units of output, the total fixed cost of $100 becomes $50 of AFC or fixed cost per unit; then it becomes $33.33 per unit as $100 is spread over 3 units, and $25 per unit when spread over 4 units. This process is sometimes referred to as "spreading the overhead." Figure 6.3 shows that AFC graphs as a continuously declining curve as total output is increased.

AVC Average variable cost (AVC) for any output level is calculated by dividing total variable cost (TVC) by that output (Q):

$$AVC = \frac{TVC}{Q}$$

Due to increasing and then diminishing returns, AVC declines initially, reaches a minimum, and then increases again. A graph of AVC is a U-shaped or saucer-shaped curve, as shown in Figure 6.3.

Because total variable cost reflects the law of diminishing returns, so must AVC, which is derived from total variable cost. Because marginal returns increase initially, it takes fewer and fewer additional variable resources to produce each of the first 4 units of output. As a result, variable cost per unit declines. AVC hits a minimum with the fifth unit of output, and beyond that point AVC rises because diminishing returns require more and more variable resources to produce each additional unit of output.

You can verify the U or saucer shape of the AVC curve by returning to the production table in Figure 6.2. Assume the price of labor is $10 per unit. Labor cost per unit of output is then $10 (the price per unit of labor in this example) divided by average product (output per labor unit). Because we have assumed labor to be the only variable input, the labor cost per unit of output is the variable cost per unit of output, or AVC. When average product is initially low, AVC is high. As workers are added, average product rises and AVC falls. When average product is at its maximum, AVC is at its minimum. Then, as still more workers are added and average product declines, AVC rises. The "hump" of the average-product curve is reflected in the saucer or U shape of the AVC curve.

ATC Average total cost (ATC) for any output level is found by dividing total cost (TC) by that output (Q) or by adding AFC and AVC at that output:

$$ATC = \frac{TC}{Q} = \frac{TFC}{Q} + \frac{TVC}{Q} = AFC + AVC$$

Graphically, we can find ATC by adding vertically the AFC and AVC curves, as in Figure 6.3. Thus, the vertical distance between the ATC and AVC curves measures AFC at any level of output.

---

average fixed cost (AFC)
A firm's total fixed cost divided by output.

average variable cost (AVC)
A firm's total variable cost divided by output.

average total cost (ATC)
A firm's total cost (= total fixed costs + total variable costs) divided by output.

Marginal Cost

One final and very crucial cost concept remains: **Marginal cost (MC)** is *the extra, or additional, cost of producing 1 more unit of output.* MC can be determined for each added unit of output by noting the change in total cost that that unit's production entails:

$$MC = \frac{\text{change in TC}}{\text{change in } Q}$$

Calculations   In column 4 of Figure 6.3's table, production of the first unit of output increases total cost from $100 to $190. Therefore, the additional, or marginal, cost of that first unit is $90 (column 8). The marginal cost of the second unit is $80 (= $270 − $190); the MC of the third is $70 (= $340 − $270); and so forth. The MC for each of the 10 units of output is shown in column 8.

MC can also be calculated from the total-variable-cost column because the only difference between total cost and total variable cost is the constant amount of fixed costs ($100). Thus, the change in total cost and the change in total variable cost accompanying each additional unit of output are always the same.

Marginal Decisions   Marginal costs are costs the firm can control directly and immediately. Specifically, MC designates all the cost incurred in producing the last unit of output. Thus, it also designates the cost that can be "saved" by not producing that last unit. Average-cost figures do not provide this information. For example, suppose the firm is undecided whether to produce 3 or 4 units of output. At 4 units the table in Figure 6.3 indicates that ATC is $100. But the firm does not increase its total costs by $100 by producing the fourth unit, nor does it save $100 by not producing that unit. Rather, the change in costs involved here is only $60, as the MC column in the table reveals.

A firm's decisions as to what output level to produce are typically marginal decisions, that is, decisions to produce a few more or a few less units. Marginal cost is the change in costs when 1 more or 1 less unit of output is produced. When coupled with marginal revenue (which, as you will see in Chapter 7, indicates the change in revenue from 1 more or 1 less unit of output), marginal cost allows a firm to determine if it is profitable to expand or contract its production. The analysis in the next three chapters focuses on those marginal calculations.

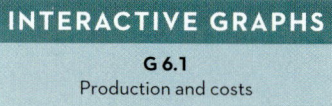

WORKED PROBLEMS
W 6.3
Per-unit cost

Graphical Portrayal   Marginal cost is shown graphically in Figure 6.3. Marginal cost at first declines sharply, reaches a minimum, and then rises rather abruptly. This reflects the fact that variable costs, and therefore total cost, increase first by decreasing amounts and then by increasing amounts.

INTERACTIVE GRAPHS
G 6.1
Production and costs

Relation of MC to AVC and ATC   Figure 6.3 shows that the marginal-cost curve MC intersects both the AVC and the ATC curves at their minimum points. As noted earlier, this marginal-average relationship is a mathematical necessity. When the amount (the marginal cost) added to total cost is less than the current average total cost, ATC will fall. Conversely, when the marginal cost exceeds ATC, ATC will rise. This means in Figure 6.3 that as long as MC lies below ATC, ATC will fall, and whenever MC lies above ATC, ATC will rise. Therefore, at the point of intersection where MC equals ATC, ATC has just ceased to fall but has not yet begun to rise. This, by definition, is the minimum point on the ATC curve. The marginal-cost curve intersects the average-total-cost curve at the ATC curve's minimum point.

Marginal cost can be defined as the addition either to total cost or to total variable cost resulting from 1 more unit of output; thus, this same rationale explains why the MC curve also crosses the AVC curve at the AVC curve's minimum point. No such relationship exists between the MC curve and the average-fixed-cost curve because the two are not related; marginal cost includes only those costs that change with output, and fixed costs by definition are those that are independent of output.

Rising Gasoline Prices

Applying the Analysis

Changes in supply and demand often lead to rapid increases in the price of gasoline. Because gasoline is used to power nearly all motor vehicles, including those used by businesses, increases in the price of gasoline lead to increases in firms' short-run variable costs, marginal costs, and average total costs. In terms of our analysis, their AVC, MC, and ATC curves all shift upward when an increase in the price of gasoline increases their production costs.

The extent of these upward shifts depends upon the relative importance of gasoline as a variable input in the various firms' individual production processes. Package-delivery companies like FedEx that use a lot of gasoline-powered vehicles will see substantial upward shifts while software companies like Symantec (Norton) that mainly deliver their products through Internet downloads may see only small upward shifts.

Question:
If rising gasoline prices increase the cost for delivery to firms such as FedEx, how would that affect the cost curves for Internet retailers such as Amazon that ship a lot of packages?

Long-Run Production Costs

In the long run, an industry and its individual firms can undertake all desired resource adjustments. That is, they can change the amount of all inputs used. The firm can alter its plant capacity; it can build a larger plant or revert to a smaller plant than that assumed in Figures 6.2 and 6.3. The industry also can change its overall capacity; the long run allows sufficient time for new firms to enter or for existing firms to leave an industry. We will discuss the impact of the entry and exit of firms to and from an industry in the next chapter; here we are concerned only with changes in plant capacity made by a single firm. Let's couch our analysis in terms of average total cost (ATC), making no distinction between fixed and variable costs because all resources, and therefore all costs, are variable in the long run.

FIGURE 6.4

The long-run average-total-cost curve: five possible plant sizes. The long-run average-total-cost curve is made up of segments of the short-run cost curves (ATC-1, ATC-2, etc.) of the various-size plants from which the firm might choose. Each point on the bumpy planning curve shows the lowest unit cost attainable for any output when the firm has had time to make all desired changes in its plant size.

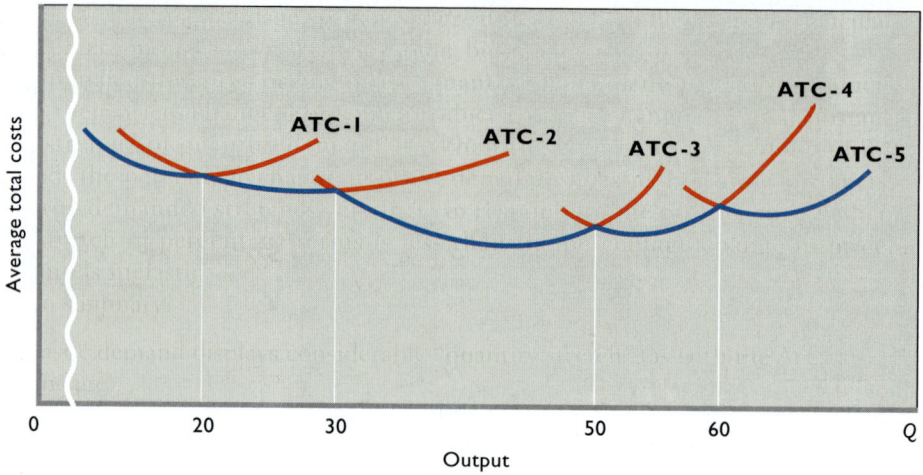

Firm Size and Costs

Suppose a manufacturer with a single plant begins on a small scale and, as the result of successful operations, expands to successively larger plant sizes with larger output capacities. What happens to average total cost as this occurs? For a time, successively larger plants will reduce average total cost. However, eventually the building of a still larger plant may cause ATC to rise.

Figure 6.4 illustrates this situation for five possible plant sizes. ATC-1 is the short-run average-total-cost curve for the smallest of the five plants, and ATC-5, the curve for the largest. Constructing larger plants will lower the minimum average total costs through plant size 3. But then larger plants will mean higher minimum average total costs.

The Long-Run Cost Curve

The vertical lines perpendicular to the output axis in Figure 6.4 indicate the outputs at which the firm should change plant size to realize the lowest attainable average total costs of production. These are the outputs at which the per-unit costs for a larger plant drop below those for the current, smaller plant. For all outputs up to 20 units, the lowest average total costs are attainable with plant size 1. However, if the firm's volume of sales expands beyond 20 units but less than 30, it can achieve lower per-unit costs by constructing a larger plant, size 2. Although total cost will be higher at the expanded levels of production, the cost per unit of output will be less. For any output between 30 and 50 units, plant size 3 will yield the lowest average total costs. From 50 to 60 units of output, the firm must build the size-4 plant to achieve the lowest unit costs. Lowest average total costs for any output over 60 units require construction of the still larger plant, size 5.

Tracing these adjustments, we find that the long-run ATC curve for the enterprise is made up of segments of the short-run ATC curves for the various plant sizes that can be constructed. The long-run ATC curve shows the lowest average total cost at

FIGURE 6.5

The long-run average-total-cost curve: unlimited number of plant sizes. If the number of possible plant sizes is very large, the long-run average-total-cost curve approximates a smooth curve. Economies of scale, followed by diseconomies of scale, cause the curve to be U-shaped.

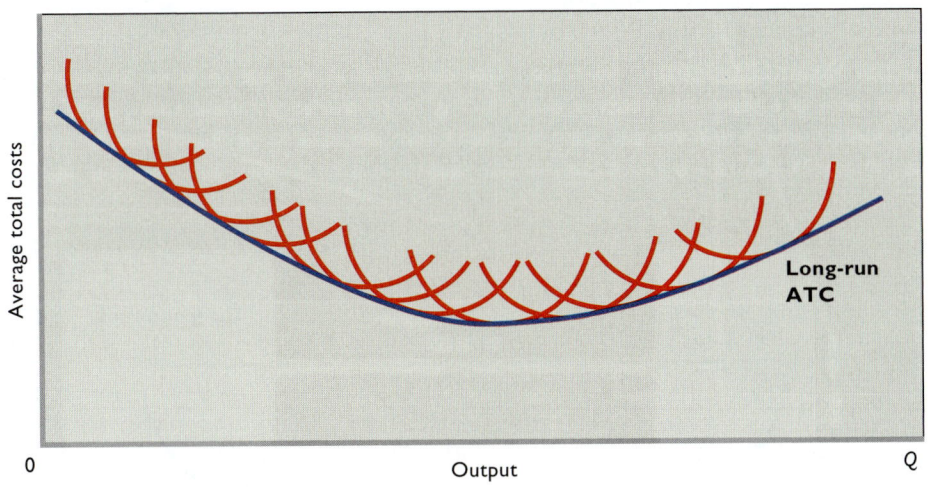

which *any output level* can be produced after the firm has had time to make all appropriate adjustments in its plant size. In Figure 6.4 the red, bumpy curve is the firm's long-run ATC curve or, as it is often called, the firm's *planning curve*.

In most lines of production, the choice of plant size is much wider than in our illustration. In many industries the number of possible plant sizes is virtually unlimited, and in time quite small changes in the volume of output will lead to changes in plant size. Graphically, this implies an unlimited number of short-run ATC curves, one for each output level, as suggested by Figure 6.5. Then, rather than being made up of segments of short-run ATC curves as in Figure 6.4, the long-run ATC curve is made up of all the points of tangency of the unlimited number of short-run ATC curves from which the long-run ATC curve is derived. Therefore, the planning curve is smooth rather than bumpy. Each point on it tells us the minimum ATC of producing the corresponding level of output.

Economies and Diseconomies of Scale

We have assumed that, for a time, larger and larger plant sizes will lead to lower unit costs but that, beyond some point, successively larger plants will mean higher average total costs. That is, we have assumed the long-run ATC curve is U-shaped. But why should this be? It turns out that the U shape is caused by economies and diseconomies of large-scale production, as we explain in a moment. But before we do, please understand that the U shape of the long-run average-total-cost curve *cannot* be the result of rising resource prices or the law of diminishing returns. First, our discussion assumes that resource prices are constant. Second, the law of diminishing returns does not apply to production in the long run. This is true because the law of diminishing returns only deals with situations in which a productive resource or input is held constant. Under our definition of "long run," all resources and inputs are variable.

economies of scale
Reductions in the average total cost of producing a product as the firm expands the size of its operations (output) in the long run.

Economies of Scale   **Economies of scale,** or *economies of mass production,* explain the downsloping part of the long-run ATC curve, as indicated in Figure 6.6, graphs (a), (b), and (c). As plant size increases, a number of factors will, for a time, lead to lower average costs of production.

Labor Specialization   Increased specialization in the use of labor becomes more achievable as a plant increases in size. Hiring more workers means jobs can be divided and subdivided. Each worker may now have just one task to perform instead of five or six. Workers can work full time on the tasks for which they have special skills. By

FIGURE 6.6
Various possible long-run average-total-cost curves. In (a), economies of scale are rather rapidly obtained as plant size rises, and diseconomies of scale are not encountered until a considerably large scale of output has been achieved. Thus, long-run average total cost is constant over a wide range of output. In (b), economies of scale are extensive, and diseconomies of scale occur only at very large outputs. Average total cost therefore declines over a broad range of output. In (c), economies of scale are exhausted quickly, followed immediately by diseconomies of scale. Minimum ATC thus occurs at a relatively low output.

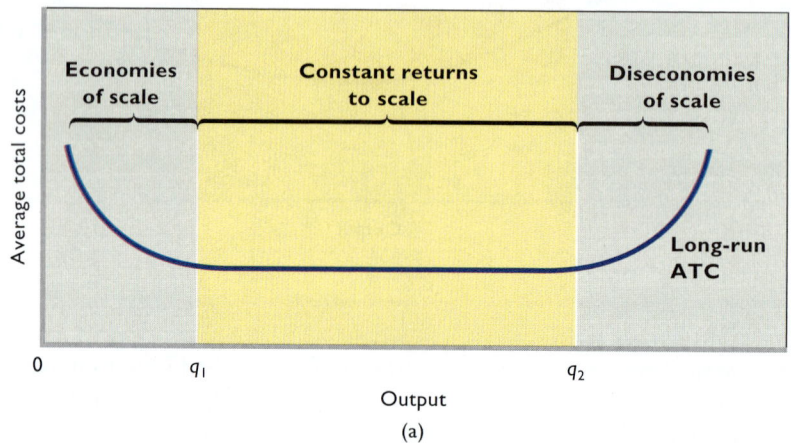

(a)

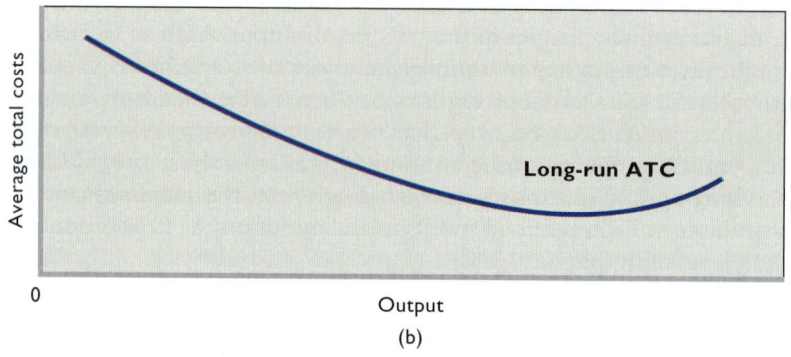

(b)

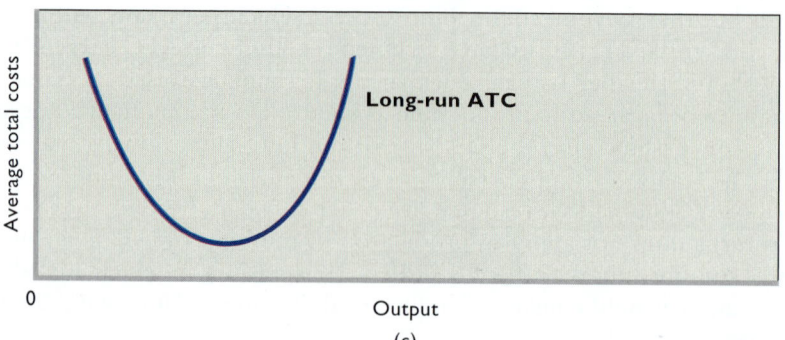

(c)

contrast, skilled machinists in a small plant may spend half their time performing unskilled tasks, leading to higher production costs.

Further, by working at fewer tasks, workers become even more proficient at those tasks. The jack-of-all-trades doing five or six jobs is not likely to be efficient in any of them. Concentrating on one task, the same worker may become highly efficient.

Finally, greater labor specialization eliminates the loss of time that occurs whenever a worker shifts from one task to another.

Managerial Specialization   Large-scale production also means better use of, and greater specialization in, management. A supervisor who can handle 20 workers is underused in a small plant that employs only 10 people. The production staff could be doubled with no increase in supervisory costs.

Small firms cannot use management specialists to best advantage. For example, a sales specialist working in a small plant may have to spend some of her time on functions outside of her area of expertise—marketing, personnel, and finance. A larger scale of operations would allow her to supervise marketing full time, while different specialists perform other managerial functions. Greater efficiency and lower unit costs are the net result.

Efficient Capital   Small firms often cannot afford the most efficient equipment. In many lines of production, such machinery is available only in very large and extremely expensive units. Furthermore, effective use of the equipment demands a high volume of production, and that again requires large-scale producers.

In the automobile industry, the most efficient fabrication method employs robotics and elaborate assembly-line equipment. Effective use of this equipment demands an annual output of perhaps 200,000 to 400,000 automobiles. Only very-large-scale producers can afford to purchase and use this equipment efficiently. The small-scale producer is faced with a dilemma. To fabricate automobiles using other equipment is inefficient and therefore more costly per unit. But so, too, is buying and underutilizing the equipment used by the large manufacturers. Because it cannot spread the high equipment cost over very many units of output, the small-scale producer will be stuck with high costs per unit of output.

Other Factors   Many products entail design and development costs, as well as other "start-up" costs, which must be incurred irrespective of projected sales. These costs decline per unit as output is increased. Similarly, advertising costs decline per auto, per computer, per stereo system, and per box of detergent as more units are produced and sold. Also, the firm's production and marketing expertise usually rises as it produces and sells more output. This *learning by doing* is a further source of economies of scale.

All these factors contribute to lower average total costs for the firm that is able to expand its scale of operations. Where economies of scale are possible, an increase in all resources of, say, 10 percent will cause a more-than-proportionate increase in output of, say, 20 percent. The result will be a decline in ATC.

In many U.S. manufacturing industries, economies of scale have been of great significance. Firms that have expanded their scale of operations to obtain economies of mass production have survived and flourished. Those unable to expand have become relatively high-cost producers, doomed to a struggle to survive.

© Getty Images   © Bryan Mullennix/Getty Images

Photo Op Economies of Scale

Economies of scale are extensive in the automobile industry, where the capital required is large and expensive and many workers are needed to perform the numerous, highly specialized tasks. Economies of scale in copying keys are exhausted at low levels of output; production usually occurs in small shops, the capital involved is relatively small and inexpensive, and a small number of workers (often only one) perform all of the labor and managerial functions of the business. There would be little, if any, cost advantage to establishing a key copying "factory" with hundreds of stations.

Applying the Analysis

The Verson Stamping Machine

In 1996 Verson (a U.S. firm located in Chicago) introduced a 49-foot-tall metal-stamping machine that is the size of a house and weighs as much as 12 locomotives. This $30 million machine, which cuts and sculpts raw sheets of steel into automobile hoods and fenders, enables automakers to make new parts in just 5 minutes compared with 8 hours for older stamping presses. A single machine is designed to make 5 million auto parts per year. So, to achieve the cost saving from the machine, an auto manufacturer must have sufficient auto production to use all these parts. By allowing the use of this cost-saving piece of equipment, large firm size achieves economies of scale.

Question:
Do you see any potential problems for a company that relies too heavily on just a few large machines for fabricating millions of its critical product parts?

Diseconomies of Scale   In time the expansion of a firm may lead to diseconomies and therefore higher average total costs.

The main factor causing **diseconomies of scale** is the difficulty of efficiently controlling and coordinating a firm's operations as it becomes a large-scale producer. In a small plant, a single key executive may make all the basic decisions for the plant's operation. Because of the firm's small size, the executive is close to the production line, understands the firm's operations, and can make efficient decisions because the small plant size requires only a relatively small amount of information to be examined and understood in optimizing production.

diseconomies of scale
Increases in the average total cost of producing a product as the firm expands the size of its operations (output) in the long run.

This neat picture changes as a firm grows. One person cannot assemble, digest, and understand all the information essential to decision making on a large scale. Authority must be delegated to many vice presidents, second vice presidents, and so forth. This expansion of the management hierarchy leads to problems of communication and cooperation, bureaucratic red tape, and the possibility that decisions will not be coordinated. At the same time, each new manager must be paid a salary. Thus, declining efficiency in making and executing decisions goes hand-in-hand with rising average total costs as bureaucracy expands beyond a certain point.

Also, in massive production facilities, workers may feel alienated from their employers and care little about working efficiently. Opportunities to shirk, by avoiding work in favor of on-the-job leisure, may be greater in large plants than in small ones. Countering worker alienation and shirking may require additional worker supervision, which increases costs.

Where diseconomies of scale are operative, an increase in all inputs of, say, 10 percent will cause a less-than-proportionate increase in output of, say, 5 percent. As a consequence, ATC will increase. The rising portion of the long-run cost curves in Figure 6.6 illustrates diseconomies of scale.

Constant Returns to Scale   In some industries there may exist a rather wide range of output between the output at which economies of scale end and the output at which diseconomies of scale begin. That is, there may be a range of **constant returns to scale** over which long-run average cost does not change. The q_1q_2 output range of Figure 6.6a is an example. Here a given percentage increase in all inputs of, say, 10 percent will cause a proportionate 10 percent increase in output. Thus, in this range ATC is constant.

Minimum Efficient Scale and Industry Structure

Economies and diseconomies of scale are an important determinant of an industry's structure. Here we introduce the concept of **minimum efficient scale (MES),** which is the lowest level of output at which a firm can minimize long-run average costs. In Figure 6.6a that level occurs at q_1 units of output. Because of the extended range of constant returns to scale, firms producing substantially greater outputs could also realize the minimum attainable long-run average costs. Specifically, firms within the q_1q_2 range would be equally efficient. So we would not be surprised to find an industry with such cost conditions to be populated by firms of quite different sizes. The apparel, banking, furniture, snowboard, wood products, food processing, and small-appliance industries are examples. With an extended range of constant returns to scale, relatively large and relatively small firms can coexist in an industry and be equally successful.

Compare this with Figure 6.6b, where economies of scale continue over a wide range of outputs and diseconomies of scale appear only at very high levels of output. This pattern of declining long-run average total cost occurs in the automobile, aluminum, steel, and other heavy industries. The same pattern holds in several of the new industries related to information technology, for example, computer microchips, operating system software, and Internet service provision. Given consumer demand, efficient production will be achieved with a few large-scale producers. Small firms cannot realize the minimum efficient scale and will not be able to compete.

Where economies of scale are few and diseconomies come into play quickly, the minimum efficient size occurs at a low level of output, as shown in Figure 6.6c. In such industries, a particular level of consumer demand will support a large number of relatively small producers. Many retail trades and some types of farming fall into this category. So do certain kinds of light manufacturing, such as the baking, clothing, and shoe industries. Fairly small firms are more efficient than larger-scale producers would be if they were present in such industries.

constant returns to scale
No changes in the average total cost of producing a product as the firm expands the size of its operations (output) in the long run.

minimum efficient scale (MES)
The lowest level of output at which a firm can minimize long-run average total cost.

Our point here is that the shape of the long-run average-total-cost curve is determined by technology and the economies and diseconomies of scale that result. The shape of the long-run ATC curve, in turn, can be significant in determining whether an industry is populated by a relatively large number of small firms or is dominated by a few large producers, or lies somewhere in between.

But we must be cautious in our assessment because industry structure does not depend on cost conditions alone. Government policies, the geographic size of markets, managerial strategy and skill, and other factors must be considered in explaining the structure of a particular industry.

> **ORIGIN OF THE IDEA**
> **O 6.4**
> Minimum efficient scale

Applying the Analysis

Aircraft Assembly Plants versus Concrete Plants

Why are there only three plants in the United States (all operated by Boeing) that produce large commercial aircraft and thousands of plants (owned by hundreds of firms) that produce ready-mix concrete? The simple answer is that MES is radically different in the two industries. Why is that? First, while economies of scale are extensive in assembling large commercial aircraft, they are only very modest in mixing concrete. Manufacturing airplanes is a complex process that requires huge facilities, thousands of workers, and very expensive, specialized machinery. Economies of scale extend to huge plant sizes. But mixing Portland cement, sand, gravel, and water to produce concrete requires only a handful of workers and relatively inexpensive equipment. Economies of scale are exhausted at a relatively small size.

The differing MES also derives from the vastly different sizes of the geographic markets. The market for commercial airplanes is global, and aircraft manufacturers can deliver new airplanes anywhere in the world by flying them there. In contrast, the geographic market for a concrete plant is roughly the 50-mile radius within which the concrete can be delivered before it "sets up." So in the ready-mix concrete industry, thousands of small concrete plants are positioned close to their customers in hundreds of small and large cities.

Question:
Speculate as to why the MES of firms in the Portland cement industry is considerably larger than the MES of single ready-mix concrete plants.

Summary

1. Corporations—the dominant form of business organizations—are legal entities, distinct and separate from the individuals who own them. They often have thousands, or even millions, of stockholders who jointly own them. They finance their operations and purchases of new plant and equipment partly through the issuance of stocks and bonds. Stocks are ownership shares of a corporation, and bonds are promises to repay a loan, usually at a set rate of interest.

2. A principal-agent problem may occur in corporations when the agents (managers) hired to represent the interest of the principals (stockholders) pursue their own objectives to the detriment of the objectives of the principals.

3. The economic cost of using a resource to produce a good or service is the value or worth that the resource would have had in its best alternative use. Economic costs include explicit costs, which flow to resources

owned and supplied by others, and implicit costs, which are payments for the use of self-owned and self-employed resources. One implicit cost is a normal profit to the entrepreneur. Economic profit occurs when total revenue exceeds total cost (= explicit costs + implicit costs, including a normal profit).

4. In the short run, a firm's plant capacity is fixed. The firm can use its plant more or less intensively by adding or subtracting units of variable resources, but it does not have sufficient time in the short run to alter plant size.

5. The law of diminishing returns describes what happens to output as a fixed plant is used more intensively. As successive units of a variable resource, such as labor, are added to a fixed plant, beyond some point the marginal product associated with each additional unit of a resource declines.

6. Because some resources are variable and others are fixed, costs can be classified as variable or fixed in the short run. Fixed costs are independent of the level of output; variable costs vary with output. The total cost of any output is the sum of fixed and variable costs at that output.

7. Average fixed, average variable, and average total costs are fixed, variable, and total costs per unit of output. Average fixed cost declines continuously as output increases because a fixed sum is being spread over a larger and larger number of units of production. A graph of average variable cost is U-shaped, reflecting the law of diminishing returns. Average total cost is the sum of average fixed and average variable costs; its graph is also U-shaped.

8. Marginal cost is the extra, or additional, cost of producing 1 more unit of output. It is the amount by which total cost and total variable cost change when 1 more or 1 less unit of output is produced. Graphically, the marginal-cost curve intersects the ATC and AVC curves at their minimum points.

9. The long run is a period of time sufficiently long for a firm to vary the amounts of all resources used, including plant size. In the long run, all costs are variable. The long-run ATC, or planning, curve is composed of segments of the short-run ATC curves, and it represents the various plant sizes a firm can construct in the long run.

10. The long-run ATC curve is generally U-shaped. Economies of scale are first encountered as a small firm expands. Greater specialization in the use of labor and management, the ability to use the most efficient equipment, and the spreading of start-up costs among more units of output all contribute to economies of scale. As the firm continues to grow, it will encounter diseconomies of scale stemming from the managerial complexities that accompany large-scale production. The ranges of output over which economies and diseconomies of scale occur in an industry are often an important determinant of the structure of that industry.

11. A firm's minimum efficient scale (MES) is the lowest level of output at which it can minimize its long-run average cost. In some industries, MES occurs at such low levels of output that numerous firms can populate the industry. In other industries, MES occurs at such high output levels that only a few firms can exist in the long run.

Terms and Concepts

stocks

bonds

limited liability

principal-agent problem

economic cost

explicit costs

implicit costs

accounting profit

normal profit

economic profit

short run

long run

total product (TP)

marginal product (MP)

average product (AP)

law of diminishing returns

fixed costs

variable costs

total cost

average fixed cost (AFC)

average variable cost (AVC)

average total cost (ATC)

marginal cost (MC)

economies of scale

diseconomies of scale

constant returns to scale

minimum efficient scale (MES)

Questions

1. Distinguish between a plant, a firm, and an industry. Contrast a vertically integrated firm, a horizontally integrated firm, and a conglomerate. Cite an example of a horizontally integrated firm from which you have recently made a purchase. **LO1**

2. What major advantages of corporations have given rise to their dominance as a form of business organization? **LO1**

3. What is the principal-agent problem as it relates to corporate managers and stockholders? How did firms try to solve this problem in the 1990s? In what way did the "solution" backfire on some firms? **LO1**

4. Distinguish between explicit and implicit costs, giving examples of each. What are some explicit and implicit costs of attending college? **LO2**

5. Distinguish between accounting profit, economic profit, and normal profit. Does accounting profit or economic profit determine how entrepreneurs allocate resources between different business ventures? Explain. **LO2**

6. Which of the following are short-run and which are long-run adjustments? **LO3**
   a. Wendy's builds a new restaurant.
   b. Harley-Davidson Corporation hires 200 more production workers.
   c. A farmer increases the amount of fertilizer used on his corn crop.
   d. An Alcoa aluminum plant adds a third shift of workers.

7. Complete the following table by calculating marginal product and average product from the data given: **LO3**

Inputs of Labor	Total Product	Marginal Product	Average Product
0	0	_____	
1	15	_____	_____
2	34	_____	_____
3	51	_____	_____
4	65	_____	_____
5	74	_____	_____
6	80	_____	_____
7	83	_____	_____
8	82	_____	_____

Explain why marginal product eventually declines and ultimately becomes negative. What bearing does the law of diminishing returns have on marginal costs? Be specific.

8. Why can the distinction between fixed costs and variable costs be made in the short run? Classify the following as fixed or variable costs: advertising expenditures, fuel, interest on company-issued bonds, shipping charges, payments for raw materials, real estate taxes, executive salaries, insurance premiums, wage payments, sales taxes, and rental payments on leased office machinery. **LO4**

9. A firm has fixed costs of $60 and variable costs as indicated in the accompanying table. **LO4**
   Complete the table and check your calculations by referring to question 3 at the end of Chapter 7.
   a. Graph the AFC, ATC, and MC curves. Why does the AFC curve slope continuously downward? Why does the MC curve eventually slope upward? Why does the MC curve intersect the ATC curve at its minimum point?
   b. Explain how the location of each curve graphed in question 9a would be altered if (1) total fixed cost had been $100 rather than $60 and (2) total variable cost had been $10 less at each level of output.

10. Indicate how each of the following would shift the (1) marginal-cost curve, (2) average-variable-cost curve, (3) average-fixed-cost curve, and (4) average-total-cost curve of a manufacturing firm. In each case, specify the direction of the shift. **LO4**
    a. A reduction in business property taxes.
    b. An increase in the hourly wage rates of production workers.
    c. A decrease in the price of electricity.
    d. An increase in transportation costs.

11. Suppose a firm has only three possible plant-size options, represented by the ATC curves shown in the accompanying figure. What plant size will the firm choose

Table for question 9

Total Product	Total Fixed Cost	Total Variable Cost	Total Cost	Average Fixed Cost	Average Variable Cost	Average Total Cost	Marginal Cost
0	$_____	$ 0	$___			$_____	
1	_____	45	___	$_____	$_____	_____	$_____
2	_____	85	___	_____	_____	_____	_____
3	_____	120	___	_____	_____	_____	_____
4	_____	150	___	_____	_____	_____	_____
5	_____	185	___	_____	_____	_____	_____
6	_____	225	___	_____	_____	_____	_____
7	_____	270	___	_____	_____	_____	_____
8	_____	325	___	_____	_____	_____	_____
9	_____	390	___	_____	_____	_____	_____
10	_____	465	___	_____	_____	_____	_____

in producing (a) 50, (b) 130, (c) 160, and (d) 250 units of output? Draw the firm's long-run average-cost curve on the diagram and describe this curve. **LO5**

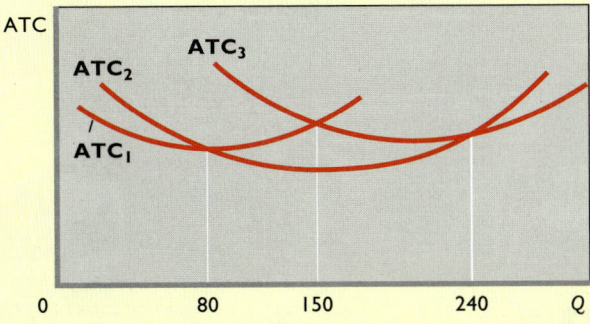

12. Use the concepts of economies and diseconomies of scale to explain the shape of a firm's long-run ATC curve. What is the concept of minimum efficient scale? What bearing can the shape of the long-run ATC curve have on the structure of an industry? **LO5**

Problems

1. Gomez runs a small pottery firm. He hires one helper at $12,000 per year, pays annual rent of $5000 for his shop, and spends $20,000 per year on materials. He has $40,000 of his own funds invested in equipment (pottery wheels, kilns, and so forth) that could earn him $4000 per year if alternatively invested. He has been offered $15,000 per year to work as a potter for a competitor. He estimates his entrepreneurial talents are worth $3000 per year. Total annual revenue from pottery sales is $72,000. Calculate the accounting profit and the economic profit for Gomez's pottery firm. **LO2**

2. Imagine you have some workers and some handheld computers that you can use to take inventory at a warehouse. There are diminishing returns to taking inventory. If one worker uses one computer, he can inventory 100 items per hour. Two workers sharing a computer can together inventory 150 items per hour. Three workers sharing a computer can together inventory 160 items per hour. And four or more workers sharing a computer can together inventory fewer than 160 items per hour. Computers cost $100 each and you must pay each worker $25 per hour. If you assign one worker per computer, what is the cost of inventorying a single item? What if you assign two workers per computer? Three? How many workers per computer should you assign if you wish to minimize the cost of inventorying a single item? **LO3**

3. You are a newspaper publisher. You are in the middle of a one-year rental contract for your factory that requires you to pay $500,000 per month, and you have contractual labor obligations of $1 million per month that you can't get out of. You also have a marginal printing cost of $.25 per paper as well as a marginal delivery cost of $.10 per paper. If sales fall by 20 percent from 1 million papers per month to 800,000 papers per month, what happens to the AFC per paper, the MC per paper, and the minimum amount that you must charge to break even on these costs? **LO4**

4. There are economies of scale in ranching, especially with regard to fencing land. Suppose that barbed-wire fencing costs $10,000 per mile to set up. How much would it cost to fence a single property whose area is one square mile if that property also happens to be perfectly square, with sides that are each one mile long? How much would it cost to fence exactly four such properties, which together would contain four square miles of area? Now, consider how much it would cost to fence in four square miles of ranch land if, instead, it comes as a single large square that is two miles long on each side. Which is more costly—fencing in the four, one-square-mile properties or the single four-square-mile property? **LO5**

FURTHER TEST YOUR KNOWLEDGE AT
www.brue3e.com

At the text's Online Learning Center, **www.brue3e.com,** you will find one or more web-based questions that require information from the Internet to answer. We urge you to check them out, since they will familiarize you with websites that may be helpful in other courses and perhaps even in your career. The OLC also features multiple-choice quizzes that give instant feedback and provides other helpful ways to further test your knowledge of the chapter.

CHAPTER SEVEN

Pure Competition

After reading this chapter, you should be able to:

1. Give the names and summarize the main characteristics of the four basic market models.
2. List the conditions required for purely competitive markets.
3. Describe how purely competitive firms maximize profits or minimize losses.
4. Explain why the marginal-cost curve and supply curve of competitive firms are identical.
5. Discuss how industry entry and exit produce economic efficiency.
6. Identify the differences between constant-cost, increasing-cost, and decreasing-cost industries.

In Chapter 4 we examined the relationship between product demand and total revenue, and in Chapter 6 we discussed businesses and their production costs. Now we want to connect revenues and costs to see how a business decides what price to charge and how much output to produce. But a firm's decisions concerning price and production depend greatly on the character of the industry in which it is operating. There is no "average" or "typical" industry. At one extreme is a single producer that dominates the market; at the other extreme are industries in which thousands of firms each produces a tiny fraction of market supply. Between these extremes are many other industries.

Since we cannot examine each industry individually, our approach will be to look at four basic *models* of market structure. Together, these models will help you understand how price, output, and profit are determined in the many product markets in the economy. They also will help you evaluate the efficiency or inefficiency of those markets. Finally, these four models will provide a crucial background for assessing public policies (such as antitrust policy) relating to certain firms and industries.

Four Market Models

Economists group industries into four distinct market structures: pure competition, pure monopoly, monopolistic competition, and oligopoly. These four market models differ in several respects: the number of firms in the industry, whether those firms produce a standardized product or try to distinguish their products from those of other firms, and how easy or how difficult it is for firms to enter the industry.

The four models are as follows, presented in order of degree of competition (most to least):

- *Pure competition* involves a very large number of firms producing a standardized product (that is, a product like cotton for which each producer's output is virtually identical to that of every other producer). New firms can enter or exit the industry very easily.
- *Monopolistic competition* is characterized by a relatively large number of sellers producing differentiated products (clothing, furniture, books). Present in this model is widespread *nonprice competition*, a selling strategy in which one firm tries to distinguish its product or service from all competing products on the basis of attributes such as design and workmanship (an approach called *product differentiation*). Either entry to or exit from monopolistically competitive industries is quite easy.
- *Oligopoly* involves only a few sellers of a standardized or differentiated product, so each firm is affected by the decisions of its rivals and must take those decisions into account in determining its own price and output.

© Getty Images

© PRNewsFoto/Dove

Photo Op Standardized versus Differentiated Products

Wheat is an example of a standardized product, whereas Dove shampoo is an example of a differentiated product.

- *Pure monopoly* is a market structure in which one firm is the sole seller of a product or service for which there is no good substitute (for example, a local electric utility or patented medical device). Since the entry of additional firms is blocked, one firm constitutes the entire industry. The pure monopolist produces a single unique product, so product differentiation is not an issue.

Pure Competition: Characteristics and Occurrence

pure competition
A market structure in which a very large number of firms produce a standardized product and there are no restrictions on entry.

Let's take a fuller look at **pure competition,** the focus of the remainder of this chapter:

- *Very large numbers* A basic feature of a purely competitive market is the presence of a large number of independently acting sellers, often offering their products in large national or international markets. Examples: markets for farm commodities, the stock market, and the foreign exchange market.
- *Standardized product* Purely competitive firms produce a standardized (identical or homogeneous) product. As long as the price is the same, consumers will be indifferent about which seller to buy the product from. Buyers view the products of firms B, C, D, and E as perfect substitutes for the product of firm A. Because purely competitive firms sell standardized products, they make no attempt to differentiate their products and do not engage in other forms of nonprice competition.
- *"Price takers"* In a purely competitive market, individual firms do not exert control over product price. Each firm produces such a small fraction of total output that increasing or decreasing its output will not perceptibly influence total supply or, therefore, product price. In short, the competitive firm is a **price taker:** It cannot change market price; it can only adjust to it. That means that the individual competitive producer is at the mercy of the market. Asking a price higher than the market price would be futile. Consumers will not buy from firm A at $2.05 when its 9999 competitors are selling an identical product, and therefore a perfect substitute, at $2 per unit. Conversely, because firm A can sell as much as it chooses at $2 per unit, it has no reason to charge a lower price, say, $1.95. Doing that would shrink its profit.

price taker
A competitive firm that cannot change the market price, but can only accept it as "given" and adjust to it.

- *Free entry and exit* New firms can freely enter and existing firms can freely leave purely competitive industries. No significant legal, technological, financial, or other obstacles prohibit new firms from selling their output in any competitive market.

Although pure competition is somewhat rare in the real world, this market model is highly relevant to several industries. In particular, we can learn much about markets for agricultural goods, fish products, foreign exchange, basic metals, and stock shares by studying the pure-competition model. Also, pure competition is a meaningful starting point for any discussion of how prices and output are determined. Moreover, the operation of a purely competitive economy provides a norm for evaluating the efficiency of the real-world economy.

Demand as Seen by a Purely Competitive Seller

To develop a model of pure competition, we first examine demand from a purely competitive seller's viewpoint and see how it affects revenue. This seller might be a wheat farmer, a strawberry grower, a sheep rancher, a foreign-currency broker, or some other pure competitor. Because each purely competitive firm offers only a negligible fraction of total market supply, it must accept the price predetermined by the market. Pure competitors are price takers, not price makers.

Perfectly Elastic Demand

The demand schedule faced by the *individual firm* in a purely competitive industry is perfectly elastic at the market price, as demonstrated in Figure 7.1. As shown in column 1 of the table in Figure 7.1, the market price is $131. The firm represented cannot obtain a higher price by restricting its output, nor does it need to lower its price to increase its sales volume. Columns 1 and 2 show that the firm can produce and sell as many or as few units as it likes at the market price of $131.

We are *not* saying that *market* demand is perfectly elastic in a competitive market. Rather, market demand graphs as a downsloping curve. An entire industry (all firms producing a particular product) can affect price by changing industry output. For example, all firms, acting independently but simultaneously, can increase price by reducing output. But the individual competitive firm cannot do that because its output represents such a small fraction of its industry's total output. For the individual competitive firm, the market price is therefore a fixed value at which it can sell as many or as few units as it cares to. Graphically, this implies that the individual competitive firm's demand curve will plot as a straight, horizontal line such as *D* in Figure 7.1.

Average, Total, and Marginal Revenue

The firm's demand schedule is also its average-revenue schedule. Price per unit to the purchaser is also revenue per unit, or average revenue, to the seller. To say that all buyers must pay $131 per unit is to say that the revenue per unit, or **average revenue,** received by the seller is $131. Price and average revenue are the same thing.

The **total revenue** for each sales level is found by multiplying price by the corresponding quantity the firm can sell. (Column 1 multiplied by column 2 in the table in Figure 7.1 yields column 3.) In this case, total revenue increases by a constant amount, $131, for each additional unit of sales. Each unit sold adds exactly its constant price to total revenue.

When a firm is pondering a change in its output, it will consider how its total revenue will change as a result. **Marginal revenue** is the change in total revenue (or the extra revenue) that results from selling 1 more unit of output. In column 3 of the table in Figure 7.1, total revenue is zero when zero units are sold. The first unit of output sold increases total revenue from zero to $131, so marginal revenue for that unit is $131. The second unit sold increases total revenue from $131 to $262, and marginal revenue is again $131. Note in column 4 that marginal revenue is a constant $131, as is price. *In pure competition, marginal revenue and price are equal.*

Figure 7.1 shows the purely competitive firm's total-revenue, demand, marginal-revenue, and average-revenue curves. Total revenue (TR) is a straight line that slopes

average revenue
Total revenue from the sale of a product divided by the quantity of the product sold.

total revenue
The total number of dollars received by a firm from the sale of a product.

marginal revenue
The change in total revenue that results from selling 1 more unit of a firm's product.

FIGURE 7.1

A purely competitive firm's demand and revenue curves. The demand curve (*D*) of a purely competitive firm is a horizontal line (perfectly elastic) because the firm can sell as much output as it wants at the market price (here, $131). Because each additional unit sold increases total revenue by the amount of the price, the firm's total-revenue curve (TR) is a straight upward-sloping line and its marginal-revenue curve (MR) coincides with the firm's demand curve. The average-revenue curve (AR) also coincides with the demand curve.

Firm's Demand Schedule		Firm's Revenue Data	
(1) **Product Price (*P*)** **(Average Revenue)**	**(2)** **Quantity** **Demanded (*Q*)**	**(3)** **Total Revenue** **(TR), (1) × (2)**	**(4)** **Marginal** **Revenue (MR)**
$131	0	$ 0	
131	1	131	$131
131	2	262	131
131	3	393	131
131	4	524	131
131	5	655	131
131	6	786	131
131	7	917	131
131	8	1048	131
131	9	1179	131
131	10	1310	131

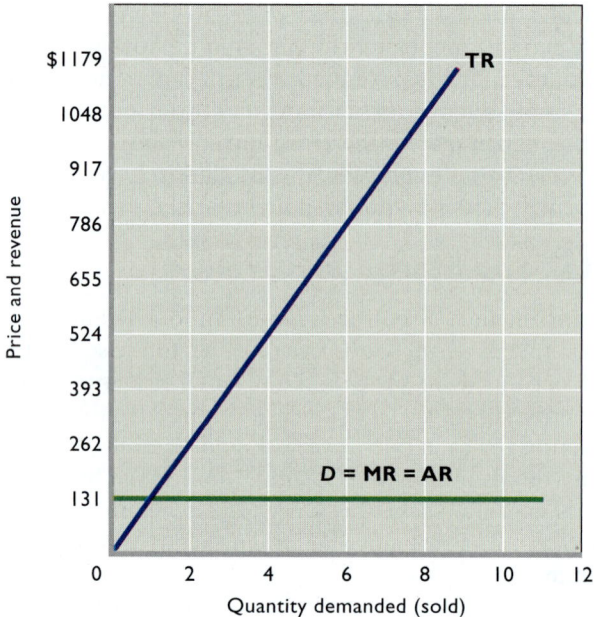

upward to the right. Its slope is constant because each extra unit of sales increases TR by $131. The demand curve (*D*) is horizontal, indicating perfect price elasticity. The marginal-revenue curve (MR) coincides with the demand curve because the product price (and hence MR) is constant. The average revenue equals price and therefore also coincides with the demand curve.

Profit Maximization in the Short Run

Because the purely competitive firm is a price taker, it cannot attempt to maximize its profit by raising or lowering the price it charges. With its price set by supply and demand in the overall market, the only variable that the firm can control is its output. As a result, the purely competitive firm attempts to maximize its economic profit (or minimize its economic loss) by adjusting its *output*. And, in the short run, the firm has a fixed plant. Thus, it can adjust its output only through changes in the amount of variable resources (materials, labor) it uses. It adjusts its variable resources to achieve the output level that maximizes its profit.

More specifically, the firm compares the amounts that each *additional* unit of output would add to total revenue and to total cost. In other words, the firm compares the *marginal revenue* (MR) and the *marginal cost* (MC) of each successive unit of output. Assuming that producing is preferable to shutting down, the firm should produce any unit of output whose marginal revenue exceeds its marginal cost because the firm would gain more in revenue from selling that unit than it would add to its costs by producing it. Conversely, if the marginal cost of a unit of output exceeds its marginal revenue, the firm should not produce that unit. Producing it would add more to costs than to revenue, and profit would decline or loss would increase.

In the initial stages of production, where output is relatively low, marginal revenue will usually (but not always) exceed marginal cost. So it is profitable to produce through this range of output. But at later stages of production, where output is relatively high, rising marginal costs will exceed marginal revenue. Obviously, a profit-maximizing firm will want to avoid output levels in that range. Separating these two production ranges is a unique point at which marginal revenue equals marginal cost. This point is the key to the output-determining rule: *In the short run, the firm will maximize profit or minimize loss by producing the output at which marginal revenue equals marginal cost (as long as producing is preferable to shutting down)*. This profit-maximizing guide is known as the **MR = MC rule**. (For most sets of MR and MC data, MR and MC will be precisely equal at a fractional level of output. In such instances the firm should produce the last complete unit of output for which MR exceeds MC.)

Keep in mind these three features of the MR = MC rule:

MR = MC rule
A method of determining the total output at which economic profit is at a maximum (or losses at a minimum).

- As noted, the rule applies only if producing is preferable to shutting down. We will show shortly that if marginal revenue does not equal or exceed average variable cost, the firm will shut down rather than produce the amount of output at which MR = MC.
- The rule is an accurate guide to profit maximization for all firms whether they are purely competitive, monopolistic, monopolistically competitive, or oligopolistic.
- We can restate the rule as $P = MC$ when applied to a purely competitive firm. Because the demand schedule faced by a competitive seller is perfectly elastic at the going market price, product price and marginal revenue are equal. So under pure competition (and only under pure competition), we may substitute P for MR in the rule: *When producing is preferable to shutting down, the competitive firm that wants to maximize its profit or minimize its loss should produce at that point where price equals marginal cost ($P = MC$)*.

Now let's apply the MR = MC rule or, because we are considering pure competition, the $P = MC$ rule.

Profit Maximization

The first five columns in the table in Figure 7.2 reproduce the AFC, AVC, ATC, and MC data derived for our product in Chapter 6. Here, we will compare the marginal-cost data of column 5 with price (equals marginal revenue) for each unit of output. Suppose first that the market price, and therefore marginal revenue, is $131, as shown in column 6.

FIGURE 7.2

Short-run profit maximizing for a purely competitive firm. The MR = MC output enables the purely competitive firm to maximize profits or to minimize losses. In this case MR (= P in pure competition) and MC are equal at 9 units of output, Q. There P exceeds the average total cost A = $97.78, so the firm realizes an economic profit of P − A per unit. The total economic profit is represented by the green rectangle and is 9 × (P − A).

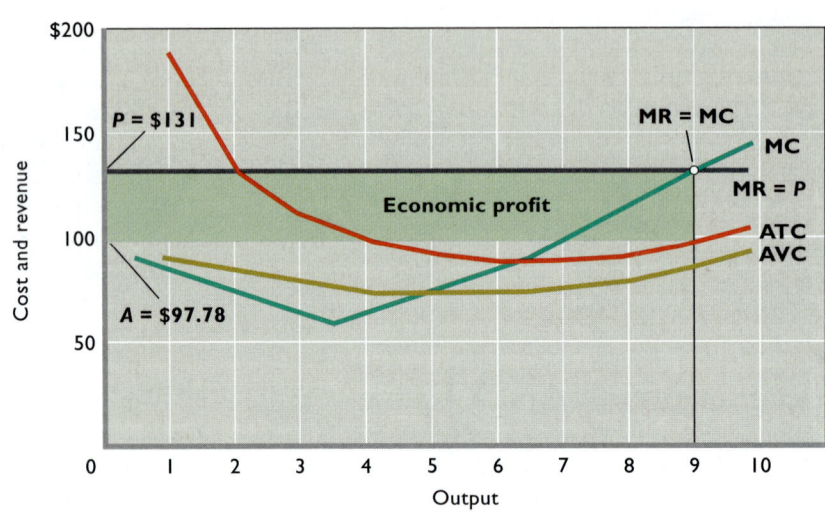

(1)	(2)	(3)	(4)	(5)	(6)	(7)
Total Product (Output)	Average Fixed Cost (AFC)	Average Variable Cost (AVC)	Average Total Cost (ATC)	Marginal Cost (MC)	$ 131 Price = Marginal Revenue (MR)	Total Economic Profit (+) or Loss (−)
0						$−100
				$ 90	$131	
1	$100.00	$90.00	$190.00			−59
				80	131	
2	50.00	85.00	135.00			−8
				70	131	
3	33.33	80.00	113.33			+53
				60	131	
4	25.00	75.00	100.00			+124
				70	131	
5	20.00	74.00	94.00			+185
				80	131	
6	16.67	75.00	91.67			+236
				90	131	
7	14.29	77.14	91.43			+277
				110	131	
8	12.50	81.25	93.75			+298
				130	131	
9	11.11	86.67	97.78			+299
				150	131	
10	10.00	93.00	103.00			+280

What is the profit-maximizing output? Every unit of output up to and including the ninth unit represents greater marginal revenue than marginal cost of output. Each of the first 9 units therefore adds to the firm's profit and should be produced. The firm, however, should not produce the tenth unit. It would add more to cost ($150) than to revenue ($131).

We can calculate the economic profit realized by producing 9 units from the average-total-cost data. Price ($131) multiplied by output (9) yields total revenue of $1179. Multiplying average total cost ($97.78) by output (9) gives us total cost of $880.[1] The difference of $299 (= $1179 − $880) is the economic profit. Clearly, this firm will prefer to operate rather than shut down.

An alternative, and perhaps easier, way to calculate the economic profit is to determine the profit per unit by subtracting the average total cost ($97.78) from the product price ($131). Then multiply the difference (a per-unit profit of $33.22) by output (9). Take some time

now to verify the numbers in column 7. You will find that any output other than that which adheres to the MR = MC rule will yield either profits below $299 or losses.

Figure 7.2 also shows price (= MR) and marginal cost graphically. Price equals marginal cost at the profit-maximizing output of 9 units. There the per-unit economic profit is $P − A$, where P is the market price and A is the average total cost of 9 units of output. The total economic profit is $9 \times (P − A)$, shown by the green rectangular area.

Loss Minimization and Shutdown

Now let's assume that the market price is $81 rather than $131. Should the firm still produce? If so, how much? And what will be the resulting profit or loss? The answers, respectively, are "Yes," "Six units," and "A loss of $64."

The first five columns of the table in Figure 7.3 are the same as the first five columns of the table in Figure 7.2. But column 6 of the table in Figure 7.3 shows the new price (equal to MR) of $81. Looking at columns 5 and 6, notice that the first unit of output adds $90 to total cost but only $81 to total revenue. One might conclude: "Don't produce—close down!" But that would be hasty. Remember that in the very early stages of production, marginal product is low, making marginal cost unusually high. The price–marginal cost relationship improves with increased production. For units 2 through 6, price exceeds marginal cost. Each of these 5 units adds more to revenue than to cost, and as shown in column 7, they decrease the total loss. Together they more than compensate for the "loss" taken on the first unit. Beyond 6 units, however, MC exceeds MR (= P). The firm should therefore produce 6 units. In general, the profit-seeking producer should always compare marginal revenue (or price under pure competition) with the rising portion of the marginal-cost schedule or curve.

Loss Minimization   Will production be profitable? No, because at 6 units of output the average total cost of $91.67 exceeds the price of $81 by $10.67 per unit. If we multiply that by the 6 units of output, we find the firm's total loss is $64. Alternatively,

---

[1]Most of the unit-cost data are rounded figures from the total-cost figures presented in the previous chapter. Therefore, economic profits calculated from the unit-cost figures will typically vary by a few cents from the profits determined by subtracting actual total cost from total revenue. Here we simply ignore the few-cents differentials.

FIGURE 7.3

Short-run loss minimization for a purely competitive firm. If price *P* exceeds the minimum AVC (here, $74 at *Q* = 5) but is less than ATC, the MR = MC output (here, 6 units) will permit the firm to minimize its losses. In this instance the loss is *A* − *P* per unit, where *A* is the average total cost at 6 units of output. The total loss is shown by the red area and is equal to 6 × (*A* − *P*).

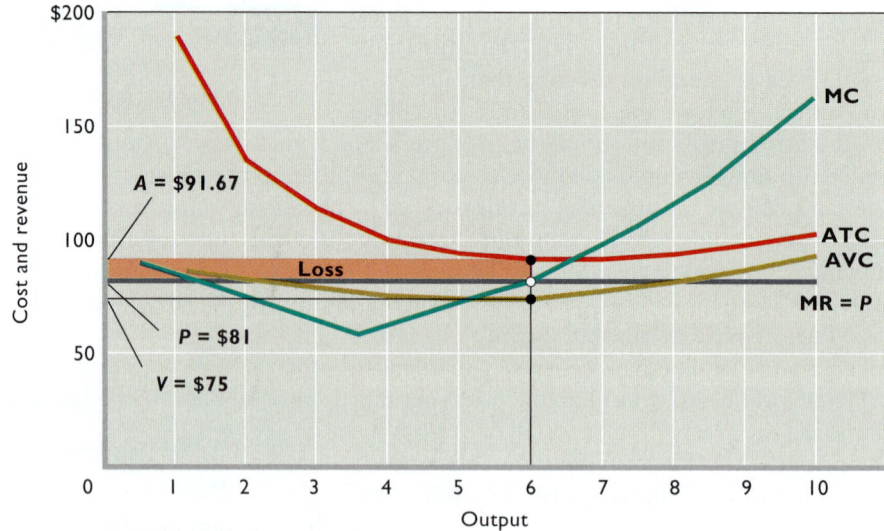

(1) Total Product (Output)	(2) Average Fixed Cost (AFC)	(3) Average Variable Cost (AVC)	(4) Average Total Cost (ATC)	(5) Marginal Cost (MC)	(6) $81 Price = Marginal Revenue (MR)	(7) Profit (+) or Loss (−), $81 Price
0						$−100
1	$100.00	$90.00	$190.00	$ 90	$81	−109
2	50.00	85.00	135.00	80	81	−108
3	33.33	80.00	113.33	70	81	− 97
4	25.00	75.00	100.00	60	81	− 76
5	20.00	74.00	94.00	70	81	− 65
6	16.67	75.00	91.67	80	81	−64
7	14.29	77.14	91.43	90	81	− 73
8	12.50	81.25	93.75	110	81	−102
9	11.11	86.67	97.78	130	81	−151
10	10.00	93.00	103.00	150	81	−220

comparing the total revenue of $486 (= 6 × $81) with the total cost of $550 (= 6 × $91.67), we see again that the firm's loss is $64.

Then why produce? Because this loss is less than the firm's $100 of fixed costs, which is the $100 loss the firm would incur in the short run by closing down. The firm receives enough revenue per unit ($81) to cover its average variable costs of $75 and also provide $6 per unit, or a total of $36, to apply against fixed costs. Therefore, the firm's loss is only $64 (= $100 − $36), not $100.

This loss-minimizing case is illustrated in the graph in Figure 7.3. Wherever price *P* exceeds AVC but is less than ATC, the firm can pay part, but not all, of its fixed costs

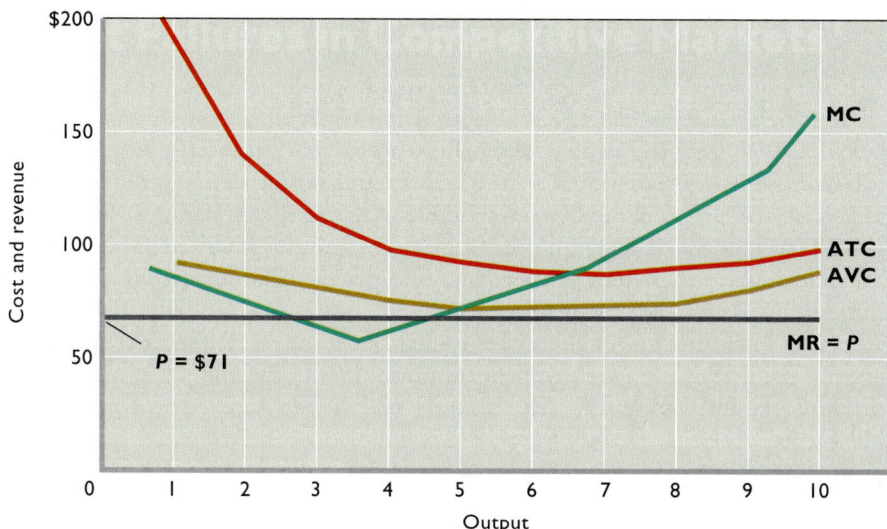

FIGURE 7.4
The short-run shut-down case for a purely competitive firm. If price *P* (here, $71) falls below the minimum AVC (here, $74 at *Q* = 5), the competitive firm will minimize its losses in the short run by shutting down. There is no level of output at which the firm can produce and realize a loss smaller than its total fixed cost.

(1) Total Product (Output)	(2) Average Fixed Cost (AFC)	(3) Average Variable Cost (AVC)	(4) Average Total Cost (ATC)	(5) Marginal Cost (MC)	(6) $71 Price = Marginal Revenue (MR)	(7) Profit (+) or Loss (−), $81 Price
0						$−100
1	$100.00	$90.00	$190.00	$ 90	$71	−119
2	50.00	85.00	135.00	80	71	−128
3	33.33	80.00	113.33	70	71	−127
4	25.00	75.00	100.00	60	71	−116
5	20.00	74.00	94.00	70	71	−115
6	16.67	75.00	91.67	80	71	−124
7	14.29	77.14	91.43	90	71	−143
8	12.50	81.25	93.75	110	71	−182
9	11.11	86.67	97.78	130	71	−241
10	10.00	93.00	103.00	150	71	−320

by producing. The firm minimizes its loss by producing the output at which MC = MR (here, 6 units). At that output, each unit contributes *P* − *V* to covering fixed cost, where *V* is the AVC at 6 units of output. The per-unit loss is *A* − *P* = $10.67, and the total loss is 6 × (*A* − *P*), or $64, as shown by the red area.

Shutdown   Suppose now that the market yields a price of only $71. Should the firm produce? No, because at every output level the firm's average variable cost is greater than the price (compare columns 3 and 6 of the table in Figure 7.4). The smallest loss the firm can incur by producing is greater than the $100 fixed cost it will lose by shutting down (as shown by column 7). The best action is to shut down.

You can see this shutdown situation in the graph in Figure 7.4, where the MR = P line lies below AVC at all points. The $71 price comes closest to covering average variable costs at the MR (= P) = MC output of 5 units. But even here, the table reveals that price or revenue per unit would fall short of average variable cost by $3 (= $74 − $71). By producing at the MR (= P) = MC output, the firm would lose its $100 worth of fixed cost plus $15 (= $3 of variable cost on each of the 5 units), for a total loss of $115. This compares unfavorably with the $100 fixed-cost loss the firm would incur by shutting down and producing no output. So it will make sense for the firm to shut down rather than produce at a $71 price—or at any price less than the minimum average variable cost of $74.

The shutdown case reminds us of the qualifier to our MR (= P) = MC rule. A competitive firm will maximize profit or minimize loss in the short run by producing that output at which MR (= P) = MC, *provided that market price exceeds minimum average variable cost.*

Applying the Analysis

The Still There Motel

Have you ever driven by a poorly maintained business facility and wondered why the owner does not either fix up the property or go out of business? The somewhat surprising reason is that it may be unprofitable to improve the facility yet profitable to continue for a time to operate the business as it deteriorates. Seeing why will aid your understanding of the "stay open or shut down" decision facing firms experiencing declining demand.

Consider the Still There Motel on Old Highway North, Anytown, USA. The owner built the motel on the basis of traffic patterns and competition existing several decades ago. But as interstate highways were built, the motel found itself located on a relatively untraveled stretch of road. Also, it faced severe competition from "chain" motels located much closer to the interstate highway.

As demand and revenue fell, Still There moved from profitability to loss (P < ATC). But at first its room rates and annual revenue were sufficient to cover its total variable costs and contribute some to the payment of fixed costs such as insurance and property taxes (P > AVC). By staying open, Still There lost less than it would have if it shut down. But since its total revenue did not cover its total costs (or P < ATC), the owner realized that something must be done in the long run. The owner decided to lower average total costs by reducing annual maintenance. In effect, the owner opted to allow the motel to deteriorate as a way of regaining temporary profitability.

This renewed profitability of Still There cannot last because in time no further reduction in maintenance costs will be possible. The further deterioration of the motel structure will produce even lower room rates, and therefore even less total revenue. The owner of Still There knows that sooner or later total revenue will again fall below total cost (or P will again fall below ATC), even with an annual maintenance expense of zero. When that occurs, the owner will close down the business, tear down the structure, and sell the vacant property. But, in the meantime, the motel is still there—open, deteriorating, and profitable.

Question:
Why might even a well-maintained, profitable motel shut down in the long run if the land on which it is located becomes extremely valuable due to surrounding economic development?

Marginal Cost and Short-Run Supply

In the preceding section, we simply selected three different prices and asked what quantity the profit-seeking competitive firm, faced with certain costs, would choose to offer in the market at each price. This set of product prices and corresponding quantities supplied constitutes part of the supply schedule for the competitive firm.

Table 7.1 summarizes the supply schedule data for those three prices ($131, $81, and $71) and four others. This table confirms the direct relationship between product price and quantity supplied that we identified in Chapter 3. Note first that the firm will not produce at price $61 or $71 because both are less than the $74 minimum AVC. Then note that quantity supplied increases as price increases. Observe finally that economic profit is higher at higher prices.

Generalized Depiction

Figure 7.5 generalizes the MR = MC rule and the relationship between short-run production costs and the firm's supply behavior. The ATC, AVC, and MC curves are shown, along with several marginal-revenue lines drawn at possible market prices. Let's observe quantity supplied at each of these prices:

- Price P_1 is below the firm's minimum average variable cost, so at this price the firm won't operate at all. Quantity supplied will be zero, as it will be at all other prices below P_2.
- Price P_2 is just equal to the minimum average variable cost. The firm will supply Q_2 units of output (where MR_2 = MC) and just cover its total variable cost. Its loss will equal its total fixed cost. (Actually, the firm would be indifferent as to shutting down or supplying Q_2 units of output, but we assume it produces.)
- At price P_3 the firm will supply Q_3 units of output to minimize its short-run losses. At any other price between P_2 and P_4 the firm will minimize its losses by producing and supplying the MR = MC quantity.
- The firm will just break even at price P_4. There it will supply Q_4 units of output (where MR_4 = MC), earning a normal profit but not an economic profit. (Recall that a normal profit is a cost and included in the cost curves.) Total revenue will just cover total cost, including a normal profit, because the revenue per unit ($MR_4 = P_4$) and the total cost per unit (ATC) are the same.
- At price P_5 the firm will realize an economic profit by producing and supplying Q_5 units of output. In fact, at any price above P_4, the firm will obtain economic profit by producing to the point where MR (= P) = MC.

Price	Quantity Supplied	Maximum Profit (+) or Minimum Loss (−)
$151	10	$+480
131	9	+299
111	8	+138
91	7	−3
81	6	−64
71	0	−100
61	0	−100

TABLE 7.1

The Supply Schedule of a Competitive Firm Confronted with the Cost Data in the Table in Figure 7.2

FIGURE 7.5
The *P* = MC rule and the competitive firm's short-run supply curve. Application of the *P* = MC rule, as modified by the shut-down case, reveals that the (solid) segment of the firm's MC curve that lies above AVC is the firm's short-run supply curve.

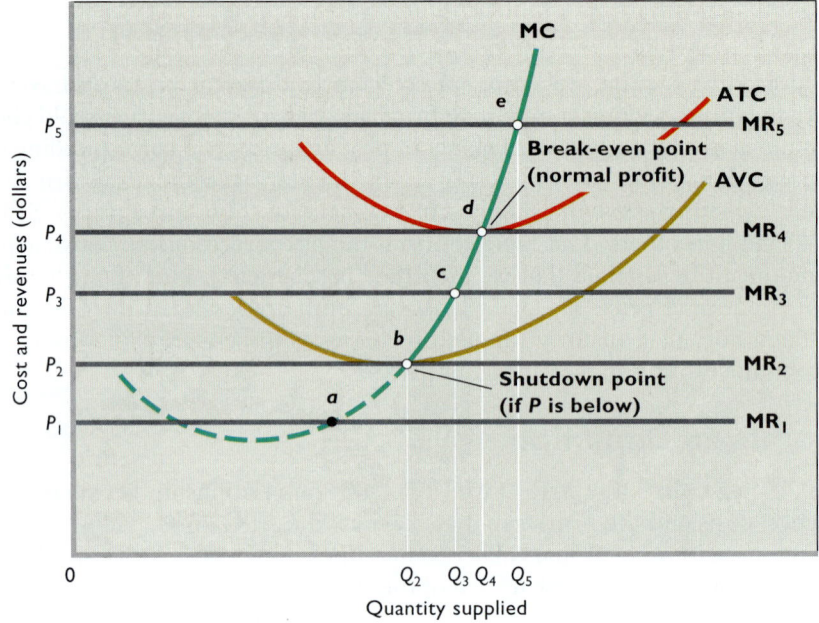

Note that each of the MR (= *P*) = MC intersection points labeled *b, c, d,* and *e* in Figure 7.5 indicates a possible product price (on the vertical axis) and the corresponding quantity that the firm would supply at that price (on the horizontal axis). Thus, points such as these are on the upsloping supply curve of the competitive firm. Note too that quantity supplied would be zero at any price below the minimum average variable cost (AVC). *We can conclude that the portion of the firm's marginal-cost curve lying above its average-variable-cost curve is its short-run supply curve.* In Figure 7.5, the solid segment of the marginal-cost curve MC *is* this firm's **short-run supply curve.** It tells us the amount of output the firm will supply at each price in a series of prices. It slopes upward because of the law of diminishing returns.

short-run supply curve
A curve that shows the quantity of a product a firm in a purely competitive industry will offer to sell at various prices in the short run.

Table 7.2 summarizes the MR = MC approach to determining the competitive firm's profit-maximizing output level. It also shows the conditions under which a firm should decide to produce, and the circumstances that will generate economic profits.

Firm and Industry: Equilibrium Price

In the preceding section we established the competitive firm's short-run supply curve by applying the MR (= *P*) = MC rule. But which of the various possible prices will actually be the market equilibrium price?

TABLE 7.2

Output Determination in Pure Competition in the Short Run

Question	Answer
Should this firm produce?	Yes, if price is equal to, or greater than, minimum average variable cost. This means that the firm is profitable or that its losses are less than its fixed cost.
What quantity should this firm produce?	Produce where MR (= *P*) = MC; there, profit is maximized (TR exceeds TC by a maximum amount) or loss is minimized.
Will production result in economic profit?	Yes, if price exceeds average total cost (so that TR exceeds TC). No, if average total cost exceeds price (so that TC exceeds TR).

(1) Quantity Supplied, Single Firm	(2) Total Quantity Supplied, 1000 Firms	(3) Product Price	(4) Total Quantity Demanded
10	10,000	$151	4,000
9	9,000	131	6,000
8	**8,000**	**111**	**8,000**
7	7,000	91	9,000
6	6,000	81	11,000
0	0	71	13,000
0	0	61	16,000

TABLE 7.3

Firm and Market Supply and Market Demand

From Chapter 3 we know that the market equilibrium price will be the price at which the total quantity supplied of the product equals the total quantity demanded. So to determine the equilibrium price, we first need to obtain a total supply schedule and a total demand schedule. We find the total supply schedule by assuming a particular number of firms in the industry and supposing that each firm has the same individual supply schedule as the firm represented in Figure 7.5. Then we sum the quantities supplied at each price level to obtain the total (or market) supply schedule. Columns 1 and 3 in Table 7.3 repeat the supply schedule for the individual competitive firm, as derived in Table 7.1. Suppose 1000 firms compete in this industry, all having the same total and unit costs as the single firm we discussed. This lets us calculate the market supply schedule (columns 2 and 3) by multiplying the quantity-supplied figures of the single firm (column 1) by 1000.

Market Price and Profits   To determine the equilibrium price and output, we must compare these total-supply data with total-demand data. Let's assume that total demand is as shown in columns 3 and 4 in Table 7.3. By comparing the total quantity supplied and the total quantity demanded at the seven possible prices, we determine that the equilibrium price is $111 and the equilibrium quantity is 8000 units for the industry—8 units for each of the 1000 identical firms.

Will these conditions of market supply and demand make this a profitable or unprofitable industry? Multiplying product price ($111) by output (8 units), we find that the total revenue of each firm is $888. The total cost is $750, found by looking at column 4 of the table in Figure 6.3. The $138 difference is the economic profit of each firm. For the industry, total economic profit is $138,000. This, then, is a profitable industry.

Another way of calculating economic profit is to determine per-unit profit by subtracting average total cost ($93.75) from product price ($111) and multiplying the difference (per-unit profit of $17.25) by the firm's equilibrium level of output (8). Again we obtain an economic profit of $138 per firm and $138,000 for the industry.

Figure 7.6 shows this analysis graphically. The individual supply curves of each of the 1000 identical firms—one of which is shown as $s = $ MC in Figure 7.6a—are summed horizontally to get the total-supply curve $S = \Sigma$MC's of Figure 7.6b. With total-demand curve D, it yields the equilibrium price $111 and equilibrium quantity (for the industry) 8000 units. This equilibrium price is given and unalterable to the individual firm; that is, each firm's demand curve is perfectly elastic at the equilibrium price, as indicated by d in Figure 7.6a. Because the individual firm is a price taker, the marginal-revenue curve coincides with the firm's demand curve d. This $111 price

FIGURE 7.6

Short-run competitive equilibrium for (a) a firm and (b) the industry. The horizontal sum of the 1000 firms' individual supply curves (s) determines the industry (market) supply curve (S). Given industry (market) demand (D), the short-run equilibrium price and output for the industry are $111 and 8000 units. Taking the equilibrium price as given, the individual firm establishes its profit-maximizing output at 8 units and, in this case, realizes the economic profit represented by the green area.

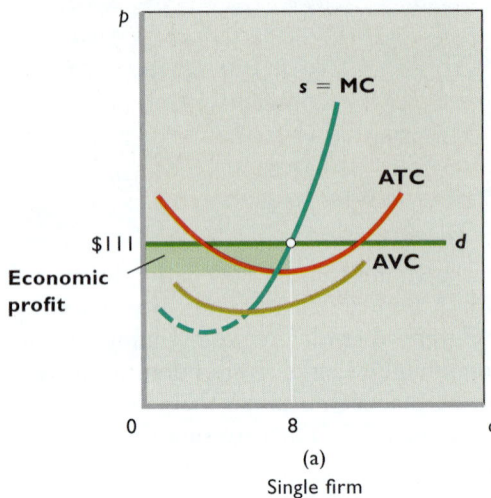
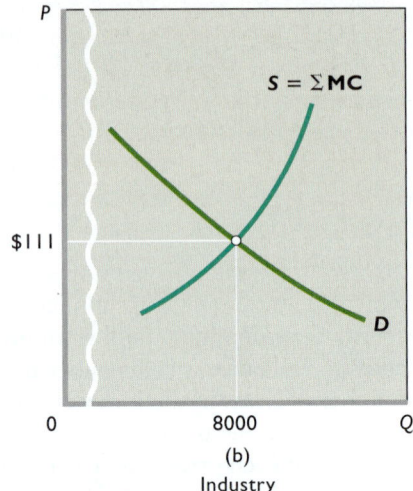

(a)
Single firm

(b)
Industry

exceeds the average total cost at the firm's equilibrium MR = MC output of 8 units, so the firm earns an economic profit represented by the green area in Figure 7.6a.

Assuming no changes in costs or market demand, these diagrams reveal a genuine equilibrium in the short run. There are no shortages or surpluses in the market to cause price or total quantity to change. Nor can any firm in the industry increase its profit by altering its output. Note, however, that weaker market demand or stronger market supply (and therefore lower prices) could shift the line d downward and change the situation to losses (P < ATC) or even to shutdown (P < AVC).

> **WORKED PROBLEMS**
>
> **W 7.2**
> Short-run competitive equilibrium

Firm versus Industry   Figure 7.6 underscores a point made earlier: Product price is a given fact to the individual competitive firm, but the supply plans of all competitive producers as a group are a basic determinant of product price. There is no inconsistency here. One firm, supplying a negligible fraction of total supply, cannot affect price. But the sum of the supply curves of all the firms in the industry constitutes the market supply curve, and that curve (along with demand) does have an important bearing on equilibrium price.

Profit Maximization in the Long Run

The entry and exit of firms in our market models can only take place in the long run. In the short run, the industry is composed of a specific number of firms, each with a plant size that is fixed and unalterable in the short run. Firms may shut down in the sense that they can produce zero units of output in the short run, but they do not have sufficient time to liquidate their assets and go out of business.

In the long run, by contrast, the firms already in an industry have sufficient time to either expand or contract their capacities. More important, the number of firms in the industry may either increase or decrease as new firms enter or existing firms leave.

The length of time constituting the long run varies substantially by industry, however, so that you should not fix in your mind any specific number of years, months, or days. Instead, focus your attention on the incentives provided by profits and losses for the entry and exit of firms into any purely competitive industry and, later in the chapter, on how those incentives lead to productive and allocative efficiency. The time horizons are far less important than how these long-run adjustments affect price, quantity, and profits, and the process by which profits and losses guide business managers toward the efficient use of society's resources.

Assumptions

We make three simplifying assumptions, none of which alters our conclusions:

- *Entry and exit only* The only long-run adjustment in our graphical analysis is caused by the entry or exit of firms. Moreover, we ignore all short-run adjustments in order to concentrate on the effects of the long-run adjustments.
- *Identical costs* All firms in the industry have identical cost curves. This assumption lets us discuss an "average," or "representative," firm, knowing that all other firms in the industry are similarly affected by any long-run adjustments that occur.
- *Constant-cost industry* The industry is a constant-cost industry. This means that the entry and exit of firms do not affect resource prices or, consequently, the locations of the average-total-cost curves of individual firms.

Goal of Our Analysis

The basic conclusion we seek to explain is this: After all long-run adjustments are completed in a purely competitive industry, product price will be exactly equal to, and production will occur at, each firm's minimum average total cost.

This conclusion follows from two basic facts: (1) Firms seek profits and shun losses and (2) under pure competition, firms are free to enter and leave an industry. If market price initially exceeds minimum average total costs, the resulting economic profits will attract new firms to the industry. But this industry expansion will increase supply until price is brought back down to equality with minimum average total cost. Conversely, if price is initially less than minimum average total cost, resulting losses will cause firms to leave the industry. As they leave, total supply will decline, bringing the price back up to equality with minimum average total cost.

Long-Run Equilibrium

Consider the average firm in a purely competitive industry that is initially in long-run equilibrium. This firm is represented in Figure 7.7a, where MR = MC and price and minimum average total cost are equal at $50. Economic profit here is zero; the industry is in equilibrium or "at rest" because there is no tendency for firms to enter or to leave. The existing firms are just covering the explicit and implicit costs that are represented by their cost curves. Recall that the firm's cost curves include the normal profits that owners could expect to receive in their best alternative business ventures. The $50 market price is determined in Figure 7.7b by market or industry demand D_1 and supply S_1.

FIGURE 7.7

Temporary profits and the reestablishment of long-run equilibrium in (a) a representative firm and (b) the industry. A favorable shift in demand (D_1 to D_2) will upset the original industry equilibrium and produce economic profits. But those profits will entice new firms to enter the industry, increasing supply (S_1 to S_2) and lowering product price until economic profits are once again zero.

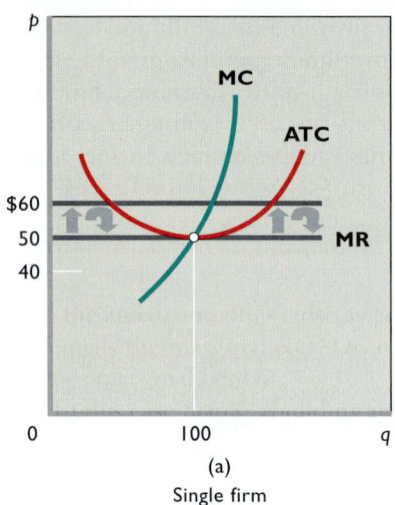

(a)
Single firm

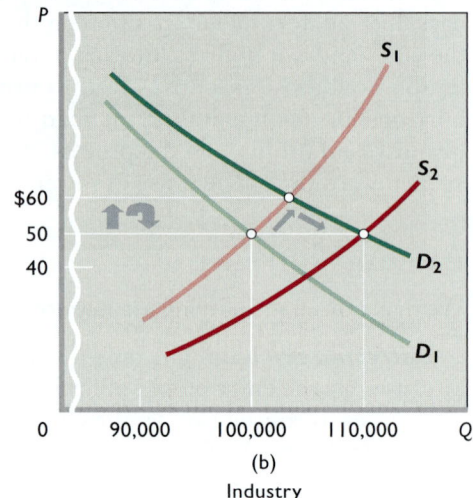

(b)
Industry

(S_1 is a short-run supply curve; we will develop the long-run industry supply curve in our discussion.)

As shown on the quantity axes of the two graphs, equilibrium output in the industry is 100,000 while equilibrium output for the single firm is 100. If all firms in the industry are identical, there must be 1000 firms (=100,000/100).

Entry Eliminates Economic Profits   Let's upset the long-run equilibrium in Figure 7.7 and see what happens. Suppose a change in consumer tastes increases product demand from D_1 to D_2. Price will rise to $60, as determined at the intersection of D_2 and S_1, and the firm's marginal-revenue curve will shift upward to $60. This $60 price exceeds the firm's average total cost of $50 at output 100, creating an economic profit of $10 per unit. This economic profit will lure new firms into the industry. Some entrants will be newly created firms; others will shift from less-prosperous industries.

As firms enter, the market supply of the product increases and the product price falls below $60. Economic profits persist, and entry continues until short-run supply increases to S_2. Market price falls to $50, as does marginal revenue for the firm. Price and minimum average total cost are again equal at $50. The economic profits caused by the boost in demand have been eliminated, and, as a result, the previous incentive for more firms to enter the industry has disappeared because the firms that remain are earning only a normal profit (zero economic profit). Entry ceases and a new long-run equilibrium is reached.

Observe in Figure 7.7a and 7.7b that total quantity supplied is now 110,000 units and each firm is producing 100 units. Now 1100 firms rather than the original 1000 populate the industry. Economic profits have attracted 100 more firms.

FIGURE 7.8

Temporary losses and the reestablishment of long-run equilibrium in (a) a representative firm and (b) the industry. An unfavorable shift in demand (D_1 to D_3) will upset the original industry equilibrium and produce losses. But those losses will cause firms to leave the industry, decreasing supply (S_1 to S_3) and increasing product price until all losses have disappeared.

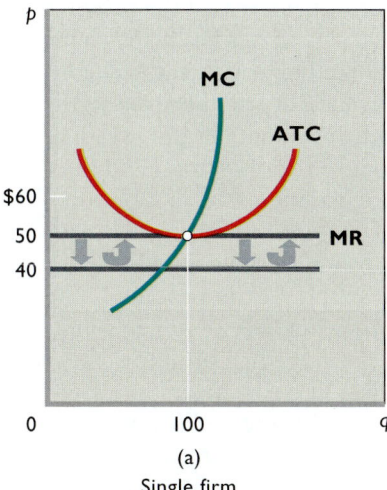

(a)
Single firm

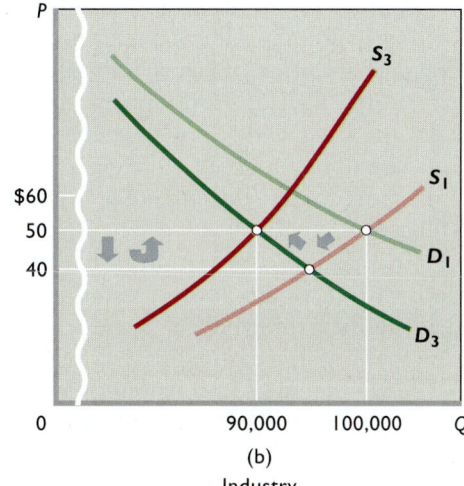

(b)
Industry

Exit Eliminates Losses   Now let's consider a shift in the opposite direction. We begin in Figure 7.8b with curves S_1 and D_1 setting the same initial long-run equilibrium situation as in our previous analysis, including the $50 price.

Suppose consumer demand declines from D_1 to D_3. This forces the market price and marginal revenue down to $40, making production unprofitable at the minimum ATC of $50. In time the resulting economic losses will induce firms to leave the industry. Their owners will seek a normal profit elsewhere rather than accept the below-normal profits (losses) now confronting them. As this exodus of firms proceeds, however, industry supply decreases, pushing the price up from $40 toward $50. Losses continue and more firms leave the industry until the supply curve shifts to S_3. Once this happens, price is again $50, just equal to the minimum average total cost. Losses have been eliminated so that the firms that remain are earning only a normal profit (zero economic profit). Since this is no better or worse than entrepreneurs could expect to earn in other business ventures, there is no longer any incentive to exit the industry. Long-run equilibrium is restored.

In Figure 7.8a and 7.8b, total quantity supplied is now 90,000 units and each firm is producing 100 units. Only 900 firms, not the original 1000, populate the industry. Losses have forced 100 firms out.

You may have noted that we have sidestepped the question of which firms will leave the industry when losses occur by assuming that all firms have identical cost curves. In the "real world," of course, managerial talents differ. Even if resource prices and technology are the same for all firms, less skillfully managed firms tend to incur higher costs and therefore are the first to leave an industry when demand declines. Similarly, firms with less-productive labor forces or higher transportation costs will be higher-cost producers and likely candidates to quit an industry when demand decreases.

Applying the Analysis

The Exit of Farmers from U.S. Agriculture

The U.S. agricultural industry serves as a good example of how losses resulting from declining prices received by individual producers create an exit of producers from an industry.

A rapid rate of technological advance has significantly increased the *supply* of U.S. agricultural products over time. This technological progress has many roots: the mechanization of farms, improved techniques of land management, soil conservation, irrigation, development of hybrid crops, availability of improved fertilizers and insecticides, polymer-coated seeds, and improvements in the breeding and care of livestock. In 1950 each farmworker produced enough food and fiber to support about a dozen people. By 2011 that figure had increased to more than 100 people!

Increases in *demand* for agricultural products, however, have failed to keep pace with technologically created increases in the supply of the products. The demand for farm products in the United States is *income-inelastic*. Estimates indicate that a 10 percent increase in real per capita after-tax income produces about a 2 percent increase in consumption of farm products. Once consumers' stomachs are filled, they turn to the amenities of life that manufacturing and services, not agriculture, provide. So, as the incomes of Americans rise, the demand for farm products increases far less rapidly than the demand for products in general.

The consequences of the long-run supply and demand conditions just outlined have been those predicted by the long-run pure-competition model. Financial losses in agriculture have triggered a large decline in the number of farms and a massive exit of workers to other sectors of the economy. In 1950 there were about 5.4 million farms in the United States employing 9.3 million people. Today there are just over 2 million farms employing 1.8 million people. Since 1950, farm employment has declined from 15.8 percent of the U.S. workforce to just 1.2 percent. Moreover, the exodus of farmers would have been even larger in the absence of government subsidies that have enabled many farmers to remain in agriculture. Such subsidies were traditionally in the form of government price supports (price floors) but have more recently evolved to direct subsidy payments to farmers. Such payments have averaged more than $16 billion annually over the last decade.

Question:
Why is the exit of farmers from U.S. agriculture bad for the farmers who must leave but good for the farmers who remain?

Long-Run Supply for a Constant-Cost Industry

long-run supply curve
A curve that shows the prices at which a purely competitive industry will make various quantities of the product available in the long run.

constant-cost industry
An industry in which the entry of new firms has no effect on resource prices and thus no effect on production costs.

We have established that changes in market supply through entry and exit create a long-run equilibrium in purely competitive markets. Although our analysis has dealt with the long run, we have noted that the market supply curves in Figures 7.7b and 7.8b are short-run curves. What then is the character of the **long-run supply curve** of a competitive industry? Our analysis points us toward an answer. The crucial factor here is the effect, if any, that changes in the number of firms in the industry will have on costs of the individual firms in the industry.

In our discussion of long-run competitive equilibrium, we assumed that the industry under discussion was a **constant-cost industry.** This means that industry expansion or contraction will not affect resource prices and therefore production costs.

Graphically, it means that the entry or exit of firms does not shift the long-run ATC curves of individual firms. This is the case when the industry's demand for resources is small in relation to the total demand for those resources. Then the industry can expand or contract without significantly affecting resource prices and costs.

What does the long-run supply curve of a constant-cost industry look like? The answer is contained in our previous analysis. There we saw that the entry and exit of firms changes industry output but always brings the product price back to its original level, where it is just equal to the constant minimum ATC. Specifically, we discovered that the industry would supply 90,000, 100,000, or 110,000 units of output, all at a price of $50 per unit. In other words, the long-run supply curve of a constant-cost industry is perfectly elastic.

Figure 7.9a demonstrates this graphically. Suppose industry demand is originally D_1, industry output is Q_1 (100,000 units), and product price is P_1 ($50). This situation, from Figure 7.7, is one of long-run equilibrium. We saw that when demand increases to D_2, upsetting this equilibrium, the resulting economic profits attract new firms. Because this is a constant-cost industry, entry continues and industry output expands until the price is driven back down to the level of the unchanged minimum ATC. This is at price P_2 ($50) and output Q_2 (110,000).

From Figure 7.8, we saw that a decline in market demand from D_1 to D_3 causes an exit of firms and ultimately restores equilibrium at price P_3 ($50) and output Q_3 (90,000 units). The points Z_1, Z_2, and Z_3 in Figure 7.9a represent these three price-quantity combinations. A line or curve connecting all such points shows the various price-quantity combinations that firms would produce if they had enough time to make all desired adjustments to changes in demand. This line or curve is the industry's long-run supply curve. In a constant-cost industry, this curve (straight line) is horizontal, as in Figure 7.9a, thus representing perfectly elastic supply.

FIGURE 7.9

Long-run supply: constant-cost industry versus increasing-cost industry. (a) In a constant-cost industry, the entry of firms does not affect resource prices or, therefore, unit costs. So an increase in demand (D_1 to D_2) or a decrease in demand (D_1 to D_3) causes a change in industry output (Q_1 to Q_2 or Q_1 to Q_3) but no alteration in price ($50). This means that the long-run industry supply curve (S) is horizontal through points Z_3, Z_1, and Z_2. (b) In an increasing-cost industry, the entry of new firms in response to an increase in demand (D_3 to D_1 to D_2) will bid up resource prices and thereby increase unit costs. As a result, an increased industry output (Q_3 to Q_1 to Q_2) will be forthcoming only at higher prices ($45 to $50 to $55). The long-run industry supply curve (S) therefore slopes upward through points Y_3, Y_1, and Y_2.

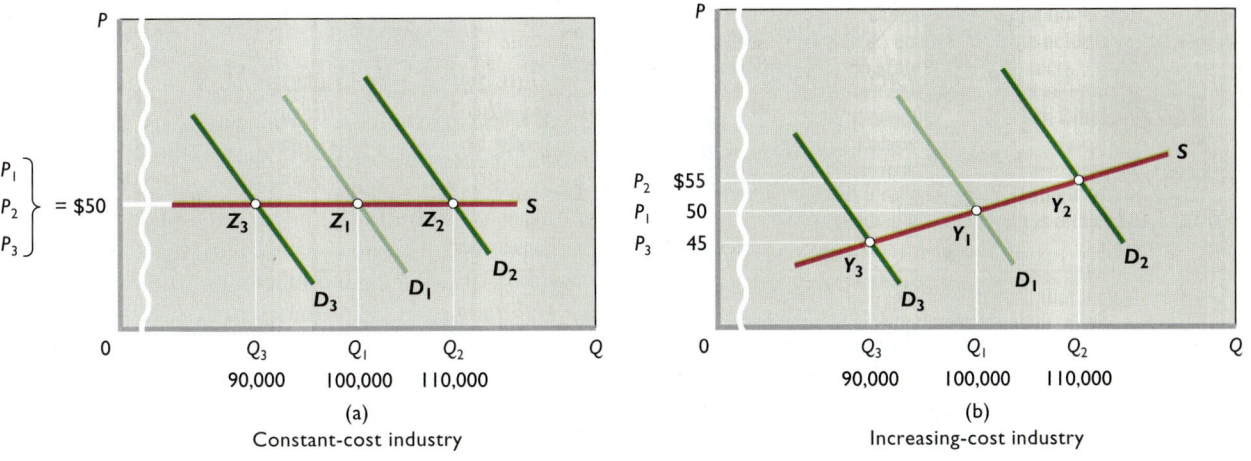

(a)
Constant-cost industry

(b)
Increasing-cost industry

Long-Run Supply for an Increasing-Cost Industry

increasing-cost industry
An industry in which the entry of new firms raises the prices for resources and thus increases their production costs.

Constant-cost industries are a special case. Most industries are **increasing-cost industries,** in which firms' ATC curves shift upward as the industry expands and downward as the industry contracts. The construction industry and medical care industries are examples.

Usually, the entry of new firms will increase resource prices, particularly in industries using specialized resources whose long-run supplies do not readily increase in response to increases in resource demand. Higher resource prices result in higher long-run average total costs for all firms in the industry. These higher costs cause upward shifts in each firm's long-run ATC curve.

Thus, when an increase in product demand results in economic profits and attracts new firms to an increasing-cost industry, a two-way squeeze works to eliminate those profits. As before, the entry of new firms increases market supply and lowers the market price. But now each firm's ATC curve also shifts upward. The overall result is a higher-than-original equilibrium price. The industry produces a larger output at a higher product price because the industry expansion has increased resource prices and the minimum average total cost.

Since greater output will be supplied at a higher price, the long-run industry supply curve is upsloping. Instead of supplying 90,000, 100,000, or 110,000 units at the same price of $50, an increasing-cost industry might supply 90,000 units at $45, 100,000 units at $50, and 110,000 units at $55. A higher price is required to induce more production because costs per unit of output increase as production increases.

Figure 7.9b nicely illustrates the situation. Original market demand is D_1 and industry price and output are P_1 ($50) and Q_1 (100,000 units), respectively, at equilibrium point Y_1. An increase in demand to D_2 upsets this equilibrium and leads to economic profits. New firms enter the industry, increasing both market supply and production costs of individual firms. A new price is established at point Y_2, where P_2 is $55 and Q_2 is 110,000 units.

Conversely, a decline in demand from D_1 to D_3 makes production unprofitable and causes firms to leave the industry. The resulting decline in resource prices reduces the minimum average total cost of production for firms that stay. A new equilibrium price is established at some level below the original price, say, at point Y_3, where P_3 is $45 and Q_3 is 90,000 units. Connecting these three equilibrium positions, we derive the upsloping long-run supply curve S in Figure 7.9b.

Long-Run Supply for a Decreasing-Cost Industry

decreasing-cost industry
An industry in which the entry of new firms lowers the prices of resources and thus decreases production costs.

In **decreasing-cost industries,** firms experience lower costs as their industry expands. The personal computer industry is an example. As demand for personal computers increased, new manufacturers of computers entered the industry and greatly increased the resource demand for the components used to build them (for example, memory chips, hard drives, monitors, and operating software). The expanded production of the components enabled the producers of those items to achieve substantial economies of scale. The decreased production costs of the components reduced their prices, which greatly lowered the computer manufacturers' average costs of production. The supply of personal computers increased by more than demand, and the price of personal computers declined. Although not shown in Figure 7.9, the long-run supply curve of a decreasing-cost industry is *downsloping*.

© Craig Aurness/CORBIS   © Compassionate Eye Foundation/Getty Images

Photo Op Increasing-Cost versus Decreasing-Cost Industries

Mining is an example of an increasing-cost industry, whereas electronics is an example of a decreasing-cost industry.

Unfortunately, the industries that show decreasing costs also show increasing costs if output contracts. A decline in demand (say from foreign competition) makes production unprofitable and causes firms to leave the industry. Firms that remain face a greater minimum average total cost of production, implying a higher long-run equilibrium price in the market.

Pure Competition and Efficiency

Our final goal in this chapter is to examine the efficiency aspects of pure competition. Assuming a constant- or increasing-cost industry, the final long-run equilibrium positions of all firms have the same basic efficiency characteristics. As shown in Figure 7.10, price (and marginal revenue) will settle where it is equal to minimum average total cost: P (and MR) = minimum ATC. Moreover, since the marginal-cost curve intersects the average-total-cost curve at its minimum point, marginal cost and average total cost are equal: MC = minimum ATC. So in long-run equilibrium, a multiple equality occurs: P (and MR) = MC = minimum ATC. Thus, in long-run equilibrium, each firm produces at the output level that is associated with this triple equality.[2]

The triple equality tells us two very important things about long-run equilibrium. First, it tells us that although a competitive firm may realize economic profit or loss in the short run, it will earn only a normal profit by producing in accordance with the MR (= P) = MC rule in the long run. Second, the triple equality tells us that in long-run equilibrium, the profit-maximizing decision rule that leads each firm to produce the quantity at which P = MR also implies that each firm will produce at the output level that is associated with the minimum point on each identical firm's ATC curve.

---

[2]This triple equality does not hold for decreasing-cost industries because MC always remains below ATC if average costs are decreasing. We will discuss this situation of "natural monopoly" in Chapter 8.

FIGURE 7.10

Long-run equilibrium of a competitive firm. The equality of price (*P*), marginal cost (MC), and minimum average total cost (ATC) at output Q*f* indicates that the firm is achieving productive efficiency and allocative efficiency. It is using the most efficient technology, charging the lowest price, and producing the greatest output consistent with its costs. It is receiving only a normal profit, which is incorporated into the ATC curve. The equality of price and marginal cost indicates that society allocated its scarce resources in accordance with consumer preferences.

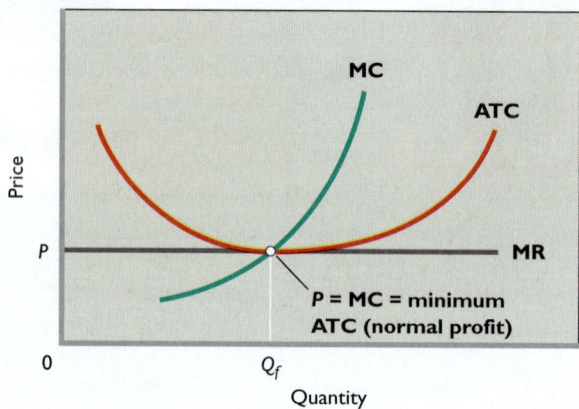

This is very important because it suggests that pure competition leads to the most efficient possible use of society's resources. Indeed, subject only to Chapter 5's qualifications relating to public goods and externalities, an idealized purely competitive market economy composed of constant- or increasing-cost industries will generate both productive efficiency and allocative efficiency.

Productive efficiency requires that goods be produced in the least costly way. Allocative efficiency requires that resources be apportioned among firms and industries so as to yield the mix of products and services that is most wanted by society (least-cost production assumed). Allocative efficiency has been realized when it is impossible to alter the combination of goods produced and achieve a net gain for society. Let's look at how productive and allocative efficiency would be achieved under purely competitive conditions.

Productive Efficiency: *P* = Minimum ATC

In the long run, pure competition forces firms to produce at the minimum average total cost of production and to charge a price that is just consistent with that cost. This is true because firms that do not use the best-available (least-cost) production methods and combinations of inputs will not survive.

To see why that is true, let's suppose that Figure 7.10 has to do with pure competition in the cucumber industry. In the final equilibrium position shown in Figure 7.10, suppose each firm in the cucumber industry is producing 100 units (say, pickup truckloads) of output by using $5000 (equal to average total cost of $50 × 100 units) worth of resources. If any firm produced that same amount of output at any higher total cost, say $7000, it would be wasting resources because all of the other firms in the industry are able to produce that same amount of output using only $5000 worth of resources. Society would be faced with a net loss of $2000 worth of alternative products. But this cannot happen in pure competition; this firm would incur a loss of $2000, requiring it either to reduce its costs or go out of business.

Note, too, that consumers benefit from productive efficiency by paying the lowest product price possible under the prevailing technology and cost conditions. And the firm receives only a normal profit, which is part of its economic costs and thus incorporated in its ATC curve.

Allocative Efficiency: $P = MC$

Productive efficiency alone does not ensure the efficient allocation of resources. It does not guarantee that anyone will want to buy the items that are being produced in the least-cost manner. For all we know,

consumers might prefer that the resources used to produce those items be redirected toward producing other products instead.

Fortunately, long-run equilibrium in pure competition also guarantees *allocative efficiency*, so we can be certain that society's scarce resources are directed toward producing the goods and services that people most want to consume. Stated formally, allocative efficiency occurs when it is impossible to produce any net gains for society by altering the combination of goods and services that are produced from society's limited supply of resources. There are two critical elements here:

- The money price of any product is society's measure of the relative worth of an additional unit of that product—for example, cucumbers. So the price of a unit of cucumbers is the marginal benefit derived from that unit of the product.
- Similarly, recalling the idea of opportunity cost, we see that the marginal cost of an additional unit of a product measures the value, or relative worth, of the other goods sacrificed to obtain it. In producing cucumbers, resources are drawn away from producing other goods. The marginal cost of producing a unit of cucumbers measures society's sacrifice of those other products.

Efficient Allocation   In pure competition, when profit-motivated firms produce each good or service to the point where price (marginal benefit) and marginal cost are equal, society's resources are being allocated efficiently. Each item is being produced to the point at which the value of the last unit is equal to the value of the alternative goods sacrificed by its production. Altering the production of cucumbers would reduce consumer satisfaction. Producing cucumbers beyond the $P = MC$ point in Figure 7.10 would sacrifice alternative goods whose value to society exceeds that of the extra cucumbers. Producing cucumbers short of the $P = MC$ point would sacrifice cucumbers that society values more than the alternative goods its resources could produce.

Dynamic Adjustments   A further attribute of purely competitive markets is their ability to restore efficiency when disrupted by changes in the economy. A change in consumer tastes, resource supplies, or technology will automatically set in motion the appropriate realignments of resources. For example, suppose that cucumbers and pickles become dramatically more popular. First, the price of cucumbers will increase, and so, at current output, the price of cucumbers will exceed their marginal cost. At this point efficiency will be lost, but the higher price will create economic profits in the cucumber industry and stimulate its expansion. The profitability of cucumbers will permit the industry to bid resources away from now less-pressing uses, say, watermelons. Expansion of the industry will end only when the price of cucumbers and their marginal cost are equal—that is, when allocative efficiency has been restored.

Similarly, a change in the supply of a particular resource—for example, the field laborers who pick cucumbers—or in a production technique will upset an existing price–marginal-cost equality by either raising or lowering marginal cost. The resulting inequality will cause business managers, in either pursuing profit or avoiding loss, to reallocate resources until price once again equals marginal cost. In so doing, they will correct any inefficiency in the allocation of resources that the original change may have temporarily imposed on the economy.

"Invisible Hand" Revisited   The highly efficient allocation of resources that a purely competitive economy promotes comes about because businesses and resource suppliers seek to further their self-interest. For private goods with no externalities (Chapter 5), the "invisible hand" (Chapter 2) is at work. The competitive system not only maximizes profits for individual producers but also, at the same time, creates a pattern of resource allocation that maximizes consumer satisfaction. The invisible hand thus organizes the private interests of producers in a way that is fully in sync with society's interest in using scarce resources efficiently. Striving for profit (and avoiding losses) produces highly desirable economic outcomes.

Summary

1. Economists group industries into four models based on their market structures: (a) pure competition, (b) monopolistic competition, (c) oligopoly, and (d) pure monopoly.

2. A purely competitive industry consists of a large number of independent firms producing a standardized product. Pure competition assumes that firms and resources are mobile among different industries.

3. In a competitive industry, no single firm can influence market price. This means that the firm's demand curve is perfectly elastic and price equals both marginal revenue and average revenue.

4. Provided price exceeds minimum average variable cost, a competitive firm maximizes profit or minimizes loss in the short run by producing the output at which price or marginal revenue equals marginal cost.

5. If price is less than minimum average variable cost, a competitive firm minimizes its loss by shutting down. If price is greater than average variable cost but is less than average total cost, a competitive firm minimizes its loss by producing the $P = MC$ amount of output. If price also exceeds average total cost, the firm maximizes its economic profit at the $P = MC$ amount of output.

6. Applying the MR $(= P) = MC$ rule at various possible market prices leads to the conclusion that the segment of the firm's short-run marginal-cost curve that lies above the firm's average-variable-cost curve is its short-run supply curve.

7. In the long run, the market price of a product will equal the minimum average total cost of production. At a higher price, economic profits would entice firms to enter the industry until those profits had been competed away. At a lower price, losses would force firms to exit the industry until the product price rose to equal average total cost.

8. The long-run supply curve is horizontal for a constant-cost industry, upsloping for an increasing-cost industry, and downsloping for a decreasing-cost industry.

9. The long-run equality of price and minimum average total cost means that competitive firms will use the most efficient known technology and charge the lowest price consistent with their production costs. That is, purely competitive firms will achieve productive efficiency.

10. The long-run equality of price and marginal cost implies that resources will be allocated in accordance with consumer tastes. The competitive price system will reallocate resources in response to a change in consumer tastes, in technology, or in resource supplies and will thereby maintain allocative efficiency over time.

Terms and Concepts

pure competition

price taker

average revenue

total revenue

marginal revenue

MR = MC rule

short-run supply curve

long-run supply curve

constant-cost industry

increasing-cost industry

decreasing-cost industry

Questions

1. Briefly state the basic characteristics of pure competition, pure monopoly, monopolistic competition, and oligopoly. Under which of these market classifications does each of the following most accurately fit? (a) a supermarket in your hometown; (b) the steel industry; (c) a Kansas wheat farm; (d) the commercial bank in which you or your family has an account; (e) the automobile industry. In each case, justify your classification. **LO1**

2. Use the demand schedule that follows to determine total revenue and marginal revenue for each possible level of sales: **LO2**

Product Price	Quantity Demanded	Total Revenue	Marginal Revenue
$2	0	$_____	
			$_____
2	1	_____	
			_____
2	2	_____	
			_____
2	3	_____	
			_____
2	4	_____	
			_____
2	5	_____	

a. What can you conclude about the structure of the industry in which this firm is operating? Explain.

b. Graph the demand, total-revenue, and marginal-revenue curves for this firm.

c. Why do the demand, marginal-revenue, and average-revenue curves coincide?

d. "Marginal revenue is the change in total revenue associated with additional units of output." Explain verbally and graphically, using the data in the table.

3. "Even if a firm is losing money, it may be better to stay in business in the short run." Is this statement ever true? Under what condition(s)? **LO3**

4. Why is the equality of marginal revenue and marginal cost essential for profit maximization in all market structures? Explain why price can be substituted for marginal revenue in the MR = MC rule when an industry is purely competitive. **LO3**

5. "That segment of a competitive firm's marginal-cost curve that lies above its average-variable-cost curve constitutes the short-run supply curve for the firm." Explain using a graph and words. **LO4**

6. Explain: "The short-run rule for operating or shutting down is $P > AVC$, operate; $P < AVC$, shut down. The long-run rule for continuing in business or exiting the industry is $P \geq ATC$, continue; $P < ATC$, exit." **LO5**

7. Using diagrams for both the industry and a representative firm, illustrate competitive long-run equilibrium. Assuming constant costs, employ these diagrams to show how (a) an increase and (b) a decrease in market demand will upset that long-run equilibrium. Trace graphically and describe verbally the adjustment processes by which long-run equilibrium is restored. Now rework your analysis for increasing- and decreasing-cost industries, and compare the three long-run supply curves. **LO6**

8. In long-run equilibrium, $P =$ minimum ATC = MC. What is the significance of the equality of P and minimum ATC for society? The equality of P and MC? Distinguish between productive efficiency and allocative efficiency in your answer. **LO5**

9. Suppose that purely competitive firms producing cashews discover that P exceeds MC. Will their combined output of cashews be too little, too much, or just right to achieve allocative efficiency? In the long run, what will happen to the supply of cashews and the price of cashews? **LO5**

Problems

1. A purely competitive firm finds that the market price for its product is $20. It has a fixed cost of $100 and a variable cost of $10 per unit for the first 50 units and then $25 per unit for all successive units. Does price exceed average variable cost for the first 50 units? What about for the first 100 units? What is the marginal cost per unit for the first 50 units? What about for units 51 and higher? For each of the first 50 units, does MR exceed MC? What about for units 51 and higher? What output level will yield the largest possible profit for this purely competitive firm? **LO3**

2. A purely competitive wheat farmer can sell any wheat he grows for $10 per bushel. His five acres of land show diminishing returns because some are better suited for wheat production than others. The first acre can produce 1000 bushels of wheat, the second acre 900, the third 800, and so on. Draw a table with multiple columns to help you answer the following questions. How many bushels will each of the farmer's five acres produce? How much revenue will each acre generate? What are the TR and MR for each acre? If the marginal cost of planting and harvesting an acre is $7000 per acre for each of the five acres, how many acres should the farmer plant and harvest? **LO3**

3. Karen runs a print shop that makes posters for large companies. It is a very competitive business. The market price is currently $1 per poster. She has fixed costs of $250.

Her variable costs are $1000 for the first thousand posters, $800 for the second thousand, and then $750 for each additional thousand posters. What is her AFC per poster (not per thousand!) if she prints 1000 posters? 2000? 10,000? What is her ATC per poster if she prints 1000? 2000? 10,000? If the market price fell to 70 cents per poster, would there be *any* output level at which Karen would *not* shut down production immediately? **LO3**

4. Assume that the cost data in the table below are for a purely competitive producer: **LO3**

   a. At a product price of $56, will this firm produce in the short run? If it is preferable to produce, what will be the profit-maximizing or loss-minimizing output? What economic profit or loss will the firm realize per unit of output?

Total Product	Average Fixed Cost	Average Variable Cost	Average Total Cost	Marginal Cost
0				
1	$60.00	$45.00	$105.00	$45
2	30.00	42.50	72.50	40
3	20.00	40.00	60.00	35
4	15.00	37.50	52.50	30
5	12.00	37.00	49.00	35
6	10.00	37.50	47.50	40
7	8.57	38.57	47.14	45
8	7.50	40.63	48.13	55
9	6.67	43.33	50.00	65
10	6.00	46.50	52.50	75

   b. Answer the questions of 4a assuming product price is $41.
   c. Answer the questions of 4a assuming product price is $32.
   d. In the accompanying table, complete the short-run supply schedule for the firm (columns 1 and 2) and indicate the profit or loss incurred at each output (column 3).

(1) Price	(2) Quantity Supplied, Single Firm	(3) Profit (+) or Loss (−)	(4) Quantity Supplied, 1500 Firms
$26	_____	$_____	_____
32	_____	_____	_____
38	_____	_____	_____
41	_____	_____	_____
46	_____	_____	_____
56	_____	_____	_____
66	_____	_____	_____

   e. Now assume that there are 1500 identical firms in this competitive industry; that is, there are 1500 firms, each of which has the cost data shown in the table. Complete the industry supply schedule (column 4).
   f. Suppose the market demand data for the product are as follows:

Price	Total Quantity Demanded
$26	17,000
32	15,000
38	13,500
41	12,000
46	10,500
56	9500
66	8000

What will be the equilibrium price? What will be the equilibrium output for the industry? For each firm? What will profit or loss be per unit? Per firm? Will this industry expand or contract in the long run?

FURTHER TEST YOUR KNOWLEDGE AT
www.brue3e.com

At the text's Online Learning Center, **www.brue3e.com,** you will find one or more web-based questions that require information from the Internet to answer. We urge you to check them out, since they will familiarize you with websites that may be helpful in other courses and perhaps even in your career. The OLC also features multiple-choice quizzes that give instant feedback and provides other helpful ways to further test your knowledge of the chapter.

CHAPTER EIGHT

Pure Monopoly

After reading this chapter, you should be able to:

1. List the characteristics of pure monopoly and discuss several barriers to entry that relate to monopoly.
2. Explain how a pure monopoly sets its profit-maximizing output and price.
3. Discuss the economic effects of monopoly.
4. Describe why a monopolist might prefer to charge different prices in different markets.
5. Identify the antitrust laws that are used to deal with monopoly.

We turn now from pure competition to pure monopoly (a single seller). You deal with monopolies—or near-monopolies—more often than you might think. This happens when you see the Microsoft Windows logo after you turn on your computer and when you swallow a prescription drug that is under patent. Depending on where you live, you may be patronizing a local or regional monopoly when you make a local telephone call, turn on your lights, or subscribe to cable TV.

What precisely do we mean by "pure monopoly," and what conditions enable it to arise and survive? How does a pure monopolist determine what price to charge? Does a pure monopolist achieve the efficiency associated with pure competition? If not, what should the government try to do about it? A model of pure monopoly will help us answer these questions.

An Introduction to Pure Monopoly

pure monopoly
An industry in which one firm is the sole producer or seller of a product or service for which there are no close substitutes.

Pure monopoly exists when a single firm is the sole producer of a product for which there are no close substitutes. Here are the main characteristics of **pure monopoly:**

- *Single seller* A pure, or absolute, monopoly is an industry in which a single firm is the sole producer of a specific good or the sole supplier of a service; the firm and the industry are synonymous.

- *No close substitutes* A pure monopoly's product is unique in that there are no close substitutes. The consumer who chooses not to buy the monopolized product must do without it.

- *Price maker* The pure monopolist controls the total quantity supplied and thus has considerable control over price; it is a *price maker*. (Unlike a pure competitor, which has no such control and therefore is a *price taker*.) The pure monopolist confronts the usual downward-sloping product demand curve. It can change its product price by changing the quantity of the product it produces. The monopolist will use this power whenever it is advantageous to do so.

- *Blocked entry* A pure monopolist faces no immediate competition because certain barriers keep potential competitors from entering the industry. Those barriers may be economic, technological, legal, or of some other type. But entry is totally blocked in pure monopoly.

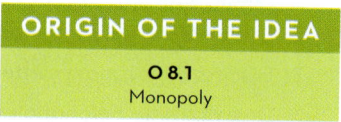

ORIGIN OF THE IDEA

O 8.1
Monopoly

Examples of *pure* monopoly are relatively rare, but there are excellent examples of less pure forms. In many cities, government-owned or government-regulated public utilities—natural gas and electric companies, the water company, the cable TV company, and the local telephone company—are all monopolies or virtually so.

There are also many "near-monopolies" in which a single firm has the bulk of sales in a specific market. Intel, for example, produces 80 percent of the central microprocessors used in personal computers. First Data Corporation, via its Western Union subsidiary, accounts for 80 percent of the market for money order transfers. Brannock Device Company has an 80 percent market share of the shoe-sizing devices found in shoe stores. Wham-O, through its Frisbee brand, sells 90 percent of plastic throwing disks. The De Beers diamond syndicate effectively controls 55 percent of the world's supply of rough-cut diamonds.

Professional sports teams are, in a sense, monopolies because they are the sole suppliers of specific services in large geographic areas. With a few exceptions, a single major-league team in each sport serves each large American city. If you want to see a live major-league baseball game in St. Louis or Seattle, you must patronize the Cardinals or the Mariners, respectively. Other geographic monopolies exist. For example, a small town may be served by only one airline or railroad. In a small, extremely isolated community, the local barber shop, dry cleaner, or grocery store may approximate a monopoly.

Of course, there is almost always some competition. Satellite television is a substitute for cable, and amateur softball is a substitute for professional baseball. The Linux operating system can substitute for Windows, and so on. But such substitutes are typically in some way less appealing.

Barriers to Entry

The factors that prohibit firms from entering an industry are called **barriers to entry.** In pure monopoly, strong barriers to entry effectively block all potential competition. Somewhat weaker barriers may permit *oligopoly*, a market structure dominated by a few firms. Still weaker barriers may permit the entry of a fairly large number of competing firms, giving rise to *monopolistic competition.* And the absence of any effective entry barriers permits the entry of a very large number of firms, which provide the basis of pure competition. So barriers to entry are pertinent not only to the extreme case of pure monopoly but also to other market structures in which there are monopoly-like characteristics or monopoly-like behavior.

We will now discuss the four most prominent barriers to entry.

barriers to entry
Any conditions that prevent the entry of firms into an industry.

Economies of Scale

Modern technology in some industries is such that economies of scale—declining average total cost with added firm size—are extensive. In such cases, a firm's long-run average-cost schedule will decline over a wide range of output. Given market demand, only a few large firms or, in the extreme, only a single large firm can achieve low average total costs.

If a pure monopoly exists in such an industry, economies of scale will serve as an entry barrier and will protect the monopolist from competition. New firms that try to enter the industry as small-scale producers cannot realize the cost economies of the monopolist. They therefore will be undercut and forced out of business by the monopolist, which can sell at a much lower price and still make a profit because of its lower per-unit cost associated with its economies of scale. A new firm might try to start out big, that is, to enter the industry as a large-scale producer so as to achieve the necessary economies of scale. But the massive plant facilities required would necessitate huge amounts of financing, which a new and untried enterprise would find difficult to secure. In most cases, the financial obstacles and risks to "starting big" are prohibitive. This explains why efforts to enter such industries as automobiles, computer operating software, commercial aircraft, and basic steel are so rare.

> **ORIGIN OF THE IDEA**
>
> **O 8.2**
> Minimum efficient scale

In the extreme circumstance, in which the market demand curve cuts the long-run ATC curve where average total costs are still declining, the single firm is called a **natural monopoly.** It might seem that a natural monopolist's lower unit cost would enable it to charge a lower price than if the industry were more competitive. But that won't necessarily happen. As with any monopolist, a natural monopolist may, instead, set its price far above ATC and obtain substantial economic profit. In that event, the lowest-unit-cost advantage of a natural monopolist would accrue to the monopolist as profit and not as lower prices to consumers.

natural monopoly
An industry in which economies of scale are so great that only a single firm can achieve minimum efficient scale.

Legal Barriers to Entry: Patents and Licenses

Government also creates legal barriers to entry by awarding patents and licenses.

Patents   A *patent* is the exclusive right of an inventor to use, or to allow another to use, her or his invention. Patents and patent laws aim to protect the inventor from rivals who would use the invention without having shared in the effort and expense of developing it. At the same time, patents provide the inventor with a monopoly position for the life of the patent. The world's nations have agreed on a uniform patent length of 20 years from the time of application. Patents have figured prominently in the growth of modern-day giants such as IBM, Pfizer, Kodak, Xerox, Intel, General Electric, and DuPont.

Research and development (R&D) is what leads to most patentable inventions and products. Firms that gain monopoly power through their own research or by purchasing the patents of others can use patents to strengthen their market position. The profit from one patent can finance the research required to develop new patentable products. In the pharmaceutical industry, patents on prescription drugs have produced large monopoly profits that have helped finance the discovery of new patentable medicines. So monopoly power achieved through patents may well be self-sustaining, even though patents eventually expire and generic drugs then compete with the original brand.

Licenses   Government may also limit entry into an industry or occupation through *licensing*. At the national level, the Federal Communications Commission licenses only so many radio and television stations in each geographic area. In many large cities, one of a limited number of municipal licenses is required to drive a taxicab. The consequent restriction of the supply of cabs creates economic profit for cab owners and drivers. New cabs cannot enter the industry to drive down prices and profits. In a few instances, the government might "license" itself to provide some product and thereby create a public monopoly. For example, in some states only state-owned retail outlets can sell liquor. Similarly, many states have "licensed" themselves to run lotteries.

Ownership or Control of Essential Resources

A monopolist can use private property as an obstacle to potential rivals. For example, a firm that owns or controls a resource essential to the production process can prohibit the entry of rival firms. At one time the International Nickel Company of Canada (now called Inco) controlled a large percentage of the world's known nickel reserves. A local firm may own all the nearby deposits of sand and gravel. And it is very difficult for new sports leagues to be created because existing professional sports leagues have contracts with the best players and have long-term leases on the major stadiums and arenas.

Pricing and Other Strategic Barriers to Entry

Even if a firm is not protected from entry by, say, extensive economies of scale or ownership of essential resources, entry may effectively be blocked by the way the monopolist responds to attempts by rivals to enter the industry. Confronted with a new entrant, the monopolist may "create an entry barrier" by slashing its price, stepping up its advertising, or taking other strategic actions to make it difficult for the entrant to succeed.

Examples of entry deterrence: In 2005 Dentsply, the dominant American maker of false teeth (70 percent market share) was found to have unlawfully precluded independent distributors of false teeth from carrying competing brands. The lack of access to the distributors deterred potential foreign competitors from entering the U.S. market. As another example, in 2001 a U.S. court of appeals upheld a lower court's finding that Microsoft used a series of illegal actions to maintain its monopoly in Intel-compatible PC operating systems (95 percent market share). One such action was charging higher prices for its Windows operating system to computer manufacturers that featured Netscape's Navigator rather than Microsoft's Internet Explorer.

Monopoly Demand

Now that we have explained the sources of monopoly, we want to build a model of pure monopoly so that we can analyze its price and output decisions. Let's start by making three assumptions:

- Patents, economies of scale, or resource ownership secure our firm's monopoly.
- No unit of government regulates the firm.
- The firm is a single-price monopolist; it charges the same price for all units of output.

The crucial difference between a pure monopolist and a purely competitive seller lies on the demand side of the market. The purely competitive seller faces a perfectly elastic demand at the price determined by market supply and demand. It is a price taker that can sell as much or as little as it wants at the going market price. Each additional unit sold will add the amount of the constant product price to the firm's total revenue. That means that marginal revenue for the competitive seller is constant and equal to product price. (Review Figure 7.1 for price, marginal-revenue, and total-revenue relationships for the purely competitive firm.)

The demand curve for the monopolist (or oligopolist or monopolistic competitor) is quite different from that of the pure competitor. Because the pure monopolist *is* the industry, its demand curve is *the market demand curve*. And because market demand is not perfectly elastic, the monopolist's demand curve is downsloping. Columns 1 and 2 in the table in Figure 8.1 illustrate this fact. Note that quantity demanded increases as price decreases.

In Chapter 7 we drew separate demand curves for the purely competitive industry and for a single firm in such an industry. But only a single demand curve is needed in pure monopoly because the firm and the industry are one and the same. We have graphed part of the demand data in the table in Figure 8.1 as demand curve *D* in Figure 8.1a. This is the monopolist's demand curve *and* the market demand curve. The downward-sloping demand curve has two implications that are essential to understanding the monopoly model.

Marginal Revenue Is Less Than Price

With a fixed downsloping demand curve, the pure monopolist can increase sales only by charging a lower price. Consequently, marginal revenue is less than price (average revenue) for every unit of output except the first. Why so? The reason is that the lower price of the extra unit of output also applies to all prior units of output. The monopolist could have sold these prior units at a higher price if it had not produced and sold the extra output. Each additional unit of output sold increases total revenue by an amount equal to its own price less the sum of the price cuts that apply to all prior units of output.

Figure 8.1a confirms this point. There, we have highlighted two price-quantity combinations from the monopolist's demand curve. The monopolist can sell 1 more unit at $132 than it can at $142 and that way obtain $132 of extra revenue (the blue area). But to sell that fourth unit for $132, the monopolist must also sell the first 3 units at $132 rather than $142. The $10 reduction in revenue on 3 units results in a $30 revenue loss (the red area). The net difference in total revenue from selling a fourth unit is $102: the $132 gain from the fourth unit minus the $30 forgone on the first 3 units. This net gain (marginal revenue) of $102 from the fourth unit is clearly less than the $132 price of the fourth unit.

FIGURE 8.1

Demand, price, and marginal revenue in pure monopoly. (a) A pure monopolist (or any other imperfect competitor) must set a lower price in order to sell more output. Here, by charging $132 rather than $142, the monopolist sells an extra unit (the fourth unit) and gains $132 from that sale. But from this gain $30 is subtracted, which reflects the $10 less the monopolist received for each of the first 3 units. Thus, the marginal revenue of the fourth unit is $102 (= $132 − $30), considerably less than its $132 price. (b) Because a monopolist must lower the price on all units sold in order to increase its sales, its marginal-revenue curve (MR) lies below its downsloping demand curve (D).

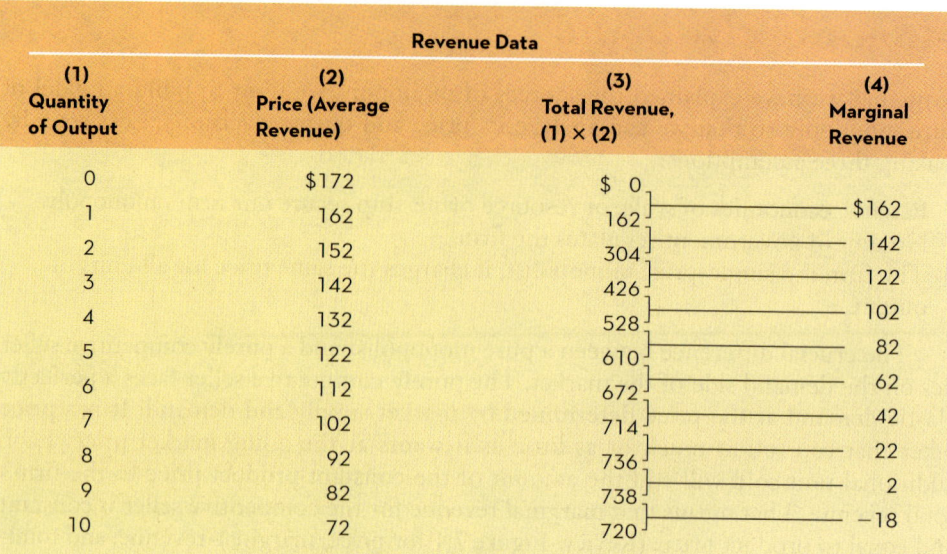

Revenue Data			
(1) Quantity of Output	**(2)** Price (Average Revenue)	**(3)** Total Revenue, (1) × (2)	**(4)** Marginal Revenue
0	$172	$ 0	
1	162	162	$162
2	152	304	142
3	142	426	122
4	132	528	102
5	122	610	82
6	112	672	62
7	102	714	42
8	92	736	22
9	82	738	2
10	72	720	−18

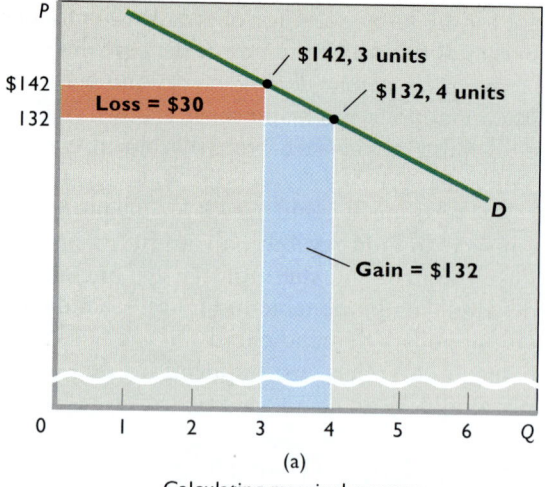

(a)
Calculating marginal revenue

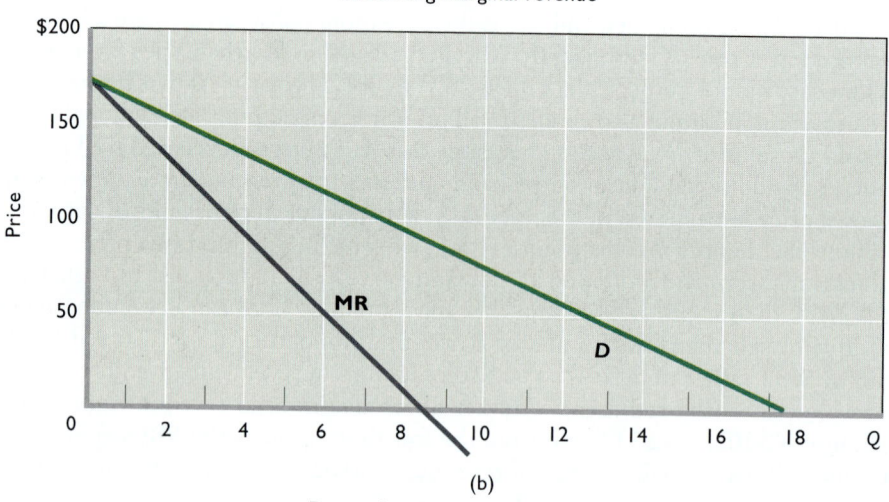

(b)
Demand and marginal-revenue curves

Column 4 in the table shows that marginal revenue is always less than the corresponding product price in column 2, except for the first unit of output. We show the relationship between the monopolist's demand curve and marginal-revenue curve in Figure 8.1b. For this figure, we extended the demand and marginal-revenue data of columns 1, 2, and 4 in the table, assuming that successive $10 price cuts each elicits 1 additional unit of sales. That is, the monopolist can sell 11 units at $62, 12 units at $52, and so on. Note that the monopolist's MR curve lies below the demand curve, indicating that marginal revenue is less than price at every output quantity except the very first unit.

The Monopolist Is a Price Maker

All imperfect competitors, whether they are pure monopolists, oligopolists, or monopolistic competitors, face downsloping demand curves. As a result, any change in quantity produced causes a movement along their respective demand curves and a change in the price they can charge for their respective products. Economists summarize this fact by saying that firms with downsloping demand curves are *price makers*.

This is most evident in pure monopoly, where an industry consists of a single monopoly firm so that total industry output is exactly equal to whatever the single monopoly firm chooses to produce. As we just mentioned, the monopolist faces a downsloping demand curve in which each amount of output is associated with some unique price. Thus, in deciding on the quantity of output to produce, the monopolist is also indirectly determining the price it will charge. Through control of output, it can "make the price." From columns 1 and 2 in the table in Figure 8.1 we find that the monopolist can charge a price of $72 if it produces and offers for sale 10 units, a price of $82 if it produces and offers for sale 9 units, and so forth.

Output and Price Determination

At what specific price-quantity combination will a profit-maximizing monopolist choose to operate? To answer this question, we must add production costs to our analysis.

Cost Data

On the cost side, we will assume that although the firm is a monopolist in the product market, it hires resources competitively and employs the same technology and, therefore, has the same cost structure as the purely competitive firm that we studied in Chapter 7. By using the same cost data that we developed in Chapter 6 and applied to the competitive firm in Chapter 7, we will be able to directly compare the price and output decisions of a pure monopoly with those of a pure competitor. Columns 5 through 7 in the table in Figure 8.2 restate the pertinent cost data from the table in Figure 7.2.

MR = MC Rule

A monopolist seeking to maximize total profit will employ the same rationale as a profit-seeking firm in a competitive industry. If producing is preferable to shutting down, it will produce up to the output at which marginal revenue equals marginal cost (MR = MC).

A comparison of columns 4 and 7 in the table in Figure 8.2 indicates that the profit-maximizing output is 5 units because the fifth unit is the last unit of output

FIGURE 8.2

Profit maximization by a pure monopolist. The pure monopolist maximizes profit by producing the MR = MC output, here $Q_m = 5$ units. Then, as seen from the demand curve, it will charge price $P_m = \$122$. Average total cost is $A = \$94$, so per-unit profit is $P_m - A$ and total profit is $5 \times (P_m - A)$. Total economic profit is thus $\$140$, as shown by the green rectangle.

	Revenue Data				Cost Data		
(1) Quantity of Output	**(2)** Price (Average Revenue)	**(3)** Total Revenue, (1) × (2)	**(4)** Marginal Revenue	**(5)** Average Total Cost	**(6)** Total Cost, (1) × (5)	**(7)** Marginal Cost	**(8)** Profit (+) or Loss (−)
0	$172	$ 0		$ 100			$−100
			$162		$ 90		
1	162	162		$190.00	190		− 28
			142		80		
2	152	304		135.00	270		+ 34
			122		70		
3	142	426		113.33	340		+ 86
			102		60		
4	132	528		100.00	400		+ 128
			82		**70**		
5	**122**	**610**		**94.00**	**470**		**+140**
			62		80		
6	112	672		91.67	550		+ 122
			42		90		
7	102	714		91.43	640		+ 74
			22		110		
8	92	736		93.75	750		− 14
			2		130		
9	82	738		97.78	880		− 142
			−18		150		
10	72	720		103.00	1030		− 310

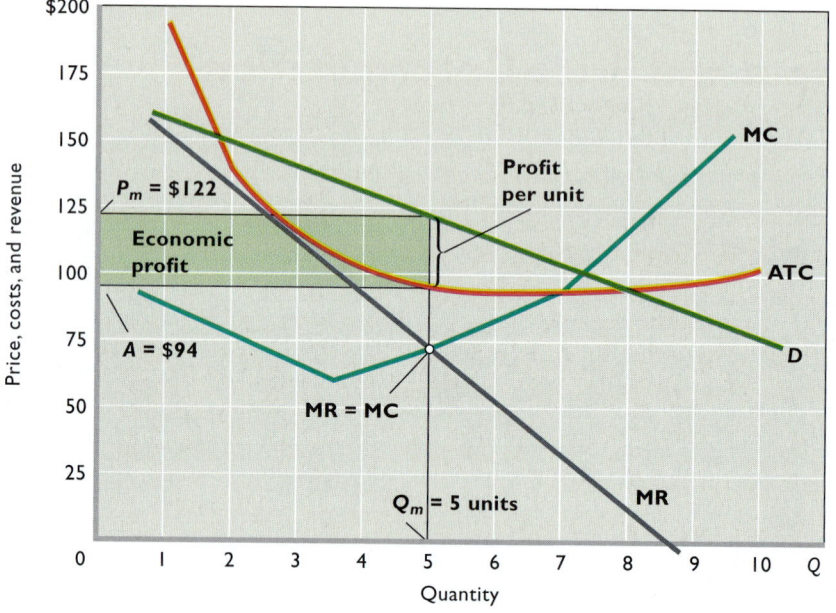

whose marginal revenue exceeds its marginal cost. What price will the monopolist charge? The demand schedule shown as columns 1 and 2 in the table indicates there is only one price at which 5 units can be sold: $122.

This analysis is shown in Figure 8.2, where we have graphed the demand, marginal-revenue, average-total-cost, and marginal-cost data from the table. The profit-maximizing output occurs at 5 units of output (Q_m), where the marginal-revenue (MR) and marginal-cost (MC) curves intersect. There, MR = MC.

To find the price the monopolist will charge, we extend a vertical line from Q_m up to the demand curve D. The unique price P_m at which Q_m units can be sold is $122. In this case, $122 is the profit-maximizing price. So the monopolist sets the quantity at Q_m to charge its profit-maximizing price of $122.

WORKED PROBLEMS

W 8.1
Monopoly price and output

INTERACTIVE GRAPHS

G 8.1
Monopoly

Columns 2 and 5 of the table show that at 5 units of output, the product price ($122) exceeds the average total cost ($94). The monopolist thus obtains an economic profit of $28 per unit, and the total economic profit is then $140 (= 5 units × $28). In the graph in Figure 8.2, per-unit profit is $P_m - A$, where A is the average total cost of producing Q_m units. Total economic profit of $140 (the green rectangle) is found by multiplying this per-unit profit by the profit-maximizing output Q_m.

Misconceptions Concerning Monopoly Pricing

Our analysis exposes three fallacies concerning monopoly behavior.

Not Highest Price   Because a monopolist can manipulate output and price, people often believe it "will charge the highest price possible." That is incorrect. There are many prices above P_m in Figure 8.2, but the monopolist shuns them because they yield a smaller-than-maximum total profit. The monopolist seeks maximum total profit, not maximum price. Some high prices that could be charged would reduce sales and total revenue too severely to offset any decrease in total cost.

Total, Not Unit, Profit   The monopolist seeks maximum *total* profit, not maximum *unit* profit. In Figure 8.2 a careful comparison of the vertical distance between average total cost and price at various possible outputs indicates that per-unit profit is greater at a point slightly to the left of the profit-maximizing output Q_m. This is seen in the table, where unit profit at 4 units of output is $32 (= $132 − $100) compared with $28 (= $122 − $94) at the profit-maximizing output of 5 units. Here the monopolist accepts a lower-than-maximum per-unit profit because additional sales more than compensate for the lower unit profit. A profit-seeking monopolist would rather sell 5 units at a profit of $28 per unit (for a total profit of $140) than 4 units at a profit of $32 per unit (for a total profit of only $128).

Possibility of Losses   The likelihood of economic profit is greater for a pure monopolist than for a pure competitor. In the long run, the pure competitor is destined to have only a normal profit, whereas barriers to entry mean that any economic profit realized by the monopolist can persist. In pure monopoly there are no new entrants to increase supply, drive down price, and eliminate economic profit.

But pure monopoly does not guarantee profit. Despite dominance in its market (as, say, a seller of home sewing machines), a monopoly enterprise can suffer a loss because of weak demand and relatively high costs. If the demand and cost situation faced by the monopolist is far less favorable than that in Figure 8.2, the monopolist can incur losses. Like the pure competitor, the monopolist will not persist in operating at a loss in the long run. Faced with continuing losses, the firm's owners will move their resources to alternative industries that offer better profit opportunities. Like any firm, a monopolist must obtain a minimum of a normal profit in the long run or it will go out of business.

Economic Effects of Monopoly

Let's now evaluate pure monopoly from the standpoint of society as a whole. Our reference for this evaluation will be the outcome of long-run efficiency in a purely competitive market, identified by the triple equality $P = MC = \text{minimum ATC}$.

Price, Output, and Efficiency

Figure 8.3 graphically contrasts the price, output, and efficiency outcomes of pure monopoly and a purely competitive *industry*. The $S = MC$ curve in Figure 8.3a reminds us that the market supply curve S for a purely competitive industry is the horizontal sum of the marginal-cost curves of all the firms in the industry. Suppose there are 1000 such firms. Comparing their combined supply curve S with market demand D, we see that the purely competitive price and output are P_c and Q_c.

Recall that this price-output combination results in both productive efficiency and allocative efficiency. *Productive efficiency* is achieved because free entry and exit force firms to operate where their average total cost is at a minimum. The sum of the minimum-ATC outputs of the 1000 pure competitors is the industry output, here, Q_c. Product price is at the lowest level consistent with minimum average total cost. The *allocative efficiency* of pure competition results because production occurs up to that output at which price (the measure of a product's value or marginal benefit to society) equals marginal cost (the worth of the alternative products forgone by society in producing any given commodity). In short: $P = MC = \text{minimum ATC}$.

FIGURE 8.3

Inefficiency of pure monopoly relative to a purely competitive industry. (a) In a purely competitive industry, entry and exit of firms ensure that price (P_c) equals marginal cost (MC) and that the minimum average-total-cost output (Q_c) is produced. Both productive efficiency ($P = \text{minimum ATC}$) and allocative efficiency ($P = MC$) are obtained. (b) In pure monopoly, the MR curve lies below the demand curve. The monopolist maximizes profit at output Q_m, where $MR = MC$, and charges price P_m. Thus, output is lower (Q_m rather than Q_c) and price is higher (P_m rather than P_c) than they would be in a purely competitive industry. Monopoly is inefficient, since output is less than that required for achieving minimum ATC (here, at Q_c) and because the monopolist's price exceeds MC.

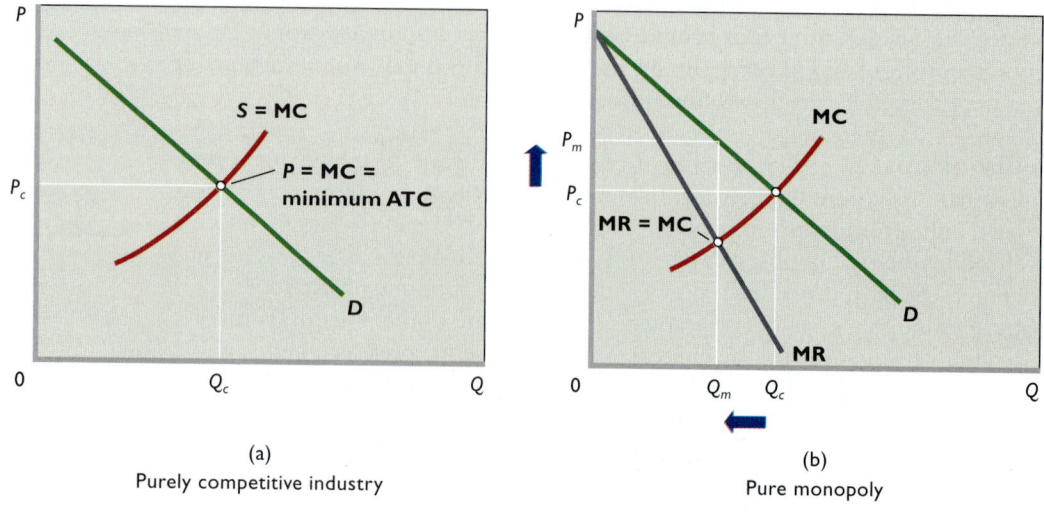

(a)
Purely competitive industry

(b)
Pure monopoly

Now let's suppose that this industry becomes a pure monopoly (Figure 8.3b) as a result of one firm acquiring all its competitors. We also assume that no changes in costs or market demand result from this dramatic change in the industry structure. What formerly were 1000 competing firms are now a single pure monopolist consisting of 1000 noncompeting branches.

The competitive market supply curve S has become the marginal-cost curve (MC) of the monopolist, the summation of the individual marginal-cost curves of its many branch plants. The important change, however, is on the demand side. From the viewpoint of each of the 1000 individual competitive firms, demand was perfectly elastic, and marginal revenue was therefore equal to the market equilibrium price P_c. So each firm equated its marginal revenue of P_c dollars per unit with its individual marginal cost curve to maximize profits. But market demand and individual demand are the same to the pure monopolist. The firm *is* the industry, and thus the monopolist sees the downsloping demand curve D shown in Figure 8.3b.

This means that marginal revenue is less than price, that graphically the MR curve lies below demand curve D. In using the MR = MC rule, the monopolist selects output Q_m and price P_m. A comparison of both graphs in Figure 8.3 reveals that the monopolist finds it profitable to sell a smaller output at a higher price than do the competitive producers.

Monopoly yields neither productive nor allocative efficiency. The lack of productive efficiency can be understood most directly by noting that the monopolist's output Q_m is less than Q_c, the output at which average total cost is lowest. In addition, the monopoly price P_m is higher than the competitive price P_c that we know in long-run equilibrium in pure competition equals minimum average total cost. Thus, the monopoly price exceeds minimum average total cost, thereby demonstrating in another way that the monopoly will not be productively efficient.

The monopolist's underproduction also implies allocative inefficiency. One way to see this is to note that at the monopoly output level Q_m, the monopoly price P_m that consumers are willing to pay exceeds the marginal cost of production. This means that consumers value additional units of this product more highly than they do the alternative products that could be produced from the resources that would be necessary to make more units of the monopolist's product.

The monopolist's allocative inefficiency can also be understood by noting that for every unit between Q_m and Q_c, marginal benefit exceeds marginal cost because the demand curve lies above the supply curve. By choosing not to produce these units, the monopolist reduces allocative efficiency because the resources that should have been used to make these units will be redirected instead toward producing items that bring lower net benefits to society. In monopoly, then

- P exceeds MC.
- P exceeds minimum ATC.

Income Transfer

In general, a monopoly transfers income from consumers to the owners of the monopoly. The income is received by the owners as revenue. Because a monopoly has market power, it can charge a higher price than would a purely competitive firm with the same costs. So the monopoly in effect levies a "private tax" on consumers. This private tax can often generate substantial economic profits that can persist because entry to the industry is blocked. Because, on average, monopoly owners have more income than buyers, monopoly increases income inequality.

Cost Complications

Our conclusion has been that, given identical costs, a purely monopolistic industry will charge a higher price, produce a smaller output, and allocate economic resources less efficiently than a purely competitive industry. These inferior results are rooted in the entry barriers present in monopoly.

Now we must recognize that costs may not be the same for purely competitive and monopolistic producers. The unit cost incurred by a monopolist may be either larger or smaller than that incurred by a purely competitive firm. There are four reasons why costs may differ: (1) economies of scale, (2) a factor called "X-inefficiency," (3) the need for monopoly-preserving expenditures, and (4) the "very long run" perspective, which allows for technological advance.

Economies of Scale Once Again   Where economies of scale are extensive, market demand may not be sufficient to support a large number of competing firms, each producing at minimum efficient scale (MES). In such cases, an industry of one or two firms would have a lower average total cost than would the same industry made up of numerous competitive firms. At the extreme, only a single firm—a natural monopoly—might be able to achieve the lowest long-run average total cost.

Some firms relating to new information technologies—for example, computer software, Internet service, and wireless communications—have displayed extensive economies of scale. As these firms have grown, their long-run average total costs have declined because of greater use of specialized inputs, the spreading of product development costs, and learning by doing. Also, *simultaneous consumption* and *network effects* have reduced costs.

A product's ability to satisfy a large number of consumers at the same time is called **simultaneous consumption.** Dell Inc. needs to produce a personal computer for each customer, but Microsoft needs to produce its Windows program only once. Then, at very low marginal cost, Microsoft delivers its program by disk or Internet to millions of consumers. Others able to deliver to additional consumers at low cost include Internet service providers, music producers, and wireless communication firms. Because marginal costs are so low, the average total cost of output typically declines as more customers are added.

Network effects are present if the value of a product to each user, including existing users, increases as the total number of users rises. Good examples are computer software, cell phones, and websites like Facebook where the content is provided by users. When other people have Internet service and devices to access it, a person can conveniently send e-mail messages to them. And when they have similar software, then documents, spreadsheets, and photos can be attached to the e-mail messages. The greater the number of persons connected to the system, the greater are the benefits of the product to each person.

Such network effects may drive a market toward monopoly because consumers tend to choose standard products that everyone else is using. The focused demand for these products permits their producers to grow rapidly and thus achieve economies of scale. Smaller firms, which have either higher-cost "right" products or "wrong" products, get acquired or go out of business.

Economists generally agree that some new information firms have not yet exhausted their economies of scale. But most economists question whether such firms are truly natural monopolies. Most firms eventually achieve their minimum efficient scale at less than the full size of the market. That means competition among firms is possible.

simultaneous consumption
A product's ability to satisfy a large number of consumers at the same time.

network effects
Increases in the value of a product to each user as the total number of users rises.

But even if natural monopoly develops, it's unlikely that the monopolist will pass cost reductions along to consumers as price reductions. So, with perhaps a handful of exceptions, economies of scale do not change the general conclusion that monopoly industries are inefficient relative to competitive industries.

X-Inefficiency In constructing all the average-total-cost curves used in this book, we have assumed that the firm uses the most efficient existing technology. This assumption is only natural because firms cannot maximize profits unless they are minimizing costs. **X-inefficiency** occurs when a firm produces output at a higher cost than is necessary to produce it. For example, in Figure 8.2 the ATC and MC curves might be located above those shown, indicating higher costs at each level of output.

> **ORIGIN OF THE IDEA**
>
> **O 8.3**
> X-inefficiency

X-inefficiency
The production of output, whatever its level, at higher than the lowest average (and total) cost possible.

Why is X-inefficiency allowed to occur if it reduces profits? The answer harks back to our early discussion of the principal-agent problem. Managers may have goals, such as expanding power, having an easier work life, avoiding business risk, or giving jobs to incompetent relatives, that conflict with cost minimization. Or X-inefficiency may arise because a firm's workers are poorly motivated or ineffectively supervised. Or a firm may simply become lethargic and inert, relying on rules of thumb or intuition in decision making as opposed to relevant calculations of costs and revenues.

Presumably, monopolistic firms tend more toward X-inefficiency than competitive producers do. Firms in competitive industries are continually under pressure from rivals, forcing them to be internally efficient to survive. But monopolists are sheltered from such competitive forces by entry barriers, and that lack of pressure may lead to X-inefficiency.

Rent-Seeking Expenditures Economists define **rent-seeking behavior** as any activity designed to transfer income or wealth to a particular firm or resource supplier at someone else's, or even society's, expense. We have seen that a monopolist can obtain an economic profit even in the long run. Therefore, it is no surprise that a firm may go to great expense to acquire or maintain a monopoly granted by government through legislation or an exclusive license. Such rent-seeking expenditures add nothing to the firm's output, but they clearly increase its costs. Taken alone, rent-seeking implies that monopoly involves higher costs and less efficiency than suggested in Figure 8.3b.

rent-seeking behavior
Any action designed to gain special benefits from government at taxpayers' or someone else's expense.

Technological Advance In the very long run, firms can reduce their costs through the discovery and implementation of new technology. If monopolists are more likely than competitive producers to develop more efficient production techniques over time, then the inefficiency of monopoly might be overstated. The general view of economists is that a pure monopolist will not be technologically progressive. Although its economic profit provides ample means to finance research and development, it has little incentive to implement new techniques (or products). The absence of competitors means that there is no external pressure for technological advance in a monopolized market. Because of its sheltered market position, the pure monopolist can afford to be inefficient and lethargic; there is no major penalty for not being more efficient.

One caveat: Recall that entirely new products and new methods of production can suddenly supplant existing monopoly through the process of creative destruction (Chapter 2). Recognizing this threat, the monopolist may continue to engage in R&D

and seek technological advance to avoid falling prey to future rivals. In this case technological advance is essential to the maintenance of monopoly. But forestalling creative destruction means that it is *potential* competition, not the monopoly market structure, that is driving the technological advance. By assumption, no such competition exists in the pure-monopoly model because entry is entirely blocked.

Applying the Analysis

Is De Beers' Diamond Monopoly Forever?

De Beers, a Swiss-based company controlled by a South African corporation, produces about 45 percent of the world's rough-cut diamonds and purchases for resale a sizable number of the rough-cut diamonds produced by other mines worldwide. As a result, De Beers markets about 55 percent of the world's diamonds to a select group of diamond cutters and dealers. But that percentage has declined from 80 percent in the mid-1980s. Therein lies the company's problem.

De Beers' past monopoly behavior is a classic example of the monopoly model illustrated in Figure 8.2. No matter how many diamonds it mined or purchased, it sold only the quantity of diamonds that would yield an "appropriate" (monopoly) price. That price was well above production costs, and De Beers and its partners earned monopoly profits.

When demand fell, De Beers reduced its sales to maintain price. The excess of production over sales was then reflected in growing diamond stockpiles held by De Beers. It also attempted to bolster demand through advertising ("Diamonds are forever"). When demand was strong, it increased sales by reducing its diamond inventories.

De Beers used several methods to control the production of many mines it did not own. First, it convinced a number of independent producers that "single-channel" or monopoly marketing through De Beers would maximize their profit. Second, mines that circumvented De Beers often found their market suddenly flooded with similar diamonds from De Beers' vast stockpiles. The resulting price decline and loss of profit often would encourage a "rogue" mine into the De Beers fold. Finally, De Beers simply purchased and stockpiled diamonds produced by independent mines to keep their added supplies from undercutting the market.

Several factors have come together to unravel the monopoly. New diamond discoveries resulted in a growing leakage of diamonds into world markets outside De Beers' control. For example, significant prospecting and trading in Angola occurred. Recent diamond discoveries in Canada's Northwest Territories posed another threat. Although De Beers is a participant in that region, a large uncontrolled supply of diamonds has begun to emerge. Another challenge has been technological improvements that now allow chemical firms to manufacture flawless artificial diamonds. To prevent consumers from switching to synthetic diamonds, De Beers had to launch a costly campaign to promote "mined diamonds" over synthetics.

Moreover, the international media began to focus heavily on the role that diamonds play in financing bloody civil wars in Africa. Fearing a consumer boycott of diamonds, De Beers pledged that it would not buy these "conflict" diamonds or do business with any firms that did. These diamonds, however, continue to find their way into the marketplace, eluding De Beers' control.

In mid-2000 De Beers abandoned its attempt to control the supply of diamonds. Since then it has tried to transform itself from a diamond cartel to a modern international corporation selling "premium" diamonds under the De Beers label. It has gradually reduced its $4 billion stockpile of diamonds and turned its efforts to increasing the demand for its "branded" diamonds through advertising. De Beers' new strategy is to establish itself as "the diamond supplier of choice."

Diamonds may be forever, but the De Beers diamond monopoly was not. Nevertheless, with its high market share and ability to control its own production levels, De Beers continues to wield considerable influence over the price of rough-cut diamonds.

Question:
De Beers' advertising is trying to establish the tradition of giving diamond anniversary rings. What is the logic behind its efforts? Use Figure 8.2 to demonstrate this graphically.

Price Discrimination

We have thus far assumed that the monopolist charges a single price to all buyers. But under certain conditions the monopolist can increase its profit by charging different prices to different buyers. In so doing, the monopolist is engaging in **price discrimination,** the practice of selling a specific product at more than one price when the price differences are not justified by cost differences.

ORIGIN OF THE IDEA
O 8.4
Price discrimination

price discrimination
The selling of a product to different buyers at different prices when the price differences are not justified by differences in costs.

Price discrimination is a common business practice that rarely reduces competition and therefore is rarely challenged by government. The exception occurs when a firm engages in price discrimination as part of a strategy to block entry or drive out competitors.

Conditions

The opportunity to engage in price discrimination is not readily available to all sellers. Price discrimination is possible when the following conditions are met:

- *Monopoly power* The seller must be a monopolist or, at least, must possess some degree of monopoly power, that is, some ability to control output and price.
- *Market segregation* At relatively low cost to itself, the seller must be able to segregate buyers into distinct classes, each of which has a different willingness or ability to pay for the product. This separation of buyers is usually based on different price elasticities of demand, as the examples below will make clear.
- *No resale* The original purchaser cannot resell the product or service. If buyers in the low-price segment of the market could easily resell in the high-price segment, the monopolist's price-discrimination strategy would create competition in the high-price segment. This competition would reduce the price in the high-price segment and undermine the monopolist's price-discrimination policy. This condition suggests that service industries such as the transportation industry or legal and medical services, where resale is impossible, are candidates for price discrimination.

Examples

Price discrimination is widely practiced in the U.S. economy. For example, airlines charge high fares to business travelers, whose demand for travel is inelastic, and offer lower highly restricted, nonrefundable fares to attract vacationers and others whose demands are more elastic.

Electric utilities frequently segment their markets by end uses, such as lighting and heating. The absence of reasonable lighting substitutes means that the demand for electricity for illumination is inelastic and that the price per kilowatt-hour for such use is high. But the availability of natural gas and petroleum for heating makes the demand for electricity for this purpose less inelastic and the price lower.

Movie theaters and golf courses vary their charges on the basis of time (for example, higher evening and weekend rates) and age (for example, lower rates for children, senior discounts). Railroads vary the rate charged per ton-mile of freight according to the market value of the product being shipped. The shipper of 10 tons of television sets or refrigerators is charged more than the shipper of 10 tons of gravel or coal.

The issuance of discount coupons, redeemable at purchase, is a form of price discrimination. It enables firms to give price discounts to their most price-sensitive customers who have elastic demand. Less price-sensitive consumers who have less elastic demand are not as likely to take the time to clip and redeem coupons. The firm thus makes a larger profit than if it had used a single-price, no-coupon strategy.

Finally, price discrimination often occurs in international trade. A Russian aluminum producer, for example, might sell aluminum for less in the United States than in Russia. In the United States, this seller faces an elastic demand because several substitute suppliers are available. But in Russia, where the manufacturer dominates the market and trade barriers impede imports, consumers have fewer choices and thus demand is less elastic.

Graphical Analysis

Figure 8.4 demonstrates price discrimination graphically. The two graphs are for a single pure monopolist selling its product, say, software, in two segregated parts of the market. For example, one segment might be small-business customers and the other students. Student versions of the software are identical to the versions sold to businesses but are available (1 per person) only to customers with a student ID. Presumably, students have lower ability to pay for the software and are charged a discounted price.

The demand curve D_b, in Figure 8.4a, represents the relatively inelastic demand for the product of business customers. The demand curve D_s, in Figure 8.4b, reflects the elastic demand of students. The marginal revenue curves (MR_b and MR_s) lie below their respective demand curves, reflecting the demand–marginal revenue relationship previously described.

For visual clarity, we have assumed that average total cost (ATC) is constant. Therefore, marginal cost (MC) equals average total cost (ATC) at all quantities of output. These costs are the same for both versions of the software and therefore appear as the single straight line labeled "MC = ATC."

What price will the pure monopolist charge to each set of customers? Using the MR = MC rule for profit maximization, the firm will offer Q_b units of the software for sale to small businesses. It can sell that profit-maximizing output by charging price P_b. Again using the MR = MC rule, the monopolist will offer Q_s units of software to students. To sell those Q_s units, the firm will charge students the lower price P_s.

FIGURE 8.4

Price discrimination to different groups of buyers. The price-discriminating monopolist represented here maximizes its total profit by dividing the market into two segments based on differences in elasticity of demand. It then produces and sells the MR = MC output in each market segment. (For visual clarity, average total cost (ATC) is assumed to be constant. Therefore, MC equals ATC at all output levels.) (a) The firm charges a higher price (here, P_b) to customers who have a less elastic demand curve and (b) a lower price (here, P_s) to customers with a more elastic demand. The price discriminator's total profit is larger than it would be with no discrimination and therefore a single price.

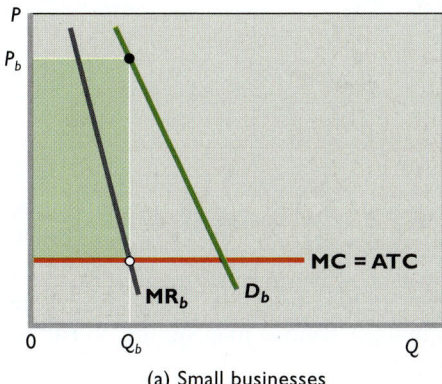

(a) Small businesses

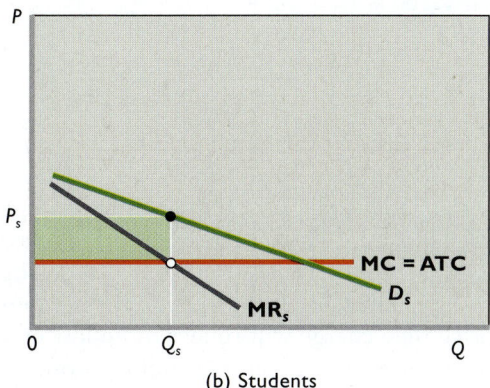

(b) Students

Firms engage in price discrimination because it enhances their profit. The numbers (not shown) behind the curves in Figure 8.4 would reveal that the sum of the two profit rectangles shown in green exceeds the single profit rectangle the firm would obtain from a single monopoly price. How do consumers fare? In this case, students clearly benefit by paying a lower price than they would if the firm charged a single monopoly price; in contrast, the price discrimination results in a higher price for business customers. Therefore, compared to the single-price situation, students buy more of the software and small businesses buy less.

WORKED PROBLEMS

W 8.2

Price discrimination

Price Discrimination at the Ballpark

Professional baseball teams earn substantial revenues through ticket sales. To maximize profit, they offer significantly lower ticket prices for children (whose demand is elastic) than for adults (whose demand is inelastic). This discount may be as much as 50 percent.

If this type of price discrimination increases revenue and profit, why don't teams also price-discriminate at the concession stands? Why don't they offer half-price hot dogs, soft drinks, peanuts, and Cracker Jack to children? The answer involves the three requirements for successful price discrimination. All three requirements are met for game tickets: (1) The team has monopoly power; (2) it can segregate ticket buyers by age group, each group having a different elasticity of demand; and (3) children cannot resell their discounted tickets to adults.

It's a different situation at the concession stands. Specifically, the third condition is *not* met. If the team had dual prices, it could not prevent the exchange or

Applying the Analysis

"resale" of the concession goods from children to adults. Many adults would send children to buy food and soft drinks for them: "Here's some money, Billy. Go buy *10* hot dogs for all of us." In this case, price discrimination would reduce, not increase, team profit. Thus, children and adults are charged the same high prices at the concession stands.

Question:
Why are the prices for concessions at the games quite high compared to prices for the same or similar items at the local convenience store?

Monopoly and Antitrust Policy

Monopoly is a legitimate concern. Monopolists can charge higher-than-competitive prices that result in an underallocation of resources to the monopolized product. They can stifle innovation, engage in rent-seeking behavior, and foster X-inefficiency. Even when their costs are low because of economies of scale, there is no guarantee that the price they charge will reflect those low costs. The cost savings may simply accrue to the monopoly as greater economic profit.

Not Widespread

Fortunately, however, monopoly is not widespread in the United States. Barriers to entry are seldom completely successful. Although research and technological advances may strengthen the market position of a monopoly, technology may also undermine monopoly power. Over time, the creation of new technologies may work to destroy monopoly positions (creative destruction). For example, the development of courier delivery, fax machines, and e-mail has eroded the monopoly power of the U.S. Postal Service. Cable television monopolies are now challenged by satellite TV and by new technologies that permit the transmission of audio and visual signals over the Internet.

Similarly, patents eventually expire; and even before they do, the development of new and distinct substitutable products often circumvents existing patent advantages. New sources of monopolized resources sometimes are found, and competition from foreign firms may emerge. (See Global Snapshot 8.1.) Finally, if a monopoly is sufficiently fearful of future competition from new products, it may keep its prices relatively low so as to discourage rivals from developing such products. If so, consumers may pay nearly competitive prices even though competition is currently lacking.

Antitrust Policy

What should government do about monopoly when it arises and persists in the real world? Economists agree that government needs to look carefully at monopoly on a case-by-case basis. If the monopoly appears to be unsustainable over a long period of time, say, because of emerging new technology, society can simply choose to ignore it. In contrast, the government may want to file charges against a monopoly under the antitrust laws if the monopoly was achieved through anticompetitive actions, creates substantial economic inefficiency, and appears to be long-lasting. (Monopolies were once called "trusts.") The relevant antitrust law is the Sherman Act of 1890, which has two main provisions:

Competition from Foreign Multinational Corporations

Global Snapshot 8.1

Competition from foreign multinational corporations diminishes the market power of firms in the United States. Here are just a few of the hundreds of foreign multinational corporations that compete strongly with U.S. firms in certain American markets.

Company (Country)	Main Products
Bayer (Germany)	chemicals
BP Amoco (United Kingdom)	gasoline
Michelin (France)	tires
NEC (Japan)	computers
Nestlé (Switzerland)	food products
Nokia (Finland)	wireless phones
Royal Dutch/Shell (Netherlands)	gasoline
Royal Philips (Netherlands)	electronics
Sony (Japan)	electronics
Toyota (Japan)	automobiles
Unilever (Netherlands)	food products

Source: Compiled from "Global 500," Fortune, July 26, 2010. © Time Inc., used under license.

- *Section 1* "Every contract, combination in the form of a trust or otherwise, or conspiracy, in restraint of trade or commerce among the several States, or with foreign nations is declared to be illegal."
- *Section 2* "Every person who shall monopolize, or attempt to monopolize, or combine or conspire with any person or persons, to monopolize any part of the trade or commerce among the several States, or with foreign nations, shall be deemed guilty of a felony . . ." (as later amended from "misdemeanor").

In the 1911 Standard Oil case, the Supreme Court found Standard Oil guilty of monopolizing the petroleum industry through a series of abusive and anticompetitive actions. The Court's remedy was to divide Standard Oil into several competing firms. But the Standard Oil case left open an important question: Is every monopoly in violation of Section 2 of the Sherman Act or just those created or maintained by anticompetitive actions?

In the 1920 U.S. Steel case, the courts established a **rule of reason** interpretation of Section 2, saying that it is not illegal to be a monopoly. Only monopolies that "unreasonably" restrain trade violate Section 2 of the Sherman Act and are subject to antitrust action. Size alone was not an offense. Although U.S. Steel clearly possessed monopoly power, it was innocent of "monopolizing" because it had not resorted to illegal acts against competitors in obtaining that power nor had it unreasonably used its monopoly power. Unlike Standard Oil, which was a "bad trust," U.S. Steel was a "good trust" and therefore not in violation of the law. The rule of reason was attacked and once reversed by the courts, but today it is the accepted legal interpretation of the Sherman Act's monopoly provisions.

Today, the U.S. Department of Justice, the Federal Trade Commission, injured private parties, or state attorney generals can file antitrust suits against alleged violators

rule of reason
The court ruling that only monopolies unreasonably attained or maintained are illegal.

of the Sherman Act. The courts can issue injunctions to prohibit anticompetitive practices (a behavioral remedy) or, if necessary, break up monopolists into competing firms (a structural remedy). Courts also can fine and imprison violators. Also, parties injured by monopolies can sue for *treble damages*—an award of three times the amount of the monetary injury done to them. In some cases, these damages have summed to millions or even billions of dollars.

The largest and most significant monopoly case of recent times is the Microsoft case, which is the subject of the application that follows.

Applying
the Analysis

United States v. Microsoft

In May 1998 the U.S. Justice Department, 19 individual states, and the District of Columbia (hereafter, "the government") filed antitrust charges against Microsoft under the Sherman Antitrust Act. The government charged that Microsoft had violated Section 2 of the act through a series of unlawful actions designed to maintain its "Windows" monopoly. It also charged that some of that conduct violated Section 1 of the Sherman Act, which prohibits actions that restrain trade or commerce.

Microsoft denied the charges, arguing it had achieved its success through product innovation and lawful business practices. Microsoft contended it should not be penalized for its superior foresight, business acumen, and technological prowess. It also insisted that its monopoly was highly transitory because of rapid technological advance.

In June 2000 the district court ruled that the relevant market was software used to operate Intel-compatible personal computers (PCs). Microsoft's 95 percent share of that market clearly gave it monopoly power. The court pointed out, however, that being a monopoly is not illegal. The violation of the Sherman Act occurred because Microsoft used anticompetitive means to maintain its monopoly power.

According to the court, Microsoft feared that the success of Netscape's Navigator, which allowed people to browse the Internet, might allow Netscape to expand its software to include a competitive PC operating system—software that would threaten the Windows monopoly. It also feared that Sun's Internet applications of its Java programming language might eventually threaten Microsoft's Windows monopoly.

To counter these and similar threats, Microsoft illegally signed contracts with PC makers that required them to feature its Internet Explorer on the PC desktop and penalized companies that promoted software products that competed with Microsoft products. Moreover, it gave friendly companies coding that linked Windows to software applications and withheld such coding from companies featuring Netscape. Finally, under license from Sun, Microsoft developed Windows-related Java software that made Sun's own software incompatible with Windows.

The district court ordered Microsoft to split into two competing companies, one initially selling the Windows operating system and the other initially selling Microsoft applications (such as Word, Hotmail, MSN, PowerPoint, and Internet Explorer). Both companies would be free to develop new products that compete with each other, and both could derive those products from the intellectual property embodied in the common products existing at the time of divestiture.

In late 2000 Microsoft appealed the district court decision to a U.S. court of appeals. In 2001 the higher court affirmed that Microsoft illegally maintained its monopoly, but tossed out the district court's decision to break up Microsoft. It agreed with Microsoft that the company was denied due process during the penalty phase of the trial and concluded that the district court judge had displayed an appearance of bias by holding extensive interviews with the press. The appeals court sent the remedial phase of the case to a new district court judge to determine appropriate remedies. The appeals court also raised issues relating to the wisdom of a structural remedy.

At the urging of the new district court judge, the federal government and Microsoft negotiated a proposed settlement. With minor modification, the settlement became the final court order in 2002. The breakup was rescinded and replaced with a behavioral remedy. It (1) prevents Microsoft from retaliating against any firm that is developing, selling, or using software that competes with Microsoft Windows or Internet Explorer or is shipping a personal computer that includes both Windows and a non-Microsoft operating system; (2) requires Microsoft to establish uniform royalty and licensing terms for computer manufacturers wanting to include Windows on their PCs; (3) requires that manufacturers be allowed to remove Microsoft icons and replace them with other icons on the Windows desktop; and (4) calls for Microsoft to provide technical information to other companies so those firms can develop programs that work as well with Windows as Microsoft's own products.

Microsoft's actions and conviction have indirectly resulted in billions of dollars of fines and payouts by Microsoft. Main examples: To AOL Time Warner (Netscape), $750 million; to the European Commission, $600 million in 2004 and $1.35 billion in 2008; to Sun Microsystems, $1.6 billion; to Novell, $536 million; to Brust.com, $60 million; to Gateway; $150 million; to interTrust, $440 million; to RealNetworks, $761 million; and to IBM, $850 million.

Question:
Why is the 2002 Microsoft settlement a behavioral remedy rather than a structural remedy?

Source: United States v. Microsoft (District Court Conclusions of Law), April 2000; *United States v. Microsoft* (court of appeals), June 2001; *United States v. Microsoft* (Final Judgment), November 2002; and Reuters and Associated Press news services.

Summary

1. A pure monopolist is the sole producer of a good or service for which there are no close substitutes.

2. The existence of pure monopoly is explained by barriers to entry in the form of (a) economies of scale, (b) patent ownership and research, (c) ownership or control of essential resources, and (d) pricing and other strategic behavior.

3. The pure monopolist's market situation differs from that of a competitive firm in that the monopolist's demand curve is downsloping, causing the marginal-revenue curve to lie below the demand curve. Like the competitive seller, the pure monopolist will maximize profit by equating marginal revenue and marginal cost. Barriers to entry may permit a monopolist to acquire economic profit even in the long run. However, (a) the monopolist does not charge "the highest price possible"; (b) the price that yields maximum total profit to the monopolist rarely coincides with the price that yields maximum unit profit; and (c) high costs and a weak demand may prevent the monopolist from realizing any profit at all.

4. With the same costs, the pure monopolist will find it profitable to restrict output and charge a higher price than would sellers in a purely competitive industry. This

restriction of output causes a misallocation of resources, as is evidenced by the fact that price exceeds marginal cost in monopolized markets.

5. Monopoly transfers income from consumers to monopolists because monopolists can charge a higher price than would a purely competitive firm with the same costs. So monopolists, in effect, levy a "private tax" on consumers and, if demand is strong enough, obtain substantial economic profits.

6. The costs monopolists and competitive producers face may not be the same. On the one hand, economies of scale may make lower unit costs available to monopolists but not to competitors. Also, pure monopoly may be more likely than pure competition to reduce costs via technological advance because of the monopolist's ability to realize economic profit, which can be used to finance research. On the other hand, X-inefficiency—the failure to produce with the least costly combination of inputs—is more common among monopolists than among competitive firms. Also, monopolists may make

costly expenditures to maintain monopoly privileges that are conferred by government. Finally, the blocked entry of rival firms weakens the monopolist's incentive to be technologically progressive.

7. A firm can increase its profit through price discrimination provided it (a) has monopoly pricing power, (b) can segregate buyers on the basis of elasticities of demand, and (c) can prevent its product or service from being readily transferred between the segregated markets.

8. The cornerstone of antimonopoly law is the Sherman Act of 1890, particularly Section 2. According to the rule of reason, possession of monopoly power is not illegal. But monopoly that is unreasonably gained or unreasonably maintained is a violation of the law.

9. If a company is found guilty of violating the Sherman Act, the government can either break up the monopoly into competing firms (a structural remedy) or prohibit it from engaging in specific anticompetitive business practices (a behavioral remedy).

Terms and Concepts

pure monopoly	simultaneous consumption	rent-seeking behavior
barriers to entry	network effects	price discrimination
natural monopoly	X-inefficiency	rule of reason

Questions

1. "No firm is completely sheltered from rivals; all firms compete for consumer dollars. If that is so, then pure monopoly does not exist." Do you agree? Explain. **LO1**

2. Discuss the major barriers to entry into an industry. Explain how each barrier can foster either monopoly or oligopoly. Which barriers, if any, do you feel give rise to monopoly that is socially justifiable? **LO1**

3. How does the demand curve faced by a purely monopolistic seller differ from that confronting a purely competitive firm? Why does it differ? Of what significance is the difference? Why is the pure monopolist's demand curve typically not perfectly inelastic? **LO2**

4. Use the following demand schedule for a pure monopolist to calculate total revenue and marginal revenue at each quantity. Plot the monopolist's demand curve and marginal-revenue curve, and explain the relationships between them. Explain why the marginal revenue of the fourth unit of output is $3.50, even though its price is $5. What generalization can you make as to the relationship between the monopolist's demand and its marginal revenue? Suppose the marginal cost of successive

units of output was zero. What output would the single-price monopolist produce, and what price would it charge? **LO2**

Price (P)	Quantity Demanded (Q)	Price (P)	Quantity Demanded (Q)
$7.00	0	$4.50	5
6.50	1	4.00	6
6.00	2	3.50	7
5.50	3	3.00	8
5.00	4	2.50	9

5. Assume a monopolistic publisher has agreed to pay an author 10 percent of the total revenue from the sales of a text. Will the author and the publisher want to charge the same price for the text? Explain. **LO2**

6. Assume that a pure monopolist and a purely competitive firm have the same unit costs. Contrast the two with respect to (a) price, (b) output, (c) profits,

(d) allocation of resources, and (e) impact on the distribution of income. Since both monopolists and competitive firms follow the MR = MC rule in maximizing profits, how do you account for the different results? Why might the costs of a purely competitive firm and those of a monopolist be different? What are the implications of such a cost difference? **LO3**

7. Critically evaluate and explain each statement: **LO3**
   a. Because they can control product price, monopolists are always assured of profitable production by simply charging the highest price consumers will pay.
   b. The pure monopolist seeks the output that will yield the greatest per-unit profit.
   c. An excess of price over marginal cost is the market's way of signaling the need for more production of a good.
   d. The more profitable a firm, the greater its monopoly power.
   e. The monopolist has a pricing policy; the competitive producer does not.

f. With respect to resource allocation, the interests of the seller and of society coincide in a purely competitive market but conflict in a monopolized market.

8. U.S. pharmaceutical companies charge different prices for prescription drugs to buyers in different nations, depending on elasticity of demand and government-imposed price ceilings. Explain why these companies, for profit reasons, oppose laws allowing reimportation of their drugs back into the United States. **LO4**

9. How was De Beers able to control the world price of diamonds over the past several decades even though it produced only 45 percent of the diamonds? What factors ended its monopoly? What is its new profit strategy? **LO5**

10. Under what law and on what basis did the federal district court find Microsoft guilty of violating the Sherman Act? What was the initial district court's remedy? How did Microsoft fare with its appeal to the court of appeals? What was the final negotiated remedy? **LO5**

Problems

1. Assume that the most efficient production technology available for making vitamin pills has the cost structure given in the following table. Note that output is measured as the number of bottles of vitamins produced per day and that costs include a normal profit. **LO1**

Output	TC	MC
25,000	$100,000	$0.50
50,000	150,000	1.00
75,000	187,500	2.50
100,000	275,500	3.00

   a. What is ATC per unit for each level of output listed in the table?
   b. Is this a decreasing-cost industry? (Answer yes or no).
   c. Suppose that the market price for a bottle of vitamins is $2.50 and that at that price the total market quantity demanded is 75,000,000 bottles. How many firms will there be in this industry?
   d. Suppose that, instead, the market quantity demanded at a price of $2.50 is only 75,000. How many firms do you expect there to be in this industry?
   e. Review your answers to parts b, c, and d. Does the level of demand determine this industry's market structure?

2. A new production technology for making vitamins is invented by a college professor who decides not to patent it. Thus, it is available for anybody to copy and put into

use. The TC per bottle for production up to 100,000 bottles per day is given in the following table. **LO1**

Output	TC
25,000	$50,000
50,000	70,000
75,000	75,000
100,000	80,000

   a. What is ATC for each level of output listed in the table?
   b. Suppose that for each 25,000-bottle-per-day increase in production above 100,000 bottles per day, TC increases by $5000 (so that, for instance, 125,000 bottles per day would generate total costs of $85,000 and 150,000 bottles per day would generate total costs of $90,000). Is this a decreasing-cost industry?
   c. Suppose that the price of a bottle of vitamins is $1.33 and that at that price the total quantity demanded by consumers is 75,000,000 bottles. How many firms will there be in this industry?
   d. Suppose that, instead, the market quantity demanded at a price of $1.33 is only 75,000. How many firms do you expect there to be in this industry?
   e. Review your answers to parts b, c, and d. Does the level of demand determine this industry's market structure?
   f. Compare your answer to part d of this problem with your answer to part d of problem 1. Do both production technologies show constant returns to scale?

3. Suppose a pure monopolist is faced with the demand schedule shown below and the same cost data as the competitive producer discussed in problem 4 at the end of Chapter 7. Calculate the missing total-revenue and marginal-revenue amounts, and determine the profit-maximizing price and profit-maximizing output for this monopolist. What is the monopolist's profit? Verify your answer graphically and by comparing total revenue and total cost. **LO2**

Price	Quantity Demanded	Total Revenue	Marginal Revenue
$115	0	$ __	
100	1	__	$ __
83	2	__	__
71	3	__	__
63	4	__	__
55	5	__	__
48	6	__	__
42	7	__	__
37	8	__	__
33	9	__	__
29	10	__	__

4. Suppose that a price-discriminating monopolist has segregated its market into two groups of buyers. The first group is described by the demand and revenue data that you developed for problem 3. The demand and revenue data for the second group of buyers is shown in the table. Assume that MC is $13 in both markets and MC = ATC at all output levels. What price will the firm charge in each market? Based solely on these two prices, which market has the higher price elasticity of demand? What will be this monopolist's total economic profit? **LO4**

Price	Quantity Demanded	Total Revenue	Marginal Revenue
$71	0	$ 0	
63	1	63	$63
55	2	110	47
48	3	144	34
42	4	168	24
37	5	185	17
33	6	198	13
29	7	203	5

FURTHER TEST YOUR KNOWLEDGE AT
www.brue3e.com

At the text's Online Learning Center, **www.brue3e.com,** you will find one or more web-based questions that require information from the Internet to answer. We urge you to check them out, since they will familiarize you with websites that may be helpful in other courses and perhaps even in your career. The OLC also features multiple-choice quizzes that give instant feedback and provides other helpful ways to further test your knowledge of the chapter.

CHAPTER NINE

Monopolistic Competition and Oligopoly

After reading this chapter you should be able to:

1. List the characteristics of monopolistic competition.
2. Explain why monopolistic competitors earn only a normal profit in the long run.
3. Describe the characteristics of oligopoly.
4. Discuss how game theory relates to oligopoly.
5. Relate why the demand curve of an oligopolist may be kinked.
6. Compare the incentives and obstacles to collusion among oligopolists.
7. Contrast the positive and potential negative effects of advertising.

In the United States, most industries have a market structure that falls somewhere between the two poles of pure competition (Chapter 7) and pure monopoly (Chapter 8). To begin with, most real-world industries usually have fewer than the large number of producers required for pure competition but more than the single producer that defines pure monopoly. In addition, most firms in most industries have both distinguishable rather than standardized products as well as some discretion over the prices they charge. As a result, competition often occurs on the basis of price, quality, location, service, and advertising.

Finally, entry to most real-world industries ranges from easy to very difficult but is rarely completely blocked.

This chapter examines two models that more closely approximate these widespread industry structures. You will discover that *monopolistic competition* mixes a small amount of monopoly power with a large amount of competition. *Oligopoly,* in contrast, blends a large amount of monopoly power with both considerable rivalry among existing firms and the threat of increased future competition due to foreign firms and new technologies.

© Robert Landau/CORBIS

© Royalty-Free/CORBIS

Photo Op Monopolistic Competition versus Oligopoly

Furniture is produced in a monopolistically competitive industry, whereas refrigerators are produced in an oligopolistic industry.

Monopolistic Competition

monopolistic competition
A market structure in which many firms sell a differentiated product and entry into and exit from the market are relatively easy.

Let's begin by examining **monopolistic competition,** which is characterized by (1) a relatively large number of sellers, (2) differentiated products (often promoted by heavy advertising), and (3) easy entry into, and exit from, the industry. The first and third characteristics provide the "competitive" aspect of monopolistic competition; the second characteristic provides the "monopolistic" aspect. In general, however, monopolistically competitive industries are much more competitive than they are monopolistic.

Relatively Large Number of Sellers

Monopolistic competition is characterized by a fairly large number of firms, say, 25, 35, 60, or 70, not by the hundreds or thousands of firms in pure competition. Consequently, monopolistic competition involves:

ORIGIN OF THE IDEA
O 9.1
Monopolistic competition

- *Small market shares*   Each firm has a comparatively small percentage of the total market and consequently has limited control over market price.
- *No collusion*   The presence of a relatively large number of firms ensures that collusion by a group of firms to restrict output and set prices is unlikely.

- *Independent action*   With numerous firms in an industry, there is no feeling of interdependence among them; each firm can determine its own pricing policy without considering the possible reactions of rival firms. A single firm may realize a modest increase in sales by cutting its price, but the effect of that action on competitors' sales will be nearly imperceptible and will probably trigger no response.

Differentiated Products

In contrast to pure competition, in which there is a standardized product, monopolistic competition is distinguished by **product differentiation.** Monopolistically competitive firms turn out variations of a particular product. They produce products with slightly different physical characteristics, offer varying degrees of customer service, provide varying amounts of locational convenience, or proclaim special qualities, real or imagined, for their products.

   These aspects of product differentiation require more attention.

product differentiation A form of nonprice competition in which a firm tries to distinguish its product or service from all competing ones on the basis of attributes such as design and quality.

Product Attributes   Product differentiation may entail physical or qualitative differences in the products themselves. Real differences in functional features, materials, design, and workmanship are vital aspects of product differentiation. Personal computers, for example, differ in terms of storage capacity, speed, graphic displays, and included software. There are dozens of competing principles of economics textbooks that differ in content, organization, presentation and readability, pedagogical aids, and graphics and design. Most cities have a variety of retail stores selling men's and women's clothes that differ greatly in styling, materials, and quality of work. Similarly, one pizza place may feature its thin crust Neapolitan style pizza, while another may tout its thick-crust Chicago-style pizza.

Service   Service and the conditions surrounding the sale of a product are forms of product differentiation too. One shoe store may stress the fashion knowledge and helpfulness of its clerks. A competitor may leave trying on shoes and carrying them to the register to its customers but feature lower prices. Customers may prefer 1-day over 3-day dry cleaning of equal quality. The prestige appeal of a store, the courteousness and helpfulness of clerks, the firm's reputation for servicing or exchanging its products, and the credit it makes available are all service aspects of product differentiation.

Location   Products may also be differentiated through the location and accessibility of the stores that sell them. Small convenience stores manage to compete with large supermarkets, even though these minimarts have a more limited range of products and charge higher prices. They compete mainly on the basis of location—being close to customers and situated on busy streets. A motel's proximity to an interstate highway gives it a locational advantage that may enable it to charge a higher room rate than nearby motels in less convenient locations.

Brand Names and Packaging   Product differentiation may also be created through the use of brand names and trademarks, packaging, and celebrity connections. Most aspirin tablets are very much alike, but many headache sufferers believe that one brand—for example, Bayer, Anacin, or Bufferin—is superior and worth a higher price than a generic substitute. A celebrity's name associated with watches, perfume, or athletic apparel may enhance the appeal of those products for some buyers. Many customers prefer one style of ballpoint pen to another. Packaging that touts "natural spring" bottled water may attract additional customers.

Some Control over Price   Despite the relatively large number of firms, monopolistic competitors do have some control over their product prices because of product differentiation. If consumers prefer the products of specific sellers, then within limits they will pay more to satisfy their preferences. Sellers and buyers are not linked randomly, as in a purely competitive market. But the monopolistic competitor's control over price is quite limited since there are numerous potential substitutes for its product.

Easy Entry and Exit

Entry into monopolistically competitive industries is relatively easy compared to oligopoly or pure monopoly. Because monopolistic competitors are typically small firms, both absolutely and relatively, economies of scale are few and capital requirements are low. On the other hand, compared with pure competition, financial barriers may result from the need to develop and advertise a product that differs from rivals' products. Some firms may have trade secrets relating to their products or hold trademarks on their brand names, making it difficult and costly for other firms to imitate them.

Exit from monopolistically competitive industries is relatively easy. Nothing prevents an unprofitable monopolistic competitor from holding a going-out-of-business sale and shutting down.

Advertising

The expense and effort involved in product differentiation would be wasted if consumers were not made aware of product differences. Thus, monopolistic competitors advertise their products, often heavily. The goal of product differentiation and advertising—so-called **nonprice competition**—is to make price less of a factor in consumer purchases and make product differences a greater factor. If successful, the demand for the firm's product will increase. The firm's demand may also become less elastic because of the greater loyalty to the firm's product.

nonprice competition
A selling strategy in which one firm tries to distinguish its product or service from all competing ones on the basis of attributes other than price.

Monopolistically Competitive Industries

Several manufacturing industries approximate monopolistic competition. Examples of manufactured goods produced in monopolistically competitive industries are jewelry, asphalt, wood pallets, commercial signs, leather goods, plastic pipes, textile bags, and kitchen cabinets. In addition, many retail establishments in metropolitan areas are monopolistically competitive, including grocery stores, gasoline stations, hair salons, dry cleaners, clothing stores, and restaurants. Also, many providers of professional services such as medical care, legal assistance, real estate sales, and basic bookkeeping are monopolistic competitors.

Price and Output in Monopolistic Competition

How does a monopolistically competitive firm decide what quantity to produce and what price to charge? Initially, we assume that each firm in the industry is producing a specific differentiated product and engaging in a particular amount of advertising. Later we'll see how changes in the product and in the amount of advertising modify our conclusions.

The Firm's Demand Curve

Our explanation is based on Figure 9.1, which shows that the demand curve faced by a monopolistically competitive seller is highly, but not perfectly, elastic. It is precisely this feature that distinguishes monopolistic competition from both pure monopoly and pure competition. The monopolistic competitor's demand is more elastic than the demand faced by a pure monopolist because the monopolistically competitive seller has many competitors producing closely substitutable goods. The pure monopolist has no rivals at all. Yet, for two reasons, the monopolistic competitor's demand is not perfectly elastic like that of the pure competitor. First, the monopolistic competitor has fewer rivals; second, its products are differentiated, so they are not perfect substitutes.

FIGURE 9.1

A monopolistically competitive firm: short run and long run. The monopolistic competitor maximizes profit or minimizes loss by producing the output at which MR = MC. The economic profit shown in (a) will induce new firms to enter, eventually eliminating economic profit. The loss shown in (b) will cause an exit of firms until normal profit is restored. After such entry and exit, the price will settle in (c) to where it just equals average total cost at the MR = MC output. At this price P_3 and output Q_3, the monopolistic competitor earns only a normal profit, and the industry is in long-run equilibrium.

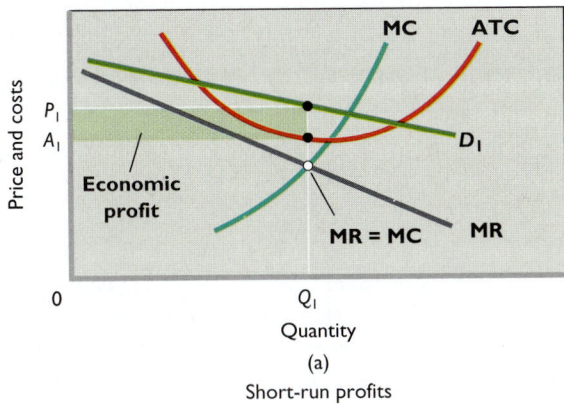

(a)
Short-run profits

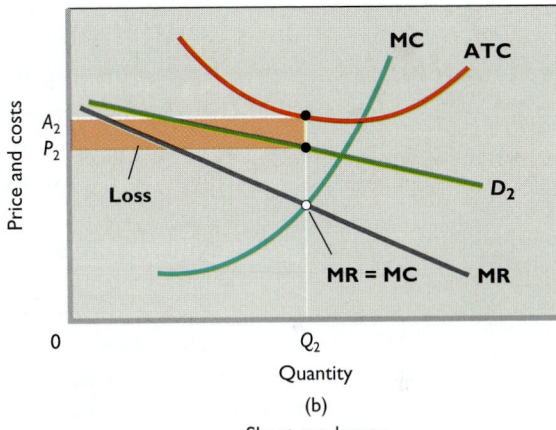

(b)
Short-run losses

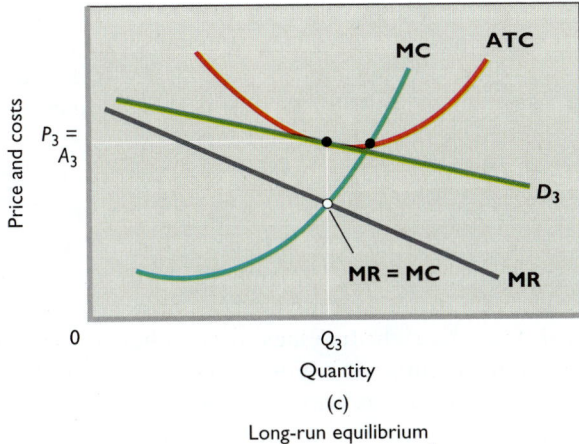

(c)
Long-run equilibrium

The price elasticity of demand faced by the monopolistically competitive firm depends on the number of rivals and the degree of product differentiation. The larger the number of rivals and the weaker the product differentiation, the greater the price elasticity of each seller's demand, that is, the closer monopolistic competition will be to pure competition.

The Short Run: Profit or Loss

In the short run, monopolistically competitive firms maximize profit or minimize loss using exactly the same strategy as pure competitors and monopolists: They produce the level of output at which marginal revenue equals marginal cost (MR = MC). Thus, the monopolistically competitive firm in Figure 9.1a produces output Q_1, where MR = MC. As shown by demand curve D_1, it then can charge price P_1. It realizes an economic profit, shown by the green area $[= (P_1 - A_1) \times Q_1]$.

But with less favorable demand or costs, the firm may incur a loss in the short run. We show this possibility in Figure 9.1b, where the firm's best strategy is to minimize its loss. It does so by producing output Q_2 (where MR = MC) and, as determined by demand curve D_2, by charging price P_2. Because price P_2 is less than average total cost A_2, the firm incurs a per-unit loss of $A_2 - P_2$ and a total loss represented as the red area $[= (A_2 - P_2) \times Q_2]$.

The Long Run: Only a Normal Profit

In the long run, firms will enter a profitable monopolistically competitive industry and leave an unprofitable one. So a monopolistic competitor will earn only a normal profit in the long run or, in other words, will only break even. (Remember that the cost curves include both explicit and implicit costs, including a normal profit.)

Profits: Firms Enter　In the case of short-run profit (Figure 9.1a), economic profits attract new rivals because entry to the industry is relatively easy. As new firms enter, the demand curve faced by the typical firm shifts to the left (falls). Why? Because each firm has a smaller share of total demand and now faces a larger number of close-substitute products. This decline in the firm's demand reduces its economic profit. When entry of new firms has reduced demand to the extent that the demand curve is tangent to the average-total-cost curve at the profit-maximizing output, the firm is just making a normal profit. This situation is shown in Figure 9.1c, where demand is D_3 and the firm's long-run equilibrium output is Q_3. As Figure 9.1c indicates, any greater or lesser output will entail an average total cost that exceeds product price P_3, meaning a loss for the firm. At the tangency point between the demand curve and ATC, total revenue equals total costs. With the economic profit gone, there is no further incentive for additional firms to enter.

Losses: Firms Leave　When the industry suffers short-run losses, as in Figure 9.1b, some firms will exit in the long run. Faced with fewer substitute products and blessed with an expanded share of total demand, the surviving firms will see their demand

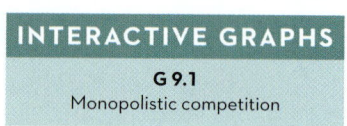

INTERACTIVE GRAPHS

G 9.1
Monopolistic competition

curves shift to the right (rise), as to D_3. Their losses will disappear and give way to normal profits (Figure 9.1c). (For simplicity we have assumed a constant-cost industry; shifts in the cost curves as firms enter or leave would complicate our discussion slightly but would not alter our conclusions.)

Monopolistic Competition and Efficiency

We know from Chapter 7 that economic efficiency requires each firm to produce the amount of output at which $P = MC = $ minimum ATC. The equality of P and ATC yields *productive efficiency*. The good is being produced in the least costly way, and the price is just sufficient to cover average total cost, including a normal profit. The equality of P and MC yields *allocative efficiency*. The right amount of output is being produced, and thus the right amount of society's scarce resources is being devoted to this specific use.

How efficient is monopolistic competition, as measured against this triple equality? In particular, do monopolistically competitive firms produce the efficient output level associated with $P = MC = $ minimum ATC?

Neither Productive nor Allocative Efficiency

In monopolistic competition, neither productive nor allocative efficiency occurs in long-run equilibrium. Figure 9.2 enlarges part of Figure 9.1c and clearly shows this. First note that the profit-maximizing price P_3 slightly exceeds the lowest average total cost, A_4. In producing the profit-maximizing output Q_3, the firm's average total cost therefore is slightly higher than optimal from society's perspective—productive efficiency is not achieved. Also note that the profit-maximizing price P_3 exceeds marginal cost (here M_3), meaning that monopolistic competition causes an underallocation of resources. Society values each unit of output between Q_3 and Q_4 more highly than the goods it would have to forgo to produce those units. Thus, to a modest extent,

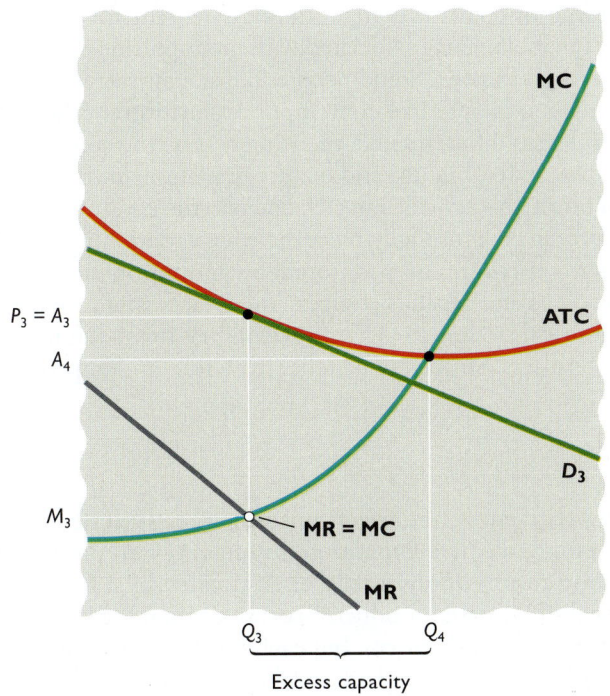

FIGURE 9.2

The inefficiency of monopolistic competition. In long-run equilibrium a monopolistic competitor achieves neither productive nor allocative efficiency. Productive efficiency is not realized because production occurs where the average total cost A_3 exceeds the minimum average total cost A_4. Allocative efficiency is not achieved because the product price P_3 exceeds the marginal cost M_3. The results are an underallocation of resources and excess production capacity of $Q_4 - Q_3$.

monopolistic competition also fails the allocative-efficiency test. Consumers pay a higher-than-competitive price and obtain a less-than-optimal output. Indeed, monopolistic competitors must charge a higher-than-competitive price in the long run in order to achieve a normal profit.

Excess Capacity

excess capacity
Plant or equipment that is underused because the firm is producing less than the minimum-ATC output.

In monopolistic competition, the gap between the minimum-ATC output and the profit-maximizing output identifies **excess capacity:** plant and equipment that are underused because firms are producing less than the minimum-ATC output. This gap is shown as the distance between Q_4 and Q_3 in Figure 9.2. Note in the figure that the minimum ATC is at point b. If each monopolistic competitor could profitably produce at this point on its ATC curve, the lower average total cost would enable a lower price than P_3. More importantly, if each firm produced at b rather than at a, fewer firms would be needed to produce the industry output. But because monopolistically competitive firms produce at a in long-run equilibrium, monopolistically competitive industries are overpopulated with firms, each operating below its optimal capacity. This situation is typified by many kinds of retail establishments. For example, in most cities there is an abundance of small motels and restaurants that operate well below half capacity.

Product Variety and Improvement

But monopolistic competition also has two notable virtues. It promotes product variety and product improvement. A monopolistic competitor is rarely satisfied with the situation portrayed in Figure 9.1c because it means only a normal profit. Instead, it may try to regain its economic profit through further product differentiation and better advertising. By developing or improving its product, it may be able to re-create, at least for a while, the profit outcome of Figure 9.1a.

The product variety and product improvement that accompany the drive to regain economic profit in monopolistic competition are benefits for society—ones that may offset the cost of the inefficiency associated with monopolistic competition. Consumers have a wide diversity of tastes: Some people like Italian salad dressing, others prefer French dressing; some people like contemporary furniture, others prefer traditional furniture. If a product is differentiated, then at any time the consumer will be offered a wide range of types, styles, brands, and quality gradations of that product. Compared with pure competition, this provides an advantage to the consumer. The range of choice is widened, and producers more fully meet the wide variation in consumer tastes.

The product improvement promoted by monopolistic competition further differentiates products and expands choices. And a successful product improvement by one firm obligates rivals to imitate or improve on that firm's temporary market advantage or else lose business. So society benefits from new and improved products.

Oligopoly

oligopoly
A market structure dominated by a few large producers of homogeneous or differentiated products.

In terms of competitiveness, the spectrum of market structures reaches from pure competition, to monopolistic competition, to oligopoly, to pure monopoly. We now direct our attention to **oligopoly,** a market dominated by a few large producers of a homogeneous or differentiated product. Because of their "fewness," oligopolists have considerable control over their prices, but each must consider the possible reaction of rivals to its own pricing, output, and advertising decisions.

A Few Large Producers

The phrase "a few large producers" is necessarily vague because the market model of oligopoly covers much ground, ranging between pure monopoly, on the one hand, and monopolistic competition, on the other. Oligopoly encompasses the U.S. aluminum industry, in which three huge firms dominate an entire national market, and the situation in which four or five much smaller auto-parts stores enjoy roughly equal shares of the market in a medium-size town. Generally, however, when you hear a term such as "Big Three," "Big Four," or "Big Six," you can be sure it refers to an oligopolistic industry. Examples of U.S. industries that are oligopolies are tires, beer, cigarettes, copper, greeting cards, lightbulbs, aircraft, motor vehicles, gypsum products, and breakfast cereals. There are numerous others.

Either Homogeneous or Differentiated Products

An oligopoly may be either a **homogeneous oligopoly** or a **differentiated oligopoly**, depending on whether the firms in the oligopoly produce standardized (homogeneous) or differentiated products. Many industrial products (steel, zinc, copper, aluminum, lead, cement, industrial alcohol) are virtually standardized products that are produced in oligopolies. Alternatively, many consumer goods industries (automobiles, tires, household appliances, electronic equipment, breakfast cereals, cigarettes, and many sporting goods) are differentiated oligopolies. These differentiated oligopolies typically engage in considerable nonprice competition supported by heavy advertising.

homogeneous oligopoly
An oligopoly in which the firms produce a standardized product.

differentiated oligopoly
An oligopoly in which the firms produce a differentiated product.

Control over Price, but Mutual Interdependence

Because firms are few in oligopolistic industries, each firm is a "price maker"; like the monopolist, it can set its price and output levels to maximize its profit. But unlike the monopolist, which has no rivals, the oligopolist must consider how its rivals will react to any change in its price, output, product characteristics, or advertising. Oligopoly is thus characterized by *strategic behavior* and *mutual interdependence*. By **strategic behavior,** we simply mean self-interested behavior that takes into account the reactions of others. Firms develop and implement price, quality, location, service, and advertising strategies to "grow their business" and expand their profits. But because rivals are few, there is **mutual interdependence:** a situation in which each firm's profit depends not just on its own price and sales strategies but also on those of the other firms in its highly concentrated industry. So oligopolistic firms base their decisions on how they think rivals will react. Example: In deciding whether to increase the price of its cosmetics, L'Oreal will try to predict the response of the other major producers, such as Clinique. Second example: In deciding on its advertising strategy, Burger King will take into consideration how McDonald's might react.

strategic behavior
Self-interested behavior that takes into account the reactions of others.

mutual interdependence
A situation in which a change in strategy (usually price) by one firm will affect the sales and profits of other firms.

Creative Strategic Behavior

Illustrating the Idea

The following story, offered with tongue in cheek, illustrates a localized market that exhibits some characteristics of oligopoly, including strategic behavior.

Tracy Martinez's Native American Arts and Crafts store is located in the center of a small tourist town that borders on a national park. In its early days, Tracy had a minimonopoly. Business was brisk, and prices and profits were high.

To Tracy's annoyance, two "copycat" shops opened adjacent to her store, one on either side of her shop. Worse yet, the competitors named their shops to take advantage of Tracy's advertising. One was "Native Arts and Crafts"; the other, "Indian Arts and Crafts." These new sellers drew business away from Tracy's store, forcing her to lower her prices. The three side-by-side stores in the small, isolated town constituted a localized oligopoly for Native American arts and crafts.

Tracy began to think strategically about ways to boost profit. She decided to distinguish her shop from those on either side by offering a greater mix of high-quality, expensive products and a lesser mix of inexpensive souvenir items. The tactic worked for a while, but the other stores eventually imitated her product mix.

Then, one of the competitors next door escalated the rivalry by hanging up a large sign proclaiming "We Sell for Less!" Shortly thereafter, the other shop put up a large sign stating "We Won't Be Undersold!"

Not to be outdone, Tracy painted a colorful sign of her own and hung it above her door. It read "Main Entrance."

Question:
How do you think the two rivals will react to Tracy's strategy?

Entry Barriers

The same barriers to entry that create pure monopoly also contribute to the creation of oligopoly. Economies of scale are important entry barriers in a number of oligopolistic industries, such as the aircraft, rubber, and copper industries. In those industries, three or four firms might each have sufficient sales to achieve economies of scale, but new firms would have such a small market share that they could not do so. They would then be high-cost producers, and as such they could not survive. A closely related barrier is the large expenditure for capital—the cost of obtaining necessary plant and equipment—required for entering certain industries. The jet engine, automobile, commercial aircraft, and petroleum-refining industries, for example, are all characterized by very high capital requirements.

The ownership and control of raw materials help explain why oligopoly exists in many mining industries, including gold, silver, and copper. In the computer, chemicals, consumer electronics, and pharmaceutical industries, patents have served as entry barriers. Moreover, oligopolists can sometimes preclude the entry of new competitors through preemptive and retaliatory pricing and advertising strategies.

Mergers

Some oligopolies have emerged mainly through the growth of the dominant firms in a given industry (examples: breakfast cereals, chewing gum, candy bars). But for other industries the route to oligopoly has been through mergers (examples: steel, in its early history; and, more recently, airlines, banking, and entertainment). Section 7 of the Clayton Act (1914) outlaws mergers that *substantially* lessen competition. But the implied "rule of reason" leaves room for considerable interpretation. As a result, many mergers between firms in the same industry go unchallenged by government.

The combining of two or more firms in the same industry may significantly increase their market share, which may allow the new firm to achieve greater economies of scale. The merger also may increase the firm's monopoly power (pricing power) through greater control over market supply. Finally, because the new firm is a larger buyer of inputs, it may be able to obtain lower prices (costs) on its production inputs.

Oligopoly Behavior: A Game-Theory Overview

Oligopoly pricing behavior has the characteristics of certain games of strategy, such as poker, chess, and bridge. The best way to play such a game depends on the way one's opponent plays. Players (and oligopolists) must pattern their actions according to the actions and expected reactions of rivals. The study of how people or firms behave in strategic situations is called **game theory.**

game theory
The study of how people or firms behave in strategic situations.

The Prisoner's Dilemma

Illustrating the Idea

Games come in different forms, with many possible strategies and outcomes, and have numerous business, political, and personal applications. One frequently observed type of game is known as a *prisoner's dilemma game* because it is similar to a situation in which two people—let's call them Betty and Al—have committed a diamond heist and are being detained by the police as prime suspects. Unknown to the two, the evidence against them is weak so that the best hope that the police have for getting a conviction is if one or both of the thieves confess to the crime. The police place Betty and Al in separate holding cells and offer each the same deal: Confess to the crime and receive a lighter prison sentence.

Each detainee therefore faces a dilemma. If Betty remains silent and Al confesses, Betty will end up with a long prison sentence. If Betty confesses and Al says nothing, Al will receive a long prison sentence. What happens? Fearful that the other person will confess, both confess, even though they each would be better off saying nothing. In business, a form of the "confess–confess outcome" can occur when two oligopolists escalate their advertising budgets to high levels, even though both would earn higher profits at agreed-upon lower levels. In politics, it occurs when two candidates engage in negative advertising, despite claiming that, in principle, they are opposed to its use.

Question:
How might the prisoners' strategies or decisions be affected if the general prison population tends to punish those who are known to "rat out" (confess against) their partners?

Now let's look at a more detailed prisoner's dilemma game, using the tools of game theory to analyze the pricing behavior of oligopolists. We assume that a duopoly, or two-firm oligopoly, is producing athletic shoes. Each of the two firms—for example, RareAir and Uptown—has a choice of two pricing strategies: price high or price low. The profit each firm earns will depend on the strategy it chooses *and* the strategy its rival chooses.

There are four possible combinations of strategies for the two firms, and a lettered cell in Figure 9.3 represents each combination. For example, cell C

ORIGIN OF THE IDEA

O 9.2
Game theory

Profit payoff (in millions) for a two-firm oligopoly. Each firm has two possible pricing strategies. RareAir's strategies are shown in the top margin, and Uptown's in the left margin. Each lettered cell of this four-cell payoff matrix represents one combination of a RareAir strategy and an Uptown strategy and shows the profit that combination would earn for each firm. Assuming no collusion, the outcome of this game is cell D, with both parties using low-price strategies and earning $8 million of profits.

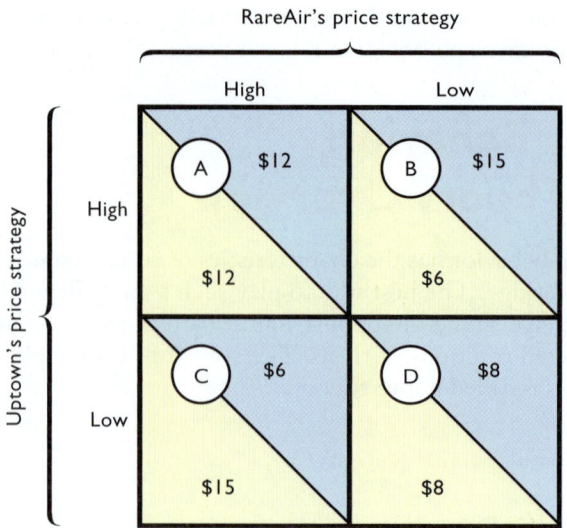

represents a low-price strategy for Uptown along with a high-price strategy for RareAir. Figure 9.3 is called a *payoff matrix* because each cell shows the payoff (profit) to each firm that would result from each combination of strategies. Cell C shows that if Uptown adopts a low-price strategy and RareAir a high-price strategy, then Uptown will earn $15 million (yellow portion) and RareAir will earn $6 million (blue portion).

Mutual Interdependence Revisited

The data in Figure 9.3 are hypothetical, but their relationships are typical of real situations. Recall that oligopolistic firms can increase their profits, and influence their rivals' profits, by changing their pricing strategies. Each firm's profit depends on its own pricing strategy and that of its rivals. This mutual interdependence of oligopolists is the most obvious point demonstrated by Figure 9.3. If Uptown adopts a high-price strategy, its profit will be $12 million provided that RareAir also employs a high-price strategy (cell A). But if RareAir uses a low-price strategy against Uptown's high-price strategy (cell B), RareAir will increase its market share and boost its profit from $12 million to $15 million. RareAir's higher profit will come at the expense of Uptown, whose profit will fall from $12 million to $6 million. Uptown's high-price strategy is a good strategy only if RareAir also employs a high-price strategy.

Collusion

collusion
A situation in which firms act together and in agreement to fix prices, divide markets, or otherwise restrict competition.

Figure 9.3 also suggests that oligopolists often can benefit from **collusion**—that is, cooperation with rivals. Collusion occurs whenever firms in an industry reach an agreement to fix prices, divide up the market, or otherwise restrict competition among them. To see the benefits of collusion, first suppose that both firms in Figure 9.3 are acting independently and following high-price strategies. Each realizes a $12 million profit (cell A).

Note that either RareAir or Uptown could increase its profit by switching to a low-price strategy (cell B or C). The low-price firm would increase its profit to $15 million, and the profit of the high-price firm would fall to $6 million. The high-price firm would be better off if it, too, adopted a low-price policy because its profit would rise from $6 million to $8 million (cell D). The effect of all this independent strategy shifting would be the reduction of both firms' profits from $12 million (cell A) to $8 million (cell D).

In real situations, too, independent action by oligopolists may lead to mutually "competitive" low-price strategies: Independent oligopolists compete with respect to price, and this leads to lower prices and lower profits. This outcome is clearly beneficial to consumers but not to the oligopolists, whose profits decrease.

How could oligopolists avoid the low-profit outcome of cell D? The answer is that they could collude, rather than establish prices competitively or independently. In our example, the two firms could agree to establish and maintain a high-price policy. So each firm will increase its profit from $8 million (cell D) to $12 million (cell A).

Incentive to Cheat

The payoff matrix also explains why an oligopolist might be strongly tempted to cheat on a collusive agreement. Suppose Uptown and RareAir agree to maintain high-price policies, with each earning $12 million in profit (cell A). Both are tempted to cheat

> **INTERACTIVE GRAPHS**
>
> **G 9.2**
> Game theory

on this collusive pricing agreement because either firm can increase its profit to $15 million by lowering its price. For instance, if Uptown secretly cheats and sells at the low price while RareAir keeps on charging the high price, the payoff would move from cell A to cell C so that Uptown's profit would rise to $15 million while RareAir's profit would fall to $6 million. On the other hand, if RareAir cheats and sets a low price while Uptown keeps the agreement and charges the high price, the payoff matrix would move from cell A to cell B so that RareAir would get $15 million while Uptown would get only $6 million. As you can see, cheating is both very lucrative to the cheater as well as very costly to the firm that gets cheated on. As a result, both firms will probably cheat so that the game will settle back to cell D, with each firm using its low-price strategy. This is another example of the prisoner's dilemma illustrated previously.

Kinked-Demand Model

Our game-theory discussion is helpful in understanding more traditional, graphical oligopoly models. We begin by examining a model in which rivals do not overtly collude to fix a common price. Such collusion is, in fact, illegal in the United States. Specifically, Section 1 of the Sherman Act of 1890 outlaws conspiracies to restrain trade. In antitrust law, these violations are known as **per se violations;** they are "in and of themselves" illegal, and therefore not subject to the rule of reason (Chapter 8). To gain a conviction, the government needs to show only that there was a conspiracy to fix prices, rig bids, or divide up markets, not that the conspiracy succeeded or caused serious damage to other parties.

per se violation
A collusive action, such as an attempt to fix prices or divide a market, that violates the antitrust laws, even if the action is unsuccessful.

Kinked-Demand Curve

Imagine an oligopolistic industry made up of three law-abiding firms (Arch, King, and Dave's), each having about one-third of the total market for a differentiated product. The question is, "What does each firm's demand curve look like?"

Let's focus on Arch, understanding that the analysis is applicable to each firm. Assume that the going price for the product is P_0 and Arch is currently selling output Q_0, as shown in Figure 9.4. Suppose Arch is considering a price increase. But if Arch

FIGURE 9.4

The kinked-demand curve. In all likelihood an oligopolist's rivals will ignore a price increase above the going price P_0 but follow a price cut below P_0. This causes the oligopolist's demand curve (D_2eD_1) to be kinked at e (price P_0) and the marginal-revenue curve to have a vertical break, or gap (fg). The firm will be highly reluctant to raise or lower its price. Moreover, any shift in marginal costs between MC_1 and MC_2 will cut the vertical (dashed) segment of the marginal-revenue curve and produce no change in price P_0 or output Q_0.

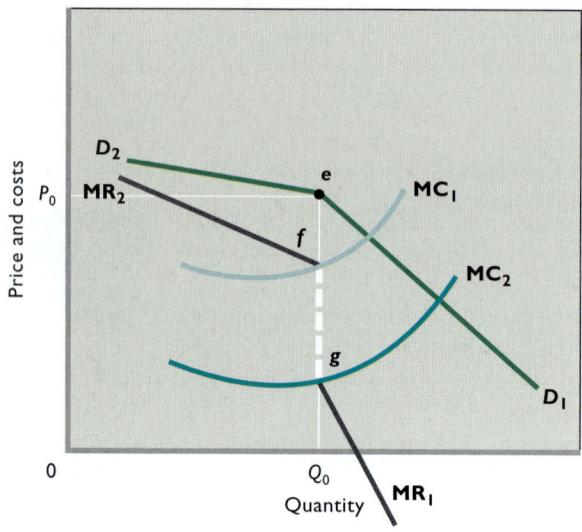

raises its price above P_0 and its rivals ignore the price increase, Arch will lose sales significantly to its two rivals, who will be underpricing it. If that is the case, the demand and marginal-revenue curves faced by Arch will resemble the straight lines D_2 and MR_2 in Figure 9.4. Demand in this case is quite elastic: Arch's total revenue will fall. Because of product differentiation, however, Arch's sales and total revenue will not fall to zero when it raises its price; some of Arch's customers will pay the higher price because they have a strong preference for Arch's product.

And what about a price cut? It is reasonable to expect that King's and Dave's will exactly match any price cut to prevent Arch from gaining an advantage over them. Arch's sales will increase only modestly. The small increase in sales that Arch (and its two rivals) will realize is at the expense of other industries; Arch will gain no sales from King's and Dave's. So Arch's demand and marginal-revenue curves below price P_0 will look like the straight lines labeled D_1 and MR_1 in Figure 9.4.

Graphically, the D_2e "rivals ignore" segment of Arch's demand curve seems relevant for price increases, and the D_1e "rivals match" segment of demand seems relevant for price cuts. It is logical, then, or at least a reasonable assumption, that the noncollusive oligopolist faces the **kinked-demand curve** D_2eD_1, as shown in Figure 9.4. Demand is highly elastic above the going price P_0 but much less elastic or even inelastic below that price.

Note also that if rivals ignore a price increase but match a price decrease, the marginal-revenue curve of the oligopolist also will have an odd shape. It, too, will be made up of two segments: the left-hand marginal-revenue curve MR_2f in Figure 9.4 and the right-hand marginal-revenue curve MR_1g. Because of the sharp difference in elasticity of demand above and below the going price, there is a gap, or what we can simply treat as a vertical segment, in the marginal-revenue curve. This gap is the dashed segment fg in the combined marginal-revenue curve MR_2fgMR_1.

kinked-demand curve
A demand curve based on the assumption that rivals will ignore a price increase and follow a price decrease.

Price Inflexibility

This analysis helps explain why prices are generally stable in noncollusive oligopolistic industries. There are both demand and cost reasons.

On the demand side, the kinked-demand curve gives each oligopolist reason to believe that any change in price will be for the worse. If it raises its price, many of its customers will desert it. If it lowers its price, its sales will increase very modestly since rivals will match the lower price. Even if a price cut increases the oligopolist's total revenue somewhat, its costs may increase by a greater amount, depending on the price elasticity of demand. For instance, if its demand is inelastic to the right of Q_0, as it may well be, then the firm's profit will surely fall. Its total revenue will decline at the same time that the production of a larger output increases its total cost.

On the cost side, the broken marginal-revenue curve suggests that even if an oligopolist's costs change substantially, the firm may have no reason to change its price. In particular, all positions of the marginal-cost curve between MC_1 and MC_2 in Figure 9.4 will result in the firm's deciding on exactly the same price and output. For all those positions, MR equals MC at output Q_0; at that output, it will charge price P_0.

Price Leadership

The uncertainties of the reactions of rivals create a major problem for oligopolists. There are times when wages and other input prices rise beyond the marginal costs associated with MC_1 in Figure 9.4. If no oligopolist dare raise its price, profits for all rivals will be severely squeezed. In many industries, a pattern of price leadership has emerged to handle these situations. **Price leadership** involves an implicit understanding by which oligopolists can coordinate prices without engaging in outright collusion based on formal agreements and secret meetings. Rather, a practice evolves whereby the "dominant firm"—usually the largest or most efficient in the industry—initiates price changes and all other firms more or less automatically follow the leader. Many industries, including farm machinery, cement, copper, newsprint, glass containers, steel, beer, fertilizer, cigarettes, and tin, practice, or have in the recent past practiced, price leadership.

price leadership
An implicit understanding that other firms will follow the lead when a certain firm in the industry initiates a price change.

An examination of price leadership in a variety of industries suggests that the price leader is likely to observe the following tactics.

- *Infrequent price changes*   Because price changes always carry the risk that rivals will not follow the lead, price adjustments are made only infrequently. The price leader does not respond to minuscule day-to-day changes in costs and demand. Price is changed only when cost and demand conditions have been altered significantly and on an industry basis as the result of, for example, industry wage increases, an increase in excise taxes, or an increase in the price of some basic input such as energy. In the automobile industry, price adjustments traditionally have been made when new models are introduced each fall.
- *Communications*   The price leader often communicates impending price adjustments to the industry through speeches by major executives, trade publication interviews, or press releases. By publicizing "the need to raise prices," the price leader seeks agreement among its competitors regarding the actual increase.
- *Avoidance of price wars*   Price leaders try to prevent price wars that can damage industry profits. Such wars can lead to successive rounds of price cuts as rivals attempt to maintain their market shares.

Challenges to Price Leadership

Despite attempts to maintain orderly price leadership, price wars occasionally break out in oligopolistic industries. Sometimes price wars result from attempts to establish new price leaders; other times, they result from attempts to "steal" business from rivals.

Consider the breakfast cereal industry, in which Kellogg traditionally had been the price leader. General Mills countered Kellogg's leadership in 1995 by reducing the prices of its cereals by 11 percent. In 1996, another rival, Post, responded to General Mills' action with a 20 percent price cut. Kellogg then followed with a 20 percent cut of its own. Not to be outdone, Post reduced its prices by another 11 percent. In short, a full-scale price war broke out between General Mills, Post, and Kellogg.

As another example, in October 2009 with the Christmas shopping season just getting underway, Walmart cut its price on 10 highly anticipated new books to just $10 each. Within hours, Amazon.com matched the price cut. Walmart then retaliated by cutting its price for the books to just $9 each. Amazon.com matched that reduction—at which point Walmart went to $8.99! Then, out of nowhere, Target jumped in at $8.98, a price that Amazon.com and Walmart immediately matched. And that is where the price finally came to rest—at a level so low that each company was losing money on each book it sold.

Most price wars eventually run their course. After a period of low or negative profits, they again yield price leadership to one of the industry's dominant firms. That firm then begins to raise prices back to their previous levels, and the other firms willingly follow. Orderly pricing is then restored.

Question:
How might a low-cost price leader "enforce" its leadership through implied threats to rivals?

Collusion

The disadvantages and uncertainties of kinked-demand oligopolies and price leadership make collusion tempting. By controlling price through collusion, oligopolists may be able to reduce uncertainty, increase profits, and perhaps even prohibit the entry of new rivals. Collusion may assume a variety of forms. The most comprehensive form is the **cartel,** a group of producers that typically creates a formal written agreement specifying how much each member will produce and charge. The cartel members must control output—divide up the market—in order to maintain the agreed-upon price. The collusion is *overt*, or open to view, and typically involves a group of foreign nations or foreign producers. More common forms of collusion are *covert*, or hidden from view. They include conspiracies to fix prices, rig bids, and divide up markets. Such conspiracies sometimes occur even though they are illegal.

cartel
A formal agreement among producers to set the price and the individual firm's output levels of a product.

Joint-Profit Maximization

To see the benefits of a cartel or other form of collusion, assume there are three hypothetical oligopolistic firms (Gypsum, Sheetrock, and GSR) producing, in this instance, gypsum drywall panels for finishing interior walls. Suppose all three firms produce a

FIGURE 9.5

Collusion and the tendency toward joint-profit maximization. If oligopolistic firms face identical or highly similar demand and cost conditions, they may collude to limit their joint output and to set a single, common price. Thus, each firm acts as if it were a pure monopolist, setting output at Q_0 and charging price P_0. This price and output combination maximizes each firm's profit (green area) and thus the joint profits of all.

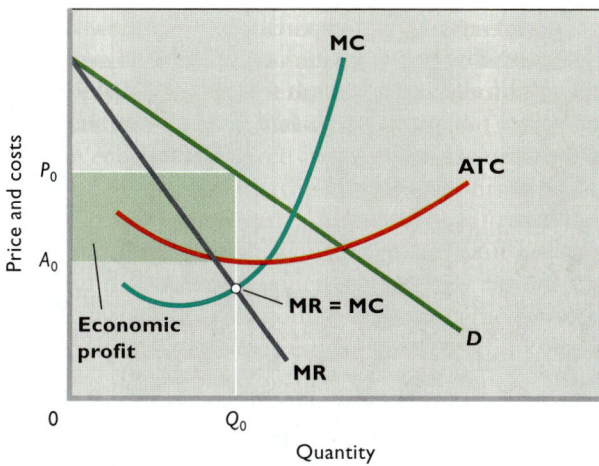

homogeneous product and have identical cost, demand, and marginal-revenue curves. Figure 9.5 represents the position of each of our three oligopolistic firms.

What price and output combination should, say, Gypsum select? If Gypsum were a pure monopolist, the answer would be clear: Establish output at Q_0, where marginal revenue equals marginal cost; charge the corresponding price P_0; and enjoy the maximum profit attainable. However, Gypsum does have two rivals selling identical products, and if Gypsum's assumption that its rivals will match its price of P_0 proves to be incorrect, the consequences could be disastrous for Gypsum. Specifically, if Sheetrock and GSR actually charge prices below P_0, then Gypsum's demand curve D will shift sharply to the left as its potential customers turn to its rivals, which are now selling the same product at a lower price. Of course, Gypsum can retaliate by cutting its price too, but this will move all three firms down their demand curves, lowering their profits. It may even drive them to a point where average total cost exceeds price and losses are incurred.

So the question becomes, "Will Sheetrock and GSR want to charge a price below P_0?" Under our assumptions, and recognizing that Gypsum has little choice except to match any price they may set below P_0, the answer is no. Faced with the same demand and cost circumstances, Sheetrock and GSR will find it in their interest to produce Q_0 and charge P_0. This is a curious situation; each firm finds it most profitable to charge the same price, P_0, but only if its rivals actually do so! How can the three firms ensure the price P_0 and quantity Q_0 solution in which each is keenly interested? How can they avoid the less profitable outcomes associated with either higher or lower prices?

The answer is evident: They can collude. They can get together, talk it over, and agree to charge the same price, P_0. In addition to reducing the possibility of price wars, this will give each firm the maximum profit. For society, the result will be the same as would occur if the industry were a pure monopoly composed of three identical plants.

Cartels and Collusion

Undoubtedly the most significant international cartel is the Organization of Petroleum Exporting Countries (OPEC), comprising 12 oil-producing nations (Saudi Arabia, Iran, Venezuela, UAE, Nigeria, Kuwait, Libya, Algeria, Angola, Ecuador, Qatar, and Iraq). OPEC produces about 41 percent of the world's oil and supplies about 43 percent of all oil traded internationally. OPEC has in some cases been able to drastically alter oil prices by increasing or decreasing supply. In the late 1990s, for instance, it caused oil prices to rise from $11 per barrel to $34 per barrel over a 15-month period.

That being said, most increases in the price of oil are not caused by OPEC. Between 2005 and 2008, for example, oil prices went from $40 per barrel to $140 per barrel due to rapidly rising demand from China and supply uncertainties related to armed conflict in the Middle East. But as the recession that began in December 2007 took hold, demand slumped and oil prices collapsed back down to about $40 per barrel. OPEC was largely a non-factor in this rise and fall in the price of oil. But in those cases where OPEC can effectively enforce its production agreements, there is little doubt that it can hold the price of oil substantially above the marginal cost of production.

Because cartels among domestic firms are illegal in the United States, any collusion that exists is covert or secret. Yet there are numerous examples of collusion, as shown by evidence from antitrust (antimonopoly) cases. In 1993 Borden, Pet, and Dean Food, among others, either pleaded guilty to or were convicted of rigging bids on the prices of milk products sold to schools and military bases. By phone or at luncheons, company executives agreed in advance on which firm would submit the low bid for each school district or military base. In 1996 American agribusiness Archer Daniels Midland and three Japanese and South Korean firms were found to have conspired to fix the worldwide price and sales volume of a livestock feed additive. Executives for the firms secretly met in Hong Kong, Paris, Mexico City, Vancouver, and Zurich to discuss their plans.

There are many other relatively recent examples of price-fixing: ConAgra and Hormel agreed to pay more than $21 million to settle their roles in a nationwide price-fixing case involving catfish. The U.S. Justice Department fined UCAR International $110 million for scheming with rivals to fix prices and divide the world market for graphite electrodes used in steel mills. The auction houses Sotheby's and Christy's were found guilty of conspiring over a 6-year period to set the same commission rates for sellers at auctions. Bayer AG pleaded guilty to, and was fined $66 million for, taking part in a conspiracy to divide up the market and set prices for chemicals used in rubber manufacturing.

Question:
In what way might mergers be an alternative to illegal collusion? In view of your answer, why is it important to enforce laws that outlaw mergers that substantially reduce competition?

Obstacles to Collusion

Normally, cartels and similar collusive arrangements are difficult to establish and maintain. Below are several barriers to collusion beyond the antitrust laws.

Demand and Cost Differences   When oligopolists face different costs and demand curves, it is difficult for them to agree on a price. This is particularly the case in industries where products are differentiated and change frequently. Even with highly standardized products, firms usually have somewhat different market shares and operate with differing degrees of productive efficiency. Thus, it is unlikely that even homogeneous oligopolists would have the same demand and cost curves.

In either case, differences in costs and demand mean that the profit-maximizing price will differ among firms; no single price will be readily acceptable to all, as we assumed was true in Figure 9.5. So price collusion depends on compromises and concessions that are not always easy to obtain and hence act as an obstacle to collusion.

Number of Firms   Other things equal, the larger the number of firms, the more difficult it is to create a cartel or some other form of price collusion. Agreement on price by three or four producers that control an entire market may be relatively easy to accomplish. But such agreement is more difficult to achieve where there are, say, 10 firms, each with roughly 10 percent of the market, or where the Big Three have 70 percent of the market while a competitive fringe of 8 or 10 smaller firms battles for the remainder.

Cheating   As the game-theory model makes clear, there is a temptation for collusive oligopolists to engage in secret price-cutting to increase sales and profit. The difficulty with such cheating is that buyers who are paying a high price for a product may become aware of the lower-priced sales and demand similar treatment. Or buyers receiving a price concession from one producer may use the concession as a wedge to get even larger price concessions from a rival producer. Buyers' attempts to play producers against one another may precipitate price wars among the producers. Although secret price concessions are potentially profitable, they threaten collusive oligopolies over time. Collusion is more likely to succeed when cheating is easy to detect and punish. Then the conspirators are less likely to cheat on the price agreement.

Recession   Long-lasting recession usually serves as an enemy of collusion because slumping markets increase average total cost. In technical terms, as the oligopolists' demand and marginal-revenue curves shift to the left in Figure 9.5 in response to a recession, each firm moves leftward and upward to a higher operating point on its average-total-cost curve. Firms find they have substantial excess production capacity, sales are down, unit costs are up, and profits are being squeezed. Under such conditions, businesses may feel they can avoid serious profit reductions (or even losses) by cutting price and thus gaining sales at the expense of rivals.

Potential Entry   The greater prices and profits that result from collusion may attract new entrants, including foreign firms. Since that would increase market supply and reduce prices and profits, successful collusion requires that colluding oligopolists block the entry of new producers.

Oligopoly and Advertising

We have noted that oligopolists would rather not compete on the basis of price and may become involved in price collusion. Nonetheless, each firm's share of the total market is typically determined through product development and advertising, for two reasons:

- Product development and advertising campaigns are less easily duplicated than price cuts. Price cuts can be quickly and easily matched by a firm's rivals to cancel any potential gain in sales derived from that strategy. Product improvements and successful advertising, however, can produce more permanent gains in market share because they cannot be duplicated as quickly and completely as price reductions.

TABLE 9.1

The Largest
U.S. Advertisers, 2011

Company	Advertising Spending Millions of $
Procter & Gamble	$2949
AT&T	1925
General Motors	1784
Verizon	1637
Comcast	1577
L'Oréal	1344
Time Warner	1279
Pfizer	1204
Chrysler	1193
News Corp	1171

Source: Kantar Media, **www.kantarmediana.com**

• Oligopolists have sufficient financial resources to engage in product development and advertising. For most oligopolists, the economic profits earned in the past can help finance current advertising and product development.

In 2011, U.S. firms spent an estimated $144 billion on advertising in the United States. *Advertising is prevalent in both monopolistic competition and oligopoly.* Table 9.1 lists the 10 leading U.S. advertisers in 2011.

Advertising may affect prices, competition, and efficiency either positively or negatively, depending on the circumstances. While our focus here is on advertising by oligopolists, the analysis is equally applicable to advertising by monopolistic competitors.

Positive Effects of Advertising

In order to make rational (efficient) decisions, consumers need information about product characteristics and prices. Media advertising may be a low-cost means for consumers to obtain that information. Suppose you are in the market for a high-quality camera and there is no advertising of such a product in newspapers or magazines. To make a rational choice, you may have to spend several days visiting stores to determine the availability, prices, and features of various brands. This search entails both direct costs (gasoline, parking fees) and indirect costs (the value of your time). By providing information about the available options, advertising reduces your search time and minimizes these direct and indirect costs.

By providing information about the various competing goods that are available, advertising diminishes monopoly power. In fact, advertising is frequently associated with the introduction of new products designed to compete with existing brands. Could Toyota and Honda have so strongly challenged U.S. auto producers without advertising? Could FedEx have sliced market share away from UPS and the U.S. Postal Service without advertising?

Viewed this way, advertising is an efficiency-enhancing activity. It is a relatively inexpensive means of providing useful information to consumers and thus lowering their search costs. By enhancing competition, advertising results in greater economic efficiency. By facilitating the introduction of new products, advertising speeds up technological progress. By increasing sales and output, advertising can reduce long-run average total cost by enabling firms to obtain economies of scale.

Potential Negative Effects of Advertising

Not all the effects of advertising are positive, of course. Much advertising is designed simply to manipulate or persuade consumers—that is, to alter their preferences in favor of the advertiser's product. A television commercial that indicates that a popular personality drinks a particular brand of soft drink—and therefore that you should too—conveys little or no information to consumers about price or quality. In addition, advertising is sometimes based on misleading and extravagant claims that confuse consumers rather than enlighten them. Indeed, in some cases advertising may well persuade consumers to pay high prices for much-acclaimed but inferior products, forgoing better but unadvertised products selling at lower prices. Example: *Consumer Reports* has found that heavily advertised premium motor oils and fancy additives provide no better engine performance and longevity than do cheaper brands.

Firms often establish substantial brand-name loyalty and thus achieve monopoly power via their advertising (see Global Snapshot 9.1). As a consequence, they are able to increase their sales, expand their market shares, and enjoy greater profits. Larger profits permit still more advertising and further enlargement of the firm's market share and profit. In time, consumers may lose the advantages of competitive markets and face the disadvantages of monopolized markets. Moreover, new entrants to the industry need to incur large advertising costs in order to establish their products in the marketplace; thus, advertising costs may be a barrier to entry.

The World's Top 10 Brand Names

Global Snapshot 9.1

Here are the world's top 10 brands, based on four criteria: the brand's market share within its category, the brand's world appeal across age groups and nationalities, the loyalty of customers to the brand, and the ability of the brand to "stretch" to products beyond the original product.

World's Top 10 Brands

Coca-Cola
IBM
Microsoft
Google
General Electric
McDonald's
Intel
Apple
Disney
Hewlett-Packard

Source: Interbrand's Top 100 Best Global Brands, 2011, **www.BestGlobalBrands.com.** Used with permission of Interbrand.

Advertising can also be self-canceling. The advertising campaign of one fast-food hamburger chain may be offset by equally costly campaigns waged by rivals, so each firm's demand actually remains unchanged. Few, if any, extra burgers will be purchased, and all firms will experience higher costs, and either their profits will fall or, through successful price leadership, their product prices will rise.

When advertising either leads to increased monopoly power or is self-canceling, economic inefficiency results.

Oligopoly and Efficiency

Is oligopoly, then, an efficient market structure from society's standpoint? How do the price and output decisions of the oligopolist measure up to the triple equality $P = MC = $ minimum ATC that occurs in pure competition?

Inefficiency

Many economists believe that the outcome of some oligopolistic markets is approximately as shown in Figure 9.5. This view is bolstered by evidence that many oligopolists sustain sizable economic profits year after year. In that case, the oligopolist's production occurs where price exceeds marginal cost and average total cost. Moreover, production is below the output at which average total cost is minimized. In this view, neither productive efficiency ($P = $ minimum ATC) nor allocative efficiency ($P = MC$) is likely to occur under oligopoly. A few observers assert that oligopoly is actually less desirable than pure monopoly because government usually regulates pure monopoly in the United States to guard against abuses of monopoly power. Informal collusion among oligopolists may yield price and output results similar to those under pure monopoly yet give the outward appearance of competition involving independent firms.

Qualifications

We should note, however, three qualifications to this view:

- *Increased foreign competition*   In recent decades foreign competition has increased rivalry in a number of oligopolistic industries—steel, automobiles, video games, electric shavers, outboard motors, and copy machines, for example. This has helped to break down such cozy arrangements as price leadership and to stimulate much more competitive pricing.
- *Limit pricing*   Recall that some oligopolists may purposely keep prices below the short-run profit-maximizing level in order to bolster entry barriers. In essence, consumers and society may get some of the benefits of competition—prices closer to marginal cost and minimum average total cost—even without the competition that free entry would provide.
- *Technological advance*   Over time, oligopolistic industries may foster more rapid product development and greater improvement of production techniques than would be possible if they were purely competitive. Oligopolists have large economic profits from which they can fund expensive research and development (R&D). Moreover, the existence of barriers to entry may give the oligopolist some assurance that it will reap the rewards of successful R&D. Oligopolists account for the bulk of the more than $200 billion that U.S. businesses spend on R&D each year. Thus, the short-run economic inefficiencies of oligopolists may be partly or wholly offset by the oligopolists' contributions to better products, lower prices, and lower costs over time.

Oligopoly in the Beer Industry

Applying the Analysis

The beer industry serves as a good case study for oligopoly. This industry was once populated by hundreds of firms and an even larger number of brands. But it now is an oligopoly dominated by a handful of producers.

Since the Second World War, profound changes have increased the level of concentration in the U.S. beer industry. In 1947 more than 400 independent brewing companies resided in the United States. By 1967, the number had declined to 124 and by 1980 it had dropped to just 33. In 1947 the largest five brewers sold only 19 percent of the nation's beer. In 2007, the Big Three brewers (Anheuser-Busch, SABMiller, and Molson/Coors) sold 76 percent. In 2007, Anheuser-Bush (48 percent) and SABMiller (18 percent) alone combined for 66 percent of industry sales. And, in late 2007, SABMiller acquired the U.S. operations of Molson/Coors, thus creating MillerCoors and turning the Big Three into the Big Two. In 2008, Belgian brewer InBev purchased Anheuser-Busch, thereby forming international brewing giant A-B. The U.S. beer industry clearly meets all the criteria of oligopoly.

Changes on the demand side of the market have contributed to the "shakeout" of small brewers from the industry. First, consumer tastes in the mass market have generally shifted from the stronger-flavored beers of the small brewers to the light products of the larger brewers. Second, there has been a shift from the consumption of beer in taverns to consumption of it in the home. The beer consumed in taverns was mainly "draft" or "tap" beer from kegs, supplied by local and regional brewers that could deliver the kegs in a timely fashion at relatively low transportation cost. But the large increase in the demand for beer consumed at home opened the door for large brewers that sold their beer in bottles and aluminum cans. The large brewers could ship their beer by truck or rail over long distances and compete directly with the local brewers.

Developments on the supply side of the market have been even more profound. Technological advances speeded up the bottling and canning lines. Today, large brewers can fill and close 2000 cans per line per minute. Large plants are also able to reduce labor costs through the automating of brewing and warehousing. Furthermore, plant construction costs per barrel of production capacity are about one-third less for a 4.5-million-barrel plant than for a 1.5-million-barrel plant. As a consequence of these and other factors, the minimum efficient scale in brewing is a plant size of about 4.5 million barrels. Additionally, studies indicate that further cost savings are available to brewing firms that have two or more separate large breweries in different regions of the country. Between the economies of scale from plant size and these cost savings from multiple plants, cost considerations deter entry to the mainline beer industry.

"Blindfold" taste tests confirm that most mass-produced American beers taste alike. Undaunted, brewers spend large amounts of money touting the supposed differences between their brands in order to build brand loyalty. And here Anheuser-Busch InBev and MillerCoors, which sell national brands, enjoy major cost advantages over producers such as Pabst that have many regional brands (for example, Lonestar, Rainer, Schaefer, and Schmidts). The reason is that national television advertising is less costly *per viewer* than local TV advertising.

Up until the recent combination of Molson/Coors and SABMiller, mergers had not been the dominant factor in explaining the industry consolidation. Rather, that was largely caused by failing smaller breweries' (such as Heileman's) selling out. Dominant firms have expanded by heavily advertising their main brands and by creating new brands such as Miller Lite, Bud Light, Genuine Draft, Keystone, and Icehouse rather than acquiring other brewers. This has sustained significant product differentiation, despite the declining number of major brewers.

The story of the last three decades has been Anheuser-Busch InBev (A-B), which has greatly expanded its market share. A-B now makes the nation's top two brands: Bud Light and Budweiser account for nearly half the beer sold in the United States. Part of A-B's success owes to the demise of regional competitors. But part also is the result of A-B's competitive prowess. It has constructed state-of-the-art breweries, created effective advertising campaigns, and forged strong relationships with regional distributors. Meanwhile, Miller's market share has declined slightly in recent years. In 2002 Philip Morris sold Miller to London-based SAB. SABMiller, as the combined firm was called, redesigned Miller's labeling to enhance its appeal both domestically and overseas. Perhaps of greater importance, SABMiller's acquisition of Coors to form MillerCoors immediately expanded its U.S. market share from 18 percent to 29 percent. MillerCoors thus became the number two brewer in the United States after A-B, which controls 49 percent of the market.

Imported beers such as Heineken, Corona, and Guinness constitute about 9 percent of the market, with individual brands seeming to wax and wane in popularity. Some local or regional microbreweries such as Samuel Adams and Pyramid, which brew "craft" or specialty beers and charge super-premium prices, have whittled into the sales of the major brewers. Craft and specialty beers account for only 6 percent of beer consumed in the United States, but they are the fastest-growing segment of the U.S. industry. A-B and and MillerCoors have taken notice, responding with specialty brands of their own (for example, Red Wolf, Red Dog, Killarney's, Icehouse, and Blue Moon) and buying stakes in microbrewers Redhook Ale and Celis.

Source: Based on Kenneth G. Elzinga, "Beer," in Walter Adams and James Brock (eds.), *The Structure of American Industry*, 10th ed. (Upper Saddle River, N.J.: Prentice-Hall, 2001), pp. 85–113; and Douglas F. Greer, "Beer: Causes of Structural Change," in Larry Duetsch (ed.), *Industry Studies*, 2d ed. (New York: M. E. Sharpe, 1998), pp. 28–64. Updated data and information are mainly from *Beer Marketer's Insights*, **www.beerinsights.com**, and the Association of Brewers, **www.beertown.com**.

Summary

1. The distinguishing features of monopolistic competition are (a) there are enough firms in the industry to ensure that each firm has only limited control over price, mutual interdependence is absent, and collusion is nearly impossible; (b) products are characterized by real or perceived differences so that economic rivalry entails both price and nonprice competition; and (c) entry to the industry is relatively easy. Many aspects of retailing, and some manufacturing industries in which economies of scale are few, approximate monopolistic competition.

2. Monopolistically competitive firms may earn economic profits or incur losses in the short run. The easy entry and exit of firms result in only normal profits in the long run.

3. The long-run equilibrium position of the monopolistically competitive producer is less efficient than that of the pure competitor. Under monopolistic competition, price exceeds marginal cost, suggesting an underallocation of resources to the product, and price exceeds minimum average total cost, indicating that consumers do not get the product at the lowest price that cost conditions might allow.

4. Nonprice competition provides a way that monopolistically competitive firms can offset the long-run tendency for economic profit to fall to zero. Through product differentiation, product development, and advertising, a firm may strive to increase the demand for its product more

than enough to cover the added cost of such nonprice competition. Consumers benefit from the wide diversity of product choice that monopolistic competition provides.

5. In practice, the monopolistic competitor seeks the specific combination of price, product, and advertising that will maximize profit.

6. Oligopolistic industries are characterized by the presence of few firms, each having a significant fraction of the market. Firms thus situated engage in strategic behavior and are mutually interdependent: The behavior of any one firm directly affects, and is affected by, the actions of rivals. Products may be either virtually uniform or significantly differentiated. Various barriers to entry, including economies of scale, underlie and maintain oligopoly.

7. Game theory (a) shows the interdependence of oligopolists' pricing policies, (b) reveals the tendency of oligopolists to collude, and (c) explains the temptation of oligopolists to cheat on collusive arrangements.

8. Noncollusive oligopolists may face a kinked-demand curve. This curve and the accompanying marginal-revenue curve help explain the price rigidity that often characterizes oligopolies; they do not, however, explain how the actual prices of products were first established.

9. Price leadership is an informal means of overcoming difficulties relating to kinked-demand curves whereby one firm, usually the largest or most efficient, initiates price changes and the other firms in the industry follow the leader.

10. Collusive oligopolists such as cartels maximize joint profits—that is, they behave like pure monopolists. Demand and cost differences, a "large" number of firms, cheating through secret price concessions, recessions, and the antitrust laws are all obstacles to collusive oligopoly.

11. Market shares in oligopolistic industries are usually determined on the basis of product development and advertising. Oligopolists emphasize nonprice competition because (a) advertising and product variations are less easy for rivals to match and (b) oligopolists frequently have ample resources to finance nonprice competition.

12. Advertising may affect prices, competition, and efficiency either positively or negatively. Positive: It can provide consumers with low-cost information about competing products, help introduce new competing products into concentrated industries, and generally reduce monopoly power and its attendant inefficiencies. Negative: It can promote monopoly power via persuasion and the creation of entry barriers. Moreover, it can be self-canceling when engaged in by rivals; then it boosts costs and creates inefficiency while accomplishing little else.

13. Neither productive nor allocative efficiency is realized in oligopolistic markets, but oligopoly may be superior to pure competition in promoting research and development and technological progress.

Terms and Concepts

monopolistic competition

product differentiation

nonprice competition

excess capacity

oligopoly

homogeneous oligopoly

differentiated oligopoly

strategic behavior

mutual interdependence

game theory

collusion

per se violation

kinked-demand curve

price leadership

cartel

Questions

1. How does monopolistic competition differ from pure competition in its basic characteristics? How does it differ from pure monopoly? Explain fully what product differentiation may involve. Explain how the entry of firms into its industry affects the demand curve facing a monopolistic competitor and how that, in turn, affects its economic profit. **LO1**

2. Compare the elasticity of the monopolistic competitor's demand with that of a pure competitor and a pure monopolist. Assuming identical long-run costs, compare graphically the prices and outputs that would result in the long run under pure competition and under monopolistic competition. Contrast the two market structures in terms of

productive and allocative efficiency. Explain: "Monopolistically competitive industries are characterized by too many firms, each of which produces too little." **LO2**

3. "Monopolistic competition is monopolistic up to the point at which consumers become willing to buy close-substitute products and competitive beyond that point." Explain. **LO1, LO2**

4. "Competition in quality and service may be just as effective as price competition in giving buyers more for their money." Do you agree? Why? Explain why monopolistically competitive firms frequently prefer nonprice competition to price competition. **LO2**

5. Why do oligopolies exist? List five or six oligopolists whose products you own or regularly purchase. What distinguishes oligopoly from monopolistic competition? **LO3**

6. Explain the general meaning of the following profit payoff matrix for oligopolists X and Y. All profit figures are in thousands. **LO4**

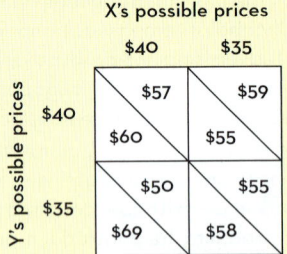

X's possible prices

		$40	$35
Y's possible prices	$40	$57 / $60	$59 / $55
	$35	$50 / $69	$55 / $58

a. Use the payoff matrix to explain the mutual interdependence that characterizes oligopolistic industries.

b. Assuming no collusion between X and Y, what is the likely pricing outcome?

c. In view of your answer to part b, explain why price collusion is mutually profitable. Why might there be a temptation to cheat on the collusive agreement?

7. Construct a game-theory matrix to illustrate the text example of two firms and their decisions on high versus low advertising budgets and the effects of each on profits. Show a circumstance in which both firms select high advertising budgets even though both would be more profitable with low advertising budgets. Why won't they unilaterally cut their advertising budgets? Explain why this is an example of the prisoner's dilemma. **LO4, LO7**

8. What assumptions about a rival's response to price changes underlie the kinked-demand curve for oligopolists? Why is there a gap in the oligopolist's marginal-revenue curve? How does the kinked-demand curve explain price rigidity in oligopoly? **LO5**

9. Why might price collusion occur in oligopolistic industries? Assess the economic desirability of collusive pricing. What are the main obstacles to collusion? Speculate as to why price leadership is legal in the United States, whereas price-fixing is not. **LO6**

10. Why is there so much advertising in monopolistic competition and oligopoly? How does such advertising help consumers and promote efficiency? Why might it be excessive at times? **LO7**

11. What firm dominates the beer industry? What demand and supply factors have contributed to "fewness" in this industry? **LO3**

Problems

1. Assume that in short-run equilibrium, a particular monopolistically competitive firm charges $12 for each unit of its output and sells 52 units of output per day. How much revenue will it take in each day? If its average total cost (ATC) for those 52 units is $10, will the firm (a) earn a short-run economic profit, (b) break even with only a normal profit, or (c) suffer an economic loss? If a profit or loss, what will be the amount? Next, suppose that entry or exit occurs in this monopolistic industry and establishes a long-run equilibrium. If the firm's daily output remains at 52 units, what price will it be able to charge? What will be its economic profit? **LO2**

2. Suppose that a restaurant in an oligopolistic part of that industry is currently serving 230 meals per day (the output where MR = MC). At that output level, ATC per meal is $10 and consumers are willing to pay $12 per meal. What is the size of this firm's profit or loss? Will there be

entry or exit? Will this restaurant's demand curve shift left or right? In long-run equilibrium, suppose that this restaurant charges $11 per meal for 180 meals and that the marginal cost of the 180th meal is $8. What is the size of the firm's profit? **LO3**

3. Suppose than an oligopolist is charging $21 per unit of output and selling 31 units each day. What is its daily total revenue? Also suppose that previously it had lowered its price from $21 to $19, rivals matched the price cut, and the firm's sales increased from 31 to 32 units. It also previously raised its price from $21 to $23, rivals ignored the price hike, and the firm's daily total revenue came in at $482. Which of the following is most logical to conclude? The firm's demand curve is (a) inelastic over the $21 to $23 price range, (b) elastic over the $19 to $21 price range, (c) a linear (straight) downsloping line, or (d) a curve with a kink in it? **LO5**

FURTHER TEST YOUR KNOWLEDGE AT
www.brue3e.com

At the text's Online Learning Center, **www.brue3e.com**, you will find one or more web-based questions that require information from the Internet to answer. We urge you to check them out, since they will familiarize you with websites that may be helpful in other courses and perhaps even in your career. The OLC also features multiple-choice quizzes that give instant feedback and provides other helpful ways to further test your knowledge of the chapter.

Wage Determination

Web Chapter A is a bonus chapter found at the book's website, **www.brue3e.com.** It extends the analysis of Part 3, "Product Markets," by using the same tools to examine the market for labor. Your instructor may (or may not) assign all or part of this chapter.

Income Inequality and Poverty

Web Chapter B is a bonus chapter found at the book's website, **www.brue3e.com.** It extends the analysis of Part 3, "Product Markets," by using the same tools to examine the market for labor. Your instructor may (or may not) assign all or part of this chapter.

CHAPTER TEN

GDP and Economic Growth

After reading this chapter, you should be able to:

1. Explain how gross domestic product (GDP) is defined and measured.
2. Describe how economists distinguish between nominal GDP and real GDP.
3. List two ways that economic growth is measured.
4. Identify the general supply, demand, and efficiency forces that give rise to economic growth.
5. Describe "growth accounting" and the specific factors accounting for economic growth in the United States.
6. Explain why the trend rate of U.S. productivity growth has increased since the earlier 1973–1995 period.
7. Discuss differing perspectives as to whether growth is desirable and sustainable.

As you learned in Chapter 2, economists represent the economy as a circular flow of output (goods and services), income, and spending (Figure 2.2, p. 41). In our discussion of microeconomics, we examined how society can maximize output and income at any point in time by using the market system and government decisions to allocate society's limited resources to their highest valued uses.

We now want to turn to macroeconomics: the part of economics concerned with the economy as a whole. In this chapter we are interested in how economists measure the overall (aggregate) flow of goods and services in the circular flow diagram, both in total and on a per-person basis. Once that is established, we can examine the factors that expand the flow of goods and services over time and thus improve a society's standard of living. What are the main sources of such economic growth? Is economic growth desirable?

Gross Domestic Product

To examine the level of total output, total income, and total spending, we need to combine and measure the production, income, and spending of all the participants in the economy. The Bureau of Economic Analysis (BEA), an agency of the Commerce Department, does just that when it compiles the **national income and product accounts (NIPA)** for the U.S. economy. The BEA derives the NIPA data from Census Bureau surveys and information available from government agencies.

The primary measure of the economy's performance is its annual total output of goods and services. This output is called **gross domestic product (GDP):** the total market value of all final goods and services produced within the borders of a country during a specific period of time, typically a year. GDP includes all goods and services produced by either citizen-supplied or foreign-supplied resources employed within the country. If a final good or service is produced in the United States, it is part of U.S. GDP.[1]

A Monetary Measure

If the economy produces three sofas and two computers in year 1 and two sofas and three computers in year 2, in which year is output greater? We can't answer that question until we attach a price tag to each of the two products to indicate how society evaluates their relative worth.

That's what GDP does. It is a *monetary measure*. Without such a measure we would have no way of comparing the relative values of the vast number of goods and services produced in different years. In Table 10.1 the price of sofas is $500 and the price of computers is $2000. GDP would gauge the output of year 2 ($7000) as greater than the output of year 1 ($5500) because society places a higher monetary value on the output of year 2. Society is willing to pay $1500 more for the combination of goods produced in year 2 than for the combination of goods produced in year 1.

Avoiding Multiple Counting

To measure aggregate output accurately, all goods and services produced in a particular year must be counted once and only once. Because most products go through a series of production stages before they reach the market, some of their components are bought and sold many times. To avoid counting those components each time, GDP includes only the market value of *final goods* and ignores *intermediate goods* altogether.

Intermediate goods are goods and services that are purchased for resale or for further processing or manufacturing. **Final goods** are products that are purchased by their end users. Crude oil is an intermediate good; gasoline used for personal transportation is

---

[1] In contrast to GDP, U.S. gross *national* product (GNP) consists of the total value of all the final goods and services produced by American-supplied resources, whether those goods and services are produced within the borders of the United States or abroad. The United States switched from GNP to GDP accounting in 1992 to match the type of accounting used by other countries worldwide.

national income and product accounts (NIPA)
The national accounts that measure the overall production and income of the economy for the nation as a whole.

gross domestic product (GDP)
The total market value of all final goods and services produced annually within the borders of the United States, whether by U.S. or foreign-supplied resources.

intermediate goods
Products that are purchased for resale or further processing or manufacturing.

final goods
Products, capital goods, and services that have been purchased for final use and not for resale or further processing or manufacturing.

TABLE 10.1

Comparing Heterogeneous Output by Using Money Prices

Year	Annual Output	Market Value
1	3 sofas and 2 computers	3 at $500 + 2 at $2000 = $5500
2	2 sofas and 3 computers	2 at $500 + 3 at $2000 = $7000

© Brand X Pictures/Punchstock   © Royalty-Free/CORBIS

Photo Op Intermediate versus Final Goods

Lumber is an intermediate good and a new townhouse is a final good.

a final good. Steel beams are intermediate goods; completed high-rise apartments are final goods. Lettuce, carrots, and vinegar in restaurant salads are intermediate goods; restaurant salads are final goods. Other examples of final goods are sunglasses bought by consumers, assembly machinery purchased by businesses, surveillance satellites bought by government, and smartphones purchased by foreign buyers.

Including the value of intermediate goods in calculating GDP would amount to *multiple counting*, and that would distort the value of GDP. For example, suppose that among other inputs an automobile manufacturer uses $4000 of steel, $2000 of glass, and $1000 of tires in producing a new automobile that sells for $20,000. The $20,000 final good already includes the $7000 of steel, glass, and tires. We would be greatly overstating GDP if we added the $7000 of components to the $20,000 price of the auto and obtained $27,000 of output.

Excluding Secondhand Sales and Financial Transactions

Secondhand sales do not contribute to current production and therefore are excluded from GDP. If you sell your 1965 Ford Mustang to a friend, that transaction would be ignored in determining this year's GDP because it generates no current production. The same would be true if you sold a brand-new Mustang to a neighbor a week after you purchased it. It has already been counted in GDP.

Likewise, purely financial transactions do not contribute to current production. These transactions include public transfer payments, such as social security and welfare payments, and private transfers, including the cash gifts that parents give children. Money changes hands but not in exchange for anything produced in the present. The sales of stocks and bonds are also excluded from GDP as they simply transfer pieces of paper that represent company ownership (stocks) or loans (bonds). Note, however, that the services of the stockbroker who facilitates the exchange of stock are included in GDP, as those services are part of the economy's current production.

© PhotoLink/Getty Images

© Colin Young-Wolff/PhotoEdit

Photo Op New Goods versus Secondhand Goods

The goods offered for sale at a shopping mall are new goods and therefore included in current GDP. In contrast, many of the goods sold through eBay are secondhand items and thus not part of current GDP.

Measuring GDP

The simplest way to measure GDP is to add up all that was spent to buy total output in a certain year. Economists use precise terms for the four categories of spending.

Personal Consumption Expenditures (C)

The symbol C designates the **personal consumption expenditures** component of GDP. That term covers all expenditures by households on *durable consumer goods* (automobiles, refrigerators, cameras) that have lives of more than 3 years, *nondurable consumer goods* (bread, milk, toothpaste), and *consumer expenditures for services* (of lawyers, doctors, mechanics).

Gross Private Domestic Investment (I_g)

Under the heading **gross private domestic investment** are included (1) all final purchases of machinery, equipment, and tools by business enterprises; (2) all construction; and (3) changes in inventories.

Notice that this list, except for the first item, includes more than we have meant by "economic investment" so far. The second item includes residential construction as well as the construction of new factories, warehouses, and stores. Why is residential construction investment rather than consumption? Because apartment buildings and houses, like factories and stores, earn income when they are rented or leased. Owner-occupied houses are treated as investment goods because they *could be* rented to bring in an income return. So all residential construction is treated as investment. Finally, an increase in inventories (unsold goods) is investment because it is "unconsumed output." For economists, all new output either is consumed or is capital. An increase in inventories is an addition (although temporary) to the stock of capital goods, and such additions are precisely how we define investment.

personal consumption expenditures (C)
Expenditures by households for durable goods, nondurable goods, and services.

gross private domestic investment (I_g)
Expenditures for newly produced capital goods (such as plant and equipment) and for additions to inventories.

Positive and Negative Changes in Inventories   We need to look at changes in inventories more closely. Inventories can either increase or decrease over some period. Suppose inventories rose by $10 billion between December 31, 2010, and December 31, 2011. That means the economy produced $10 billion more output than was purchased in 2011. We need to count all output produced in 2011 as part of that year's GDP, even though some of it remained unsold at the end of the year. This is accomplished by including the $10 billion increase in inventories as investment in 2011. That way the expenditures in 2011 will correctly measure the output produced that year.

Alternatively, suppose inventories fell by $10 billion in 2011. This "drawing down of inventories" means that the economy sold $10 billion more of output in 2011 than it produced that year. It did this by selling goods produced in prior years—goods already counted as GDP in those years. Unless corrected, expenditures in 2011 will overstate GDP for 2011. So in 2011 we consider the $10 billion decline in inventories as "negative investment" and subtract it from total investment that year. Thus, expenditures in 2011 will correctly measure the output produced in 2011.

Noninvestment Transactions   So much for what investment *is*. You also need to know what it *isn't*. For economists and NIPA accountants, investment does *not* include noninvestment transactions such as the transfer of paper assets (stocks, bonds) or the resale of tangible assets (houses, factories). Such financial transactions merely transfer the ownership of existing assets. The investment in the GDP accounts is economic investment—the creation of *new* capital assets. The mere transfer (sale) of claims to existing capital goods does not produce new capital goods. Therefore, such transactions (so-called financial investments) are not included as investment in the GDP accounts.

Gross Investment   As we have seen, the category "gross private domestic investment" includes (1) all final purchases of machinery, equipment, and tools; (2) all construction; and (3) changes in inventories. The words "private" and "domestic" mean that we are speaking of spending by private businesses, not by government (public) agencies, and that the investment is taking place inside the country, not abroad.

The word "gross" means that we are referring to *all* investment goods—both those that replace machinery, equipment, and buildings that were used up (worn out or made obsolete) in producing the current year's output and any net additions to the economy's stock of capital. Gross investment includes investment in replacement capital *and* in added capital [as opposed to net investment, for which replacement capital (depreciation) is subtracted from gross investment].

The symbol *I* represents private domestic investment spending, along with the subscript *g* to signify gross investment.

Government Purchases (G)

government purchases (G)
Government expenditures on final goods, services, and publicly owned capital.

The third category of expenditures in the national income accounts is **government purchases,** officially labeled "government consumption expenditures and gross investment." These expenditures have two components: (1) expenditures for goods and services that government consumes in providing public services and (2) expenditures for *publicly owned capital* such as schools and highways, which have long lifetimes. Government purchases (federal, state, and local) include all government expenditures on final goods and all direct purchases of resources, including labor. It does *not* include government transfer payments such as Social Security payments, unemployment compensation, and veterans' benefits because they merely transfer government receipts to certain households and generate no *current* production. The symbol G signifies government purchases.

Net Exports (X_n)

International trade transactions are a significant item in national income accounting. But when calculating U.S. GDP, we must keep in mind that we want to total up only those expenditures that are used to purchase goods and services produced *within the borders of the United States.* Thus, we must add in the value of exports, X, since exports are by definition goods and services produced within the borders of the United States. Don't be confused by the fact that the expenditures made to buy up our exports are made by foreigners. The definition of GDP does not care about *who* is making expenditures on U.S.-made goods and services—only that the goods and services that they buy are made within the borders of the United States. Thus, foreign spending on our exports must be included in GDP.

At this point, you might incorrectly think that GDP should be equal to the sum of $C + I_g + G + X$. But this sum overstates GDP. The problem is that, once again, we must consider only expenditures made on *domestically produced* goods and services. As it stands, C, I_g, and G count up expenditures on consumption, investment, and government purchases regardless of where those goods and services are made. Crucially, not all of the C, I_g, or G expenditures are for domestically produced goods and services. Some of the expenditures are for imports—goods and services produced outside of the United States. Thus, since we wish to count *only* the part of C, I_g, and G that goes to purchasing domestically produced goods and services, we must subtract off the spending that goes to imports, M. Doing so yields the correct formula for calculating gross domestic product:

$$GDP = C + I_g + G + X - M$$

Accountants simplify this formula for GDP by defining **net exports,** X_n, to be equal to exports minus imports:

net exports (X_n)
Exports minus imports.

$$\text{Net exports } (X_n) = \text{exports } (X) - \text{imports } (M)$$

Using this definition of net exports, the formula for gross domestic product simplifies to

$$GDP = C + I_g + G + X_n$$

In 2011 Americans spent $579 billion more on imports than foreigners spent on U.S. exports. That is, net exports in 2011 were a negative $579 billion.

Adding It Up: GDP = $C + I_g + G + X_n$

Taken together, these four categories of expenditures provide a measure of the market value of a given year's total output—its GDP. For the United States in 2011,

GDP = $10,726 + 1916 + 3031 − 579 = $15,094 billion (or $15.094 trillion)

Global Snapshot 10.1 compares GDP in the United States to GDP in several other countries for 2011.

Global Snapshot 10.1

Comparative GDPs in Trillions of U.S. Dollars, Selected Nations, 2011

The United States, China, and Japan have the world's highest GDPs. The GDP data charted below have been converted to dollars via international exchange rates.

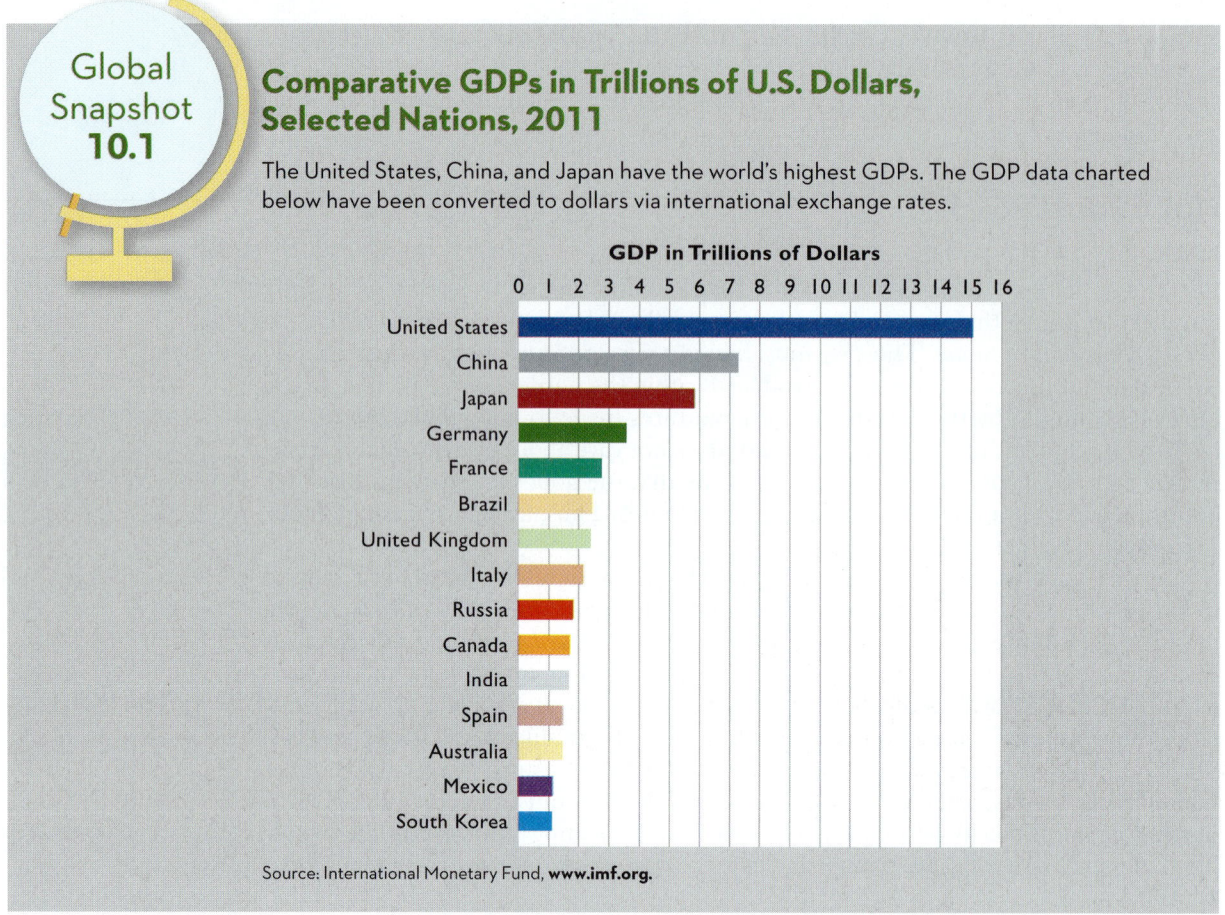

Source: International Monetary Fund, **www.imf.org.**

Nominal GDP versus Real GDP

Recall that GDP is a measure of the market or money value of all final goods and services produced by the economy in a given year. We use money or nominal values as a common denominator in order to sum that heterogeneous output into a meaningful total. But that creates a problem: How can we compare the market values of GDP from year to year if the value of money itself changes in response to inflation or deflation? After all, we determine the value of GDP by multiplying total output by market prices.

Whether there is a 5 percent increase in output with no change in prices or a 5 percent increase in prices with no change in output, the change in the monetary value of GDP will be the same. And yet it is the *quantity* of goods that get produced and distributed to households that affects our standard of living, not the price of the goods. The McDonald's hamburger that sold for 99 cents in 2011 yielded the same satisfaction as the nearly identical McDonald's hamburger that sold for 18 cents in 1967.

The way around this problem is to *deflate* GDP when prices rise and to *inflate* GDP when prices fall. These adjustments give us a measure of GDP for various years as if the value of the dollar had always been the same as it was in some reference year. A GDP based on the prices that prevailed when the output was produced is called *unadjusted GDP*, or **nominal GDP.** A GDP that has been deflated or inflated to reflect changes in the price level is called *adjusted GDP*, or **real GDP.**

nominal GDP
Gross domestic product measured in terms of the price level at the time of measurement (i.e., GDP that is unadjusted for inflation).

real GDP
Gross domestic product measured in terms of the price level in a base period (i.e., GDP that is adjusted for inflation).

TABLE 10.2

**Calculating Real GDP
(Base Year = Year 1)**

Year	(1) Units of Output	(2) Price of Pizza per Unit	(3) Unadjusted, or Nominal, GDP, (1) × (2)	(4) Adjusted, or Real, GDP
1	5	$10	$ 50	$50
2	7	20	140	70
3	8	25	200	80
4	10	30	——	——
5	11	28	——	——

Let's see how real GDP can be found. For simplicity, suppose the economy produces only one good, pizza, in the amounts indicated in Table 10.2 for years 1, 2, 3, 4, and 5. Also assume that we gather output and price data directly from the pizza business in various years. That is, we collect separate data on physical outputs (as in column 1) and their prices (as in column 2).

We can then determine the unadjusted, or nominal, GDP in each year by multiplying the number of units of output by the price per unit. Nominal GDP—here, the market value of pizza—is shown for each year in column 3.

We can also determine adjusted, or real, GDP from the data in Table 10.2. We want to know the market value of outputs in successive years *if the base-year price ($10) had prevailed.* In year 2, the 7 units of pizza would have a value of $70 (= 7 units × $10) at the year-1 price. As column 4 shows, that $70 worth of output is year 2's real GDP. Similarly, we can determine the real GDP for year 3 by multiplying the 8 units of output that year by the $10 price in the base year. You should check your understanding of nominal versus real GDP by completing columns 3 and 4, where we purposely left the last rows blank.

WORKED PROBLEMS

W 10.1
Real GDP and price indexes

Let's return to the real economy. As previously determined, nominal GDP in the United States was $15,094 billion in 2011. What was real GDP that year? Because prices rose between the 2005 base year and 2011, real GDP in 2011 turned out to be $13,315 billion. Or, in the language of economics, "GDP in 2011 was $13,315 billion in 2005 (base-year) prices."

The Underground Economy

Real GDP is a reasonably accurate and highly useful measure of how well or how poorly the economy is performing. But some production never shows up in GDP, which measures only the *market value* of output. Embedded in the U.S. economy is a flourishing, productive underground sector. Some of the people who conduct business there are gamblers, smugglers, prostitutes, "fences" of stolen goods, drug producers, and drug dealers. They have good reason to conceal their economic activities. When they do, their "contributions" to output do not show up in GDP.

Most participants in the underground economy, however, engage in perfectly legal activities but choose not to report their full incomes to the Internal Revenue Service (IRS). A bell captain at a hotel may report just a portion of the tips received from customers. Storekeepers may report only a portion of their sales receipts.

Applying the Analysis

Workers who want to hold on to their unemployment compensation benefits may take an "off-the-books" or "cash-only" job. A brick mason may agree to rebuild a neighbor's fireplace in exchange for the neighbor's repairing his boat engine. The value of none of these transactions shows up in GDP.

The value of underground transactions is estimated to be about 8 percent of the recorded GDP in the United States. That would mean that GDP in 2011 was understated by about $1.21 trillion. Global Snapshot 10.2 shows estimates of the relative sizes of underground economies in selected nations.

Question:
How would decriminalization of drugs instantly increase a nation's real GDP? What might be the downside of decriminalization of drugs for growth of real GDP over time?

Economic Growth

economic growth
The expansion of real GDP (or real GDP per capita) over time.

real GDP per capita
Real output divided by population.

The NIPA data enable economists to calculate and analyze economic growth rates. Economists define and measure **economic growth** as either an *increase in real GDP* occurring over time or an *increase in real GDP per capita* occurring over time. **Real GDP per capita** (or output per person) is found by dividing real GDP by the size of the population. With either definition, economic growth is calculated as a percentage rate of growth per quarter (3-month period) or per year.

Global Snapshot 10.2

The Underground Economy as a Percentage of GDP, Selected Nations

Underground economies vary in size worldwide. Three factors that help explain the variation are (1) the extent and complexity of regulation, (2) the type and degree of taxation, and (3) the effectiveness of law enforcement.

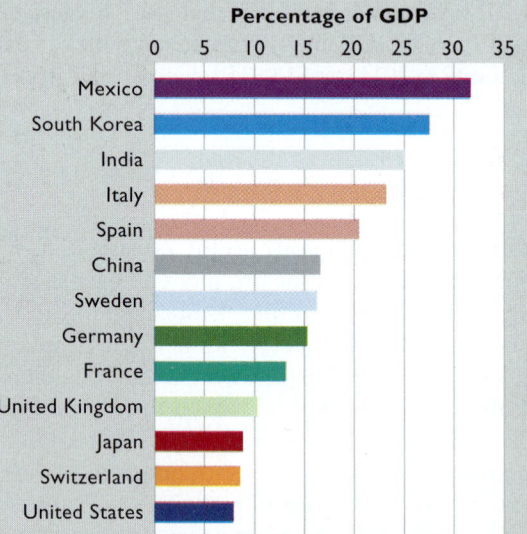

Source: Friedrich Schneider, "Shadow Economies and Corruption All over the World: New Estimates for 145 Countries," *Economics: The Open Access—Open Assessment, E-Journal,* vol. 1, 2007–9. Used with permission of Friedrich Schneider.

For measuring expansion of military potential or political preeminence, the growth of real GDP is more useful. Unless specified otherwise, growth rates reported in the news and by international agencies use this definition of economic growth. For comparing living standards, however, the second definition is superior. While China's GDP in 2011 was $7298 billion compared with Denmark's $333 billion, Denmark's real GDP per capita was $59,928 compared with China's $5414.

Growth as a Goal

Economic growth is a widely held economic goal. The expansion of total output relative to population results in rising real wages and incomes and thus higher standards of living. An economy that is experiencing economic growth is better able to meet people's wants and resolve socioeconomic problems. Rising real wages and income provide richer opportunities to individuals and families—a vacation trip, a personal computer, a higher education—without sacrificing other opportunities and pleasures. A growing economy can undertake new programs to alleviate poverty and protect the environment without impairing existing levels of consumption, investment, and public goods production.

In short, *growth lessens the burden of scarcity*. A growing economy, unlike a static economy, can consume more today while increasing its capacity to produce more in the future. By easing the burden of scarcity—by relaxing society's constraints on production—economic growth enables a nation to attain its economic goals more readily and to undertake new endeavors that require the use of goods and services to be accomplished.

Arithmetic of Growth

The mathematical approximation called the *rule of 70* shows the effect of compounding of economic growth rates over time. It tells us that we can find the number of years it will take for some measure to double, given its annual percentage increase, by dividing that percentage increase into the number 70. So

WORKED PROBLEMS

W 10.2
GDP growth

$$\text{Approximate number of years required to double real GDP} = \frac{70}{\text{annual percentage rate of growth}}$$

Examples: A 3 percent annual rate of growth will double real GDP in about 23 (= 70/3) years. Growth of 8 percent per year will double it in about 9 (= 70/8) years.

Growth Rates Matter!

Small absolute differences in rates of economic growth add up to substantial differences in real GDP and standards of living. Consider three hypothetical countries—Slogo, Sumgo, and Speedo. Suppose that in 2012 these countries have identical levels of real GDP ($6 trillion), population (200 million), and real GDP per capita ($30,000). Also, assume that annual real GDP growth is 2 percent in Slogo, 3 percent in Sumgo, and 4 percent in Speedo.

How will these alternative growth rates affect real GDP and real GDP per capita over a long period, say, the 70-year average life span of an American? By 2082 the 2, 3,

Illustrating the Idea

and 4 percent growth rates would boost real GDP from $6 trillion to $24 trillion in Slogo, $47 trillion in Sumgo, and $93 trillion in Speedo.

For illustration, let's assume that each country experienced an average annual population growth of 1 percent over the 70 years. Then, in 2082 real GDP per capita would be about $60,000 in Slogo, $118,000 in Sumgo, and $233,000 in Speedo.

No wonder economists pay so much attention to small changes in the rate of economic growth. For the United States, with a current real GDP of about $12 trillion, the difference between a 3 percent and a 4 percent rate of growth is about $120 billion of output each year. For a poor country, a difference of one-half of a percentage point in the rate of growth may mean the difference between starvation and mere hunger. Economic growth rates matter!

Question:
Why would gaps in GDP per capita for Slogo and Speedo be even more dramatic if population growth was faster in Slogo than in Speedo?

Growth in the United States

Table 10.3 gives an overview of economic growth in the United States over past periods. Column 2 reveals strong growth as measured by increases in real GDP. Note that real GDP increased more than sixfold between 1950 and 2010. But the U.S. population also increased over these years. Nevertheless, in column 4 we find that real GDP per capita rose more than threefold.

What has been the *rate* of U.S. growth? Real GDP grew at an annual rate of about 3.2 percent between 1950 and 2010. Real GDP per capita increased about 2 percent per year over that time.

Viewed from the perspective of the last half-century, economic growth in the United States lagged behind that in Japan, Germany, Italy, Canada, and France. Japan's annual growth rate, in fact, averaged twice that of the United States. But economic growth since 2000 is quite another matter. As shown in Global Snapshot 10.3, until 2007, the U.S. growth rate generally topped the rates of growth in Japan and other major industrial nations.

TABLE 10.3

Real GDP and per Capita Real GDP, Selected Years, 1950–2010

(1) Year	(2) Real GDP, Billions of 2005 $	(3) Population, Millions	(4) Real Per Capita GDP, 2005 $ (2) ÷ (3)
1950	$ 2006	152	$13,197
1960	2831	181	15,640
1970	4270	205	20,829
1980	5839	228	25,610
1990	8034	250	32,136
2000	11,226	282	39,809
2010	13,248	309	43,456

Source: Bureau of Economic Analysis, **www.bea.doc.gov**, and U.S. Census Bureau, **www.census.gov**.

Global
Snapshot
10.3

Average Annual Growth Rates, 2000–2011, Selected Nations

Between 2000 and 2006, economic growth in the United States exceeded that of several other major countries. U.S. economic growth greatly slowed in 2001 and 2002 before rising again in 2003 and 2004. U.S. growth slowed again in 2007, and many countries experienced recession in 2008 and 2009.

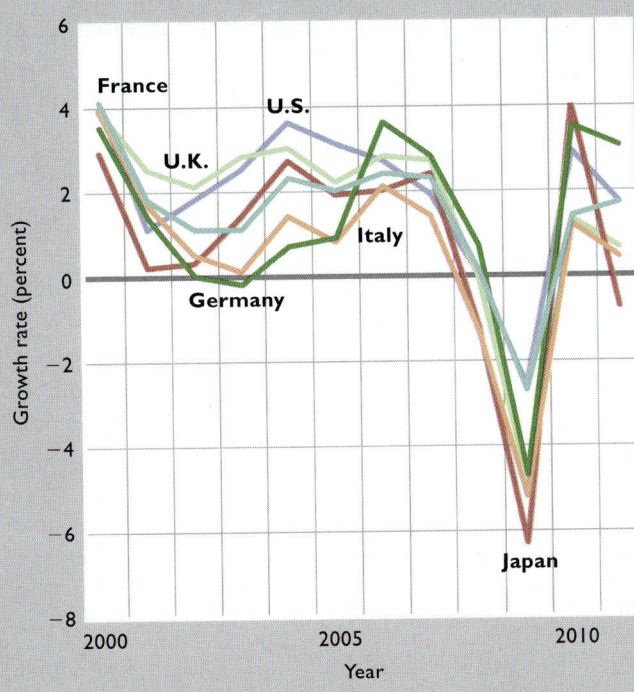

Source: Organization for Economic Cooperation and Development, **stats.oecd.org.**

Determinants of Growth

There are six main determinants of economic growth. We can group them as supply, demand, and efficiency factors.

Supply Factors

Four of the determinants of economic growth relate to the physical ability of the economy to expand. They are

- Increases in the quantity and quality of natural resources.
- Increases in the quantity and quality of human resources.
- Increases in the supply (or stock) of capital goods.
- Improvements in technology.

These *supply factors*—changes in the physical and technical agents of production—enable an economy to expand its potential GDP.

Demand Factor

The fifth determinant of economic growth is the *demand factor:*

- To achieve the higher production potential created by the supply factors, households, businesses, and government must *purchase* the economy's expanding output of goods and services.

When that occurs, there will be no unplanned increases in inventories and resources will remain fully employed. Economic growth requires increases in total spending to realize the output gains made available by increased production capacity.

Efficiency Factor

The sixth determinant of economic growth is the *efficiency factor:*

- To reach its full production potential, an economy must achieve economic efficiency as well as full employment.

The economy must use its resources in the least costly way (productive efficiency) to produce the specific mix of goods and services that maximizes people's well-being (allocative efficiency). The ability to expand production, together with the full use of available resources, is not sufficient for achieving maximum possible growth. Also required is the efficient use of those resources.

The supply, demand, and efficiency factors in economic growth are related. Unemployment caused by insufficient total spending (the demand factor) may lower the rate of new capital accumulation (a supply factor) and delay expenditures on research

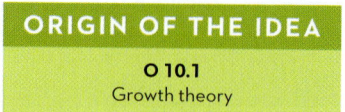

ORIGIN OF THE IDEA

O 10.1
Growth theory

(also a supply factor). Conversely, low spending on investment (a supply factor) may cause insufficient spending (the demand factor) and unemployment. Widespread inefficiency in the use of resources (the efficiency factor) may translate into higher costs of goods and services and thus lower profits, which in turn may slow innovation and reduce the accumulation of capital (supply factors). Economic growth is a dynamic process in which the supply, demand, and efficiency factors all interact.

Production Possibilities Analysis

To put the six factors affecting the rate of economic growth into better perspective, let's use the production possibilities analysis introduced in Chapter 1.

Growth and Production Possibilities

Recall that a curve like *AB* in Figure 10.1 is a production possibilities curve. It indicates the various *maximum* combinations of products an economy can produce with its fixed quantity and quality of natural, human, and capital resources and its stock of technological knowledge. An improvement in any of the supply factors will push the production possibilities curve outward, as from *AB* to *CD*.

But the demand factor reminds us that an increase in total spending is needed to move the economy from a point like *a* on curve *AB* to any of the points on the higher curve *CD*. And the efficiency factor reminds us that we need least-cost production and an optimal location on *CD* for the resources to make their maximum possible dollar

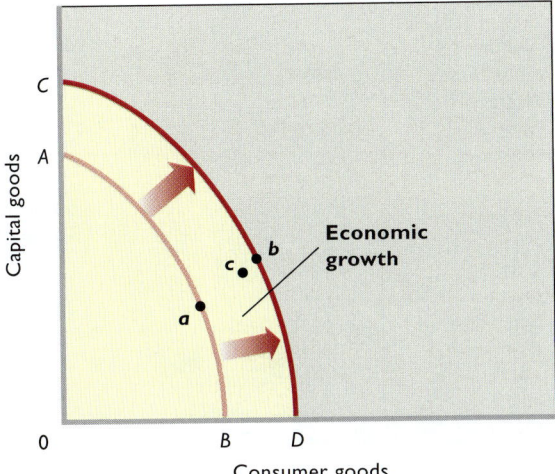

FIGURE 10.1
**Economic growth
and the production
possibilities curve.**
Economic growth is
made possible by the
four supply factors that
shift the production
possibilities curve
outward, as from *AB* to
CD. Economic growth is
realized when the
demand factor and the
efficiency factor move
the economy from
point *a* to *b*.

contribution to total output. You will recall from Chapter 1 that this "best allocation" is determined by expanding production of each good until its marginal cost equals its marginal benefit. Here, we assume that this optimal combination of capital and consumer goods occurs at point *b*.

Example: The net increase in the size of the labor force in the United States in recent years has been 1.5 million to 2 million workers per year. That increment raises the economy's production capacity. But obtaining the extra output that these added workers could produce depends on their success in finding jobs. It also depends on whether or not the jobs are in firms and industries where the workers' talents are fully and optimally used. Society does not want new labor-force entrants to be unemployed. Nor does it want pediatricians working as plumbers or pediatricians producing services for which marginal costs exceed marginal benefits.

Normally, increases in total spending match increases in production capacity, and the economy moves from a point on the previous production possibilities curve to a point on the expanded curve. Moreover, the competitive market system tends to drive the economy toward productive and allocative efficiency. Occasionally, however, the economy may end up at some point such as *c* in Figure 10.1. That kind of outcome occurred in the United States during the severe recession of 2007–2009. Real output fell far below the real output that the economy would have produced if it had achieved full employment and operated on its production possibilities curve.

Inputs and Productivity

Society can increase its output and income in two fundamental ways: (1) by increasing its inputs of resources and (2) by raising the productivity of those inputs. Figure 10.2 concentrates on the input of *labor* and provides a useful framework for discussing the role of supply factors in growth. A nation's real GDP in any year depends on the input of labor (measured in hours of work) multiplied by **labor productivity** (measured as real output per hour of work).

WORKED PROBLEMS

W 10.3
Productivity and economic growth

labor productivity
Real output per hour
of work.

FIGURE 10.2
The supply determinants of real output. Real GDP is usefully viewed as the product of the quantity of labor inputs (hours of work) multiplied by labor productivity.

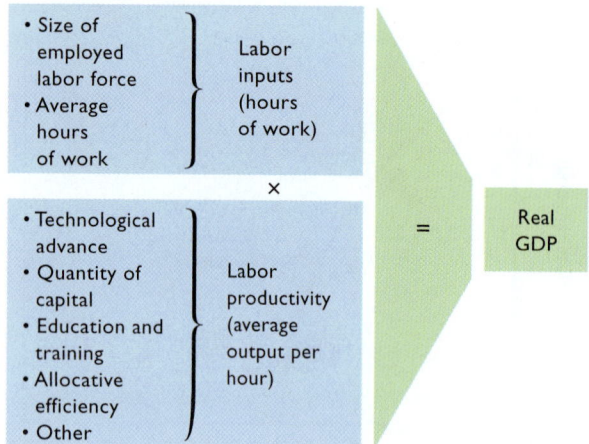

So, thought of this way, a nation's economic growth from one year to the next depends on its *increase* in labor inputs (if any) and its *increase* in labor productivity (if any).

Illustration: Assume that the cool economy of Rapland has 10 workers in year 1, each working 2000 hours per year (50 weeks at 40 hours per week). The total input of labor therefore is 20,000 hours. If productivity (average real output per hour of work) is $10, then real GDP in Rapland will be $200,000 (= 20,000 × $10). If work hours rise to 20,200 and labor productivity rises to $10.40, Rapland's real GDP will increase to $210,080 in year 2. Rapland's rate of economic growth will be about 5 percent [= ($210,080 − $200,000)/$200,000] for the year.

Hours of Work   What determines the number of hours worked each year? As shown in Figure 10.2, the hours of labor input depend on the size of the employed labor force and the length of the average workweek. Labor-force size depends on the size of the working-age population and the **labor-force participation rate**—the percentage of the working-age population actually in the labor force. The length of the average workweek is governed by legal and institutional considerations and by collective bargaining.

labor-force participation rate
The percentage of the working-age population actually in the labor force.

Labor Productivity   Figure 10.2 tells us that labor productivity is determined by technological progress, the quantity of capital goods available to workers, the quality of the labor itself, and the efficiency with which inputs are allocated, combined, and managed. Productivity rises when the health, training, education, and motivation of workers improve; when workers have more and better machinery and natural resources with which to work; when production is better organized and managed; and when labor is reallocated from less efficient industries to more efficient industries.

Accounting for Growth

growth accounting
The bookkeeping of the supply-side elements that contribute to changes in real GDP.

The Council of Economic Advisers uses a system called **growth accounting** to assess the relative importance of the supply-side elements that contribute to changes in real GDP. This system groups these elements into the two main categories we have just discussed:

- Increases in hours of work.
- Increases in labor productivity.

TABLE 10.4

Accounting for the Growth of U.S. Real GDP, 1953–2007 Plus Projection from 2010 to 2021 (Average Annual Percentage Changes)

Item	Actual				Projected
	1953 Q2 to 1973 Q4	1973 Q4 to 1995 Q2	1995 Q2 to 2001 Q1	2001 Q1 to 2007 Q3	2010 Q1 to 2021 Q4
Increase in real GDP	3.6	2.8	3.8	2.6	2.5
Increase in quantity of labor	1.1	1.3	1.4	−0.1	0.2
Increase in labor productivity	2.5	1.5	2.4	2.7	2.3

Source: Derived from *Economic Report of the President, 2008*, p. 45; and *Economic Report of the President, 2011*, p. 52.

Labor Inputs versus Labor Productivity

Table 10.4 provides the relevant data for four periods. The symbol "Q" in the table stands for "quarter" of the year. The beginning points for three of the four periods are business-cycle peaks, and the last column includes future projections by the Council of Economic Advisers. It is clear from the table that both increases in the quantity of labor and rises in labor productivity are important sources of economic growth. Between 1953 and 2011, the labor force increased from 63 million to 154 million workers. Over that period the average length of the workweek remained relatively stable. Falling birthrates slowed the growth of the native population, but increased immigration partly offset that slowdown. Of particular significance was a surge of women's participation in the labor force, from 34 percent in 1953 to 59 percent in 2010. Partly as a result, U.S. labor-force growth averaged about 1.6 million workers per year over the past 58 years.

The growth of labor productivity has also been important to economic growth. In fact, productivity growth has usually been the more significant factor, with the exception of 1973–1995 when productivity growth greatly slowed. For example, between 2001 and 2007, productivity growth was responsible for all of the 2.6 percent average annual economic growth. Productivity growth is projected to account for 92 percent of the growth of real GDP between 2010 and 2021.

Because increases in labor productivity are so important to economic growth, economists go to the trouble of investigating and assessing the relative importance of the factors that contribute to productivity growth. There are five factors that, together, appear to explain changes in productivity growth rates. They are technological advance, the amount of capital each worker has to work with, education and training, economies of scale, and resource allocation. We will examine each factor in turn, noting how much each factor contributes to productivity growth.

Technological Advance

The largest contributor to productivity growth is technological advance, which is thought to account for about 40 percent of productivity growth. As economist Paul Romer has stated, "Human history teaches us that economic growth springs from better recipes, not just from more cooking."

Technological advance includes not only innovative production techniques but new managerial methods and new forms of business organization that improve the process of production. Generally, technological advance is generated by the discovery of new knowledge, which allows resources to be combined in improved ways that increase output. Once discovered and implemented, new knowledge soon becomes available to entrepreneurs and firms at relatively low cost. Technological advance therefore eventually spreads through the entire economy, boosting productivity and economic growth.

Technological advance and capital formation (investment) are closely related because technological advance usually promotes investment in new machinery and equipment. In fact, technological advance is often *embodied* within new capital. For example, the purchase of new computers brings into industry speedier, more powerful computers that incorporate new technology.

Technological advance has been both rapid and profound. Gas and diesel engines, conveyor belts, and assembly lines are significant developments of the past. So, too, are fuel-efficient commercial aircraft, integrated microcircuits, personal computers, digital photography, and containerized shipping. More recently, technological advance has exploded, particularly in the areas of computers, wireless communications, and the Internet. Other fertile areas of recent innovation are medicine and biotechnology.

Quantity of Capital

A second major contributor to productivity growth is increased capital, which explains roughly 30 percent of productivity growth. More and better plant and equipment make workers more productive. And a nation acquires more capital by saving some of its income and using that saving to invest in plant and equipment.

Although some capital substitutes for labor, most capital is complementary to labor—it makes labor more productive. A key determinant of labor productivity is the amount of capital goods available *per worker*. If both the aggregate stock of capital goods and the size of the labor force increase over a given period, the individual worker is not necessarily better equipped and productivity will not necessarily rise. But the quantity of capital equipment available per U.S. worker has increased greatly over time. (In 2008 it was about $118,200 per worker.)

infrastructure
Public and private capital goods that buttress an economy's production capacity (for example, highways, bridges, airports, public transit systems, wastewater treatment facilities, educational facilities, and telecommunications systems that complement private capital).

Public investment in the U.S. **infrastructure** (highways and bridges, public transit systems, water and sewage systems, airports, industrial parks, educational facilities, and so on) has also grown over the years. This publicly owned capital complements private capital. Investments in new highways promote private investment in new factories and retail stores along their routes. Industrial parks developed by local governments attract manufacturing and distribution firms.

Private investment in infrastructure also plays a large role in economic growth. One example is the tremendous growth of private capital relating to communications systems over the years.

Education and Training

human capital
The knowledge and skills that make a worker productive.

Ben Franklin once said, "He that hath a trade hath an estate," meaning that education and training contribute to a worker's stock of **human capital**—the knowledge and skills that make a worker productive. Investment in human capital includes not only formal education but also on-the-job training. Like investment in physical capital, investment in human capital is an important means of increasing labor productivity and earnings. An estimated 15 percent of productivity growth derives from investments in people's education and skills.

© Medioimages/Superstock

© Royalty-Free/CORBIS

Photo Op Public and Private Investment in Infrastructure

Both public infrastructure investments (such as highways and bridges) and private infrastructure investments (such as wireless communications systems) have increased the nation's stock of private and public capital and help expand real GDP.

One measure of a nation's quality of labor is its level of educational attainment. Figure 10.3 shows large gains in educational attainment over the past several decades. In 1960 only 41 percent of the U.S. population age 25 or older had at least a high school education; and only 8 percent had a college education (bachelor's degree) or more. By 2010, those numbers had increased to over 85 and 28 percent, respectively. Clearly, more people are receiving an education than ever before.

But all is not upbeat with education in the United States. Many observers think that the quality of education in the United States has declined. For example, U.S. students in science and mathematics perform poorly on tests on those subjects relative to students in many other nations. The United States has been producing fewer native-born engineers and scientists, a problem that may trace back to inadequate training in math and science in elementary and high schools. For these reasons, much recent public policy discussion and legislation have been directed toward improving the quality of the U.S. education and training system.

Economies of Scale and Resource Allocation

Economies of scale and improved resource allocation are a fourth and fifth source of productivity growth, and together they explain about 15 percent of productivity growth.

FIGURE 10.3

Changes in the educational attainment of the U.S. adult population. The percentage of the U.S. adult population, age 25 or more, completing high school and college (bachelor's degree or higher) has been rising over recent decades.

Source: U.S. Census Bureau, **www.census.gov**.

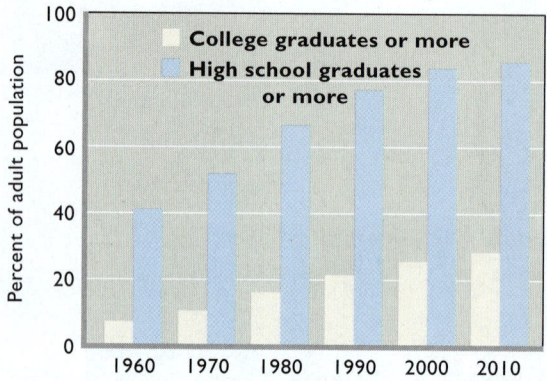

Economies of Scale   Reductions in per-unit production costs that result from increases in output levels are called **economies of scale.** Markets have increased in size over time, allowing firms to increase output levels and thereby achieve production advantages associated with greater size. As firms expand their size and output, they are able to use larger, more productive equipment and employ methods of manufacturing and delivery that increase productivity. They also are better able to recoup substantial investments in developing new products and production methods. Examples: A large manufacturer of autos can use elaborate assembly lines with computerization and robotics, while smaller producers must settle for less-advanced technologies using more labor inputs. Large pharmaceutical firms greatly reduce the average amount of labor (researchers, production workers) needed to produce each pill as they increase the number of pills produced. Accordingly, economies of scale result in greater real GDP and thus contribute to economic growth.

Improved Resource Allocation   Improved resource allocation means that workers over time have moved from low-productivity employment to high-productivity employment. Historically, many workers have shifted from agriculture, where labor productivity is low, to manufacturing, where it is quite high. More recently, labor has shifted away from some manufacturing industries to even higher-productivity industries such as computer software, business consulting, and pharmaceuticals. As a result of such shifts, the average productivity of U.S. workers has increased.

Also, things such as tariffs, import quotas, and other barriers to international trade tend to relegate resources to relatively unproductive pursuits. The long-run movement toward liberalized international trade through international agreements has improved the allocation of resources, increased labor productivity, and expanded real output, both here and abroad.

Finally, discrimination in education and the labor market has historically deterred some women and minorities from entering high-productivity jobs. With the decline of such discrimination over time, many members of those groups have shifted from low-productivity jobs to higher-productivity jobs. The result has been higher overall labor productivity and real GDP.

economies of scale
Reductions in per-unit production costs that result from increases in the size of markets and firms.

Institutional Structures That Promote Growth

Economic historians have identified several institutional structures that promote and sustain modern economic growth. Some structures increase the savings and investment that are needed to fund the construction and maintenance of the huge amounts of infrastructure required to run modern economies. Other institutional structures promote the development of new technologies. And still others act to ensure that resources flow efficiently to their most productive uses. These growth-promoting institutional structures include

- *Strong property rights* These appear to be absolutely necessary for rapid and sustained economic growth. People will not invest if they believe that thieves, bandits, or a rapacious and tyrannical government will steal their investments or their expected returns.
- *Patents and copyrights* These are necessary if a society wants a constant flow of innovative new technologies and sophisticated new ideas. Before patents and copyrights were first issued and enforced, inventors and authors usually saw their ideas stolen before they could profit from them. By giving inventors and authors the exclusive right to market and sell their creations, patents and copyrights give a strong financial incentive to invent and create.
- *Efficient financial institutions* These are needed to channel the savings generated by households towards the businesses, entrepreneurs, and inventors that do most of society's investing and inventing. Banks as well as stock and bond markets appear to be institutions crucial to modern economic growth.
- *Free trade* Free trade promotes economic growth by allowing countries to specialize so that different types of output can be produced in the countries where they can be made most efficiently. In addition, free trade promotes the rapid spread of new ideas so that innovations made in one country quickly spread to other countries.
- *A competitive market system* Under a market system, prices and profits serve as the signals that tell firms what to make and how much of it to make. Rich leader countries vary substantially in terms of how much government regulation they impose on markets, but in all cases, firms have substantial autonomy to follow market signals not only in terms of current production but also in terms of the investments they will currently make to produce what they believe consumers will demand in the future.

Other Factors

Several other difficult-to-measure factors also influence a nation's capacity for economic growth. The overall social-cultural-political environment of the United States, for example, has encouraged economic growth. Beyond the market system that has prevailed in the United States, the nation also has had a stable political system characterized by democratic principles, internal order, the right of property ownership, the legal status of enterprise, and the enforcement of contracts. Economic freedom and political freedom have been "growth-friendly."

In addition, and unlike some nations, there are virtually no social or moral taboos on production and material progress in the United States. The nation's social philosophy has embraced wealth creation as an attainable and desirable goal and the inventor, the innovator, and the businessperson are accorded high degrees of prestige and respect in American society. Finally, Americans have a positive attitude toward work and risk taking, resulting in an ample supply of willing workers and innovative entrepreneurs. A flow of energetic immigrants has greatly augmented that supply.

The Rise in the Average Rate of Productivity Growth

Figure 10.4 shows the growth of labor productivity (as measured by changes in the index of labor productivity for the full business sector) in the United States from 1973 to 2009, along with separate trend lines for 1973–1995 and 1995–2009. Labor productivity in the business sector grew by an average of only 1.5 percent yearly over the 1973–1995 period. But productivity growth averaged 2.8 percent between 1995 and 2009. Many economists believe that this higher productivity growth resulted from a significant new wave of technological advance, coupled with global competition. Some economists think there is a good chance that the higher trend rates of productivity growth could continue for many years to come.

This increase in productivity growth is important because real output, real income, and real wages are linked to labor productivity. To see why, suppose you are alone on an uninhabited island. The number of fish you can catch or coconuts you can pick per hour—your productivity—is your real wage (or real income) per hour. By *increasing* your productivity, you can improve your standard of living because greater output per hour means there are more fish and coconuts (goods) available to consume.

So it is for the economy as a whole: Over long periods, the economy's labor productivity determines its average real hourly wage, which includes fringe benefits such as health care insurance and contributions to pensions. The economy's income per hour is equal to its output per hour. So productivity growth is the economy's main route for improving the living standards for its workers.

FIGURE 10.4

Growth of labor productivity in the United States, 1973–2009. U.S. labor productivity (here, for the business sector) increased at an average annual rate of only 1.5 percent from 1973 to 1995. But between 1995 and 2009, it rose to an annual rate of 2.8 percent.

Source: U.S. Bureau of Labor Statistics, **www.bls.gov**.

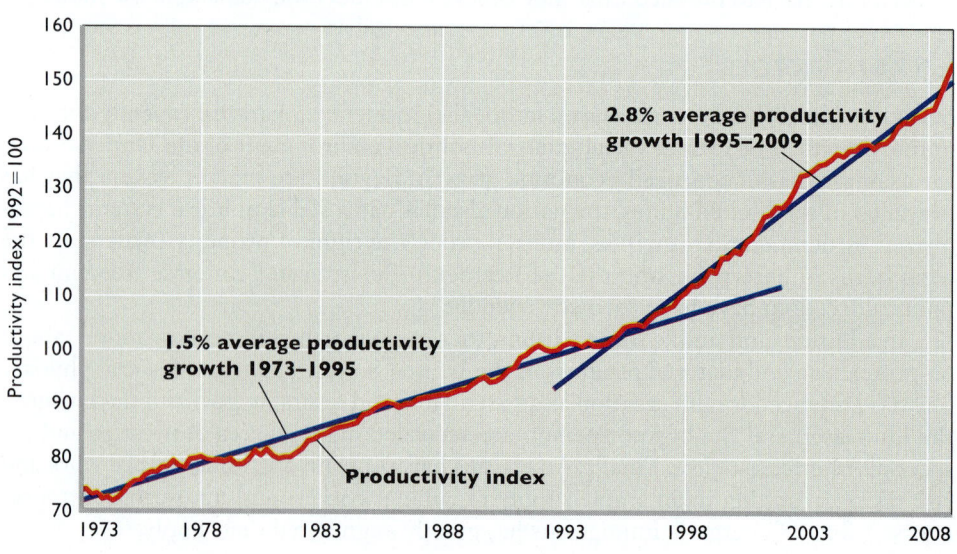

Reasons for the Rise in the Average Rate of Productivity Growth

Why has productivity growth increased relative to earlier periods?

The Microchip and Information Technology   The core element of the productivity speedup is an explosion of entrepreneurship and innovation based on the microprocessor, or *microchip*, which bundles transistors on a piece of silicon. Some observers liken the invention of the microchip to that of electricity, the automobile, air travel, the telephone, and television in importance and scope.

The microchip has found its way into thousands of applications. It has helped create a wide array of new products and services and new ways of doing business. Its immediate results were the pocket calculator, the bar-code scanner, the personal computer, the laptop computer, and more powerful business computers. But the miniaturization of electronic circuits also advanced the development of many other products such as cell phones and pagers, computer-guided lasers, deciphered genetic codes, global positioning equipment, energy conservation systems, Doppler radar, and digital cameras.

Perhaps of greatest significance, the widespread availability of personal and laptop computers stimulated the desire to tie them together. That desire promoted rapid development of the Internet and all its many manifestations, such as business-to-household and business-to-business electronic commerce *(e-commerce)*. The combination of the computer, fiber optic cable, wireless technology, and the Internet constitutes a spectacular advance in **information technology,** which has been used to connect all parts of the world.

New Firms and Increasing Returns   Hundreds of new **start-up firms** advanced various aspects of the new information technology. Many of these firms created more "hype" than goods and services and quickly fell by the wayside. But a number of firms flourished, eventually to take their places among the nation's largest firms. Examples of those firms include Intel (microchips); Apple and Dell (personal computers); Microsoft and Oracle (computer software); Cisco Systems (Internet switching systems); Yahoo and Google (Internet search engines); and Amazon.com (electronic commerce). There are scores more! Most of these firms were either "not on the radar" or "a relatively small blip on the radar" 30 years ago. Today each of them has large annual revenue and employs thousands of workers.

Successful new firms often experience **increasing returns,** a situation in which a given percentage increase in the amount of inputs a firm uses leads to an even larger percentage increase in the amount of output the firm produces. For example, suppose that a company called Techco decides to double the size of its operations to meet the growing demand for its services. After doubling its plant and equipment and doubling its workforce, say, from 100 workers to 200 workers, it finds that its total output has tripled from 8000 units to 24,000 units. Techco has experienced increasing returns; its output has increased by 200 percent, while its inputs have increased by only 100 percent. That is, its labor productivity has gone up from 80 units per worker (= 8000 units/100 workers) to 120 units per worker (= 24,000 units/200 workers). Increasing returns boost labor productivity and lower per-unit production costs. Since these cost reductions result from increases in output levels, they are examples of *economies of scale*.

information technology
New and more efficient methods of delivering and receiving information through use of computers, fax machines, wireless phones, and the Internet.

start-up firms
New firms focused on creating and introducing particular new products or employing specific new production or distribution methods.

increasing returns
A firm's output increases by a larger percentage than the increase in its inputs.

Both emerging firms as well as established firms can exploit several different sources of increasing returns and economies of scale:

- *More specialized inputs* Firms can use more specialized and thus more productive capital and workers as they expand their operations. A growing new e-commerce business, for example, can purchase highly specialized inventory management systems and hire specialized personnel such as accountants, marketing managers, and system maintenance experts.
- *Spreading of development costs* Firms can spread high product development costs over greater output. For example, suppose that a new software product costs $100,000 to develop and only $2 per unit to manufacture and sell. If the firm sells 1000 units of the software, its cost per unit will be $102 [= ($100,000 + $2000)/1000], but if it sells 500,000 units, that cost will drop to only $2.20 [= ($100,000 + $1 million)/500,000].
- *Simultaneous consumption* Many recently developed products and services can satisfy large numbers of customers at the same time. Unlike a gallon of gas that needs to be produced for each buyer, a software program needs to be produced only once. It then becomes available at very low expense to thousands or even millions of buyers. The same is true of books delivered to electronic reading devices, movies distributed on DVDs, and information disseminated through the Internet.
- *Network effects* Software and Internet service become more beneficial to a buyer the greater the number of households and businesses that also buy them. When others have Internet service, you can send e-mail messages to them. And when they also have software that allows display of documents and photos, you can attach those items to your e-mail messages. These system advantages are called **network effects,** which are increases in the value of the product to each user, including existing users, as the total number of users rises. The domestic and global expansion of the Internet in particular has produced network effects, as have cell phones, pagers, palm computers, and other aspects of wireless communication. Network effects magnify the value of output well beyond the costs of inputs.
- *Learning by doing* Finally, firms that produce new products or pioneer new ways of doing business experience increasing returns through **learning by doing.** Tasks that initially may have taken firms hours may take them only minutes once the methods are perfected.

Whatever the particular source of increasing returns, the result is higher productivity, which tends to reduce the per-unit cost of producing and delivering products.

network effects
Increases in the value of a product to each user, including existing users, as the total number of users rises.

learning by doing
Achieving greater productivity and lower average total costs through gains in knowledge and skill that accompany repetition of a task.

Global Competition The recent economy is characterized not only by information technology and increasing returns but also by heightened global competition. The collapse of the socialist economies in the late 1980s and early 1990s, together with the success of market systems, has led to a reawakening of capitalism throughout the world. The new information technologies have "shrunk the globe" and made it imperative for all firms to lower their costs and prices and to innovate in order to remain competitive. Free-trade zones such as those created by the North American Free Trade Agreement (NAFTA) and the European Union (EU) also have heightened competition internationally by removing trade protection from domestic firms. So, too, has trade liberalization through the World Trade Organization (WTO). The larger geographic markets and lower tariffs, in turn, have enabled emerging and old-line firms to expand beyond their national borders.

Implications for Economic Growth

Other things equal, stronger productivity growth and heightened global competition allow the economy to achieve a higher rate of economic growth. A glance back at Figure 10.1 will help make this point. Suppose that the shift of the production possibilities curve from *AB* to *CD* reflects annual changes in potential output levels before the recent increase in growth rates. Then the higher growth rates of the more recent period of accelerated productivity growth would be depicted by a *larger* outward shift of the economy's production possibilities from *AB* to a curve beyond *CD*. When coupled with economic efficiency and increased total spending, the economy's real GDP would rise by more than that shown.

Two cautions: Although the trend line of productivity growth seems to be steeper than in the past and bodes well for long-term economic growth, fluctuations of the rate of economic growth will still occur. Because of demand factors, real output periodically deviates below and above the growth trend—as it certainly did during the very severe recession of 2007–2009. Also, you need to know that the growth of the U.S. labor force may be declining. That slowing may offset some or all of the extra potential for economic growth that would arise from greater productivity growth.

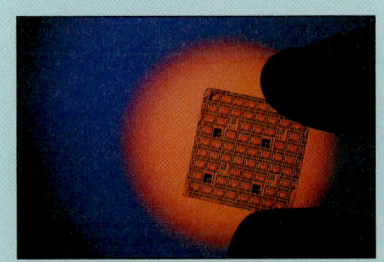
© Royalty-Free/CORBIS

Courtesy of Google Inc.

© age fotostock/SuperStock

Photo Op Key Elements of the Rise in U.S. Productivity

A combination of information technology, emerging new firms, and globalization helps explain the speedup in U.S. productivity growth since 1995.

Skepticism About Longevity

Although most macroeconomists have revised their forecasts for long-term productivity growth upward, at least slightly, others are still skeptical and urge a "wait-and-see" approach. These macroeconomists acknowledge that the economy has experienced a rapid advance of new technology, some new firms have experienced increasing returns, and global competition has increased. But they wonder if these factors are sufficiently profound to produce a 15- to 20-year period of substantially higher rates of productivity growth and real GDP growth.

They also point out that productivity surged between 1975 and 1978 and between 1983 and 1986 but in each case soon reverted to its lower long-run trend. The higher trend line of productivity inferred from the short-run spurt of productivity could prove to be an illusion. Only by looking backward over long periods can economists distinguish the start of a new long-run trend from a shorter-term boost in productivity related to the business cycle and temporary factors.

What Can We Conclude?

Given the different views on the recent productivity acceleration, what should we conclude? Perhaps the safest conclusions are these:

- The prospects for a lasting increase in productivity growth are good (see Global Snapshot 10.4). Studies indicate that productivity increases related to information technology have spread to a wide range of industries, including services. Even in the recession year 2001 and in 2002, when the economy was sluggish, productivity growth remained strong. Specifically, it averaged about 3.3 percent in the business sector over those two years. Productivity rose by 3.8 percent in 2003, 2.9 percent in 2004, and 2.0 percent in 2005 as the economy vigorously expanded.
- Time will tell. Productivity growth was 0.7 percent in 2008, 2.5 percent in 2009, 4.0 percent in 2010, and 0.2 percent in 2011. The average for these rates for the latest four years is lower than the 2.8 percent rate shown by the trend line in Figure 10.4, but it is higher than the 1.5 percent rate for the 1973–1995 period. Clearly many more years must elapse before economists will be ready to declare the post-1995 productivity acceleration to be a sustained, long-term trend.

Global Snapshot 10.4

Global Competitiveness Index

The Global Competitiveness Index published annually by the World Economic Forum measures each country's potential for economic growth. The index uses various factors—such as innovativeness, the capability to transfer technology among sectors, the efficiency of the financial system, rates of investment, and the degree of integration with the rest of the world—to measure a country's ability to achieve economic growth over time. Here is the top 10 list for 2010–2011.

Country	Global Competitiveness Ranking, 2010–2011
Switzerland	1
Singapore	2
Sweden	3
Finland	4
United States	5
Germany	6
Netherlands	7
Denmark	8
Japan	9
United Kingdom	10

Source: Copyright World Economic Forum, The Global Competitiveness Report, 2011–2012, **www.weforum.org.**

Is Growth Desirable and Sustainable?

Economists typically see economic growth as desirable and sustainable. But not all social observers agree.

The Antigrowth View

Critics of growth say industrialization and growth result in pollution, climate change, ozone depletion, and other environmental problems. These adverse spillover costs occur because inputs in the production process reenter the environment as some form of waste. The more rapid our growth and the higher our standard of living, the more waste the environment must absorb—or attempt to absorb. In an already wealthy society, further growth usually means satisfying increasingly trivial wants at the cost of mounting threats to the ecological system.

Critics of growth also argue that there is little compelling evidence that economic growth has solved sociological problems such as poverty, homelessness, and discrimination. Consider poverty: In the antigrowth view, American poverty (and, for that matter, world poverty) is a problem of distribution, not production. The requisite for solving the problem is commitment and political courage to redistribute wealth and income, not further increases in output.

Antigrowth sentiment also says that while growth may permit us to "make a better living," it does not give us "the good life." We may be producing more and enjoying it less. Growth means frantic paces on jobs, worker burnout, and alienated employees who have little or no control over decisions affecting their lives. The changing technology at the core of growth poses new anxieties and new sources of insecurity for workers. Both high-level and low-level workers face the prospect of having their hard-earned skills and experience rendered obsolete by an onrushing technology. High-growth economies are high-stress economies, which may impair our physical and mental health.

Finally, critics of high rates of growth doubt that they are sustainable. The planet Earth has finite amounts of natural resources available, and they are being consumed at alarming rates. Higher rates of economic growth simply speed up the degradation and exhaustion of the earth's resources. In this view, slower economic growth that is sustainable is preferable to faster growth.

In Defense of Economic Growth

The primary defense of growth is that it is the path to the greater material abundance and higher living standards desired by the vast majority of people. Rising output and incomes allow people to buy

> more education, recreation, and travel, more medical care, closer communications, more skilled personal and professional services, and better-designed as well as more numerous products. It also means more art, music, and poetry, theater, and drama. It can even mean more time and resources devoted to spiritual growth and human development.[2]

Growth also enables society to improve the nation's infrastructure, enhance the care of the sick and elderly, provide greater access for the disabled, and provide more police and fire protection. Economic growth may be the only realistic way to reduce poverty, since there is little political support for greater redistribution of

---

[2]Alice M. Rivlin, *Reviving the American Dream* (Washington, D.C.: Brookings Institution, 1992), p. 36.

income. The way to improve the economic position of the poor is to increase household incomes through higher productivity and economic growth. Also, a no-growth policy among industrial nations might severely limit growth in poor nations. Foreign investment and development assistance in those nations would fall, keeping the world's poor in poverty longer.

Economic growth has not made labor more unpleasant or hazardous, as critics suggest. New machinery is usually less taxing and less dangerous than the machinery it replaces. Air-conditioned workplaces are more pleasant than steamy workshops. Furthermore, why would an end to economic growth reduce materialism or alienation? The loudest protests against materialism are heard in those nations and groups that now enjoy the highest levels of material abundance! The high standard of living that growth provides has increased our leisure and given us more time for reflection and self-fulfillment.

Does growth threaten the environment? The connection between growth and environment is tenuous, say growth proponents. Increases in economic growth need not mean increases in pollution. Pollution is not so much a by-product of growth as it is a "problem of the commons." Much of the environment—streams, lakes, oceans, and the air—is treated as "common property," with insufficient or no restrictions on its use. The commons have become our dumping grounds; we have overused and debased them. Environmental pollution is a case of spillover or external costs, and correcting this problem involves regulatory legislation, specific taxes ("effluent charges"), or market-based incentives to remedy misuse of the environment.

Those who support growth admit there are serious environmental problems but say that limiting growth is the wrong solution. Growth has allowed economies to reduce pollution, be more sensitive to environmental considerations, set aside wilderness, create national parks and monuments, and clean up hazardous waste, while still enabling rising household incomes.

Is growth sustainable? Yes, say the proponents of growth. If we were depleting natural resources faster than their discovery, we would see the prices of those resources rise. That has not been the case for most natural resources; in fact, the prices of most of them have declined. And if one natural resource becomes too expensive, another resource will be substituted for it. Moreover, say economists, economic growth has to do with the expansion and application of human knowledge and information, not of extractable natural resources. In this view, economic growth—and solving any problems it may create—is limited only by human imagination.

Summary

1. Gross domestic product (GDP) is the market value of all final goods and services produced within the borders of a nation in a year. Intermediate goods and secondhand sales are purposely excluded in calculating GDP.

2. GDP can be calculated by adding consumer purchases of goods and services, gross investment spending by businesses, government purchases, and net exports: $GDP = C + I_g + G + X_n$.

3. Nominal (current-dollar) GDP measures each year's output valued in terms of the prices prevailing in that year. Real (constant-dollar) GDP measures each year's output in terms of the prices that prevailed in a selected base

year. Because real GDP is adjusted for price-level changes, differences in real GDP are due only to differences in output.

4. Economic growth is either (a) an increase of real GDP over time or (b) an increase in real GDP per capita over time. Growth lessens the burden of scarcity and provides increases in real GDP that can be used to resolve socioeconomic problems.

5. The supply factors in economic growth are (a) the quantity and quality of a nation's natural resources, (b) the quantity and quality of its human resources, (c) its stock of capital facilities, and (d) its technology. Two other

factors—a sufficient level of aggregate demand and economic efficiency—are necessary for the economy to realize its growth potential.

6. The growth of production capacity is shown graphically as an outward shift of a nation's production possibilities curve. Growth is realized when total spending rises sufficiently to match the growth of production capacity.

7. U.S. real GDP has grown partly because of increased inputs of labor and primarily because of increases in the productivity of labor. The increases in productivity have resulted mainly from technological progress, increases in the quantity of capital per worker, improvements in the quality of labor, economies of scale, and an improved allocation of labor.

8. Over long time periods, the growth of labor productivity underlies an economy's growth of real wages and its standard of living.

9. Productivity rose by 2.8 percent annually between 1995 and 2009, compared to 1.5 percent annually between 1973 and 1995. Some economists think this productivity acceleration will be long-lasting and allow the economy to experience greater noninflationary economic growth.

10. The post-1995 increase in the average rate of productivity growth is based on (a) rapid technological change in the form of the microchip and information technology, (b) increasing returns and lower per-unit costs, and (c) heightened global competition that holds down prices.

11. The main sources of increasing returns in recent years are (a) the use of more specialized inputs as firms grow, (b) the spreading of development costs, (c) simultaneous consumption by consumers, (d) network effects, and (e) learning by doing. Increasing returns mean higher productivity and lower per-unit production costs.

12. Some economists wonder if the recent rise in the average rate of productivity growth is permanent, and therefore they urge a wait-and-see approach. They point out that surges in productivity and real GDP growth have previously occurred but do not necessarily represent long-lived trends.

13. Critics of rapid growth say that it adds to environmental degradation, increases human stress, and exhausts the earth's finite supply of natural resources. Defenders of rapid growth say that it is the primary path to the rising living standards nearly universally desired by people, that it need not debase the environment, and that there are no indications that we are running out of resources. Growth is based on the expansion and application of human knowledge, which is limited only by human imagination.

Terms and Concepts

national income and product accounts (NIPA)

gross domestic product (GDP)

intermediate goods

final goods

personal consumption expenditures (C)

gross private domestic investment (I_g)

government purchases (G)

net exports (X_n)

nominal GDP

real GDP

economic growth

real GDP per capita

labor productivity

labor-force participation rate

growth accounting

infrastructure

human capital

economies of scale

information technology

start-up firms

increasing returns

network effects

learning by doing

Questions

1. Why do national income accountants compare the market value of the total outputs in various years rather than actual physical volumes of production? What problem is posed by any comparison over time of the market values of various total outputs? How is this problem resolved? **LO1**

2. Why are only final goods counted in measuring GDP for a particular year? Why is the value of used furniture that's bought and sold not counted? **LO1**

3. What are the three main types of consumption expenditures? Why are purchases of new houses considered to be investment expenditures rather than consumption expenditures? **LO1**

4. Why are changes in inventories included as part of investment spending? Suppose inventories declined by $1 billion during 2012. How would this affect the size of gross private domestic investment and gross domestic product in 2012? Explain. **LO1**

5. Define net exports. Explain how U.S. exports and imports each affects domestic production. How are net exports determined? Explain how net exports might be a negative amount. **LO1**

6. Which of the following are included in this year's GDP? Explain your answer in each case. **LO1**
   a. The services of a commercial painter in painting the family home.
   b. An auto dealer's sale of a new car to a nonbusiness customer.
   c. The money received by Smith when she sells her biology textbook to a used-book buyer.
   d. The publication and sale of a new economics textbook.
   e. A $2 billion increase in business inventories.
   f. Government purchases of newly produced aircraft.

7. What are the four supply factors of economic growth? What is the demand factor? What is the efficiency factor? Illustrate these factors in terms of the production possibilities curve. **LO4**

8. To what extent have increases in U.S. real GDP resulted from more labor inputs? From higher labor productivity? Rearrange the following contributors to the growth of real GDP in order of their quantitative importance: economies of scale, quantity of capital, improved resource allocation, education and training, technological advance. **LO5**

9. True or false? If false, explain why. **LO5**
   a. Technological advance, which to date has played a relatively small role in U.S. economic growth, is destined to play a more important role in the future.
   b. Many public capital goods are complementary to private capital goods.
   c. Immigration has slowed economic growth in the United States.

10. Explain why there is such a close relationship between changes in a nation's rate of productivity growth and changes in its average real hourly wage. **LO6**

11. Relate each of the following to the recent productivity speedup: **LO6**
    a. Information technology
    b. Increasing returns
    c. Network effects
    d. Global competition

12. Provide three examples of products or services that can be simultaneously consumed by many people. Explain why labor productivity greatly rises as the firm sells more units of the product or service. Explain why the higher level of sales greatly reduces the per-unit cost of the product. **LO6**

Problems

1. Suppose that annual output in year 1 in a 3-good economy is 3 quarts of ice cream, 1 bottle of shampoo, and 3 jars of peanut butter. In year 2, the output mix changes to 5 quarts of ice cream, 2 bottles of shampoo, and 2 jars of peanut butter. If the prices in both years are $4 per quart for ice cream, $3 per bottle of shampoo, and $2 per jar of peanut butter, what was the economy's GDP in year 1? What was its GDP in year 2? **LO1**

2. If in some country personal consumption expenditures in a specific year are $50 billion, purchases of stocks and bonds are $30 billion, net exports are −$10 billion, government purchases are $20 billion, sales of secondhand items are $8 billion, and gross investment is $25 billion, what is the country's GDP for the year? **LO1**

3. Assume that a grower of flower bulbs sells its annual output of bulbs to an Internet retailer for $70,000. The retailer, in turn, brings in $160,000 from selling the bulbs directly to final customers. What amount would these two transactions add to personal consumption expenditures and thus to GDP during the year? **LO1**

4. Using the NIPA data below, compute GDP. All figures are in billions. **LO1**

Personal consumption expenditures	$245
Wages and salaries	223
Imports	18
Corporate profits	42
Depreciation	28
Gross private domestic investment	86
Government purchases	82
Exports	9

5. Suppose that in 1984 the total output in a single-good economy was 7000 buckets of chicken. Also suppose that in 1984 each bucket of chicken was priced at $10. Finally, assume that in 2004 the price per bucket of chicken was $16 and that 22,000 buckets were produced. Determine real GDP for 1984 and 2004, in 1984 prices. **LO2**

6. Suppose an economy's real GDP is $30,000 in year 1 and $31,200 in year 2. What is the growth rate of its real GDP? Assume that population is 100 in year 1 and 102 in year 2. What is the growth rate of GDP per capita? **LO3**

7. What annual growth rate is needed for a country to double its output in 7 years? In 35 years? In 70 years? In 140 years? **LO3**

8. Assume that a "leader country" has real GDP per capita of $40,000, whereas a "follower country" has real GDP per capita of $20,000. Next suppose that the growth of real GDP per capita falls to zero percent in the leader country and rises to 7 percent in the follower country. If these rates continue for long periods of time, how many years will it take for the follower country to catch up to the living standard of the leader country? **LO3**

9. Suppose that work hours in New Zombie are 200 in year 1 and productivity is $8 per hour worked. What is New Zombie's real GDP? If work hours increase to 210 in year 2 and productivity rises to $10 per hour, what is New Zombie's rate of economic growth? **LO5**

FURTHER TEST YOUR KNOWLEDGE AT
www.brue3e.com

At the text's Online Learning Center, **www.brue3e.com**, you will find one or more web-based questions that require information from the Internet to answer. We urge you to check them out, since they will familiarize you with websites that may be helpful in other courses and perhaps even in your career. The OLC also features multiple-choice quizzes that give instant feedback and provides other helpful ways to further test your knowledge of the chapter.

CHAPTER ELEVEN

Business Cycles, Unemployment, and Inflation

After reading this chapter, you should be able to:

1. Describe the business cycle and its primary phases.

2. Illustrate how unemployment and inflation are measured.

3. Explain the types of unemployment and inflation and their various economic impacts.

As indicated in Chapter 10, the United States has experienced remarkable economic growth over time. But this growth has not been smooth, steady, or predictable from year to year. At various times the United States has experienced recessions, high unemployment rates, or high inflation rates. For example, U.S. unemployment rose by 8 million workers and the unemployment rate increased from 4.7 percent to 10.1 percent during the Great Recession. Other nations also have suffered high unemployment rates at times. As just one example, Spain's unemployment rate was over 21 percent in 2011. Also, inflation has occasionally plagued the United States and other nations. For instance, the U.S. inflation rate in 1980 was 13.5 percent. Zimbabwe's inflation soared to 26,000 percent in 2007!

Our goal in this chapter is to examine the concepts, terminology, and facts relating to macroeconomic instability. Specifically, we want to discuss the business cycle, unemployment, and inflation. The concepts discussed are extremely important for understanding subsequent chapters on economic theory and economic policy.

Business Cycles

The long-run growth trend of the U.S. economy is one of expansion, as stylized by the upsloping line labeled "Growth Trend" in Figure 11.1. But growth has been interrupted by periods of economic insta-

ORIGIN OF THE IDEA

O 11.1
Business cycles

bility usually associated with *business cycles*. **Business cycles** are alternating rises and declines in the level of economic activity, sometimes over several years. Individual cycles (one "up" followed by one "down") vary substantially in duration and intensity.

As shown in Figure 11.1, the two primary phases of business cycles are recessions and expansions ("peaks" and "troughs" are merely turning points). A **recession** is a period of decline in total output, income, and employment. This downturn, which lasts 6 months or more, is marked by the widespread contraction of business activity in many sectors of the economy. Along with declines in real GDP, significant increases in unemployment occur. Table 11.1 documents the 10 recessions in the United States since 1950.

business cycles
Recurring increases and decreases in the level of economic activity over periods of time.

recession
A period of declining real GDP, accompanied by lower income and higher unemployment.

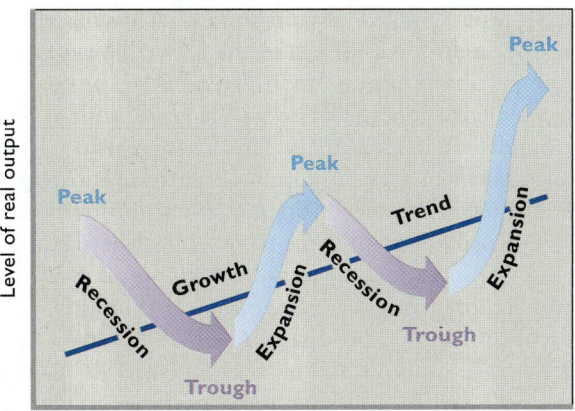

FIGURE 11.1
The business cycle. Economists distinguish two primary phases of the business cycle (recession and expansion); the duration and strength of each phase may vary.

TABLE 11.1

U.S. Recessions since 1950

Period	Duration, Months	Depth (Decline in Real Output)
1953–54	10	−3.7%
1957–58	8	−3.9
1960–61	10	−1.6
1969–70	11	−1.0
1973–75	16	−4.9
1980	6	−2.3
1981–82	16	−3.3
1990–91	8	−1.8
2001	8	−0.5
2007–2009	18	−3.7

Source: National Bureau of Economic Research, **www.nber.org,** and Minneapolis Federal Reserve Bank, "The Recession and Recovery in Perspective," **www.minneapolis-fed.gov.** Output data are in 2000 dollars.

expansion
A generalized increase in output, income, and business activity.

A recession is usually followed by a recovery and **expansion,** a period in which real GDP, income, and employment rise. At some point, full employment is again achieved. If spending then expands more rapidly than does production capacity, prices of nearly all goods and services will rise. In other words, inflation will occur.

The Business Cycle Dating Committee of the National Bureau of Economic Research (NBER)—a nonprofit economic research organization—declares the start and end of recessions in the United States. Citing evidence of declining real output and falling employment, the NBER officially declared that the latest recession, the Great Recession, began in December 2007. The NBER subsequently declared that this recession ended in June 2009, 18 months after it began. In making this announcement, the NBER pointed out that its declaration was not a forecast for the future path of the economy.

Causes of Business Cycles

The long-run trend of the U.S. economy is expansion and growth. That is why the business cycles in Figure 11.1 are drawn against a trend of economic growth. A key issue in macroeconomics is why the economy sees business cycle fluctuations rather than slow, smooth growth. In terms of Figure 11.1, why does output go up and down rather than just staying on the smooth growth trend line?

shocks
Situations in which events don't meet expectations.

Economists have developed several possible explanations for business cycles. These theories are founded on the idea that fluctuations are driven by **shocks**—situations in which individuals and firms were expecting one thing to happen but then something else happened. For instance, consider a situation in which a firm decides to build a high-speed railroad that will shuttle passengers between Washington, D.C., and New York. They do so expecting it to be very popular and make a handsome profit. But if it unexpectedly turns out to be unpopular and loses money, the railroad must figure out how to respond. Should the railroad go out of business, change the service it provides, or spend millions on a massive advertising campaign? These sorts of decisions are necessitated by the shock and surprise of having to deal with an unexpected situation.

demand shocks
Unexpected changes in the demand for goods and services.

supply shocks
Unexpected changes in the supply of goods and services.

Economies are exposed to both demand shocks and supply shocks. **Demand shocks** are unexpected changes in the demand for goods and services. **Supply shocks** are unexpected changes in the supply of goods and services. Please note that the word *shock* only tells us that something unexpected has happened. It does not tell us whether what has happened is unexpectedly good or unexpectedly bad. To make things more clear, economists use more specific terms. For instance, a *positive demand shock* refers to a situation in which demand turns out to be higher than expected, while a *negative demand shock* refers to a situation in which demand turns out to be lower than expected.

Shocks to the economy, particularly those with significant negative impacts, often lead to calls for government action. But why are shocks a big enough problem to justify calling in the government for help? Why can't firms deal with shocks on their own? Why don't product and resource markets respond quickly to correct imbalances?

sticky prices
A situation where prices of goods and services are slow to respond to changes in supply and demand.

The answer to these questions is that the prices of many goods and services are inflexible (slow to change, also known as **sticky prices**) in the short run. This implies that price changes do not quickly equalize the quantities demanded of such goods and services with their respective quantities supplied. Instead, because prices are inflexible, the economy is forced to respond in the short run to demand shocks primarily through changes in output and employment rather than through changes in prices. If negative effects on output and employment effects are severe and/or long-lasting, government is generally called upon to take corrective action. We will address government policy options in upcoming chapters; for now we resume our focus on business cycles.

Economists cite several possible general sources of shocks that can cause business cycles.

- *Irregular innovation* Significant new products or production methods, such as those associated with the railroad, automobile, computer, and the Internet, can rapidly spread through the economy, sparking sizable increases in investment, consumption, output, and employment. After the economy has largely absorbed the new innovation, the economy may for a time slow down or possibly decline. Because such innovations occur irregularly and unexpectedly, they may contribute to the variability of economic activity.

- *Productivity changes* When productivity—output per unit of input—unexpectedly increases, the economy booms; when productivity unexpectedly decreases, the economy recedes. Such changes in productivity can result from unexpected changes in resource availability (of, say, oil or agricultural commodities) or from unexpected changes in the general rate of technological advance.

- *Monetary factors* Some economists see business cycles as purely monetary phenomena. When a nation's central bank shocks the economy by creating more money than people were expecting, an inflationary boom in output occurs. By contrast, printing less money than people were expecting triggers an output decline and, eventually, a price-level fall.

- *Political events* Unexpected political events, such as peace treaties, new wars, or the 9/11 terrorist attacks, can create economic opportunities or strains. In adjusting to these shocks, the economy may experience upswings or downswings.

- *Financial instability* Unexpected financial bubbles (rapid asset price increases) or bursts (abrupt asset price decreases) can spill over to the general economy by expanding or contracting lending, and boosting or eroding the confidence of consumers and businesses. Booms and busts in the rest of the economy may follow.

The severe recession of 2007–2009 was precipitated by a combination of excessive money and a financial frenzy that led to overvalued real estate and unsustainable mortgage debt. Institutions bundled this debt into new securities ("derivatives") that were sold to financial investors. Some of the investors, in turn, bought insurance against losses that might arise from the securities. As real estate prices plummeted and mortgage defaults unexpectedly rocketed, the securitization and insurance structure buckled and nearly collapsed. Credit markets froze, pessimism prevailed, and spending by businesses and households declined.

Whatever the source of economic shocks, most economists agree that the *immediate* cause of the large majority of cyclical changes in the levels of real output and employment is unexpected changes in the level of total spending. If total spending unexpectedly sinks and firms cannot lower prices, firms will find themselves selling fewer units of output (since, with prices fixed, a decreased amount of spending implies fewer items purchased). Slower sales will cause firms to cut back on production. As they do, GDP will fall. And because fewer workers will be needed to produce less output, employment also will fall. The economy will contract and enter a recession.

By contrast, if the level of spending unexpectedly rises, output, employment, and incomes will rise. This is true because with prices sticky, the increased spending will mean that consumers will be buying a larger volume of goods and services (since, with prices fixed, more spending means more items purchased). Firms will respond by increasing output. This will increase GDP. And because they will need to hire more workers to produce the larger volume of output, employment also will increase. The economy will boom and enjoy an expansion. Eventually, as time passes and prices become more flexible, prices are also likely to rise as a result of the increased spending.

Cyclical Impact: Durables and Nondurables

Although the business cycle is felt everywhere in the economy, it affects different segments in different ways and to different degrees.

Firms and industries producing *capital goods* (for example, housing, commercial buildings, heavy equipment, and farm implements) and *consumer durables* (for example, automobiles, personal computers, refrigerators) are affected most by the business cycle. Within limits, firms can postpone the purchase of capital goods. For instance, when the economy goes into recession, producers frequently delay the purchase of new equipment and the construction of new plants. The business outlook simply does not warrant increases in the stock of capital goods. In good times, capital goods are usually replaced before they depreciate completely. But when recession strikes, firms patch up their old equipment and make do. As a result, investment in capital goods declines sharply. Firms that have excess plant capacity may not even bother to replace all the capital that is depreciating. For them, net investment may be negative. The pattern is much the same for consumer durables such as automobiles and major appliances. When recession occurs and households must trim their budgets, purchases of these goods are often deferred. Families repair their old cars and appliances rather than buy new ones, and the firms producing these products suffer. (Of course, producers of capital goods and consumer durables also benefit most from expansions.)

In contrast, *service* industries and industries that produce *nondurable consumer goods* are somewhat insulated from the most severe effects of recession. People find it difficult to cut back on needed medical and legal services, for example. And a recession actually helps some service firms, such as pawnbrokers and law firms that specialize in bankruptcies. Nor are the purchases of many nondurable goods such as food and clothing easy to postpone. The quantity and quality of purchases of nondurables will decline, but not so much as will purchases of capital goods and consumer durables.

Applying the Analysis

Stock Prices and Macroeconomic Instability

Every day, the individual stocks (ownership shares) of thousands of corporations are bought and sold in the stock market. The owners of the individual stocks receive dividends—a portion of the firm's profit. Supply and demand in the stock market determine the price of each firm's stock, with individual stock prices generally rising and falling in concert with the collective expectations for each firm's profits. Greater profits normally result in higher dividends to the stock owners, and, in anticipation of higher dividends, people are willing to pay a higher price for the stock.

The media closely monitor and report stock market averages such as the Dow Jones Industrial Average (DJIA)—the weighted-average price of the stocks of 30 major

U.S. industrial firms. It is common for these price averages to change over time or even to rise or fall sharply during a single day. On "Black Monday," October 19, 1987, the DJIA fell by 20 percent. In contrast, the stock market averages rose spectacularly in 1998 and 1999, with the DJIA rising 16 and 25 percent in those two years. In 2002, the DJIA fell 17 percent. In 2003, it rose by 25 percent. In the last three months of 2008, the DJIA plummeted by 34 percent, the steepest decline since the 1930s.

The volatility of the stock market raises this question: Do changes in stock price averages and thus stock market wealth cause macroeconomic instability? Linkages between the stock market and the economy might lead us to answer "yes." Consider a sharp increase in stock prices. Feeling wealthier, stock owners respond by increasing their spending (the *wealth effect*). Firms react by increasing their purchases of new capital goods because they can finance such purchases through issuing new shares of high-valued stock (the *investment effect*). Of course, sharp declines in stock prices would produce the opposite results.

Studies find that changes in stock prices do affect consumption and investment but that these consumption and investment impacts are relatively weak. For example, a 10 percent sustained increase in stock market values in 1 year is associated with a 4 percent increase in consumption spending over the next 3 years. The investment response is even weaker. So typical day-to-day and year-to-year changes in stock market values have little impact on the macroeconomy.

In contrast, *stock market bubbles* can be detrimental to an economy. Such bubbles are huge run-ups of overall stock prices, caused by excessive optimism and frenzied buying. The rising stock values are unsupported by realistic prospects of the future strength of the economy and the firms operating in it. Rather than slowly decompress, such bubbles may burst and cause harm to the economy. The free fall of stock values, if long-lasting, causes reverse wealth effects. The stock market crash also may create an overall pessimism about the economy that undermines consumption and investment spending even further. Indeed, the plunge of the stock market in 2007 and 2008 contributed to the severe recession of 2007–2009 by stressing financial institutions and creating a tremendous amount of pessimism about the direction of the economy.

Question:
Suppose that your college savings fund of $100,000, all invested in stocks, was reduced in value to $25,000 because of a stock market crash. Explain how that would affect your spending for college (including your choice of school) and spending for other goods and services.

Unemployment

Two problems that arise over the course of the business cycle are unemployment and inflation. Let's look at unemployment first.

Measurement of Unemployment

The U.S. Bureau of Labor Statistics (BLS) conducts a nationwide random survey of some 60,000 households each month to determine who is employed and who is not employed. In a series of questions it asks which members of the household are working, unemployed and looking for work, not looking for work, and so on. From the answers it determines an unemployment rate for the entire nation.

FIGURE 11.2

The labor force, employment, and unemployment, 2011. The labor force consists of persons 16 years of age or older who are not in institutions and who are (1) employed or (2) unemployed but seeking employment.
Source: Bureau of Labor Statistics, **www.bls.gov** (civilian labor force data, which excludes military employment).

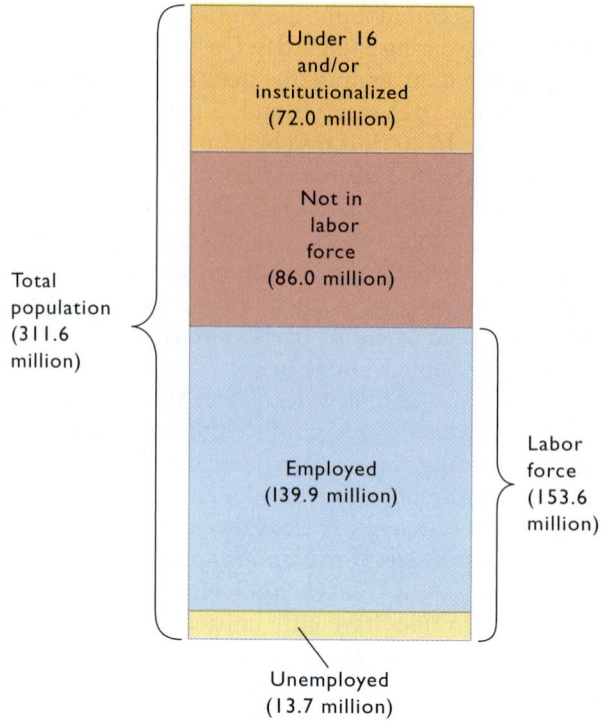

Total population (311.6 million)

Under 16 and/or institutionalized (72.0 million)

Not in labor force (86.0 million)

Employed (139.9 million)

Labor force (153.6 million)

Unemployed (13.7 million)

labor force
Persons 16 years and older who are not in institutions and who are either employed or unemployed and seeking work.

unemployment rate
The percentage of the labor force unemployed.

Figure 11.2 helps explain the mathematics. It divides the total U.S. population into three groups. One group is made up of people less than 16 years of age and people who are institutionalized, for example, in mental hospitals or correctional institutions. Such people are not considered potential members of the labor force. A second group, labeled "Not in labor force," is composed of adults who are potential workers but are not employed and are not seeking work. For example, they are homemakers, full-time students, or retirees. The third group is the **labor force,** which constituted about 49 percent of the total population in 2011. The labor force consists of people who are able and willing to work. Both those who are employed full-time and part-time and those who are unemployed but actively seeking work are counted as being in the labor force. The **unemployment rate** is the percentage of the labor force unemployed:

$$\text{Unemployment rate} = \frac{\text{unemployed}}{\text{labor force}} \times 100$$

The statistics underlying the rounded numbers in Figure 11.2 show that in 2011 the unemployment rate averaged

$$\frac{13,747,000}{153,617,000} \times 100 = 8.9\%$$

WORKED PROBLEMS

W 11.1
Unemployment rate

Types of Unemployment

There are three *types* of unemployment: frictional, structural, and cyclical.

Frictional Unemployment   At any moment some workers are "between jobs." Some of them will be moving voluntarily from one job to another. Others will have been fired and will be seeking reemployment. Still others will have been laid off temporarily because of seasonal demand. In addition to those between jobs, many young workers will be searching for their first jobs.

As these unemployed people find jobs or are called back from temporary layoffs, other job seekers and laid-off workers will replace them in the "unemployment pool." It is important to keep in mind that while the pool itself persists because there are always newly unemployed workers flowing into it, most workers do *not* stay in the unemployment pool for very long. Indeed, when the economy is strong, the majority of unemployed workers find new jobs within a couple of months. One should be careful not to make the mistake of confusing the permanence of the pool itself with the false ideal that the pool's membership is permanent, too. On the other hand, there *are* workers who do remain unemployed and in the pool for very long periods of time—sometimes for many years. As we discuss the different types of unemployment below, notice that certain types tend to be transitory while others are associated with much longer spells of unemployment.

Economists use the term **frictional unemployment**—consisting of *search unemployment* and *wait unemployment*—for workers who are either searching for jobs or waiting to take jobs in the near future. The word "frictional" implies that the labor market does not operate perfectly and instantaneously (without friction) in matching workers and jobs.

Frictional unemployment is inevitable and, at least in part, desirable. Many people who are frictionally unemployed are moving into the labor force or from low-paying, low-productivity jobs to higher-paying, higher-productivity positions. That means greater income for the workers, a better allocation of labor resources, and a larger real GDP for the economy.

> **frictional unemployment**
> Unemployment that is associated with people searching for jobs or waiting to take jobs in the near future.

Structural Unemployment

Structural Unemployment   Frictional unemployment blurs into a category called **structural unemployment.** Here, economists use "structural" in the sense of "compositional." Changes over time in consumer demand and in technology alter the "structure" of the total demand for labor, both occupationally and geographically.

Occupationally, the demand for certain skills (for example, sewing clothes or working on farms) may decline or even vanish. The demand for other skills (for example, designing software or maintaining computer systems) will intensify. Unemployment results because the composition of the labor force does not respond immediately or completely to the new structure of job opportunities. Workers who find that their skills and experience have become obsolete or unneeded thus find that they have no marketable talents. They are structurally unemployed until they adapt or develop skills that employers want.

Geographically, the demand for labor also changes over time. An example: migration of industry and thus of employment opportunities from the Snow Belt to the Sun Belt over the past few decades. Another example is the movement of jobs from inner-city factories to suburban industrial parks. And a final example is the so-called *offshoring* of jobs that occurs when the demand for a particular type of labor shifts from domestic firms to foreign firms. As job opportunities shift from one place to another, some workers become structurally unemployed.

> **structural unemployment**
> Unemployment that is associated with a mismatch between available jobs and the skills or locations of those unemployed.

Cyclical Unemployment

Cyclical Unemployment   Unemployment caused by a decline in total spending is called **cyclical unemployment** and typically begins in the recession phase of the business cycle. As the demand for goods and services decreases, employment falls and unemployment rises. The 25 percent unemployment rate in 1933 reflected mainly cyclical unemployment, as did significant parts of the 9.7 percent unemployment rate in 1982, the 7.5 percent rate in 1992, and the 8.9 percent rate in 2011.

Cyclical unemployment is a very serious problem when it occurs. To understand its costs, we need to define "full employment."

> **cyclical unemployment**
> Unemployment that is associated with the recessionary phase of a business cycle.

Definition of Full Employment

Because frictional and structural unemployment are largely unavoidable in a dynamic economy, *full employment* is something less than 100 percent employment of the labor force. Economists say that the economy is "fully employed" when it is experiencing only frictional and structural unemployment. That is, full employment occurs when there is no cyclical unemployment. Today, most economists believe that the economy is fully employed when the unemployment rate is less than 5 percent. The level of real GDP that would occur precisely at "full employment" is called **potential output** (or *potential GDP*).

potential output
The level of real GDP that would occur if there was full employment.

Economic Cost of Unemployment

The basic economic cost of unemployment is forgone output. When the economy fails to create enough jobs for all who have the necessary skills and are willing to work, potential production of goods and services is irretrievably lost. In terms of Chapter 1's analysis, cyclical unemployment means that society is operating at some point inside its production possibilities curve. Economists call this sacrifice of output a **GDP gap**—the difference between actual and potential GDP. That is:

GDP gap
The negative or positive difference between actual GDP and potential GDP.

$$\text{GDP gap} = \text{actual GDP} - \text{potential GDP}$$

The GDP gap can be either a negative number (actual GDP is less than potential GDP) or a positive number (actual GDP exceeds potential GDP). There is a close correlation between the actual unemployment rate and the GDP gap. The higher the unemployment rate, the greater is the negative GDP gap.

Society's cost of unemployment—its forgone output—translates to forgone income for individuals. This loss of income is borne unequally. Some groups have higher unemployment rates than others and bear the brunt of rising rates during recessions. For instance, workers in lower-skilled occupations (for example, laborers) have higher unemployment rates than workers in higher-skilled occupations (for example, professionals). Lower-skilled workers have more and longer spells of structural unemployment than higher-skilled workers. They also are less likely to be self-employed than are higher-skilled workers. Moreover, lower-skilled workers usually bear the brunt of recessions. Businesses generally retain most of their higher-skilled workers, in whom they have invested the expense of training.

Also, teenagers have much higher unemployment rates than adults. Teenagers have lower skill levels, quit their jobs more frequently, are more frequently "fired," and have less geographic mobility than adults. Many unemployed teenagers are new in the labor market, searching for their first jobs. Male African-American teenagers, in particular, have very high unemployment rates.

Finally, the overall unemployment rate for African Americans and Hispanics is higher than that for whites and Asians. The causes of the higher rates include lower rates of educational attainment, greater concentration in lower-skilled occupations, and discrimination in the labor market. In general, the unemployment rate for African Americans is twice that of whites.

International Comparisons

Unemployment rates differ greatly among nations at any given time. One reason is that nations have different unemployment rates when their economies are fully employed. Another is that nations may be in recessions or expansions. Global Snapshot 11.1 shows unemployment rates for five industrialized nations for the years 2000 through 2011. Prior to the Great Recession, the U.S. unemployment rate was considerably lower than that of countries such as France and Germany.

Unemployment Rates in Five Industrial Nations, 2000–2011

Global Snapshot 11.1

Prior to the severe recession of 2007–2009, compared with France and Germany, the United States had a relatively low unemployment rate. For many years Japan has had one of the lowest unemployment rates among industrial nations.

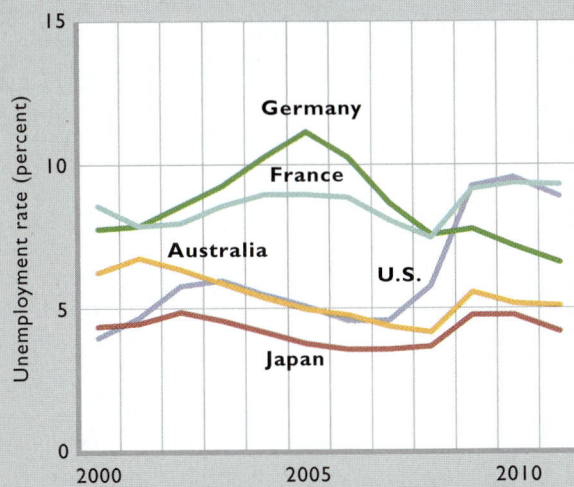

Source: Bureau of Labor Statistics, **www.bls.gov.** Based on U.S. unemployment concepts.

Inflation

We now turn to inflation, another aspect of macroeconomic instability. The problems inflation poses are subtler than those posed by unemployment.

Meaning of Inflation

Inflation is a rise in the *general level of prices*. When inflation occurs, each dollar of income will buy fewer goods and services than before. Inflation reduces the "purchasing power" of money. But inflation does not mean that *all* prices are rising. Even during periods of rapid inflation, some prices may be relatively constant and others may even fall. For example, although the United States experienced high rates of inflation in the 1970s and early 1980s, the prices of video recorders, digital watches, and personal computers declined.

inflation
A rise in the general level of prices in an economy.

Measurement of Inflation

The main measure of inflation in the United States is the **Consumer Price Index (CPI),** compiled by the Bureau of Labor Statistics (BLS). The government uses this index to report inflation rates each month and each year. It also uses the CPI to adjust Social Security benefits and income tax brackets for inflation. The CPI reports the price of a "market basket" of some 300 consumer goods and services that are purchased by a typical urban consumer.

Consumer Price Index (CPI)
An index that compares the price of a market basket of consumer goods and services in one period with the price of the same (or highly similar) market basket in a base period.

The composition of the market basket for the CPI is based on spending patterns of urban consumers in a specific period, presently 2009–2010. The BLS updates the composition of the market basket every 2 years so that it reflects the most recent patterns of consumer purchases and captures the inflation that consumers are currently experiencing. The BLS arbitrarily sets the CPI equal to 100 for 1982–1984. So the CPI for any particular year is found as follows:

$$\text{CPI} = \frac{\text{price of the most recent market basket in the particular year}}{\text{price of the same market basket in 1982–1984}}$$

The rate of inflation for a certain year is found by comparing, in percentage terms, that year's index with the index in the previous year. For example, the CPI rose from 218.1 in 2010 to 224.9 in 2011. So the rate of inflation for 2011 was 3.1 percent.

$$\text{Rate of inflation} = \frac{224.9 - 218.1}{218.1} \times 100 = 3.1\%$$

In rare cases, the CPI declines from one year to the next. For example, the CPI fell from 215.3 in 2008 to 214.5 in 2009. The rate of inflation for 2009 therefore was −0.4 percent. Such price level declines are called **deflation.**

In Chapter 10 we discussed the mathematical approximation called the *rule of 70*, which tells us that we can find the number of years it will take for some measure to double, given its annual percentage increase, by dividing that percentage increase into the number 70. For example, annual rates of inflation of 3 percent will double the price level in about 23 (= 70/3) years.

deflation
A decline in the general level of prices in an economy.

Facts of Inflation

Figure 11.3 shows December-to-December rates of annual inflation in the United States between 1960 and 2011. Observe that inflation reached double-digit rates in the 1970s and early 1980s but has since declined and has been relatively mild recently.

FIGURE 11.3

Annual inflation rates in the United States, 1960–2011 (December-to-December changes in the CPI). The major periods of inflation in the United States in the past 50 years were in the 1970s and 1980s.
Source: Bureau of Labor Statistics, **www.bls.gov**.

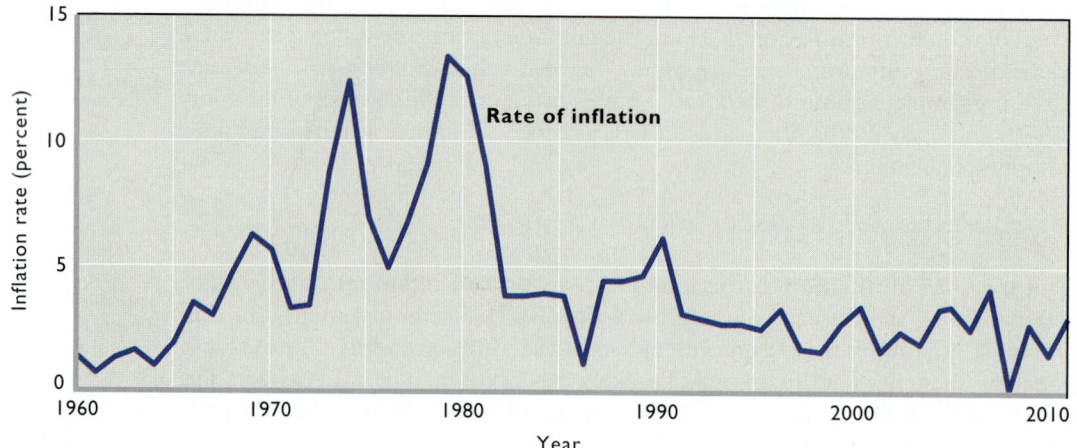

In recent years U.S. inflation has been neither unusually high nor unusually low relative to inflation in several other industrial countries (see Global Snapshot 11.2). Some nations (not shown) have had double-digit or even higher annual rates of inflation in recent years. In 2009, for example, the annual inflation rate in the Democratic Republic of Congo was 46 percent; Eritrea, 35 percent; Afghanistan, 31 percent; and Venezuela, 27 percent. Zimbabwe's inflation rate was 14.9 billion percent in 2008 before Zimbabwe did away with its existing currency.

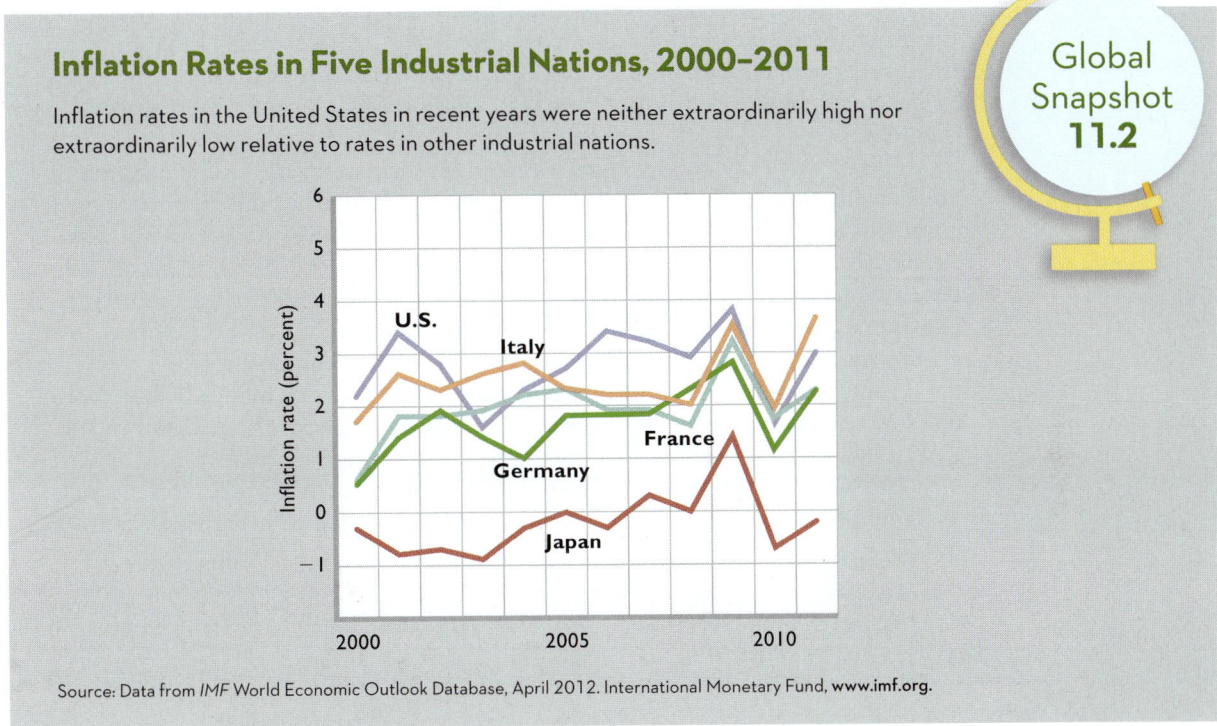

Inflation Rates in Five Industrial Nations, 2000–2011

Inflation rates in the United States in recent years were neither extraordinarily high nor extraordinarily low relative to rates in other industrial nations.

Global Snapshot 11.2

Source: Data from *IMF* World Economic Outlook Database, April 2012. International Monetary Fund, **www.imf.org.**

Types of Inflation

Nearly all prices in the economy are set by supply and demand. Consequently, if the economy is experiencing inflation and the overall level of prices is rising, we need to look for an explanation in terms of supply and demand. Reflecting this, economists distinguish between two types of inflation: *demand-pull inflation* and *cost-push inflation*.

Demand-Pull Inflation   Usually, increases in the price level are caused by an excess of total spending beyond the economy's capacity to produce. Where inflation is rapid and sustained, the cause invariably is an overissuance of money by the central bank (the Federal Reserve in the United States). When resources are already fully employed, the business sector cannot respond to excess demand by expanding output. So the excess demand bids up the prices of the limited output, producing **demand-pull inflation.** The essence of this type of inflation is "too much spending chasing too few goods."

demand-pull inflation
Inreases in the price level (inflation) caused by excessive spending.

Clipping Coins

Some interesting early episodes of demand-pull inflation occurred in Europe during the ninth to the fifteenth centuries under feudalism. In that economic system, *lords* (or *princes*) ruled individual fiefdoms, and their *vassals* (or *peasants*) worked the fields. The peasants initially paid parts of their harvest as taxes to the princes. Later, when the princes began issuing "coins of the realm," peasants began paying their taxes with gold coins.

Some princes soon discovered a way to transfer purchasing power from their vassals to themselves without explicitly increasing taxes. As coins came into the treasury, princes clipped off parts of the gold coins, making them slightly smaller. From the clippings they minted new coins and used them to buy more goods for themselves.

This practice of clipping coins was a subtle form of taxation. The quantity of goods being produced in the fiefdom remained the same, but the number of gold coins increased. With "too much money chasing too few goods," inflation occurred. Each gold coin earned by the peasants therefore had less purchasing power than previously because prices were higher. The increase of the money supply shifted purchasing power away from the peasants and toward the princes just as surely as if the princes had increased taxation of the peasants.

In more recent eras, some dictators have simply printed money to buy more goods for themselves, their relatives, and their key loyalists. These dictators, too, have levied hidden taxes on their population by creating inflation.

The moral of the story is quite simple: A society that values price-level stability should not entrust the control of its money supply to people who benefit from inflation.

Question:
Why might a government with a huge foreign debt be tempted to increase its domestic money supply and cause inflation?

Cost-Push Inflation   Inflation may also arise on the supply, or cost, side of the economy. During some periods in U.S. economic history, including the mid-1970s, the price level increased even though total spending was not excessive. These were periods when output and employment were both *declining* (evidence that total spending was not excessive) while the general price level was *rising*.

The theory of **cost-push inflation** explains rising prices in terms of factors that raise the average cost of a particular level of output. Rising average production costs squeeze profits and reduce the economy's supply of goods and services. In this scenario, costs are *pushing* the price level upward, whereas in demand-pull inflation demand is *pulling* it upward.

The major source of cost-push inflation has been so-called *supply shocks*. Specifically, abrupt increases in the costs of raw materials or energy inputs have on occasion driven up per-unit production costs and thus product prices. The rocketing prices of imported oil in 1973–1974 and again in 1979–1980 are good illustrations. As energy prices surged upward during these periods, the costs of producing and transporting virtually every product in the economy rose. Cost-push inflation ensued.

cost-push inflation
Increases in the price level (inflation) caused by sharp rises in the cost of key resources.

274

Redistribution Effects of Inflation

Inflation redistributes real income. This redistribution helps some people and hurts others, while leaving many people largely unaffected. Who gets hurt? Who benefits? Before we can answer, we need some terminology. There is a difference between money (or nominal) income and real income. **Nominal income** is the number of dollars received as wages, rent, interest, or profits. **Real income** is a measure of the amount of goods and services nominal income can buy; it is the purchasing power of nominal income, or income adjusted for inflation. That is,

$$\text{Real income} = \frac{\text{nominal income}}{\text{price index (in hundredths)}}$$

Inflation need not alter an economy's overall real income—its total purchasing power. It is evident from the above equation that real income will remain the same when nominal income and the price index rise at the same percentage rate.

But when inflation occurs, not everyone's nominal income rises at the same pace as the price level. Therein lies the potential for redistribution of real income from some to others. If the change in the price level differs from the change in a person's nominal income, his or her real income will be affected. The following approximation (shown by the ≅ sign) tells us roughly how much real income will change:

WORKED PROBLEMS

W 11.2
Nominal and real income

$$\begin{matrix} \text{Percentage} \\ \text{change in} \\ \text{real income} \end{matrix} \cong \begin{matrix} \text{percentage} \\ \text{change in} \\ \text{nominal income} \end{matrix} - \begin{matrix} \text{percentage} \\ \text{change in} \\ \text{price level} \end{matrix}$$

For example, suppose that the price level rises by 6 percent in some period. If Bob's nominal income rises by 6 percent, his real income will *remain unchanged*. But if his nominal income instead rises by 10 percent, his real income will *increase* by about 4 percent. And if Bob's nominal income rises by only 2 percent, his real income will *decline* by about 4 percent.

The redistribution effects of inflation depend on whether or not it is expected. With fully expected or *anticipated inflation*, an income receiver may be able to avoid or lessen the adverse effects of inflation on real income. The generalizations that follow assume *unanticipated inflation*—inflation whose full extent was not expected.

Who Is Hurt by Inflation?

Unanticipated inflation hurts fixed-income recipients, savers, and creditors. It redistributes real income away from them and toward others.

Fixed-Income Receivers   People whose incomes are fixed see their real incomes fall when inflation occurs. The classic case is the elderly couple living on a private pension or annuity that provides a fixed amount of nominal income each month. They may have retired on what appeared to be an adequate pension. However, years later they discover that inflation has severely cut the purchasing power of that pension—their real income.

Similarly, landlords who receive lease payments of fixed dollar amounts will be hurt by inflation as they receive dollars of declining value over time. Likewise, public sector workers whose incomes are dictated by fixed pay schedules may suffer from

nominal income
The number of dollars received as wages, rent, interest, and profit.

real income
The purchasing power of nominal income; the amount of goods and services that nominal income can buy.

inflation. The fixed "steps" (the upward yearly increases) in their pay schedules may not keep up with inflation. Minimum-wage workers and families living on fixed welfare incomes also will be hurt by inflation.

Savers   Unanticipated inflation hurts savers. As prices rise, the real value, or purchasing power, of an accumulation of savings deteriorates. Paper assets such as savings accounts, insurance policies, and annuities, which once were adequate to meet rainy-day contingencies or provide for a comfortable retirement, decline in real value during periods of inflation.

Creditors   Unanticipated inflation harms creditors (lenders). Suppose Chase Bank lends Bob $1000, to be repaid in 2 years. If in that time the price level doubles, the $1000 that Bob repays will have only half the purchasing power of the $1000 he borrowed. True, if we ignore interest charges, the same number of dollars will be repaid as was borrowed. But because of inflation, each of those dollars will buy only half as much as it did when the loan was negotiated. As prices go up, the value of the dollar goes down. So the borrower pays back less-valuable dollars than those received from the lender. The owners of Chase Bank suffer a loss of real income.

Who Is Unaffected or Helped by Inflation?

Some people are unaffected by inflation, and others are actually helped by it. For the second group, inflation redistributes real income toward them and away from others.

Flexible-Income Receivers   People who have flexible incomes may escape inflation's harm or even benefit from it. For example, individuals who derive their incomes solely from Social Security are largely unaffected by inflation because Social Security payments are *indexed* to the CPI. Benefits automatically increase when the CPI increases, preventing erosion of benefits from inflation. Some union workers also get automatic *cost-of-living adjustments (COLAs)* in their pay when the CPI rises, although such increases rarely equal the full percentage rise in inflation.

Some flexible-income receivers are helped by unanticipated inflation. The strong product demand and labor shortages implied by rapid demand-pull inflation may cause some nominal incomes to spurt ahead of the price level, thereby enhancing real incomes. As an example, property owners faced with an inflation-induced real estate boom may be able to boost rents more rapidly than the rate of inflation. Also, some business owners may benefit from inflation. If their product prices rise faster than their resource prices, business revenues will increase more rapidly than costs. In those cases, the growth rate of profit incomes will outpace the rate of inflation.

Debtors   Unanticipated inflation benefits debtors (borrowers). In our earlier example, Chase Bank's loss of real income from inflation is Bob's gain of real income. Debtor Bob borrows "dear" dollars but, because of inflation, pays back the principal and interest with "cheap" dollars whose purchasing power has been eroded by inflation. Real income is redistributed away from the owners of Chase Bank toward borrowers such as Bob.

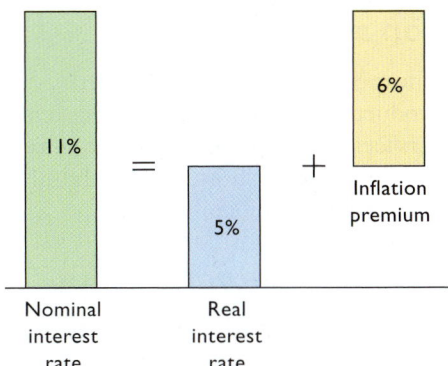

FIGURE 11.4
The inflation premium and nominal and real interest rates. The inflation premium—the expected rate of inflation—gets built into the nominal interest rate. Here, the nominal interest rate of 11 percent comprises the real interest rate of 5 percent plus the inflation premium of 6 percent.

Anticipated Inflation

The redistribution effects of inflation are less severe or are eliminated altogether if people anticipate inflation and can adjust their nominal incomes to reflect the expected price-level rises. The prolonged inflation that began in the late 1960s prompted many workers in the 1970s to insist on high wage and salary increases that would protect them from expected inflation.

Similarly, if inflation is anticipated, the redistribution of income from lender to borrower may be altered. Suppose a lender (perhaps a bank) and a borrower (a household) both agree that 5 percent is a fair rate of interest on a 1-year loan provided the price level is stable. But assume that inflation has been occurring and is expected to be 6 percent over the next year. The lender will neutralize inflation by charging an *inflation premium* of 6 percent, the amount of the anticipated inflation.

Our example reveals the difference between the real rate of interest and the nominal rate of interest. The **real interest rate** is the percentage increase in *purchasing power* that the borrower pays the lender. In our example, the real interest rate is 5 percent. The **nominal interest rate** is the percentage increase in *money* that the borrower pays the lender, including that resulting from the built-in expectation of inflation, if any. In equation form:

ORIGIN OF THE IDEA
O 11.2
Real interest rates

Nominal interest rate = real interest rate + inflation premium
(the expected rate of inflation)

As illustrated in Figure 11.4, the nominal interest rate in our example is 11 percent.

real interest rate
The percentage increase in purchasing power that a borrower pays a lender; the nominal interest rate less the expected rate of inflation.

nominal interest rate
The percentage increase in money that a borrower pays a lender.

Does Inflation Affect Output?

Thus far, our discussion has focused on how inflation redistributes a given level of total real income. But inflation also may affect an economy's level of real output (and thus its level of real income). The direction and significance of this effect on output depends on the type of inflation and its severity.

Cost-Push Inflation and Real Output

Recall that abrupt and unexpected rises in key resource prices such as oil can sufficiently drive up overall production costs to cause cost-push inflation. As prices rise, the quantity of goods and services demanded falls. So firms respond by producing less output, and unemployment goes up. In short, cost-push inflation reduces real output. It redistributes a decreased level of real income.

Demand-Pull Inflation and Real Output

Economists do not fully agree on the effects of mild inflation (less than 3 percent) on real output. One perspective is that even low levels of inflation reduce real output because inflation diverts time and effort toward activities designed to hedge against inflation. For example, businesses must incur the cost of changing thousands of prices on their shelves and in their computers simply to reflect inflation. Also, households and businesses must spend considerable time and effort obtaining the information they need to distinguish between real and nominal values such as prices, wages, and interest rates. Further, to limit the loss of purchasing power from inflation, people try to limit the amount of money they hold in their billfolds and checking accounts at any one time and instead put more money into interest-bearing accounts and stock and bond funds. But cash and checking deposits are needed in even greater amounts to buy the higher-priced goods and services. Therefore, people must make more frequent trips, phone calls, or Internet visits to financial institutions to transfer funds to checking accounts and billfolds, when needed. Bottom line: From this perspective even mild inflation reduces total output.

In contrast, other economists point out that full employment and economic growth depend on strong levels of total spending. Such spending creates high profits, strong demand for labor, and a powerful incentive for firms to expand their plants and equipment. In this view, the mild inflation that is a by-product of strong spending is a small price to pay for full employment and continued economic growth. Defenders of mild inflation say that it is much better for an economy to err on the side of strong spending, full employment, economic growth, and mild inflation than on the side of weak spending, unemployment, recession, and deflation.

Applying the Analysis

Hyperinflation

All economists agree that *hyperinflation*, which is extraordinarily rapid inflation, can have a devastating impact on real output and employment.

As prices shoot up sharply and unevenly during hyperinflation, normal economic relationships are disrupted. Business owners do not know what to charge for their products. Consumers do not know what to pay. Resource suppliers want to be paid with actual output, rather than with rapidly depreciating money. Money eventually becomes almost worthless and ceases to do its job as a medium of exchange. The economy may be thrown into a state of barter, and production and exchange drop dramatically. The net result is economic, social, and possibly political chaos.

Examples of hyperinflation are Germany after the First World War and Japan after the Second World War. In Germany, "prices increased so rapidly that waiters changed the prices on the menu several times during the course of a lunch. Sometimes customers had to pay double the price listed on the menu when they ordered."[*] In postwar Japan, in 1947 "fishermen and farmers...used scales to weigh currency and change, rather than bothering to count it."[†]

There are also more recent examples: Between June 1986 and March 1991 the cumulative inflation in Nicaragua was 11,895,866,143 percent. From November 1993 to December 1994 the cumulative inflation rate in the Democratic Republic of Congo was 69,502 percent. From February 1993 to January 1994 the cumulative inflation rate in Serbia was 156,312,790 percent.[‡]

Such dramatic hyperinflations are always the consequence of highly imprudent expansions of the money supply by government. The rocketing money supply produces frenzied total spending and severe demand-pull inflation. Zimbabwe's 14.9 billion percent in 2008 is just the latest example.

Question:
How would you alter your present spending plans if you were quite certain that the prices of everything were going to double in the coming week?

[*]Theodore Morgan, *Income and Employment*, 2nd ed. (Englewood Cliffs, N.J.: Prentice-Hall, 1952), p. 361.
[†]Raburn M. Williams, *Inflation! Money, Jobs, and Politicians* (Arlington Heights, Ill.: AHM Publishing, 1980), p. 2.
[‡]Stanley Fischer, Ratna Sahay, and Carlos Végh, "Modern Hyper- and High Inflations," *Journal of Economic Literature*, September 2002, p. 840.

Summary

1. Business cycles are recurring ups and downs in economic activity. Their two primary phases are expansions and recessions.

2. Economists distinguish between frictional, structural, and cyclical unemployment. The rate of unemployment at full employment consists of frictional and structural unemployment and currently is about 5 percent.

3. The economic cost of unemployment, as measured by the negative GDP gap, consists of the goods and services forgone by society when its resources are involuntarily idle.

4. Inflation is a rise in the general price level and is measured in the United States by the Consumer Price Index (CPI). When inflation occurs, each dollar of income will buy fewer goods and services than before. That is, inflation reduces the purchasing power of money. Deflation is a decline in the general price level.

5. Economists discern both demand-pull and cost-push (supply-side) inflation. Demand-pull inflation results from an excess of total spending relative to the economy's capacity to produce. The main source of cost-push inflation is abrupt and rapid increases in the prices of key resources. These supply shocks push up per-unit production costs and ultimately the prices of consumer goods.

6. Unanticipated inflation arbitrarily redistributes real income at the expense of fixed-income receivers, creditors, and savers. If inflation is anticipated, individuals and businesses may be able to take steps to lessen or eliminate adverse redistribution effects.

7. Cost-push inflation reduces real output and employment. Proponents of zero inflation argue that even mild demand-pull inflation (1 to 3 percent) reduces the economy's real output. Other economists say that mild inflation may be a necessary by-product of the high and growing spending that produces high levels of output, full employment, and economic growth.

8. Hyperinflation, caused by highly imprudent expansions of the money supply, may undermine the monetary system and cause severe declines in real output.

Terms and Concepts

business cycles

recession

expansion

shocks

demand shocks

supply shocks

sticky prices

labor force

unemployment rate

frictional unemployment

structural unemployment

cyclical unemployment

potential output

GDP gap

inflation

Consumer Price Index (CPI)

deflation

demand-pull inflation

cost-push inflation

nominal income

real income

real interest rate

nominal interest rate

Questions

1. What are the two primary phases of the business cycle? What tends to happen to real GDP, unemployment, and inflation during these phases? **LO1**

2. How many recessions has the United States experienced since 1950? Which ones were the longest in duration? Which ones were the most severe in terms of declines in real output? **LO1**

3. Because the United States has an unemployment compensation program that provides income for those out of work, why should we worry about unemployment? **LO3**

4. What are the three types of unemployment? Unemployment is seen by some as undesirable. Are all three types of unemployment undesirable? Explain. **LO3**

5. What is the Consumer Price Index (CPI), and how is it determined each month? What effect does inflation have on the purchasing power of a dollar? How does it explain differences between nominal and real interest rates? How does deflation differ from inflation? **LO2**

6. Briefly distinguish between demand-pull inflation and cost-push inflation. **LO3**

7. How does unanticipated inflation hurt creditors and help borrowers? How can anticipating the inflation make these effects less severe? **LO3**

8. Explain how hyperinflation might lead to a severe decline in total output. **LO3**

Problems

1. Suppose that a country's annual growth rates were 5, 3, 4, −1, −2, 2, 3, 4, 6, and 3 in yearly sequence over a 10-year period. What was the country's trend rate of growth over this period? Which set of years most clearly demonstrates an expansionary phase of the business cycle? Which set of years best illustrates a recessionary phase of the business cycle? **LO1**

2. Assume the following data for a country: total population, 500; population under 16 years of age or institutionalized, 120; not in labor force, 150; unemployed, 23; part-time workers looking for full-time jobs, 10. What is the size of the labor force? What is the official unemployment rate? **LO2**

3. If the CPI was 110 last year and is 121 this year, what is this year's rate of inflation? In contrast, suppose that the CPI was 110 last year and is 108 this year. What is this

year's rate of inflation? What term do economists use to describe this second outcome? **LO3**

4. How long would it take for the price level to double if inflation persisted at (a) 2 percent per year, (b) 5 percent per year, and (c) 10 percent per year? **LO3**

5. If your nominal income rose by 5.3 percent and the price level rose by 3.8 percent in some year, by what percentage would your real income (approximately) increase? If your nominal income rose by 2.8 percent and your real income rose by 1.1 percent in some year, what must have been the (approximate) rate of inflation? **LO3**

6. Suppose that the nominal rate of interest is 4 percent and the inflation premium is 2 percent. What is the real interest rate? Alternatively, assume that the real interest rate is 1 percent and the nominal interest rate is 6 percent. What is the inflation premium? **LO3**

FURTHER TEST YOUR KNOWLEDGE AT
www.brue3e.com

At the text's Online Learning Center, **www.brue3e.com,** you will find one or more web-based questions that require information from the Internet to answer. We urge you to check them out, since they will familiarize you with websites that may be helpful in other courses and perhaps even in your career. The OLC also features multiple-choice quizzes that give instant feedback and provides other helpful ways to further test your knowledge of the chapter.

CHAPTER TWELVE

Aggregate Demand and Aggregate Supply

After reading this chapter, you should be able to:

1. Define aggregate demand (AD) and explain the factors that cause it to change.
2. Define aggregate supply (AS) and explain the factors that cause it to change.
3. Discuss how AD and AS determine an economy's equilibrium price level and level of real GDP.
4. Describe how the AD-AS model explains periods of demand-pull inflation, cost-push inflation, and recession.

During the recession of 2007–2009, the economic terms *aggregate demand* and *aggregate supply* moved from the obscurity of economic journals and textbooks to the spotlight of national newspapers, websites, radio, and television.

The media and public asked: Why had *aggregate demand* declined, producing the deepest recession and highest rate of unemployment since 1982? Why hadn't the reductions in interest rates by the Federal Reserve boosted *aggregate demand*? Would the federal government's $787 billion stimulus package increase *aggregate demand* and reduce unemployment, as intended? Would a resurgence of oil prices and other energy prices reduce *aggregate supply,* choking off an economic expansion?

Aggregate demand and aggregate supply are the featured elements of the **aggregate demand–aggregate supply model (AD-AS model),** the focus of this chapter. The AD-AS model enables us to analyze change in real GDP and the price level simultaneously. The model therefore provides keen insights on inflation, recession, unemployment, and economic growth. In later chapters, we will see that the AD-AS model easily depicts fiscal and monetary policies such as those used in 2008 and 2009 to try to halt the downward slide of the economy and promote its recovery.

Aggregate Demand

**aggregate demand–
aggregate supply
(AD-AS) model**
The macroeconomic
model that uses
aggregate demand and
aggregate supply to
determine and explain
the price level and level
of real domestic output.

aggregate demand
A schedule or curve that
shows the total quantity of
goods and services
demanded (purchased) at
different price levels.

Aggregate demand is a schedule or curve that shows the quantities of a nation's output (real GDP) that buyers collectively want to purchase at each possible price level. These buyers include the nation's households, businesses, and government along with consumers located abroad (households, businesses, and governments in other nations). The relationship between the price level (as measured by the GDP price index) and the amount of real output demanded is inverse or negative: When the price level rises, the quantity of real GDP demanded falls; when the price level falls, the quantity of real GDP demanded rises.

Figure 12.1 shows the inverse relationship between the price level and real GDP. The downward slope of the AD curve reflects the fact that higher U.S. price levels discourage domestic buyers (households and businesses) and foreign buyers from purchasing U.S. real GDP. Lower price levels encourage them to buy more U.S. real output.

Changes in Aggregate Demand

Other things equal, a change in the price level will change the amount of total spending and therefore change the amount of real GDP demanded by the economy. Movements along a fixed aggregate demand curve represent these changes in real GDP. However, if one or more of those "other things" change, the entire aggregate demand curve will shift. We call these other things **determinants of aggregate demand.** When they change, they shift the AD curve. These AD shifters are listed in the table in Figure 12.2. In that figure, the rightward shift of the curve from AD_1 to AD_2 shows an increase in aggregate demand. The leftward shift from AD_1 to AD_3 shows a decrease in aggregate demand. Notice that the categories of spending are the same as those in the national income and product accounts (Chapter 10). To provide a clear understanding of these AD shifters, we need to elaborate on them.

**determinants of
aggregate demand**
Factors that shift the
aggregate demand
curve when they change.

Consumer Spending

If consumers decide to buy more output at each price level, the aggregate demand curve will shift to the right, as from AD_1 to AD_2 in Figure 12.2. If they decide to buy less output, the aggregate demand curve will shift to the left, as from AD_1 to AD_3.

FIGURE 12.1
The aggregate demand curve. The downsloping aggregate demand curve AD indicates an inverse (or negative) relationship between the price level and the amount of real output purchased.

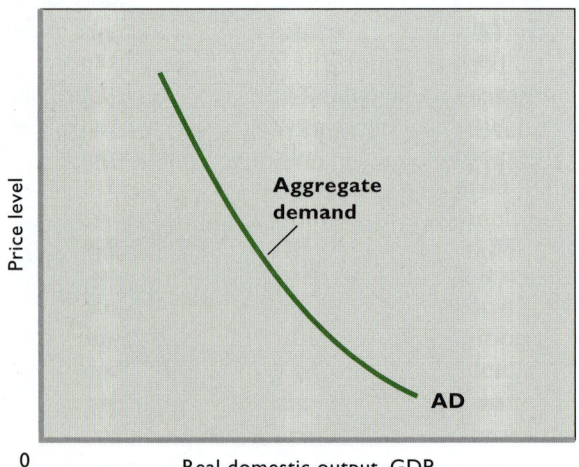

FIGURE 12.2

Changes in aggregate demand. A change in one or more of the listed determinants of aggregate demand will shift the aggregate demand curve. The rightward shift from AD$_1$ to AD$_2$ represents an increase in aggregate demand; the leftward shift from AD$_1$ to AD$_3$ shows a decrease in aggregate demand.

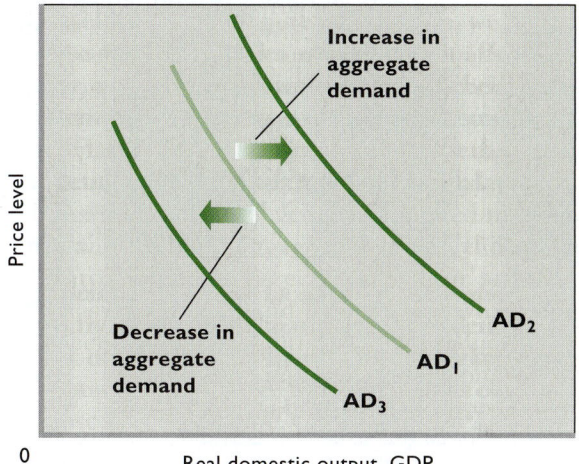

Determinants of Aggregate Demand: Factors That Shift the Aggregate Demand Curve
1. Change in consumer spending
a. Consumer wealth
b. Household borrowing
c. Consumer expectations
d. Personal taxes
2. Change in investment spending
a. Interest rates
b. Expected returns
• Expected future business conditions
• Technology
• Degree of excess capacity
• Business taxes
3. Change in government spending
4. Change in net export spending
a. National income abroad
b. Exchange rates

Several factors can change consumer spending and therefore shift the aggregate demand curve. As the table in Figure 12.2 shows, those factors are real consumer wealth, household borrowing, consumer expectations, and personal taxes.

Consumer Wealth Consumer wealth is the total dollar value of all assets owned by consumers in the economy less the dollar value of their liabilities (debts). Assets include stocks, bonds, and real estate. Liabilities include mortgages, car loans, and credit card balances.

Consumer wealth sometimes changes suddenly and unexpectedly due to surprising changes in asset values. An unforeseen increase in the stock market is a good example. The increase in wealth prompts pleasantly surprised consumers to save less and buy more out of their current incomes than they had previously been planning. The resulting increase in consumer spending—the so-called *wealth effect*—shifts the aggregate demand curve to the right. In contrast, an unexpected decline in asset values will cause an unanticipated reduction in consumer wealth at each price level. As consumers tighten their belts in response to the bad news, a "reverse wealth effect" sets in. Unpleasantly surprised consumers increase savings and reduce consumption, thereby shifting the aggregate demand curve to the left.

Household Borrowing Consumers can increase their consumption spending by borrowing. Doing so shifts the aggregate demand curve to the right. By contrast, a decrease in borrowing for consumption purposes shifts the aggregate demand curve to the left. The aggregate demand curve also will shift to the left if consumers increase their savings rates in order to pay off their debts. With more money flowing to debt repayment, consumption expenditures decline and the AD curve shifts left.

Consumer Expectations   Changes in expectations about the future may alter consumer spending. When people expect their future real incomes to rise, they tend to spend more of their current incomes. Thus, current consumption spending increases (current saving falls), and the aggregate demand curve shifts to the right. Similarly, a widely held expectation of surging inflation in the near future may increase aggregate demand today because consumers will want to buy products before their prices escalate. Conversely, expectations of lower future income or lower future prices may reduce current consumption and shift the aggregate demand curve to the left.

Personal Taxes   A reduction in personal income tax rates raises take-home income and increases consumer purchases at each possible price level. Tax cuts shift the aggregate demand curve to the right. Tax increases reduce consumption spending and shift the curve to the left.

Applying the Analysis

What Wealth Effect?

The consumption component of aggregate demand is usually relatively stable even during rather extraordinary times. Between March 2000 and July 2002, the U.S. stock market lost a staggering $3.7 trillion of value (yes, trillion). Yet consumption spending was greater at the end of that period than at the beginning. How can that be? Why didn't a negative wealth effect reduce consumption?

There are a number of reasons. Of greatest importance, the amount of consumption spending in the economy depends mainly on the *flow* of income, not the *stock* of wealth. Disposable income (after-tax income) in the United States is nearly $9 trillion annually, and consumers spend a large portion of it. Even though there was a mild recession in 2001, disposable income and consumption spending were both greater in July 2002 than in March 2000. Second, the federal government cut personal income tax rates during this period, and that bolstered consumption spending. Third, household wealth did not fall by the full amount of the $3.7 trillion stock market loss because the value of houses increased dramatically over this period. Finally, lower interest rates during this period enabled many households to refinance their mortgages, reduce monthly loan payments, and increase their current consumption. For all these offsetting reasons, the consumption component of aggregate demand held up in the face of the extraordinary loss of stock market value.

The 2007–2009 recession tells a somewhat different story, with consumption falling but not enough to definitively establish the presence of a wealth effect. Between losses in both the housing and stock markets, U.S. household wealth decreased by about $14 trillion from June 2007 to March 2009, and economic contraction began in December 2007. However, in part because of federal government policies to stimulate spending, household disposable income did not fall until the second half of 2008, reaching a low point in early 2009 and then beginning a slow but steady increase. Consumption spending followed a similar pattern, declining in the latter part of 2008 and bottoming out in the first quarter of 2009. While most economists agree that wealth losses from the housing and financial market crises contributed to lower consumption (or, at the very least, slower growth in consumption spending), the reductions in household expenditures appear to have been far less substantial than one might have anticipated.

Question:
Which do you think will decrease consumption more: a 10 percent decrease in after-tax income or a 10 percent decrease in stock market values? Explain.

Investment Spending

Investment spending (the purchase of capital goods) is a second major determinant of aggregate demand. Increases in investment spending at each price level boost aggregate demand, and decreases in investment spending reduce it.

The investment decision is a marginal-benefit–marginal-cost decision. The marginal benefit of the investment is a stream of higher profits that is expected to result from the investment. In percentage terms, economists call these higher profits (net of new operation expenses) the *expected return on the investment, r.* For example, suppose the owner of a small cabinetmaking shop is considering whether to invest in a new sanding machine that costs $1000, expands output, and has a useful life of only 1 year. (Extending the life of the machine beyond 1 year complicates the economic calculation but does not change the fundamental analysis.) Suppose the net expected revenue from the machine (that is, after such operating costs as power, lumber, labor, and certain taxes have been subtracted) is $1100. Then the expected net revenue is sufficient to cover the initial $1000 cost of the machine and leave a profit of $100. Comparing this $100 to the $1000 initial cost of the machine, we find that the expected rate of return, *r,* on the investment is 10 percent (= $100/$1000).

It is important to note that the return just discussed is an *expected* rate of return, not a *guaranteed* rate of return. Investment involves risk, so the investment may or may not pay off as anticipated. Moreover, investment faces diminishing returns. As more of it occurs, the best investment projects are completed and the subsequent projects produce lower expected rates of return. So, the expected return, *r,* tends to fall as firms undertake more and more investment.

The marginal cost of the investment to a firm is reflected in either the explicit costs of borrowing money from others or the implicit cost of using its own retained earnings to make the investment. In percentage terms, and adjusted for expected inflation, this cost is the real interest rate, *i.*

The business firm compares the real interest rate (marginal cost) with the expected return on investment (marginal benefit). If the expected rate of return (for example, 6 percent) exceeds the interest rate (say, 5 percent), the investment is undertaken. The firm expects the investment to be profitable. But if the interest rate (for example, 7 percent) exceeds the expected rate of return (6 percent), the investment will not be undertaken. The firm expects the investment to be unprofitable. The profit-maximizing firm will undertake all investment that it thinks will be profitable. That means it will invest up to the point where *r* = *i* in order to exhaust all investment possibilities for which *r* exceeds *i.*

> **ORIGIN OF THE IDEA**
> **O 12.1**
> Interest-rate–investment relationship

So real interest rates and expected returns are the two main determinants of investment spending.

Real Interest Rates   We will discover that a nation's central bank—the Federal Reserve in the United States—can take monetary actions to increase and decrease interest rates. When it takes those actions, it shifts the nation's aggregate demand curve. Other things equal, increases in real interest rates will raise borrowing costs, lower investment spending, and reduce aggregate demand. Declines in interest rates will have the opposite effects.

Expected Returns   Higher expected returns on investment projects will increase the demand for capital goods and shift the aggregate demand curve to the right. Alternatively, declines in expected returns will decrease investment and shift the curve to the left. Expected returns are influenced by several factors:

- *Future business conditions*   If firms are generally optimistic about future business conditions, they are more likely to forecast high rates of return on current investment and therefore may invest more today. In contrast, if they think the economy will deteriorate in the future, they will forecast low rates of return and perhaps will invest less today.

- *Technology*   New and improved technologies enhance expected returns on investment and thus increase aggregate demand. For example, recent advances in microbiology have motivated pharmaceutical companies to establish new labs and production facilities.
- *Degree of excess capacity*   A rise in excess capacity—unused capital—will reduce the expected return on new investment and hence decrease aggregate demand. Other things equal, firms operating factories at well below capacity have little incentive to build new factories. But when firms realize that their excess capacity is dwindling or has completely disappeared, their expected returns on new investment in factories and capital equipment rise. Thus, they increase their investment spending, and the aggregate demand curve shifts to the right.
- *Business taxes*   An increase in business taxes will reduce after-tax profits from capital investment and lower expected returns. So investment and aggregate demand will decline. A decrease in business taxes will have the opposite effects.

The variability of interest rates and investment expectations makes investment quite volatile. In contrast to consumption, investment spending rises and falls quite often, independent of changes in total income. Investment, in fact, is the least stable component of aggregate demand.

Global Snapshot 12.1 compares investment spending relative to GDP for several nations in 2011.

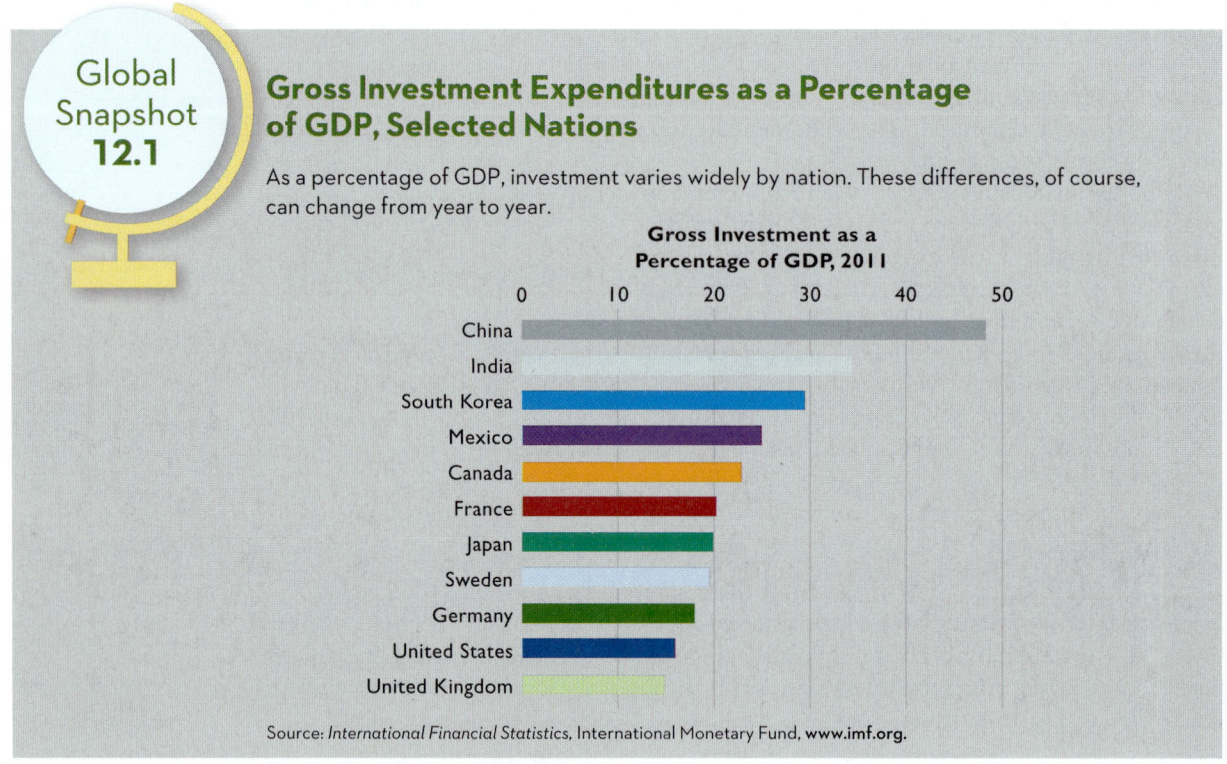

Global Snapshot 12.1

Gross Investment Expenditures as a Percentage of GDP, Selected Nations

As a percentage of GDP, investment varies widely by nation. These differences, of course, can change from year to year.

Gross Investment as a Percentage of GDP, 2011

Source: *International Financial Statistics*, International Monetary Fund, www.imf.org.

Government Spending

Government purchases are the third determinant of aggregate demand. An increase in government purchases (for example, more transportation projects) will shift the aggregate demand curve to the right, as long as tax collections and interest rates do not change as a result. In contrast, a reduction in government spending (for example, less military equipment) will shift the curve to the left.

Net Export Spending

The final determinant of aggregate demand is net export spending. Other things equal, higher U.S. *exports* mean an increased foreign demand for U.S. goods. So a rise in net exports (higher exports relative to imports) shifts the aggregate demand curve to the right. In contrast, a decrease in U.S. net exports shifts the aggregate demand curve leftward.

What might cause net exports to change, other than the price level? Two possibilities are changes in national income abroad and changes in exchange rates.

National Income Abroad Rising national income abroad encourages foreigners to buy more products, some of which are made in the United States. So U.S. net exports rise, and the U.S. aggregate demand curve shifts to the right. Declines in national income abroad do the opposite: They reduce U.S. net exports and shift the U.S. aggregate demand curve to the left.

Exchange Rates Changes in **exchange rates**—the prices of foreign currencies in terms of one's own currency—may affect U.S. net exports and therefore aggregate demand. When the dollar *depreciates* (declines in value) against foreign currencies, it takes more dollars to buy foreign goods. So foreign goods become more expensive in dollar terms, and Americans reduce their imports. On the opposite side, the depreciation of the dollar means that other currencies *appreciate* (rise in value) relative to the dollar. U.S. exports rise because those foreign currencies can buy more American goods. Conclusion: Dollar depreciation increases net exports (imports go down; exports go up) and therefore increases aggregate demand.

exchange rates
The prices of foreign currencies in terms of one's own currency.

Dollar appreciation has the opposite effects: Net exports fall (imports go up; exports go down) and aggregate demand declines.

As shown in Global Snapshot 12.2, net exports vary greatly among the major industrial nations.

Net Exports of Goods, Selected Nations, 2010

Some nations, such as Germany and China, have positive net exports; other countries, such as the United States and the United Kingdom, have negative net exports.

Global Snapshot 12.2

Source: World Trade Organization, WTO Statistics Database, **stat.wto.org.** Used with permission.

Aggregate Supply

aggregate supply
A schedule or curve that shows the total quantity of goods and services supplied (produced) at different price levels.

Aggregate supply is a schedule or curve showing the relationship between a nation's price level and the amount of real domestic output that firms in the economy produce. This relationship varies depending on the time horizon and how quickly output prices and input prices can change. We will define three time horizons.

- In the *immediate short run*, both input prices as well as output prices are fixed.
- In the *short run*, input prices are fixed, but output prices can vary.
- In the *long run*, input prices as well as output prices can vary.

In Chapter 11, we introduced the concept of inflexible (or "sticky") prices. Here we consider different degrees of stickiness in order to discuss how total output varies with the price level in the immediate short run, the short run, and the long run. As you will see, the relationship between the price level and total output is different in each of the three time horizons because input prices are stickier than output prices. While both become more flexible as time passes, output prices usually adjust more rapidly.

Aggregate Supply in the Immediate Short Run

Depending on the type of firm, the immediate short run can last anywhere from a few days to a few months. It lasts as long as *both* input prices and output prices stay fixed. Input prices are fixed in both the immediate short run and the short run by contractual agreements. In particular, 75 percent of the average firm's costs are wages and salaries—and these are almost always fixed by labor contracts for months or years at a time. As a result, they are usually fixed for a much longer duration than output prices, which can begin to change within a few days or a few months depending upon the type of firm.

That being said, output prices are also typically fixed in the immediate short run. This is most often caused by firms setting fixed prices for their customers and then agreeing to supply whatever quantity demanded results at those fixed prices. For instance, once an appliance manufacturer sets its annual list prices for refrigerators, stoves, ovens, and microwaves, it is obligated to supply however many or few appliances customers want to buy at those prices. Similarly, a catalogue company is obliged to sell however much customers want to buy of its products at the prices listed in its current catalogue. And it is obligated to supply those quantities demanded until it sends out its next catalogue.

immediate-short-run aggregate supply curve
The aggregate supply curve associated with a period of time in which neither input nor output prices respond to changes in the level of spending or production.

With output prices fixed and firms selling however much customers want to purchase at those fixed prices, the **immediate-short-run aggregate supply curve** AS_{ISR} is a horizontal line, as shown in Figure 12.3. The AS_{ISR} curve is horizontal at the overall price level P_1, which is calculated from all of the individual prices set by the various firms in the economy. Its horizontal shape implies that the total amount of output supplied in the economy depends directly on the volume of spending that results at price level P_1. If total spending is low at price level P_1, firms will supply a small amount to match the low level of spending. If total spending is high at price level P_1, they will supply a high level of output to match the high level of spending. The amount of output that results may be higher than or lower than the economy's full-employment output level Q_f.

Notice, however, that firms will respond in this manner to changes in total spending only as long as output prices remain fixed. As soon as firms are able to change their product prices, they can respond to changes in aggregate spending not only by increasing or decreasing output but also by raising or lowering prices. This is the situation that leads to the upward-sloping short-run aggregate supply curve that we discuss next.

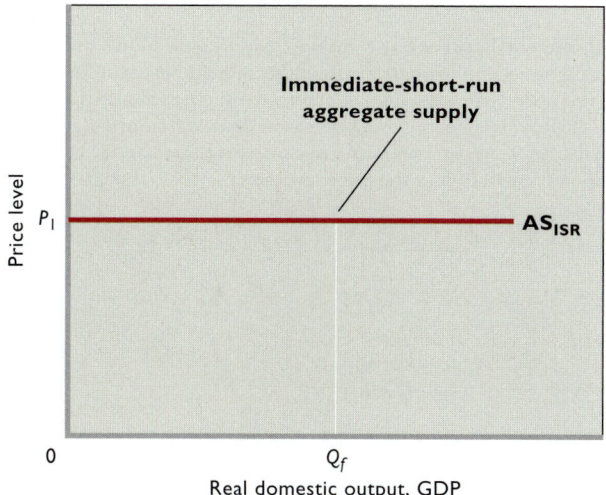

FIGURE 12.3
Aggregate supply in the immediate short run. In the immediate short-run, the aggregate supply curve AS_{ISR} is horizontal at the economy's current price level, P_1. With output prices fixed, firms collectively supply the level of output that is demanded at those prices.

Immediate-short-run aggregate supply

Price level

P_1

AS_{ISR}

0

Q_f

Real domestic output, GDP

Aggregate Supply in the Short Run

The short run begins after the immediate short run ends. As it relates to macroeconomics, the short run is a period of time during which output prices are flexible but input prices are either totally fixed or highly inflexible.

These assumptions about output prices and input prices are general—they relate to the economy in the aggregate. Naturally, some input prices are more flexible than others. Since gasoline prices are quite flexible, a package delivery firm like UPS that uses gasoline as an input will have at least one very flexible input price. On the other hand, wages at UPS are set by five-year labor contracts negotiated with its drivers' union, the Teamsters. Because wages are the firm's largest and most important input cost, it is the case that, overall, UPS faces input prices that are inflexible for several years at a time. Thus, its "short run"—during which it can change the shipping prices that it charges its customers but during which it must deal with substantially fixed input prices—is actually quite long. Keep this in mind as we derive the short-run aggregate supply for the entire economy. Its applicability does not depend on some arbitrary definition of how long the "short run" should be. Instead, the short run for which the model is relevant is any period of time during which output prices are flexible but input prices are fixed or nearly fixed.

As illustrated in Figure 12.4, the **short-run aggregate supply curve** AS slopes upward because, with input prices fixed, changes in the price level will raise or lower real firm profits. To see how this works, consider an economy that has only a single multiproduct firm called Mega Buzzer and in which the firm's owners must receive a real profit of $20 in order to produce the full-employment output of 100 units. Assume the owner's only input (aside from entrepreneurial talent) is 10 units of hired labor at $8 per worker, for a total wage cost of $80. Also, assume that the 100 units of output sell for $1 per unit, so total revenue is $100. Mega Buzzer's nominal profit is $20 (= $100 − $80), and using the $1 price to designate the base-price index of 100, its real profit is also $20 (= $20/1.00). Well and good; the full-employment output is produced.

Next, consider what will happen if the price of Mega Buzzer's output doubles. The doubling of the price level will boost total revenue from $100 to $200, but since we are discussing the short run during which input prices are fixed, the $8 nominal wage for each of the 10 workers will remain unchanged so that total costs stay at $80. Nominal

short-run aggregate supply curve
An aggregate supply curve relevant to a time period in which output prices are flexible, but input prices are sticky.

FIGURE 12.4

The aggregate supply curve (short run). The upsloping aggregate supply curve AS indicates a direct (or positive) relationship between the price level and the amount of real output that firms will offer for sale. The AS curve is relatively flat below the full-employment output because unemployed resources and unused capacity allow firms to respond to price-level rises with large increases in real output. It is relatively steep beyond the full-employment output because resource shortages and capacity limitations make it difficult to expand real output as the price level rises.

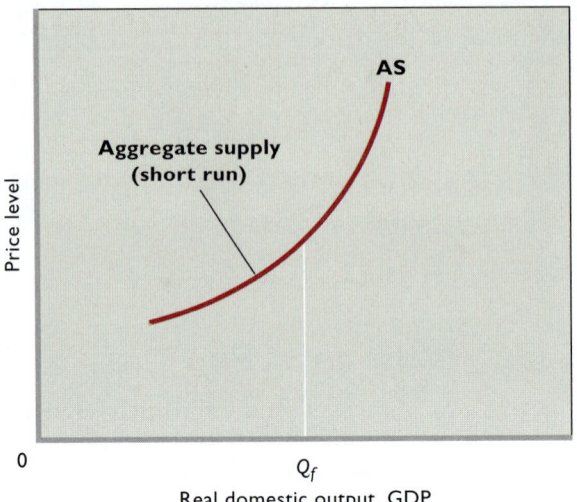

profit will rise from \$20 (= \$100 − \$80) to \$120 (= \$200 − \$80). Dividing that \$120 profit by the new price index of 200 (= 2.0 in hundredths), we find that Mega Buzzer's real profit is now \$60. The rise in the real reward from \$20 to \$60 prompts the firm (economy) to produce more output. Conversely, price-level declines reduce real profits and cause the firm (economy) to reduce its output. So, in the short run, there is a direct, or positive, relationship between the price level and real output. When the price level rises, real output rises and when the price level falls, real output falls. The result is an upward-sloping short-run aggregate supply curve.

Notice, however, that the upslope of the short-run aggregate supply curve is not constant. It is flatter at outputs below the full-employment output level Q_f and steeper at outputs above it. This has to do with the fact that per-unit production costs underlie the short-run aggregate supply curve. In equation form,

$$\text{Per-unit production cost} = \frac{\text{total input cost}}{\text{units of output}}$$

The per-unit production cost of any specific level of output establishes that output's price level because the associated price level must cover all the costs of production, including profit "costs."

As the economy expands in the short run, per-unit production costs generally rise because of reduced efficiency. But the extent of that rise depends on where the economy is operating relative to its capacity. When the economy is operating below its full-employment output, it has large amounts of unused machinery and equipment and large numbers of unemployed workers. Firms can put these idle human and property resources back to work with little upward pressure on per-unit production costs.

And as output expands, few if any shortages of inputs or production bottlenecks will arise to raise per-unit production costs. That is why the slope of the short-run aggregate supply curve increases only slowly at output levels below the full-employment output level Q_f.

On the other hand, when the economy is operating beyond Q_f, the vast majority of its available resources are already employed. Adding more workers to a relatively fixed number of highly used capital resources such as plant and equipment creates congestion in the workplace and reduces the efficiency (on average) of workers. Adding more capital, given the limited number of available workers, leaves equipment idle and reduces the efficiency of capital. Adding more land resources when capital and labor are highly constrained reduces the efficiency of land resources. Under these circumstances, total input costs rise more rapidly than total output. The result is rapidly rising per-unit production costs that give the short-run aggregate supply curve its rapidly increasing slope at output levels beyond Q_f.

Aggregate Supply in the Long Run

In macroeconomics, the long run is the time horizon over which both input prices as well as output prices are flexible. It begins after the short run ends. Depending on the type of firm and industry, this may be from a couple of weeks to several years in the future. But for the economy as a whole, it is the time horizon over which all output and input prices—including wage rates—are fully flexible.

The **long-run aggregate supply curve** AS_{LR} is vertical at the economy's full-employment output Q_f, as shown in Figure 12.5. The vertical curve means that in the long run the economy will produce the full employment output level no matter what the price level is. How can this be? Shouldn't higher prices cause firms to increase output? The explanation lies in the fact that in the long run, when both input prices as well as output prices are flexible, profit levels will always adjust so as to give firms exactly the right profit incentive to produce exactly the full-employment output level, Q_f.

To see why this is true, look back at the short-run aggregate supply curve AS shown in Figure 12.4. Suppose that the economy starts out producing at the full-employment

long-run aggregate supply curve
The aggregate supply curve associated with a period of time in which both input and output prices are fully flexible.

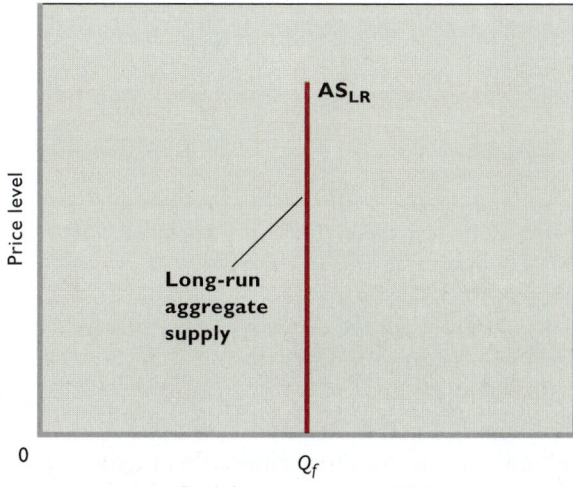

FIGURE 12.5
Aggregate supply in the long run. The long-run aggregate supply curve AS_{LR} is vertical at the full-employment level of real GDP (Q_f) because in the long run wages and other input prices rise and fall to match changes in the price level. So price-level changes do not affect firms' profits, and thus they create no incentive for firms to alter their output.

output level Q_f and that the price level at that moment has an index value of $P = 100$. Now suppose that output prices double, so that the price index goes to $P = 200$. We previously demonstrated for our single-firm economy that this doubling of the price level would cause profits to rise in the short run and that the higher profits would motivate the firm to increase output.

This outcome, however, is totally dependent upon the fact that input prices are fixed in the short run. Consider what will happen in the long run when they are free to change. Firms can only produce beyond the full-employment output level by running factories and businesses at extremely high rates. This creates a great deal of demand for the economy's limited supply of productive resources. In particular, labor is in great demand because the only way to produce beyond full employment is if workers are working overtime.

As time passes and input prices are free to change, the high demand will start to raise input prices. In particular, overworked employees will demand and receive raises as employers scramble to deal with the labor shortages that arise when the economy is producing at above its full-employment output level. As input prices increase, firm profits will begin to fall. And as they decline, so does the motive firms have to produce more than the full-employment output level. This process of rising input prices and falling profits continues until the rise in input prices exactly matches the initial change in output prices (in our example, they both double). When that happens, firm profits in real terms return to their original level so that firms are once again motivated to produce at exactly the full-employment output level. This adjustment process means that in the long run the economy will produce at full employment regardless of the price level (in our example, at either $P = 100$ or $P = 200$). That is why the long-run aggregate supply curve AS_{LR} is vertical above the full-employment output level. Every possible price level on the vertical axis is associated with the economy producing at the full-employment output level in the long run once input prices adjust to exactly match changes in output prices.

Focusing on the Short Run

The immediate-short-run aggregate supply curve, the short-run aggregate supply curve, and the long-run aggregate supply curve are all important. Each curve is appropriate to situations that match their respective assumptions about the flexibility of input and output prices. But our focus in the rest of this chapter and the chapters that immediately follow will be on short-run aggregate supply curves such as the AS curve shown in Figure 12.4. Indeed, unless explicitly stated otherwise, all references to "aggregate supply" will be to aggregate supply in the short run.

Our emphasis on the short-run aggregate supply curve stems from our interest in understanding the business cycle in the simplest possible way. It is a fact that real-world economies typically manifest simultaneous changes in both their price levels and their levels of real output. The upward-sloping short-run AS curve is the only version of aggregate supply that can handle simultaneous movements in both of these variables. By contrast, the price level is assumed fixed in the immediate-short-run version of aggregate supply illustrated in Figure 12.3 and the economy's output is always equal to the full-employment output level in the long-run version of aggregate supply shown in Figure 12.5. This renders these versions of the aggregate supply curve less useful as part of a core model for analyzing business cycles and demonstrating the short-run government policies designed to deal with them.

Changes in Aggregate Supply

An existing aggregate supply curve identifies the relationship between the price level and real output, other things equal. But when other things change, the curve itself shifts. The rightward shift of the curve from AS₁ to AS₂ in Figure 12.6 represents an increase in aggregate supply, indicating that firms are willing to produce and sell more real output at each price level. A decrease in aggregate supply is shown by the leftward shift of the curve from AS₁ to AS₃. At each price level, firms produce less output than before.

The table in Figure 12.6 lists the factors that collectively position the aggregate supply curve. They are called the **determinants of aggregate supply** and shift the curve when they change. Changes in these determinants raise or lower per-unit production costs *at each price level (or each level of output)*. These changes in per-unit production costs affect profits, thereby leading firms to alter the amount of output they are willing to produce *at each price level*. For example, firms may collectively offer $7 trillion of real output at a price level of 1.0 (= 100 in index-value terms), rather than $6.8 trillion. Or they may offer $6.5 trillion rather than $7 trillion. The point is that when one of the determinants listed in Figure 12.6 changes, the aggregate supply curve shifts to the right or left. Changes that reduce per-unit production costs shift the aggregate supply curve to the right, as from AS₁ to AS₂; changes that increase per-unit production costs shift it to the left, as from AS₁ to AS₃. *When per-unit production costs change for reasons other than changes in real output, the aggregate supply curve shifts.*

The aggregate supply determinants listed in Figure 12.6 are very important and therefore require more discussion.

> **determinants of aggregate supply**
> Factors that shift the aggregate supply curve when they change.

Input Prices

Input or resource prices—to be distinguished from the output prices that make up the price level—are a major ingredient of per-unit production costs and therefore a key determinant of aggregate supply. These resources can be either domestic or imported.

FIGURE 12.6

Changes in aggregate supply. A change in one or more of the listed determinants of aggregate supply will shift the aggregate supply curve. The rightward shift of the aggregate supply curve from AS₁ to AS₂ represents an increase in aggregate supply; the leftward shift of the curve from AS₁ to AS₃ shows a decrease in aggregate supply.

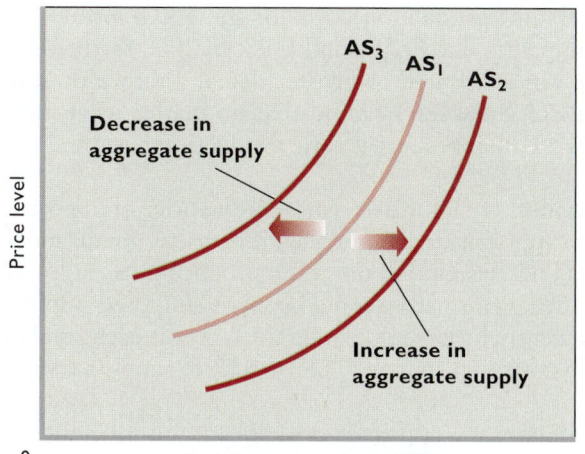

Determinants of Aggregate Supply: Factors That Shift the Aggregate Supply Curve
1. Change in input prices
a. Domestic resource prices
b. Prices of imported resources
2. Change in productivity
3. Change in legal-institutional environment
a. Business taxes
b. Government regulations

Domestic Resource Prices   As stated earlier, wages and salaries make up about 75 percent of all business costs. Other things equal, decreases in wages reduce per-unit production costs. So the aggregate supply curve shifts to the right. Increases in wages shift the curve to the left. Examples:

- Labor supply increases because of substantial immigration. Wages and per-unit production costs fall, shifting the AS curve to the right.
- Labor supply decreases because a rapid increase in pension income causes many older workers to opt for early retirement. Wage rates and per-unit production costs rise, shifting the AS curve to the left.

Similarly, the aggregate supply curve shifts when the prices of land and capital inputs change. Examples:

- The price of machinery and equipment falls because of declines in the prices of steel and electronic components. Per-unit production costs decline, and the AS curve shifts to the right.
- The supply of available land resources expands through discoveries of mineral deposits, irrigation of land, or technical innovations that transform "nonresources" (say, vast desert lands) into valuable resources (productive lands). The price of land declines, per-unit production costs fall, and the AS curve shifts to the right.

Prices of Imported Resources   Just as foreign demand for U.S. goods contributes to U.S. aggregate demand, resources imported from abroad (such as oil, tin, and copper) add to U.S. aggregate supply. Added supplies of resources—whether domestic or imported—typically reduce per-unit production costs. A decrease in the price of imported resources increases U.S. aggregate supply, while an increase in their price reduces U.S. aggregate supply.

A good example of the major effect that changing resource prices can have on aggregate supply is the oil price hikes of the 1970s. At that time, a group of oil-producing nations called the Organization of Petroleum Exporting Countries (OPEC) worked in concert to decrease oil production in order to raise the price of oil. The 10-fold increase in the price of oil that OPEC achieved during the 1970s drove up per-unit production costs and jolted the U.S. aggregate supply curve leftward. By contrast, a sharp decline in oil prices in the mid-1980s resulted in a rightward shift of the U.S. aggregate supply curve. In 1999 OPEC again reasserted itself, raising oil prices and therefore per-unit production costs for some U.S. producers including airlines and shipping companies like FedEx and UPS. In 2008 the price of oil shot upward, but this increase was attributed to greater demand rather than to decreases in supply caused by OPEC. But keep in mind that no matter what their cause, increases in the price of oil and other resources raise production costs and decrease aggregate supply.

Exchange-rate fluctuations are another factor that may alter the price of imported resources. Suppose that the dollar appreciates, enabling U.S. firms to obtain more foreign currency with each dollar. This means that domestic producers face a lower *dollar* price of imported resources. U.S. firms will respond by increasing their imports of foreign resources, thereby lowering their per-unit production costs at each level of output. Falling per-unit production costs will shift the U.S. aggregate supply curve to the right.

A depreciation of the dollar will have the opposite set of effects and will shift the aggregate supply curve to the left.

Productivity

The second major determinant of aggregate supply is **productivity,** which is a measure of the relationship between a nation's level of real output and the amount of resources used to produce that output. Thus productivity is a measure of average real output, or of real output per unit of input:

$$\text{Productivity} = \frac{\text{total output}}{\text{total inputs}}$$

With no change in resource prices, increases in productivity affect aggregate supply by reducing the per-unit production cost of output. Recall that this cost is determined by dividing the total cost of production by the dollar amount of output. For

WORKED PROBLEMS

W 12.1
Productivity and costs

example, if the total cost of production is $20 billion and total output is $40 billion, per-unit production cost is $.50. If productivity rises such that output increases from $40 billion to $60 billion, the per-unit production cost will fall from $.50 (= $20/$40) to $.33 (= $20/$60).

The generalization is this: By reducing per-unit production costs, increases in productivity shift the aggregate supply curve to the right. The main source of productivity advance is improved production technology, often embodied within new plant and equipment that replaces old plant and equipment. Other sources of productivity increases are a better-educated and better-trained workforce, improved forms of business enterprises, and the reallocation of labor resources from lower-productivity to higher-productivity uses.

Much rarer, decreases in productivity increase per-unit production costs and therefore reduce aggregate supply (shift the AS curve to the left).

Legal-Institutional Environment

Changes in the legal-institutional setting in which businesses operate are the final determinant of aggregate supply. Such changes may alter the per-unit costs of output and, if so, shift the aggregate supply curve. Two changes of this type are (1) changes in business taxes and (2) changes in the extent of regulation.

Business Taxes   Higher business taxes, such as sales, excise, and payroll taxes, increase per-unit costs and reduce short-run aggregate supply in much the same way as a wage increase does. An increase in such taxes paid by businesses will increase per-unit production costs and shift aggregate supply to the left.

Government Regulation   It is usually costly for businesses to comply with government regulations. More regulation therefore tends to increase per-unit production costs and shift the aggregate supply curve to the left. "Supply-side" proponents of deregulation of the economy have argued forcefully that, by increasing efficiency and reducing the paperwork associated with complex regulations, deregulation will reduce per-unit costs and shift the aggregate supply curve to the right. Other economists are less certain. Deregulation that results in accounting manipulations, monopolization, and business failures is likely to shift the AS curve to the left rather than to the right.

Equilibrium Price Level and Real GDP

equilibrium price level
The price level at which the aggregate demand curve and the aggregate supply curve intersect.

equilibrium real output
The level of real GDP at which the aggregate demand curve and aggregate supply curve intersect.

Of all the possible combinations of price levels and levels of real GDP, which combination will the economy gravitate toward, at least in the short run? Figure 12.7 and its accompanying table provide the answer. Equilibrium occurs at the price level that equalizes the amounts of real output demanded and supplied. The intersection of the aggregate demand curve AD and the aggregate supply curve AS establishes the economy's **equilibrium price level** and **equilibrium real output.** So aggregate demand and aggregate supply jointly establish the price level and level of real GDP.

In Figure 12.7 the equilibrium price level and level of real output are 100 and $510 billion, respectively. To illustrate why, suppose the price level is 92 rather than 100. We see from the table that the lower price level will encourage businesses to produce real output of $502 billion. This is shown by point *a* on the AS curve in the graph. But, as revealed by the table and point *b* on the aggregate demand curve, buyers will want to purchase $514 billion of real output at price level 92. Competition among buyers to purchase the lesser available real output of $502 billion will eliminate the $12 billion (= $514 billion − $502 billion) shortage and pull up the price level to 100.

As the table and graph show, the rise in the price level from 92 to 100 encourages producers to increase their real output from $502 billion to $510 billion and causes buyers to scale back their purchases from $514 billion to $510 billion. When equality occurs between the amounts of real output produced and purchased, as it does at price level 100, the economy has achieved equilibrium (here, at $510 billion of real GDP). Note that although the equilibrium price level happens to be 100 in our example, nothing special is implied by that. Any price level can be an equilibrium price level.

> **INTERACTIVE GRAPHS**
>
> **G 12.1**
> Aggregate demand–aggregate supply

FIGURE 12.7

The equilibrium price level and equilibrium real GDP. The intersection of the aggregate demand curve and the aggregate supply curve determines the economy's equilibrium price level. At the equilibrium price level of 100 (in index-value terms), the $510 billion of real output demanded matches the $510 billion of real output supplied. So equilibrium real GDP is $510 billion.

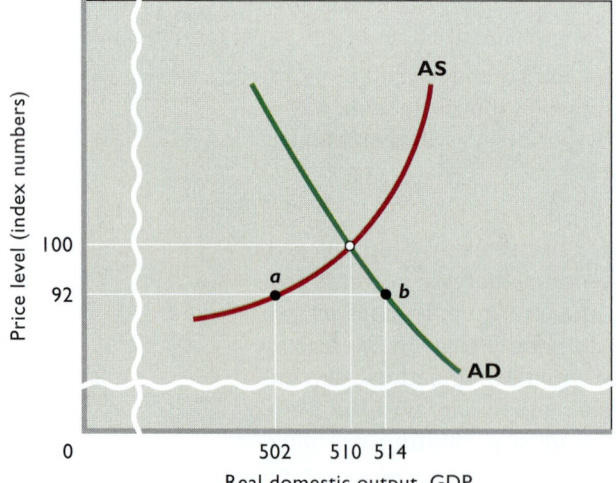

Real Output Demanded (Billions)	Price Level (Index Number)	Real Output Supplied (Billions)
$506	108	$513
508	104	512
510	**100**	**510**
512	96	507
514	92	502

Changes in the Price Level and Real GDP

Aggregate demand and aggregate supply typically change from one period to the next. If aggregate demand and aggregate supply increase proportionately over time, real GDP will expand and neither demand-pull inflation nor cyclical unemployment will occur. But we know from our discussion of the business cycle that macroeconomic stability is not always certain. A number of less-desirable situations can confront the economy. Let's apply the model to several such situations. For simplicity we will use P and Q symbols, rather than actual numbers. Remember that these symbols represent price index values and amounts of real GDP.

Demand-Pull Inflation

Suppose the economy is operating at its full-employment output and businesses and government increase their spending—actions that shift the aggregate demand curve to the right. Our list of determinants of aggregate demand (Figure 12.2) provides several reasons why this shift might occur. Perhaps firms boost their investment spending because they anticipate higher future profits from investments in new capital. Those profits are predicated on having new equipment and facilities that incorporate a number of new technologies. And perhaps government increases spending to expand national defense.

As shown by the rise in the price level from P_1 to P_2 in Figure 12.8, the increase in aggregate demand beyond the full-employment level of output moves the economy from a to b and causes inflation. This is *demand-pull inflation* because the price level is being pulled up by the increase in aggregate demand. Also, observe that the increase in demand expands real output from the full-employment level Q_f to Q_1. The distance between Q_1 and Q_f is a positive, or "inflationary," *GDP gap:* Actual GDP exceeds potential GDP.*

*This positive GDP gap cannot last forever because eventually the price of labor and other inputs will increase and therefore shift the short-run AS curve leftward. The economy will eventually return to its full-employment output, Q_f, along its vertical long-run aggregate supply curve (not shown) that is located there.

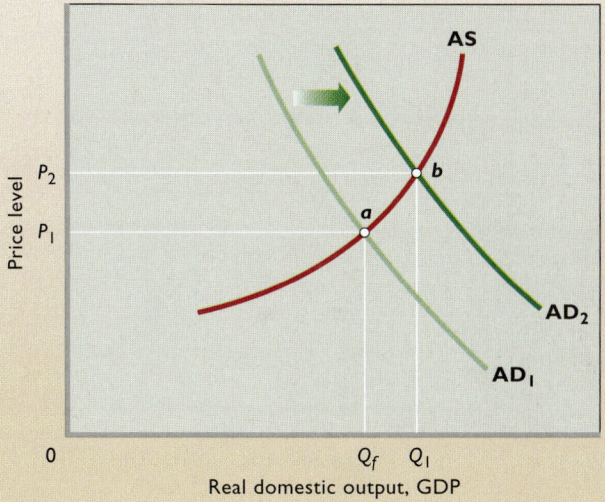

Applying the Analysis

FIGURE 12.8
Demand-pull inflation. The increase of aggregate demand from AD$_1$ to AD$_2$ moves the economy from a to b, causing demand-pull inflation of P_1 to P_2. It also causes a positive GDP gap of Q_1 minus Q_f.

A classic American example of demand-pull inflation occurred in the late 1960s. The escalation of the war in Vietnam resulted in a 40 percent increase in defense spending between 1965 and 1967 and another 15 percent increase in 1968. The rise in government spending, imposed on an already growing economy, shifted the economy's aggregate demand curve to the right, producing the worst inflation in two decades. Actual GDP exceeded potential GDP, thereby creating an inflationary GDP gap. Inflation jumped from 1.6 percent in 1965 to 5.7 percent by 1970.

A more recent example of demand-pull inflation occurred in the late 1980s. As aggregate demand expanded beyond its full-employment level between 1986 and 1990, the price level rose at an increasing rate. Specifically, the annual rate of inflation increased from 1.9 percent in 1986 to 3.6 percent in 1987 to 4.1 percent in 1988 to 4.8 percent in 1989. In terms of Figure 12.8, the aggregate demand curve moved rightward from year to year, raising the price level and the size of the positive GDP gap. The gap closed and the rate of inflation fell as the expansion gave way to the recession of 1990–1991.

Question:
How is the upward slope of the aggregate supply curve important in explaining demand-pull inflation?

Applying the Analysis

Cost-Push Inflation

Inflation also can arise on the aggregate supply side of the economy. Suppose that warfare in the Middle East severely disrupts world oil supplies and drives up oil prices by some huge amount, say, 300 percent. Higher energy prices would spread through the economy, driving up production and distribution costs on a wide variety of goods. The U.S. aggregate supply curve would spring to the left, say, from AS_1 to AS_2 in Figure 12.9. The resulting increase in the price level would be *cost-push inflation*.

FIGURE 12.9
Cost-push inflation. A leftward shift of aggregate supply from AS_1 to AS_2 moves the economy from *a* to *b*, raises the price level from P_1 to P_2, and produces cost-push inflation. Real output declines and a negative GDP gap (of Q_1 minus Q_f) occurs.

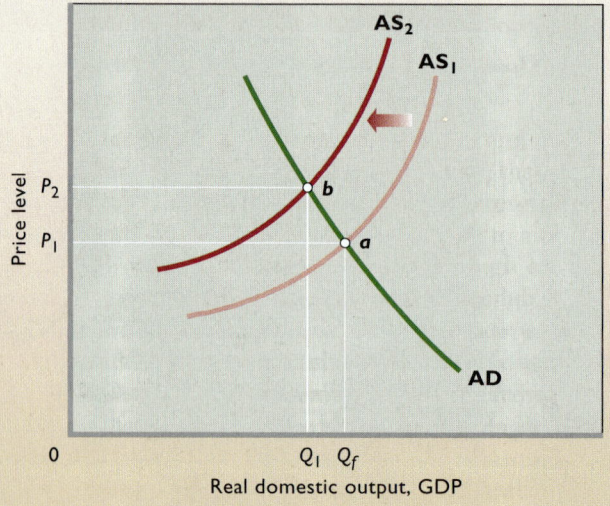

The effects of a leftward shift in aggregate supply are doubly bad. When aggregate supply shifts from AS_1 to AS_2, the economy moves from a to b. The price level rises from P_1 to P_2 and real output declines from Q_f to Q_1. Along with the cost-push inflation, a recession (and negative GDP gap) occurs. That is exactly what happened in the United States in the mid-1970s when the price of oil rocketed upward.

Today, the effect of oil prices on the U.S. economy has weakened relative to earlier periods. In the mid-1970s, oil expenditures were about 10 percent of U.S. GDP, compared to only 3 percent today. So the U.S. economy is now less vulnerable to cost-push inflation arising from oil-related "aggregate supply shocks."

Question:
Which is costlier to an economy in terms of lost real output, an equal degree of demand-pull inflation or cost-push inflation?

© Royalty-Free/CORBIS

© Photodisc/Getty Images

Photo Op Demand-Pull versus Cost-Push Inflation

A boom in investment spending, such as that for new construction, can cause demand-pull inflation. Soaring prices of key resources, such as oil, can cause cost-push inflation.

Downward Price-Level Inflexibility

We have just seen examples where, despite what we have learned about price "stickiness," the price level is readily flexible upward. But in the U.S. economy, deflation (a decline in the price level) rarely occurs even though the rate of inflation rises and falls. Why is the price level "sticky" or inflexible, particularly on the downside? Economists have offered several possible reasons for this:

- *Fear of price wars* Some oligopolists may be concerned that if they reduce their prices, rivals not only will match their price cuts but may retaliate by making even deeper cuts. An initial price cut may touch off an unwanted *price war:* successively deeper and deeper rounds of price cuts. In such a situation, all the firms end up with far less profit or higher losses than would be the case if they had simply maintained their prices. For this reason, each firm may resist making the initial price cut, choosing instead to reduce production and lay off workers.

- *Menu costs* Firms that think a recession will be relatively short-lived may be reluctant to cut their prices. One reason is what economists metaphorically call *menu costs*, named after their most obvious example: the cost of printing new menus when a restaurant decides to reduce its prices. But lowering prices also creates other costs. There are the costs of (1) estimating the magnitude and duration of the shift in demand to determine whether prices should be lowered, (2) repricing items held in inventory, (3) printing and mailing new catalogs, and (4) communicating new prices to customers, perhaps through advertising. When menu costs are present, firms may choose to avoid them by retaining current prices. That is, they may wait to see if the decline in aggregate demand is permanent.

- *Wage contracts* It usually is not profitable for firms to cut their product prices if they cannot also cut their wage rates. Wages are usually inflexible downward because large parts of the labor force work under contracts prohibiting wage cuts for the duration of the contract. (It is not uncommon for collective bargaining agreements in major industries to run for 3 years.) Similarly, the wages and salaries of nonunion workers are usually adjusted once a year, rather than quarterly or monthly.

- *Morale, effort, and productivity* Wage inflexibility downward is reinforced by the reluctance of many employers to reduce wage rates. If worker productivity (output per hour of work) remains constant, lower wages *do* reduce labor costs per unit of output. But lower wages might impair worker morale and work effort, thereby reducing productivity. Considered alone, lower productivity raises labor costs per unit of output because less output is produced. If the higher labor costs resulting from reduced productivity exceed the cost savings from the lower wage, then wage cuts will increase rather than reduce labor costs per unit of output. In such situations, firms will resist lowering wages when they are faced with a decline in aggregate demand.

- *Minimum wage* The minimum wage imposes a legal floor under the wages of the least skilled workers. Firms paying those wages cannot reduce that wage rate when aggregate demand declines.

Conclusion: In the United States, the price level readily rises but only reluctantly falls.

The Ratchet Effect

Illustrating the Idea

A *ratchet analogy* is a good way to think about the asymmetry of price-level changes. A ratchet is a tool or mechanism such as a winch, car jack, or socket wrench that cranks a wheel forward but does not allow it to go backward. Properly set, each allows the operator to move an object (boat, car, or nut) in one direction while preventing it from moving in the opposite direction.

The price level, wage rates, and per-unit production costs readily rise when aggregate demand increases along the aggregate supply curve. In the United States, the price level has increased in every year but one since 1950.

But the price level, wage rates, and per-unit production costs are inflexible downward when aggregate demand declines. The U.S. price level has fallen in only a single year (1955) since 1950, even though aggregate demand and real output have declined in a number of years.

In terms of our analogy, increases in aggregate demand ratchet the U.S. price level upward. Once in place, the higher price level remains until it is ratcheted up again. The higher price level tends to remain even with declines in aggregate demand. Inflation rates *do* rise and fall in the United States, but the price level mainly rises.

Question:
Does the ratchet analogy also apply to changes in real GDP? Why or why not?

Recession and Cyclical Unemployment

Applying the Analysis

Decreases in aggregate demand, combined with downward price-level inflexibility, can create recessions. For example, suppose that for some reason investment spending sharply declines. In Figure 12.10 we show the resulting decline in aggregate demand as a leftward shift from AD_1 to AD_2.

With the price level inflexible downward at P_1, the decline in aggregate demand moves the economy from a to b and reduces real output from Q_f to Q_1. The distance between Q_1 and Q_f measures the negative GDP gap—the amount by

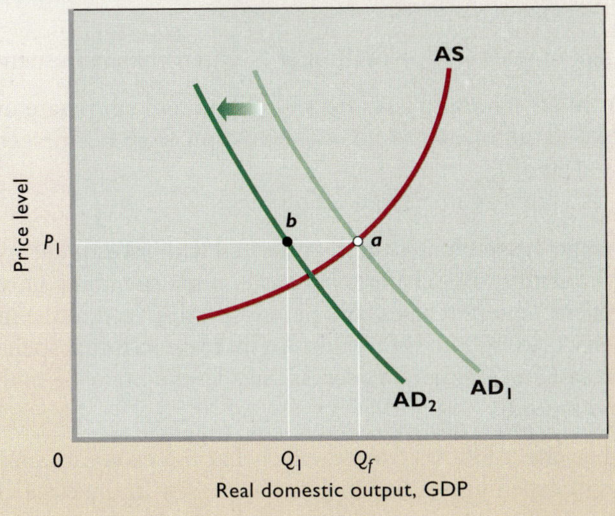

FIGURE 12.10

A recession. If the price level is downwardly inflexible, a decline of aggregate demand from AD_1 to AD_2 will move the economy from a to b and reduce real GDP from Q_f to Q_1. Idle production capacity, cyclical unemployment, and a negative GDP gap (of Q_1 minus Q_f) will result.

which actual output falls short of potential output. Because fewer workers are needed to produce the lower output, *cyclical unemployment* arises.

All recent demand-caused recessions in the United States have mimicked the "GDP gap but no deflation" scenario shown in Figure 12.10. Consider the recession that began in December 2007. In 2008, home foreclosures skyrocketed, several major financial institutions failed, and credit became very tight. New construction and other investment spending plummeted. Because of the resulting decline of aggregate demand, GDP fell short of potential output. The nation's unemployment rate rose from 4.7 percent in December 2007 to 10.1 percent in October 2009. The price level fell in some months and the rate of inflation declined (an outcome called *disinflation*). Considering the full period, however, *deflation* did not occur.

Question:
How can a decline in expected investment returns on the construction of new houses, condominiums, and office buildings contribute to a recession?

The Multiplier Effect

Before leaving the topic of aggregate demand and aggregate supply, we need to supply two additional insights. First, shifts in the aggregate demand curves such as those in Figures 12.8 and 12.10 embody an "initial change" in spending, say, an increase in investment, followed by successive rounds of additional spending by businesses and households that are on the receiving end of the prior spending. Our shifts from one AD curve to another AD curve simply show the final results.

Assuming an economy has room to expand, an initial change in investment spending changes aggregate demand and GDP (and thus income) by more than the initial spending change. That surprising result is called the *multiplier effect*. The **multiplier** measures how much larger the final change in GDP will be; it is the ratio of a change in GDP to the initial change in spending (in this case, investment). Stated generally,

multiplier
The ratio of a change in GDP to an initial change in spending.

$$\text{Multiplier} = \frac{\text{change in real GDP}}{\text{initial change in spending}}$$

By rearranging this equation, we can also say that

$$\text{Change in real GDP} = \text{multiplier} \times \text{initial change in spending}$$

So if investment in an economy rises by $30 billion and aggregate demand and real GDP increase by $90 billion as a result, we then know from our first equation that the multiplier is 3 (= $90/30).

Note these two points about the multiplier:

- The initial change in spending is often associated with investment spending because of investment's volatility. But changes in consumption spending (unrelated to change in income), government purchases, and net exports also lead to the multiplier effect.
- The multiplier works in both directions. An increase in initial spending may create a multiple increase in GDP, and a decrease in spending may be multiplied into a larger decrease in GDP.

The multiplier effect follows from the fact that the economy supports repetitive, continuous flows of expenditures and income, as we saw in the circular flow model in Chapter 2. Through this process, dollars spent by Smith are received as income by

Chin, who then spends a portion that is received as income by Gonzales, and so on. Because a portion of new income is saved (not spent), the amount of new spending in each successive round declines, eventually bringing the multiplier process to an end.

Self-Correction?

The second insight is a caution: There is some evidence that the price level and average level of wages are becoming more flexible downward in the United States. Intense international competition and the declining power of unions in the United States seem to be undermining the ability of firms and workers to resist price and wage cuts when faced with falling aggregate demand. This increased flexibility of some prices and wages may be one reason the recession of 2001 was relatively mild. The U.S. auto manufacturers, for example, maintained output in the face of falling demand by offering zero-interest loans on auto purchases. This, in effect, was a disguised price cut.

In theory, fully flexible downward prices and wages would automatically "self-correct" a recession. Reduced aggregate demand, with its accompanying negative GDP gap and greater unemployment, would reduce the price level and level of (nominal) wages. In Figure 12.10, the lower wages would reduce per-unit production costs and shift the AS curve rightward. Eventually the economy would return to its full-employment output, but at a considerably lower price level than before. That is, the economy would move back to its long-run aggregate supply curve, like the one shown in Figure 12.5.

In reality, the government and monetary authorities have been reluctant to wait for these slow and uncertain "corrections." Instead, they focus on trying to move the aggregate demand curve to its prerecession location. For example, throughout 2001 the Federal Reserve lowered interest rates to try to halt the recession and promote recovery. Those Fed actions, along with large federal tax cuts, increased military spending, and strong demand for new housing, helped increase aggregate demand and spur recovery. The economy haltingly resumed its economic growth in 2002 and 2003, and then expanded rapidly in 2004 and 2005. Robust growth continued in 2006 and for the first three quarters of 2007.

Toward the end of 2007, however, crises in the housing and credit markets precipitated a new recession, prompting the Fed to begin a series of interest rate cuts to try to boost spending. In February 2008, the federal government passed a tax rebate package, which it followed in February 2009 with $787 billion in spending increases and tax cuts, also in an effort to support aggregate demand and deal with the recession. We will examine stabilization policies such as these in the chapters that follow.

Summary

1. The aggregate demand–aggregate supply model (AD-AS model) enables analysis of simultaneous changes of real GDP and the price level.

2. The aggregate demand curve shows the level of real output that the economy will purchase at each price level. It slopes downward because higher price levels dissuade U.S. businesses and households, along with foreign buyers, from purchasing as much output as before.

3. The determinants of aggregate demand consist of spending by domestic consumers, businesses, and government and by foreign buyers. Changes in the factors listed in Figure 12.2 alter the spending by these groups and shift the aggregate demand curve.

4. The aggregate supply curve shows the levels of real output that businesses will produce at various possible price levels. The slope of the aggregate supply curve depends upon the flexibility of input and output prices.

Since these vary over time, aggregate supply curves are categorized into three time horizons, each having different underlying assumptions about the flexibility of input and output prices.

5. The *immediate-short-run aggregate supply* curve assumes that both input prices and output prices are fixed. With output prices fixed, the aggregate supply curve is a horizontal line at the current price level. The *short-run aggregate supply* curve assumes nominal wages and other input prices remain fixed while output prices vary. The aggregate supply curve is generally upsloping because per-unit production costs, and hence the prices that firms must receive, rise as real output expands. The aggregate supply curve is relatively steep to the right of the full-employment output level and relatively flat to the left of it. The *long-run aggregate supply* curve assumes that nominal wages and other input prices fully match any change in the price level. The curve is vertical at the full-employment output level.

6. Because the short-run aggregate supply curve is the only version of aggregate supply that can handle simultaneous changes in the price level and real output, it serves well as the core aggregate supply curve for analyzing the business cycle and economic policy. Unless stated otherwise, all references to "aggregate supply" refer to the short-run aggregate supply curve.

7. Figure 12.6 lists the determinants of aggregate supply: input prices, productivity, and the legal-institutional environment. A change in any one of these factors will change per-unit production costs at each level of output and therefore will shift the aggregate supply curve.

8. The intersection of the aggregate demand and aggregate supply curves determines an economy's equilibrium price level and real GDP. At the intersection, the quantity of real GDP demanded equals the quantity of real GDP supplied.

9. Increases in aggregate demand beyond the full-employment output cause inflation and positive GDP gaps (actual GDP exceeds potential GDP). Such gaps eventually evaporate as wages and other input prices rise to match the increase in the price level.

10. Leftward shifts of the aggregate supply curve reflect increases in per-unit production costs at each level of output and cause cost-push inflation, with accompanying negative GDP gaps.

11. Shifts of the aggregate demand curve to the left of the full-employment output cause recession, negative GDP gaps, and cyclical unemployment. The price level typically does not fall during U.S. recessions because of downwardly inflexible prices and wages. This inflexibility results from fear of price wars, menu costs, wage contracts, morale concerns, and minimum wages.

12. In theory, price and wage flexibility would allow the economy automatically to self-correct from a recession. In reality, downward price and wage flexibility make the process slow and uncertain. Recessions usually prompt the federal government and the Federal Reserve to take actions to try to increase aggregate demand.

13. Changes in spending (consumption, investment, government purchases, and net exports) will lead to larger changes in GDP through the multiplier effect.

Terms and Concepts

aggregate demand–aggregate supply (AD-AS) model

aggregate demand

determinants of aggregate demand

exchange rates

aggregate supply

immediate-short-run aggregate supply curve

short-run aggregate supply curve

long-run aggregate supply curve

determinants of aggregate supply

productivity

equilibrium price level

equilibrium real output

multiplier

Questions

1. What is the general relationship between a country's price level and the quantity of its domestic output (real GDP) demanded? Who are the buyers of U.S. real GDP? **LO1**

2. What assumptions cause the immediate-short-run aggregate supply curve to be horizontal? Why is the long-run aggregate supply curve vertical? Explain the shape of the short-run aggregate supply curve. Why is the short-run curve relatively flat to the left of the full-employment output and relatively steep to the right? **LO2**

3. Other things equal, what effects would each of the following have on aggregate demand or aggregate supply? In each case use a diagram to show the expected effects on the equilibrium price level and the level of real output. **LO3**
   a. A reduction in the economy's real interest rate.
   b. A major increase in federal spending for health care (with no increase in taxes).
   c. The complete disintegration of OPEC, causing oil prices to fall by one-half.

d. A 10 percent reduction in personal income tax rates (with no change in government spending).
e. A sizable increase in labor productivity (with no change in nominal wages).
f. A 12 percent increase in nominal wages (with no change in productivity).
g. A sizable depreciation in the international value of the dollar.

4. Other things equal, what effect will each of the following have on the equilibrium price level and level of real output? **LO3**
   a. An increase in aggregate demand in the steep portion of the aggregate supply curve.
   b. An increase in aggregate supply, with no change in aggregate demand (assume that prices and wages are flexible upward and downward).
   c. Equal increases in aggregate demand and aggregate supply.

d. A reduction in aggregate demand in the relatively flat portion of the aggregate supply curve.
e. An increase in aggregate demand and a decrease in aggregate supply.

5. Why does a reduction in aggregate demand tend to reduce real output, rather than the price level? **LO4**
6. Explain: "Unemployment can be caused by a decrease of aggregate demand or a decrease of aggregate supply." In each case, specify the price-level outcomes. **LO4**
7. In early 2001 investment spending sharply declined in the United States. In the 2 months following the September 11, 2001, attacks on the United States, consumption also declined. Use AD-AS analysis to show the two impacts on real GDP. **LO4**
8. Using the concept of the multiplier, explain why mass layoffs by large companies such as Boeing or General Motors are a concern to the citizens and leaders where those firms are located. **LO4**

Problems

1. Suppose that consumer spending initially rises by $5 billion for every 1 percent rise in household wealth and that investment spending initially rises by $20 billion for every 1 percentage point fall in the real interest rate. Also assume that the economy's multiplier is 4. If household wealth falls by 5 percent because of declining house values, and the real interest rate falls by 2 percentage points, in what direction and by how much will the aggregate demand curve initially shift at each price level? In what direction and by how much will it eventually shift? **LO1**

2. Answer the following questions on the basis of the three sets of data below for the country of North Vaudeville: **LO2**
   a. Which set of data illustrates aggregate supply in the immediate short run in North Vaudeville? The short run? The long run?
   b. Assuming no change in hours of work, if real output per hour of work increases by 10 percent, what will be the new levels of real GDP in the right column of A? Do the new data reflect an increase in aggregate supply or do they indicate a decrease in aggregate supply?

3. Suppose that the aggregate demand and aggregate supply schedules for a hypothetical economy are as shown in the table to the right. **LO3**

Amount of Real GDP Demanded, Billions	Price Level (Price Index)	Amount of Real GDP Supplied, Billions
$100	300	$450
200	250	400
300	200	300
400	150	200
500	100	100

a. Use the data above to graph the aggregate demand and aggregate supply curves. What is the equilibrium price level and the equilibrium level of real output in this hypothetical economy? Is the equilibrium real output also necessarily the full-employment real output?
b. If the price level in this economy is 150, will quantity demanded equal, exceed, or fall short of quantity supplied? By what amount? If the price level is 250, will quantity demanded equal, exceed, or fall short of quantity supplied? By what amount?

(A)		(B)		(C)	
Price Level	Real GDP	Price Level	Real GDP	Price Level	Real GDP
110	275	100	200	110	225
100	250	100	225	100	225
95	225	100	250	95	225
90	200	100	275	90	225

c. Suppose that buyers desire to purchase $200 billion of extra real output at each price level. Sketch in the new aggregate demand curve as AD$_1$. What is the new equilibrium price level and level of real output?

4. Suppose that the following table shows an economy's relationship between real output and the inputs needed to produce that output: **LO3**

Input Quantity	Real GDP
150.0	$400
112.5	300
75.00	200

a. What is productivity in this economy?
b. What is the per-unit cost of production if the price of each input unit is $2?
c. Assume that the input price increases from $2 to $3 with no accompanying change in productivity. What is the new per-unit cost of production? In what direction would the $1 increase in input price push

the economy's aggregate supply curve? What effect would this shift of aggregate supply have on the price level and the level of real output?

d. Suppose that the increase in input price does not occur but, instead, that productivity increases by 100 percent. What would be the new per-unit cost of production? What effect would this change in per-unit production cost have on the economy's aggregate supply curve? What effect would this shift of aggregate supply have on the price level and the level of real output?

5. Refer to the data in the table that accompanies problem 2. Suppose that the present equilibrium price level and level of real GDP are 100 and $225, and that data set B represents the relevant aggregate supply schedule for the economy. **LO4**

a. What must be the current amount of real output demanded at the 100 price level?
b. If the amount of output demanded declined by $25 at the 100 price levels shown in B, what would be the new equilibrium real GDP? In business cycle terminology, what would economists call this change in real GDP?

FURTHER TEST YOUR KNOWLEDGE AT
www.brue3e.com

At the text's Online Learning Center, **www.brue3e.com**, you will find one or more web-based questions that require information from the Internet to answer. We urge you to check them out, since they will familiarize you with websites that may be helpful in other courses and perhaps even in your career. The OLC also features multiple-choice quizzes that give instant feedback and provides other helpful ways to further test your knowledge of the chapter.

CHAPTER THIRTEEN

Fiscal Policy, Deficits, and Debt

After reading this chapter, you should be able to:

1. Identify and explain the purposes, tools, and limitations of fiscal policy.
2. Explain the role of built-in stabilizers in dampening business cycles.
3. Describe how the cyclically adjusted budget reveals the status of U.S. fiscal policy.
4. Discuss the size, composition, and consequences of the U.S. public debt.
5. Explain why there is a long-run fiscal imbalance in the Social Security system.

In the previous chapter we saw that an excessive increase in aggregate demand can cause demand-pull inflation and that a significant decline in aggregate demand can cause recession and cyclical unemployment. For those reasons, central governments sometimes use budgetary actions to try to "stimulate the economy" or "rein in inflation." Such countercyclical **fiscal policy** consists of deliberate changes in government spending and tax collections designed to achieve full employment, control inflation, and encourage economic growth. (The adjective "fiscal" simply means "financial.")

ORIGIN OF THE IDEA

O 13.1
Fiscal policy

We begin this chapter by examining the logic behind fiscal policy, its current status, and its limitations. Then we examine two related topics: the U.S. public debt and the Social Security funding problem.

Our discussion of fiscal policy and public debt is very timely. In 2009, the Congress and the Obama administration began a $787 billion stimulus program designed to help lift the U.S. economy out of a deep recession. This fiscal policy contributed to a $1.4 trillion federal budget deficit in 2009, which increased the size of the U.S. public debt to $11.9 trillion. Continued deficits increased the public debt to over $15.6 trillion in April 2012, and it has become a major political issue.

Fiscal Policy and the AD-AS Model

fiscal policy
Changes in government spending or taxation to promote full employment, price-level stability, and economic growth.

Council of Economic Advisers (CEA)
A group of three economists appointed by the U.S. president to provide advice and assistance on economic matters.

expansionary fiscal policy
An increase in government spending, a decrease in taxes, or some combination of the two for the purpose of increasing aggregate demand and real output.

budget deficit
The amount by which expenditures of the federal government exceed its revenues in any year.

The fiscal policy that we have been describing is *discretionary* (or "active"). It is often initiated on the advice of the president's **Council of Economic Advisers (CEA),** a group of three economists appointed by the president to provide expertise and assistance on economic matters. Such changes in government spending and taxes are *at the option* of the federal government. They do not occur automatically, independent of congressional action. The latter changes are *nondiscretionary* (or "passive" or "automatic"), and we will examine them later in this chapter.

Expansionary Fiscal Policy

When recession occurs, an **expansionary fiscal policy** may be in order. This policy consists of government spending increases, tax reductions, or both, designed to increase aggregate demand and therefore raise real GDP. Consider Figure 13.1, where we suppose that a sharp decline in investment spending has shifted the economy's aggregate demand curve to the left from AD$_1$ to AD$_2$. (Disregard the arrow for now.) The cause of the recession may be that profit expectations on investment projects have dimmed, curtailing investment spending and reducing aggregate demand.

Suppose the economy's potential or full-employment output is $510 billion in Figure 13.1. If the price level is inflexible downward at P_1, the aggregate demand curve slides leftward at that price level and reduces real GDP to $490 billion. A negative GDP gap of $20 billion (= $490 billion − $510 billion) arises. An increase in unemployment accompanies this negative GDP gap because fewer workers are needed to produce the reduced output. In short, the economy depicted is suffering both recession and cyclical unemployment.

What fiscal policy should the federal government adopt to try to remedy the situation? It has three main options: (1) government-spending increases, (2) tax reductions, or (3) some combination of the two. If the federal budget is balanced at the outset, expansionary fiscal policy will create a government **budget deficit** (government spending in excess of tax revenues).

FIGURE 13.1
Expansionary fiscal policy. Expansionary fiscal policy uses increases in government spending, tax cuts, or a combination of both to increase aggregate demand and push the economy out of recession. Here, this policy increases aggregate demand from AD$_2$ to AD$_1$, increases real GDP from $490 billion to $510 billion, and restores full employment.

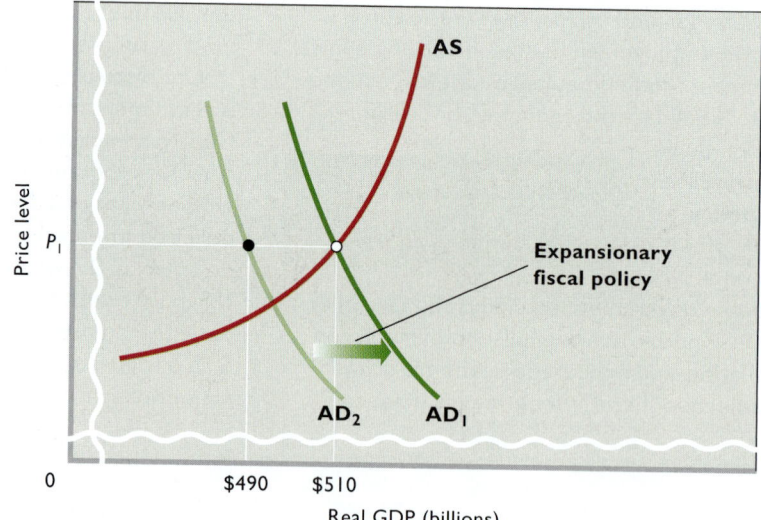

Government Spending Increases   To increase aggregate demand, the federal government can increase its spending. For example, it might boost spending on highways, education, and health care. Other things equal, a sufficient increase in government spending will shift an economy's aggregate demand curve to the right, as from AD_2 to AD_1 in Figure 13.1. Observe that real output rises to $510 billion, up $20 billion from its recessionary level of $490 billion. Firms increase their employment to the full-employment level, output increases, and the negative GDP gap disappears.

Tax Reductions   Alternatively, the government could reduce taxes to shift the aggregate demand curve rightward, as from AD_2 to AD_1. Suppose the government cuts personal income taxes, which increases disposable income. Households will spend a large part of that income and save the rest. The part spent—the new consumption spending—will increase aggregate demand. In Figure 13.1, this increase in aggregate demand from AD_2 to AD_1 expands real GDP by $20 billion, eliminating the negative GDP gap. Employment increases accordingly, and the unemployment rate falls.

A tax cut must be larger than an increase in government spending to achieve the same rightward shift of the aggregate demand curve. This is because households save part of the higher after-tax income provided by the tax cut. Only the part of the tax cut that increases consumption spending shifts the aggregate demand curve to the right.

Combined Government Spending Increases and Tax Reductions   The government may combine spending increases and tax cuts to produce the desired initial increase in spending and the eventual increase in aggregate demand and real GDP. In the economy depicted in Figure 13.1, there is some combination of greater government spending and lower taxes (increased consumption spending) that will shift the aggregate demand curve from AD_2 to AD_1 and remove the negative GDP gap.

Contractionary Fiscal Policy

When demand-pull inflation occurs, a restrictive or **contractionary fiscal policy** may help control it. This policy consists of government spending reductions, tax increases, or both, designed to decrease aggregate demand and therefore lower or eliminate inflation. Take a look at Figure 13.2, where the full-employment level of real GDP is $510 billion. Suppose a sharp increase in investment and net export spending shifts the aggregate demand curve from AD_3 to AD_4. The outcomes are demand-pull inflation, as shown by the rise of the price level from P_1 to P_2, and a positive GDP gap of $12 billion (=$522 billion − $510 billion).

If the government decides on fiscal policy to control this inflation, its options are the opposite of those used to combat recession. It can (1) decrease government spending, (2) raise taxes, or (3) use some combination of those two policies. When the economy faces demand-pull inflation, fiscal policy should move toward a government **budget surplus** (tax revenues in excess of government spending).

Government Spending Decreases   Reduced government spending shifts the aggregate demand curve leftward to control demand-pull inflation. In Figure 13.2, this spending cut shifts the aggregate demand curve leftward from AD_4 to AD_3. If the price level were downwardly flexible, the price level would return to P_1, where it was before demand-pull inflation occurred. That is, deflation would occur.

Unfortunately, the actual economy is not as simple and tidy as Figure 13.2 suggests. Increases in aggregate demand tend to ratchet the price level upward, but

contractionary fiscal policy
A decrease in government spending, an increase in taxes, or some combination of the two for the purpose of decreasing aggregate demand and halting inflation.

budget surplus
The amount by which revenues of the federal government exceed its expenditures in any year.

FIGURE 13.2

Contractionary fiscal policy. Contractionary fiscal policy uses decreases in government spending, increases in taxes, or a combination of both to reduce aggregate demand and slow or eliminate demand-pull inflation. Here, this policy shifts the aggregate demand curve from AD_4 to AD_3, removes the upward pressure on the price level, and halts the demand-pull inflation. Note, however, that even though the inflation is stopped, the presence of inflexible ("sticky") prices may prevent the price level from falling to P_1.

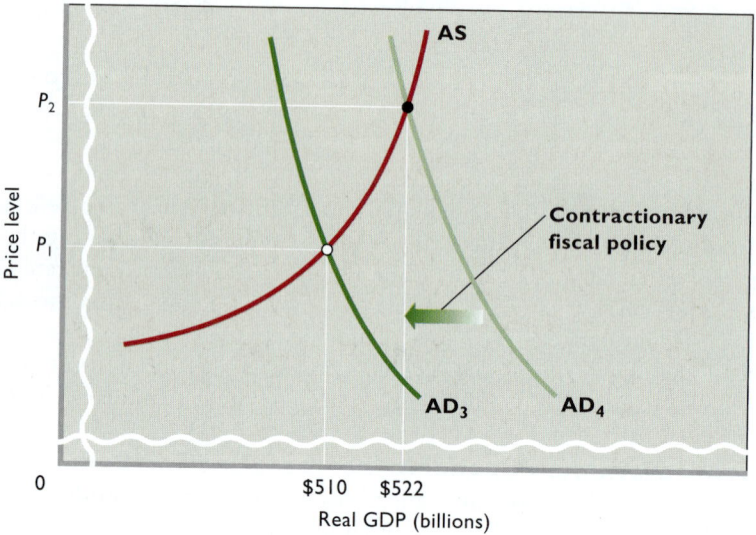

declines in aggregate demand do not seem to push the price level downward. So stopping inflation is a matter of halting the rise of the price level, not trying to lower it to the previous level. Demand-pull inflation usually is experienced as a continual rightward shifting of the aggregate demand curve. Contractionary fiscal policy is designed to stop a further shift, not to restore a lower price level. Successful fiscal policy eliminates a continuing positive (and thus inflationary) GDP gap and prevents the price level from continuing its inflationary rise. Nevertheless, Figure 13.2 displays the basic principle: Reductions in government expenditures can be used as a fiscal policy action to tame demand-pull inflation.

Tax Increases   Just as government can use tax cuts to increase consumption spending, it can use tax increases to reduce consumption spending. In the economy in Figure 13.2, the government must raise taxes sufficiently to reduce consumption such that the aggregate demand curve will shift leftward from AD_4 to AD_3. That way, the demand-pull inflation will have been controlled.

Because part of any tax increase reduces saving rather than consumption, a tax increase must exceed a decrease in government spending to cause the same leftward shift of the aggregate demand curve. Only the part of the tax increase that lowers consumption spending reduces aggregate demand.

Combined Government Spending Decreases and Tax Increases   The

government may choose to combine spending decreases and tax increases in order to reduce aggregate demand and check inflation. Some combination of lower government spending and higher taxes will shift the aggregate demand curve from AD_4 to AD_3.

Built-In Stability

To some degree, government tax revenues change automatically over the course of the business cycle and in ways that stabilize the economy. This automatic response, or built-in stability, constitutes nondiscretionary (or "passive" or "automatic") budgetary policy and results from the makeup of most tax systems. We did not include this built-in stability in our discussion of fiscal policy because we implicitly assumed that the same amount of tax revenue was being collected at each level of GDP. But the actual U.S. tax system is such that *net tax revenues* vary directly with GDP. (*Net taxes* are tax revenues less transfers and subsidies. From here on, we will use the simpler "taxes" to mean "net taxes.")

Virtually any tax will yield more tax revenue as GDP (and therefore total income) rises. In particular, personal income taxes have progressive rates and thus generate more-than-proportionate increases in tax revenues as GDP expands. Furthermore, as GDP rises and more goods and services are purchased, revenues from corporate income taxes and from sales taxes and excise taxes also increase. And, similarly, revenues from payroll taxes rise as economic expansion creates more jobs and income. Conversely, when GDP declines, tax receipts from all these sources also decline.

Transfer payments (or "negative taxes") behave in the opposite way from tax revenues. For example, welfare and unemployment compensation payments decline during an economic expansion and increase during an economic contraction.

Automatic or Built-In Stabilizers

A **built-in stabilizer** is anything that increases the government's budget deficit (or reduces its budget surplus) during a recession and increases its budget surplus (or reduces its budget deficit) during inflation without requiring explicit action by policymakers. As Figure 13.3 reveals, this is precisely what the U.S. tax system does. Government expenditures G are fixed and assumed to be independent of the level of GDP. Congress decides on a particular level of spending, but it does not determine the magnitude of tax revenues. Instead, it establishes tax rates, and the tax revenues then vary directly with the level of GDP that the economy achieves. Line T represents that direct relationship between tax revenues and GDP.

built-in stabilizer
Anything that increases the government's budget deficit (or reduces its budget surplus) during a recession and increases its budget surplus (or reduces its budget deficit) during expansion without requiring explicit action by policymakers.

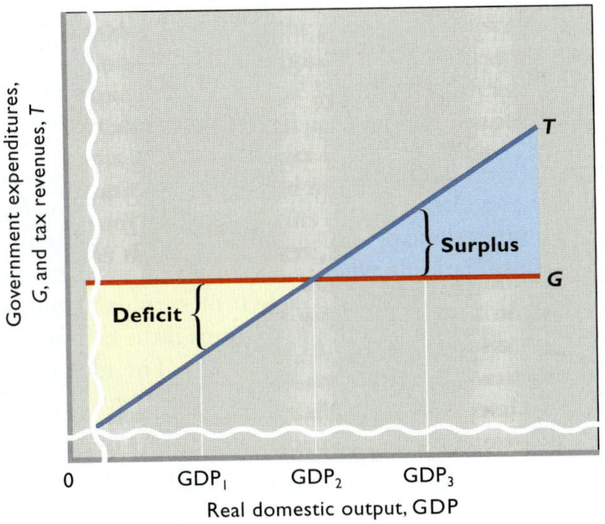

FIGURE 13.3
Built-in stability. Tax revenues T vary directly with GDP, and government spending G is assumed to be independent of GDP. As GDP falls in a recession, deficits occur automatically and help alleviate the recession. As GDP rises during expansion, surpluses occur automatically and help offset possible inflation.

Economic Importance

The economic importance of the direct relationship between tax receipts and GDP becomes apparent when we consider that

- Taxes reduce spending and aggregate demand.
- Reductions in spending are desirable when the economy is moving toward inflation, whereas increases in spending are desirable when the economy is slumping.

As shown in Figure 13.3, tax revenues automatically increase as GDP rises during prosperity, and since taxes reduce household and business spending, they restrain the economic expansion. That is, as the economy moves toward a higher GDP, tax revenues automatically rise and move the budget from deficit toward surplus. In Figure 13.3, observe that the high and perhaps inflationary income level GDP_3 automatically generates a contractionary budget surplus.

Conversely, as output and income fall during recession, tax revenues automatically decline, increasing spending by households and businesses and thus cushioning the economic contraction. With a falling GDP, tax receipts decline and move the government's budget from surplus toward deficit. In Figure 13.3, the low level of income GDP_1 will automatically yield an expansionary budget deficit.

Built-in stability has reduced the severity of U.S. business fluctuations, perhaps by as much as 8 to 10 percent of the change in GDP that otherwise would have occurred.[1] In recession year 2009, for example, revenues from the individual income tax fell by a staggering 22 percent. This decline helped keep household spending and real GDP from falling even more than they did. But built-in stabilizers can only dampen, not counteract, swings in real GDP. Discretionary fiscal policy (changes in tax rates and expenditures) or monetary policy (central bank–caused changes in interest rates) may be needed to correct recession or inflation of any appreciable magnitude.

Evaluating Fiscal Policy

How can we determine whether a government's discretionary fiscal policy is expansionary, neutral, or contractionary? We cannot simply examine the actual budget deficits or surpluses that take place under the current policy because they will necessarily include the automatic changes in tax revenues that accompany every change in GDP. In addition, the expansionary or contractionary strength of any change in discretionary fiscal policy depends not on its absolute size but on how large it is relative to the size of the economy. So, in evaluating the status of fiscal policy, we must adjust deficits and surpluses to eliminate automatic changes in tax revenues and also compare the sizes of the adjusted budget deficits and surpluses to the level of potential GDP.

cyclically adjusted budget
A measure of what the federal budget deficit or surplus would be with existing tax rates and government spending programs if the economy had achieved its full-employment GDP in the year.

Economists use the **cyclically adjusted budget** (or *full-employment budget*) to adjust actual federal budget deficits and surpluses to account for the changes in tax revenues that happen automatically whenever GDP changes. The cyclically adjusted budget measures what the federal budget deficit or surplus would have been under existing tax rates and government spending programs if the economy had achieved its full-employment level of GDP (its potential output). The idea is to compare *actual* government expenditures with the tax revenues *that would have occurred* if the economy

[1]Alan J. Auerbach and Daniel Feenberg, "The Significance of Federal Taxes as Automatic Stabilizers," *Journal of Economic Perspectives*, Summer 2000, p. 54.

had achieved full-employment GDP. That procedure removes budget deficits or surpluses that arise simply because of cyclical changes in GDP and thus tell us nothing about whether the government's current discretionary fiscal policy is fundamentally expansionary, contractionary, or neutral.

Consider Figure 13.4, where line G represents government expenditures and line T represents tax revenues. In full-employment year 1, government expenditures of $500 billion equal tax revenues of $500 billion, as indicated by the intersection of lines G and T at point a. The actual budget deficit and the cyclically adjusted budget deficit in year 1 are zero—government expenditures equal tax revenues, and government spending equals the tax revenues forthcoming at the full-employment output GDP_1. Obviously, the cyclically adjusted budget deficit *as a percentage of potential GDP* is also zero. The government's fiscal policy is neutral.

Now suppose that a recession occurs and GDP falls from GDP_1 to GDP_2, as shown in Figure 13.4. Let's also assume that the government takes no discretionary action, so lines G and T remain as shown in the figure. Tax revenues automatically fall to $450 billion (point c) at GDP_2, while government spending (we assume) remains unaltered at $500 billion (point b). A $50 billion actual budget deficit (represented by distance bc) arises. But this **cyclical deficit** is simply a by-product of the economy's slide into recession, not the result of discretionary fiscal actions by the government. We would be wrong to conclude from this deficit that the government is engaging in an expansionary fiscal policy. The government's fiscal policy has not changed; it is still neutral.

That fact is highlighted when we consider the cyclically adjusted budget deficit for year 2 in Figure 13.4. The $500 billion of government expenditures in year 2 is

cyclical deficit
A federal budget deficit that is caused by a recession and the consequent decline in tax revenues.

FIGURE 13.4

Cyclically adjusted budget deficits. The cyclically adjusted budget deficit is zero at the full-employment output GDP_1. But it is also zero at the recessionary output GDP_2 because the $500 billion of government expenditures at GDP_2 equals the $500 billion of tax revenues that would be forthcoming at the full-employment GDP_1. Here, fiscal policy did not change as the economy slid into recession. The deficit that arose is simply a cyclical deficit.

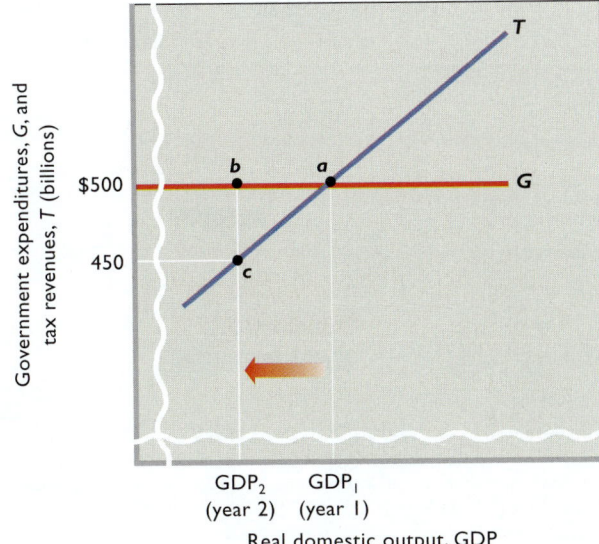

shown by *b* on line *G*. And, as shown by *a* on line *T*, $500 billion of tax revenues would have occurred if the economy had achieved its full-employment GDP. Because both *b* and *a* represent $500 billion, the cyclically adjusted budget deficit in year 2 is zero, as is this deficit as a percentage of potential GDP. Since the full-employment deficits are zero in both years, we know that government did not change its discretionary fiscal policy, even though a recession occurred and an actual deficit of $50 billion resulted.

In contrast, if we observed a cyclically adjusted deficit of zero in a specific year, followed by a cyclically adjusted budget deficit in the next, we could conclude that fiscal policy is expansionary. Because the cyclically adjusted budget adjusts for automatic changes in tax revenues, the increase in the cyclically adjusted budget deficit reveals that government either increased its spending (*G*) or decreased tax rates such that tax revenues (*T*) decreased. In Figure 13.4, the government either shifted the line *G* upward or the line *T* downward. These changes in *G* and *T* are precisely the discretionary actions that we have identified as elements of an *expansionary* fiscal policy. Similarly, if we observed a cyclically adjusted deficit of zero in one year, followed by a cyclically adjusted budget surplus in the next, we could conclude that fiscal policy is contractionary. Government either decreased its spending (*G*) or increased tax rates such that tax revenues (*T*) increased. We know that these changes in *G* and *T* are elements of a *contractionary* fiscal policy.

Global Snapshot 13.1 shows the extent of the cyclically adjusted budget deficits or surpluses of a number of countries in 2010.

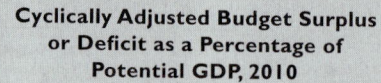

Global Snapshot 13.1

Cyclically Adjusted Budget Deficits or Surpluses as a Percentage of Potential GDP, Selected Nations

Because of the global recession, in 2010 all but a few of the world's major nations had cyclically adjusted budget deficits. These deficits varied as percentages of potential GDP, but they each reflected some degree of expansionary fiscal policy.

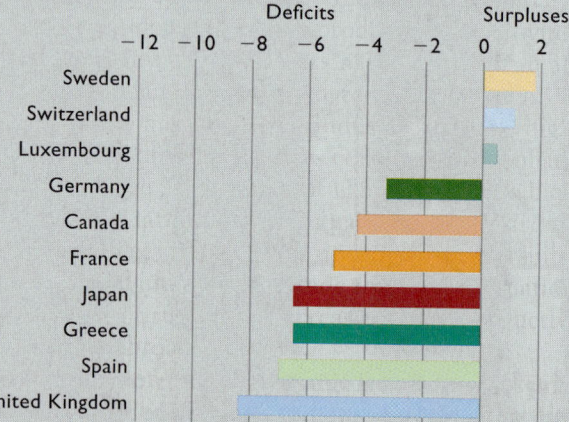

Cyclically Adjusted Budget Surplus or Deficit as a Percentage of Potential GDP, 2010

Source: Organization for Economic Cooperation and Development, *OECD Economic Outlook*, November 2011, **www.oecd.org**. Accessed April 22, 2012.

Recent U.S. Fiscal Policy

Table 13.1 lists the actual federal budget deficits and surpluses (column 2) and the cyclically adjusted deficits and surpluses (column 3), as percentages of actual GDP and potential GDP, respectively, between 2000 and 2010. Observe that the cyclically adjusted deficits are generally smaller than the actual deficits. This is because the actual deficits include cyclical deficits, whereas the cyclically adjusted deficits eliminate them. Only cyclically adjusted surpluses and deficits as percentages of potential GDP (column 3) provide the information needed to assess discretionary fiscal policy and determine whether it is expansionary, contractionary, or neutral.

Take a look at the data for 2000, for example, which shows that fiscal policy was contractionary that year. Note that the actual budget surplus was 2.5 percent of GDP in 2000 and the cyclically adjusted budget surplus was 1.0 percent of potential GDP. Because the economy was fully employed and corporate profits were strong, tax revenues poured into the federal government and exceeded government expenditures.

But not all was well in 2000. Specifically, the so-called dot-com stock market bubble burst that year, and the U.S. economy noticeably slowed over the latter half of the year. In March 2001 the economy slid into a recession. Congress and the Bush administration responded by cutting taxes by $44 billion in 2001 and scheduling an additional $52 billion of cuts for 2002. These stimulus policies helped boost the economy and offset the recession as well as cushion the economic blow delivered by the September 11, 2001, terrorist attacks. In March 2002 Congress passed further tax cuts totaling $122 billion over two years and extended unemployment benefits.

As Table 13.1 reveals, the cyclically adjusted budget moved from a surplus of 1.0 percent of potential GDP in 2000 to a deficit of −1.3 percent two years later in 2002. Fiscal policy had definitely turned expansionary. Nevertheless, the economy remained sluggish through 2002 and into 2003. In June 2003 Congress again cut taxes, this time by a much larger $350 billion over several years. Specifically, the tax legislation accelerated the reduction of marginal tax rates already scheduled for

TABLE 13.1

Federal Deficits (−) and Surpluses (+) as Percentages of GDP, 2000–2010

(1) Year	(2) Actual Deficit − or Surplus +	(3) Cyclically Adjusted Deficit − or Surplus +*
2000	+2.5	+1.0
2001	+1.3	+0.5
2002	−1.5	−1.3
2003	−3.4	−2.8
2004	−3.5	−3.3
2005	−2.6	−2.7
2006	−1.9	−2.2
2007	−1.2	−1.3
2008	−3.2	−2.9
2009	−9.4	−7.3
2010	−8.4	−6.1

*As a percentage of potential GDP.
Source: Congressional Budget Office, **www.cbo.gov**.

future years and slashed tax rates on income from dividends and capital gains. It also increased tax breaks for families and small businesses. Note from the table that this tax package increased the cyclically adjusted budget deficit as a percentage of potential GDP to −2.8 percent in 2003. The economy strengthened and both real output and employment grew between 2003 and 2007. By 2007 full employment had been restored, although a −1.3 percent cyclically adjusted budget deficit still remained.

As pointed out in previous chapters, major economic trouble began in 2007. In the summer of 2007, a crisis in the market for mortgage loans flared up. Later in 2007 that crisis spread rapidly to other financial markets, threatened the survival of several major U.S. financial institutions, and severely disrupted the entire financial system. As credit markets began to freeze, general pessimism spread beyond the financial markets to the overall economy. Businesses and households retrenched on their borrowing and spending, and in December 2007 the economy entered a recession. Over the following two years, it became known as the Great Recession—one of the steepest and longest economic downturns since the 1930s.

In 2008 Congress acted rapidly to pass an economic stimulus package. This law provided a total of $152 billion in stimulus, with some of it coming as tax breaks for businesses, but most of it delivered as checks of up to $600 each to taxpayers, veterans, and Social Security recipients.

As a percentage of GDP, the *actual* federal budget deficit jumped from −1.2 percent in 2007 to −3.2 percent in 2008. This increase resulted from an automatic drop-off of tax revenues during the recession, along with the tax rebates (fiscal stimulus checks) paid out in 2008. As shown in Table 13.1, the *cyclically adjusted* budget deficit rose from −1.3 percent of potential GDP in 2007 to −2.9 percent in 2008. This increase in the cyclically adjusted budget reveals that fiscal policy in 2008 was expansionary.

The government hoped that those receiving checks would spend the money and thus boost consumption and aggregate demand. But households instead saved substantial parts of the money from the checks or used some of the money to pay down credit card loans. Although this stimulus plan boosted output somewhat in mid-2008, it was neither as expansionary nor long-lasting as policymakers had hoped. The continuing forces of the Great Recession simply overwhelmed the policy.

With the economy continuing its precipitous slide, the Obama administration and Congress enacted the American Recovery and Reinvestment Act of 2009. This gigantic $787 billion program—coming on top of a $700 billion rescue package for financial institutions—consisted of low- and middle-income tax rebates, plus large increases in expenditures on infrastructure, education, and health care. The idea was to flood the economy with additional spending to try to boost aggregate demand and get people back to work.

The tax cuts in the package were aimed at lower- and middle-income individuals and households, who were thought to be more likely than high-income people to spend (rather than save) the extra income from the tax rebates. Rather than sending out lump-sum stimulus checks as in 2008, the new tax rebates showed up as small increases in workers' monthly payroll checks. With smaller amounts per month rather than a single large check, the government hoped that people would spend the bulk of their enhanced income—rather than save it as they had done with the one-time-only, lump-sum checks received in 2008. The second part of the fiscal policy (60 percent of the funding) consisted of increases in government expenditures on a wide assortment of programs, including transportation, education, and aid to state governments. The highly stimulative fiscal

FIGURE 13.5

Federal budget deficits and surpluses, actual and projected, fiscal years 1994–2014 (in billions of nominal dollars). The annual budget deficits of 1992 through 1997 gave way to budget surpluses from 1998 through 2001. Deficits reappeared in 2002 and declined through 2007. They greatly ballooned in recessionary years 2008 and 2009 and are projected to remain high for many years to come.

Source: Congressional Budget Office, **www.cbo.gov.**

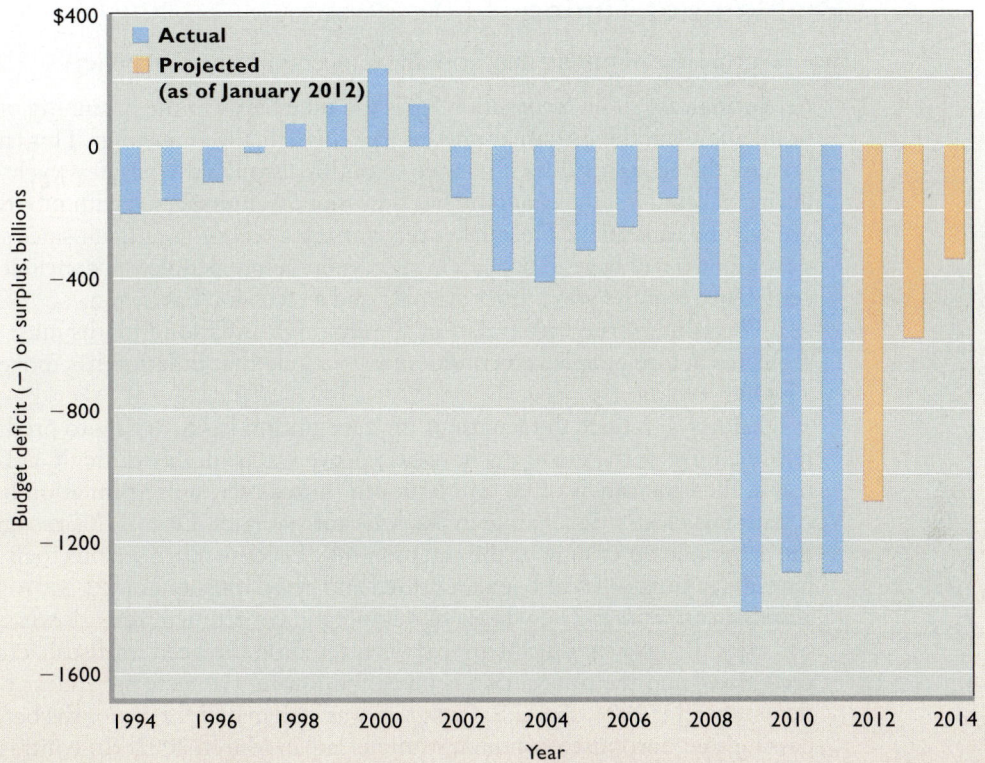

policy for 2009 is fully reflected in column 3 of Table 13.1. The cyclically adjusted budget deficit rose dramatically from −2.9 percent of potential GDP in 2008 to a very high −7.3 percent of potential GDP in 2009.

Figure 13.5 shows the absolute magnitudes of actual (not cyclically adjusted) U.S. budget surpluses and deficits, here from 1994 through 2011. It also shows the projected future deficits through 2014, as estimated by the Congressional Budget Office (CBO). In recession year 2009, the federal budget deficit reached $1413 billion, mainly but not totally due to reduced tax revenues from lower income and record amounts of stimulus spending. The CBO projects high deficits for several years to come. But projected deficits and surpluses are subject to large and frequent changes, as government alters its fiscal policy and GDP growth accelerates or slows. So we suggest that you update this figure by going to the Congressional Budget Office website, **www.cbo.gov**, and selecting Budget and Economic Outlook: Fiscal Years 2012 to 2022 (or more recent) and then Budget Projections. The relevant numbers are in Table 1-1 in the row labeled Total Deficit.

Question:

Use Figure 13.5 to demonstrate how each of the following contributed to increased actual budget deficits in recent years: (a) the recession of 2007–2009, (b) the war on terrorism in the United States and abroad, and (c) the Bush administration tax cuts.

Problems, Criticisms, and Complications

Economists recognize that governments may encounter a number of significant problems in enacting and applying fiscal policy.

Problems of Timing

Several problems of timing may arise in connection with fiscal policy:

- *Recognition lag* The recognition lag is the time between the beginning of recession or inflation and the certain awareness that it is actually happening. This lag arises because the economy does not move smoothly through the business cycle. Even during good times, the economy has slow months interspersed with months of rapid growth and expansion. This makes recognizing a recession difficult since several slow months will have to happen in succession before people can conclude with any confidence that the good times are over and a recession has begun.

  The same is true with inflation. Several high-inflation months must come in sequence before people can confidently conclude that inflation has moved to a higher level.

  Efforts to reduce the length of the recognition lag by trying to predict the future course of the economy have also proven to be highly difficult, at best. As a result, the economy is often 4 to 6 months into a recession or inflation before the situation is clearly discernible in the relevant statistics. Due to this recognition lag, the economic downslide or the inflation may become more serious than it would have if the situation had been identified and acted on sooner.

- *Administrative lag* The wheels of democratic government turn slowly. There will typically be a significant lag between the time the need for fiscal action is recognized and the time action is taken. Following the terrorist attacks of September 11, 2001, the U.S. Congress was stalemated for 5 months before passing a compromise economic stimulus law in March 2002. (In contrast, the Federal Reserve began lowering interest rates the week after the attacks.)

- *Operational lag* A lag also occurs between the time fiscal action is taken and the time that action affects output, employment, or the price level. Although changes in tax rates can be put into effect relatively quickly once new laws are passed, government spending on public works—new dams, interstate highways, and so on—requires long planning periods and even longer periods of construction. Such spending is of questionable use in offsetting short (for example, 6- to 12-month) periods of recession. Consequently, discretionary fiscal policy has increasingly relied on tax changes rather than on changes in spending as its main tool.

Political Considerations

Fiscal policy is conducted in a political arena. That reality not only may slow the enactment of fiscal policy but also may create the potential for political considerations swamping economic considerations in its formulation. It is a human trait to rationalize actions and policies that are in one's self-interest. Politicians are very human—they want to get reelected. A strong economy at election time will certainly help them. So they may favor large tax cuts under the guise of expansionary fiscal policy even though that policy is economically inappropriate. Similarly, they may rationalize increased government spending on popular items such as farm subsidies, health care, education, and homeland security.

At the extreme, elected officials and political parties might collectively "hijack" fiscal policy for political purposes, cause inappropriate changes in aggregate demand,

and thereby cause (rather than avert) economic fluctuations. For instance, before an election they may try to stimulate the economy to improve their reelection hopes. And then after the election they may try to use contractionary fiscal policy to dampen the excessive aggregate demand that they caused with their pre-election stimulus. Such **political business cycles**—swings in overall economic activity and real GDP resulting from election-motivated fiscal policy, rather than from inherent instability in the private sector—are difficult to document and prove, but there is little doubt that political considerations weigh heavily in the formulation of fiscal policy. The question is how often, if ever, those political considerations run counter to "sound economics."

An example of the interaction of political and economic considerations—and a notable exception to the administrative lag mentioned previously—was the Economic Stimulus Act of 2008. The proposal was unveiled by President Bush on January 28, 2008; passed through both houses of Congress less than two weeks later; and signed into law on February 14, 2008. While there seemed to be strong consensus among lawmakers that the U.S. economy needed a boost, some have also suggested that the looming 2008 elections provided additional motivation to act quickly.

Future Policy Reversals

Fiscal policy may fail to achieve its intended objectives if households expect future reversals of policy. Consider a tax cut, for example. If taxpayers believe the tax reduction is temporary, they may save a large portion of their tax cut, reasoning that rates will return to their previous level in the future. They save more now so that they will be able to draw on this extra savings to maintain their future consumption levels if taxes do indeed rise again in the future. So a tax reduction thought to be temporary may not increase present consumption spending and aggregate demand by as much as our simple model (Figure 13.1) suggests.

The opposite may be true for a tax increase. If taxpayers think it is temporary, they may reduce their saving to pay the tax while maintaining their present consumption. They may reason that they can restore their saving when the tax rate again falls. So the tax increase may not reduce current consumption and aggregate demand by as much as policymakers intended.

To the extent that this so-called *consumption smoothing* occurs over time, fiscal policy will lose some of its strength. The lesson is that tax-rate changes that households view as permanent are more likely to alter consumption and aggregate demand than tax changes they view as temporary.

Offsetting State and Local Finance

The fiscal policies of state and local governments are frequently *pro-cyclical*, meaning that they worsen rather than correct recession or inflation. Unlike the federal government, most state and local governments face constitutional or other legal requirements to balance their budgets. Like households and private businesses, state and local governments increase their expenditures during prosperity and cut them during recession.

During the Great Depression of the 1930s, most of the increase in federal spending was offset by decreases in state and local spending. During and immediately following the recession of 2001, many state and local governments had to offset lower tax revenues resulting from the reduced personal income and spending of their citizens. They offset the decline in revenues by raising tax rates, imposing new taxes, and reducing spending.

In view of these past experiences, the $787 billion fiscal package of 2009 made a special effort to reduce this problem by giving substantial aid dollars to state governments. Because of the sizeable federal aid, the states did not have to increase taxes and

political business cycle
The alleged tendency of presidential administrations and Congress to create macroeconomic instability by reducing taxes and increasing government spending before elections, and by raising taxes and reducing expenditures after elections.

reduce expenditures by as much as otherwise. So their collective fiscal actions did not fight as much against the increase in aggregate demand that the federal government wanted to achieve with its tax cuts and expenditure increases.

Crowding-Out Effect

crowding-out effect
A decrease in private investment caused by higher interest rates that result from the federal government's increased borrowing to finance deficits (or debt).

Another potential flaw of fiscal policy is the so-called **crowding-out effect:** An expansionary fiscal policy (deficit spending) may increase the interest rate and reduce investment spending, thereby weakening or canceling the stimulus of the expansionary policy. The rising interest rate might also potentially crowd out interest-sensitive consumption spending (such as purchasing automobiles on credit). But since investment is the most volatile component of GDP, the crowding-out effect focuses its attention on investment and whether the stimulus provided by deficit spending may be partly or even fully neutralized by an offsetting reduction in investment spending.

To see the potential problem, realize that whenever the government borrows money (as it must if it is deficit spending), it increases the overall demand for money. If the monetary authorities are holding the money supply constant, this increase in demand will raise the price paid for borrowing money: the interest rate. Because investment spending varies inversely with the interest rate, some investment will be choked off or "crowded out."

INTERACTIVE GRAPHS

G 13.1
Crowding out

ORIGIN OF THE IDEA

O 13.2
Crowding out

Economists vary in their opinions about the strength of the crowding-out effect. An important thing to keep in mind is that crowding out is likely to be less of a problem when the economy is in recession because investment demand tends to be low. Why? Because the sale of products slows down during recessions, so that most businesses end up with substantial amounts of excess capacity. As a result, they do not have much incentive to add new machinery or build new factories. After all, why should they add capacity when some of the capacity they already have is lying idle?

With investment demand low during a recession, the crowding-out effect is likely to be very small. Simply put, there isn't much investment for the government to crowd out. Even if deficit spending does increase the interest rate, investment spending cannot fall by that much for the simple reason that it is only a small number to begin with.

By contrast, when the economy is operating at or near full capacity, investment demand is likely to be quite high so that crowding out will probably be a much more serious problem. When the economy is booming, factories will be running at or near full capacity and firms will have investment demand for two reasons. First, equipment running at full capacity wears out fast, so that firms will be doing a lot of investment just to replace machinery and equipment that wears out and depreciates. Second, the economy is likely to be growing overall so that firms will be investing to *add* to their production capacity so they can meet anticipated demand.

Current Thinking on Fiscal Policy

Where do these complications leave us as to the advisability and effectiveness of discretionary fiscal policy? In view of the complications and uncertain outcomes of fiscal policy, some economists argue that it is better not to engage in it at all. Those holding that view point to the superiority of monetary policy (changes in interest rates engineered by the Federal Reserve) as a stabilizing device or believe that most economic fluctuations tend to be mild and self-correcting.

But most economists believe that fiscal policy remains an important, useful policy lever in the government's macroeconomic toolkit. The current popular view is that fiscal policy can help "push the economy" in a particular direction but cannot "fine-tune it" to a precise macroeconomic outcome. Mainstream economists generally agree that monetary policy is the best month-to-month stabilization tool for the U.S. economy. If monetary policy is doing its job, the government should maintain a relatively neutral fiscal policy, with a cyclically adjusted budget deficit or surplus of no more than 2 percent of potential GDP. It should hold major discretionary fiscal policy in reserve to help counter situations where recession threatens to be deep and long-lasting (as in 2008 and 2009) or where a substantial reduction in aggregate demand might help the Federal Reserve to quell a major bout of inflation.

Finally, there is general agreement that proposed fiscal policy should be evaluated for its potential positive and negative impacts on long-run productivity growth. The short-run policy tools used for conducting active fiscal policy often have long-run impacts. Countercyclical fiscal policy should be shaped to strengthen, or at least not impede, the growth of long-run aggregate supply (shown as a rightward shift of the long-run aggregate supply curve in Figure 12.5). For example, a tax cut might be structured to enhance work effort, strengthen investment, and encourage innovation. Or an increase in government spending might center on preplanned projects for "public capital" (highways, mass transit, ports, airports) that are complementary to private investment and thus conducive to long-term economic growth.

The U.S. Public Debt

The U.S. national debt, or **public debt,** is essentially the accumulation of all past federal deficits and surpluses. The deficits have greatly exceeded the surpluses and have emerged mainly from war financing, recessions, and fiscal policy. In 2011 the total public debt was $14.8 trillion—$8.5 trillion held by the public, excluding the Federal Reserve, and $6.3 trillion held by federal agencies and the Federal Reserve. Between 2007 and 2009, the public debt expanded by a huge $2.9 trillion. During the Great Recession, federal tax revenues plummeted because incomes and profit fell, and federal expenditures jumped because of huge spending to rescue failing financial institutions and to stimulate the shrinking economy.

public debt
The total amount of money owed by the federal government to the owners of government securities; equal to the sum of past government budget deficits less government budget surpluses.

You can find the current size of the public debt at the website of the Department of Treasury, Bureau of the Public Debt, at **www.treasurydirect.gov/NP/BPDLogin?application=np.** At this site, you will see that the U.S. Treasury defines "the public" to include the Federal Reserve. But because the Federal Reserve is the nation's central bank, economists view it as essentially part of the federal government and not part of the public. Economists typically focus on the part of the debt that is not owned by the federal government and the Federal Reserve.

Ownership

The total public debt of $14.8 trillion represents the total amount of money owed by the federal government to the holders of **U.S. securities:** financial instruments issued by the federal government to borrow money to finance expenditures that exceed tax revenues. These U.S. securities (loan instruments) are of four types: *Treasury bills* (short-term securities), *Treasury notes* (medium-term securities), *Treasury bonds* (long-term securities), and *U.S. savings bonds* (long-term, nonmarketable bonds).

U.S. securities
Treasury bills, Treasury notes, Treasury bonds, and U.S. savings bonds issued by the federal government to finance expenditures that exceed tax revenues.

FIGURE 13.6
Ownership of the total public debt, 2011. The $14.8 trillion public debt can be divided into the proportion held by the public, excluding the Federal Reserve (57 percent), and the proportion held by federal agencies and the Federal Reserve System (43 percent). Of the total debt, 32 percent is foreign-owned.

Source: *Economic Report of the President, 2012,* **www.white-house.gov/administration/eop/cea/economic-report-of-the-President;** authors' derivation from Tables B-81 and B89, September 2011 data.

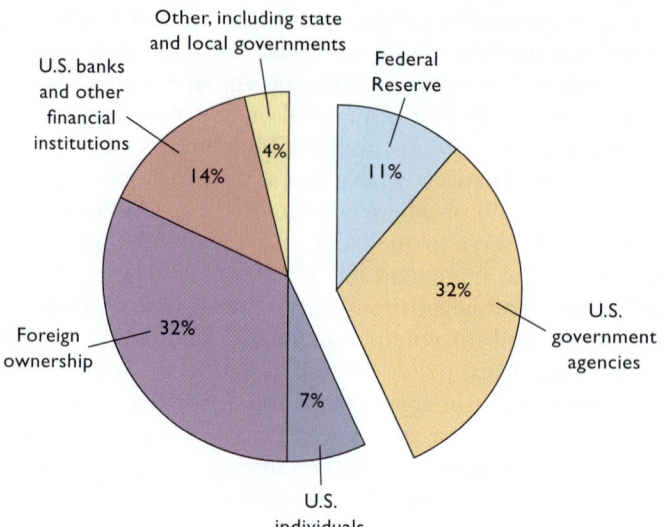

Total debt: $14.8 trillion

Figure 13.6 shows that the public, sans the Federal Reserve, held 57 percent of the federal debt in 2011 and that federal government agencies and the Federal Reserve held the remaining 43 percent. Observe that "the public" in the pie chart consists of individuals here and abroad, state and local governments, and U.S. financial institutions. Foreigners held about 32 percent of the total U.S. public debt in 2011, meaning that most of the U.S. public debt is held internally and not externally. Americans owed 68 percent of the public debt to Americans.

Debt and GDP

A simple statement of the absolute size of the debt ignores the fact that the wealth and productive ability of the U.S. economy are also vast. A wealthy, highly productive nation can incur and carry a large public debt much more easily than a poor nation can. A more meaningful measure of the public debt relates it to an economy's GDP. Figure 13.7 shows the yearly relative sizes of the U.S. public debt held outside the Federal Reserve and federal agencies. In 2011 the percentage was 57 percent. Most noticeably, the percentage rose dramatically in 2008 through 2011 because of huge budget deficits together with declining real GDP in 2008 and 2009.

International Comparisons

It is not uncommon for countries to have sizable public debts. As shown in Global Snapshot 13.2, the public debt as a percentage of real GDP in the United States is neither particularly high nor low relative to such debt percentages in other advanced industrial nations.

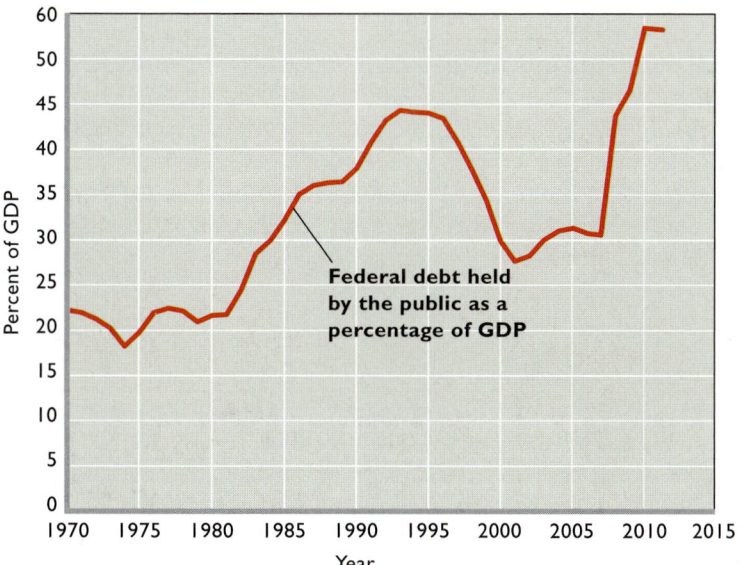

FIGURE 13.7
Federal debt held by the public, excluding the Federal Reserve, as a percentage of GDP, 1970–2011. As a percentage of GDP, the federal debt held by the public (held outside the Federal Reserve and federal government agencies) increased sharply over the 1980–1995 period and declined significantly between 1995 and 2001. Since 2001, the percentage has gone up again, and jumped abruptly and sharply from 2008 through 2010.

Source: *Economic Report of the President, 2012,* **www.whitehouse. gov/administration/eop/cea/ economic-report-of-the-President,** from Tables B-78 and B-81.

Publicly Held Debt: International Comparisons

Although the United States has the world's largest public debt, a number of other nations have larger debts as percentages of their GDPs.

Global Snapshot 13.2

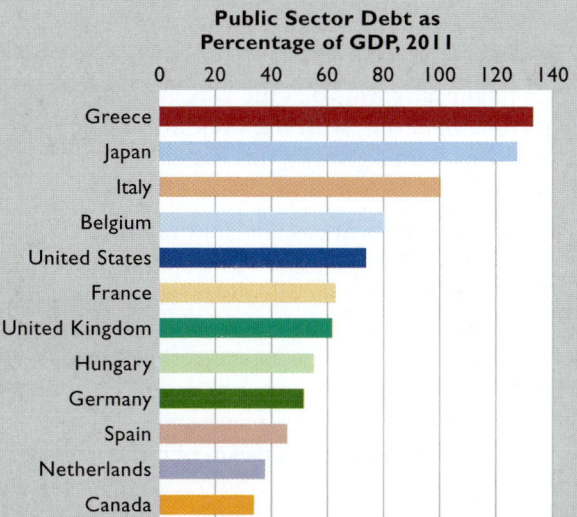

Source: Organization for Economic Cooperation and Development, OECD Economic Outlook, November 2011, **www.oecd.org.** Accessed April 22, 2012. These debt calculations encompass federal, state, and local debt, including the debt of government-owned enterprises (not just federal debt as in Figure 13.7).

Interest Charges

Many economists conclude that the primary burden of the debt is the annual interest charge accruing on the bonds sold to finance the debt. In 2011 interest on the total public debt was $230 billion. Although this amount is sizable in absolute terms, it was only 1.5 percent of GDP for 2011. So, the federal government had to collect taxes equal to 1.5 percent of GDP to service the total public debt. This percentage was down from 3.2 percent in 1990 and 2.3 percent in 2000, mainly because interest rates in 2011 were extremely low.

False Concerns?

You may wonder if the large public debt might bankrupt the United States or at least place a tremendous burden on your children and grandchildren. Fortunately, these are largely false concerns. People were wondering the same things 50 years ago!

Bankruptcy

The large U.S. public debt does not threaten to bankrupt the federal government, leaving it unable to meet its financial obligations. There are two main reasons: refinancing and taxation.

Refinancing   As long as the U.S. public debt is viewed by lenders as manageable and sustainable, the public debt is easily refinanced. As portions of the debt come due on maturing Treasury bills, notes, and bonds each month, the government does not cut expenditures or raise taxes to provide the funds required. Rather, it refinances the debt by selling new bonds and using the proceeds to pay holders of the maturing bonds. The new bonds are in strong demand because lenders can obtain a market-determined interest return with no risk of default by the federal government.

Of course, refinancing could become an issue with a high enough debt-to-GDP ratio. Some countries such as Greece have run into this problem. High and rising ratios in the United States might raise fears that the U.S. government might be unable to pay back loans as they come due. But, with the present U.S. debt-to-GDP ratio and the prospects of long-term economic growth, this is a false concern for the United States.

Taxation   The federal government has the constitutional authority to levy and collect taxes. A tax increase is a government option for gaining sufficient revenue to pay interest and principal on the public debt. Financially distressed private households and corporations cannot extract themselves from their financial difficulties by taxing the public. If their incomes or sales revenues fall short of their expenses, they can indeed go bankrupt. But the federal government does have the option to impose new taxes or increase existing tax rates if necessary to finance its debt. Such tax hikes may be politically unpopular and may weaken incentives to work and invest, but they *are* a means of raising funds to finance the debt.

Burdening Future Generations

In 2011 public debt per capita was $47,428. Was each child born in 2011 handed a $47,428 bill from the federal government? Not really. The public debt does not impose as much of a burden on future generations as commonly thought.

FIGURE 13.8

The investment demand curve and the crowding-out effect. If the investment demand curve (ID_1) is fixed, the increase in the interest rate from 6 percent to 10 percent caused by financing a large public debt will move the economy from a to b, crowding out $10 billion of private investment and decreasing the size of the capital stock inherited by future generations. However, if the public goods enabled by the debt improve the investment prospects of businesses, the private investment demand curve will shift rightward, as from ID_1 to ID_2. That shift may offset the crowding-out effect wholly or in part. In this case, it moves the economy from a to c.

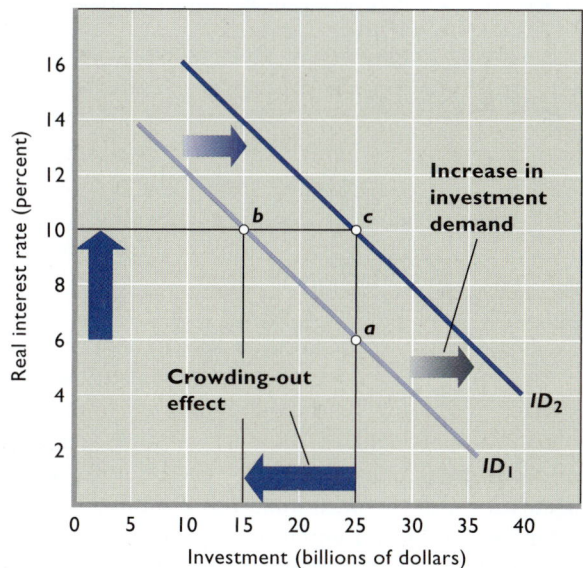

by the public debt is for public investment outlays (for example, highways, mass transit systems, and electric power facilities) and "human capital" (for example, investments in education, job training, and health). Like private expenditures on machinery and equipment, those **public investments** increase the economy's future production capacity. Because of the financing through debt, the stock of public capital passed on to future generations may be higher than otherwise. That greater stock of public capital may offset the diminished stock of private capital resulting from the crowding-out effect, leaving overall production capacity unimpaired.

So-called public-private complementarities are a second factor that could reduce the crowding-out effect. Some public and private investments are complementary. Thus, the public investment financed through debt could spur some private-sector investment by increasing its expected rate of return. For example, a federal building in a city may encourage private investment in the form of nearby office buildings, shops, and restaurants. Through its complementary effect, the spending on public capital may shift the private investment demand curve to the right, as from ID_1 to ID_2 in Figure 13.8. Even though the government borrowing boosts the interest rate from 6 percent to 10 percent, total private investment need not fall. In the case shown as the move from a to c in Figure 13.8, it remains at $25 billion. Of course, the increase in investment demand might be smaller than that shown. If it were smaller, the crowding-out effect would not be fully offset. But the point is that an increase in investment demand may counter the decline in investment that would otherwise result from the higher interest rate.

public investments
Government expenditures on public capital (such as highways, bridges, mass-transit systems, and electric power facilities) and on human capital (such as education, training, and health).

The Long-Run Fiscal Imbalance: Social Security

The most significant fiscal issue in the United States is not the budget deficit or the public debt but, rather, the long-term funding imbalance in the Social Security and Medicare programs. Over the next 75 years, benefits to Social Security and Medicare beneficiaries are expected to exceed program revenues by trillions of dollars. We will focus our attention on Social Security.

The Future Funding Shortfall

The Social Security program (excluding Medicare) has grown from less than one-half of 1 percent of U.S. GDP in 1950 to 4.9 percent of GDP in 2011. That percentage is projected to grow to 6.2 percent of GDP in 2035 and level off at around 6.0 percent of GDP by 2050. There is a severe long-run shortfall in Social Security funding because of growing payments to retiring baby boomers.

The $731 billion Social Security program is largely a "pay-as-you-go" plan, meaning that most of the current revenues from the 12.4 percent Social Security tax (the rate when the 2.9 percent Medicare tax is excluded) are paid out to current Social Security retirees. In anticipation of the large benefits owed to the baby boomers when they retire, however, the Social Security Administration has been placing an excess of current revenues over current payouts into the **Social Security trust fund,** consisting of U.S. Treasury securities. But the accumulation of money in the trust fund will be greatly inadequate for paying the retirement benefits promised to all future retirees.

Social Security trust fund
A federal fund that saves excessive Social Security tax revenues received in one year to meet Social Security benefit obligations that exceed Social Security tax revenues in some subsequent year.

In 2010, because of the weakened economy, payroll tax revenues fell $49 billion short of program expenditures. Interest earnings on trust fund assets were sufficient to overcome this deficit, so the trust fund continued to grow, but at a slower pace than during more robust economic times. In 2022, Social Security retirement revenues (including interest earnings) will fall below Social Security retirement benefits, and the system will begin dipping into the trust fund to make up the difference. The trust fund will be exhausted in 2036, after which the annual tax revenues will cover only 75 percent of the promised benefits. The federal government faces a several-trillion-dollar shortfall of long-run revenues for funding Social Security.

As shown in Figure 13.9, the problem is one of demographics. The percentage of the American population age 62 or older will rise substantially over the next several decades, with the greatest increases for people who are age 75 and older. High fertility rates during the "baby boom" (1946–1964), declining birthrates thereafter, and rising life expectancies have combined to produce an aging population. In the future, more people will be receiving Social Security benefits for longer periods, and fewer workers will pay for each person's benefits. The number of workers per Social Security beneficiary was 5:1 in 1960. Today it is 3:1, and by 2040 it will be only 2:1.

There is no easy way to restore long-run balance to Social Security funding. Either benefits must be reduced or revenues must be increased. The Social Security Administration concludes that bringing projected Social Security revenues and payments into balance over the next 75 years would require a 14 percent permanent reduction in Social Security benefits, a 17 percent permanent increase in tax revenues, or some combination of the two.[2]

---

[2]Social Security Board of Trustees, "Status of the Social Security and Medicare Programs: A Summary of the 2011 Annual Reports," **www.ssa.gov.**

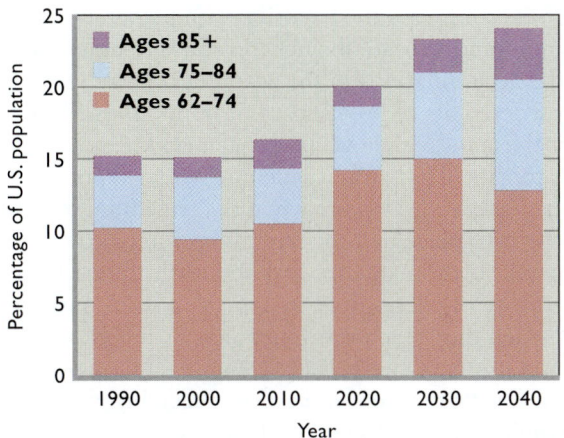

FIGURE 13.9
The aging U.S. population. The percentage of the U.S. population that is age 62 or older is rapidly rising. Depending on policy responses, this could result in a severe funding shortfall for Social Security in the decades ahead.

Photo Op Will Social Security Be There for You?

Social Security is largely a "pay-as-you-go" plan, in which current retirement benefits are paid out of current payroll taxes. But the number of retirees in the United States is growing faster than the number of workers, foretelling a future funding shortfall.

Policy Options

Several suggestions have been offered to help make Social Security financially sound. These ideas include increasing the retirement age, subjecting a larger portion of total earnings to the Social Security tax, and reducing benefits for wealthy retirees.

Other ideas are more novel. For example, one suggestion is to boost the trust fund by investing all or part of it in corporate stocks and bonds. The federal government would own the stock investments, and an appointed panel would oversee the direction of those investments. The presumed higher returns on the investments relative to the lower returns on U.S. securities would stretch out the life of the trust fund. Nevertheless, a substantial increase in the payroll tax would still be needed to cover the shortfalls after the trust fund is exhausted.

Another option is to increase the payroll tax immediately—perhaps by as much as 1.5 percentage points—and allocate the new revenues to individual accounts. Government would own the accumulations in the accounts, but individuals could direct their investments to a restricted list of broad stock or bond funds. When they retire, recipients could convert these individual account balances to annuities—securities paying monthly payments for life. That annuity income would supplement reduced monthly benefits from the pay-as-you-go system when the trust fund is exhausted.

A different route is to place half the payroll tax into accounts that individuals, not the government, would own, maintain, and bequeath. Individuals could invest these funds in bank certificates of deposit or in approved stock and bond funds and draw upon the accounts when they reach retirement age. A flat monthly benefit would supplement the accumulations in the private accounts. The personal security accounts would be phased in over time, so people now receiving or about to receive Social Security benefits would continue to receive benefits.

These general ideas do not exhaust the possible reforms, since the variations on each plan are nearly endless. Reaching consensus on Social Security reform will be difficult because every citizen has a direct economic stake in the outcome and little agreement is present among them on the proper magnitude of the benefits, how the program should be structured, and how we should pay for the projected funding shortfall. Nevertheless, Americans will eventually need to confront the problem of trillions of dollars of unfunded Social Security liabilities.

Summary

1. Fiscal policy consists of deliberate changes in government spending, taxes, or some combination of both to promote full employment, price-level stability, and economic growth. Fiscal policy requires increases in government spending, decreases in taxes, or both—a budget deficit—to increase aggregate demand and push an economy from a recession. Decreases in government spending, increases in taxes, or both—a budget surplus—are appropriate fiscal policy for dealing with demand-pull inflation.

2. Built-in stability arises from net tax revenues, which vary directly with the level of GDP. During recession, the federal budget automatically moves toward a stabilizing deficit; during expansion, the budget automatically moves toward an anti-inflationary surplus. Built-in stability lessens, but does not fully correct, undesired changes in real GDP.

3. Actual federal budget deficits can go up or down because of changes in GDP, changes in fiscal policy, or both. Deficits caused by changes in GDP are called cyclical deficits. The cyclically adjusted budget removes cyclical deficits from the budget and therefore measures the budget deficit or surplus (if either) that would occur if the economy operated at its full-employment output throughout the year. Changes in the cyclical budget deficit or surplus provide meaningful information as to whether the government's fiscal policy is expansionary, neutral, or contractionary. Changes in the actual budget deficit or surplus do not, since such deficits or surpluses can include cyclical deficits or surpluses.

4. In 2001 the Bush administration and Congress chose to reduce marginal tax rates and phase out the federal estate tax. A recession occurred in 2001, the stock market crashed, and federal spending for the war on terrorism rocketed. The federal budget swung from a surplus of $127 billion in 2001 to a deficit of $158 billion in 2002. In 2003 the Bush administration and Congress accelerated the tax reductions scheduled under the 2001 tax law and cut tax rates on capital gains and dividends. The purposes were to stimulate a sluggish economy. By 2007 the economy had reached its full-employment level of output.

5. The federal government responded to the deep recession of 2007–2009 by implementing highly expansionary fiscal policy. In 2008 the federal government passed a tax rebate program that sent $600 checks to qualified individuals. Later that year, it created a $700

billion emergency fund to keep key financial institutions from failing. These and other programs increased the cyclically adjusted budget deficit from −1.3 percent of potential GDP in 2007 to −2.9 percent in 2008. When the economy continued to plunge, the Obama administration and Congress enacted a massive $787 billion stimulus program to be implemented over 2 years. The cyclically adjusted budget deficit shot up from −2.9 percent of potential GDP in 2008 to −7.3 percent in 2009.

6. Certain problems complicate the enactment and implementation of fiscal policy. They include (a) timing problems associated with recognition, administrative, and operational lags; (b) the potential for misuse of fiscal policy for political rather than economic purposes; (c) the fact that state and local finances tend to be procyclical; (d) potential ineffectiveness if households expect future policy reversals; and (e) the possibility of fiscal policy crowding out private investment.

7. Most economists believe that fiscal policy can help move the economy in a desired direction but cannot reliably be used to fine-tune the economy to a position of price stability and full employment. Nevertheless, fiscal policy is a valuable backup tool for aiding monetary policy in fighting significant recession or inflation.

8. The public debt is the total accumulation of the government's deficits (minus surpluses) over time and consists of Treasury bills, Treasury notes, Treasury bonds, and U.S. savings bonds. In 2011 the U.S. public debt was $14.8 trillion, or $47,428 per person. The public (which here includes banks and state and local governments) holds 57 percent of that federal debt; the Federal Reserve and federal agencies hold the other 43 percent. Foreigners hold 32 percent of the federal debt. Interest payments as a percentage of GDP were about 1.5 percent in 2011. This is down from 3.2 percent in 1990.

9. The concern that a large public debt may bankrupt the government is a false worry because (a) the debt need only be refinanced rather than refunded and (b) the federal government has the power to increase taxes to make interest payments on the debt.

10. In general, the public debt is not a vehicle for shifting economic burdens to future generations. Americans inherit not only most of the public debt (a liability) but also most of the U.S. securities (an asset) that finance the debt.

11. More substantive problems associated with public debt include the following: (a) Payment of interest on the debt may increase income inequality. (b) Interest payments on the debt require higher taxes, which may impair incentives. (c) Paying interest or principal on the portion of the debt held by foreigners means a transfer of real output to abroad. (d) Government borrowing to refinance or pay interest on the debt may increase interest rates and crowd out private investment spending, leaving future generations with a smaller stock of capital than they would have otherwise.

12. The increase in investment in public capital that may result from debt financing may partly or wholly offset the crowding-out effect of the public debt on private investment. Also, the added public investment may stimulate private investment, where the two are complements.

13. The Social Security system has a significant long-run funding problem. The number of Social Security beneficiaries is projected to significantly rise in future years, and those retirees, on average, are expected to live longer than current retirees. Meanwhile, the number of workers paying Social Security taxes will increase relatively slowly. So a large gap between Social Security revenues and payments will eventually arise. This problem has created calls for various kinds of Social Security reform.

Terms and Concepts

fiscal policy

Council of Economic Advisers (CEA)

expansionary fiscal policy

budget deficit

contractionary fiscal policy

budget surplus

built-in stabilizer

cyclically adjusted budget

cyclical deficit

political business cycle

crowding-out effect

public debt

U.S. securities

external public debt

investment demand curve

public investments

Social Security trust fund

Questions

1. The federal government establishes its budget to decide what programs to provide and how to pay for them. How does fiscal policy differ from this ordinary fiscal activity of budgeting? **LO1**

2. What are government's fiscal policy options for moving the economy out of a recession? Speculate on which of these fiscal options might be favored by (a) a person who wants to preserve the size of government and (b) a person who thinks the public sector is too large. How does the "ratchet effect" affect anti-inflationary fiscal policy? **LO1**

3. Explain how built-in (or automatic) stabilizers work. What are the differences between proportional, progressive, and regressive tax systems as they relate to an economy's built-in stability? **LO2**

4. Briefly state and evaluate the problem of time lags in enacting and applying fiscal policy. How might "politics" complicate fiscal policy? How might expectations of a near-term policy reversal weaken fiscal policy based on changes in tax rates? What is the crowding-out effect, and why might it be relevant to fiscal policy? **LO1**

5. Define the cyclically adjusted budget, explain its significance, and state why it may differ from the actual budget. Suppose the full-employment, noninflationary level of real output is GDP_3 (not GDP_2) in the economy depicted in Figure 13.3. If the economy is operating at GDP_2, instead of GDP_3, what is the status of its cyclically adjusted budget? The status of its current fiscal policy? What change in fiscal policy would you recommend? How would you accomplish that in terms of the G and T lines in the figure? **LO3**

6. Use Figure 13.4 to explain why the deliberate increase of the cyclically adjusted budget deficit (resulting from the tax cut) will reduce the size of the actual budget deficit if the fiscal policy succeeds in pushing the economy to its full-employment output of GDP_1. In requesting a tax cut in the early 1960s, President Kennedy said, "It is a paradoxical truth that tax rates are too high today and tax revenues are too low and the soundest way to raise tax revenues in the long run is to cut tax rates now." Relate this quotation to your previous answer in this question. **LO3**

7. Why did the budget surpluses in 2000 and 2001 give way to a series of budget deficits beginning in 2002? Why did those deficits increase substantially beginning in 2008? **LO3**

8. Distinguish between the total U.S. debt and the debt held by the public. Why is the debt as a percentage of GDP more relevant than the total debt? Contrast the effects of paying off an internally held debt and paying off an externally held debt. **LO4**

9. True or false? If the statement is false, explain why: **LO4**
   a. An internally held public debt is like a debt of the left hand owed to the right hand.
   b. The Federal Reserve and federal government agencies hold more than half the public debt.
   c. As a percentage of GDP, the federal debt held by the public was smaller in 2011 than it was in 1990.
   d. As a percentage of GDP, the total U.S. public debt is the highest such debt among the world's advanced industrial nations.

10. Why might economists be quite concerned if the annual interest payments on the debt sharply increased as a percentage of GDP? **LO4**

11. Trace the cause-and-effect chain through which financing and refinancing of the public debt might affect real interest rates, private investment, the stock of capital, and economic growth. How might investment in public capital and complementarities between public capital and private capital alter the outcome of the cause-effect chain? **LO4**

12. What do economists mean when they refer to Social Security as a pay-as-you-go plan? What is the Social Security trust fund? What is the nature of the long-run fiscal imbalance in the Social Security retirement system? What are the broad options for fixing the long-run problem? **LO5**

Problems

1. Refer back to the table in Figure 12.7 in the previous chapter. Suppose that aggregate demand increases such that the amount of real output demanded rises by $7 billion at each price level. By what percentage will the price level increase? Will this inflation be demand-pull inflation or will it be cost-push inflation? If potential real GDP (that is, full-employment GDP) is $510 billion, what will be the size of the positive GDP gap after the change in aggregate demand? If government wants to use fiscal policy to counter the resulting inflation without changing tax rates, would it increase government spending or decrease it? **LO1**

2. Refer to the accompanying table for Waxwania: **LO2, LO3**

Government Expenditures, G	Tax Revenues, T	Real GDP
$160	$100	$500
160	120	600
160	140	700
160	160	800
160	180	900

a. What is the marginal tax rate in Waxwania? The average tax rate? Which of the following describes the tax system: proportional, progressive, regressive?

b. Suppose Waxwania is producing $600 of real GDP, whereas the potential real GDP (or full-employment real GDP) is $700. How large is its budget deficit? Its cyclically adjusted budget deficit? Its cyclically adjusted budget deficit as a percentage of potential real GDP? Is Waxwania's fiscal policy expansionary or is it contractionary?

3. Suppose that a country has no public debt in year 1 but experiences a budget deficit of $40 billion in year 2, a budget deficit of $20 billion in year 3, a budget surplus of $10 billion in year 4, and a budget deficit of $2 billion in year 5. What is the absolute size of its public debt in year 5? If its real GDP in year 5 is $104 billion, what is this country's public debt as a percentage of real GDP in year 5? **LO4**

4. Suppose that the investment demand curve in a certain economy is such that investment declines by $100 billion for every 1 percentage point increase in the real interest rate. Also, suppose that the investment demand curve shifts rightward by $150 billion at each real interest rate for every 1 percentage point increase in the expected rate of return from investment. If stimulus spending (an expansionary fiscal policy) by government increases the real interest rate by 2 percentage points, but also raises the expected rate of return on investment by 1 percentage point, how much investment, if any, will be crowded out? **LO4**

FURTHER TEST YOUR KNOWLEDGE AT
www.brue3e.com

At the text's Online Learning Center, **www.brue3e.com**, you will find one or more web-based questions that require information from the Internet to answer. We urge you to check them out, since they will familiarize you with websites that may be helpful in other courses and perhaps even in your career. The OLC also features multiple-choice quizzes that give instant feedback and provides other helpful ways to further test your knowledge of the chapter.

CHAPTER FOURTEEN

Money, Banking, and Financial Institutions

After reading this chapter, you should be able to:

1. Identify and explain the functions of money and the components of the U.S. money supply.

2. Describe what "backs" the money supply, making us willing to accept it as payment.

3. Discuss the makeup of the Federal Reserve and the U.S. banking system.

4. Identify the functions and responsibilities of the Federal Reserve.

5. Identify and explain the main factors that contributed to the financial crisis of 2007–2008.

6. Discuss the actions of the U.S. Treasury that helped keep the banking and financial crisis of 2007–2008 from worsening.

7. Identify the main subsets of the financial services industry in the United States and provide examples of some firms in each category.

8. Describe how banks create money in a "fractional reserve" banking system.

Money is a fascinating aspect of the economy:

> Money bewitches people. They fret for it, and they sweat for it. They devise most ingenious ways to get it, and most ingenious ways to get rid of it. Money is the only commodity that is good for nothing but to be gotten rid of. It will not feed you, clothe you, shelter you, or amuse you unless you spend it or invest it. It imparts value only in parting. People will do almost anything for money, and money will do almost anything for people. Money is a captivating, circulating, masquerading puzzle.[1]

In this chapter and the next we want to unmask the critical role of money and the monetary system in the economy. When the monetary system is working properly, it provides the lifeblood of the circular flows of income and expenditure. A well-operating monetary system helps the economy achieve both full employment and the efficient use of resources. A malfunctioning monetary system distorts the allocation of resources and creates severe fluctuations in the economy's levels of output, employment, and prices.

---

[1] Federal Reserve Bank of Philadelphia, "Creeping Inflation," *Business Review*, August 1957, p. 3. Used with permission.

The Functions of Money

There is an old saying that "money *is* what money *does.*" In a conceptual sense, anything that performs the functions of money *is* money. Here are those functions:

- *Medium of exchange* First and foremost, money is a **medium of exchange** that is usable for buying and selling goods and services. A bakery worker does not want to be paid 200 bagels per week. Nor does the bakery owner want to receive, say, halibut in exchange for bagels. Money, however, is readily acceptable as payment. As we saw in Chapter 2, money is a social invention with which resource suppliers and producers can be paid and that can be used to buy any of the full range of items available in the marketplace. As a medium of exchange, money allows society to escape the complications of barter. And because it provides a convenient way of exchanging goods, money enables society to gain the advantages of geographic and human specialization.

medium of exchange
An item that sellers generally accept and buyers generally use to pay for goods and services.

- *Unit of account* Money is also a **unit of account.** Society uses monetary units—dollars, in the United States—as a yardstick for measuring the relative worth of a wide variety of goods, services, and resources. Just as we measure distance in miles or kilometers, we gauge the value of goods in dollars. With money as an acceptable unit of account, the price of each item need be stated only in terms of the monetary unit. We need not state the price of cows in terms of corn, crayons, and cranberries. Money aids rational decision making by enabling buyers and sellers to easily compare the prices of various goods, services, and resources. It also permits us to define debt obligations, determine taxes owed, and calculate the nation's GDP.

unit of account
A standard measurement unit in terms of which prices can be stated and the relative value of goods and services compared.

- *Store of value* Money also serves as a **store of value** that allows people to transfer purchasing power from the present to the future. People normally do not spend all their incomes on the day they receive them. In order to buy things later, they store some of their wealth as money. The money you place in a safe or a checking account will still be available to you a few weeks or months from now. When inflation is nonexistent or mild, holding money is a relatively risk-free way to store wealth for later use.

store of value
An asset set aside to purchase items in the future.

People can, of course, choose to hold some or all of their wealth in a wide variety of assets besides money. These include real estate, stocks, bonds, precious metals such as gold, and even collectible items like fine art or comic books. But a key advantage that money has over all other assets is that it has the most *liquidity*, or spendability.

An asset's **liquidity** is the ease with which it can be converted quickly into the most widely accepted and easily spent form of money, cash, with little or no loss of purchasing power. The more liquid an asset is, the more quickly it can be converted into cash and used for either purchases of goods and services or purchases of other assets.

liquidity
The ease with which an asset can be converted into cash.

Levels of liquidity vary radically. By definition, cash is perfectly liquid. By contrast, a house is highly illiquid for two reasons. First, it may take several months before a willing buyer can be found and a sale negotiated so that its value can be converted into cash. Second, there is a loss of purchasing power when the house is sold because numerous fees have to be paid to real estate agents and other individuals in order to complete the sale.

As we are about to discuss, our economy uses several different types of money including cash, coins, checking account deposits, savings account deposits, and even more exotic things like deposits in money market mutual funds. As we describe the various forms of money in detail, take the time to compare their relative levels of liquidity—both with each other and with other assets like stocks, bonds, and real estate. Cash is perfectly liquid. Other forms of money are highly liquid, but less liquid than cash.

The Components of the Money Supply

Money is a "stock" of some item or group of items (unlike income, for example, which is a "flow"). Societies have used many items as money, including whales' teeth, circular stones, elephant-tail bristles, gold coins, furs, and pieces of paper. Anything that is widely accepted as a medium of exchange can serve as money. In the United States, currency is not the only form of money. As you will see, certain debts of government and financial institutions are also used as money.

Money Definition: M1

The narrowest definition of the U.S. money supply is called **M1.** It consists of

M1
The most narrowly defined money supply, equal to currency (outside banks) plus the checkable deposits of commercial banks and thrift institutions.

- Currency (coins and paper money) in the hands of the nonbank public.
- All checkable deposits (all deposits in commercial banks and "thrift" or savings institutions on which checks of any size can be drawn).[2]

Government and government agencies supply coins and paper money. Commercial banks and savings institutions provide checkable deposits.

Federal Reserve Notes
Paper bills issued by the Federal Reserve Banks.

Currency: Coins + Paper Money   The currency of the United States consists of metal coins and paper money. The coins are issued by the U.S. Treasury while the paper money consists of **Federal Reserve Notes** issued by the Federal Reserve System (the U.S. central bank). Coins are minted by the U.S. Mint while the paper money is printed by the Bureau of Engraving and Printing. Both the U.S. Mint and the Bureau of Engraving and Printing are part of the U.S. Department of the Treasury.

token money
Currency that has a face value greater than the materials used to produce it.

As with the currencies of other countries, the currency of the United States is **token money**. This means that the face value of any piece of currency is unrelated to its *intrinsic value*—the value of the physical material (metal or paper and ink) out of which that currency is constructed. Governments make sure that face values exceed intrinsic values in order to discourage people from destroying coins and bills in order to resell the material that they are made out of. For instance, if 50-cent pieces each contained 75 cents' worth of metal, then it would be profitable to melt them down and sell the metal. Fifty-cent pieces would disappear from circulation very quickly!

Figure 14.1 shows that coins and paper money (currency) constitute half of the U.S. economy's *M*1 money supply.

checkable deposits
Deposits in banks or thrifts against which checks may be written.

Checkable Deposits   The safety and convenience of checks has made checkable deposits a large component of the *M*1 money supply. You would not think of stuffing $4896 in bills in an envelope and dropping it in a mailbox to pay a debt. But writing and mailing a check for a large sum is commonplace. The person cashing a check must endorse it (sign it on the reverse side); the writer of the check subsequently receives a record of the cashed check as a receipt attesting to the fulfillment of the obligation. Similarly, because the writing of a check requires a signature, the theft or loss of your checkbook is not nearly as calamitous as losing an identical amount of currency. Finally, it is more convenient to write a check than to transport and count out a large sum of currency. For all these reasons, **checkable deposits** (checkbook money) are a

---

[2]In order to avoid a maze of details in the ensuing discussion, we do not discuss several of the quantitatively less significant components of the definitions of money. For example, traveler's checks are included in the *M*1 money supply. The statistical appendix of any recent *Federal Reserve Bulletin* provides more comprehensive definitions.

FIGURE 14.1

Components of money supply M1 and money supply M2, in the United States. *M1* is a narrow definition of the money supply that includes currency (in circulation) and checkable deposits. *M2* is a broader definition that includes *M1* along with several other relatively liquid account balances.
* These categories include other, quantitatively smaller components such as traveler's checks.
Source: Federal Reserve System, **www.federalreserve.gov**. Data are for March 2012.

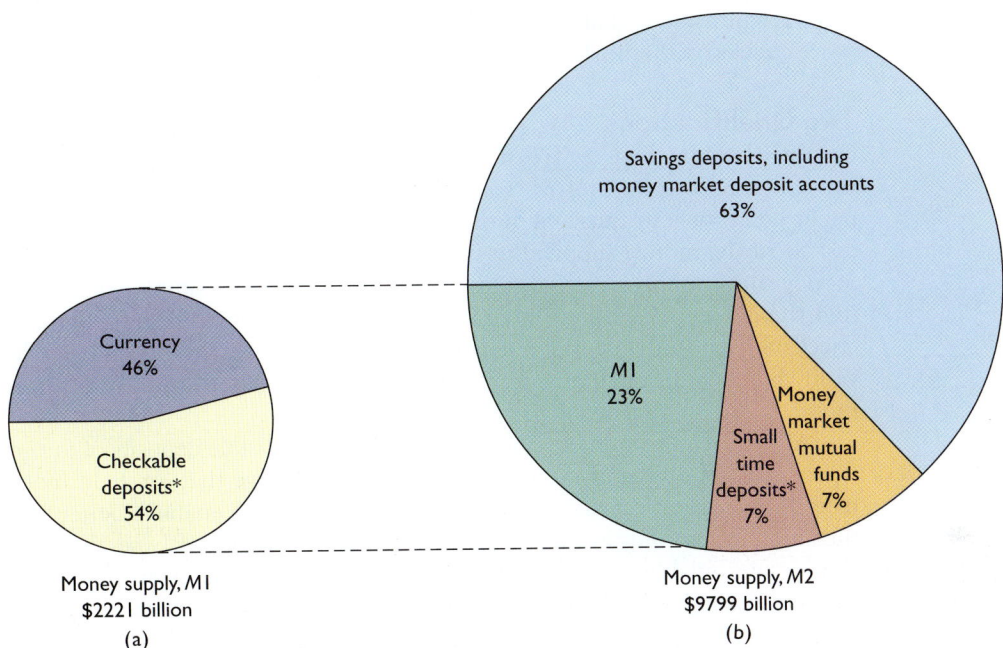

Money supply, *M1*
$2221 billion
(a)

Money supply, *M2*
$9799 billion
(b)

large component of the stock of money in the United States. About half of *M1* is in the form of checkable deposits, on which checks can be drawn.

It might seem strange that checking account balances are regarded as part of the money supply. But the reason is clear: Checks are nothing more than a way to transfer the ownership of deposits in banks and other financial institutions and are generally acceptable as a medium of exchange. Although checks are less generally accepted than currency for small purchases, for major purchases most sellers willingly accept checks as payment. Moreover, people can convert checkable deposits into paper money and coins on demand; checks drawn on those deposits are thus the equivalent of currency.

To summarize:

$$\text{Money, } M1 = \text{Curency} + \text{Checkable Deposits}$$

Institutions That Offer Checkable Deposits

In the United States, a variety of financial institutions allow customers to write checks in any amount on the funds they have deposited. **Commercial banks** are the primary depository institutions. They accept the deposits of households and businesses, keep the money safe until it is demanded via checks, and in the meantime use it to make available a wide variety of loans. Commercial bank loans provide short-term financial capital to businesses, and they finance consumer purchases of automobiles and other durable goods.

Savings and loan associations (S&Ls), mutual savings banks, and credit unions supplement the commercial banks and are known collectively as savings or **thrift institutions,**

commercial banks
Firms that engage in the business of banking (accepting deposits, offering checking accounts, and making loans).

thrift institutions
Savings and loan associations, mutual savings banks, or credit unions that offer savings and checking accounts.

or simply "thrifts." *Savings and loan associations* and *mutual savings banks* accept the deposits of households and businesses and then use the funds to finance housing mortgages and to provide other loans. *Credit unions* accept deposits from and lend to "members," who usually are a group of people who work for the same company.

The checkable deposits of banks and thrifts are known variously as demand deposits, NOW (negotiable order of withdrawal) accounts, ATS (automatic transfer service) accounts, and share draft accounts. Their commonality is that depositors can write checks on them whenever, and in whatever amount, they choose.

Two Qualifications   We must qualify our discussion in two important ways. First, currency held by the U.S. Treasury, the Federal Reserve Banks, commercial banks, and thrift institutions is *excluded* from M1 and other measures of the money supply. A paper dollar or four quarters in the billfold of, say, Emma Buck obviously constitutes just $1 of the money supply. But if we counted currency held by banks as part of the money supply, the same $1 would count for $2 of money supply when Emma deposited the currency into her checkable deposit in her bank. It would count for $1 of checkable deposit owned by Buck and also $1 of currency in the bank's cash drawer or vault. By excluding currency held by banks when determining the total supply of money, we avoid this problem of double counting.

Also *excluded* from the money supply are any checkable deposits of the government (specifically, the U.S. Treasury) or the Federal Reserve that are held by commercial banks or thrift institutions. This exclusion is designed to enable a better assessment of the amount of money available *to the private sector* for potential spending. The amount of money available to households and businesses is of keen interest to the Federal Reserve in conducting its monetary policy (a topic we cover in the next chapter).

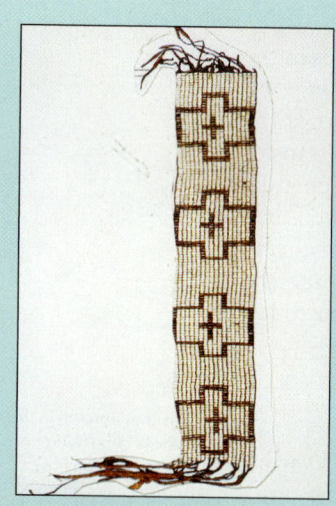
© Getty Images

© Getty Images/Stockbyte

© Getty Images

Photo Op Money: Then and Now

Items such as wampum belts were once used as money. Today, bills and coins, along with checkable deposits, constitute the *M1* money supply.

Money Definition: *M2*

A second and broader definition of money includes *M1* plus several near-monies. **Near-monies** are certain highly liquid financial assets that do not function directly or fully as a medium of exchange but can be readily converted into currency or checkable deposits. Three categories of near-monies owned by individuals are included in the *M2* definition of money:

- *Savings deposits, including money market deposit accounts* A depositor can withdraw funds from an interest-earning **savings account** at a bank or thrift or simply request that the funds be transferred to a checkable account. A person can also withdraw funds from a **money market deposit account (MMDA),** which is an interest-earning account containing interest-earning short-term securities. MMDAs, however, have a minimum-balance requirement and a limit on how often a person can withdraw funds.

- *Small-denominated (less than $100,000) time deposits* Funds from **time deposits** become available at their maturity. For example, a person can convert a 6-month time deposit ("certificate of deposit" or simply "CD") to currency without penalty 6 months or more after it has been deposited. In return for this withdrawal limitation, the financial institution pays a higher interest rate on such deposits than it does on its MMDAs. Also, a person can "cash in" a CD before its maturity but must pay a severe penalty.

- *Money market mutual funds* By making a telephone call, using the Internet, or writing a check for $500 or more, a depositor can redeem shares in a **money market mutual fund (MMMF)** offered by a mutual fund company. Such companies combine the funds of individual shareholders to buy interest-bearing short-term credit instruments such as certificates of deposit and U.S. government securities. Then they can offer interest on the MMMF accounts of the shareholders (depositors) who jointly own those financial assets.

All three categories of near-monies imply substantial liquidity. In summary, *M2* includes the immediate medium-of-exchange items (currency and checkable deposits) that constitute *M1* plus certain near-monies that can be easily converted into currency and checkable deposits. In Figure 14.1 we see that the addition of all these items yields an *M2* money supply that is about five times larger than the narrower *M1* money supply. Thus, to summarize in equation form,

$$\text{Money, } M2 = M1 + \text{savings deposits, including MMDAs} + \text{small-denominated}$$
$$\text{(less than \$100,000) time deposits} + \text{MMMFs}$$

Actually, there is an entire spectrum of assets that vary slightly in terms of their liquidity or "moneyness" that are not included in *M1* or *M2*. Because the simple *M1* definition includes only items directly and immediately usable as a medium of exchange, it is often cited in discussions of the money supply. But, for some purposes, economists prefer the broader *M2* definition. For example, *M2* is used as one of the 10 trend variables in the index of leading indicators (an economic forecasting tool). Still broader definitions of money are so inclusive that they have limited usefulness.

We will use the narrow *M1* definition of the money supply in our discussion and analysis, unless stated otherwise. The important principles we will develop relating to *M1* also apply to *M2* because *M1* is included in *M2*.

---

near-monies
Financial assets that do not directly serve as a medium of exchange but readily can be converted into narrowly defined money (currency + checkable deposits).

M2
A more broadly defined money supply, equal to *M1* plus noncheckable savings accounts (including money market deposit accounts), time deposits of less than $100,000, and individual money market mutual fund balances.

savings account
An interest-earning account (at a bank or thrift) from which funds normally can be withdrawn at any time.

money market deposit account (MMDA)
An interest-earning account (at a bank or thrift) consisting of short-term securities and on which a limited number of checks can be written each year.

time deposits
Interest-earning deposits (at a bank or thrift) such as certificates of deposit (CDs) that depositors can withdraw without penalty after the end of a specified period.

money market mutual fund (MMMF)
An interest-earning account at an investment company, which pools the funds of depositors to purchase short-term securities.

What "Backs" the Money Supply?

The money supply in the United States essentially is "backed" (guaranteed) by government's ability to keep the value of money relatively stable. Nothing more! Paper currency and checkable deposits have no intrinsic value. A $5 bill is just an inscribed piece of paper. A checkable deposit is merely a bookkeeping entry. And coins, we know, have less intrinsic value than their face value. Nor will government redeem the paper money you hold for anything tangible, such as gold.

To many people, the fact that the government does not back the currency with anything tangible seems implausible and insecure. But the decision not to back the currency with anything tangible was made for a very good reason. If the government backed the currency with something tangible like gold, then the supply of money would vary with how much gold was available. By not backing the currency, the government avoids this constraint and indeed receives a key freedom—the ability to provide as much or as little money as needed to maintain the value of money and to best suit the economic needs of the country. In effect, by choosing not to back the currency, the government has chosen to give itself the ability to freely "manage" the nation's money supply. Its monetary authorities attempt to provide the amount of money needed for the particular volume of business activity that will promote full employment, price-level stability, and economic growth.

Nearly all today's economists agree that managing the money supply is more sensible than linking it to gold or to some other commodity whose supply might change arbitrarily and capriciously. For instance, if we used gold to back the money supply so that gold was redeemable for money, and *vice versa*, then a large increase in the nation's gold stock as the result of a new gold discovery might increase the money supply too rapidly and thereby trigger rapid inflation. Or a long-lasting decline in gold production might reduce the money supply to the point where recession and unemployment resulted.

In short, people cannot convert paper money into a fixed amount of gold or any other precious commodity. Money is exchangeable only for paper money. If you ask the government to redeem $5 of your paper money, it will swap one paper $5 bill for another bearing a different serial number. That is all you can get. Similarly, checkable deposits can be redeemed not for gold but only for paper money, which, as we have just seen, the government will not redeem for anything tangible.

Value of Money

So why are currency and checkable deposits money, whereas, say, Monopoly (the game) money is not? What gives a $20 bill or a $100 checking account entry its value? The answer to these questions has three parts.

Acceptability   Currency and checkable deposits are money because people accept them as money. By virtue of long-standing business practice, currency and checkable deposits perform the basic function of money: They are acceptable as a medium of exchange. We accept paper money in exchange because we are confident it will be exchangeable for real goods, services, and resources when we spend it.

legal tender
A legal designation of a nation's official currency (bills and coins).

Legal Tender   Our confidence in the acceptability of paper money undoubtedly is strengthened because government has designated currency as **legal tender.** Specifically, each bill contains the statement "This note is legal tender for all debts, public and private." That means paper money is a valid and legal means of payment of any debt that was contracted in dollars. (But private firms and government are not mandated to accept cash. It is not illegal for them to specify payment in noncash forms such as checks, cashier's checks, money orders, or credit cards.)

The general acceptance of paper currency as money is more important than the government's decree that money is legal tender, however. The government has never decreed checks to be legal tender, and yet they serve as such in many of the economy's exchanges of goods, services, and resources. But it is true that government agencies—the Federal Deposit Insurance Corporation (FDIC) and the National Credit Union Administration (NCUA)—insure individual deposits of up to $250,000 at commercial banks and thrifts. That fact enhances our willingness to store money in checkable accounts and write checks on those accounts to buy goods, services, and resources.

Illustrating
the Idea

Are Credit Cards Money?

You may wonder why we have ignored credit cards such as Visa and MasterCard in our discussion of the money supply. After all, credit cards are a convenient way to buy things and account for about 25 percent of the dollar value of all transactions in the United States. The answer is that a credit card is not money. Rather, it is a convenient means of obtaining a short-term loan from the financial institution that issued the card.

What happens when you purchase an item with a credit card? The bank that issued the card will reimburse the seller by making a money payment, charging the establishment a transaction fee, and later you will reimburse the bank for its loan to you by also making a money payment. Rather than reduce your cash or checking account with each purchase, you bunch your payments once a month. You may have to pay an annual fee for the services provided, and if you pay the bank in installments, you will pay a sizable interest charge on the loan. Credit cards are merely a means of deferring or postponing payment for a short period. Your checking account balance used to pay your monthly credit card bill *is* money; the credit card is *not* money.[*]

Although credit cards are not money, they allow individuals and businesses to "economize" in the use of money. Credit cards enable people to hold less currency in their billfolds and have smaller checkable deposit balances (prior to the due date for paying the credit card bill) in their bank accounts. Credit cards also help people coordinate the timing of their expenditures with their receipt of income.

Question:
If credit cards are not money, why are they so popular?

[*]A bank debit card, however, is very similar to a blank check in your checkbook. Unlike a purchase with a credit card, a purchase with a debit card creates a direct "debit" (a subtraction) from your checking account balance. That checking account balance *is* money—it is part of *M1*.

Relative Scarcity   The value of money, like the economic value of anything else, depends on its supply and demand. Money derives its value from its scarcity relative to its utility (its want-satisfying power). The utility of money lies in its capacity to be exchanged for goods and services, now or in the future. The economy's demand for money thus depends on the total dollar volume of transactions in any period plus the amount of money individuals and businesses want to hold for future transactions. With a reasonably constant demand for money, the supply of money provided by the monetary authorities will determine the value or "purchasing power" of the monetary unit (dollar, yen, peso, or whatever).

Money and Prices

The purchasing power of money is the amount of goods and services a unit of money will buy. When money rapidly loses its purchasing power, it loses its role as money.

The Purchasing Power of the Dollar   The amount a dollar will buy varies inversely with the price level, meaning a reciprocal relationship exists between the general price level and the purchasing power of the dollar. When the Consumer Price Index or "cost-of-living" index goes up, the purchasing power of the dollar goes down, and vice versa. Higher prices lower the purchasing power of the dollar because more dollars are needed to buy a particular amount of goods, services, or resources. For example, if the price level doubles, the purchasing power of the dollar declines by one-half, or 50 percent.

Conversely, lower prices increase the purchasing power of the dollar because fewer dollars are needed to obtain a specific quantity of goods and services. If the price level falls by, say, one-half, or 50 percent, the purchasing power of the dollar doubles.

Inflation and Acceptability   In Chapter 11 we noted situations in which a nation's currency became worthless and unacceptable in exchange. These instances of runaway inflation, or *hyperinflation*, happened when the government issued so many pieces of paper currency that the purchasing power of each of those units of money was almost totally undermined. The infamous post–World War I hyperinflation in Germany is an example. In December 1919 there were about 50 billion marks in circulation. Four years later there were 496,585,345,900 billion marks in circulation! The result? The German mark in 1923 was worth an infinitesimal fraction of its 1919 value.[3]

Runaway inflation may significantly depreciate the purchasing power of money between the time it is received and the time it is spent. Rapid declines in the purchasing power of a currency may cause it to cease being used as a medium of exchange. Businesses and households may refuse to accept paper money in exchange because they do not want to bear the loss in its value that will occur while it is in their possession. (All this despite the fact that the government says that paper currency is legal tender!) Without an acceptable domestic medium of exchange, the economy may simply revert to barter. Alternatively, more internally stable currencies such as the U.S. dollar may come into widespread use.

Similarly, people will use money as a store of value only as long as there is no sizable deterioration in the value of that money because of inflation. And an economy can effectively employ money as a unit of account only when its purchasing power is relatively stable. A monetary yardstick that no longer measures a yard (in terms of purchasing power) does not permit buyers and sellers to establish the terms of trade clearly. When the value of the dollar is declining rapidly, sellers do not know what to charge and buyers do not know what to pay.

---

[3]Frank G. Graham, *Exchange, Prices and Production in Hyperinflation Germany, 1920–1923* (Princeton, N.J.: Princeton University Press, 1930), p. 13.

The Federal Reserve and the Banking System

A key element of the U.S. banking system is the **Federal Reserve System** (the "Fed"). As shown in Figure 14.2, a Board of Governors directs the activities of 12 Federal Reserve Banks, which in turn control the lending activity of the nation's banks and thrift institutions. The Fed's major goal is to control the money supply. But since checkable deposits in banks are such a large part of the money supply, an important part of its duties involves assuring the stability of the banking system.

Board of Governors

The central authority of the U.S. money and banking system is the **Board of Governors** of the Federal Reserve System. The U.S. president, with the confirmation of the Senate, appoints the seven Board members. Terms are 14 years and staggered so that one member is replaced every 2 years. In addition, new members are appointed when resignations occur. The president selects the chairperson and vice-chairperson of the Board from among the members. Those officers serve 4-year terms and can be reappointed to new 4-year terms by the president. The long-term appointments provide the Board with continuity, experienced membership, and independence from political pressures that could result in inflation.

The 12 Federal Reserve Banks

The 12 **Federal Reserve Banks,** which blend private and public control, collectively serve as the nation's "central bank." These banks also serve as bankers' banks.

Central Banks   Most nations have a single central bank—for example, Britain's Bank of England or Japan's Bank of Japan. The United States' central bank consists of 12 banks whose policies are coordinated by the Fed's Board of Governors.

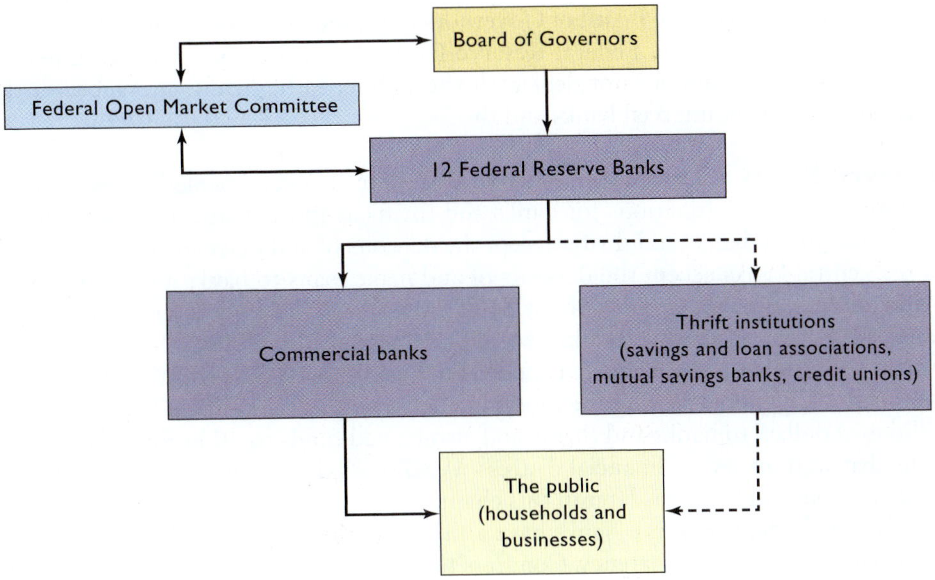

Federal Reserve System
A central component of the U.S. banking system, consisting of the Board of Governors of the Federal Reserve and 12 regional Federal Reserve Banks.

Board of Governors
The seven-member group that supervises and controls the money and banking system of the United States; the Board of Governors of the Federal Reserve System; the Federal Reserve Board.

Federal Reserve Banks
The 12 banks chartered by the U.S. government to control the money supply and perform other functions. (See central bank, quasi-public bank, and bankers' bank.)

FIGURE 14.2
The framework of the Federal Reserve System and its relationship to the nonbank public. The Board of Governors makes the basic policy decisions that provide monetary control of the U.S. money and banking system. The 12 Federal Reserve Banks implement these decisions. Both the Board of Governors and the 12 Federal Reserve Banks are aided by the Federal Open Market Committee (FOMC).

FIGURE 14.3
The 12 Federal Reserve Districts. The Federal Reserve System divides the United States into 12 districts, each having one central bank and in some instances one or more branches of the central bank. Hawaii and Alaska are included in the 12th district.

Source: *Federal Reserve Bulletin*, **www.federalreserve. gov/pubs/bulletin.**

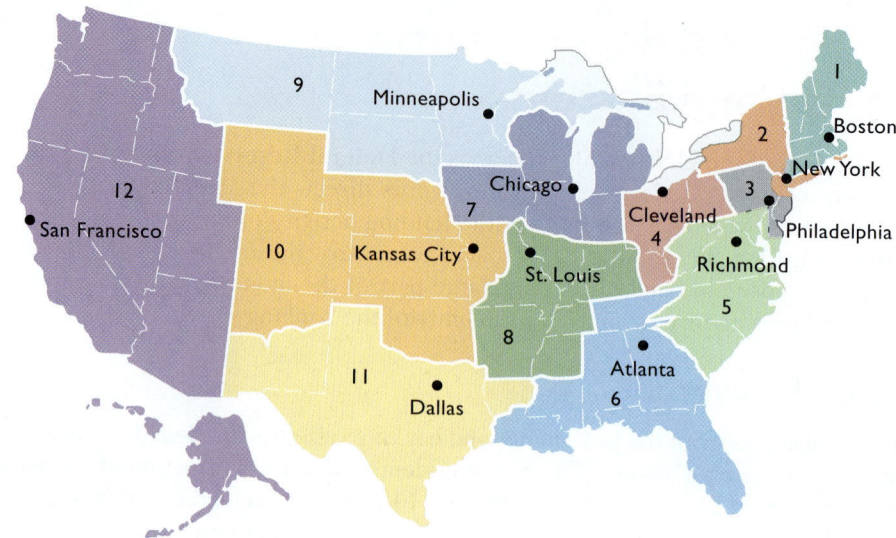

The 12 Federal Reserve Banks accommodate the geographic size and economic diversity of the United States and the nation's large number of commercial banks and thrifts.

Figure 14.3 locates the 12 Federal Reserve Banks and indicates the district that each serves. These banks implement the basic policy of the Board of Governors.

Quasi-Public Banks The 12 Federal Reserve Banks are quasi-public banks, which blend private ownership and public control. Each Federal Reserve Bank is owned by the private commercial banks in its district. (Federally chartered commercial banks are required to purchase shares of stock in the Federal Reserve Bank in their district.) But the Board of Governors is an independent, quasi-government body that sets the basic policies that the Federal Reserve Banks pursue.

Despite their private ownership, the Federal Reserve Banks are in practice public institutions. Unlike private firms, they are not motivated by profit. The policies they follow are designed by the Board of Governors to promote the well-being of the economy as a whole. Also, the Federal Reserve Banks do not compete with commercial banks. In general, they do not deal with the public; rather, they interact with the government and commercial banks and thrifts.

Bankers' Banks The Federal Reserve Banks are "bankers' banks." They perform essentially the same functions for banks and thrifts as those institutions perform for the public. Just as banks and thrifts accept the deposits of and make loans to the public, so the central banks accept the deposits of and make loans to banks and thrifts. Normally, these loans average only about $150 million a day. But in emergency circumstances the Federal Reserve Banks become the "lender of last resort" to the banking system and can lend out as much as needed to ensure that banks and thrifts can meet their cash obligations. During the mortgage debt crisis of 2007–2008, the Fed loaned billions of dollars to banks and thrifts and also loaned funds to other financial institutions that were in severe financial distress. We discuss that crisis and the Fed's emergency response to the crisis later in this chapter.

But the Federal Reserve Banks have a third function, which banks and thrifts do not perform: They issue currency. Congress has authorized the Federal Reserve Banks to put into circulation Federal Reserve Notes, which constitute the economy's paper money supply.

FOMC

The **Federal Open Market Committee (FOMC)** aids the Board of Governors in conducting monetary policy. The FOMC is made up of 12 individuals:

- The seven members of the Board of Governors.
- The president of the New York Federal Reserve Bank.
- Four of the remaining presidents of Federal Reserve Banks on a 1-year rotating basis.

The FOMC meets regularly to direct the purchase and sale of government securities (bills, notes, bonds) in the open market in which such securities are bought and sold on a daily basis. We will find in Chapter 15 that the purpose of these aptly named *open-market operations* is to control the nation's money supply and influence interest rates. The Federal Reserve Bank in New York City conducts most of the Fed's open-market operations.

Federal Open Market Committee (FOMC)
The 12-member Federal Reserve group that determines the purchase and sale policies of the Federal Reserve Banks in the market for U.S. government securities.

Commercial Banks and Thrifts

There are about 6200 commercial banks. Roughly three-fourths are *state banks*, which are chartered (authorized) by individual states to operate within those states. The other one-fourth of all banks are *national banks*, chartered by the federal government to operate nationally. Some of the U.S. national banks are very large, ranking among the world's largest financial institutions (see Global Snapshot 14.1). The 8700 thrift institutions—the vast majority of which are credit unions—are regulated by agencies separate and apart from the Board of Governors and the Federal Reserve Banks. For example, the operations of savings and loan associations are regulated and monitored by the Treasury Department's Office of Thrift Supervision. But the thrifts *are* subject to monetary control by the Federal Reserve System. In particular, like the banks, thrifts are required to keep a certain percentage of their checkable deposits as reserves. In Figure 14.2 we use dashed arrows to indicate that the thrift institutions are partially subject to the control of the Board of Governors and the central banks. Decisions concerning monetary policy affect the thrifts along with the commercial banks.

Fed Functions and Responsibilities

The Fed performs several functions, some of which we have already mentioned. They and other functions are worth summarizing:

- *Issuing currency* The Federal Reserve Banks issue Federal Reserve Notes, the paper currency used in the U.S. monetary system. (The Federal Reserve Bank that issued a particular bill is identified in black in the upper left of the front of the newly designed bills. "A1," for example, identifies the Boston bank; "B2," the New York bank; and so on.)
- *Setting reserve requirements and holding reserves* The Fed sets legal reserve ratios, which are the fractions of checking account balances that banks must maintain as currency reserves. The central banks accept as deposits from the banks and thrifts any portion of their mandated reserves not held as vault cash.
- *Lending money to financial institutions* The Fed routinely lends money to banks and thrifts. Additionally, in times of national emergency, the Fed serves as a *lender of last resort* not only to banks and thrifts but also to other critical firms in the financial industry.

The World's 12 Largest Financial Institutions

The world's 12 largest private sector financial institutions are headquartered mainly in Europe, China, Japan, and the United States (2012 data).

Assets (billions of U.S. dollars)

Institution	Assets
Deutsche Bank (Germany)	2,809
HSBC Holdings (U.K.)	2,550
BNP Paris (France)	2,539
Mitsubishi UFJ (Japan)	2,479
Barclays (U.K.)	2,425
Royal Bank of Scotland (U.K.)	2,336
JP Morgan Chase (U.S.)	2,266
Crédit Agricole (France)	2,238
Bank of America (U.S.)	2,129
ICBC (China)	2,039
Citigroup (U.S.)	1,974
Mizuho Financial (Japan)	1,934

Source: Forbes Global 2000, www.forbes.com. Used with permission of Forbes Media LLC © 2012.

- **Providing for check collection** The Fed provides the banking system with a means for collecting checks. If Sue writes a check on her Miami bank or thrift to Joe, who deposits it in his Dallas bank or thrift, how does the Dallas bank collect the money represented by the check drawn against the Miami bank? Answer: The Fed handles it in 2 or 3 days by adjusting the reserves (deposits) of the two banks.

- **Acting as fiscal agent** The Fed acts as the fiscal agent (provider of financial services) for the federal government. The government collects huge sums through taxation, spends equally large amounts, and sells and redeems bonds. To carry out these activities, the government uses the Fed's facilities as its bank.

- **Supervising banks** The Fed supervises the operations of banks. It makes periodic examinations to assess bank profitability, to ascertain that banks perform in accordance with the many regulations to which they are subject, and to uncover questionable practices or fraud.[4]

- **Controlling the money supply** Finally, the major task of the Fed is to manage the nation's money supply, and thus indirectly set interest rates, according to the needs of the economy. This involves making an amount of money available that is consistent with high and rising levels of output and employment *and* a relatively constant price level. While all the other functions of the Fed are routine activities or have a service nature, managing the nation's money supply requires making basic, but unique, policy decisions. (We discuss those decisions in detail in Chapter 15.)

---

[4]The Fed is not alone in this task of supervision. The individual states supervise the banks that they charter. The Comptroller of the Currency supervises the national banks, and the Office of Thrift Supervision supervises the thrifts. Also, the Federal Deposit Insurance Corporation supervises the banks and thrifts whose deposits it insures.

Federal Reserve Independence

Congress purposely established the Fed as an independent agency of government. The objective was to protect the Fed from political pressures so that it could effectively control the money supply and interest rates in order to maintain price-level stability. Political pressures on Congress and the executive branch may at times result in inflationary fiscal policies, including tax cuts and special-interest spending. If Congress and the executive branch also controlled the nation's monetary policy, citizens and lobbying groups undoubtedly would pressure elected officials to keep interest rates low even though at times high interest rates are necessary to reduce aggregate demand and thus control inflation. An independent monetary authority (the Fed) can take actions to increase interest rates when higher rates are needed to stem inflation. Studies show that countries that have independent central banks like the Fed have lower rates of inflation, on average, than countries that have little or no central bank independence.

The Financial Crisis of 2007 and 2008

A properly functioning monetary system supports the continuous circular flows of income and expenditures in the economy. In contrast, a malfunctioning monetary system causes major problems in credit markets and can cause severe fluctuations in the economy's levels of output, employment, and prices.

"Malfunctioning" is too gentle an adjective to describe the monetary system in late 2007 and 2008. In that period, the U.S. financial system faced its most serious crisis since the Great Depression of the 1930s. The financial crisis soon spread to the entire economy, culminating in the severe recession of 2007–2009. We discussed the recession in detail in previous chapters, and we now want to examine the financial crisis that led up to it. What was the nature of the financial crisis? What caused it? How has it changed the structure of the U.S. financial services industry?

The Mortgage Default Crisis

In 2007 a major wave of defaults on home mortgage loans threatened the health of not only the original mortgage lenders but of any financial institution that had made such loans or invested in such loans either directly or indirectly. A majority of these mortgage defaults were on **subprime mortgage loans**—high-interest-rate loans to home buyers with higher-than-average credit risk. Several of the biggest indirect investors in these subprime loans had been banks. The banks had lent money to investment companies that had purchased many of the mortgages from mortgage lenders. When the mortgages started to go bad, many investment funds "blew up" and could not repay the loans they had taken out from the banks. The banks thus had to "write off" (declare unrecoverable) the loans they had made to the investment companies, but doing that meant reducing their banks' reserves and limiting their ability to generate new loans. This greatly threatened the economy because both consumers and businesses rely on loans to finance consumption and investment expenditures.

A strange thing about the crisis was that before it happened, banks and government regulators had mistakenly believed that an innovation known as the "mortgage-backed security" had eliminated most of the bank exposure to mortgage defaults. **Mortgage-backed securities** are bonds backed by mortgage payments. To create them, banks and other mortgage lenders first made mortgage loans. But then instead of holding all of those loans as assets on their balance sheets and collecting the

subprime mortgage loans
High-interest-rate loans to home buyers with above-average credit risk.

mortgage-backed securities
Bonds that represent claims to all or part of the monthly mortgage payments from the pools of mortgage loans made by lenders to borrowers to help them purchase residential property.

monthly mortgage payments, the banks and other mortgage lenders bundled hundreds or thousands of them together and sold them off as bonds—in essence selling the right to collect all the future mortgage payments. The banks obtained a single, up-front cash payment for the bond and the bond buyer started to collect the mortgage payments as the return on the investment.

From the banks' perspective, this seemed like a smart business decision because it transferred any future default risk on those mortgages to the buyer of the bond. The banks thought that they were off the hook for these mortgages. Unfortunately for them, however, they lent a substantial portion of the money they received from selling the bonds to investment funds that invested in mortgage-backed bonds. They also purchased large amounts of mortgage-backed securities as financial investments to help meet bank capital requirements set by bank regulators. So while the banks were no longer directly exposed to major portions of the mortgage default risk, they were still indirectly exposed to it. When many homebuyers started to default on their mortgages, the banks lost money on the mortgages they still held. The banks also lost money on the loans they had made to the investors who had purchased mortgage-backed securities, and also on the mortgage-backed securities the banks had purchased from investment firms.

But what caused the skyrocketing mortgage default rates in the first place? There were many causes, including certain government programs that greatly encouraged and subsidized home ownership for former renters. Also contributing were declining real estate values that arrived at the end of a long housing boom during which house prices had greatly increased. But an equally important factor was the bad incentives provided by the previously discussed mortgage-backed bonds. Because the banks and other mortgage lenders thought that they were no longer exposed to large portions of their mortgage default risk, they became lax in their lending practices—so much so that people were granted subprime mortgage loans that they were unlikely to be able to repay. Some mortgage companies were so eager to sign up new homebuyers (in order to bundle their loans together to sell bonds) that they stopped running credit checks and even allowed applicants to claim higher incomes than they were actually earning in order to qualify them for big loans. The natural result was that many people took on "too much mortgage" and were soon failing to make their monthly payments.

Securitization

securitization
The process of aggregating many individual financial debts into a pool and then issuing new securities (financial instruments) backed by the pool. The holders of the new securities are entitled to receive debt payments made on the individual financial debts in the pool.

The problems just described relate to **securitization**—the process of slicing up and bundling groups of loans, mortgages, corporate bonds, or other financial debts into distinct new securities. This process was not new and was viewed favorably by government regulators, who thought securitization made the banking system safer by allowing banks to shed risk. As noted in our discussion of mortgages, these securities were sold to financial investors, who purchased them to obtain the interest payments and the eventual return of principal generated by the underlying securities. For example, the mortgage loans provided to the subprime borrowers were bundled together as mortgage-backed securities and sold to private investors, mutual fund firms, and pension funds. These securities were attractive to many private investors and financial institutions alike because they offered higher-interest returns than securities backed by less-risky mortgages or other safer investments.

Once created, loan-backed securities are bought and sold in financial markets just like other securities such as stocks and bonds. These sorts of securities can therefore end up worldwide in the investment portfolios of banks, thrifts, insurance companies, and pensions, as well as in personal accounts.

To reduce the risk for holders of these securities, a few large insurance companies developed other securities that the holders of loan-backed securities could purchase to insure against losses from defaults. American International Group (AIG), in particular, issued billions of dollars of *collateralized default swaps*—essentially insurance policies— that were designed to compensate the holders of loan-backed securities if the loans underlying these investments went into default and did not pay off. Thus, collateralized default swaps became yet another category of investment security that was highly exposed to mortgage-loan risk.

Securitization is so widespread and so critical to the modern financial system that economists sometimes refer to it as the *shadow banking system*. All sorts of securities backed by loans or other securities are issued, bought, sold, and resold each day in a process that helps to keep credit flowing to the households and firms that rely on it for their personal and business needs. In general, securitization therefore is a positive financial innovation. But mortgage-backed securities, in particular, turned out to contain much more risk than most people thought.

Investors and government regulators failed to ask three related questions about mortgage-backed securities: What would happen if the value of one of the types of loans (say, mortgages) that underlies part of the securitization process unexpectedly plunged? And what then would happen if some of the largest holders of the securities based on these mortgages were major U.S. financial institutions that are vitally important to the day-to-day financing of the credit needed to keep the American economy running smoothly? And what would happen after that if the main insurer of these securities not only was the largest insurance company in the United States but in the world?

All three seemingly improbable "what ifs?" occurred! As previously explained, interest rates on adjustable-rate mortgages increased and house prices fell. Borrowers who had made relatively small down payments on home purchases or had previously cashed out home equity through refinancing discovered that they owed more on their mortgages than their properties were worth. Their loans were said to be "underwater." As interest rates adjusted upward and the economy slowed, borrowers began falling behind on their monthly mortgage payments. Lenders began to foreclose on many houses, while other borrowers literally handed in their house keys and walked away from their houses *and* their mortgages.

Failures and Near-Failures of Financial Firms

When the mortgage loan "card" underpinning mortgage-based securitization fell, the securitization layers above it collapsed like a house of cards. First, the big mortgage lenders faced demise because they still held large amounts of the bad debt. Three huge mortgage lenders collapsed or nearly collapsed. Countrywide, the second largest mortgage lender, was saved from bankruptcy by Bank of America. Regulators also seized Washington Mutual bank, the nation's largest mortgage lender, and arranged a quick takeover by JPMorgan Chase. Wachovia bank's heavy exposure to mortgages through its Golden West subsidiary resulted in near bankruptcy, and it was rescued through acquisition by Wells Fargo.

The exposure to the growing problem of loan defaults quickly jumped from direct mortgage lenders to other financial institutions. Securities firms and investment banks that held large amounts of loan-backed securities began to suffer huge losses. Merrill Lynch lost more in two years than it made in the prior decade and was acquired at a fire-sale price by Bank of America. Lehman Brothers, a major holder of mortgage-backed securities, declared bankruptcy. Goldman Sachs, Morgan Stanley, and other financial firms that had heavy exposures to mortgage-backed securities and collateralized default swaps rushed to become bank holding companies so they could qualify for the massive emergency loans that the Federal Reserve was making available to banks and bank holding companies. Citibank survived through infusions of federal government loans. Insurance company AIG suffered enormous losses because it had not set aside sufficient reserves to pay off the unexpectedly large losses that accrued on the insurance policies that it had sold to holders of mortgage-backed securities. The nightmarish thought of a total collapse of the U.S. financial system suddenly became a realistic possibility.

The Treasury Bailout: TARP

Troubled Asset Relief Program (TARP)
A 2008 federal government program that authorized the U.S. Treasury to loan up to $700 billion to critical financial institutions and other U.S. firms that were in extreme financial trouble and therefore at high risk of failure.

In late 2008 Congress passed the **Troubled Asset Relief Program (TARP),** which allocated $700 billion to the U.S. Treasury to make emergency loans to critical financial and other U.S. firms. Of that $700 billion, $415 billion was distributed before lending from TARP ended in October 2010. As of March 2012, approximately $293 billion had been repaid, and the U.S. Treasury estimates that the final cost of the program will be less than $50 billion (and may even generate a positive return). The federal government and Federal Reserve spent $182 billion just keeping insurer AIG afloat. Other major recipients of TARP funds included Citibank, Bank of America, JPMorgan Chase, and Goldman Sachs. Later, nonfinancial firms such as General Motors and Chrysler also received several billion dollars of TARP loans.

TARP indeed saved several financial institutions whose bankruptcy would have caused a tsunami of secondary effects that probably would have brought down other financial firms and frozen credit throughout the economy. But this very fact demonstrates the problem of **moral hazard**—a situation where individuals or institutions may change their behavior as the result of a contract or agreement. As it relates to financial investment, moral hazard is the tendency for financial investors and financial services firms to take on greater risks because they assume they are at least partially insured against losses. Without TARP, several firms would have gone bankrupt and their stockholders, bondholders, and executives all would have suffered large personal losses. With TARP, those outcomes were at least partially avoided. TARP and similar government bailouts were essentially government-provided insurance payouts to financial firms that never had to pay a single cent in insurance premiums for the massive bailouts that kept them afloat.

moral hazard
The possibility that individuals or institutions will change their behavior as the result of a contract or agreement.

The correct assumption by large firms that they were simply too big for government to let them fail may have given them an incentive to make riskier investments than if no government bailouts were likely to be forthcoming.

The Postcrisis U.S. Financial Services Industry

financial services industry
The broad category of firms that provide financial products and services to help households and businesses earn *interest,* receive *dividends,* obtain *capital gains,* insure against losses, and plan for retirement.

Table 14.1 lists the major categories of firms within the U.S. financial services industry and gives examples of firms in each category. Note that the main categories of the **financial services industry** are commercial banks, thrifts, insurance companies, mutual fund companies, pension funds, securities firms, and investment banks. Even before the financial crisis of 2007–2008, the financial services industry was consolidating into fewer, larger firms, each offering a wider spectrum of services. In 1999 Congress ended the Depression-era prohibition against banks selling stocks, bonds, and mutual funds. Thus, the lines between the subsets of the financial industry began to blur. Many banks acquired stock brokerage firms and, in a few cases, insurance companies. For example,

TABLE 14.1

Major Categories of Financial Institutions within the U.S. Financial Services Industry

Institution	Description	Examples
Commercial banks	State and national banks that provide checking and savings accounts, sell certificates of deposit, and make loans. The Federal Deposit Insurance Corporation (FDIC) insures checking and savings accounts up to $250,000.	JPMorgan Chase, Bank of America, Citibank, Wells Fargo
Thrifts	Savings and loan associations (S&Ls), mutual saving banks, and credit unions that offer checking and savings accounts and make loans. Historically, S&Ls made mortgage loans for houses while mutual savings banks and credit unions made small personal loans, such as automobile loans. Today, major thrifts offer the same range of banking services as commercial banks. The Federal Deposit Insurance Corporation and the National Credit Union Administration insure checking and savings deposits up to $250,000.	Charter One, New York Community Bank, Pentagon Federal Credit Union, Boeing Employees Credit Union (BECU)
Insurance companies	Firms that offer policies (contracts) through which individuals pay premiums to insure against some loss, say, disability or death. In some life insurance policies and annuities, the funds are invested for the client in stocks and bonds and paid back after a specified number of years. Thus, insurance sometimes has a saving or financial-investment element.	Prudential, New York Life, Northwestern Mutual, Hartford, MetLife
Mutual fund companies	Firms that pool deposits by customers to purchase stocks or bonds (or both). Customers thus indirectly own a part of a particular set of stocks or bonds, say stocks in companies expected to grow rapidly (a growth fund) or bonds issued by state governments (a municipal bond fund).	Fidelity, Vanguard, Putnam, Janus, T. Rowe Price
Pension funds	For-profit or nonprofit institutions that collect savings from workers (or from employers on their behalf) throughout their working years and then buy stocks and bonds with the proceeds and make monthly retirement payments.	TIAA-CREF, Teamsters' Union, CalPERS
Securities firms	Firms that offer security advice and buy and sell stocks and bonds for clients. More generally known as *stock brokerage firms*.	Merrill Lynch, Smith Barney, Charles Schwab
Investment banks	Firms that help corporations and governments raise money by selling stocks and bonds. They also typically offer advisory services for corporate mergers and acquisitions as well as brokerage services and advice.	Goldman Sachs, Morgan Stanley, Deutsche Bank, Nomura Securities

Citigroup, which was once only into banking, now owns Smith Barney, a large securities firm. Many large banks (for example, Wells Fargo) and pension funds (for example, TIAA-CREF) now provide mutual funds, including money market mutual funds that pay relatively high interest and on which checks of $500 or more can be written.

The upheaval in the financial markets caused by the financial crisis of 2007–2008 further consolidated the industry and further blurred the lines between its segments. Between September 2007 and April 2012, the FDIC shut down more than 430 U.S. banks and transferred their bank deposits to other, usually larger, banks. In 2010 the three largest U.S. banks (JPMorgan Chase, Bank of America, and Wells Fargo) held roughly $3 of every $10 on deposit in the United States.

Also, during the financial crisis of 2007–2008, major investment banks Goldman Sachs and Morgan Stanley opted to become commercial banks to gain access to emergency Federal Reserve loans (we will discuss these emergency loans in Chapter 15). The nation's largest thrift—Washington Mutual—was absorbed by commercial bank JPMorgan Chase. But even with all this blending, the categories in Table 14.1 remain helpful. The main lines of a firm's businesses often are in one category or another. For example, even though Goldman Sachs is licensed and regulated as a bank, it is first and foremost an investment company. And the insurance companies and pension funds do most of their business as such.

The financial crisis of 2007–2008 generated much introspection about what went wrong and how to prevent anything like it from happening again. Politicians and financial regulators tightened lending rules to offset the "pass the buck" incentives created by mortgage-backed securities and prevent loans from being issued to people who are unlikely to be able to make the required monthly payments. They also passed legislation to help homeowners who were "underwater" on mortgage loans remain in their homes.

In mid-2010 Congress passed and the president signed the **Wall Street Reform and Consumer Protection Act.** This sweeping law includes provisions that

- eliminate the Office of Thrift Supervision and give broader authority to the Federal Reserve to regulate all large financial institutions;
- create a Financial Stability Oversight Council to be on the lookout for risks to the financial system;
- establish a process for the federal government to liquidate (sell off) the assets of large failing financial institutions, much like the FDIC does with failing banks;
- provide federal regulatory oversight of mortgage-backed securities and other derivatives and require that they be traded on public exchanges;
- require companies selling asset-backed securities to retain a portion of those securities so the sellers share part of the risk; and
- establish a stronger consumer financial protection role for the Fed through creation of the Bureau of Consumer Financial Protection.

Proponents of the new law say that it will help prevent many of the practices that led up to the financial crisis of 2007–2008. They also contend that the law will send a strong message to stockholders, bondholders, and executives of large financial firms that they will suffer unavoidable and extremely high personal financial losses if they allow their firms to ever again get into serious financial trouble.

Skeptics of the new law say that regulators already had all the tools they needed to prevent the financial crisis. They also point out that the government's own efforts to promote home ownership, via quasi-government institutions that purchased mortgage-backed securities, greatly contributed to the financial crisis. Critics of the new law say that it will simply impose heavy new regulatory costs on the financial industry while doing little to prevent future government bailouts.

The Fractional Reserve System

We have seen that the $M1$ money supply consists of currency (coins and Federal Reserve Notes) and checkable deposits. The U.S. Mint creates the coins and the U.S. Bureau of Engraving creates the Federal Reserve Notes. So who creates the checkable deposits that make up about half the nation's $M1$ money supply? Surprisingly, it is loan officers at banks and thrifts!

The United States, like most other countries today, has a **fractional reserve banking system** in which only a portion (fraction) of the total money supply is held in reserve as currency. Our goal is to explain how commercial banks and thrifts can create checkable deposits by issuing loans. Our examples will involve commercial banks, but remember that thrift institutions also provide checkable deposits. So the analysis applies to banks and thrifts alike.

Wall Street Reform and Consumer Protection Act of 2010
A law that gave authority to the Federal Reserve to regulate all large financial institutions, created an oversight council to look for growing risk to the financial system, established a process for the federal government to sell off the assets of large failing financial institutions, provided federal regulatory oversight of asset-backed securities, and created a financial consumer protection bureau within the Fed.

fractional reserve banking system
A banking system in which banks and thrifts are required to hold less than 100 percent of their checkable-deposit liabilities as reserves.

The Goldsmiths

Here is the history behind the idea of the fractional reserve system.

When early traders began to use gold in making transactions, they soon realized that it was both unsafe and inconvenient to carry gold and to have it weighed and assayed (judged for purity) every time they negotiated a transaction. So by the 16th century they had begun to deposit their gold with goldsmiths, who would store it in vaults for a fee. On receiving a gold deposit, the goldsmith would issue a receipt to the depositor. Soon people were paying for goods with goldsmiths' receipts, which served as one of the first types of paper money.

At this point the goldsmiths—embryonic bankers—used a 100 percent reserve system; they backed their circulating paper money receipts fully with the gold that they held "in reserve" in their vaults. But because of the public's acceptance of the goldsmiths' receipts as paper money, the goldsmiths soon realized that owners rarely redeemed the gold they had in storage. In fact, the goldsmiths observed that the amount of gold being deposited with them in any week or month was likely to exceed the amount that was being withdrawn.

Then some clever goldsmith hit on the idea that paper "receipts" could be issued in excess of the amount of gold held. Goldsmiths would put these receipts, which were redeemable in gold, into circulation by making interest-earning loans to merchants, producers, and consumers. A borrower might, for instance, borrow $10,000 worth of gold receipts today with the promise to repay $10,500 worth of gold receipts in one year (a five percent interest rate). Borrowers were willing to accept loans in the form of gold receipts because the receipts were accepted as a medium of exchange in the marketplace.

This was the beginning of the fractional reserve system of banking, in which reserves in bank vaults are a fraction of the total money supply. If, for example, the goldsmith issued $1 million in receipts for actual gold in storage and another $1 million in receipts as loans, then the total value of paper money in circulation would be $2 million—twice the value of the gold. Gold reserves would be a fraction (one-half) of outstanding paper money.

Question:
Explain how the gold receipts issued by goldsmiths performed the three major functions of money.

The goldsmith story highlights two significant characteristics of fractional reserve banking. First, banks can create money through lending. In fact, goldsmiths created money when they made loans by giving borrowers paper money that was not fully backed by gold reserves. The quantity of such money goldsmiths could create depended on the amount of reserves they deemed prudent to have available. The smaller the amount of reserves thought necessary, the larger the amount of paper money the goldsmiths could create. Today, gold is no longer used as bank reserves. Instead, currency itself serves as bank reserves so that the creation of checkable-deposit money by banks (via their lending) is limited by the amount of *currency reserves* that the banks feel obligated, or are required by law, to keep.

A second reality is that banks operating on the basis of fractional reserves are vulnerable to "panics" or "runs." A goldsmith who issued paper money equal to twice the value of his gold reserves would be unable to convert all that paper money into gold in the event that all the holders of that money appeared at his door at the same time demanding their gold. In fact, many European and U.S. banks were once ruined by this unfortunate circumstance. However, a bank panic is highly unlikely if the banker's reserve and lending policies are prudent. Indeed, one reason why banking systems are highly regulated industries is to prevent runs on banks. This is also the reason why the United States has a system of deposit insurance.

A Single Commercial Bank

To illustrate the workings of the modern fractional reserve banking system, we need to examine a commercial bank's balance sheet.

balance sheet
A statement of the assets, liabilities, and net worth of a firm, individual, or institution at some time.

The **balance sheet** of a commercial bank (or thrift) is a statement of assets—things owned by the bank or owed to the bank—and claims on those assets. A bank balance sheet summarizes the financial position of the bank at a certain time. Every balance sheet must balance; this means that the value of *assets* must equal the amount of claims against those assets. The claims shown on a balance sheet are divided into two groups: the claims of nonowners of the bank against the firm's assets, called *liabilities*, and the claims of the owners of the firm against the firm's assets, called *net worth*. Liabilities are things owed by the bank to depositors or others. A balance sheet is balanced because

$$\text{Assets} = \text{liabilities} + \text{net worth}$$

For every \$1 change in assets, there must be an offsetting \$1 change in liabilities + net worth. For every \$1 change in liabilities + net worth, there must be an offsetting \$1 change in assets.

Now let's work through a series of bank transactions involving balance sheets to establish how individual banks can create money.

Transaction 1: Creating a Bank

Suppose some farsighted citizens of the town of Somewhere decide their town needs a new commercial bank to provide banking services for that growing community. Once they have secured a state or national charter for their bank, they turn to the task of selling, say, \$250,000 worth of stock certificates (equity shares) to buyers, both in and out of the community. Their efforts meet with success and the Bank of Somewhere comes into existence—at least on paper. What does its balance sheet look like at this stage?

The founders of the bank have sold \$250,000 worth of shares of stock in the bank—some to themselves, some to other people. As a result, the bank now has \$250,000 in cash on hand and \$250,000 worth of stock certificates outstanding. The cash is an asset to the bank. Cash held by a bank is sometimes called *vault cash* or *till money*. The shares of stock outstanding constitute an equal amount of claims that the owners have against the bank's assets. Those shares of stock constitute the net worth of the bank. The bank's balance sheet reads:

Creating a Bank			
Balance Sheet 1: Somewhere Bank			
Assets		Liabilities and net worth	
Cash	\$250,000	Stock shares	\$250,000

Each item listed in a balance sheet such as this is called an *account*.

Transaction 2: Acquiring Property and Equipment

The board of directors (who represent the bank's owners) must now get the new bank off the drawing board and make it a reality. First, property and equipment must be acquired. Suppose the directors, confident of the success of their venture, purchase a building for $220,000 and pay $20,000 for office equipment. This simple transaction changes the composition of the bank's assets. The bank now has $240,000 less in cash and $240,000 of new property assets. Using blue to denote accounts affected by each transaction, we show that the bank's balance sheet at the end of transaction 2 appears as follows:

Acquiring Property and Equipment Balance Sheet 2: Somewhere Bank		
Assets	Liabilities and net worth	
Cash	$ 10,000	Stock shares $250,000
Property	240,000	

Note that the balance sheet still balances, as it must.

Transaction 3: Accepting Deposits

Commercial banks have two basic functions: to accept deposits of money and to make loans. Now that the bank is operating, suppose that the citizens and businesses of Somewhere decide to deposit $100,000 in the Somewhere bank. What happens to the bank's balance sheet?

The bank receives cash, which is an asset to the bank. Suppose this money is deposited in the bank as checkable deposits (checking account entries), rather than as savings accounts or time deposits. These newly created *checkable deposits* constitute claims that the depositors have against the assets of the Somewhere bank and thus are a new liability account. The bank's balance sheet now looks like this:

Accepting Deposits Balance Sheet 3: Somewhere Bank			
Assets		Liabilities and net worth	
Cash	$110,000	Checkable deposits	$100,000
Property	240,000	Stock shares	250,000

There has been no change in the economy's total supply of money as a result of transaction 3, but a change has occurred in the composition of the money supply. Bank money, or checkable deposits, has increased by $100,000, and currency held by the public has decreased by $100,000. Currency held by a bank, you will recall, is not part of the economy's money supply.

A withdrawal of cash will reduce the bank's checkable-deposit liabilities and its holdings of cash by the amount of the withdrawal. This, too, changes the composition, but not the total supply, of money in the economy.

Transaction 4: Depositing Reserves in a Federal Reserve Bank

All commercial banks and thrift institutions that provide checkable deposits must by law keep **required reserves.** Required reserves are an amount of funds equal to a specified percentage of the bank's own deposit liabilities. A bank must keep these

required reserves
The funds that banks and thrifts must deposit with the Federal Reserve Bank (or hold as vault cash) to meet the Fed's reserve requirement.

reserves on deposit with the Federal Reserve Bank in its district or as cash in the bank's vault. To simplify, we suppose the Bank of Somewhere keeps its required reserves entirely as deposits in the Federal Reserve Bank of its district. But remember that vault cash is counted as reserves and real-world banks keep a significant portion of their own reserves in their vaults.

The "specified percentage" of checkable-deposit liabilities that a commercial bank must keep as reserves is known as the **reserve ratio**—the ratio of the required reserves the commercial bank must keep to the bank's own outstanding checkable-deposit liabilities:

reserve ratio
The legally required percentage of reserves for every $1 of a bank or thrift's checkable deposits.

$$\text{Reserve ratio} = \frac{\text{commercial bank's requied reserves}}{\text{commercial bank's checkable-deposit liabilities}}$$

If the reserve ratio is $\frac{1}{10}$, or 10 percent, the Somewhere bank, having accepted $100,000 in deposits from the public, would have to keep $10,000 as reserves. If the ratio is $\frac{1}{5}$, or 20 percent, $20,000 of reserves would be required. If $\frac{1}{2}$, or 50 percent, $50,000 would be required.

The Fed has the authority to establish and vary the reserve ratio within limits legislated by Congress. A 10 percent reserve is required on checkable deposits over $55.2 million, although the Fed can vary that percentage between 8 and 14 percent. Also, after consultation with appropriate congressional committees, the Fed for 180 days may impose reserve requirements outside the 8–14 percent range. Beginning in late 2008, the Fed began paying banks interest on their required reserves and on their excess reserves held at the Federal Reserve Banks.

In order to simplify, we will suppose that the reserve ratio for checkable deposits in commercial banks is $\frac{1}{5}$, or 20 percent. Although 20 percent obviously is higher than the requirement really is, the figure is convenient for calculations. The main point is that reserve requirements are fractional, meaning that they are less than 100 percent.

By depositing $20,000 in the Federal Reserve Bank, the Somewhere bank will just be meeting the required 20 percent ratio between its reserves and its own deposit liabilities. We will use "reserves" to mean the funds commercial banks deposit in the Federal Reserve Banks, to distinguish those funds from the public's deposits in commercial banks.

But suppose the Somewhere bank anticipates that its holdings of checkable deposits will grow in the future. Then, instead of sending just the minimum amount, $20,000, it sends an extra $90,000, for a total of $110,000. In so doing, the bank will avoid the inconvenience of sending additional reserves to the Federal Reserve Bank each time its own checkable-deposit liabilities increase. And, as you will see, it is these extra reserves that enable banks to lend money and earn interest income.

Actually, a real-world bank would not deposit *all* its cash in the Federal Reserve Bank. However, because (1) banks as a rule hold vault cash only in the amount of $1\frac{1}{2}$ or 2 percent of their total assets and (2) vault cash can be counted as reserves, we will assume for simplicity that all of Somewhere's cash is deposited in the Federal Reserve Bank and therefore constitutes the commercial bank's actual reserves. By making this simplifying assumption, we do not need to bother adding two assets—"cash" and "deposits in the Federal Reserve Bank"—to determine reserves.

After the Somewhere bank deposits $110,000 of reserves at the Fed, its balance sheet becomes:

Depositing Reserves at the Fed **Balance Sheet 4: Somewhere Bank**			
Assets		Liabilities and net worth	
Cash	$ 0	Checkable deposits	$100,000
Reserves	110,000		
Property	240,000	Stock shares	250,000

There are three things to note about this latest transaction.

Excess Reserves   A bank's **excess reserves** are found by subtracting its *required reserves* (or legally required reserves) from its **actual reserves:**

$$\text{Excess reserves} = \text{actual reserves} - \text{required reserves}$$

In this case,

Actual reserves	$110,000
Required reserves	−20,000
Excess reserves	$ 90,000

The only reliable way of computing excess reserves is to multiply the bank's checkable-deposit liabilities by the reserve ratio to obtain required reserves ($100,000 × 20 percent = $20,000) and then to subtract the required reserves from the actual reserves listed on the asset side of the bank's balance sheet.

To test your understanding, compute the bank's excess reserves from balance sheet 4, assuming that the reserve ratio is (1) 10 percent, (2) $33\frac{1}{3}$ percent, and (3) 50 percent.

We will soon demonstrate that the ability of a commercial bank to make loans depends on the existence of excess reserves. Understanding this concept is crucial in seeing how the banking system creates money.

Control   You might think the basic purpose of reserves is to enhance the liquidity of a bank and protect commercial bank depositors from losses. Reserves would constitute a ready source of funds from which commercial banks could meet large, unexpected cash withdrawals by depositors.

But this reasoning breaks down under scrutiny. Although historically reserves have been seen as a source of liquidity and therefore as protection for depositors, a bank's required reserves are not great enough to meet sudden, massive cash withdrawals. If the banker's nightmare should materialize—everyone with checkable deposits appearing at once to demand those deposits in cash—the legal reserves held as vault cash or at the Federal Reserve Bank would be insufficient. The banker simply could not meet this "bank panic." Because reserves are fractional, checkable deposits are usually much greater than a bank's required reserves.

So commercial bank deposits must be protected by other means. Periodic bank examinations are one way of promoting prudent commercial banking practices. Furthermore, as we have mentioned, government-sponsored deposit insurance funds insure individual deposits in banks and thrifts up to $250,000.

If it is not the purpose of reserves to provide for commercial bank liquidity, then what is their function? *Control* is the answer. Required reserves help the Fed control the lending ability of commercial banks. The Fed can take certain actions that either increase or decrease commercial bank reserves and affect the ability of banks to grant

excess reserves
Actual bank or thrift reserves minus legally required reserves.

actual reserves
The funds that a bank or thrift has on deposit at a Federal Reserve Bank or is holding as vault cash.

credit. The objective is to prevent banks from overextending or underextending bank credit. To the degree that these policies successfully influence the volume of commercial bank credit, the Fed can help the economy avoid business fluctuations. Another function of reserves is to facilitate the collection or "clearing" of checks.

Transaction 5: Clearing a Check Drawn against the Bank

Assume that Fred Bradshaw, a Somewhere farmer, deposited a substantial portion of the $100,000 in checkable deposits that the Somewhere bank received in transaction 3. Now suppose that Bradshaw buys $50,000 of farm machinery from the Ajax Farm Implement Company of Elsewhere. Bradshaw pays for this machinery by writing a $50,000 check against his deposit in the Somewhere bank. He gives the check to the Ajax Company. What are the results?

Ajax deposits the check in its account with the Elsewhere bank. The Elsewhere bank increases Ajax's checkable deposits by $50,000 when Ajax deposits the check. Ajax is now paid in full. Bradshaw is pleased with his new machinery.

Now the Elsewhere bank has Bradshaw's check. This check is simply a claim against the assets of the Somewhere bank. The Elsewhere bank will collect this claim by sending the check (along with checks drawn on other banks) to the regional Federal Reserve Bank. Here a clerk will clear, or collect, the check for the Elsewhere bank by increasing Elsewhere's reserve in the Federal Reserve Bank by $50,000 and decreasing the Somewhere bank's reserve by that same amount. The check is "collected" merely by making bookkeeping notations to the effect that Somewhere's claim against the Federal Reserve Bank is reduced by $50,000 and Elsewhere's claim is increased by $50,000.

Finally, the Federal Reserve Bank sends the cleared check back to the Somewhere bank, and for the first time the Somewhere bank discovers that one of its depositors has drawn a check for $50,000 against his checkable deposit. Accordingly, the Somewhere bank reduces Bradshaw's checkable deposit by $50,000 and notes that the collection of this check has caused a $50,000 decline in its reserves at the Federal Reserve Bank. All the balance sheets balance: The Somewhere bank has reduced both its assets (reserves) and its liabilities (checkable deposits) by $50,000. The Elsewhere bank has $50,000 more both assets (reserves) and liabilities (checkable deposits). Ownership of reserves at the Federal Reserve Bank has changed—with Somewhere owning $50,000 less and Elsewhere owning $50,000 more—but total reserves stay the same.

Whenever a check is drawn against one bank and deposited in another bank, collection of that check will reduce both the reserves and the checkable deposits of the bank on which the check is drawn. Conversely, if a bank receives a check drawn on another bank, the bank receiving the check will, in the process of collecting it, have its reserves and deposits increased by the amount of the check. In our example, the Somewhere bank loses $50,000 in both reserves and deposits to the Elsewhere bank. But there is no loss of reserves or deposits for the banking system as a whole. What one bank loses, another bank gains.

If we bring all the other assets and liabilities back into the picture, the Somewhere bank's balance sheet looks like this at the end of transaction 5:

Clearing a Check			
Balance Sheet 5: Somewhere Bank			
Assets		Liabilities and net worth	
Reserves	$ 60,000	Checkable deposits	$ 50,000
Property	240,000	Stock shares	250,000

Verify that with a 20 percent reserve requirement, the bank's excess reserves now stand at $50,000.

Transaction 6: Granting a Loan (Creating Money)

In addition to accepting deposits, commercial banks grant loans to borrowers. What effect does lending by a commercial bank have on its balance sheet?

Suppose the Gristly Meat Packing Company of Somewhere decides it is time to expand its facilities. Suppose, too, that the company needs exactly $50,000—which just happens to be equal to the Somewhere bank's excess reserves—to finance this project.

Gristly goes to the Somewhere bank and requests a loan for this amount. The Somewhere bank knows the Gristly Company's fine reputation and financial soundness and is convinced of its ability to repay the loan. So the loan is granted. In return, the president of Gristly hands a promissory note—a fancy IOU—to the Somewhere bank. Gristly wants the convenience and safety of paying its obligations by check. So, instead of receiving a bushel basket full of currency from the bank, Gristly gets a $50,000 increase in its checkable-deposit account in the Somewhere bank.

The Somewhere bank has acquired an interest-earning asset (the promissory note, which it files under "Loans") and has created checkable deposits (a liability) to "pay" for this asset. Gristly has swapped an IOU for the right to draw an additional $50,000 worth of checks against its checkable deposit in the Somewhere bank. Both parties are pleased.

At the moment the loan is completed, the Somewhere bank's position is shown by balance sheet 6a:

When a Loan Is Negotiated Balance Sheet 6a: Somewhere Bank			
Assets		Liabilities and net worth	
Reserves	$ 60,000	Checkable	
Loans	50,000	deposits	$100,000
Property	240,000	Stock shares	250,000

All this looks simple enough. But a close examination of the Somewhere bank's balance statement reveals a startling fact: *When a bank makes loans, it creates money.* The president of Gristly went to the bank with something that is *not* money—her IOU—and walked out with something that *is* money—a checkable deposit.

Contrast transaction 6a with transaction 3, in which checkable deposits were created but only as a result of currency having been taken out of circulation. There was a change in the *composition* of the money supply in that situation but no change in the *total supply* of money. But when banks lend, they create checkable deposits that *are* money. By extending credit, the Somewhere bank has "monetized" an IOU. Gristly and the Somewhere bank have created and then swapped claims. The claim created by Gristly and given to the bank is not money; an individual's IOU is not acceptable as a medium of exchange. But the claim created by the bank and given to Gristly *is* money; checks drawn against a checkable deposit are acceptable as a medium of exchange. Checkable deposit money like this constitutes about one-half the quantity of *M*1 money in the United States and about 10 percent of *M*2.

Much of the money used in the United States, therefore, is created through the extension of credit by commercial banks. This checkable-deposit money may be thought of as "debts" of commercial banks and thrift institutions. Checkable deposits are bank debts in the sense that they are claims that banks and thrifts promise to pay "on demand."

But there are factors limiting the ability of a commercial bank to create checkable deposits ("bank money") by lending. The Somewhere bank can expect the newly created checkable deposit of $50,000 to be a very active account. Gristly would not borrow $50,000 at, say, 7, 10, or 12 percent interest for the sheer joy of knowing that funds were available if needed.

Assume that Gristly awards a $50,000 building contract to the Quickbuck Construction Company. Quickbuck, true to its name, completes the expansion promptly and is paid with a check for $50,000 drawn by Gristly against its checkable deposit in the Somewhere bank. Quickbuck does not deposit this check in the Somewhere bank but instead deposits it in the Elsewhere bank. Elsewhere now has a $50,000 claim against the Somewhere bank. The check is collected in the manner described in transaction 5. As a result, the Somewhere bank loses both reserves and deposits equal to the amount of the check; Elsewhere acquires $50,000 of reserves and deposits.

In summary, assuming a check is drawn by the borrower for the entire amount of the loan ($50,000) and is given to a firm that deposits it in some other bank, the Somewhere bank's balance sheet will read as follows *after the check has been cleared against it:*

After a Check Is Drawn on the Loan Balance Sheet 6b: Somewhere Bank			
Assets		Liabilities and net worth	
Reserves	$ 10,000	Checkable	
Loans	50,000	deposits	$ 50,000
Property	240,000	Stock shares	250,000

After the check has been collected, the Somewhere bank just meets the required reserve ratio of 20 percent (= $10,000/$50,000). The bank has *no* excess reserves. This poses a question: Could the Somewhere bank have lent more than $50,000—an amount greater than its excess reserves—and still have met the 20 percent reserve requirement when a check for the full amount of the loan was cleared against it? The answer is no; the bank is "fully loaned up."

Here is why: Suppose the Somewhere bank had lent $55,000 to the Gristly company and that the Gristly company had spent all of that money by writing a $55,000 check to Quickbuck Construction.

WORKED PROBLEMS

W 14.1
Single bank accounting

Collection of the check against the Somewhere bank would have lowered its reserves to $5000 (= $60,000 − $55,000), and checkable deposits would once again stand at $50,000 (= $105,000 − $55,000). The ratio of actual reserves to checkable deposits would then be $5000/$50,000, or 10 percent, not the 20 percent required. So the Somewhere bank could not have lent $55,000.

By experimenting with other amounts over $50,000, you will find that the maximum amount the Somewhere bank could lend at the outset of transaction 6 is $50,000. This amount is identical to the amount of excess reserves the bank had available when the loan was negotiated. *A single commercial bank in a multibank banking system can lend only an amount equal to its initial preloan excess reserves.* When it lends, the lending bank faces the possibility that checks for the entire amount of the loan will be drawn and cleared against it. If that happens, the lending bank will lose (to other banks) reserves equal to the amount it lends. So, to be safe, it limits its lending to the amount of its excess reserves.

Bank creation of money raises an interesting question: If banks create checkable deposit money when they lend their excess reserves, is money destroyed when borrowers pay off their loans? The answer is yes. When loans are paid off, the process just described works in reverse. Checkable deposits decline by the amount of the loan payment.

The Banking System: Multiple-Deposit Expansion

Thus far we have seen that a single bank in a banking system can lend one dollar for each dollar of its excess reserves. The situation is different for all commercial banks as a group. We will find that the commercial banking system can lend—that is, can create money—by a multiple of its excess reserves. This multiple lending is accomplished even though each bank in the system can lend only "dollar for dollar" with its excess reserves.

How do these seemingly paradoxical results come about? To answer this question succinctly, we will make three simplifying assumptions:

- The reserve ratio for all commercial banks is 20 percent.
- Initially all banks are meeting this 20 percent reserve requirement exactly. No excess reserves exist; or, in the parlance of banking, they are "loaned up" (or "loaned out") fully in terms of the reserve requirement.
- If any bank can increase its loans as a result of acquiring excess reserves, an amount equal to those excess reserves will be lent to one borrower, who will write a check for the entire amount of the loan and give it to someone else, who will deposit the check in another bank. This third assumption means that the worst thing possible happens to every lending bank—a check for the entire amount of the loan is drawn and cleared against it in favor of another bank.

The Banking System's Lending Potential

Suppose a junkyard owner finds a $100 bill while dismantling a car that has been on the lot for years. He deposits the $100 in bank A, which adds the $100 to its reserves. We will record only changes in the balance sheets of the various commercial banks. The deposit changes bank A's balance sheet as shown by entries (a_1):

Multiple-Deposit Expansion Process Balance Sheet: Commercial Bank A		
Assets	Liabilities and net worth	
Reserves	$+100 ($a_1$)	Checkable
	− 80 (a_3)	deposits	$+100 ($a_1$)
Loans	+ 80 (a_2)		+ 80 (a_2)
			− 80 (a_3)

Recall from transaction 3 that this $100 deposit of currency does not alter the money supply. While $100 of checkable-deposit money comes into being, it is offset by the $100 of currency no longer in the hands of the nonbank public (the junkyard owner). But bank A *has* acquired excess reserves of $80. Of the newly acquired $100 in currency, 20 percent, or $20, must be earmarked for the required reserves on the new $100 checkable deposit, and the remaining $80 goes to excess reserves. Remembering that a single commercial bank can lend only an amount equal to its excess reserves, we conclude that bank A can lend a maximum of $80. When a loan for this amount is made, bank A's loans increase by $80 and the borrower gets an $80 checkable deposit. We add these figures—entries (a_2)—to bank A's balance sheet.

But now we employ our third assumption: The borrower uses the full amount of the loan ($80) to write a check ($80) to someone else, and that person deposits the amount in bank B, a different bank. As we saw in transaction 6, bank A loses both reserves and deposits equal to the amount of the loan, as indicated in entries (a_3). The net result of these transactions is that bank A's reserves now stand at + $20 (= $100 − $80), loans at +$80, and checkable deposits at +$100 (= $100 + $80 − $80). When the dust has settled, bank A is just meeting the 20 percent reserve ratio.

Recalling our previous discussion, we know that bank B acquires both the reserves and the deposits that bank A has lost. Bank B's balance sheet is changed as shown in the entries (b_1) that follow.

Multiple-Deposit Expansion Process Balance Sheet: Commercial Bank B			
Assets		**Liabilities and net worth**	
Reserves	$+80 ($b_1$) −64 ($b_3$)	Checkable deposits	$+80 ($b_1$) +64 ($b_2$)
Loans	+64 (b_2)		−64 (b_3)

When the borrower's check is drawn and cleared, bank A loses $80 in reserves and deposits and bank B gains $80 in reserves and deposits. But 20 percent, or $16, of bank B's new reserves must be kept as required reserves against the new $80 in checkable deposits. This means that bank B has $64 (= $80 − $16) in excess reserves. It can therefore lend $64 [entries ($b_2$)]. When the new borrower writes a check for $64 to buy a product, and the seller deposits the check in bank C, the reserves and deposits of bank B both fall by $64 [entries ($b_3$)]. As a result of these transactions, bank B's reserves now stand at +$16 (= $80 − $64), loans at +$64, and checkable deposits at +$80 (= $80 + $64 − $64). After all this, bank B is just meeting the 20 percent reserve requirement.

We could go ahead with this procedure by bringing banks C, D, E, … , N and so on into the picture. In fact, the process will go on almost indefinitely, just as long as banks further down the line receive at least one penny in new reserves that they can use to back another round of lending and money creation. But that might be annoying! Instead, we summarize the entire analysis in Table 14.2. Our

TABLE 14.2

Expansion of the Money Supply by the Commercial Banking System

Bank	(1) Acquired Reserves and Deposits	(2) Required Reserves (Reserve Ratio = .2)	(3) Excess Reserves, (1) − (2)	(4) Amount Bank Can Lend; New Money Created = (3)
Bank A	$100.00 ($a_1$)	$20.00	**$80.00**	$80.00 ($a_2$)
Bank B	80.00 (a_3, b_1)	16.00	64.00	64.00 (b_2)
Bank C	64.00	12.80	51.20	51.20
Bank D	51.20	10.24	40.96	40.96
Bank E	40.96	8.19	32.77	32.77
Bank F	32.77	6.55	26.21	26.21
Bank G	26.21	5.24	20.97	20.97
Bank H	20.97	4.20	16.78	16.78
Bank I	16.78	3.36	13.42	13.42
Bank J	13.42	2.68	10.74	10.74
Bank K	10.74	2.15	8.59	8.59
Bank L	8.59	1.72	6.87	6.87
Bank M	6.87	1.37	5.50	5.50
Bank N	5.50	1.10	4.40	4.40
Other banks	21.99	4.40	17.59	17.59
Total amount of money created (sum of the amounts in column 4)				**$400.00**

conclusion is startling: On the basis of only $80 in excess reserves (acquired by the banking system when someone deposited $100 of currency in bank A), the entire commercial banking system is able to lend $400, the sum of the amounts in column 4. The banking system can lend excess reserves by a multiple of 5 (= $400/$80) when the reserve ratio is 20 percent. Yet each single bank in the banking system is lending only an amount equal to its own excess reserves. How do we explain this? How can the banking system as a whole lend by a multiple of its excess reserves, when each individual bank can lend only dollar for dollar with its excess reserves?

The answer is that reserves lost by a single bank are not lost to the banking system as a whole. The reserves lost by bank A are acquired by bank B. Those lost by B are gained by C. C loses to D, D to E, E to F, and so forth. Although reserves can be, and are, lost by individual banks in the banking system, there is no loss of reserves for the banking system as a whole.

An individual bank can safely lend only an amount equal to its excess reserves, *but the commercial banking system can lend by a multiple of its collective excess reserves.* Commercial banks as a group can create money by lending in a manner very different from that of the individual banks in the group.

The Monetary Multiplier

The **monetary multiplier** (or, less commonly, the *checkable deposit multiplier*) defines the relationship between any new excess reserves in the banking system and the magnified creation of new checkable-deposit money by banks as a group. The monetary multiplier exists because the reserves and deposits lost by one bank become reserves of another bank. It magnifies excess reserves into a larger creation of checkable-deposit money. The monetary multiplier m is the reciprocal of the required reserve ratio R (the leakage into required reserves that occurs at each step in the lending process). In short,

monetary multiplier
The multiple of its excess reserves by which the banking system can expand checkable deposits and thus the money supply by making new loans.

$$\text{Monetary multiplier} = \frac{1}{\text{required reserve ratio}}$$

or, in symbols,

$$m = \frac{1}{R}$$

In this formula, m represents the maximum amount of new checkable-deposit money that can be created by a single dollar of excess reserves, given the value of R. By multiplying the excess reserves E by m, we can find the maximum amount of new checkable-deposit money, D, that can be created by the banking system. That is,

WORKED PROBLEMS

W 14.2
Money creation

Maximum checkable-deposit creation = excess reserves × monetary multiplier or, more simply,

$$D = E \times m$$

In our example in Table 14.2, R is .20, so m is 5 (=1/.20). Then

$$D = \$80 \times 5 = \$400$$

Reversibility: The Multiple Destruction of Money

The process we have described is reversible. Just as money is created when banks make loans, money is destroyed when loans are paid off. Loan repayment, in effect, sets off a process of multiple destruction of money akin to the multiple creation process. Because loans are both made and paid off in any period, the direction of the money supply in a given period will depend on the net effect of the two processes. If the dollar amount of loans made in some period exceeds the dollar amount of loans paid off, checkable deposits will expand and the money supply will increase. In contrast, if the dollar amount of loans made in some period is less than the dollar amount of loans paid off, checkable deposits will contract and the money supply will decline.

Applying the Analysis

The Bank Panics of 1930 to 1933

In the early months of the Great Depression, before there was deposit insurance, several financially weak banks went out of business. As word spread that customers of those banks had lost their deposits, a general concern arose that something similar could happen at other banks. Depositors became frightened that their banks did not, in fact, still have all the money they had deposited. And, of course, that is a reality in a fractional reserve banking system. Acting on their fears, people en masse tried to "cash out" their bank accounts by withdrawing their money before it was all gone. This "run on the banks" caused many previously financially sound banks to declare bankruptcy. More than 9000 banks failed within 3 years.

The massive conversion of checkable deposits to currency during 1930 to 1933 reduced the nation's money supply. This might seem strange, since a check written for "cash" reduces checkable-deposit money and increases currency in the hands of the public by the same amount. So how does the money supply decline? Our discussion of the money-creation process provides the answer, but now the story becomes one of money destruction.

Suppose that people collectively cash out $10 billion from their checking accounts. As an immediate result, checkable-deposit money declines by $10 billion, while currency held by the public increases by $10 billion. But here is the catch: Assuming a reserve ratio of 20 percent, the $10 billion of currency in the banks had been supporting $50 billion of deposit money, the $10 billion of deposits plus $40 billion created through loans. The $10 billion withdrawal of currency forces banks to reduce loans (and thus checkable-deposit money) by $40 billion to continue to meet their reserve requirement. In short, a $40 billion destruction of deposit money occurs. This is the scenario that occurred in the early years of the 1930s.

Accompanying this multiple contraction of checkable deposits was the banks' "scramble for liquidity" to try to meet further withdrawals of currency. To obtain more currency, they sold many of their holdings of government securities to the public. A bank's sale of government securities to the public, like a reduction in loans, reduces the money supply. People write checks for the securities, reducing their checkable deposits, and the bank uses the currency it obtains to meet the ongoing bank run. In short, the loss of reserves from the banking system, in conjunction with the scramble for security, reduced the amount of checkable-deposit money by far more than the increase in currency in the hands of the public. Thus, the money supply collapsed.

In 1933, President Franklin Roosevelt ended the bank panic by declaring a "national bank holiday," during which all national banks were shut down for 1 week so that government inspectors could have time to go over each bank's accounting records. Only healthy banks with plenty of reserves were allowed to reopen. This meant that when the holiday was over, people could trust in any bank that had been allowed to reopen. This identification of healthy banks, along with the initiation of the federal deposit insurance program, reassured depositors and ended the bank panics.

But before these policies could begin to turn things around, the nation's money supply had plummeted by 25–33 percent, depending on how narrowly or broadly the money supply is defined. This was the largest drop in the money supply in U.S. history. This decline contributed substantially to the nation's deepest and longest depression. Simply put, less money meant less spending on goods and services as well as fewer loans for businesses. Both effects exacerbated the Great Depression.

Today, a multiple contraction of the money supply of the 1930–1933 magnitude is unthinkable. FDIC deposit insurance has kept individual bank failures from becoming general panics. For example, during the financial crisis of 2007–2008, the FDIC increased deposit insurance from $100,000 to $250,000 per account, and the federal government guaranteed the safety of all balances in money market mutual fund accounts. Also, while the Fed stood idly by during the bank panics of 1930 to 1933, in 2007–2008 it took immediate and dramatic actions to maintain the banking system's reserves and the nation's money supply. We discussed these lender-of-last-resort actions earlier. In Chapter 15 we will discuss the interest rate policies that the Fed undertook during the crisis.

QUESTION: Why do fractional reserve banking and deposit insurance closely accompany one another in modern banking systems?

Summary

1. Conceptually, money is any item that society accepts as (a) a medium of exchange, (b) a unit of monetary account, and (c) a store of value.

2. In the United States, two "official" definitions of money are M1, consisting of currency (outside banks) and checkable deposits, and M2, consisting of M1 plus savings deposits, including money market deposit accounts, small-denominated (less than $100,000) time deposits, and money market mutual fund balances.

3. Money has value because of the goods, services, and resources it will command in the market. Maintaining the purchasing power of money depends largely on the government's effectiveness in managing the money supply to prevent inflation.

4. The U.S. banking system consists of (a) the Board of Governors of the Federal Reserve System, (b) the 12 Federal Reserve Banks, and (c) some 6200 commercial banks and 8700 thrift institutions (mainly credit unions). The Board of Governors is the basic policy-making body for the entire banking system. The directives of the Board and the Federal Open Market Committee (FOMC) are made effective through the 12 Federal Reserve Banks, which are simultaneously (a) central banks, (b) quasi-public banks, and (c) bankers' banks.

5. The major functions of the Fed are to (a) issue Federal Reserve Notes, (b) set reserve requirements and hold reserves deposited by banks and thrifts, (c) lend money to financial institutions and serve as a lender of last resort in national financial emergencies, (d) provide for the rapid collection of checks, (e) act as the fiscal agent for the federal government, (f) supervise the operations of the banks, and (g) control the supply of money in the best interests of the economy.

6. The Fed is essentially an independent institution, controlled neither by the president of the United States

nor by Congress. This independence shields the Fed from political pressure and allows it to raise and lower interest rates (via changes in the money supply) as needed to promote full employment, price stability, and economic growth.

7. The financial crisis of 2007–2008 consisted of an unprecedented rise in mortgage loan defaults, the collapse or near-collapse of several major financial institutions, and the generalized freezing up of credit availability. The crisis resulted from bad mortgage loans together with declining real estate prices. It also resulted from underestimation of risk by holders of mortgage-backed securities and faulty insurance securities designed to protect holders of mortgage-backed securities from the risk of default.

8. In 2008 Congress passed the Troubled Asset Relief Program (TARP), which authorized the U.S. Treasury to spend up to $700 billion to make emergency loans and guarantees to failing financial firms.

9. The TARP loans intensified the moral hazard problem. This is the tendency of financial investors and financial firms to take on greater risk when they assume they are at least partially insured against loss.

10. The main categories of the U.S. financial services industry are commercial banks, thrifts, insurance companies, mutual fund companies, pension funds, securities firms, and investment banks. The reassembly of the wreckage from the financial crisis of 2007–2008 has further consolidated the already consolidating financial services industry and has further blurred some of the lines between the subsets of the industry.

11. In response to the financial crisis, Congress passed the Wall Street Reform and Consumer Financial Protection Act of 2010.

12. Modern banking systems are fractional reserve systems: Only a fraction of checkable deposits is backed by currency. Commercial banks keep required reserves on deposit in a Federal Reserve Bank or as vault cash. These required reserves are equal to a specified percentage of the commercial bank's checkable-deposit liabilities. Excess reserves are equal to actual reserves minus required reserves.

13. Commercial banks create money—checkable deposits, or checkable-deposit money—when they make loans. The ability of a single commercial bank to create money by lending depends on the size of its excess reserves. Generally, a commercial bank can lend only an amount equal to its excess reserves. Money creation is thus limited because, in all likelihood, checks drawn by borrowers will be deposited in other banks, causing a loss of reserves and deposits to the lending bank equal to the amount of money lent.

14. The commercial banking system as a whole can lend by a multiple of its excess reserves because the system as a whole cannot lose reserves. Individual banks, however, can lose reserves to other banks in the system. The multiple by which the banking system can lend on the basis of each dollar of excess reserves is the reciprocal of the reserve ratio.

15. The bank panics of 1930–1933 resulted in a significant contraction of the U.S. money supply, contributed to the Great Depression, and gave rise to federal deposit insurance.

Terms and Concepts

medium of exchange

unit of account

store of value

liquidity

M1

Federal Reserve Notes

token money

checkable deposits

commercial banks

thrift institutions

near-monies

M2

savings account

money market deposit account (MMDA)

time deposits

money market mutual fund (MMMF)

legal tender

Federal Reserve System

Board of Governors

Federal Reserve Banks

Federal Open Market Committee (FOMC)

subprime mortgage loans

mortgage-backed securities

securitization

Troubled Asset Relief Program (TARP)

moral hazard

financial services industry

Wall Street Reform and Consumer Protection Act of 2010

fractional reserve banking system

balance sheet

required reserves

reserve ratio

excess reserves

actual reserves

monetary multiplier

Questions

1. What are the three basic functions of money? Describe how rapid inflation can undermine money's ability to perform each of the three functions. **LO1**

2. Which two of the following financial institutions offer checkable deposits included within the *M1* money supply: mutual fund companies; insurance companies; commercial banks; securities firms; thrift institutions? Which of the following is *not* included in either *M1* or *M2*: currency held by the public; checkable deposits; money market mutual fund balances; small-denominated (less than $100,000) time deposits; currency held by banks; savings deposits? **LO1**

3. What are the components of the *M1* money supply? What is the largest component? Which of the components of *M1* is *legal tender*? Why is the face value of a coin greater than its intrinsic value? What near-monies are included in the *M2* money supply? **LO1**

4. How does the purchasing power of the dollar relate to the nation's price level? **LO2**

5. Who selects the chairperson of the Federal Reserve System? Describe the relationship between the Board of Governors of the Federal Reserve System and the 12 Federal Reserve Banks. What is the composition and purpose of the Federal Open Market Committee (FOMC)? **LO3**

6. What is meant when economists say that the Federal Reserve Banks are central banks, quasi-public banks, and bankers' banks? What are the seven basic functions of the Federal Reserve System? **LO4**

7. How do each of the following relate to the financial crisis of 2007–2008: declines in real estate values, subprime mortgage loans, mortgage-backed securities, AIG. **LO5**

8. What is TARP and how was it funded? How do government loans relate to the concept of moral hazard? **LO6**

9. What are the major categories of firms that make up the U.S. financial services industry? Are there more or fewer banks today than before the start of the financial crisis of 2007–2008? Why are the lines between the categories of financial firms even more blurred than they were before the crisis? How did the Wall Street Reform and Consumer Protection Act of 2010 try to address some of the problems that helped cause the crisis? **LO7**

10. What is the difference between an asset and a liability on a bank's balance sheet? How does net worth relate to each? Why must a balance sheet always balance? What are the major assets and claims on a commercial bank's balance sheet? **LO8**

11. Why does the Federal Reserve require that commercial banks have reserves? What are excess reserves? How do you calculate the amount of excess reserves held by a bank? What is the significance of excess reserves? **LO8**

12. "Whenever currency is deposited in a commercial bank, cash goes out of circulation and, as a result, the *M1* supply of money is reduced." Do you agree? Explain why or why not. **LO8**

13. Explain why a single commercial bank can safely lend only an amount equal to its excess reserves but the commercial banking system as a whole can lend by a multiple of its excess reserves. What is the monetary multiplier, and how does it relate to the reserve ratio? **LO8**

Problems

1. Assume that the following asset values (in millions of dollars) exist in Ironmania: Federal Reserve Notes in circulation = $700; Money market mutual funds (MMMFs) held by individuals = $400; Corporate bonds = $300; Iron ore deposits = $50; Currency in commercial banks = $100; Savings deposits, including money market deposit accounts (MMDAs) = $140; Checkable deposits = $1500; Small-denominated (less than $100,000) time deposits = $100; Coins in circulation = $40. **LO1**
   a. What is *M1* in Ironmania?
   b. What is *M2* in Ironmania?

2. Assume that Jimmy Cash has $2000 in his checking account at Folsom Bank and uses his checking account card to withdraw $200 of cash from the bank's ATM machine. By what dollar amount did the *M1* money supply change as a result of this single, isolated transaction? **LO1**

3. Suppose the price level and value of the U.S. dollar in year 1 are 1 and $1, respectively. If the price level rises to 1.25 in year 2, what is the new value of the dollar? If, instead, the price level falls to .50, what is the value of the dollar? **LO2**

4. Suppose that Lady Gaga goes to Las Vegas to play poker and at the last minute her record company says it will reimburse her for 50 percent of any gambling losses that she incurs. Will Lady Gaga wager more or less as a result of the reimbursement offer? What economic concept does your answer illustrate? **LO5**

5. Assume that securitization combined with borrowing and irrational exuberance in Hyperville have driven up the value of existing financial securities at a geometric rate, specifically from $2 to $4 to $8 to $16 to $32 to $64 over a six-year time period. Over the same period, the value of the assets underlying the securities rose at an arithmetic rate from $2 to $3 to $4 to $5 to $6 to $7. If these patterns hold for decreases as well as for increases, by how much would the value of the financial securities decline if the value of the underlying asset suddenly and unexpectedly fell by $5? **LO5**

6. Suppose the assets of the Silver Lode Bank are $100,000 higher than on the previous day and its net worth is up $20,000. By how much and in what direction must its liabilities have changed from the day before? **LO8**

7. Suppose that Serendipity Bank has excess reserves of $8000 and checkable deposits of $150,000. If the reserve ratio is 20 percent, what is the size of the bank's actual reserves? **LO8**

8. Third National Bank has reserves of $20,000 and checkable deposits of $100,000. The reserve ratio is 20 percent. Households deposit $5000 in currency into the bank and that currency is added to reserves. What level of excess reserves does the bank now have? **LO8**

9. The balance sheet below is for Big Bucks Bank. The reserve ratio is 20 percent. **LO8**
   a. What is the maximum amount of new loans that Big Bucks Bank can make? Show in columns 1 and 1′ how the bank's balance sheet will appear after the bank has lent this additional amount.
   b. By how much has the supply of money changed?
   c. How will the bank's balance sheet appear after checks drawn for the entire amount of the new loans have been cleared against the bank? Show the new balance sheet in columns 2 and 2′.
   d. Answer questions a, b, and c on the assumption that the reserve ratio is 15 percent.

10. Suppose the simplified consolidated balance sheet shown below is for the entire commercial banking system and that all figures are in billions of dollars. The reserve ratio is 25 percent. **LO8**
    a. What is the amount of excess reserves in this commercial banking system? What is the maximum amount the banking system might lend? Show in columns 1 and 1′ how the consolidated balance sheet would look after this amount has been lent. What is the size of the monetary multiplier?
    b. Answer the questions in part a assuming the reserve ratio is 20 percent. What is the resulting difference in the amount that the commercial banking system can lend?

Assets			Liabilities and net worth		
	(1)				(1′)
Reserves	$ 52	___	Checkable		
Securities	48	___	deposits	$200	___
Loans	100	___			

11. If the required reserve ratio is 10 percent, what is the monetary multiplier? If the monetary multiplier is 4, what is the required reserve ratio? **LO8**

Assets				Liabilities and net worth			
	(1)	(2)				(1′)	(2′)
Reserves	$22,000	___	___	Checkable			
Securities	38,000	___	___	deposits	$100,000	___	___
Loans	40,000	___	___				

FURTHER TEST YOUR KNOWLEDGE AT
www.brue3e.com

At the text's Online Learning Center, **www.brue3e.com**, you will find one or more web-based questions that require information from the Internet to answer. We urge you to check them out, since they will familiarize you with websites that may be helpful in other courses and perhaps even in your career. The OLC also features multiple-choice quizzes that give instant feedback and provides other helpful ways to further test your knowledge of the chapter.

CHAPTER FIFTEEN

Interest Rates and Monetary Policy

After reading this chapter, you should be able to:

1. Discuss how the equilibrium interest rate is determined in the market for money.
2. List and explain the goals and tools of monetary policy.
3. Describe the mechanisms by which monetary policy affects GDP and the price level.
4. Discuss the effectiveness of monetary policy and its shortcomings.
5. Describe how the Fed has used monetary policy in recent years to promote macroeconomic stability.

Some newspaper commentators have stated that the chairperson of the Federal Reserve Board (currently Ben Bernanke) is the second most powerful person in the United States, after the U.S. president. That is undoubtedly an exaggeration because the chair has only a single vote on the 7-person Federal Reserve Board and 12-person Federal Open Market Committee. But there can be no doubt about the chair's influence, the overall importance of the Federal Reserve, and the **monetary policy** that it conducts. Such policy consists of deliberate changes in the money supply to influence interest rates and thus the total level of spending in the economy. The goal of monetary policy is to achieve and maintain price-level stability, full employment, and economic growth.

Interest Rates

Before we examine how the Federal Reserve can influence the money supply and interest rates, we need to better understand the market in which interest rates are established. As indicated in Table 15.1, there are many different interest rates that vary by purpose, size, risk, maturity, and taxability. (Global Snapshot 15.1 compares one interest rate—the percentage rate on 3-month loans—for several countries in a recent year.) But for simplicity economists often speak of a single interest rate. As we will see, the interest rate in the economy results from the interaction of money demand and money supply.

The Demand for Money

Why does the public want to hold some of its wealth as *money?* There are two main reasons: to make purchases with it and to hold it as an asset.

Transactions Demand, D_t   People hold money because it is convenient for purchasing goods and services. Households usually are paid once a week, every 2 weeks, or monthly, whereas their expenditures are less predictable and typically more frequent. So households must have enough money on hand to buy groceries and pay mortgage and utility bills. Nor are businesses' revenues and expenditures simultaneous. Businesses need to have money available to pay for labor, materials, power, and other inputs. The demand for money as a medium of exchange is called the **transactions demand** for money.

monetary policy
A central bank's changing of the money supply to influence interest rates and assist the economy in achieving price-level stability, full employment, and economic growth.

transactions demand
The amount of money people want to hold for use as a medium of exchange.

TABLE 15.1

Selected U.S. Interest Rates, April 2012

Type of Interest Rate	Annual Percentage
20-year Treasury bond rate (interest rate on federal government security used to finance the public debt)	2.76%
90-day Treasury bill rate (interest rate on federal government security used to finance the public debt)	0.08
Prime interest rate (interest rate used as a reference point for a wide range of bank loans)	3.25
30-year mortgage rate (fixed interest rate on loans for houses)	3.82
4-year automobile loan rate (interest rate for new autos by automobile finance companies)	3.28
Tax-exempt state and municipal bond rate (interest rate paid on a low-risk bond issued by a state or local government)	3.90
Federal funds rate (interest rate on overnight loans between banks)	0.15
Consumer credit card rate (interest rate charged for credit card purchases)	16.35

Source: Federal Reserve, **www.federalreserve.gov**, and Bankrate.com, **www.bankrate.com**.

The level of nominal GDP is the main determinant of the amount of money demanded for transactions. The larger the total money value of all goods and services exchanged in the economy, the larger the amount of money needed to negotiate those transactions. The transactions demand for money varies directly with nominal GDP. We specify *nominal* GDP because households and firms will want more money for transactions if prices rise or if real output increases. In both instances there will be a need for a larger dollar volume to accomplish the desired transactions.

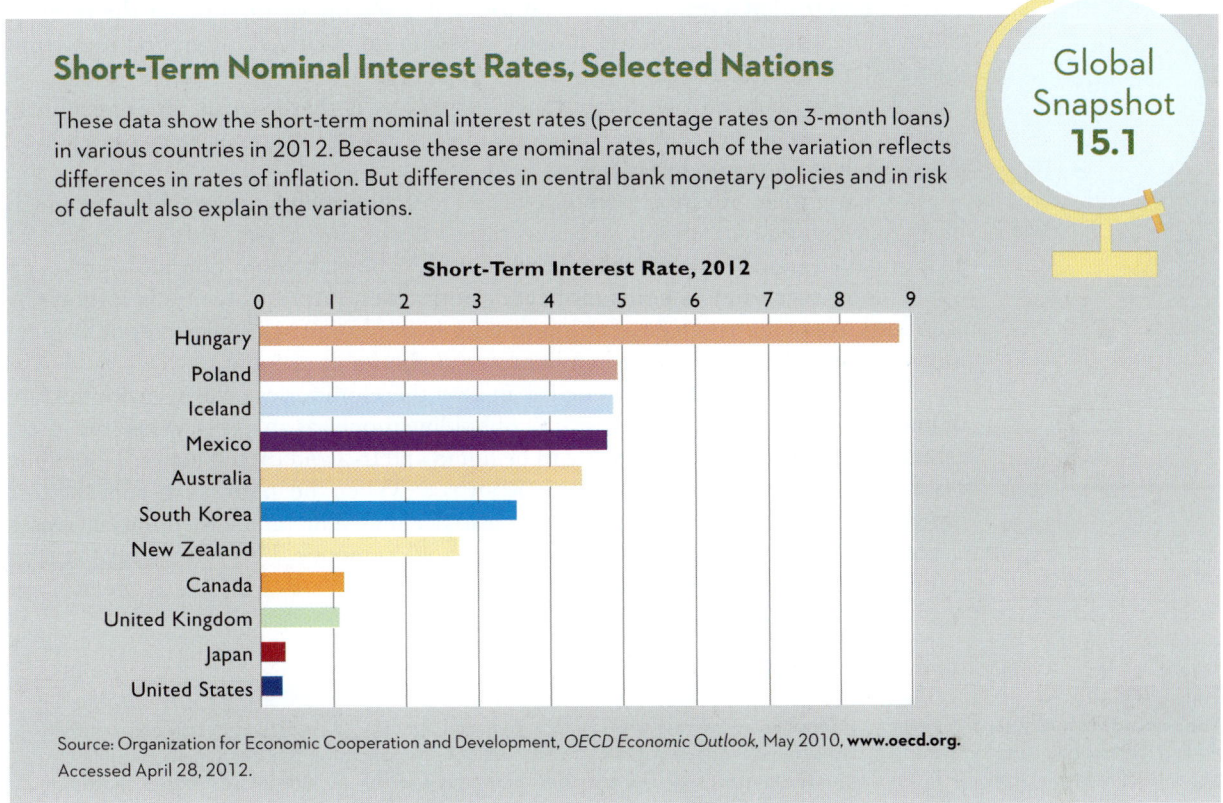

Short-Term Nominal Interest Rates, Selected Nations

Global Snapshot 15.1

These data show the short-term nominal interest rates (percentage rates on 3-month loans) in various countries in 2012. Because these are nominal rates, much of the variation reflects differences in rates of inflation. But differences in central bank monetary policies and in risk of default also explain the variations.

Short-Term Interest Rate, 2012

Source: Organization for Economic Cooperation and Development, *OECD Economic Outlook*, May 2010, **www.oecd.org.** Accessed April 28, 2012.

In Figure 15.1a we graph the quantity of money demanded for transactions against the interest rate. For simplicity, let's assume that the amount demanded depends exclusively on the level of nominal GDP and is independent of the real interest rate. (In reality, higher interest rates are associated with slightly lower volumes of money demanded for transactions.) Our simplifying assumption allows us to graph the transactions demand, D_t, as a vertical line. This demand curve is positioned at $100 billion, on the assumption that each dollar held for transactions purposes is spent an average of three times per year and that nominal GDP is $300 billion. Thus the public needs $100 billion (= $300 billion/3) to purchase that GDP.

Asset Demand, D_a   The second reason for holding money derives from money's function as a store of value. People may hold their financial assets in many forms, including corporate stocks, corporate or government bonds, or money. To the extent they want to hold money as an asset, there is an **asset demand** for money.

asset demand
The amount of money people want to hold as a store of value.

People like to hold some of their financial assets as money (apart from using it to buy goods and services) because money is the most liquid of all financial assets; it is immediately usable for purchasing other assets when opportunities arise.

Money is also an attractive asset to hold when the prices of other assets such as bonds are expected to decline. For example, when the price of a bond falls, the bondholder who sells the bond prior to the payback date of the full principal will suffer a loss (called a *capital loss*). That loss will partially or fully offset the interest received on the bond. Holding money presents no such risk of capital loss from changes in interest rates.

The disadvantage of holding money as an asset is that it earns no or very little interest. Checkable deposits pay either no interest or lower interest rates than bonds. Currency itself earns no interest at all.

Knowing these advantages and disadvantages, the public must decide how much of its financial assets to hold as money, rather than other assets such as bonds. The answer depends primarily on the rate of interest. A household or a business incurs an opportunity cost when it holds money; in both cases, interest income is forgone or sacrificed. If a bond pays 6 percent interest, for example, it costs $6 per year of forgone income to hold $100 as cash or in a noninterest checkable account.

The amount of money demanded as an asset therefore varies inversely with the rate of interest (which is the opportunity cost of holding money as an asset). When the interest rate rises, it becomes more costly to be liquid and to avoid capital losses. The public reacts by reducing its holdings of money as an asset. When the interest rate falls, the cost of being liquid and avoiding capital losses also declines. The public therefore increases the amount of financial assets that it wants to hold as money. This inverse relationship just described is shown by D_a in Figure 15.1b.

FIGURE 15.1

The demand for money, supply of money, and equilibrium interest rate. The total demand for money, D_m, is determined by horizontally adding the asset demand for money, D_a, to the transactions demand, D_t. The transactions demand is vertical because it is assumed to depend solely on nominal GDP rather than on the interest rate. The asset demand varies inversely with the interest rate because of the opportunity cost involved in holding currency and checkable deposits that pay no interest or very low interest. Combining the money supply, S_m, with the total money demand, D_m, portrays the money market and determines the equilibrium interest rate, i_e.

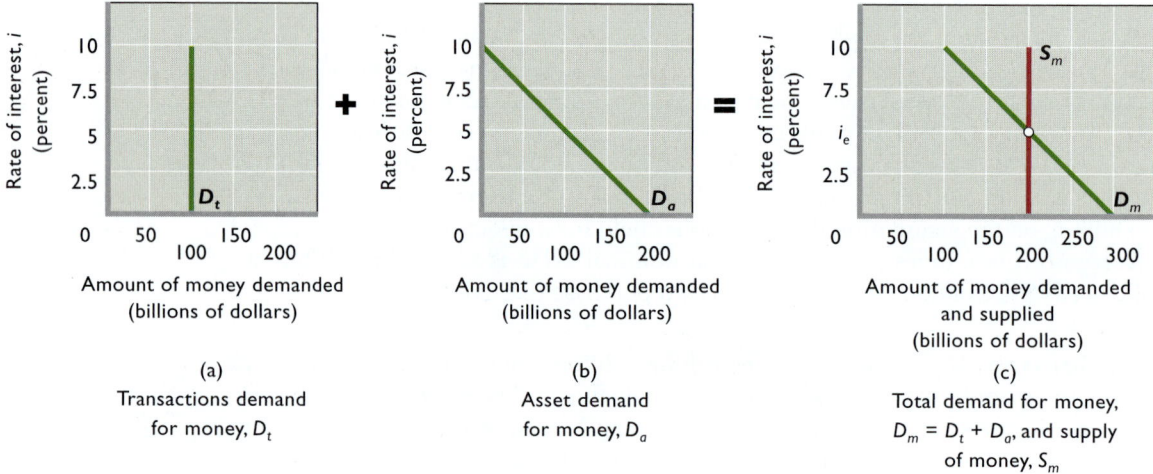

(a)	(b)	(c)
Transactions demand for money, D_t	Asset demand for money, D_a	Total demand for money, $D_m = D_t + D_a$, and supply of money, S_m

Total Money Demand, D_m   As shown in Figure 15.1, we find the **total demand for money**, D_m, by horizontally adding the asset demand to the transactions demand. The resulting downward-sloping line in Figure 15.1c represents the total amount of money the public wants to hold, both for transactions and as an asset, at each possible interest rate.

Recall that the transactions demand for money depends on the nominal GDP. A change in the nominal GDP—working through the transactions demand for money—will shift the total money demand curve. Specifically, an increase in nominal GDP means that the public wants to hold a larger amount of money for transactions, and that extra demand will shift the total money demand curve to the right. In contrast, a decline in the nominal GDP will shift the total money demand curve to the left. As an example, suppose nominal GDP increases from $300 billion to $450 billion and the average dollar held for transactions is still spent three times per year. Then the transactions demand curve will shift from $100 billion (= $300 billion/3) to $150 billion (= $450 billion/3). The total money demand curve will then lay $50 billion farther to the right at each possible interest rate.

total demand for money
The sum of the transactions demand and asset demand for money.

The Equilibrium Interest Rate

We can combine the demand for money with the supply of money to determine the equilibrium rate of interest. In Figure 15.1c the vertical line, S_m, represents the money supply. It is a vertical line because the monetary authorities and financial institutions have provided the economy with some particular stock of money. Here it is $200 billion.

Just as in a product market or a resource market, the intersection of demand and supply in the **money market** determines equilibrium price. In Figure 15.1, this equilibrium price is the equilibrium interest rate, i_e. At this interest rate, the quantity of money demanded (= $200 billion) equals the quantity of money supplied (= $200 billion). The equilibrium interest rate can be thought of as the market-determined price that borrowers must pay for using someone else's money over some period of time.

money market
The market in which the demand for and the supply of money determine the interest rate (or series of interest rates) in the economy.

That Is Interest

Interest is needed to entice individuals to give up liquidity or sacrifice their present consumption, that is, to let someone else use their money for a period of time. The following story told by economist Irving Fisher (1867–1947) helps illustrate the idea of the "time value of money." The irony is that it was Fisher who had earlier formalized this exact idea in his theory of interest.

In the process of a massage, a masseur informed Fisher that he was a socialist who believed that "interest is the basis of capitalism and is robbery." Following the massage, Fisher asked, "How much do I owe you?"
The masseur replied, "Thirty dollars."

Illustrating the Idea

"Very well," said Fisher, "I will give you a note payable a hundred years hence. I suppose you have no objections to taking this note without any interest. At the end of that time, you, or perhaps your grandchildren, can redeem it."

"But I cannot afford to wait that long," said the masseur.

"I thought you said that interest was robbery. If interest is robbery, you ought to be willing to wait indefinitely for the money. If you are willing to wait ten years, how much would you require?"

"Well, I would have to get more than thirty dollars. "

His point now made, Fisher replied, "That is interest."*

Question:
Who benefits most from lending at interest: the lender or the borrower?

*Irving Fisher, as quoted in Irving Norton Fisher, *My Father Irving Fisher* (New York: Comet, 1956), p. 77.

Tools of Monetary Policy

We can now explore how the Federal Reserve (the "Fed") can change the supply of money in the economy and therefore alter the interest rate. The Fed has three main tools of monetary control that it can use to alter the money supply: open-market operations, the reserve ratio, and the discount rate.

ORIGIN OF THE IDEA

O 15.2
Tools of monetary policy

Open-Market Operations

Bond markets are "open" to all buyers and sellers of corporate and government bonds (securities). The Federal Reserve is the largest single holder of U.S. government securities. The U.S. government, not the Fed, issued these Treasury bills (short-term securities), Treasury notes (mid-term securities), and Treasury bonds (long-term securities) to finance past budget deficits. Over the decades, the Fed has purchased these securities from major financial institutions that buy and sell government and corporate securities for themselves or their customers.

open-market operations
The buying and selling of U.S. government securities by the Fed for purposes of carrying out monetary policy.

The Fed's **open-market operations** consist of the buying of government bonds (U.S. securities) from, or the selling of government bonds to, commercial banks and the general public. The conduit for the Fed's open-market operations is the New York Federal Reserve Bank and a group of 16 or so large financial firms called "primary dealers." These financial institutions, in turn, buy the bonds from, and sell the bonds to, commercial banks and the general public. Open-market operations are the Fed's most important day-to-day instrument for influencing the money supply.

Buying Securities   Suppose the Federal Open Market Committee (FOMC) directs the Federal Reserve Bank of New York to buy $100 million of government bonds. The Federal Reserve Bank indirectly purchases these bonds from commercial banks (or thrifts) or the public. In both cases the reserves of the commercial banks will increase.

When a Federal Reserve Bank buys government bonds from *commercial banks*, those banks send some of their holdings of securities to the Federal Reserve Bank. In paying for the securities, the Federal Reserve Bank in essence writes checks for $100 million to the commercial banks. The banks deposit the $100 million of checks in their own accounts. When the checks clear against the Federal Reserve Bank, $100 million of reserves flow to the commercial banks. Because there are no new checkable deposits, the entire $100 million of new reserves in the banking system are excess reserves.

We know from Chapter 14 that excess reserves allow the banking system to make loans (expand the money supply) by a multiple of excess reserves. Suppose the reserve requirement is 20 percent, so the monetary multiplier is 5. Then commercial banks can expand the $100 million of excess reserves to $500 million of new checkable-deposit money.

The effect on commercial bank reserves is much the same when a Federal Reserve Bank purchases securities from the *general public* rather than directly from banks. The Federal Reserve Bank buys the $100 million of securities by issuing checks to the sellers, who deposit the checks in their checkable-deposit accounts at their commercial banks. When the checks clear, $100 million of new reserves flow from the Federal Reserve Bank to the commercial banks. Because the banks need only 20 percent of the new reserves for the $100 million of new checkable deposits, the commercial banks have excess reserves of $80 million (= $100 million of actual reserves − $20 million of required reserves). They lend out the excess reserves, expanding checkable deposits by $400 million (= 5 × $80 million). When added to the original checkable deposits of $100 million, the $400 million of loan-created checkable deposits result in a total of $500 million of new money in the economy.

> **WORKED PROBLEMS**
>
> **W 15.2**
> Open-market operations

Selling Securities   As you may suspect, when a Federal Reserve Bank sells government bonds, the reserves of commercial banks are reduced. Let's see why, this time dispensing with the math because it is the exact reverse of the prior examples.

When a Federal Reserve Bank sells securities in the open market to commercial banks, the Federal Reserve Bank gives up securities that the commercial banks acquire. To pay for those securities, the commercial banks in essence write checks payable to the Federal Reserve Bank. When the checks clear, reserves flow from the commercial banks to the Federal Reserve Bank. If all excess reserves are already lent out, this decline in commercial bank reserves produces a multiple decline in money created through lending. That is, the nation's money supply declines. This multiple decline in money will equal the decline in reserves times the monetary multiplier.

The outcome is the same when a Federal Reserve Bank sells securities to the public rather than directly to banks. The public pays for the securities with checks drawn on individuals' banks. When the checks clear, the commercial banks send reserves to the Federal Reserve Bank and reduce accordingly the checkable deposits of customers who wrote the checks. The lower reserves mean a multiple contraction of the money supply.

The Reserve Ratio

The Fed can also manipulate the reserve ratio in order to influence the ability of commercial banks to lend. Suppose a commercial bank's balance sheet shows that reserves are $5000 and checkable deposits are $20,000. If the reserve ratio is 20 percent (row 2, Table 15.2), the bank's required reserves are $4000. Since actual reserves are $5000, the excess reserves of this bank are $1000. On the basis of $1000 of excess reserves, this one bank can lend $1000; however, the banking system as a whole can create a maximum of $5000 of new checkable-deposit money by lending (column 7).

TABLE 15.2

The Effects of Changes in the Reserve Ratio on the Lending Ability of Commercial Banks

(1) Reserve Ratio, %	(2) Checkable Deposits	(3) Actual Reserves	(4) Required Reserves	(5) Excess Reserves, (3) − (4)	(6) Money-Creating Potential of Single Bank, = (5)	(7) Money-Creating Potential of Banking System
(1) 10	$20,000	$5000	$2000	$ 3000	$ 3000	$30,000
(2) 20	20,000	5000	4000	1000	1000	5,000
(3) 25	20,000	5000	5000	0	0	0
(4) 30	20,000	5000	6000	−1000	−1000	−3,333

Raising the Reserve Ratio   Now, what if the Fed raised the reserve ratio from 20 to 25 percent? (See row 3.) Required reserves would jump from $4000 to $5000, shrinking excess reserves from $1000 to zero. Raising the reserve ratio increases the amount of required reserves banks must keep. As a consequence, either the banks lose excess reserves, diminishing their ability to create money by lending, or they find their reserves deficient and are forced to contract checkable deposits and therefore the money supply. In the example in Table 15.2, excess reserves are transformed into required reserves, and the money-creating potential of our single bank is reduced from $1000 to zero (column 6). Moreover, the banking system's money-creating capacity declines from $5000 to zero (column 7).

What if the Fed increases the reserve requirement to 30 percent? (See row 4.) The commercial bank, to protect itself against the prospect of failing to meet this requirement, would be forced to lower its checkable deposits and at the same time increase its reserves. To reduce its checkable deposits, the bank could let outstanding loans mature and be repaid without extending new credit. This action would reduce the supply of money.

Lowering the Reserve Ratio   What would happen if the Fed lowered the reserve ratio from the original 20 percent to 10 percent? (See row 1.) In this case, required reserves would decline from $4000 to $2000 and excess reserves would jump from $1000 to $3000. The single bank's lending (money-creating) ability would increase from $1000 to $3000 (column 6) and the banking system's money-creating potential would expand from $5000 to $30,000 (column 7). Lowering the reserve ratio transforms required reserves into excess reserves and enhances the ability of banks to create new money by lending.

The examples in Table 15.2 show that a change in the reserve ratio affects the money-creating ability of the *banking system* in two ways:

- It changes the amount of excess reserves.
- It changes the size of the monetary multiplier.

For example, when the legal reserve ratio is raised from 10 to 20 percent, excess reserves are reduced from $3000 to $1000 and the monetary multiplier is reduced from 10 to 5. The money-creating potential of the banking system declines from $30,000 (= $3000 × 10) to $5000 (= $1000 × 5). Raising the reserve ratio forces banks to reduce the amount of checkable deposits they create through lending.

The Discount Rate

One of the functions of a central bank is to be a "lender of last resort." Occasionally, commercial banks have unexpected and immediate needs for additional funds. In such cases, each Federal Reserve Bank will make short-term loans to commercial banks in its district.

When a commercial bank borrows, it gives the Federal Reserve Bank a promissory note (IOU) drawn against itself and secured by acceptable collateral—typically U.S. government securities. Just as commercial banks charge interest on the loans they make to their clients, so too Federal Reserve Banks charge interest on loans they grant to commercial banks. The interest rate they charge is called the **discount rate.**

In providing the loan, the Federal Reserve Bank increases the reserves of the borrowing commercial bank. Since no required reserves need be kept against loans from Federal Reserve Banks, all new reserves acquired by borrowing from Federal Reserve Banks are excess reserves. In short, borrowing from the Federal Reserve Banks by commercial banks increases the reserves of the commercial banks and enhances their ability to extend credit.

The Fed has the power to set the discount rate at which commercial banks borrow from Federal Reserve Banks. From the commercial banks' point of view, the discount rate is a cost of acquiring reserves. A lowering of the discount rate entices commercial banks to obtain additional reserves, if needed, by borrowing from Federal Reserve Banks. When the commercial banks lend new reserves to bank customers, the money supply increases.

An increase in the discount rate discourages commercial banks from obtaining additional reserves through borrowing from the Federal Reserve Banks. So the Fed may raise the discount rate when it wants to restrict the money supply.

discount rate
The interest rate the Federal Reserve Banks charge on the loans they make to commercial banks and thrifts.

Relative Importance

All three of the Fed's primary instruments of monetary control are useful in particular economic circumstances, but open-market operations are clearly the most important of the three main tools over the course of the business cycle. The buying and selling of securities in the open market has the advantage of flexibility—government securities can be purchased or sold daily in large or small amounts—and the impact on bank reserves is prompt. And, compared with reserve-requirement changes, open-market operations work subtly and less directly. Furthermore, the ability of the Federal Reserve Banks to affect commercial bank reserves through the purchase and sale of bonds is virtually unquestionable. The Federal Reserve Banks have very large holdings of government securities ($1667 billion in April 2012, for example). The sale of those securities could theoretically reduce commercial bank reserves to zero.

Changing the reserve requirement is a potentially powerful instrument of monetary control, but the Fed has used this technique only sparingly. Normally, it can accomplish its monetary goals more easily through open-market operations. The last change in the reserve requirement was in 1992, when the Fed reduced the requirement from 12 percent to 10 percent. The main purpose was to shore up the profitability of banks and thrifts in the aftermath of the 1990–91 recession rather than to reduce interest rates by increasing reserves and expanding the money supply.

Until recently, the discount rate was mainly a passive tool of monetary control, with the Fed raising and lowering the rate simply to keep it in line with other interest rates. However, during the financial crisis of 2007–2008, the Fed aggressively lowered the discount rate independently of other interest rates in order to provide a cheap and plentiful source of reserves to banks whose reserves were being sharply reduced by unexpectedly high default rates on home mortgage loans. Banks borrowed billions at the lower discount rate. This allowed them to meet reserve requirements and thereby preserved their ability to keep extending loans.

Easy Money and Tight Money

Suppose the economy faces recession and unemployment. The Fed decides that an increase in the supply of money is needed to increase aggregate demand so as to employ idle resources. To increase the supply of money, the Fed must increase the excess reserves of commercial banks. How can it do that?

- *Buy securities* By purchasing securities in the open market, the Fed can increase commercial bank reserves. When the Fed's checks for the securities are cleared against it, the commercial banks discover that they have more reserves.
- *Lower the reserve ratio* By lowering the reserve ratio, the Fed changes required reserves into excess reserves and increases the size of the monetary multiplier.
- *Lower the discount rate* By lowering the discount rate, the Fed may entice commercial banks to borrow more reserves from the Fed.

easy money policy
Fed actions designed to increase the money supply, lower interest rates, and expand real GDP.

These actions are called an **easy money policy** (or *expansionary monetary policy*). Its purpose is to make bank loans less expensive and more available and thereby increase aggregate demand, output, and employment.

Suppose, on the other hand, excessive spending is pushing the economy into an inflationary spiral. Then the Fed should try to reduce aggregate demand by limiting or contracting the supply of money. That means reducing the reserves of commercial banks. How is that done?

- *Sell securities* By selling government bonds in the open market, the Federal Reserve Banks can reduce commercial bank reserves.
- *Increase the reserve ratio* An increase in the reserve ratio will automatically strip commercial banks of their excess reserves and decrease the size of the monetary multiplier.
- *Raise the discount rate* A boost in the discount rate will discourage commercial banks from borrowing from Federal Reserve Banks in order to build up their reserves.

tight money policy
Fed actions to reduce (or restrict) the growth of the nation's money supply, increase interest rates, and restrain inflation.

These actions are called a **tight money policy** (or *restrictive monetary policy*). The objective is to tighten the supply of money in order to reduce spending and control inflation.

Monetary Policy, Real GDP, and the Price Level

So far we have explained only how the Fed can change the money supply. Now we need to link up the money supply, the interest rate, investment spending, and aggregate demand to see how monetary policy affects the economy. How does monetary policy work?

INTERACTIVE GRAPHS

G 15.2
Monetary policy

Cause-Effect Chain

The three diagrams in Figure 15.2 will help you understand how monetary policy works toward achieving its goals.

Market for Money   Figure 15.2a represents the market for money, in which the demand curve for money and the supply curve of money are brought together. Recall that the total demand for money is made up of the transactions and asset demands. The transactions demand is directly related to the nominal GDP. The asset demand is inversely related to the interest rate. The interest rate is the opportunity cost of holding money as an asset; the higher that cost, the smaller the amount of money the public wants to hold. The total demand for money, D_m, is thus inversely related to the interest rate, as is indicated in Figure 15.2a. Also, recall that an increase in nominal GDP will shift D_m to the right and a decline in nominal GDP will shift D_m to the left.

This figure also shows three potential money supply curves, S_{m1}, S_{m2}, and S_{m3}. In each case the money supply is shown as a vertical line representing some fixed amount of money determined by the Fed. While monetary policy (specifically, the supply of money) helps determine the interest rate, the interest rate does not determine the location of the money supply curve.

The equilibrium interest rate is the rate at which the amount of money demanded and the amount supplied are equal. With money demand D_m in Figure 15.2a, if the supply of money is $125 billion ($S_{m1}$), the equilibrium interest rate is 10 percent. With a money supply of $150 billion ($S_{m2}$), the equilibrium interest rate is 8 percent; with a money supply of $175 billion ($S_{m3}$), it is 6 percent.

Investment   These 10, 8, and 6 percent real interest rates are carried rightward to the investment demand curve in Figure 15.2b. This curve shows the inverse relationship between the interest rate—the cost of borrowing to invest—and the amount of investment spending. At the 10 percent interest rate it will be profitable for the nation's businesses to invest $15 billion; at 8 percent, $20 billion; at 6 percent, $25 billion.

Changes in the interest rate mainly affect the investment component of total spending, although they also affect spending on durable consumer goods (such as autos) that are purchased on credit. The impact of changing interest rates on investment spending is great because of the large cost and long-term nature of capital purchases. Manufacturing equipment, factory buildings, and warehouses are tremendously expensive. In absolute terms, interest charges on funds borrowed for these purchases are considerable.

Similarly, the interest cost on a house purchased on a long-term contract is very large: A percentage-point change in the interest rate would amount to thousands of dollars in the total cost of a typical home.

Also, changes in the interest rate may affect investment spending by changing the relative attractiveness of purchases of capital equipment versus purchases of bonds. In purchasing capital goods, the interest rate is the cost of borrowing the funds to make the investment. In purchasing bonds, the interest rate is the return on the financial investment. If the interest rate increases, the cost of buying capital goods increases while the return on bonds increases. Businesses are then more inclined to use business savings to buy securities than to buy equipment. Conversely, a drop in the interest rate makes purchases of capital goods relatively more attractive than bond ownership.

In brief, the impact of changing interest rates is mainly on investment (and, through that, on aggregate demand, output, employment, and the price level). Moreover, as Figure 15.2b shows, investment spending varies inversely with the interest rate.

FIGURE 15.2

Monetary policy and equilibrium GDP. An easy money policy that shifts the money supply curve rightward from S_{m1} to S_{m2} lowers the interest rate from 10 percent to 8 percent. As a result, investment spending increases from $15 billion to $20 billion, shifting the aggregate demand curve rightward from AD_1 to AD_2, and real output rises from the recessionary level Q_1 to the full-employment level Q_f. A tight money policy that shifts the money supply curve leftward from S_{m3} to S_{m2} increases the interest rate from 6 percent to 8 percent. Investment spending thus falls from $25 billion to $20 billion, and the aggregate demand curve shifts leftward from AD_3 to AD_2, curtailing inflation.

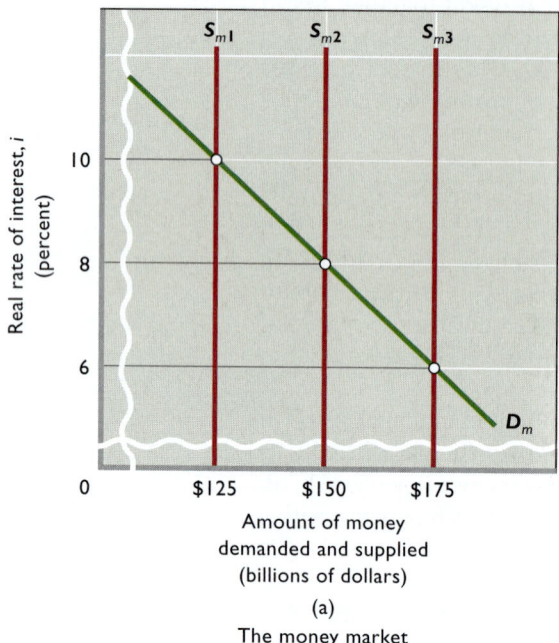

(a)
The money market

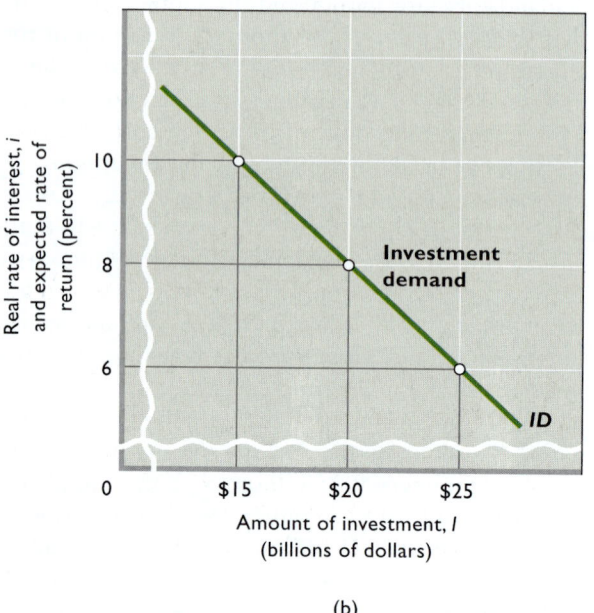

(b)
Investment demand

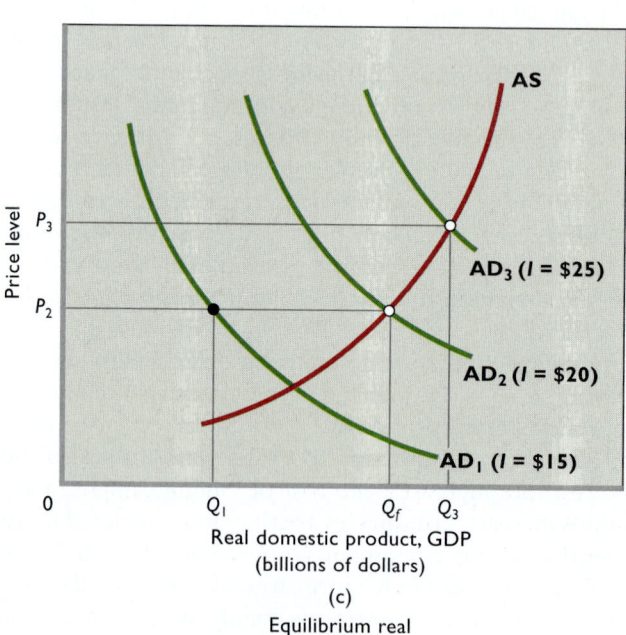

(c)
Equilibrium real
GDP and the price
level

Equilibrium GDP Figure 15.2c shows the impact of our three interest rates and corresponding levels of investment spending on aggregate demand. As noted, aggregate demand curve AD_1 is associated with the $15 billion level of investment, AD_2 with investment of $20 billion, and AD_3 with investment of $25 billion. That is, investment spending is one of the determinants of aggregate demand. Other things equal, the greater the investment spending, the farther to the right lies the aggregate demand curve.

Suppose the money supply in Figure 15.2a is $150 billion ($S_{m2}$), producing an equilibrium interest rate of 8 percent. In Figure 15.2b we see that this 8 percent interest rate will bring forth $20 billion of investment spending. This $20 billion of investment spending joins with consumption spending, net exports, and government spending to yield aggregate demand curve AD_2 in Figure 15.2c. The equilibrium levels of real output and prices are Q_f and P_2, as determined by the intersection of AD_2 and the aggregate supply curve AS.

To test your understanding of these relationships, explain why each of the other two levels of money supply in Figure 15.2a results in a different interest rate, level of investment, aggregate demand curve, and equilibrium real output.

Effects of an Easy Money Policy

Next, suppose that the money supply is $125 billion ($S_{m1}$) in Figure 15.2a. Because the resulting real output Q_1 in Figure 15.2c is far below the full-employment output, Q_f, the economy must be experiencing recession and substantial unemployment. The Fed therefore should institute an easy money policy.

To increase the money supply, the Federal Reserve Banks will take some combination of the following actions: (1) Buy government securities from banks and the public in the open market, (2) lower the legal reserve ratio, and (3) lower the discount rate. The intended outcome will be an increase in excess reserves in the commercial banking system. Because excess reserves are the basis on which commercial banks and thrifts can earn profit by lending and thus creating checkable-deposit money, the nation's money supply probably will rise. An increase in the money supply will lower the interest rate, increasing investment, aggregate demand, and equilibrium GDP.

For example, an increase in the money supply from $125 billion to $150 billion ($S_{m1}$ to S_{m2}) will reduce the interest rate from 10 to 8 percent, as indicated in Figure 15.2a, and will boost investment from $15 billion to $20 billion, as shown in Figure 15.2b. This $5 billion increase in investment will shift the aggregate demand curve rightward, as shown by the shift from AD_1 to AD_2 in Figure 15.2c. This rightward shift in the aggregate demand curve will eliminate the negative GDP gap by increasing GDP from Q_1 to the full-employment GDP of Q_f.[1]

Column 1 in Table 15.3 summarizes the chain of events associated with an easy money policy.

Effects of a Tight Money Policy

Now let's assume that the money supply is $175 billion ($S_{m3}$) in Figure 15.2a. This results in an interest rate of 6 percent, investment spending of $25 billion, and aggregate

---

[1]For simplicity we assume that the increase in real GDP does not increase the demand for money. In reality, the transactions demand for money would rise, slightly dampening the decline in the interest rate shown in Figure 15.2a. We also assume that the price level was inflexible downward at P_2 when the economy entered the recession. So the easy money policy expands real GDP from Q_1 to Q_f without causing inflation.

TABLE 15.3

Monetary Policies for Recession and Inflation

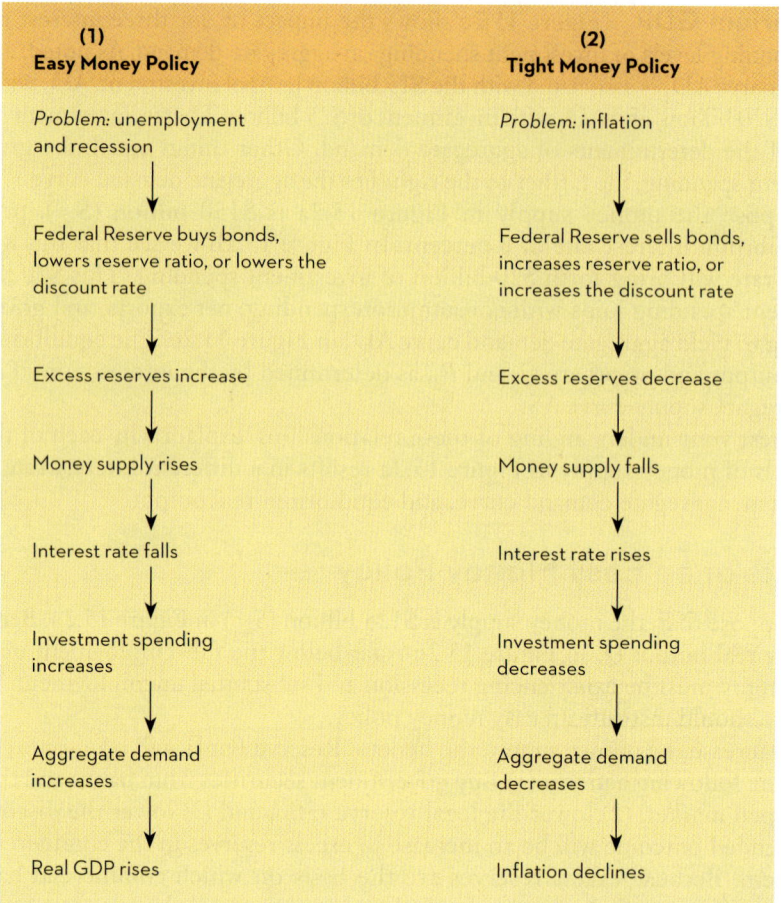

(1) Easy Money Policy	(2) Tight Money Policy
Problem: unemployment and recession	*Problem:* inflation
↓	↓
Federal Reserve buys bonds, lowers reserve ratio, or lowers the discount rate	Federal Reserve sells bonds, increases reserve ratio, or increases the discount rate
↓	↓
Excess reserves increase	Excess reserves decrease
↓	↓
Money supply rises	Money supply falls
↓	↓
Interest rate falls	Interest rate rises
↓	↓
Investment spending increases	Investment spending decreases
↓	↓
Aggregate demand increases	Aggregate demand decreases
↓	↓
Real GDP rises	Inflation declines

demand AD_3. As you can see in Figure 15.2c, we have depicted a positive GDP gap of $Q_3 - Q_f$ and demand-pull inflation. Aggregate demand AD_3 is excessive relative to the economy's full-employment level of real output Q_f. To rein in spending, the Fed will institute a tight money policy.

The Federal Reserve Board will direct Federal Reserve Banks to undertake some combination of the following actions: (1) sell government securities to banks and the public in the open market, (2) increase the legal reserve ratio, and (3) increase the discount rate. Banks then will discover that their reserves are below those required. So they will need to reduce their checkable deposits by refraining from issuing new loans as old loans are paid back. This will shrink the money supply and increase the interest rate. The higher interest rate will discourage investment, lowering aggregate demand and restraining demand-pull inflation.

If the Fed reduces the money supply from $175 billion to $150 billion ($S_{m3}$ to S_{m2} in Figure 15.2a), the interest rate will rise from 6 to 8 percent and investment will decline from $25 billion to $20 billion (Figure 15.2b). This $5 billion decrease in investment will shift the aggregate demand curve leftward from AD_3 to AD_2 (Figure 15.2c). This leftward shift of the aggregate demand curve will eliminate the excessive spending and halt the demand-pull inflation. In the real world, of course, the goal will be to stop inflation—that is, to halt further increases in the price level—

rather than to actually drive down the price level, which tends to be inflexible downward.[2] Given the downward inflexibility of prices, reducing the money supply to $150 billion would push the equilibrium GDP below its full employment level. To stop the inflation and restore output to its full employment level without causing a recession, a smaller monetary contraction would be necessary.

Column 2 in Table 15.3 summarizes the cause-effect chain of a tight money policy.

Monetary Policy in Action

We now turn from monetary policy in theory to monetary policy in action. Monetary policy has become the dominant component of U.S. national stabilization policy. It has two key advantages over fiscal policy:

- Speed and flexibility.
- Isolation from political pressure.

Compared with fiscal policy, monetary policy can be quickly altered. Recall that congressional deliberations may delay the application of fiscal policy for months. In contrast, the Fed can buy or sell securities from day to day and thus affect the money supply and interest rates almost immediately.

Also, because members of the Fed's Board of Governors are appointed and serve 14-year terms, they are relatively isolated from lobbying and need not worry about retaining their popularity with voters. Thus, the Board, more readily than Congress, can engage in politically unpopular policies (higher interest rates) that may be necessary for the long-term health of the economy. Moreover, monetary policy is a subtler and more politically neutral measure than fiscal policy. Changes in government spending directly affect the allocation of resources, and changes in taxes can have extensive political ramifications. Because monetary policy works more subtly, it is more politically palatable.

The Focus on the Federal Funds Rate

The Fed currently focuses monetary policy on altering the **Federal funds rate** as needed to stabilize the economy. Normal day-to-day flows of funds to banks rarely leave all banks with their exact levels of legally required reserves. Also, funds held at the Federal Reserve Banks are highly liquid, but they earn less interest than commercial banks can obtain from other sources. Banks therefore prefer to lend these excess reserves to other banks on an overnight basis to earn interest without sacrificing long-term liquidity. Banks that borrow in this Federal funds market—the market for immediately available reserve balances at the Federal Reserve—do so because they are temporarily short of required reserves. The interest rate paid on these overnight loans is called the *Federal funds rate*.

Because the Federal Reserve can control the supply of Federal funds—the supply of reserves in the banking system—it can control the Federal funds interest rate. The Fed is a monopoly supplier of reserves. When it wants to increase the Federal funds rate, it sells securities in the open market to reduce (or withdraw) bank reserves. This is

Federal funds rate
The interest rate banks and thrifts charge one another on overnight loans made out of their excess reserves.

---

[2]Again, we assume for simplicity that the decrease in nominal GDP does not feed back to reduce the demand for money and thus the interest rate. In reality, this would occur, slightly dampening the increase in the interest rate shown in Figure 15.2a.

FIGURE 15.3

The prime interest rate and the Federal funds rate in the United States, 1998–2011. The prime interest rate rises and falls with changes in the Federal funds rate.

Source: *Federal Reserve Statistical Release*, Historical Data, H.15, **www.federalreserve.gov.**

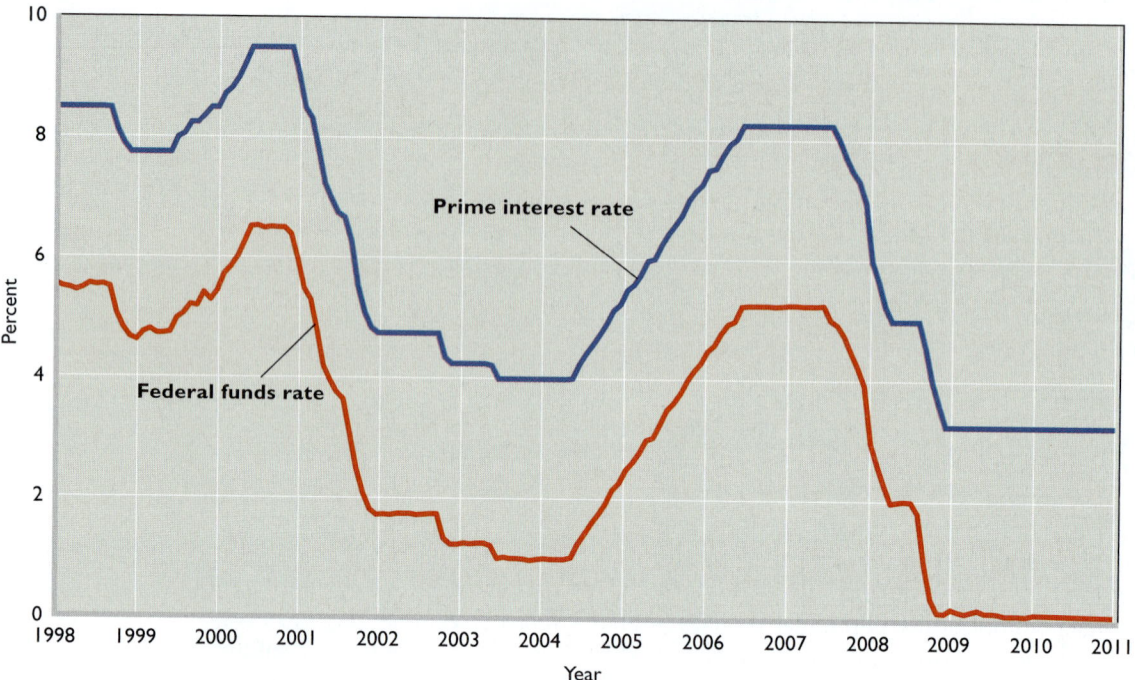

prime interest rate
The benchmark interest rate that banks and thrifts use as a reference point for a wide range of loans to businesses and individuals.

a "tighter" or "more restrictive" monetary policy. When it wants to reduce the Federal funds rate, it buys securities in the open market to increase (or inject) reserves. This is an "easier" or "more accommodating" monetary policy.

The Fed can target the Federal funds rate because it knows that interest rates in general typically rise and fall with that rate. For example, in Figure 15.3 observe that the **prime interest rate** generally parallels the Federal funds rate. The prime interest rate is the benchmark rate that banks use as a reference point for a wide range of interest rates on loans to businesses and individuals. By changing the Federal funds rate, the Fed in effect alters the economy's prime interest rate along with a wide array of other short-term interest rates.

Why the lockstep pattern between the Federal funds rate and the prime interest rate? Sales of securities by the Fed in the open market reduce excess reserves in the banking system, lessening the supply of excess reserves available for overnight loans in the Federal funds market. The decreased supply of excess reserves in that market increases the Federal funds rate. In addition, reduced excess reserves decrease the amount of bank lending and hence the amount of checkable-deposit money. Declines in the supply of money produce higher interest rates in general, including the prime interest rate.

Purchases of securities by the Fed in the open market increase the supply of reserves in the Federal funds market, reducing the Federal funds rate. The money supply rises because the increased supply of excess reserves leads to more lending and thus greater creation of checkable-deposit money. As a result, interest rates in general fall, including the prime interest rate.

Recent U.S. Monetary Policy

The Fed has been highly active in its use of monetary policy in recent decades. To demonstrate this fact, let's begin with the year 2000, when the economy abruptly slowed after a long period of full employment and strong economic growth. The Fed responded to the slowdown by cutting the Federal funds interest rate by a full percentage point in two increments in January 2001. Despite those rate cuts, the economy entered a recession in March 2001. Between March 20, 2001, and August 21, 2001, the Fed reduced the Federal funds rate from 5 percent to 3.5 percent in a series of steps. In the 3 months following the terrorist attacks of September 11, 2001, it lowered the Federal funds rate from 3.5 percent to 1.75 percent, and it left the rate there until it lowered it to 1.25 percent in November 2002. Partly because of the Fed's actions, the prime interest rate dropped from 9.5 percent at the end of 2000 to 4.25 percent in December 2002.

Economists generally give the Fed high marks for helping to keep the recession of 2001 relatively mild, particularly in view of the adverse economic impacts of the terrorist attacks of September 11, 2001, and the steep stock-market decline in 2001–2002.

The Fed left the Federal funds rate at historic lows in 2003. But as the economy began to expand robustly in 2004, the Fed engineered a gradual series of rate hikes designed to boost the prime interest rate and other interest rates to make sure that aggregate demand continued to grow at a pace consistent with low inflation. By the summer of 2006, the target for the Federal funds rate had risen to 5.25 percent and the prime rate was 8.25 percent. With the economy enjoying sustainable, noninflationary growth, the Fed left the Federal funds rate at 5.25 percent for over a year.

The mortgage default crisis (discussed in Chapter 14) began during the late summer of 2007 and posed a grave threat to the financial system and the economy. In response, the Fed took several actions. In August it lowered the discount rate by half a percentage point. Then, between September 2007 and April 2008, it lowered the target for the Federal funds rate from 5.25 percent to 2 percent. As discussed below, the Fed also took a series of extraordinary actions to prevent the failure of key financial firms.

In October 2008, the Fed first reduced the Federal funds target rate to 1.5 percent and then later that same month to 1 percent. In December 2008, the Fed lowered it further to a targeted range of 0 percent to 0.25 percent. The Federal funds rate remained in that range through September 2009. The Fed aggressively increased the supply of Federal funds to lower the actual Federal funds rate to its target level. All these monetary actions and lender-of-last-resort functions described below helped to stabilize the banking sector and keep credit flowing—thereby offsetting at least some of the damage done by the financial crisis.

The decline in the Federal funds rate to near zero during the financial and economic crisis dropped the prime interest rate (review Figure 15.3). In December 2007, the prime interest rate stood at 7.3 percent. By January 2009, it had declined to 3.25 percent, where it remained well into 2012.

In addition to lowering interest rates, the Fed engaged heavily in open-market operations, albeit with a twist. In what has come to be known as *quantitative easing*, the Fed purchased both government and private securities in an effort to expand bank reserves. However, with the economy slow to recover and with no further room to lower short-term interest rates, in November 2010 the Fed initiated a second round of quantitative easing, often termed *QE2*. QE2 differed from traditional open-market operations in that it focused on purchasing longer-term U.S. Treasury securities in an effort to lower longer-term interest rates that influence business investment and larger consumer purchases. From November 2010 until QE2's completion in June 2011, the Fed purchased $600 billion in longer-term Treasury securities. In November 2011, with the economy still sluggish, the Fed announced that it would purchase long-term securities with the proceeds from selling short-term securities. This effort to reduce long-term interest rates was known as the maturity extension program, or "operation twist."

With economic growth still anemic and with little threat of inflation increasing, the Fed announced in April 2012 its intention to keep interests rates low until late 2014. The Federal Reserve is lauded by many observers for its quick and innovative actions during the financial crisis and severe recession. Nevertheless, some economists contend that the Fed contributed to the financial crisis by holding the Federal funds interest rate too low for too long during the recovery from the 2001 recession. These critics say that the artificially low interest rates made mortgage and other loans too inexpensive and therefore contributed to the borrowing frenzy by home-owners and other financial investors. Other economists counter that the low mortgage interest rates resulted from huge inflows of savings from abroad to a wide variety of U.S. financial markets.

Question:
What is the current monetary policy stance of the Fed? Has it been increasing interest rates, decreasing them, or leaving them unchanged in recent months? (Answer this question by going to the Federal Reserve's website, www.federalreserve.gov.)

Applying the Analysis

The Financial Crisis: The Fed Responds

As noted in Chapter 14's list of Fed functions, one of the roles of the Federal Reserve is to serve as the lender of last resort to financial institutions in times of financial emergencies. The Fed performed this vital function well following the 9/11 terrorist attacks. The financial crisis of 2007–2008 presented another, broader-based financial emergency. Under Fed Chair Ben Bernanke, the Fed designed and implemented several highly creative new lender-of-last-resort facilities to pump liquidity into the financial system. These facilities, procedures, and capabilities were in addition to both the TARP efforts by the U.S. Treasury and the Fed's use of standard tools of monetary policy designed to reduce interest rates. All the new Fed facilities had the single purpose and desired outcome of keeping credit flowing.

Total Fed assets rose from $885 billion in February 2008 to $2854 billion in July 2011. This increase reflected a huge rise in the amount of securities (U.S. securities, mortgage-backed securities, and others) owned by the Fed. In undertaking its lender-of-last-resort functions, the Fed bought these securities from financial institutions. The purpose was to increase liquidity in the financial system by exchanging illiquid bonds (that the firms could not easily sell during the crisis) for cash, the most liquid of all assets.

Many economists believe that TARP and the Fed's actions helped avert a second Great Depression. The following list of new Fed credit facilities underscores the extraordinary extent of the Fed's lender-of-last-resort response to the crisis. Most of these programs terminated in 2010, but the Fed could reestablish them in the event of another financial crisis.

- *Term Auction Facility (TAF)* Provided short-term loans of reserves to commercial banks through a secret bidding process. With auctions conducted twice monthly, the Fed received written bids from commercial banks, indicating the quantity of reserves desired and the maximum interest rate the commercial bank was willing to pay. Starting with the highest interest rate bidder, commercial banks received desired reserves until the total reserves available through the auction were exhausted. (Final auction held March 8, 2010)
- *Primary Dealer Credit Facility (PDCF)* Provided overnight loans to primary dealers who were willing to post loan-backed securities as collateral. (The Fed kept the collateral on any loan not repaid on time.) Primary dealers are the 16 major financial institutions that the Fed uses to buy and sell U.S. securities. (Closed February 1, 2010)
- *Term Securities Lending Facility (TSLF)* Lent U.S. securities to primary dealers for one-month terms to promote liquidity in the markets for those U.S. securities. The financial institutions obtained the securities from the Fed through participating in competitive single-bid auctions. (Closed February 1, 2010)
- *Asset-Backed Commercial Paper Money Market Mutual Fund Liquidity Facility (AMLF)* Provided loans to U.S. banks and thrifts to finance their purchases of *commercial paper* from money market mutual funds. Commercial paper consists of asset-backed, short-term IOUs that are mainly issued by corporations. These short-term loans were vital for financing the day-to-day operations of businesses. (Closed February 1, 2010)
- *Commercial Paper Funding Facility (CPFF)* Purchased commercial paper to support the commercial paper market and therefore the short-term credit needs of businesses. (Closed February 1, 2010)
- *Money Market Investor Funding Facility (MMIFF)* Provided funding support to a private-sector initiative designed to ensure the liquidity of U.S. money market mutual funds. Many Americans rely on money market mutual funds as low-risk investments. (Expired October 30, 2009)
- *Term Asset-Backed Securities Loan Facility (TALF)* Helped households and businesses with their credit needs by providing funding support for asset-backed securities collateralized by student loans, auto loans, credit card loans, and loans guaranteed by the Small Business Administration (SBA). (Closed June 30, 2010)
- *Interest Payments on Reserves* Bolsters the profitability of banks by paying interest on the reserves they hold in their vaults or in the Federal Reserve Banks.

These extraordinary efforts, like those of the Treasury, helped prevent total disarray in the credit markets. But like TARP, the Fed efforts intensified the moral hazard problem by greatly limiting the losses that otherwise would have resulted from bad financial assumptions and decisions.

Question:
Did the Fed's actions (along with fiscal policies enacted during the same period) succeed in preventing recession or promoting a strong recovery?

Problems and Complications

Despite its recent successes in the United States, monetary policy has certain limitations and faces real-world complications.

Lags   Recall that fiscal policy is hindered by three delays, or lags—a recognition lag, an administrative lag, and an operational lag. Monetary policy also faces a recognition lag and an operational lag, but because the Fed can decide and implement policy changes within days, it avoids the long administrative lag that hinders fiscal policy.

A recognition lag affects monetary policy because normal monthly variations in economic activity and the price level mean that the Fed may not be able to quickly recognize when the economy is truly starting to recede or when inflation is really starting to rise. Once the Fed acts, an operational lag of 3 to 6 months or more affects monetary policy because that much time is typically required for interest-rate changes to have their full impacts on investment, aggregate demand, real GDP, and the price level.

Cyclical Asymmetry and the Liquidity Trap   Monetary policy may be highly effective in slowing expansions and controlling inflation but may be much less reliable in pushing the economy from a severe recession. Economists say that monetary policy may suffer from **cyclical asymmetry.** The metaphor of "pushing on a string" is often invoked to capture this problem. Imagine the Fed standing on the left-hand side of Figure 15.2c, holding one end of a "monetary-policy string." And imagine that the other end of the monetary-policy string is tied to the AD curve. Because the string would go taut if pulled on, monetary policy may be useful in *pulling* aggregate demand to the left. But because the string would go limp if pushed on, monetary policy will be rather ineffective at *pushing* aggregate demand to the right.

The reason for this asymmetry has to do with the asymmetric way in which people may act in response to changes in bank reserves. If pursued vigorously, a restrictive monetary policy can deplete commercial banking reserves to the point where banks are forced to reduce the volume of loans. That means a contraction of the money supply, higher interest rates, and reduced aggregate demand. The Fed can absorb sufficient reserves and eventually achieve its goal.

But the Fed cannot be certain of achieving its goal when it adds reserves to the banking system because of the so-called **liquidity trap,** in which adding more liquidity to banks has little or no additional positive effect on lending, borrowing, investment, or aggregate demand. For example, during the recent recession, the Fed created billions of dollars of excess reserves that drove down the Federal funds rate to as low as 0.2 percent. The prime interest rate fell from 7.3 percent (December 2007) to 3.25 percent (March 2009). Nevertheless, lending by banks stalled throughout the first 15 months of the recession. The banks were fearful that the loans they would make to households, businesses, and other financial institutions would not be paid back. Consequently, they were content to hold reserves at the Federal Reserve Banks.

To switch analogies, an expansionary monetary policy suffers from a "you can lead a horse to water, but you can't make it drink" problem. The Fed can create excess reserves, but it cannot guarantee that the banks will actually make additional loans and thus promote spending. If commercial banks seek liquidity and are unwilling to lend, the efforts of the Fed will be of little avail. Similarly, households and businesses can frustrate the intentions of the Fed by not borrowing excess reserves being made available as loans. And when the Fed buys securities from the public, people may choose to pay off existing loans with the money received, rather than increasing their spending on goods and services.

cyclical asymmetry
The potential problem of monetary policy successfully controlling inflation during the expansionary phase of the business cycle but failing to expand spending and real GDP during the recessionary phase of the cycle.

liquidity trap
A situation in a severe recession in which the Fed's injection of additional reserves into the banking system has little or no additional positive impact on lending, borrowing, investment, or aggregate demand.

Furthermore, a severe recession may so undermine business confidence that the investment demand curve shifts to the left and overwhelms the lower interest rates associated with an expansionary monetary policy. That is what happened in the most recent recession. Although the Fed drove the real interest rate down to zero percent, investment spending remained low and the economy remained mired in recession. The recent U.S. experience reminds us that active monetary policy certainly is not a cure-all for the business cycle. Under some circumstances, monetary policy may be like "pushing on a string."

The liquidity trap that occurred during the severe recession was a primary reason why public policy in the United States turned so significantly and forcefully toward fiscal policy in 2009. Recall our discussion of the American Recovery and Redevelopment Act of 2009, which authorized the infusion of $787 billion of new tax cuts and government spending in 2009 and 2010.

Up, Up, and Away

Applying the Analysis

The consolidated balance sheet of the 12 Federal Reserve Banks changed markedly as a result of the severe recession of 2007–2009. Total Fed assets increased from $885 billion in February 2008 to $2831 billion in June 2011. This increase reflected an enormous rise in the number of U.S. securities, mortgage-backed securities, and other financial assets purchased by the Federal Reserve. In undertaking its monetary policy and its lender-of-last-resort functions, the Fed bought these securities from financial institutions—purposely increasing the liquidity of the financial system. The Fed also increased its loans to financial institutions, particularly through the term auction facility. Because term auction loans are "owed to" the Fed, the accounting credits for them are assets on the Fed's balance sheet.

On the liability side, the reserves of commercial banks rose from $43 billion in February 2008 to $1706 billion in June 2011. To make sure they were liquid and the funds were safe, banks placed much of the proceeds from selling securities to the Fed into their respective reserve accounts at the Fed. This flow was strengthened because the Fed began paying interest on the reserves that banks were holding at the Fed.

In June 2011 total bank reserves held at the Fed exceeded total checkable deposits held by the banks. The severe distress in the financial system had voluntarily turned the fractional reserve system into a 100-percent-plus reserve system! The banks had enormous excess reserves from which to increase lending once the banks became more certain of their own financial viability and the likelihood that newly issued loans would be paid back.

The Fed therefore faces a challenging task of using monetary policy to absorb large portions of this overstock of excess reserves as the economy recovers and picks up momentum. It does not want the banks to lend out the full amount of these excess reserves because that would flood the economy with bank-created money and excessively expand the money supply. During a vigorous economic expansion, the excessive money and resulting very low interest rates could produce such large expansions of aggregate demand that rapid inflation would occur.

Question:
What does a 100-percent-plus reserve system imply for the monetary multiplier?

Summary

1. There is a set of interest rates that vary by loan purpose, size, risk, maturity, and taxability. Nevertheless, economists often speak of a single interest rate in order to simplify their analysis.

2. The total demand for money consists of the transactions demand and asset demand for money. The amount of money demanded for transactions varies directly with the nominal GDP; the amount of money demanded as an asset varies inversely with the interest rate. The money market combines the total demand for money with the money supply to determine equilibrium interest rates.

3. The goal of monetary policy is to help the economy achieve price stability, full employment, and economic growth.

4. The three main instruments of monetary policy are (a) open-market operations, (b) the reserve ratio, and (c) the discount rate.

5. The Fed's most often used monetary policy tool is its open-market operations. The Fed injects reserves into the banking system (and reduces interest rates) by buying securities from commercial banks and the general public. The Fed withdraws reserves from the banking system (and increases interest rates) by selling securities to commercial banks and the general public.

6. Monetary policy affects the economy through a complex cause-effect chain: (a) Policy decisions affect commercial bank reserves; (b) changes in reserves affect the money supply; (c) changes in the money supply alter the interest rate; (d) changes in the interest rate affect investment; (e) changes in investment affect aggregate demand; and (f) changes in aggregate demand affect the equilibrium real GDP and the price level. Table 15.3 draws together all the basic ideas relevant to the use of monetary policy.

7. The advantages of monetary policy include its flexibility and political acceptability. Recently, the Fed has targeted changes in the Federal funds rate as the immediate focus of its monetary policy. When it deems it necessary, the Fed uses open-market operations to change that rate, which is the interest rate banks charge one another on overnight loans of excess reserves. Interest rates in general, including the prime interest rate, rise and fall with the Federal funds rate. The prime interest rate is the benchmark rate that banks use as a reference rate for a wide range of interest rates on short-term loans to businesses and individuals.

8. In recent years, the Fed has used monetary policy to keep inflation low while helping to limit the depth of the recession of 2001, boost the economy as it recovered from that recession, help stabilize the banking sector in the wake of the mortgage debt crisis, and promote recovery from the severe recession of 2007–2009.

9. In response to the financial crisis, the Federal Reserve provided lender-of-last-resort loans to financial institutions through a series of newly established Fed facilities. Most of these facilities closed in 2010 but could be reestablished in the event of another financial crisis.

10. Monetary policy has two major limitations and potential problems: (a) Recognition and operation lags complicate the timing of monetary policy. (b) In a severe recession, the reluctance of banks to lend excess reserves and firms to borrow money to spend on capital goods may contribute to a liquidity trap that limits the effectiveness of an expansionary monetary policy.

Terms and Concepts

monetary policy	open-market operations	prime interest rate
transactions demand	discount rate	cyclical asymmetry
asset demand	easy money policy	liquidity trap
total demand for money	tight money policy	
money market	Federal funds rate	

Questions

1. What is the basic determinant of (a) the strength of the transactions demand for money (the location of the transactions demand for money curve) and (b) the amount of money demanded for assets, given a particular asset demand for money curve? How is the equilibrium interest rate in the market for money determined? Use a graph to show the impact of an increase in the total demand for money on the equilibrium interest rate (no change in money supply). Use your general knowledge of equilibrium prices to explain why the previous interest rate is no longer sustainable. **LO1**

2. What is the basic objective of monetary policy? State the cause-effect chain through which monetary policy is made effective. What are the major strengths of monetary policy? Why is monetary policy easier to undertake than fiscal policy? **LO2, LO4**

3. What is the impact of each of the following transactions on commercial bank reserves? **LO2**

   a. The New York Federal Reserve Bank purchases government securities from private businesses and consumers.

   b. Commercial banks borrow from Federal Reserve Banks at the discount rate.

   c. The Fed reduces the reserve ratio.

4. Why do changes in bank reserves resulting from open-market operations by the Fed produce *multiple* changes in checkable deposits (and therefore money) in the economy? **LO3**

5. Suppose that you are a member of the Board of Governors of the Federal Reserve System. The economy is experiencing a sharp and prolonged inflationary trend. What changes in (a) the reserve ratio, (b) the discount rate, and (c) open-market operations would you recommend? Explain in each case how the change you advocate would affect commercial bank reserves, the money supply, interest rates, and aggregate demand. **LO3**

6. What do economists mean when they say that monetary policy can exhibit cyclical asymmetry? How does the idea of a liquidity trap relate to cyclical asymmetry? Why is this possibility of a liquidity trap significant to policymakers? **LO4**

7. Distinguish between the Federal funds rate and the prime interest rate. Which of these two rates does the Fed explicitly target in undertaking its monetary policy? **LO5**

8. How did the Fed use the main tools of monetary policy to respond to the financial crisis that began in 2007? What additional programs did the Fed create and implement to facilitate its role as lender of last resort? What was the primary purpose of these new programs? **LO5**

Problems

1. Assume that the following data characterize the hypothetical economy of Trance: money supply = $200 billion; quantity of money demanded for transactions = $150 billion; quantity of money demanded as an asset = $10 billion at 12 percent interest, increasing by $10 billion for each 2-percentage-point fall in the interest rate. **LO1**

   a. What is the equilibrium interest rate in Trance?

   b. At the equilibrium interest rate, what are the quantity of money supplied, the total quantity of money demanded, the amount of money demanded for transactions, and the amount of money demanded as an asset in Trance?

2. Refer to Table 15.2 and assume that the Fed's reserve ratio is 10 percent and the economy is in a severe recession. Also suppose that the commercial banks are hoarding all excess reserves (not lending them out) because of their fear of loan defaults. Finally, suppose that the Fed is highly concerned that the banks will suddenly lend out these excess reserves and possibly contribute to inflation once the economy begins to recover and confidence is restored. By how many percentage points would the Fed need to increase the reserve ratio to eliminate one-third of the excess reserves? What would be the size of the monetary multiplier before and after the change in the reserve ratio? By how much would the lending potential of the banks decline as a result of the increase in the reserve ratio? **LO2**

3. Refer to the table for Moola at the bottom of this page to answer the following questions. What is the equilibrium interest rate in Moola? What is the level of investment at the equilibrium interest rate? Is there either a recessionary output gap (negative GDP gap) or an inflationary output gap (positive GDP gap) at the equilibrium interest rate and, if either, what is the amount? Given money demand, by how much would the Moola central bank need to change the money supply to close the output gap? What is the expenditure multiplier in Moola? **LO4**

Money Supply	Money Demand	Interest Rate	Investment at Interest (Rate Shown)	Potential Real GDP	Actual Real GDP at Interest (Rate Shown)
$500	$800	2%	$50	$350	$390
500	700	3	40	350	370
500	600	4	30	350	350
500	500	5	20	350	330
500	400	6	10	350	310

FURTHER TEST YOUR KNOWLEDGE AT
www.brue3e.com

At the text's Online Learning Center, **www.brue3e.com,** you will find one or more web-based questions that require information from the Internet to answer. We urge you to check them out, since they will familiarize you with websites that may be helpful in other courses and perhaps even in your career. The OLC also features multiple-choice quizzes that give instant feedback and provides other helpful ways to further test your knowledge of the chapter.

CHAPTER SIXTEEN

International Trade and Exchange Rates

After reading this chapter, you should be able to:

1. List and discuss several key facts about U.S. international trade.
2. Define comparative advantage and demonstrate how specialization and trade add to a nation's output.
3. Explain how exchange rates are determined in currency markets.
4. Analyze the validity of the most frequently presented arguments for protectionism.
5. Discuss the role played by free-trade zones and the World Trade Organization (WTO) in promoting international trade.

Backpackers in the wilderness like to think they are "leaving the world behind," but, like Atlas, they carry the world on their shoulders. Much of their equipment is imported—knives from Switzerland, rain gear from South Korea, cameras from Japan, aluminum pots from England, sleeping bags from China, and compasses from Finland. Moreover, they may have driven to the trailheads in Japanese-made Toyotas or German-made BMWs, sipping coffee from Brazil or snacking on bananas from Honduras.

International trade and the global economy affect all of us daily, whether we are hiking in the wilderness, driving our cars, listening to music, or working at our jobs. We cannot "leave the world behind." We are enmeshed in a global web of economic relationships—trading of goods and services, multinational corporations, cooperative ventures among the world's firms, and ties among the world's financial markets.

Trade Facts

The following facts provide an "executive summary" of U.S. international trade:

- A *trade deficit* occurs when imports exceed exports. The United States has a trade deficit in goods. In 2011, U.S. imports of goods exceeded U.S. exports of goods by $738 billion.
- A *trade surplus* occurs when exports exceed imports. The United States has a trade surplus in services (such as air transportation services and financial services). In 2011, U.S. exports of services exceeded U.S. imports of services by $178 billion.
- Principal U.S. exports include chemicals, agricultural products, consumer durables, semiconductors, and aircraft; principal imports include petroleum, automobiles, metals, household appliances, and computers.
- Canada is the United States' most important trading partner quantitatively. In 2011, 19 percent of U.S. exported goods were sold to Canadians, who in turn provided 14 percent of the U.S. imports of goods.
- The United States has a sizable trade deficit with China. In 2011, U.S. imports of goods from China exceeded exports of goods to China by $295 billion.
- The U.S. dependence on foreign oil is reflected in its trade with members of OPEC. In 2011, the United States imported $191 billion of goods (mainly oil) from OPEC members, while exporting $64 billion of goods to those countries.
- The United States leads the world in the combined volume of exports and imports, as measured in dollars. China, the United States, Germany, Japan, and the Netherlands were the top five exporters by dollar in 2010. Currently, the United States provides about 8.4 percent of the world's exports. (See Global Snapshot 16.1.)

Shares of World Exports, Selected Nations

Global Snapshot 16.1

China has the largest share of world exports, followed by the United States and Germany. The eight largest export nations account for about 45 percent of world exports.

Percentage Share of World Exports, 2010

China	~10.5
United States	~8.5
Germany	~8.5
Japan	~5
Netherlands	~3.5
France	~3.5
South Korea	~3
Italy	~3

Source: *International Trade Statistics*, WTO Publications. Used with permission of the World Trade Organization, **www.wto.org.**

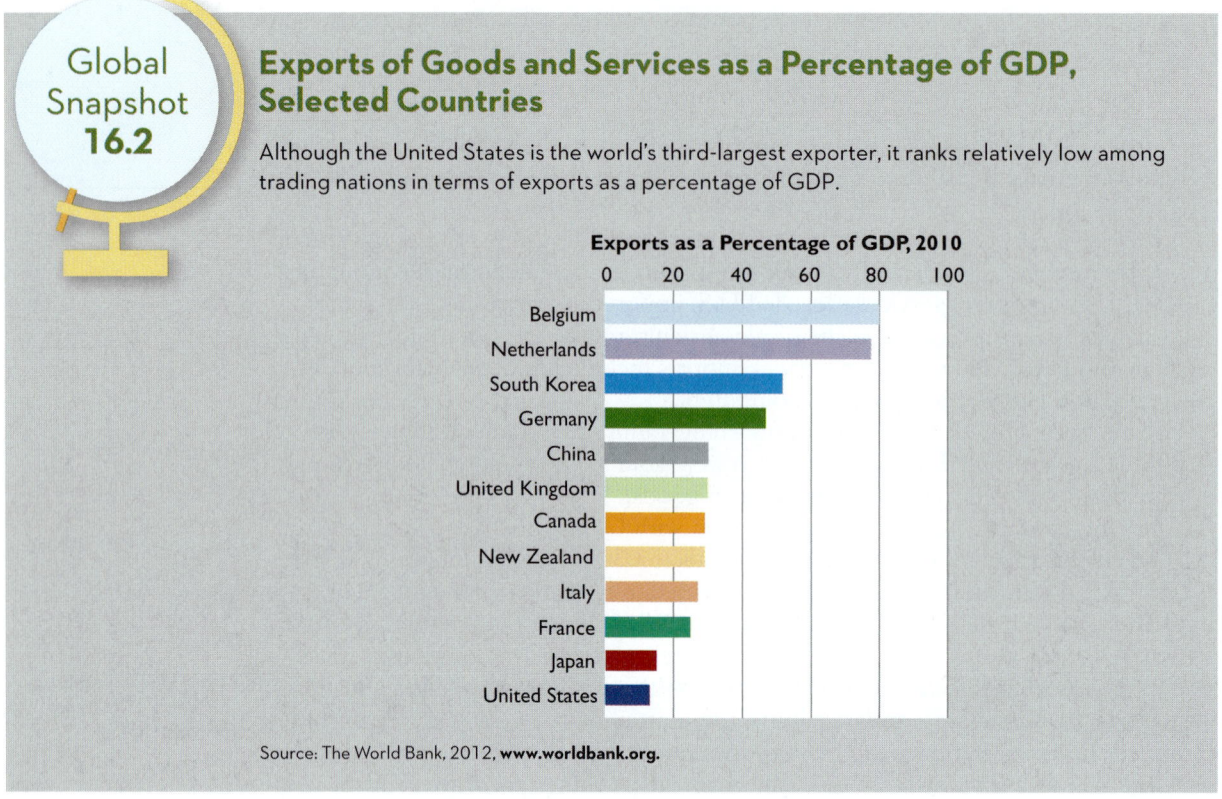

Global Snapshot 16.2

Exports of Goods and Services as a Percentage of GDP, Selected Countries

Although the United States is the world's third-largest exporter, it ranks relatively low among trading nations in terms of exports as a percentage of GDP.

Exports as a Percentage of GDP, 2010

Belgium
Netherlands
South Korea
Germany
China
United Kingdom
Canada
New Zealand
Italy
France
Japan
United States

Source: The World Bank, 2012, **www.worldbank.org.**

- Exports of goods and services make up about 13 percent of total U.S. output. That percentage is much lower than the percentage in many other nations, including Canada, Italy, France, and the United Kingdom (see Global Snapshot 16.2).
- China has become a major international trader, with an estimated $1.6 trillion of exports in 2010. Other Asian economies—including South Korea, Taiwan, and Singapore—are also active in international trade. Their combined exports exceed those of France, Britain, or Italy.
- International trade and finance are often at the center of economic policy.

With this information in mind, let's look more closely at the economics of international trade.

Comparative Advantage and Specialization

Given the presence of an *open economy*—one that includes the international sector—the United States produces more of certain goods (exports) and fewer of other goods (imports) than it would otherwise. Thus, U.S. labor and other resources are shifted toward export industries and away from import industries. For example, the United States uses more resources to make computers and to grow wheat and less to make sporting goods and clothing. So we ask: "Do shifts of resources like these make economic sense? Do they enhance U.S. total output and thus the U.S. standard of living?"

The answers are affirmative. Specialization and international trade increase the productivity of a nation's resources and allow for greater total output than would otherwise be possible. This idea is not new. Adam Smith had this to say in 1776:

> It is the maxim of every prudent master of a family, never to attempt to make at home what it will cost him more to make than to buy. The taylor does not attempt to make his own shoes, but buys them of the shoemaker. The shoemaker does not attempt to make his own clothes, but employs a taylor. The farmer attempts to make neither the one nor the other, but employs those different artificers. . . .
>
> What is prudence in the conduct of every private family, can scarce be folly in that of a great kingdom. If a foreign country can supply us with a commodity cheaper than we can make it, better buy it of them with some part of the produce of our own industry, employed in a way in which we have some advantage.[1]

Nations specialize and trade for the same reasons that individuals do: Specialization and exchange result in greater overall output and income. In the early 1800s British economist David Ricardo expanded on Smith's idea by observing that it pays for a person or a country to specialize and trade even if a nation is more productive than a potential trading partner in *all* economic activities. We demonstrate Ricardo's principle in the examples that follow.

A CPA and a House Painter

Illustrating the Idea

Consider the certified public accountant (CPA) who is also a skilled house painter. Suppose the CPA is a swifter painter than the professional painter she is thinking of hiring. Also suppose that she can earn $50 per hour as an accountant but would have to pay the painter $15 per hour. And say it would take the accountant 30 hours to paint her house but the painter would take 40 hours.

Should the CPA take time from her accounting to paint her own house, or should she hire the painter? The CPA's opportunity cost of painting her house is $1500 (= 30 hours of sacrificed CPA time × $50 per CPA hour). The cost of hiring the painter is only $600 (= 40 hours of painting × $15 per hour of painting). Although the CPA is better at both accounting and painting, she will get her house painted at lower cost by specializing in accounting and using some of her earnings from accounting to hire a house painter.

Similarly, the house painter can reduce his cost of obtaining accounting services by specializing in painting and using some of his income to hire the CPA to prepare his income tax forms. Suppose it would take the painter 10 hours to prepare his tax return, while the CPA could handle the task in 2 hours. The house painter would sacrifice $150 of income (= 10 hours of painting time × $15 per hour) to do something he could hire the CPA to do for $100 (= 2 hours of CPA time × $50 per CPA hour). By specializing in painting and hiring the CPA to prepare his tax return, the painter lowers the cost of getting his tax return prepared.

We will see that what is true for our CPA and house painter is also true for nations. Specializing on the basis of comparative advantage enables nations to reduce the cost of obtaining the goods and services they desire.

Question:
How might the specialization described above change once the CPA retires? What generalization about the permanency of a particular pattern of specialization can you draw from your answer?

---

[1] Adam Smith, *The Wealth of Nations* (New York: Modern Library, 1937), p. 424. (Originally published in 1776.)

Comparative Advantage: Production Possibilities Analysis

Our simple example shows that the reason specialization is economically desirable is that it results in more efficient production. Now let's put specialization into the context of trading nations and use the familiar concept of the production possibilities table for our analysis.

Assumptions and Comparative Costs   Suppose the production possibilities for one product in Mexico and for one product in the United States are as shown in Tables 16.1 and 16.2. Both tables reflect constant costs. Each country must give up a constant amount of one product to secure a certain increment of the other product. (This assumption simplifies our discussion without impairing the validity of our conclusions. Later we will allow for increasing costs.)

Also for simplicity, suppose that the labor forces in the United States and Mexico are of equal size. The data then tell us that the United States has an *absolute advantage* in producing both products. If the United States and Mexico use their entire (equal-size) labor forces to produce avocados, the United States can produce 90 tons compared with Mexico's 60 tons. Similarly, the United States can produce 30 tons of soybeans compared to Mexico's 15 tons. There are greater production possibilities in the United States, using the same number of workers as in Mexico. So labor productivity (output per worker) in the United States exceeds that in Mexico in producing both products.

Although the United States has an absolute advantage in producing both goods, gains from specialization and trade are possible. Specialization and trade are mutually beneficial or "profitable" to the two nations if the *comparative* costs of producing the two products within the two nations differ. What are the comparative costs of avocados and soybeans in Mexico? By comparing production alternatives A and B in Table 16.1, we see that Mexico must sacrifice 5 tons of soybeans ($= 15 - 10$) to produce 20 tons of avocados ($= 20 - 0$). Or, more simply, in Mexico it costs 1 ton of soybeans (S) to produce 4 tons of avocados (A); that is, $1S \equiv 4A$. (The "$\equiv$" sign simply means "equivalent to.") Because we assumed constant costs, this domestic opportunity cost will not change as Mexico expands the output of either product. This is evident from production possibilities B and C, where we see that 4 more tons of avocados ($= 24 - 20$) cost 1 unit of soybeans ($= 10 - 9$).

TABLE 16.1

Mexico's Production Possibilities Table (in Tons)

	Production Alternatives				
Product	A	B	C	D	E
Avocados	0	20	24	40	60
Soybeans	15	10	9	5	0

TABLE 16.2

U.S. Production Possibilities Table (in Tons)

	Production Alternatives				
Product	R	S	T	U	V
Avocados	0	30	33	60	90
Soybeans	30	20	19	10	0

Similarly, in Table 16.2, comparing U.S. production alternatives R and S reveals that in the United States it costs 10 tons of soybeans (= 30 − 20) to obtain 30 tons of avocados (= 30 − 0). That is, the domestic (internal) comparative-cost ratio for the two products in the United States is 1S ≡ 3A. Comparing production alternatives S and T reinforces this conclusion: an extra 3 tons of avocados (= 33 − 30) comes at the sacrifice of 1 ton of soybeans (= 20 − 19).

The comparative costs of the two products within the two nations are obviously different. Economists say that the United States has a **comparative advantage** over Mexico in soybeans. The United States must forgo only 3 tons of avocados to get 1 ton of soybeans, but Mexico must forgo 4 tons of avocados to get 1 ton of soybeans. In terms of opportunity costs, soybeans are relatively cheaper in the United States. *A nation has a comparative advantage in some product when it can produce that product at a lower opportunity cost than can a potential trading partner.* Mexico, in contrast, has a comparative advantage in avocados. While 1 ton of avocados costs $\frac{1}{3}$ ton of soybeans in the United States, it costs only $\frac{1}{4}$ ton of soybeans in Mexico. Comparatively speaking, avocados are cheaper in Mexico. We summarize the situation in Table 16.3. Be sure to give it a close look.

Because of these differences in comparative costs, Mexico should produce avocados and the United States should produce soybeans. If both nations specialize according to their comparative advantages, each can achieve a larger total output with the same total input of resources. Together they will be using their scarce resources more efficiently.

comparative advantage
A lower relative or comparative opportunity cost than that of another person, producer, or country.

ORIGIN OF THE IDEA

O 16.1
Absolute and comparative advantage

Terms of Trade   The United States can shift production between soybeans and avocados at the rate of 1S for 3A. Thus, the United States would specialize in soybeans only if it could obtain *more than* 3 tons of avocados for 1 ton of soybeans by trading with Mexico. Similarly, Mexico can shift production at the rate of 4A for 1S. So it would be advantageous to Mexico to specialize in avocados if it could get 1 ton of soybeans for *less than* 4 tons of avocados.

Suppose that through negotiation the two nations agree on an exchange rate of 1 ton of soybeans for $3\frac{1}{2}$ tons of avocados. These **terms of trade** are mutually beneficial to both countries since each can "do better" through such trade than through domestic production alone. The United States can get $3\frac{1}{2}$ tons of avocados by sending 1 ton of soybeans to Mexico, while it can get only 3 tons of avocados by shifting its own resources domestically from soybeans to avocados. Mexico can obtain 1 ton of soybeans at a lower cost of $3\frac{1}{2}$ tons of avocados through trade with the United States, compared to the cost of 4 tons if Mexico produced the 1 ton of soybeans itself.

terms of trade
The rate at which units of one product can be exchanged for units of another product.

TABLE 16.3
Comparative-Advantage Example: A Summary

Soybeans	Avocados
Mexico: Must give up 4 tons of avocados to get 1 ton of soybeans	**Mexico:** Must give up $\frac{1}{4}$ ton of soybeans to get 1 ton of avocados
United States: Must give up 3 tons of avocados to get 1 ton of soybeans	**United States:** Must give up $\frac{1}{3}$ ton of soybeans to get 1 ton of avocados
Comparative advantage: United States	**Comparative advantage:** Mexico

Gains from Specialization and Trade

Let's pinpoint the gains in total output from specialization and trade. Suppose that, before specialization and trade, production alternative C in Table 16.1 and alternative T in Table 16.2 were the optimal product mixes for the two countries. That is, Mexico preferred 24 tons of avocados and 9 tons of soybeans (Table 16.1) and the United States preferred 33 tons of avocados and 19 tons of soybeans (Table 16.2) to all other available domestic alternatives. These outputs are shown in column 1 in Table 16.4.

Now assume that both nations specialize according to their comparative advantages, with Mexico producing 60 tons of avocados and no soybeans (alternative E) and the United States producing no avocados and 30 tons of soybeans (alternative R). These outputs are shown in column 2 in Table 16.4. Using our $1S \equiv 3\frac{1}{2}A$ terms of trade, assume that Mexico exchanges 35 tons of avocados for 10 tons of U.S. soybeans. Column 3 in Table 16.4 shows the quantities exchanged in this trade, with a minus sign indicating exports and a plus sign indicating imports. As shown in column 4, after the trade Mexico has 25 tons of avocados and 10 tons of soybeans, while the United States has 35 tons of avocados and 20 tons of soybeans. Compared with their optimal product mixes before specialization and trade (column 1), *both* nations now enjoy more avocados and more soybeans! Specifically, Mexico has gained 1 ton of avocados and 1 ton of soybeans. The United States has gained 2 tons of avocados and 1 ton of soybeans. These gains are shown in column 5.

Specialization based on comparative advantage improves global resource allocation. The same total inputs of world resources and technology result in a larger global output. If Mexico and the United States allocate all their resources to avocados and soybeans, respectively, the same total inputs of resources can produce more output between them, indicating that resources are being allocated more efficiently.

Through specialization and international trade a nation can overcome the production constraints imposed by its domestic production possibilities table and curve. Our discussion of Tables 16.1, 16.2, and 16.4 has shown just how this is done. The domestic production possibilities data (Tables 16.1 and 16.2) of the two countries have not changed, meaning that neither nation's production possibilities curve has shifted. But specialization and trade mean that citizens of both countries can enjoy increased consumption (column 5 of Table 16.4).

> **WORKED PROBLEMS**
>
> **W 16.1**
> Gains from specialization

TABLE 16.4

Specialization According to Comparative Advantage and the Gains from Trade (in Tons)

Country	(1) Outputs before Specialization	(2) Outputs after Specialization	(3) Amounts Traded	(4) Outputs Available after Trade	(5) Gains from Specialization and Trade (4) − (1)
Mexico	24 avocados	60 avocados	−35 avocados	25 avocados	1 avocados
	9 soybeans	0 soybeans	+10 soybeans	10 soybeans	1 soybeans
United States	33 avocados	0 avocados	+35 avocados	35 avocados	2 avocados
	19 soybeans	30 soybeans	−10 soybeans	20 soybeans	1 soybeans

Trade with Increasing Costs

To explain the basic principles underlying international trade, we simplified our analysis in several ways. For example, we limited discussion to two products and two nations. But multiproduct and multinational analysis yields the same conclusions. We also assumed constant opportunity costs, which is a more substantive simplification. Let's consider the effect of allowing increasing opportunity costs to enter the picture.

As before, suppose that comparative advantage indicates that the United States should specialize in soybeans and Mexico in avocados. But now, as the United States begins to expand soybean production, its cost of soybeans will rise. It will eventually have to sacrifice more than 3 tons of avocados to get 1 additional ton of soybeans. Resources are no longer perfectly substitutable between alternative uses, as our constant-cost assumption implied. Resources less and less suitable to soybean production must be allocated to the U.S. soybean industry in expanding soybean output, and that means increasing costs—the sacrifice of larger and larger amounts of avocados for each additional ton of soybeans.

© Getty Images

© Photolink/Getty Images

Photo Op The Fruits of Free Trade*

Because of specialization and exchange, fruits and vegetables from all over the world appear in our grocery stores. For example, apples may be from New Zealand; bananas, from Ecuador; coconuts, from the Philippines; pineapples, from Costa Rica; avocados, from Mexico; plums, from Chile; and potatoes, from Peru.

*This example is from "The Fruits of Free Trade," *2002 Annual Report*, by W. Michael Cox and Richard Alm, p. 3, Federal Reserve Bank of Dallas.

Similarly, Mexico will find that its cost of producing an additional ton of avocados will rise beyond 4 tons of soybeans as it produces more avocados. Resources transferred from soybean to avocado production will eventually be less suitable to avocado production.

At some point the differing domestic cost ratios that underlie comparative advantage will disappear, and further specialization will become uneconomical. And, most importantly, this point of equal cost ratios may be reached while the United States is still producing some avocados along with its soybeans and Mexico is producing some soybeans along with its avocados. The primary effect of increasing opportunity costs is less-than-complete specialization. For this reason we often find domestically produced products competing directly against identical or similar imported products within a particular economy.

The Foreign Exchange Market

Buyers and sellers (whether individuals, firms, or nations) use money to buy products or to pay for the use of resources. Within the domestic economy, prices are stated in terms of the domestic currency and buyers use that currency to purchase domestic products. In Mexico, for example, buyers have pesos, and that is what sellers want.

International markets are different. Sellers set their prices in terms of their domestic currencies, but buyers often possess entirely different currencies. How many dollars does it take to buy a truckload of Mexican avocados selling for 3000 pesos, a German automobile selling for 50,000 euros, or a Japanese motorcycle priced at 300,000 yen? Producers in Mexico, Germany, and Japan want payment in pesos, euros, and yen, respectively, so that they can pay their wages, rent, interest, dividends, and taxes.

A **foreign exchange market,** a market in which various national currencies are exchanged for one another, serves this need. The equilibrium prices in such currency markets are called **exchange rates.** An exchange rate is the rate at which the currency of one nation can be exchanged for the currency of another nation. (See Global Snapshot 16.3.)

The market price or exchange rate of a nation's currency is an unusual price; it links all domestic prices with all foreign prices. Exchange rates enable consumers in one country to translate prices of foreign goods into units of their own currency: They need only multiply the foreign product price by the exchange rate. If the U.S. dollar–yen exchange rate is $.01 (1 cent) per yen, a Sony television set priced at ¥20,000 will cost $200 (= 20,000 × $.01) in the United States. If the exchange rate rises to $.02 (2 cents) per yen, the television will cost $400 (= 20,000 × $.02) in the United States. Similarly, all other Japanese products would double in price to U.S. buyers in response to the altered exchange rate.

foreign exchange market
A market in which foreign currencies are exchanged and relative currency prices are established.

exchange rates
The rates at which national currencies trade for one another.

Global Snapshot **16.3**

Exchange Rates: Foreign Currency per U.S. Dollar

The amount of foreign currency that a dollar will buy varies greatly from nation to nation and fluctuates in response to supply and demand changes in the foreign exchange market. The amounts shown here are for April 2012.

$1 Will Buy

51.7 Indian rupees
.62 British pounds
.99 Canadian dollars
13.1 Mexican pesos
.92 Swiss francs
.76 European euros
81.3 Japanese yen
1137 South Korean won
6.75 Swedish kronor
4.29 Venezuelan bolivares fuertes

© PhotoLink/Getty Images/DIL

© Photodisc/Getty Images

Photo Op Foreign Currencies

The world is awash with hundreds of national currencies. Currency markets determine the rates of exchange between them.

Exchange Rates

Let's examine the rate, or price, at which U.S. dollars might be exchanged for British pounds. In Figure 16.1 we show the dollar price of 1 pound on the vertical axis and the quantity of pounds on the horizontal axis. The demand for pounds is D_1 and the supply of pounds is S_1 in this market for British pounds.

The *demand-for-pounds curve* is downward-sloping because all British goods and services will be cheaper to the United States if pounds become less expensive to the United States. That is, at lower dollar prices for pounds, the United States can obtain more pounds for each dollar and therefore buy more British goods and services per dollar. To buy those cheaper British goods, U.S. consumers will increase the quantity of pounds they demand.

The *supply-of-pounds curve* is upsloping because the British will purchase more U.S. goods when the dollar price of pounds rises (that is, as the pound price of dollars falls). When the British buy more U.S. goods, they supply a greater quantity of pounds to the foreign exchange market. In other words, they must exchange pounds for dollars to purchase U.S. goods. So, when the dollar price of pounds rises, the quantity of pounds supplied goes up.

The intersection of the supply curve and the demand curve will determine the dollar price of pounds. In Figure 16.1, that price (exchange rate) is $2 for £1. At this exchange rate, the quantity of pounds supplied and demanded are equal; neither a shortage nor a surplus of pounds occurs.

Depreciation and Appreciation

An exchange rate determined by market forces can, and often does, change daily like stock and bond prices. These price changes result from changes in the supply of, or demand for, a particular currency. When the dollar price of pounds *rises*, for example,

FIGURE 16.1

The market for foreign currency (pounds). The intersection of the demand-for-pounds curve D_1 and the supply-of-pounds curve S_1 determines the equilibrium dollar price of pounds, here, $2. That means that the exchange rate is $2 = £1. Not shown, an increase in demand for pounds or a decrease in the supply of pounds will increase the dollar price of pounds and thus cause the pound to appreciate. Also not shown, a decrease in demand for pounds or an increase in the supply of pounds will reduce the dollar price of pounds, meaning that the pound has depreciated.

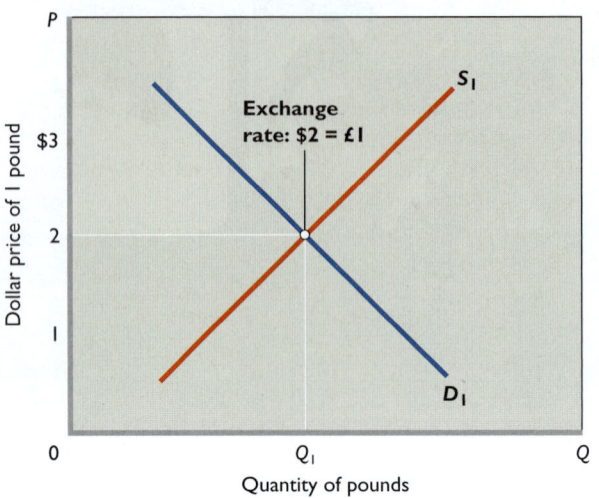

from $2 = £1 to $3 = £1, the dollar has *depreciated* relative to the pound (and the pound has appreciated relative to the dollar). A **depreciation** of a currency means that more units of it (dollars) are needed to buy a single unit of some other currency (a pound).

When the dollar price of pounds *falls*, for example, from $2 = £1 to $1 = £1, the dollar has *appreciated* relative to the pound. An **appreciation** of a currency means that it takes fewer units of it (dollars) to buy a single unit of some other currency (a pound). For example, the dollar price of pounds might decline from $2 to $1. Each British product becomes less expensive in terms of dollars, so people in the United States purchase more British goods. In general, U.S. imports from the United Kingdom rise. Meanwhile, because it takes more pounds to get a dollar, U.S. exports to the United Kingdom fall.

The central point is this: When the dollar depreciates (dollar price of foreign currencies rises), U.S. exports rise and U.S. imports fall; when the dollar appreciates (dollar price of foreign currencies falls), U.S. exports fall and U.S. imports rise.

In our U.S.-Britain illustrations, depreciation of the dollar means an appreciation of the pound, and vice versa. When the dollar price of a pound jumps from $2 = £1 to $3 = £1, the pound has appreciated relative to the dollar because it takes fewer pounds to buy $1. At $2 = £1, it took £1/2 to buy $1; at $3 = £1, it takes only £1/3 to buy $1. Conversely, when the dollar appreciates relative to the pound, the pound depreciates relative to the dollar. More pounds are needed to buy a U.S. dollar.

In general, the relevant terminology and relationships between the U.S. dollar and another currency are as follows.

- Dollar price of foreign currency increases ≡ dollar depreciates relative to the foreign currency ≡ foreign currency price of dollar decreases ≡ foreign currency appreciates relative to the dollar.
- Dollar price of foreign currency decreases ≡ dollar appreciates relative to the foreign currency ≡ foreign currency price of dollar increases ≡ foreign currency depreciates relative to the dollar.

depreciation (of a currency)
A decrease in the value of a currency relative to another currency.

appreciation (of a currency)
An increase in the value of a currency relative to another currency.

Determinants of Exchange Rates

What factors would cause a nation's currency to appreciate or depreciate in the market for foreign exchange? Here are three generalizations (other things equal):

- If the demand for a nation's currency increases, that currency will appreciate; if the demand declines, that currency will depreciate.
- If the supply of a nation's currency increases, that currency will depreciate; if the supply decreases, that currency will appreciate.
- If a nation's currency appreciates, some foreign currency depreciates relative to it.

With these generalizations in mind, let's examine the determinants of exchange rates—the factors that shift the demand or supply curve for a certain currency. As we do so, keep in mind that the other-things-equal assumption is always in force. Also note that we are discussing factors *that change the exchange rate*, not things that change *as a result of* a change in the exchange rate.

Tastes Any change in consumer tastes or preferences for the products of a foreign country may alter the demand for that nation's currency and change its exchange rate. If technological advances in U.S. MP3 players make them more attractive to British consumers and businesses, then the British will supply more pounds in the exchange market in order to purchase more U.S. MP3 players. The supply-of-pounds curve will shift to the right, causing the pound to depreciate and the dollar to appreciate.

In contrast, the U.S. demand-for-pounds curve will shift to the right if British woolen apparel becomes more fashionable in the United States. So the pound will appreciate and the dollar will depreciate.

Relative Income A nation's currency is likely to depreciate if its growth of national income is more rapid than that of other countries. Here's why: A country's imports vary directly with its income level. As total income rises in the United States, people there buy both more domestic goods and more foreign goods. If the U.S. economy is expanding rapidly and the British economy is stagnant, U.S. imports of British goods, and therefore U.S. demands for pounds, will increase. The dollar price of pounds will rise, so the dollar will depreciate.

Relative Inflation Rate Changes Other things equal, changes in the relative rates of inflation of two nations change their relative price levels and alter the exchange rate between their currencies. The currency of the nation with the higher inflation rate—the more rapidly rising price level—tends to depreciate. Suppose, for example, that inflation is zero percent in Great Britain and 5 percent in the United States so that prices, on average, are rising by 5 percent per year in the United States while, on average, remaining unchanged in Great Britain. U.S. consumers will seek out more of the now relatively lower-priced British goods, increasing the demand for pounds. British consumers will purchase less of the now relatively higher-priced U.S. goods, reducing the supply of pounds. This combination of increased demand for pounds and reduced supply of pounds will cause the pound to appreciate and the dollar to depreciate.

Relative Interest Rates Changes in relative interest rates between two countries may alter their exchange rate. Suppose that real interest rates rise in the United States but stay constant in Great Britain. British citizens will then find the United

States a more attractive place in which to loan money directly or loan money indirectly by buying bonds. To make these loans, they will have to supply pounds in the foreign exchange market to obtain dollars. The increase in the supply of pounds results in depreciation of the pound and appreciation of the dollar.

Changes in Relative Expected Returns on Stocks, Real Estate, and Production Facilities   International investing extends beyond buying foreign bonds. It includes international investments in stocks and real estate as well as foreign purchases of factories and production facilities. Other things equal, the extent of this foreign investment depends on relative expected returns. To make the investments, investors in one country must sell their currencies to purchase the foreign currencies needed for the foreign investments.

For instance, suppose that investing in England suddenly becomes more popular due to a more positive outlook regarding expected returns on stocks, real estate, and production facilities there. U.S. investors therefore will sell U.S. assets to buy more assets in England. The U.S. assets will be sold for dollars, which will then be brought to the foreign exchange market and exchanged for pounds, which will in turn be used to purchase British assets. The increased demand for pounds in the foreign exchange market will cause the pound to appreciate and the dollar to depreciate.

Speculation   Currency speculators are people who buy and sell currencies with an eye toward reselling or repurchasing them at a profit. Suppose that, as a group, speculators anticipate that the pound will appreciate and the dollar will depreciate. Speculators holding dollars will therefore try to convert them into pounds. This effort will increase the demand for pounds and cause the dollar price of pounds to rise (that is, cause the dollar to depreciate). A self-fulfilling prophecy occurs: The pound appreciates and the dollar depreciates because speculators act on the belief that these changes will in fact take place. In this way, speculation can cause changes in exchange rates.

Government and Trade

If people and nations benefit from specialization and international exchange, why do governments sometimes try to restrict the free flow of imports or encourage exports? What kinds of world trade barriers can governments erect, and why would they do so?

Trade Protections and Subsidies

tariffs
Taxes imposed by a nation on imported goods.

Trade interventions by government take several forms. Excise taxes on imported goods are called **tariffs**. A *protective tariff* is implemented to shield domestic producers from foreign competition. These tariffs impede free trade by increasing the prices of imported goods and therefore shifting sales toward domestic producers. Although protective tariffs are usually not high enough to stop the importation of foreign goods, they put foreign producers at a competitive disadvantage. A tariff on imported shoes, for example, would make domestically produced shoes more attractive to consumers.

import quotas
Limits imposed by nations on the quantities (or total values) of goods that may be imported during some period of time.

Import quotas are limits on the quantities or total value of specific items that may be imported in some period. Once a quota is "filled," further imports of that product are choked off. Import quotas are more effective than tariffs in impeding international trade. With a tariff, a product can go on being imported in large quantities; with an import quota, however, all imports are prohibited once the quota is filled.

Nontariff barriers (NTBs) include onerous licensing requirements, unreasonable standards pertaining to product quality, or excessive bureaucratic hurdles and delays in customs procedures. Some nations require that importers of foreign goods obtain licenses. By restricting the issuance of licenses, imports can be restricted. Although many nations carefully inspect imported agricultural products to prevent the introduction of potentially harmful insects, some countries use lengthy inspections to impede imports.

A **voluntary export restriction (VER)** is a trade barrier by which foreign firms "voluntarily" limit the amount of their exports to a particular country. Exporters agree to a VER, which has the effect of an import quota, to avoid more stringent trade barriers. In the late 1990s, for example, Canadian producers of softwood lumber (fir, spruce, cedar, pine) agreed to a VER on exports to the United States under the threat of a permanently higher U.S. tariff.

Export subsidies consist of government payments to domestic producers of export goods. By reducing production costs, the subsidies enable producers to charge lower prices and thus to sell more exports in world markets. Example: The United States and other nations have subsidized domestic farmers to boost the domestic food supply. Such subsidies have lowered the market price of agricultural commodities and have artificially lowered their export prices.

Economic Impact of Tariffs

Tariffs, quotas, and other trade restrictions have a series of economic effects predicted by supply and demand analysis and observed in reality. These effects vary somewhat by type of trade protection. So to keep things simple, we will focus on the effects of tariffs.

Direct Effects Because tariffs raise the price of goods imported to the United States, U.S. consumption of those goods declines. Higher prices reduce quantity demanded, as indicated by the law of demand. A tariff prompts consumers to buy fewer of the imported goods and reallocate a portion of their expenditures to less desired substitute products. U.S. consumers are clearly injured by the tariff.

ORIGIN OF THE IDEA

O 16.2
Mercantilism

U.S. producers—who are not subject to the tariff—receive the higher price (pretariff foreign price + tariff) on the imported product. Because this new price is higher than before, the domestic producers respond by producing more. Higher prices increase quantity supplied, as indicated by the law of supply. So domestic producers increase their output. They therefore enjoy both a higher price and expanded sales; this explains why domestic producers lobby for protective tariffs. But from a social point of view, the greater domestic production means the tariff allows domestic producers to bid resources away from other, more efficient, U.S. industries.

Foreign producers are hurt by tariffs. Although the sales price of the imported good is higher, that higher amount accrues to the U.S. government as tariff revenues, not to foreign producers. The after-tariff price, or the per-unit revenue to foreign producers, remains as before, but the volume of U.S. imports (foreign exports) falls.

Government gains revenue from tariffs. This revenue is a transfer of income from consumers to government and does not represent any net change in the nation's

nontariff barriers (NTBs)

All impediments other than protective tariffs that nations establish to impede imports, including import quotas, licensing requirements, unreasonable product-quality standards, and unnecessary bureaucratic detail in customs procedures.

voluntary export restriction (VER)

An agreement by countries or foreign firms to limit their exports to a certain foreign nation to avoid enactment of formal trade barriers by that nation.

export subsidies

Government payments to domestic producers to enable them to reduce the price of a product to foreign buyers.

economic well-being. The result is that government gains a portion of what consumers lose by paying more for imported goods.

Indirect Effects   Tariffs have a subtle effect beyond those just mentioned. They also hurt domestic firms that use the protected goods as inputs in their production process. For example, a tariff on imported steel boosts the price of steel girders, thus hurting firms that build bridges and office towers. Also, tariffs reduce competition in the protected industries. With less competition from foreign producers, domestic firms may be slow to design and implement cost-saving production methods and introduce new products.

Because foreigners sell fewer imported goods in the United States, they earn fewer dollars and so must buy fewer U.S. exports. U.S. export industries must then cut production and release resources. These are highly efficient industries, as we know from their comparative advantage and their ability to sell goods in world markets.

Tariffs directly promote the expansion of inefficient industries that do not have a comparative advantage; they also indirectly cause the contraction of relatively efficient industries that do have a comparative advantage. Put bluntly, tariffs cause resources to be shifted in the wrong direction—and that is not surprising. We know that specialization and world trade lead to more efficient use of world resources and greater world output. But protective tariffs reduce world trade. Therefore, tariffs also reduce efficiency and the world's real output.

Net Costs of Tariffs

Tariffs impose costs on domestic consumers but provide gains to domestic producers and revenue to the federal government. The consumer costs of trade restrictions are calculated by determining the effect the restrictions have on consumer prices. Protection raises the price of a product in three ways: (1) the price of the imported product goes up; (2) the higher price of imports causes some consumers to shift their purchases to higher-priced domestically produced goods; and (3) the prices of domestically produced goods rise because import competition has declined.

Study after study finds that the costs to consumers substantially exceed the gains to producers and government. A sizable net cost or efficiency loss to society arises from trade protection. Furthermore, industries employ large amounts of economic resources to influence Congress to pass and retain protectionist laws. Because these efforts divert resources away from more socially desirable purposes, trade restrictions also impose that cost on society.

Conclusion: The gains that U.S. trade barriers produce for protected industries and their workers come at the expense of much greater losses for the entire economy. The result is economic inefficiency, reduced consumption, and lower standards of living.

So Why Government Trade Protections?

In view of the benefits of free trade, what accounts for the impulse to impede imports and boost exports through government policy? There are several reasons—some legitimate, most not.

Misunderstanding the Gains from Trade   It is a commonly accepted myth that the greatest benefit to be derived from international trade is greater domestic sales and employment in the export sector. This suggests that exports are "good" because they increase domestic sales and employment, whereas imports are "bad" because they reduce domestic sales and deprive people of jobs at home. Actually, the true benefit created by international trade is the extra output obtained from abroad—the imports obtained for a lower opportunity cost than if they were produced at home.

A recent study suggests that the elimination of trade barriers since the Second World War has increased the income of the average U.S. household by at least $7000 and perhaps by as much as $13,000. These income gains are recurring; they happen year after year.[2]

Political Considerations   While a nation as a whole gains from trade, trade may harm particular domestic industries and particular groups of resource suppliers. In our earlier comparative-advantage example, specialization and trade adversely affected the U.S. avocado industry and the Mexican soybean industry. Understandably, those industries might seek to preserve their economic positions by persuading their respective governments to protect them from imports—perhaps through tariffs.

Those who directly benefit from import protection are relatively few in number but have much at stake. Thus, they have a strong incentive to pursue political activity to achieve their aims. Moreover, because the costs of import protection are buried in the price of goods and spread out over millions of citizens, the cost borne by each individual citizen is quite small. However, the full cost of tariffs and quotas typically greatly exceeds the benefits. It is not uncommon to find that it costs the public $250,000 or more a year to protect a domestic job that pays less than one-fourth that amount.

In the political arena, the voice of the relatively few producers and unions demanding *protectionism* is loud and constant, whereas the voice of those footing the bill is soft or nonexistent. When political deal making is added in—"You back tariffs for the apparel industry in my state, and I'll back tariffs for the steel industry in your state"—the outcome can be a network of protective tariffs.

Buy American?

Will "buying American" make Americans better off? No, says Dallas Federal Reserve economist W. Michael Cox:

> A common myth is that it is better for Americans to spend their money at home than abroad. The best way to expose the fallacy of this argument is to take it to its logical extreme. If it is better for me to spend my money here than abroad, then it is even better yet to buy in Texas than in New York, better yet to buy in Dallas than in Houston . . . in my own neighborhood . . . within my own family . . . to consume only what I can produce. Alone and poor.*

*"The Fruits of Free Trade," *2002 Annual Report*, by W. Michael Cox and Richard Alm, p. 16, Federal Reserve Bank of Dallas. Used with permission.

Illustrating the Idea

[2]Scott C. Bradford, Paul L.E. Grieco, and Gary C. Hufbauer, "The Payoff to America from Globalization," *The World Economy*, July 2006, pp. 893–916.

Three Arguments for Protection

Arguments for trade protection are many and diverse. Some—such as tariffs to protect "infant industries" or to create "military self-sufficiency"—have some legitimacy. But other arguments break down under close scrutiny. Three protectionist arguments, in particular, have persisted decade after decade in the United States.

Increased-Domestic-Employment Argument

Arguing for a tariff to "save U.S. jobs" becomes fashionable when the economy encounters a recession (such as the severe recession of 2007–2009 in the United States). In an economy that engages in international trade, exports involve spending on domestic output and imports reflect spending to obtain part of another nation's output. So, in this argument, reducing imports will divert spending on another nation's output to spending on domestic output. Thus domestic output and employment will rise. But this argument has several shortcomings.

While imports may eliminate some U.S. jobs, they create others. Imports may have eliminated the jobs of some U.S. steel and textile workers in recent years, but other workers have gained jobs unloading ships, flying imported aircraft, and selling imported electronic equipment. Import restrictions alter the composition of employment, but they may have little or no effect on the volume of employment.

The *fallacy of composition*—the false idea that what is true for the part is necessarily true for the whole—is also present in this rationale for tariffs. All nations cannot simultaneously succeed in restricting imports while maintaining their exports; what is true for one nation is not true for all nations. The exports of one nation must be the imports of another nation. To the extent that one country is able to expand its economy through an excess of exports over imports, the resulting excess of imports over exports worsens another economy's unemployment problem. It is no wonder that tariffs and import quotas meant to achieve domestic full employment are called "beggar my neighbor" policies: They achieve short-run domestic goals by making trading partners poorer.

Moreover, nations adversely affected by tariffs and quotas are likely to retaliate, causing a "trade-barrier war" that will choke off trade and make all nations worse off. The **Smoot-Hawley Tariff Act** of 1930 is a classic example. Although that act was meant to reduce imports and stimulate U.S. production, the high tariffs it authorized prompted adversely affected nations to retaliate with tariffs equally high. International trade fell, lowering the output and income of all nations. Economic historians generally agree that the Smoot-Hawley Tariff Act was a contributing cause of the Great Depression.

Finally, forcing an excess of exports over imports cannot succeed in raising domestic employment over the long run. It is through U.S. imports that foreign nations earn dollars for buying U.S. exports. In the long run a nation must import in order to export. The long-run impact of tariffs is not an increase in domestic employment but, at best, a reallocation of workers away from export industries and to protected domestic industries. This shift implies a less efficient allocation of resources.

Cheap-Foreign-Labor Argument

The cheap-foreign-labor argument says that government must shield domestic firms and workers from the ruinous competition of countries where wages are low. If protection is not provided, cheap imports will flood U.S. markets and the prices of U.S.

Smoot-Hawley Tariff Act
Legislation passed in 1930 that established very high U.S. tariffs designed to reduce imports and stimulate the domestic economy. Instead, the law resulted only in retaliatory tariffs by other nations and a decline in trade worldwide.

goods—along with the wages of U.S. workers—will be pulled down. That is, the domestic living standards in the United States will be reduced.

This argument can be rebutted at several levels. The logic of the argument suggests that it is not mutually beneficial for rich and poor persons to trade with one another. However, that is not the case. A relatively low-income mechanic may fix the Mercedes owned by a wealthy lawyer, and both may benefit from the transaction. And both U.S. consumers and Chinese workers gain when they "trade" a pair of athletic shoes priced at $30 as opposed to U.S. consumers being restricted to a similar shoe made in the United States for $60.

Also, recall that gains from trade are based on comparative advantage, not on absolute advantage. Again, think back to our U.S.-Mexico (soybean-avocado) example in which the United States had greater labor productivity than Mexico in producing both soybeans and avocados. Because of that greater productivity, wages and living standards will be higher for U.S. labor. Mexico's less productive labor will receive lower wages.

The cheap-foreign-labor argument suggests that, to maintain American living standards, the United States should not trade with low-wage Mexico. Suppose it forgoes trade with Mexico. Will wages and living standards rise in the United States as a result? Absolutely not! To obtain avocados, the United States will have to reallocate a portion of its labor from its relatively more-efficient soybean industry to its relatively less-efficient avocado industry. As a result, the average productivity of U.S. labor will fall, as will real wages and living standards for American workers. The labor forces of both countries will have diminished standards of living because without specialization and trade they will have less output available to them. Compare column 4 with column 1 in Table 16.4 to confirm this point.

Protection-against-Dumping Argument

The protection-against-dumping argument contends that tariffs are needed to protect domestic firms from "dumping" by foreign producers. **Dumping** is the sale of a product in a foreign country at prices either below cost or below the prices commonly charged at home.

dumping
The sale of products in a foreign country at prices either below costs or below the prices charged at home.

Economists cite two plausible reasons for this behavior. First, with regard to below-cost dumping, firms in country A may dump goods at below cost into country B in an attempt to drive their competitors in country B out of business. If the firms in country A succeed in driving their competitors in country B out of business, they will enjoy monopoly power and monopoly prices and profits on the goods they subsequently sell in country B. Their hope is that the longer-term monopoly profits will more than offset the losses from below-cost sales that must take place while they are attempting to drive their competitors in country B out of business.

Second, dumping that involves selling abroad at a price that is below the price commonly charged in the home country (but which is still at or above production costs) may be a form of price discrimination, which is charging different prices to different customers. As an example, a foreign seller that has a monopoly in its home market may find that it can maximize its overall profit by charging a high price in its monopolized domestic market while charging a lower price in the United States, where it must compete with U.S. producers. Curiously, it may pursue this strategy even if it makes no profit at all from its sales in the United States, where it must charge the competitive price. So why bother selling in the United States? Because the increase in overall production that comes about by exporting to the United States may allow the firm to obtain the per unit cost savings often associated with large-scale production. These cost savings imply even higher profits in the monopolized domestic market.

Because dumping is an "unfair trade practice," most nations prohibit it. For example, where dumping is shown to injure U.S. firms, the federal government imposes tariffs called *antidumping duties* on the goods in question. But relatively few documented cases of dumping occur each year, and specific instances of unfair trade do not justify widespread, permanent tariffs. Moreover, antidumping duties can be abused. Often, what appears to be dumping is simply comparative advantage at work.

Trade Adjustment Assistance

A nation's comparative advantage in the production of a certain product is not forever fixed. As national economies evolve, the size and quality of their labor forces may change, the volume and composition of their capital stocks may shift, new technologies may develop, and even the quality of land and the quantity of natural resources may be altered. As these changes take place, the relative efficiency with which a nation can produce specific goods will also change. Also, new trade agreements can suddenly leave formerly protected industries highly vulnerable to major disruption or even collapse.

Shifts in patterns of comparative advantage and removal of trade protection can hurt specific groups of workers. For example, the erosion of the United States' once strong comparative advantage in steel has caused production plant shutdowns and layoffs in the U.S. steel industry. The textile and apparel industries in the United States face similar difficulties. Clearly, not everyone wins from free trade (or freer trade). Some workers lose.

Trade Adjustment Assistance Act
A U.S. law passed in 2002 that provides cash assistance, education and training benefits, health care subsidies, and wage subsidies (for persons age 50 or more) to workers displaced by imports or plant relocations abroad.

The **Trade Adjustment Assistance Act** of 2002 introduced some innovative policies to help those hurt by shifts in international trade patterns. The law provides cash assistance (beyond unemployment insurance) for up to 78 weeks for workers displaced by imports or plant relocations abroad. To obtain the assistance, workers must participate in job searches, training programs, or remedial education. There also are relocation allowances to help displaced workers move geographically to new jobs within the United States. Refundable tax credits for health insurance serve as payments to help workers maintain their insurance coverage during the retraining and job search period. Also, workers who are 50 years of age or older are eligible for "wage insurance," which replaces some of the difference in pay (if any) between their old and new jobs.

Many economists support trade adjustment assistance because it not only helps workers hurt by international trade but also helps create the political support necessary to reduce trade barriers and export subsidies.

But not all economists are keen on trade adjustment assistance. Loss of jobs from imports or plant relocations abroad is only a small fraction (about 4 percent in recent years) of total job loss in the economy each year. Many workers also lose their jobs because of changing patterns of demand, changing technology, bad management, and other dynamic aspects of a market economy. Some critics ask, "What makes losing one's job to international trade worthy of such special treatment, compared to losing one's job to, say, technological change or domestic competition?" There is no totally satisfying answer.

Applying the Analysis

Is Offshoring of Jobs Bad?

Not only are some U.S. jobs lost because of international trade, but some are lost because of globalization of resource markets. In recent years U.S. firms have found it increasingly profitable to outsource work abroad. Economists call this business activity **offshoring:** shifting work previously done by American workers to workers located in other nations. Offshoring is not a new practice but traditionally has involved components for U.S. manufacturing goods. For example, Boeing has long offshored the production of major airplane parts for its "American" aircraft.

Recent advances in computer and communications technology have enabled U.S. firms to offshore service jobs such as data entry, book composition, software coding, call-center operations, medical transcription, and claims processing to countries such as India. Where offshoring occurs, some of the value added in the production process occurs in foreign countries rather than the United States. So part of the income generated from the production of U.S. goods is paid to foreigners, not to American workers.

Offshoring is obviously costly to Americans who lose their jobs, but it is not generally bad for the economy. Offshoring simply reflects a growing international trade in services, or, more descriptively, "tasks." That trade has been made possible by recent trade agreements and new information and communication technologies. As with trade in goods, trade in services reflects comparative advantage and is beneficial to both trading parties. Moreover, the United States has a sizable trade surplus with other nations in services. The United States gains by specializing in high-valued services such as transportation services, accounting services, legal services, and advertising services, where it still has a comparative advantage. It then "trades" to obtain lower-valued services such as call-center and data entry work, for which comparative advantage has gone abroad.

Offshoring also increases the demand for complementary jobs in the United States. Jobs that are close substitutes for existing U.S. jobs are lost, but complementary jobs in the United States are expanded. For example, the lower price of offshore maintenance of aircraft and reservation centers reduces the price of airline tickets. That means more domestic and international flights by American carriers, which in turn means more jobs for U.S.-based pilots, flight attendants, baggage handlers, and check-in personnel. Moreover, offshoring encourages domestic investment and expansion of firms in the United States by reducing their costs and keeping them competitive worldwide. Some observers equate "offshoring jobs" to "importing competitiveness."

Question:
What has enabled white-collar labor services to become the world's newest export and import commodity even though such labor itself remains in place?

offshoring
The practice of shifting work previously done by American workers to workers located in other nations.

Multilateral Trade Agreements and Free-Trade Zones

Being aware of the overall benefits of free trade, nations have worked to lower tariffs worldwide. Their pursuit of free trade has been aided by the growing power of free-trade interest groups: Exporters of goods and services, importers of foreign components used in "domestic" products, and domestic sellers of imported products all strongly support lower tariffs. And, in fact, tariffs have generally declined during the past half-century.

General Agreement on Tariffs and Trade

Following the Second World War, the major nations of the world set upon a general course of liberalizing trade. In 1947 some 23 nations, including the United States, signed the **General Agreement on Tariffs and Trade (GATT).** GATT was based on the principles of equal, nondiscriminatory trade treatment for all member nations and the reduction of tariffs and quotas by multilateral negotiation. Basically, GATT provided a continuing forum for the negotiation of reduced trade barriers on a multilateral basis among nations.

Since 1947, member nations have completed eight "rounds" of GATT negotiations to reduce trade barriers. The *Uruguay Round* agreement of 1993 phased in trade liberalizations between 1995 and 2005.

World Trade Organization

The Uruguay Round of 1993 established the **World Trade Organization (WTO)** as GATT's successor. In 2012, 153 nations belonged to the WTO, which oversees trade agreements and rules on disputes relating to them. It also provides forums for further rounds of trade negotiations. The ninth and latest round of negotiations—the **Doha Round**—was launched in Doha, Qatar, in late 2001. (The trade rounds occur over several years in several geographic venues but are named after the city or country of origination.) The negotiations are aimed at further reducing tariffs and quotas, as well as agricultural subsidies that distort trade.

GATT and the WTO have been positive forces in the trend toward liberalized world trade. The trade rules agreed upon by the member nations provide a strong and necessary bulwark against the protectionism called for by the special-interest groups in the various nations. For that reason and because current WTO agreements lack strong labor standards and environmental protections, the WTO is controversial.

European Union

Countries have also sought to reduce tariffs by creating regional *free-trade zones*—also called *trade blocs.* The most dramatic example is the **European Union (EU).** In 2007, the addition of Bulgaria and Romania expanded the EU to its present size of 27 nations.[3]

The EU has abolished tariffs and import quotas on nearly all products traded among the participating nations and established a common system of tariffs applicable to all goods received from nations outside the EU. It has also liberalized the movement of capital and labor within the EU and has created common policies in other economic matters of joint concern, such as agriculture, transportation, and business practices. The EU is now a strong **trade bloc:** a group of countries having common identity, economic interests, and trade rules. Of the 27 EU countries, 17 used the **euro** as a common currency in 2012.

EU integration has achieved for Europe what the U.S. constitutional prohibition on tariffs by individual states has achieved for the United States: increased regional specialization, greater productivity, greater output, and faster economic growth. The free flow of goods and services has created large markets for EU industries. The resulting economies of large-scale production have enabled those industries to

---

[3]The other 25 are France, Germany, the United Kingdom, Italy, Belgium, the Netherlands, Luxembourg, Denmark, Ireland, Greece, Spain, Portugal, Austria, Finland, Sweden, Poland, Hungary, Czech Republic, Slovakia, Lithuania, Latvia, Estonia, Slovenia, Malta, and Cyprus.

achieve much lower costs than they could have achieved in their small, single-nation markets.

North American Free Trade Agreement

In 1993 Canada, Mexico, and the United States formed a major trade bloc. The **North American Free Trade Agreement (NAFTA)** established a free-trade zone that has about the same combined output as the EU but encompasses a much larger geographic area. NAFTA has eliminated tariffs and other trade barriers between Canada, Mexico, and the United States for most goods and services.

Critics of NAFTA feared that it would cause a massive loss of U.S. jobs as firms moved to Mexico to take advantage of lower wages and weaker regulations on pollution and workplace safety. Also, there was concern that Japan and South Korea would build plants in Mexico and transport goods tariff-free to the United States, further hurting U.S. firms and workers.

In retrospect, critics were much too pessimistic. Since the passage of NAFTA in 1993, employment in the United States has increased by more than 20 million workers. Increased trade between Canada, Mexico, and the United States has enhanced the standard of living in all three countries.

Not all aspects of trade blocs are positive. By giving preferences to countries within their free-trade zones, trade blocs such as the EU and NAFTA tend to reduce their members' trade with non-bloc members. Thus, the world loses some of the benefits of a completely open global trading system. Eliminating that disadvantage has been one of the motivations for liberalizing global trade through the World Trade Organization. Its liberalizations apply equally to all 153 nations that belong to the WTO.

Recent U.S. Trade Deficits

As shown in Figure 16.2 the United States has experienced large and persistent trade deficits in recent years. These deficits rose rapidly between 2002 and 2006 before declining when consumers and businesses greatly curtailed their purchase of imports during the recession of 2007–2009. Even in 2009, however, the trade deficit on goods was still at $517 billion and the trade deficit on goods and services was $379 billion. As the

North American Free Trade Agreement (NAFTA)
A 1993 agreement establishing, over a 15-year period, a free-trade zone composed of Canada, Mexico, and the United States.

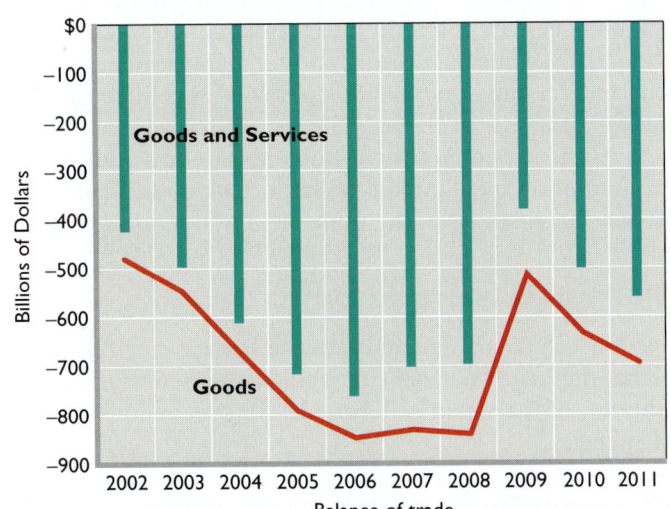

FIGURE 16.2
U.S. trade deficits, 2002–2011. The United States experienced large deficits in *goods* and in *goods and services* between 2002 and 2011. These deficits steadily increased until the recession of 2007–2009. Despite the decline, large trade deficits are expected to continue for many years to come.

Source: Bureau of Economic Analysis, **www.bea.gov.**

economy began to recover, the trade deficit on goods rose to $738 billion in 2011, and the trade deficit on goods and services rose to $560 billion. Economists expect the trade deficits to continue to expand, absolutely and relatively, toward prerecession levels when the economic recovery strengthens and U.S. income and imports rise at a faster pace.

Causes of the Trade Deficits

The large U.S. trade deficits have several causes. First, the U.S. economy expanded more rapidly between 2001 and 2007 than the economies of several U.S. trading partners. The strong U.S. income growth that accompanied that economic growth enabled Americans to greatly increase their purchases of imported products. In contrast, Japan and some European nations suffered recession or experienced relatively slow income growth over that same period. So consumers in those countries increased their purchases of U.S. exports much less rapidly than Americans increased their purchases of foreign imports.

Another factor explaining the large trade deficits is the enormous U.S. trade imbalance with China. In 2007 the United States imported $257 billion more of goods and services than it exported to China. Even in the recession year 2009, the trade deficit with China was $220 billion. That deficit was double the combined deficits with Mexico ($43 billion), Germany ($37 billion), and Japan ($28 billion). The United States is China's largest export market, and although China has greatly increased its imports from the United States, its standard of living has not yet risen sufficiently for its households to afford large quantities of U.S. products. Adding to the problem, China's government has fixed the exchange rate of it currency, the yuan, to a basket of currencies that includes the U.S. dollar. Therefore, China's large trade surpluses with the United States have not caused the yuan to appreciate much against the U.S. dollar. Greater appreciation of the yuan would have made Chinese goods more expensive in the United States and reduced U.S. imports from China. In China a stronger yuan would have reduced the dollar price of U.S. goods and increased Chinese purchases of U.S. exports. That combination—reduced U.S. imports from China and increased U.S. exports to China—would have reduced the large U.S. trade imbalance.

Another factor underlying the large U.S. trade deficits is a continuing trade deficit with oil-exporting nations. For example, in 2011 the United States had a $127 billion trade deficit with the OPEC countries.

Finally, a declining U.S. saving rate (= saving/total income) also contributed to the large U.S. trade deficits. Up until the recession of 2007–2009, the U.S. saving rate declined substantially, while its investment rate (= investment/total income) increased. The gap between U.S. investment and U.S. saving was filled by foreign purchases of U.S. real and financial assets. Because foreign savers were willing to finance a large part of U.S. investment, Americans were able to save less and consume more. Part of that added consumption spending was on imported goods. That is, the inflow of funds from abroad may be one cause of the trade deficits, not just a result of those deficits.

Implications of U.S. Trade Deficits

The prerecession U.S. trade deficits were the largest ever run by a major industrial nation. Whether the large trade deficits should be of significant concern to the United States and the rest of the world is debatable. Most economists see both benefits and costs to trade deficits.

Increased Current Consumption   At the time a trade deficit or a current account deficit is occurring, American consumers benefit. A trade deficit means that the

United States is receiving more goods and services as imports from abroad than it is sending out as exports. Taken alone, a trade deficit allows the United States to consume outside its production possibilities curve. It augments the domestic standard of living. But here is a catch: The gain in present consumption may come at the expense of reduced future consumption.

Increased U.S. Indebtedness   A trade deficit is considered "unfavorable" because it must be financed by borrowing from the rest of the world, selling off assets, or dipping into foreign currency reserves. Trade deficits are financed primarily by net inpayments of foreign currencies to the United States. When U.S. exports are insufficient to finance U.S. imports, the United States increases both its debt to people abroad and the value of foreign claims against assets in the United States. Financing of the U.S. trade deficit has resulted in a larger foreign accumulation of claims against U.S. financial and real assets than the U.S. claim against foreign assets. In 2008, foreigners owned about $3.5 trillion more of U.S. assets (corporations, land, stocks, bonds, loan notes) than U.S. citizens and institutions owned of foreign assets.

If the United States wants to regain ownership of these domestic assets, at some future time it will have to export more than it imports. At that time, domestic consumption will be lower because the United States will need to send more of its output abroad than it receives as imports. Therefore, the current consumption gains delivered by U.S. current account deficits may mean permanent debt, permanent foreign ownership, or large sacrifices of future consumption.

We say "may mean" above because the foreign lending to U.S. firms and foreign investment in the United States increase the stock of American capital. U.S. production capacity might increase more rapidly than otherwise because of a large inflow of funds to offset the trade deficits. We know that faster increases in production capacity and real GDP enhance the economy's ability to service foreign debt and buy back real capital, if that is desired.

Downward Pressure on the Dollar   Finally, the large U.S. trade deficits place downward pressure on the exchange value of the U.S. dollar. The surge of imports requires the United States to supply dollars in the currency market in order to obtain the foreign currencies required for purchasing the imported goods. That flood of dollars into the currency market causes the dollar to depreciate relative to other currencies. Between 2002 and 2008, the dollar depreciated against most other currencies, including 43 percent against the European euro, 27 percent against the British pound, 37 percent against the Canadian dollar, 15 percent against the Chinese yuan, and 25 percent against the Japanese yen. Since 2008, the U.S. dollar has continued to depreciate against the Canadian dollar, the Chinese yuan, and the Japanese yen but has appreciated relative to the euro and the pound. Some of this depreciation was fueled by the expansionary monetary policy (reduced real interest rates) undertaken by the Fed beginning in 2007 and carrying into 2011 (discussed in Chapter 15). The subsequent appreciation of the U.S. dollar relative to the European euro and British pound is largely attributed to continued economic weakness in part of the euro zone and the United Kingdom.

Economists feared that the decline in the dollar would contribute to inflation as imports became more expensive to Americans in dollar terms. Traditionally the Fed would need to react to that inflation with a tight monetary policy that raises real interest rates in the United States. However, because of the financial crisis and recession that began in 2007, the Fed chose to aggressively reduce interest rates, hoping to halt the downturn in the economy. In effect, it gambled that its actions would not ignite inflation because of the dampening effect of the severe economic recession on rising prices.

Summary

1. The United States leads the world in the volume of international trade, but trade is much larger as a percentage of GDP in many other nations.

2. Mutually advantageous specialization and trade are possible between any two nations if they have different domestic opportunity-cost ratios for any two products. By specializing on the basis of comparative advantage, nations can obtain larger real incomes with fixed amounts of resources. The terms of trade determine how this increase in world output is shared by the trading nations. Increasing costs lead to less-than-complete specialization for many tradable goods.

3. The foreign exchange market establishes exchange rates between currencies. Each nation's purchases from abroad create a supply of its own currency and a demand for foreign currencies. The resulting supply-demand equilibrium sets the exchange rate that links the currencies of all nations. Depreciation of a nation's currency reduces its imports and increases its exports; appreciation increases its imports and reduces its exports.

4. Currencies will depreciate or appreciate as a result of changes in their supply or demand, which in turn depend on changes in tastes for foreign goods, relative changes in national incomes, relative changes in inflation rates, changes in interest rates, and the extent and direction of currency speculation.

5. Trade barriers and subsidies take the form of protective tariffs, quotas, nontariff barriers, voluntary export restrictions, and export subsidies. Protective tariffs increase the prices and reduce the quantities demanded of the affected goods. Sales by foreign exporters diminish; domestic producers, however, gain higher prices and enlarged sales. Consumer losses from trade restrictions greatly exceed producer and government gains, creating an efficiency loss to society.

6. Three recurring arguments for free trade—increased domestic employment, cheap foreign labor, and protection against dumping—are either fallacies or overstatements that do not hold up under careful economic analysis.

7. Not everyone benefits from free (or freer) trade. The Trade Adjustment Assistance Act of 2002 provides cash assistance, education and training benefits, health care subsidies, and wage subsidies (for persons 50 years old or more) to workers who are displaced by imports or plant relocations abroad. But less than 4 percent of all job losses in the United States each year result from imports, plant relocations, or the offshoring of service jobs.

8. In 1947 the General Agreement on Tariffs and Trade (GATT) was formed to encourage nondiscriminatory treatment for all member nations, to reduce tariffs, and to eliminate import quotas. The Uruguay Round of GATT negotiations (1993) reduced tariffs and quotas, liberalized trade in services, reduced agricultural subsidies, reduced pirating of intellectual property, and phased out quotas on textiles.

9. GATT's successor, the World Trade Organization (WTO), had 153 member nations in 2012. It implements WTO agreements, rules on trade disputes between members, and provides forums for continued discussions on trade liberalization. The latest round of trade negotiations—the Doha Development Agenda—began in late 2001 and as of 2012 was still in progress.

10. Free-trade zones (trade blocs) liberalize trade within regions but may at the same time impede trade with non-bloc members. Two examples of free-trade arrangements are the 27-member European Union (EU) and the North American Free Trade Agreement (NAFTA), comprising Canada, Mexico, and the United States. Seventeen of the EU nations (as of 2012) have abandoned their national currencies for a common currency called the euro.

11. U.S. trade deficits have produced current increases in the living standards of U.S. consumers. But the deficits have also increased U.S. debt to the rest of the world and increased foreign ownership of assets in the United States. This greater foreign investment in the United States, however, has undoubtedly increased U.S. production possibilities. The trade deficits also place extreme downward pressure on the international value of the U.S. dollar.

Terms and Concepts

comparative advantage

terms of trade

foreign exchange market

exchange rates

depreciation

appreciation

tariffs

import quotas

nontariff barriers (NTBs)

voluntary export restriction (VER)

export subsidies

Smoot-Hawley Tariff Act

dumping

Trade Adjustment Assistance Act

offshoring

General Agreement on Tariffs and Trade (GATT)

World Trade Organization (WTO)

Doha Round

European Union (EU)

trade bloc

euro

North American Free Trade Agreement (NAFTA)

Questions

1. Quantitatively, how important is international trade to the United States relative to its importance to other nations? What country is the United States' most important trading partner, quantitatively? With what country does the United States have the largest current trade deficit? **LO1**

2. What effect do rising costs (rather than constant costs) have on the extent of specialization and trade? Explain. **LO2**

3. What is offshoring of white-collar service jobs, and how does it relate to international trade? Why has it recently increased? Why do you think more than half of all offshored jobs have gone to India? Give an example (other than that in the textbook) of how offshoring can eliminate some U.S. jobs while creating other U.S. jobs. **LO2**

4. Explain why the U.S. demand for Mexican pesos is downsloping and the supply of pesos to Americans is upsloping. Indicate whether each of the following would cause the Mexican peso to appreciate or depreciate: **LO3**
   a. The United States unilaterally reduces tariffs on Mexican products.
   b. Mexico encounters severe inflation.
   c. Deteriorating political relations reduce American tourism in Mexico.
   d. The U.S. economy moves into a severe recession.
   e. The United States engages in a high-interest-rate monetary policy.
   f. Mexican products become more fashionable to U.S. consumers.
   g. The Mexican government encourages U.S. firms to invest in Mexican oil fields.

5. Explain why you agree or disagree with the following statements: **LO3**
   a. A country that grows faster than its major trading partners can expect the international value of its currency to depreciate.
   b. A nation whose interest rate is rising more rapidly than interest rates in other nations can expect the international value of its currency to appreciate.
   c. A country's currency will appreciate if its inflation rate is less than that of the rest of the world.

6. If the European euro were to depreciate relative to the U.S. dollar in the foreign exchange market, would it be easier or harder for the French to sell their wine in the United States? Suppose you were planning a trip to Paris. How would depreciation of the euro change the dollar cost of your trip? **LO3**

7. What measures do governments take to promote exports and restrict imports? Who benefits and who loses from protectionist policies? What is the net outcome for society? **LO4**

8. Speculate as to why some U.S. firms strongly support trade liberalization while other U.S. firms favor protectionism. Speculate as to why some U.S. labor unions strongly support trade liberalization while other U.S. labor unions strongly oppose it. **LO4**

9. Explain: "Free-trade zones such as the EU and NAFTA lead a double life: They can promote free trade among members, but they pose serious trade obstacles for nonmembers." Do you think the net effects of trade blocs are good or bad for world trade? Why? How do the efforts of the WTO relate to these trade blocs? **LO5**

Problems

1. Assume that the comparative-cost ratios of two products—baby formula and tuna fish—are as follows in the nations of Canswicki and Tunata:

   Canswicki: 1 can baby formula ≡ 2 cans tuna fish
   Tunata: 1 can baby formula ≡ 4 cans tuna fish

   In what product should each nation specialize? Which of the following terms of trade would be acceptable to both nations: (a) 1 can baby formula ≡ $2\frac{1}{2}$ cans tuna fish; (b) 1 can baby formula ≡ 1 can tuna fish; (c) 1 can baby formula ≡ 5 cans tuna fish? **LO2**

2. The accompanying hypothetical production possibilities tables are for New Zealand and Spain. Each country can produce apples and plums. Plot the production possibilities data for each of the two countries separately. Referring to your graphs, answer the following: **LO2**

New Zealand's Production Possibilities Table (Millions of Bushels)

Product	Production Alternatives			
	A	B	C	D
Apples	0	20	40	60
Plums	15	10	5	0

Spain's Production Possibilities Table (Millions of Bushels)

Product	Production Alternatives			
	R	S	T	U
Apples	0	20	40	60
Plums	60	40	20	0

a. What is each country's cost ratio of producing plums and apples?

b. Which nation should specialize in which product?

c. Show the trading possibilities lines for each nation if the actual terms of trade are 1 plum for 2 apples. (Plot these lines on your graph.)

d. Suppose the optimum product mixes before specialization and trade were alternative B in New Zealand and alternative S in Spain. What would be the gains from specialization and trade?

3. The following hypothetical production possibilities tables are for China and the United States. Assume that before specialization and trade the optimal product mix for China is alternative B and for the United States is alternative U. **LO2**

Product	China Production Possibilities					
	A	**B**	**C**	**D**	**E**	**F**
Apparel (in thousands)	30	24	18	12	6	0
Chemicals (in tons)	0	6	12	18	24	30

Product	U.S. Production Possibilities					
	R	**S**	**T**	**U**	**V**	**W**
Apparel (in thousands)	10	8	6	4	2	0
Chemicals (in tons)	0	4	8	12	16	20

a. Are comparative-cost conditions such that the two areas should specialize? If so, what product should each produce?

b. What is the total gain in apparel and chemical output that would result from such specialization?

c. What are the limits of the terms of trade? Suppose that the actual terms of trade are 1 unit of apparel for $1\frac{1}{2}$ units of chemicals and that 4 units of apparel are exchanged for 6 units of chemicals. What are the gains from specialization and trade for each nation?

4. Refer to the following table, in which Q_d is the quantity of yen demanded, P is the dollar price of yen, Q_s is the quantity of yen supplied in year 1, and Q_s' is the quantity of yen supplied in year 2. All quantities are in billions and the dollar-yen exchange rate is fully flexible. **LO3**

Q_d	P	Q_s	Q_s'
10	125	30	20
15	120	25	15
20	115	20	10
25	110	15	5

a. What is the equilibrium dollar price of yen in year 1?

b. What is the equilibrium dollar price of yen in year 2?

c. Did the yen appreciate or did it depreciate relative to the dollar between years 1 and 2?

d. Did the dollar appreciate or did it depreciate relative to the yen between years 1 and 2?

e. Which one of the following could have caused the change in relative values of the dollar and yen between years 1 and 2: (1) more rapid inflation in the United States than in Japan, (2) an increase in the real interest rate in the United States but not in Japan, or (3) faster income growth in the United States than in Japan.

5. Suppose that the current Canadian dollar (CAD) to U.S. dollar exchange rate is $.85 CAD = $1 US and that the U.S. dollar price of an Apple iPhone is $300. What is the Canadian dollar price of an iPhone? Next, suppose that the CAD to U.S. dollar exchange rate moves to $.96 CAD = $1 US. What is the new Canadian dollar price of an iPhone? Other things equal, would you expect Canada to import more or fewer iPhones at the new exchange rate? **LO3**

FURTHER TEST YOUR KNOWLEDGE AT
www.brue3e.com

At the text's Online Learning Center, **www.brue3e.com**, you will find one or more web-based questions that require information from the Internet to answer. We urge you to check them out, since they will familiarize you with websites that may be helpful in other courses and perhaps even in your career. The OLC also features multiple-choice quizzes that give instant feedback and provides other helpful ways to further test your knowledge of the chapter.

Glossary

A

ability-to-pay principle The idea that those who have greater income (or wealth) should pay a greater proportion of it as taxes than those who have less income (or wealth).

accounting profit The total revenue of a firm less its explicit costs.

actual reserves The funds that a bank has on deposit at the Federal Reserve Bank of its district (plus its vault cash).

advertising A seller's activities in communicating its message about its product to potential buyers.

aggregate A collection of specific economic units treated as if they were one. For example, all prices of individual goods and services are combined into a price level, or all the units of output are aggregated into gross domestic product.

aggregate demand A schedule or curve that shows the total quantity of goods and services demanded (purchased) at different price levels.

aggregate demand–aggregate supply (AD–AS) model The macroeconomic model that uses aggregate demand and aggregate supply to determine and explain the price level and the real domestic output.

aggregate supply A schedule or curve showing the total quantity of goods and services supplied (produced) at different price levels.

aggregate supply shocks Sudden, large changes in resource costs that shift an economy's aggregate supply curve.

allocative efficiency The apportionment of resources among firms and industries to obtain the production of the products most wanted by society (consumers); the output of each product at which its marginal cost and price or marginal benefit are equal.

anticipated inflation Increases in the price level (inflation) that occur at the expected rate.

antitrust laws Legislation (including the Sherman Act) that prohibits anticompetitive business activities such as price fixing, bid rigging, monopolization, and tying contracts.

appreciation (of the dollar) An increase in the value of the dollar relative to the currency of another nation, so a dollar buys a larger amount of the foreign currency and thus of foreign goods.

asset Anything of monetary value owned by a firm or individual.

asset demand The amount of money people want to hold as a store of value; this amount varies inversely with the interest rate.

average fixed cost (AFC) A firm's total fixed cost divided by output (the quantity of product produced).

average product (AP) The total output produced per unit of a resource employed (total product divided by the quantity of that employed resource).

average revenue Total revenue from the sale of a product divided by the quantity of the product sold (demanded); equal to the price at which the product is sold when all units of the product are sold at the same price.

average tax rate Total tax paid divided by total (taxable) income, as a percentage.

average total cost (ATC) A firm's total cost divided by output (the quantity of product produced); equal to average fixed cost plus average variable cost.

average variable cost (AVC) A firm's total variable cost divided by output (the quantity of product produced).

B

balance sheet A statement of the assets, liabilities, and net worth of a firm or individual at some given time.

bank deposits The deposits that individuals or firms have at banks (or thrifts) or that banks have at the Federal Reserve Banks.

bankers' bank A bank that accepts the deposits of and makes loans to depository institutions; in the United States, a Federal Reserve Bank.

bank reserves The deposits of commercial banks and thrifts at Federal Reserve Banks plus bank and thrift vault cash.

barrier to entry Anything that artificially prevents the entry of firms into an industry.

barter The exchange of one good or service for another good or service.

base year The year with which other years are compared when an index is constructed; for example, the base year for a price index.

benefits-received principle The idea that those who receive the benefits of goods and services provided by government should pay the taxes required to finance them.

Board of Governors The seven-member group that supervises and controls the money and banking system of the United States; also called the *Board of Governors of the Federal Reserve System* and the *Federal Reserve Board*.

bond A financial device through which a borrower (a firm or government) is obligated to pay the principal and interest on a loan at a specific date in the future.

budget constraint The limit that the size of a consumer's income (and the prices that must be paid for goods and services) imposes on the ability of that consumer to obtain goods and services.

budget deficit The amount by which the expenditures of the federal government exceed its revenues in any year.

budget line A line that shows the different combinations of two products a consumer can purchase with a specific money income, given the products' prices.

budget surplus The amount by which the revenues of the federal government exceed its expenditures in any year.

built-in stabilizer A mechanism that increases government's budget deficit (or reduces its surplus) during a recession and increases government's budget surplus (or reduces its deficit) during expansion without any action by policymakers. The tax system is one such mechanism.

Bureau of Economic Analysis (BEA) An agency of the U.S. Department of Commerce that compiles the national income and product accounts.

business A firm that purchases resources and provides goods and services to the economy.

business cycles Recurring increases and decreases in the level of economic activity over periods of years; a cycle consists of peak, recession, trough, and expansion phases.

business firm (See **firm.**)

C

capital Human-made resources (buildings, machinery, and equipment) used to produce goods and services; goods that do not directly satisfy human wants; also called *capital goods* and *investment goods*.

capital gain The gain realized when securities or properties are sold for a price greater than the price paid for them.

capital goods (See **capital.**)

capitalism An economic system in which property resources are privately owned and markets and prices are used to direct and coordinate economic activities.

capital stock The total available capital in a nation.

cartel A formal agreement among firms (or countries) in an industry to set the price of a product and establish the outputs of the individual firms (or countries) or to divide the market for the product geographically.

ceiling price (See **price ceiling.**)

central bank A bank whose chief function is the control of the nation's money supply; in the United States, the Federal Reserve System.

central economic planning Government determination of the objectives of the economy and how resources will be directed to attain those goals.

ceteris paribus assumption (See **other-things-equal assumption.**)

change in demand A change in the quantity demanded of a good or service at every price; a shift of the demand curve to the left or right.

change in quantity demanded A movement from one point to another on a demand curve.

change in quantity supplied A movement from one point to another on a fixed supply curve.

change in supply A change in the quantity supplied of a good or service at every price; a shift of the supply curve to the left or right.

checkable deposit Any deposit in a commercial bank or thrift institution against which a check may be written.

check clearing The process by which funds are transferred from the checking accounts of the writers of checks to the checking accounts of the recipients of the checks.

checking account A checkable deposit in a commercial bank or thrift institution.

circular flow diagram The flow of resources from households to firms and of products from firms to households. These flows are accompanied by reverse flows of money from firms to households and from households to firms.

Coase theorem The idea, first stated by economist Ronald Coase, that externality problems may be resolved through private negotiations of the affected parties.

coincidence of wants A situation in which the good or service that one trader desires to obtain is the same as that which another trader desires to give up and an item that the second trader wishes to acquire is the same as that which the first trader desires to surrender.

collusion A situation in which firms act together and in agreement (collude) to fix prices, divide a market, or otherwise restrict competition.

command system A method of organizing an economy in which property resources are publicly owned and government uses central economic planning to direct and coordinate economic activities; command economy; communism.

commercial bank A firm that engages in the business of banking (accepts deposits, offers checking accounts, and makes loans).

commercial banking system All commercial banks and thrift institutions as a group.

communism (See **command system.**)

comparative advantage A situation in which a person or country can produce a specific product at a lower opportunity cost than some other person or country; the basis for specialization and trade.

compensating differences (Web chapter) Differences in the wages received by workers in different jobs to compensate for nonmonetary differences in the jobs.

compensation of employees Wages and salaries plus wage and salary supplements paid by employers to workers.

competition The presence in a market of independent buyers and sellers competing with one another along with the freedom of buyers and sellers to enter and leave the market.

competitive industry's short-run supply curve The horizontal summation of the short-run supply curves of the firms in a purely competitive industry (see **pure competition**); a curve that shows the total quantities offered for sale at various prices by the firms in an industry in the short run.

competitive labor market (See **purely competitive labor market.**)

complementary goods Products and services that are used together. When the price of one falls, the demand for the other increases (and conversely).

constant-cost industry An industry in which expansion by the entry of new firms has no effect on the prices firms in the industry must pay for resources and thus no effect on production costs.

constant opportunity cost An opportunity cost that remains the same for each additional unit as a consumer (or society) shifts purchases (production) from one product to another along a straight-line budget line (production possibilities curve).

constant returns to scale No changes in the average total cost of producing a product as the firm expands the size of its operations (output) in the long run.

consumer goods Products and services that satisfy human wants directly.

Consumer Price Index (CPI) An index that measures the prices of a fixed "market basket" of some 300 goods and services bought by a "typical" consumer.

consumer sovereignty Determination by consumers of the types and quantities of goods and services that will be produced with the scarce resources of the economy; consumers' direction of production through their dollar votes.

contractionary fiscal policy A decrease in government purchases for goods and services, an increase in net taxes, or some combination of the two, for the purpose of decreasing aggregate demand and thus controlling inflation.

corporate income tax A tax levied on the net income (accounting profit) of corporations.

corporation A legal entity ("person") chartered by a state or the federal government that is distinct and separate from the individuals who own it.

cost-benefit analysis A comparison of the marginal costs of a government project or program with the marginal benefits to decide whether or not to employ resources in that project or program and to what extent.

cost-of-living adjustment (COLA) An automatic increase in the incomes (wages) of workers when inflation occurs; guaranteed by a collective bargaining contract between firms and workers.

cost-push inflation Increases in the price level (inflation) resulting from an increase in resource costs (for example, raw-material prices) and hence in per-unit production costs; inflation caused by reductions in aggregate supply.

Council of Economic Advisers (CEA) A group of three persons that advises and assists the president of the United States on economic matters (including the preparation of the annual *Economic Report of the President*).

craft union A labor union that limits its membership to workers with a particular skill (craft).

creative destruction The hypothesis that the creation of new products and production methods simultaneously destroys the market power of existing monopolies.

credit union An association of persons who have a common tie (such as being employees of the same firm or members of the same labor union) that sells shares to (accepts deposits from) its members and makes loans to them.

cross-elasticity of demand The ratio of the percentage change in *quantity demanded* of one good to the percentage change in the price of some other good. A positive coefficient indicates the two products are *substitute goods*; a negative coefficient indicates they are *complementary goods*.

crowding-out effect A rise in interest rates and a resulting decrease in investment caused by the federal government's increased borrowing to finance budget deficits or debt.

currency Coins and paper money.

cyclical asymmetry The potential problem of monetary policy successfully controlling inflation during the expansionary phase of the business cycle but failing to expand spending and real GDP during the recessionary phase of the cycle.

cyclical deficit A federal budget deficit that is caused by a recession and the consequent decline in tax revenues.

cyclically adjusted budget A measure of what the federal budget deficit or budget surplus would be with the existing tax and government spending programs if the economy had achieved full-employment GDP in the year.

cyclical unemployment A type of unemployment caused by insufficient total spending (or by insufficient aggregate demand).

D

decreasing-cost industry An industry in which expansion through the entry of firms lowers the prices that firms in the industry must pay for resources and therefore decreases their production costs.

deflating Finding the real gross domestic product by decreasing the dollar value of the GDP for a year in which prices were higher than in the base year.

deflation A decline in the economy's price level.

demand A schedule showing the amounts of a good or service that buyers (or a buyer) wish to purchase at various prices during some time period.

demand curve A curve illustrating demand.

demand-pull inflation Increases in the price level (inflation) resulting from an excess of demand over output at the existing price level, caused by an increase in aggregate demand.

demand shocks Sudden, unexpected change in aggregate demand.

demand-side market failures Underallocations of resources that occur when private demand curves understate consumers' full willingness to pay for a good or service.

dependent variable A variable that changes as a consequence of a change in some other (independent) variable; the "effect" or outcome.

depository institutions Firms that accept deposits of money from the public (businesses and persons); commercial banks, savings and loan associations, mutual savings banks, and credit unions.

depreciation (of a currency) A decrease in the value of the dollar relative to another currency, so a dollar buys a smaller amount of the foreign currency and therefore of foreign goods.

derived demand (Web chapter) The demand for a resource that depends on the demand for the products it helps to produce.

determinants of aggregate demand Factors such as consumption spending, investment, government spending, and net exports that, if they change, shift the aggregate demand curve.

determinants of aggregate supply Factors such as input prices, productivity, and the legal-institutional environment that, if they change, shift the aggregate supply curve.

determinants of demand Factors other than price that determine the quantities demanded of a good or service.

determinants of supply Factors other than price that determine the quantities supplied of a good or service.

developing countries Many countries of Africa, Asia, and Latin America that are characterized by lack of capital goods, use of nonadvanced technologies, low literacy rates, high unemployment, rapid population growth, and labor forces heavily committed to agriculture.

differentiated oligopoly An oligopoly in which the firms produce a differentiated product.

differentiated product A product that differs physically or in some other way from the similar products produced by other firms; a product such that buyers are not indifferent to the seller when the price charged by all sellers is the same.

diminishing marginal returns (See **law of diminishing returns**.)

direct relationship (Web appendix) The relationship between two variables that change in the same direction, for example, product price and quantity supplied.

discount rate The interest rate that the Federal Reserve Banks charge on the loans they make to commercial banks and thrift institutions.

discretionary fiscal policy Deliberate changes in taxes (tax rates) and government spending by Congress to promote full employment, price stability, and economic growth.

discrimination The practice of according individuals or groups inferior treatment in hiring, occupational access, education and training, promotion, wage rates, or working conditions even though they have the same abilities, education, skills, and work experience as other workers.

diseconomies of scale Increases in the average total cost of producing a product as the firm expands the size of its plant (its output) in the long run.

disinflation A reduction in the rate of *inflation*.

dividends Payments by a corporation of all or part of its profit to its stockholders (the corporate owners).

division of labor The separation of the work required to produce a product into a number of different tasks that are performed by different workers; specialization of workers.

Doha Round The latest, uncompleted (as of 2011) sequence of trade negotiations by members of the World Trade Organization; named after Doha, Qatar, where the set of negotiations began.

dollar votes The "votes" that consumers and entrepreneurs cast for the production of consumer and capital goods, respectively, when they purchase those goods in product and resource markets.

dumping The sale of products in a foreign country at prices either below costs or below the prices charged at home.

durable good A consumer good with an expected life (use) of 3 or more years.

E

earned-income tax credit (Web chapter) A refundable federal tax credit for low-income working people designed to reduce poverty and encourage labor-force participation.

earnings The money income received by a worker; equal to the wage (rate) multiplied by the amount of time worked.

easy money policy Federal Reserve System actions to increase the money supply to lower interest rates and expand real GDP.

economic cost A payment that must be made to obtain and retain the services of a resource; the income a firm must provide to a resource supplier to attract the resource away from an alternative use; equal to the quantity of other products that cannot be produced when resources are instead used to make a particular product.

economic efficiency The use of the minimum necessary resources to obtain the socially optimal amounts of goods and services; entails both productive efficiency and allocative efficiency.

economic growth (1) An outward shift in the production possibilities curve that results from an increase in resource supplies or quality or an improvement in technology; (2) an increase of real output (gross domestic product) or real output per capita.

economic law An economic principle that has been tested and retested and has stood the test of time.

economic model A simplified picture of economic reality; an abstract generalization.

economic perspective A viewpoint that envisions individuals and institutions making rational decisions by comparing the marginal benefits and marginal costs associated with their actions.

economic policy A course of action intended to correct or avoid a problem.

economic principle A widely accepted generalization about the economic behavior of individuals or institutions.

economic problem The choices necessitated because society's economic wants for goods and services are unlimited but the resources available to satisfy these wants are limited (scarce).

economic profit The total revenue of a firm less its economic costs (which include both explicit costs and implicit costs); also called *pure profit* and *above-normal profit*.

economic resources The land, labor, capital, and entrepreneurial ability that are used in the production of goods and services; productive agents; factors of production.

economics The study of how people, institutions, and society make economic choices under conditions of scarcity.

economic system A particular set of institutional arrangements and a coordinating mechanism for solving the economizing problem; a method of organizing an economy, of which the market system and the command system are the two general types.

economic theory A statement of a cause-effect relationship; when accepted by nearly all economists, an economic principle.

economies of scale Reductions in the average total cost of producing a product as the firm expands the size of plant (its output) in the long run; the economies of mass production.

efficient allocation of resources That allocation of an economy's resources among the production of different products that leads to the maximum satisfaction of consumers' wants, thus producing the socially optimal mix of output with society's scarce resources.

elastic demand Product or resource demand whose price elasticity is greater than 1. This means the resulting change in quantity demanded is greater than the percentage change in price.

elasticity coefficient The number obtained when the percentage change in quantity demanded (or supplied) is divided by the percentage change in the price of the commodity.

elasticity formula (See **price elasticity of demand**.)

elasticity of labor demand (Web chapter) A measure of the responsiveness of employers to a change in the wage rate; the percentage change in labor quantity divided by the percentage change in the wage rate.

elastic supply Product or resource supply whose price elasticity is greater than 1. This means the resulting change in quantity supplied is greater than the percentage change in price.

entitlement programs (Web chapter) Government programs such as social insurance, SNAP, Medicare, and Medicaid that guarantee particular levels of transfer payments or noncash benefits to all who fit the programs' criteria.

entrepreneurial ability The human resource that combines the other resources to produce a product, makes nonroutine decisions, innovates, and bears risks.

equality-efficiency trade-off (Web chapter) The decrease in economic efficiency that may accompany a decrease in income inequality; the presumption that some income inequality is required to achieve economic efficiency.

equilibrium price The price in a competitive market at which the quantity demanded and the quantity supplied are equal, there is neither a shortage nor a surplus, and there is no tendency for price to rise or fall.

equilibrium price level The price level at which the aggregate demand curve intersects the aggregate supply curve.

equilibrium quantity (1) The quantity demanded and supplied at the equilibrium price in a competitive market; (2) the profit-maximizing output of a firm.

equilibrium real output The gross domestic product at which the total quantity of final goods and services purchased (aggregate expenditures) is equal to the total quantity of final goods and services produced (the real domestic output); the real domestic output at which the aggregate demand curve intersects the aggregate supply curve.

euro The common currency unit used by 17 European nations as of 2011 (Austria, Belgium, Cyprus, Estonia, Finland, France, Germany, Greece, Ireland, Italy, Luxembourg, Malta, the Netherlands, Portugal, Slovakia, Slovenia, and Spain).

European Union (EU) An association of 27 European nations (as of 2011) that has eliminated tariffs and quotas among them, established common tariffs for imported goods from outside the member nations, eliminated barriers to the free movement of capital, and created other common economic policies.

excess capacity Plant resources that are underused when imperfectly competitive firms produce less output than that associated with achieving minimum average total cost.

excess reserves The amount by which a bank's or thrift's actual reserves exceed its required reserves; actual reserves minus required reserves.

exchange rate The rate of exchange of one nation's currency for another nation's currency.

exchange-rate appreciation An increase in the value of a nation's currency in foreign exchange markets; an increase in the rate of exchange for foreign currencies.

exchange-rate depreciation A decrease in the value of a nation's currency in foreign exchange markets; a decrease in the rate of exchange for foreign currencies.

excise tax A tax levied on the production of a specific product or on the quantity of the product purchased.

exclusive unionism (Web chapter) The practice of a labor union of restricting the supply of skilled union labor to increase the wages received by union members; the policies typically employed by a craft union.

expansion The phase of the business cycle in which output, income, and business activity rise.

expansionary fiscal policy An increase in government purchases of goods and services, a decrease in net taxes, or some combination of the two, for the purpose of increasing aggregate demand and expanding real output.

expectations The anticipations of consumers, firms, and others about future economic conditions.

expected rate of return The increase in profit a firm anticipates it will obtain by purchasing capital (or engaging in research and development); expressed as a percentage of the total cost of the investment (or R&D) activity.

explicit cost The monetary payment a firm must make to an outsider to obtain a resource.

exports Goods and services produced in a nation and sold to buyers in other nations.

export subsidies Government payments to domestic producers to enable them to reduce the price of a good or service to foreign buyers.

external benefit A benefit obtained without compensation by third parties from the production or consumption of sellers or buyers. Example: A beekeeper benefits when a neighboring farmer plants clover.

external cost A cost imposed without compensation on third parties by the production or consumption of sellers or buyers. Example: A manufacturer dumps toxic chemicals into a river, killing the fish sought by sport fishers.

externality A benefit or cost from production or consumption, accruing without compensation to nonbuyers and nonsellers of the product (see **external benefit** and **external cost**).

external public debt Public debt owed to foreign citizens, firms, and institutions.

F

factors of production Economic resources: land, capital, labor, and entrepreneurial ability.

fallacy of composition The false idea that what is true for the individual (or part) is necessarily true for the group (or whole).

Federal Deposit Insurance Corporation (FDIC) The federally chartered corporation that insures deposit liabilities (up to $250,000 per account) of commercial banks and thrift institutions (excluding credit unions, whose deposits are insured by the National Credit Union Administration).

Federal funds rate The interest rate banks and other depository institutions charge one another on overnight loans made out of their excess reserves.

federal government The government of the United States, as distinct from the state and local governments.

Federal Open Market Committee (FOMC) The 12-member group that determines the purchase and sale policies of the Federal Reserve Banks in the market for U.S. government securities.

Federal Reserve Banks The 12 banks chartered by the U.S. government to control the money supply and perform other functions. (See **central bank, quasi-public bank,** and **bankers' bank.**)

Federal Reserve Note Paper money issued by the Federal Reserve Banks.

Federal Reserve System A central component of the U.S. banking system, consisting of the Board of Governors of the Federal Reserve and 12 regional Federal Reserve Banks.

final goods and services Goods and services that have been purchased for final use and not for resale or further processing or manufacturing.

financial capital Money available to purchase capital; simply money, as defined by economists.

financial services industry The broad category of firms that provide financial products and services to help households and businesses earn *interest*, receive *dividends*, obtain *capital gains*, insure against losses, and plan for retirement.

firm An organization that employs resources to produce a good or service for profit and owns and operates one or more plants.

fiscal policy Changes in government spending and tax collections designed to achieve a full-employment and noninflationary domestic output; also called *discretionary fiscal policy*.

fixed cost Any cost that in total does not change when the firm changes its output; the cost of fixed resources.

fixed resource Any resource whose quantity cannot be changed by a firm in the short run.

flexible prices Product prices that freely move upward or downward when product demand or supply changes.

foreign exchange market A market in which the money (currency) of one nation can be used to purchase (can be exchanged for) the money of another nation.

foreign exchange rate (See **exchange rate.**)

fractional reserve A reserve requirement that is less than 100 percent of the checkable-deposit liabilities of a commercial bank or thrift institution.

fractional reserve banking system A banking system in which banks and thrifts are required to hold less than 100 percent of their checkable deposit liabilities as cash reserves.

freedom of choice The freedom of owners of property resources to employ or dispose of them as they see fit, of workers to enter any line of work for which they are qualified, and of consumers to spend their incomes in a manner that they think is appropriate.

freedom of enterprise The freedom of firms to obtain economic resources, to use those resources to produce products of the firm's own choosing, and to sell their products in markets of their choice.

free-rider problem The inability of potential providers of an economically desirable good or service to obtain payment from those who benefit because of nonexcludability.

free trade The absence of artificial (government-imposed) barriers to trade among individuals and firms in different nations.

frictional unemployment A type of unemployment caused by workers voluntarily changing jobs and by temporary layoffs; unemployed workers between jobs.

full employment (1) The use of all available resources to produce want-satisfying goods and services; (2) the situation in which the unemployment rate is equal to the full-employment unemployment rate and where frictional and structural unemployment occur but not cyclical unemployment (and the real GDP of the economy equals potential output).

full-employment unemployment rate The unemployment rate at which there is no cyclical unemployment of the labor force; equal to between 4 and 5 percent in the United States because some frictional and structural unemployment is unavoidable.

G

gains from trade The extra output that trading partners obtain through specialization of production and exchange of goods and services.

game theory A means of analyzing the business behavior of oligopolists that uses the theory of strategy associated with games such as chess and bridge.

GDP (See **gross domestic product**.)

GDP gap Actual gross domestic product minus potential output; may be either a positive amount (a positive GDP gap) or a negative amount (a negative GDP gap).

General Agreement on Tariffs and Trade (GATT) The international agreement reached in 1947 in which 23 nations agreed to give equal and nondiscriminatory treatment to one another, to reduce tariff rates by multinational negotiations, and to eliminate import quotas. It now includes most nations and has become the World Trade Organization.

Gini ratio (Web chapter) A numerical measure of the overall dispersion of income among households, families, or individuals; found graphically by dividing the area between the diagonal line and the Lorenz curve by the entire area below the diagonal line.

government purchases Expenditures by government for goods and services that government consumes in providing public goods and for public capital that has a long lifetime; the expenditures of all governments in the economy for those final goods and services.

government transfer payment The disbursement of money (or goods and services) by government for which government receives no currently produced good or service in return.

gross domestic product (GDP) The total market value of all final goods and services produced annually within the boundaries of the United States, whether by U.S.- or foreign-supplied resources.

gross private domestic investment Expenditures for newly produced capital goods (such as machinery, equipment, tools, and buildings) and for additions to inventories.

growth accounting The bookkeeping of the supply-side elements that contribute to changes in real GDP over some specific time period.

H

homogeneous oligopoly An oligopoly in which the firms produce a standardized product.

household An economic unit (of one or more persons) that provides the economy with resources and uses the income received to purchase goods and services that satisfy economic wants.

human capital (Web chapter) The accumulation of knowledge and skills that make a worker productive.

human capital investment Any expenditure undertaken to improve the education, skills, health, or mobility of workers, with an expectation of greater productivity and thus a positive return on the investment.

hyperinflation A very rapid rise in the price level; an extremely high rate of inflation.

hypothesis A tentative explanation of cause and effect that requires testing.

I

immediate short-run aggregate supply curve An aggregate supply curve for which real output, but not the price level, changes when the aggregate demand curve shifts; a horizontal aggregate supply curve that implies an inflexible price level.

immobility The inability or unwillingness of a worker to move from one geographic area or occupation to another or from a lower-paying job to a higher-paying job.

imperfect competition Any market structure except pure competition; includes monopoly, monopolistic competition, and oligopoly.

implicit cost The monetary income a firm sacrifices when it uses a resource it owns rather than supplying the resource in the market; equal to what the resource could have earned in the best-paying alternative employment; includes a normal profit.

import quota A limit imposed by a nation on the quantity (or total value) of a good that may be imported during some period of time.

imports Spending by individuals, firms, and governments for goods and services produced in foreign nations.

inclusive unionism (Web chapter) The practice of a labor union of including as members all workers employed in an industry.

income A flow of dollars (or purchasing power) per unit of time derived from the use of human or property resources.

income elasticity of demand The ratio of the percentage change in the quantity demanded of a good to a percentage change in consumer income; measures the responsiveness of consumer purchases to income changes.

income inequality (Web chapter) The unequal distribution of an economy's total income among households or families.

income-maintenance system (Web chapter) A group of government programs designed to eliminate poverty and reduce inequality in the distribution of income.

income mobility (Web chapter) The extent to which income receivers move from one part of the income distribution to another over some period of time.

increase in demand An increase in the quantity demanded of a good or service at every price; a shift of the demand curve to the right.

increase in supply An increase in the quantity supplied of a good or service at every price; a shift of the supply curve to the right.

increasing-cost industry An industry in which expansion through the entry of new firms raises the prices firms in the industry must pay for resources and therefore increases their production costs.

increasing marginal returns An increase in the marginal product of a resource as successive units of the resource are employed.

increasing returns An increase in a firm's output by a larger percentage than the percentage increase in its inputs.

independent goods Products or services for which there is little or no relationship between the price of one and the demand for the other. When the price of one rises or falls, the demand for the other tends to remain constant.

independent variable (Web appendix) The variable causing a change in some other (dependent) variable.

industrial union A labor union that accepts as members all workers employed in a particular industry (or by a particular firm).

industry A group of (one or more) firms that produce identical or similar products.

inelastic demand Product or resource demand for which the elasticity coefficient for price is less than 1. This means the resulting percentage change in quantity demanded is less than the percentage change in price.

inelastic supply Product or resource supply for which the price elasticity coefficient is less than 1. The percentage change in quantity supplied is less than the percentage change in price.

inferior good A good or service whose consumption declines as income rises, prices held constant.

inflation A rise in the general level of prices in an economy.

inflationary expectations The belief of workers, firms, and consumers about future rates of inflation.

inflationary output gap (See **positive GDP gap.**)

inflation premium The component of the nominal interest rate that reflects anticipated inflation.

inflation targeting The annual statement of a goal for a specific range of inflation in future years, coupled with monetary policy designed to achieve the goal.

inflexible prices Product prices that remain in place (at least for a while) even though supply or demand has changed; stuck prices or sticky prices.

information technology New and more efficient methods of delivering and receiving information through use of computers, fax machines, wireless phones, and the Internet.

infrastructure The capital goods usually provided by the public sector for the use of its citizens and firms (for example, highways, bridges, transit systems, wastewater treatment facilities, municipal water systems, and airports).

in-kind transfer The distribution by government of goods and services to individuals for which the government receives no currently produced good or service in return; a government transfer payment made in goods or services rather than in money; also called *noncash transfer.*

interest The payment made for the use of money (of borrowed funds).

interest rate The annual rate at which interest is paid; a percentage of the borrowed amount.

intermediate goods Products that are purchased for resale or further processing or manufacturing.

internally held public debt Public debt owed to citizens, firms, and institutions of the same nation that issued the debt.

inventories Goods that have been produced but remain unsold.

inverse relationship (Web appendix) The relationship between two variables that change in opposite directions, for example, product price and quantity demanded.

investment Spending for the production and accumulation of capital and additions to inventories.

investment demand curve A curve that shows the amounts of investment demanded by an economy at a series of real interest rates.

investment goods (See **capital.**)

investment in human capital (See **human capital investment.**)

"invisible hand" The tendency of firms and resource suppliers that seek to further their own self-interests in competitive markets to also promote the interest of society.

K

kinked-demand curve The demand curve for a noncollusive oligopolist, which is based on the assumption that rivals will match a price decrease and will ignore a price increase.

L

labor People's physical and mental talents and efforts that are used to help produce goods and services.

labor force Persons 16 years of age and older who are not in institutions and who are employed or are unemployed and seeking work.

labor-force participation rate The percentage of the working-age population that is actually in the labor force.

labor productivity Total output divided by the quantity of labor employed to produce it; the average product of labor or output per hour of work.

labor union A group of workers organized to advance the interests of the group (to increase wages, shorten the hours worked, improve working conditions, and so on).

land Natural resources ("free gifts of nature") used to produce goods and services.

law of demand The principle that, other things equal, an increase in a product's price will reduce the quantity of it demanded, and conversely for a decrease in price.

law of diminishing marginal utility (Web chapter) The principle that as a consumer increases the consumption of a good or service, the marginal utility obtained from each additional unit of the good or service decreases.

law of diminishing returns The principle that as successive increments of a variable resource are added to a fixed resource, the marginal product of the variable resource will eventually decrease.

law of increasing opportunity costs The principle that as the production of a good increases, the opportunity cost of producing an additional unit rises.

law of supply The principle that, other things equal, an increase in the price of a product will increase the quantity of it supplied, and conversely for a price decrease.

learning by doing Achieving greater productivity and lower average total cost through gains in knowledge and skill that accompany repetition of a task; a source of economies of scale.

legal tender A legal designation of a nation's official currency (bills and coins). Payment of debts must be accepted in this monetary unit, but creditors can specify the form of payment, for example, "cash only" or "check or credit card only."

liability A debt with a monetary value; an amount owed by a firm or an individual.

limited liability Restriction of the maximum loss to a predetermined amount for the owners (stockholders) of a corporation. The maximum loss is the amount they paid for their shares of stock.

liquidity The ease with which an asset can be converted quickly into cash with little or no loss of purchasing power. Money is said to be perfectly liquid, whereas other assets have a lesser degree of liquidity.

liquidity trap A situation in a severe recession in which the Fed's injection of additional reserves into the banking system has little or no additional positive impact on lending, borrowing, investment, or aggregate demand.

long run (1) In microeconomics, a period of time long enough to enable producers of a product to change the quantities of all the resources they employ; period in which all resources and costs are variable and no resources or costs are fixed. (2) In macroeconomics, a period sufficiently long for nominal wages and other input prices to change in response to a change in the nation's price level.

long-run aggregate supply curve The aggregate supply curve associated with a time period in which input prices (especially nominal wages) are fully responsive to changes in the price level.

long-run competitive equilibrium The price at which firms in pure competition neither obtain economic profit nor suffer losses in the long run and the total quantity demanded and supplied are equal; a price equal to the minimum long-run average total cost of producing the product.

long-run supply A schedule or curve showing the prices at which a purely competitive industry will make various quantities of the product available in the long run.

long-run supply curve A curve showing the prices at which a purely competitive industry will make various quantities of the product available in the long run.

Lorenz curve (Web chapter) A curve showing the distribution of income in an economy. The cumulated percentage of families (income receivers) is measured along the horizontal axis, and cumulated percentage of income is measured along the vertical axis.

M

M1 The most narrowly defined money supply, equal to currency in the hands of the public and the checkable deposits of commercial banks and thrift institutions.

M2 A more broadly defined money supply, equal to M1 plus noncheckable savings accounts (including money market deposit accounts), small-denominated time deposits (deposits of less than $100,000), and individual money market mutual fund balances.

macroeconomics The part of economics concerned with the economy as a whole; with such major aggregates as the household, business, and government sectors; and with measures of the total economy.

marginal analysis The comparison of marginal ("extra" or "additional") benefits and marginal costs, usually for decision making.

marginal benefit The extra (additional) benefit of consuming 1 more unit of some good or service; the change in total benefit when 1 more unit is consumed.

marginal cost (MC) The extra (additional) cost of producing 1 more unit of output; equal to the change in total cost divided by the change in output (and, in the short run, to the change in total variable cost divided by the change in output).

marginal product (MP) The additional output produced when 1 additional unit of a resource is employed (the quantity of all other resources employed remaining constant); equal to the change in total product divided by the change in the quantity of a resource employed.

marginal resource cost (Web chapter) The amount the total cost of employing a resource increases when a firm employs 1 additional unit of the resource (the quantity of all other resources employed remaining constant); equal to the change in the total cost of the resource divided by the change in the quantity of the resource employed.

marginal revenue The change in total revenue that results from the sale of 1 additional unit of a firm's product; equal to the change in total revenue divided by the change in the quantity of the product sold.

marginal revenue product (Web chapter) The change in a firm's total revenue when it employs 1 additional unit of a resource (the quantity of all other resources employed remaining constant); equal to the change in total revenue divided by the change in the quantity of the resource employed.

marginal tax rate The tax rate paid on an additional dollar of income.

marginal utility The extra utility a consumer obtains from the consumption of 1 additional unit of a good or service; equal to the change in total utility divided by the change in the quantity consumed.

market Any institution or mechanism that brings together buyers (demanders) and sellers (suppliers) of a particular good or service.

market economy An economy in which only the private decisions of consumers, resource suppliers, and firms determine how resources are allocated; the market system.

market failure The inability of a market to bring about the allocation of resources that best satisfies the wants of society; in particular, the overallocation or underallocation of resources to the production of a particular good or service because of spillovers or informational problems or because markets do not provide desired public goods.

market for externality rights A market in which firms can buy rights to discharge pollutants. The price of such rights is determined by the demand for the right to discharge pollutants and a perfectly inelastic supply of such rights (the latter determined by the quantity of discharges that the environment can assimilate).

market period A period in which producers of a product are unable to change the quantity produced in response to a change in its price and in which there is a perfectly inelastic supply.

market system All the product and resource markets of a market economy and the relationships among them; a method that allows the prices determined in those markets to allocate the economy's scarce resources and to communicate and coordinate the decisions made by consumers, firms, and resource suppliers.

Medicaid (Web chapter) A federal program that helps finance the medical expenses of individuals covered by the Supplemental Security Income (SSI) and Temporary Assistance for Needy Families (TANF) programs.

Medicare (Web chapter) A federal program that is financed by payroll taxes and provides for (1) compulsory hospital insurance for senior citizens, (2) low-cost voluntary insurance to help older Americans pay physicians' fees, and (3) subsidized insurance to buy prescription drugs.

medium of exchange Any item sellers generally accept and buyers generally use to pay for a good or service; money; a convenient means of exchanging goods and services without engaging in barter.

microeconomics The part of economics concerned with such individual units as a household, a firm, or an industry and with individual markets, specific goods and services, and product and resource prices.

minimum efficient scale (MES) The lowest level of output at which a firm can minimize long-run average total cost.

minimum wage The lowest wage employers may legally pay for an hour of work.

monetary multiplier The multiple of its excess reserves by which the banking system can expand checkable deposits and thus the money supply by making new loans (or buying securities); equal to 1 divided by the reserve requirement.

monetary policy A central bank's changing of the money supply to influence interest rates and assist the economy in achieving price stability, full employment, and economic growth.

money Any item that is generally acceptable to sellers in exchange for goods and services.

money income (See **nominal income.**)

money market The market in which the demand for and the supply of money determine the interest rate (or the level of interest rates) in the economy.

money market deposit account (MMDA) An interest-earning account (at a bank or thrift) consisting of short-term securities and on which a limited number of checks may be written each year.

money market mutual funds (MMMFs) Interest-bearing accounts offered by investment companies, which pool depositors' funds for the purchase of short-term securities. Depositors may write checks in minimum amounts or more against their accounts.

money supply Narrowly defined, *M*1; more broadly defined, *M*2. (See **M1, M2.**)

monopolistic competition A market structure in which many firms sell a differentiated product, into which entry is relatively easy, in which the firm has some control over its product price, and in which there is considerable nonprice competition.

monopoly A market structure in which the number of sellers is so small that each seller is able to influence the total supply and the price of the good or service. (Also see **pure monopoly.**)

monopsony (Web chapter) A market structure in which there is only a single buyer of a good, service, or resource.

moral hazard The possibility that individuals or institutions will change their behavior as the result of a contract or agreement.

mortgage-backed securities Bonds that represent claims to all or part of the monthly mortgage payments from the pools of mortgage loans made by lenders to borrowers to help them purchase residential property.

mortgage debt crisis The period beginning in late 2007 when thousands of homeowners defaulted on mortgage loans when they experienced a combination of higher mortgage interest rates and falling home prices.

MR = MC rule The principle that a firm will maximize its profit (or minimize its losses) by producing the output at which marginal revenue and marginal cost are equal, provided product price is equal to or greater than average variable cost.

MRP = MRC rule (Web chapter) The principle that to maximize profit (or minimize losses), a firm should employ the quantity of a resource at which its marginal revenue product (MRP) is equal to its marginal resource cost (MRC), the latter being the wage rate in pure competition.

multiple counting Wrongly including the value of intermediate goods in the gross domestic product; counting the same good or service more than once.

multiplier The ratio of a change in the equilibrium GDP to the change in *investment* or in any other component of *aggregate expenditures* or *aggregate demand;* the number by which a change in any such component must be multiplied to find the resulting change in the equilibrium GDP.

multiplier effect The effect on equilibrium GDP of a change in *aggregate expenditures* or *aggregate demand* (caused by a change in the *consumption schedule, investment,* government expenditures, or *net exports*).

mutual interdependence A situation in which a change in price strategy (or in some other strategy) by one firm will affect the sales and profits of another firm (or other firms). Any firm that makes such a change can expect the other rivals to react to the change.

N

national bank A commercial bank authorized to operate by the U.S. government.

National Credit Union Administration (NCUA) The federally chartered agency that insures deposit liabilities (up to $250,000 per account) in credit unions.

national income Total income earned by resource suppliers for their contributions to gross domestic product (plus taxes on production and imports); the sum of wages and salaries, rent, interest, profit, and proprietor's income.

national income accounting The techniques used to measure the overall production of the economy and other related variables for the nation as a whole.

national income and product accounts (NIPA) The national accounts that measure overall production and income of the economy and other related aggregates for the nation as a whole.

natural monopoly An industry in which economies of scale are so great that a single firm can produce the product at a lower average total cost than would be possible if more than one firm produced the product.

natural rate of unemployment The full-employment unemployment rate; the unemployment rate occurring when there is no cyclical unemployment and the economy is achieving its potential output; the unemployment rate at which actual inflation equals expected inflation.

near-money Financial assets, the most important of which are noncheckable savings accounts, time deposits, and U.S. short-term securities and savings bonds, which are not a medium of exchange but can be readily converted into money.

negative externalities Spillover production or consumption costs imposed on third parties without compensation to them.

negative GDP gap A situation in which actual gross domestic product is less than *potential output.* Also known as a recessionary output gap.

negative relationship (See **inverse relationship.**)

net exports Exports minus imports.

net taxes The taxes collected by government less government transfer payments.

network effects Increases in the value of a product to each user, including existing users, as the total number of users rises.

net worth The total assets less the total liabilities of a firm or an individual; for a firm, the claims of the owners against the firm's total assets; for an individual, his or her wealth.

nominal GDP Gross domestic product measured in terms of the price level at the time of the measurement; GDP that is unadjusted for inflation.

nominal income The number of dollars received by an individual or group for supplying resources during some period of time; income that is not adjusted for inflation.

nominal interest rate The interest rate expressed in terms of annual amounts currently charged for interest and not adjusted for inflation.

nominal wage The amount of money received by a worker per unit of time (hour, day, etc.); money wage that is not adjusted for inflation.

noncash transfer (Web chapter) A government transfer payment in the form of goods and services rather than money, for example, food stamps, housing assistance, and job training; also called *in-kind transfer*.

noncollusive oligopoly An oligopoly in which the firms do not act together and in agreement to determine the price of the product and the output that each firm will produce.

noncompeting groups Collections of workers in the economy who do not compete with each other for employment because the skill and training of the workers in one group are substantially different from those of the workers in other groups.

nondiscretionary fiscal policy (See **built-in stabilizer.**)

nondurable good A consumer good with an expected life (use) of less than 3 years.

nonexcludability The inability to keep nonpayers (free riders) from obtaining benefits from a certain good; a public goods characteristic.

nonmarket transactions The value of the goods and services not included in the measurement of the gross domestic product because they are not bought and sold.

nonprice competition Competition based on distinguishing one's product by means of product differentiation and then advertising the distinguished product to consumers.

nonproduction transaction The purchase and sale of any item that is not a currently produced good or service.

nonrivalry The idea that one person's benefit from a certain good does not reduce the benefit available to others; a public goods characteristic.

nontariff barriers (NTBs) All barriers other than protective tariffs that nations erect to impede international trade, including import quotas, licensing requirements, unreasonable product-quality standards, unnecessary bureaucratic detail in customs procedures, and so on.

normal good A good or service whose consumption increases when income increases and falls when income decreases, price remaining constant.

normal profit The payment made by a firm to obtain and retain entrepreneurial ability; the minimum income entrepreneurial ability must receive to induce it to perform entrepreneurial functions for a firm.

North American Free Trade Agreement (NAFTA) A 1993 agreement establishing, over a 15-year period, a free-trade zone composed of Canada, Mexico, and the United States.

O

occupational licensing (Web chapter) State and local laws that require a worker to satisfy certain specific requirements and obtain a license from a licensing board before engaging in a particular occupation.

offshoring The practice of shifting work previously done by American workers to workers located abroad.

oligopoly A market structure in which a few firms sell either a standardized or a differentiated product, into which entry is difficult, in which the firm has limited control over product price because of

mutual interdependence (except when there is collusion among firms), and in which there is typically nonprice competition.

OPEC (See **Organization of Petroleum Exporting Countries.**)

open-market operations The buying and selling of U.S. government securities by the Federal Reserve Banks for purposes of carrying out monetary policy.

opportunity cost The value of the good, service, or time forgone to obtain something else.

optimal reduction of an externality The reduction of a negative externality such as pollution to a level at which the marginal benefit and marginal cost of reduction are equal.

Organization of Petroleum Exporting Countries (OPEC) A cartel of oil-producing countries (Algeria, Angola, Ecuador, Iran, Iraq, Kuwait, Libya, Nigeria, Qatar, Saudi Arabia, Venezuela, and the UAE) that attempts to control the quantity and price of crude oil exported by its members and that accounts for 60 percent of the world's export of oil.

other-things-equal assumption The assumption that factors other than those being considered are held constant; *ceteris paribus* assumption.

output effect (Web chapter) The situation in which an increase in the price of one input will increase a firm's production costs and reduce its level of output, thus reducing the demand for other inputs; conversely for a decrease in the price of the input.

P

$P = MC$ rule The principle that a purely competitive firm will maximize its profit or minimize its loss by producing that output at which the price of the product is equal to marginal cost, provided that price is equal to or greater than average variable cost in the short run and equal to or greater than average total cost in the long run.

partnership An unincorporated firm owned and operated by two or more persons.

patent An exclusive right given to inventors to produce and sell a new product or machine for 20 years from the time of patent application.

payroll tax A tax levied on employers of labor equal to a percentage of all or part of the wages and salaries paid by them and on employees equal to a percentage of all or part of the wages and salaries received by them.

per capita GDP Gross domestic product (GDP) per person; the average GDP of a population.

per capita income A nation's total income per person; the average income of a population.

perfectly elastic demand Product or resource demand in which quantity demanded can be of any amount at a particular product price; graphs as a horizontal demand curve.

perfectly elastic supply Product or resource supply in which quantity supplied can be of any amount at a particular product or resource price; graphs as a horizontal supply curve.

perfectly inelastic demand Product or resource demand in which price can be of any amount at a particular quantity of the product or resource demanded; quantity demanded does not respond to a change in price; graphs as a vertical demand curve.

perfectly inelastic supply Product or resource supply in which price can be of any amount at a particular quantity of the product or resource demanded; quantity supplied does not respond to a change in price; graphs as a vertical supply curve.

per se violations Collusive actions, such as attempts to fix prices or divide markets, that are violations of the antitrust laws, even if the actions are unsuccessful.

personal consumption expenditures The expenditures of households for durable and nondurable consumer goods and services.

personal income tax A tax levied on the taxable income of individuals, households, and unincorporated firms.

per-unit production cost The average production cost of a particular level of output; total input cost divided by units of output.

political business cycle The alleged tendency of presidential administrations and Congress to destabilize the economy by reducing taxes and increasing government expenditures before elections and to raise taxes and lower expenditures after elections.

positive externalities Spillover production or consumption benefits conferred on third parties without compensation from them.

positive GDP gap A situation in which actual gross domestic product exceeds *potential output*. Also known as an inflationary output gap.

positive relationship A direct relationship between two variables.

potential output The real output (GDP) an economy can produce when it fully employs its available resources.

poverty A situation in which the basic needs of an individual or family exceed the means to satisfy them.

poverty rate (Web chapter) The percentage of the population with incomes below the official poverty income levels that are established by the federal government.

price The amount of money needed to buy a particular good, service, or resource.

price ceiling A legally established maximum price for a good or service.

price discrimination The selling of a product to different buyers at different prices when the price differences are not justified by differences in cost.

price elasticity of demand The ratio of the percentage change in quantity demanded of a product or resource to the percentage change in its price; a measure of the responsiveness of buyers to a change in the price of a product or resource.

price elasticity of supply The ratio of the percentage change in quantity supplied of a product or resource to the percentage change in its price; a measure of the responsiveness of producers to a change in the price of a product or resource.

price-fixing The conspiring by two or more firms to set the price of their products; an illegal practice under the Sherman Act.

price floor A legally determined price above the equilibrium price.

price index An index number that shows how the weighted-average price of a "market basket" of goods changes over time.

price leadership An informal method that firms in an oligopoly may employ to set the price of their product: One firm (the leader) is the first to announce a change in price, and the other firms (the followers) soon announce identical or similar changes.

price level The weighted average of the prices of all the final goods and services produced in an economy.

price-level stability A steadiness of the price level from one period to the next; zero or low annual inflation; also called *price stability*.

price maker A seller (or buyer) that is able to affect the product or resource price by changing the amount it sells (or buys).

price support A minimum price that government allows sellers to receive for a good or service; a legally established or maintained minimum price.

price taker A seller (or buyer) that is unable to affect the price at which a product or resource sells by changing the amount it sells (or buys).

price war Successive and continued decreases in the prices charged by firms in an oligopolistic industry. Each firm lowers its price below rivals' prices, hoping to increase its sales and revenues at its rivals' expense.

prime interest rate The benchmark interest rate that banks use as a reference point for a wide range of loans to businesses and individuals.

principal-agent problem A conflict of interest that occurs when agents (workers or managers) pursue their own objectives to the detriment of the principals' (stockholders') goals.

principles Statements about economic behavior that enable prediction of the probable effects of certain actions.

private good A good or service that is individually consumed and that can be profitably provided by privately owned firms because they can exclude nonpayers from receiving the benefits.

private property The right of private persons and firms to obtain, own, control, employ, dispose of, and bequeath land, capital, and other property.

private sector The households and business firms of the economy.

product differentiation A strategy in which one firm's product is distinguished from competing products by means of its design, related services, quality, location, or other attributes (except price).

production possibilities curve A curve showing the different combinations of two goods or services that can be produced in a full-employment, full-production economy where the available supplies of resources and technology are fixed.

productive efficiency The production of a good in the least costly way; occurs when production takes place at the output at which average total cost is a minimum and marginal product per dollar's worth of input is the same for all inputs.

productivity A measure of average output or real output per unit of input. For example, the productivity of labor is determined by dividing real output by hours of work.

productivity growth The increase in productivity from one period to another.

product market A market in which products are sold by firms and bought by households.

profit The return to the resource entrepreneurial ability (see **normal profit**); total revenue minus total cost (see **economic profit**).

progressive tax A tax whose average tax rate increases as the taxpayer's income increases and decreases as the taxpayer's income decreases.

property tax A tax on the value of property (capital, land, stocks and bonds, and other assets) owned by firms and households.

proportional tax A tax whose average tax rate remains constant as the taxpayer's income increases or decreases.

proprietor's income The net income of the owners of unincorporated firms (proprietorships and partnerships).

protective tariff A tariff designed to shield domestic producers of a good or service from the competition of foreign producers.

public assistance programs Government programs that pay benefits to those who are unable to earn income (because of permanent disabilities or because they have very low income and dependent children); financed by general tax revenues and viewed as public charity (rather than earned rights).

public debt The total amount owed by the federal government to the owners of government securities; equal to the sum of past government budget deficits less government budget surpluses.

public good A good or service that is characterized by nonrivalry and nonexcludability; a good or service with these characteristics provided by government.

public investments Government expenditures on public capital (such as roads, highways, bridges, mass-transit systems, and electric power facilities) and on human capital (such as education, training, and health).

public sector The part of the economy that contains all government entities; government.

purchasing power The amount of goods and services that a monetary unit of income can buy.

pure competition A market structure in which a very large number of firms sell a standardized product, into which entry is very easy, in which the individual seller has no control over the product price, and in which there is no nonprice competition; a market characterized by a very large number of buyers and sellers.

purely competitive labor market (Web chapter) A labor market in which a large number of similarly qualified workers independently offer their labor services to a large number of employers, none of whom can set the wage rate.

pure monopoly A market structure in which one firm sells a unique product, into which entry is blocked, in which the single firm has considerable control over product price, and in which nonprice competition may or may not be found.

Q

quantity demanded The amount of a good or service that buyers (or a buyer) desire to purchase at a particular price during some period.

quantity supplied The amount of a good or service that producers (or a producer) offer to sell at a particular price during some period.

quasi-public bank A bank that is privately owned but governmentally (publicly) controlled; each of the U.S. Federal Reserve Banks.

quasi-public good A good or service to which excludability could apply but that has such a large spillover benefit that government sponsors its production to prevent an underallocation of resources.

R

rate of return The gain in net revenue divided by the cost of an investment or an R&D expenditure; expressed as a percentage.

rational behavior Human behavior based on comparison of marginal costs and marginal benefits; behavior designed to maximize total utility.

real capital (See **capital.**)

real GDP (See **real gross domestic product.**)

real GDP per capita Real output (GDP) divided by population.

real gross domestic product (GDP) Gross domestic product adjusted for inflation; gross domestic product in a year divided by the GDP price index for that year, the index expressed as a decimal.

real income The amount of goods and services that can be purchased with nominal income during some period of time; nominal income adjusted for inflation.

real interest rate The interest rate expressed in dollars of constant value (adjusted for inflation) and equal to the nominal interest rate less the expected rate of inflation.

recession A period of declining real GDP, accompanied by lower real income and higher unemployment.

recessionary output gap (See **negative GDP gap.**)

refinancing the public debt Selling new government securities to owners of expiring securities or paying them money gained from the sales of new securities to others.

regressive tax A tax whose average tax rate decreases as the taxpayer's income increases and increases as the taxpayer's income decreases.

rent-seeking behavior The actions by persons, firms, or unions to gain special benefits from government at the taxpayers' or someone else's expense.

required reserves The funds that banks and thrifts must deposit with the Federal Reserve Bank (or hold as vault cash) to meet the legal reserve requirement; a fixed percentage of the bank's or thrift's checkable deposits.

reserve ratio The specified minimum percentage of its checkable deposits that a bank or thrift must keep on deposit at the Federal Reserve Bank in its district or hold as vault cash.

resource A natural, human, or manufactured item that helps produce goods and services; a productive agent or factor of production.

resource market A market in which households sell and firms buy resources or the services of resources.

rule of reason The rule stated and applied in the U.S. Steel case that only combinations and contracts unreasonably restraining trade are subject to actions under the antitrust laws and that size and possession of monopoly power are not illegal.

rule of 70 A method for determining the number of years it will take for some measure to double, given its annual percentage increase. Example: To determine the number of years it will take for the price level to double, divide 70 by the annual rate of inflation.

S

sales tax A tax levied on the cost (at retail) of a broad group of products.

saving Disposable income not spent for consumer goods; equal to disposable income minus personal consumption expenditures.

savings account A deposit that is interest-bearing and that the depositor can normally withdraw at any time.

savings institution (See **thrift institution.**)

scarce resources The limited quantities of land, capital, labor, and entrepreneurial ability that are never sufficient to satisfy people's virtually unlimited economic wants.

scientific method The procedure for the systematic pursuit of knowledge involving the observation of facts and the formulation and testing of hypotheses to obtain theories, principles, and laws.

secular trend A long-term tendency; a change in some variable over a very long period of years.

securitization The process of aggregating many individual financial debts into a pool and then issuing new securities (financial instruments) backed by the pool. The holders of the new securities are entitled to receive debt payments made on the individual financial debts in the pool.

self-interest The most-advantageous outcome as viewed by each firm, property owner, worker, or consumer.

service An (intangible) act or use for which a consumer, firm, or government is willing to pay.

Sherman Act The federal antitrust act of 1890 that makes monopoly and conspiracies to restrain trade criminal offenses.

shocks sudden, unexpected changes in *demand* (or *aggregate demand*) or *supply* (or *aggregate supply*).

shortage The amount by which the quantity demanded of a product exceeds the quantity supplied at a particular (below-equilibrium) price.

short run (1) In microeconomics, a period of time in which producers are able to change the quantities of some but not all of the resources they employ; a period in which some resources (usually plant) are fixed and some are variable. (2) In macroeconomics, a period in which nominal wages and other input prices do not change in response to a change in the price level.

short-run aggregate supply curve An aggregate supply curve relevant to a time period in which input prices (particularly nominal wages) do not change in response to changes in the price level.

short-run competitive equilibrium The price at which the total quantity of a product supplied in the short run in a purely competitive industry equals the total quantity of the product demanded and that is equal to or greater than average variable cost.

short-run supply curve A supply curve that shows the quantity of a product a firm in a purely competitive industry will offer to sell at various prices in the short run; the portion of the firm's short-run marginal cost curve that lies above its average-variable-cost curve.

shutdown case The circumstance in which a firm would experience a loss greater than its total fixed cost if it were to produce any output greater than zero; alternatively, a situation in which a firm would cease to operate when the price at which it can sell its product is less than its average variable cost.

simultaneous consumption A product's ability to satisfy a large number of consumers at the same time.

slope of a straight line The ratio of the vertical change (the rise or fall) to the horizontal change (the run) between any two points on a line. The slope of an upward-sloping line is positive, reflecting a direct relationship between two variables; the slope of a downward-sloping line is negative, reflecting an inverse relationship between two variables.

Smoot-Hawley Tariff Act Legislation passed in 1930 that established very high tariffs. Its objective was to reduce imports and stimulate the domestic economy, but it resulted only in retaliatory tariffs by other nations.

social insurance programs Programs that replace a portion of the earnings lost when people retire or are temporarily unemployed, that are financed by payroll taxes, and that are viewed as earned rights (rather than charity).

Social Security (Web chapter) The federal program, financed by compulsory payroll taxes, that partially replaces earnings lost when workers retire, become disabled, or die.

Social Security trust fund A federal fund that saves excessive Social Security tax revenues received in one year to meet Social Security benefit obligations that exceed Social Security tax revenues in some subsequent year.

sole proprietorship An unincorporated firm owned and operated by one person.

special-interest effect Any result of government promotion of the interests (goals) of a small group at the expense of a much larger group.

specialization The use of the resources of an individual, a firm, a region, or a nation to concentrate production on one or a small number of goods and services.

speculation The activity of buying or selling with the motive of later reselling or rebuying for profit.

SSI (See **Supplemental Security Income.**)

stagflation Inflation accompanied by stagnation in the rate of growth of output and an increase in unemployment in the economy; simultaneous increases in the *inflation rate* and the *unemployment rate*.

standardized product A product whose buyers are indifferent to the seller from whom they purchase it as long as the price charged by all sellers is the same; a product all units of which are identical and thus are perfect substitutes for each other.

Standard Oil case A 1911 antitrust case in which Standard Oil was found guilty of violating the Sherman Act by illegally monopolizing the petroleum industry. As a remedy the company was divided into several competing firms.

start-up (firm) A new firm focused on creating and introducing a particular new product or employing a specific new production or distribution method.

sticky prices (See **inflexible prices.**)

stock (corporate) An ownership share in a corporation.

store of value An asset set aside for future use; one of the three functions of money.

strategic behavior Self-interested economic actions that take into account the expected reactions of others.

strike The withholding of labor services by an organized group of workers (a labor union).

structural unemployment Unemployment of workers whose skills are not demanded by employers, who lack sufficient skill to obtain employment, or who cannot easily move to locations where jobs are available.

subprime mortgage loans High-interest-rate loans to home buyers with above-average credit risk.

subsidy A payment of funds (or goods and services) by a government, firm, or household for which it receives no good or service in return. When made by a government, it is a government transfer payment.

substitute goods Products or services that can be used in place of each other. When the price of one falls, the demand for the other product falls; conversely, when the price of one product rises, the demand for the other product rises.

substitution effect (Web chapter) The effect of a change in the price of a resource on the quantity of the resource employed by a firm, assuming no change in its output.

sunk cost A cost that has been incurred and cannot be recovered.

Supplemental Nutrition Assistance Program (SNAP) (Web chapter) A government program that provides food money to low-income recipients by depositing electronic money onto special debit cards.

Supplemental Security Income (SSI) (Web chapter) A federally financed and administered program that provides a uniform nationwide minimum income for the aged, blind, and disabled who do not qualify for benefits under Social Security in the United States.

supply A schedule showing the amounts of a good or service that sellers (or a seller) will offer at various prices during some period.

supply curve A curve illustrating supply.

supply shocks Sudden, unexpected changes in *aggregate supply*.

supply-side market failures Overallocations of resources that occur when private supply curves understate the full cost of producing a good or service.

surplus The amount by which the quantity supplied of a product exceeds the quantity demanded at a specific (above-equilibrium) price.

T

tacit collusion Any method used by an oligopolist to set prices and outputs that does not involve outright (or overt) collusion. Price leadership is a frequent example.

TANF (See **Temporary Assistance for Needy Families.**)

tariff A tax imposed by a nation on an imported good.

tax An involuntary payment of money (or goods and services) to a government by a household or firm for which the household or firm receives no good or service directly in return.

tax incidence The degree to which a tax falls on a particular person or group.

technological advance New and better goods and services and new and better ways of producing or distributing them.

technology The body of knowledge and techniques that can be used to combine economic resources to produce goods and services.

Temporary Assistance for Needy Families (TANF) (Web chapter) A state-administered and partly federally funded program in the United States that provides financial aid to poor families; the basic welfare program for low-income families in the United States; contains time limits and work requirements.

terms of trade The rate at which units of one product can be exchanged for units of another product; the price of a good or service; the amount of one good or service that must be given up to obtain one unit of another good or service.

thrift institution A savings and loan association, mutual savings bank, or credit union.

tight money policy Federal Reserve System actions that contract, or restrict, the growth of the nation's money supply for the purpose of reducing or eliminating inflation.

time deposit An interest-earning deposit in a commercial bank or thrift institution that the depositor can withdraw without penalty after the end of a specified period.

token money Bills or coins for which the amount printed on the *currency* bears no relationship to the value of the paper or metal embodied within it; for currency still circulating, money for which the face value exceeds the commodity value.

total cost The sum of fixed cost and variable cost.

total demand for money The sum of the transactions demand for money and the asset demand for money.

total product (TP) The total output of a particular good or service produced by a firm (or a group of firms or the entire economy).

total revenue (TR) The total number of dollars received by a firm (or firms) from the sale of a product; equal to the total expenditures for the product produced by the firm (or firms); equal to the quantity sold (demanded) multiplied by the price at which it is sold.

total-revenue test A test to determine elasticity of demand between any two prices: Demand is elastic if total revenue moves in the opposite direction from price; it is inelastic when it moves in the same direction as price; and it is of unitary elasticity when it does not change when price changes.

total utility The total amount of satisfaction derived from the consumption of a single product or a combination of products.

Trade Adjustment Assistance Act A U.S. law passed in 2002 that provides cash assistance, education and training benefits, health care subsidies, and wage subsidies (for persons age 50 or more) to workers displaced by imports or plant relocations abroad.

trade balance The export of goods (or goods and services) of a nation less its imports of goods (or goods and services).

trade bloc A group of nations that lower or abolish trade barriers among members. Examples include the European Union and the nations of the North American Free Trade Agreement.

trade deficit The amount by which a nation's imports of goods (or goods and services) exceed its exports of goods (or goods and services).

trademark A legal protection that gives the originators of a product an exclusive right to use the brand name.

trade-off The sacrifice of some or all of one economic goal, good, or service to achieve some other goal, good, or service.

trade surplus The amount by which a nation's exports of goods (or goods and services) exceed its imports of goods (or goods and services).

transactions demand for money The amount of money people want to hold for use as a medium of exchange (to make payments); varies directly with nominal GDP.

transfer payment A payment of money (or goods and services) by a government to a household or firm for which the payer receives no good or service directly in return.

Troubled Asset Relief Program (TARP) A 2008 federal government program that authorized the U.S. Treasury to loan up to $700 billion to critical financial institutions and other U.S. firms that were in extreme financial trouble and therefore at high risk of failure.

U

unanticipated inflation Increases in the price level (inflation) at a rate greater than expected.

unemployment The failure to use all available economic resources to produce desired goods and services; the failure of the economy to fully employ its labor force.

unemployment compensation (See **unemployment insurance.**)

unemployment insurance (Web chapter) The social insurance program that in the United States is financed by state payroll taxes on employers and makes income available to workers who become unemployed and are unable to find jobs.

unemployment rate The percentage of the labor force unemployed at any time.

unfulfilled expectations Situations in which households and businesses were expecting one thing to happen but instead find that something else has happened; unrealized anticipations or plans relating to future economic conditions and outcomes.

unit elasticity Demand or supply for which the elasticity coefficient is equal to 1; means that the percentage change in the quantity demanded or supplied is equal to the percentage change in price.

unit of account A standard unit in which prices can be stated and the value of goods and services can be compared; one of the three functions of money.

unlimited wants The insatiable desire of consumers for goods and services that will give them satisfaction or utility.

U.S. securities Treasury bills, Treasury notes, Treasury bonds, and U.S. savings bonds issued by the federal government to finance expenditures that exceed tax revenues.

U.S. Steel case The antitrust action brought by the federal government against the U.S. Steel Corporation in which the courts ruled (in 1920) that only unreasonable restraints of trade were illegal and that size and the possession of monopoly power were not violations of the antitrust laws.

usury laws State laws that specify the maximum legal interest rate at which loans can be made.

utility The want-satisfying power of a good or service; the satisfaction or pleasure a consumer obtains from the consumption of a good or service (or from the consumption of a collection of goods and services).

utility-maximizing rule The principle that to obtain the greatest utility, the consumer should allocate money income so that the last dollar spent on each good or service yields the same marginal utility.

V

value of money The quantity of goods and services for which a unit of money (a dollar) can be exchanged; the purchasing power of a unit of money; the reciprocal of the price index.

variable cost A cost that in total increases when the firm increases its output and decreases when the firm reduces its output.

vault cash The currency a bank has in its vault and cash drawers.

vertical integration A group of plants engaged in different stages of the production of a final product and owned by a single firm.

voluntary export restrictions (VERs) Voluntary limitations by countries or firms of their exports to a particular foreign nation to avoid enactment of formal trade barriers by that nation.

W

wage (or **wage rate**) The price paid for the use or services of labor per unit of time (per hour, per day, and so on).

wage differential (Web chapter) The difference between the wage received by one worker or group of workers and that received by another worker or group of workers.

Wall Street Reform and Consumer Protection Act of 2010 A law that gave authority to the Federal Reserve to regulate all large financial institutions, created an oversight council to look for growing risk to the financial system, established a process for the federal government to sell off the assets of large failing financial institutions, provided federal regulatory oversight of asset-backed securities, and created a financial consumer protection bureau within the Fed.

wealth Anything that has value because it produces income or could produce income. Wealth is a stock; income is a flow. Assets less liabilities; net worth.

wealth effect The tendency for people to increase their consumption spending when the value of their financial and real assets rises and to decrease their consumption spending when the value of those assets falls.

World Trade Organization (WTO) An organization of 153 nations (as of 2011) that oversees the provisions of the current world trade agreement, resolves trade disputes stemming from it, and holds forums for further rounds of trade negotiations.

X

X-inefficiency The production of output, whatever its level, at higher than the lowest average (and total) cost.

Index

Note: Page numbers followed by n refer to notes; page numbers with W refer to web chapters.

RELEVANT ECONOMIC STATISTICS, UNITED STATES, 1991–2011

	1991	1992	1993	1994	1995	1996	1997
1 Gross domestic product (billions of dollars)	5,995.9	6,337.7	6,657.4	7,072.2	7,397.9	7,816.9	8,304.3
2 Real gross domestic product (billions of 2005 dollars)	8,008.3	8,280.0	8,516.2	8,863.1	9,086.0	9,425.8	9,845.9
3 Economic growth rate (percent change in real GDP)	−0.2	3.3	2.7	4.0	2.5	3.7	4.5
4 Consumption expenditures (billions of dollars)	3,486.1	4,235.3	4,477.9	4,743.3	4,975.8	5,256.8	5,547.4
5 Gross private domestic investment (billions of dollars)	802.9	864.8	953.4	1,097.1	1,144.0	1,240.3	1,389.8
6 Government purchases (billions of dollars)	1,234.4	1,271.0	1,291.2	1,325.5	1,369.2	1,416.0	1,468.7
7 Rate of inflation (percent change in CPI)	4.2	3.0	3.0	2.6	2.8	3.0	2.3
8 Money supply, M1	897.0	1,025.1	1,129.9	1,150.7	1,126.9	1,079.8	1,072.2
9 Federal funds interest rate (%)	5.69	3.52	3.02	4.21	5.83	5.30	5.46
10 Prime interest rate (%)	8.46	6.25	6.00	7.15	8.83	8.27	8.44
11 Population (millions)	253.5	256.9	260.2	263.4	266.6	269.7	272.9
12 Immigration (thousands)	1,827.2	974.0	904.3	804.4	720.5	915.9	798.4
13 Labor force (millions)	126.3	128.1	129.2	131.1	132.3	133.9	136.3
14 Employment (millions)	117.7	118.5	120.3	123.1	124.9	126.7	129.6
15 Unemployment rate (%)	6.8	7.5	6.9	6.1	5.6	5.4	4.9
16 Federal budget surplus (+) or deficit (−)	−269.3	−290.3	−255.1	−203.2	−164.0	−107.5	−21.9
17 Public debt (billions of dollars)	3,598.2	4,001.8	4,351.0	4,643.3	4,920.6	5,181.6	5,369.2
18 Price of crude oil (dollars per barrel)	20.20	19.25	16.75	15.66	16.75	20.46	18.64
19 Average hourly earnings, private nonagricultiral industries (dollars)	10.50	10.76	11.03	11.32	11.64	12.03	12.49
20 Average weekly hours, private nonagriculatural industries	34.1	34.2	34.3	34.5	34.3	34.3	34.5
21 After-tax manufacturing profits per dollar of sales (cents)*	2.4	0.8	2.8	5.4	5.6	6.0	6.2
22 Industry research and development expenditures (billions of dollars)	114.7	116.7	115.4	117.4	129.8	142.4	155.4
23 Net farm income (billions of dollars)	40.2	50.7	46.7	52.6	39.8	60.0	51.3
24 Federal minimum wage (dollars per hour)	4.25	4.25	4.25	4.25	4.25	4.75	5.15
25 Poverty rate (% of population)	14.2	14.8	15.1	14.5	13.8	13.7	13.3
26 Gini ratio for household income distribution**	0.428	0.434	0.454	0.456	0.450	0.455	0.459
27 Productivity growth, business sector (%)	1.5	4.3	0.4	1.0	0.2	3.0	1.9
28 Trade surplus (+) or deficit (−) (billions of dollars)	−31.1	−39.1	−70.2	−98.4	−96.3	−104.0	−108.3

*Revised definition of this series beginning in 1973.

**Revised definitions have occurred within this series.

*** National Income and Product Account data for 2007 and immediately prior years are subject to change because of further government revisions.

Sources: Bureau of Economic Analysis; Bureau of Labor Statistics; *Economic Report of the President, 2012;* U.S. Bureau of the Census; Federal Reserve System; National Science Foundation; U.S. Citizenship and Immigration Services; U.S. Department of Energy.